THE STORY OF RECONSTRUCTION

President Lincoln entering the White House of the Confederacy two days after the departure
of President Davis.
From *Leslie's Illustrated Newspaper.*

The STORY *of* RECONSTRUCTION

By ROBERT SELPH HENRY

AUTHOR OF

The Story of the Confederacy

ILLUSTRATED

KONECKY&KONECKY

Konecky & Konecky
150 Fifth Ave.
New York, NY 10011

ISBN: 1-56852-254-1

Printed and bound in the USA

To the Memory of E. J. S. H.

CONTENTS

LIST OF ILLUSTRATIONS

The Illustrations in this Volume, from drawings by J. Wells Champney,
were originally published in Edward King's *Southern States of North America.*

THE STORY OF RECONSTRUCTION

BOOK ONE

RESTORATION

THE STORY OF RECONSTRUCTION

CHAPTER I

THE HARDER PART OF WAR

ON APRIL 2, 1865, the day being Sunday, the civil government of the Confederate States of America, warned by General Lee that the place could be held no longer, abandoned its capital of Richmond. During a night of fire and terror, the President and his Cabinet started their southward wanderings, to end in scattered flight, in prison or in exile. The rear guard of Lee's army followed, to march and to fight one last week more, on the way that was to end at an obscure Virginia country courthouse, Appomattox.

On the same Sunday night remnants of Forrest's broken command picked their way out of Selma, second only to Richmond as a Confederate munitions center, by the glare on the sky from the buildings burning behind them. In North Carolina, Johnston's battered army, after its last flare of attack at Bentonville, was slowly falling back before Sherman's mighty invading force.

The power of resistance was gone out of the Confederacy; the will to resist, fast going.

Little more than twenty-four hours after the last armed Confederate marched out, President Lincoln came up the river to Richmond in a navy barge rowed by twelve sailors, through floating wreckage of boats, broken ordnance, dead horses. From the landing he walked the two miles to the building which two days before had been the White House of the Confederacy, and now was army headquarters. Union soldiers had barely succeeded in stopping the conflagration spreading from the magazines, the cotton and tobacco warehouses fired by order of the retreating Confederate government, and others fired by looting mobs. The streets through which Mr. Lincoln walked were deep with dust and acrid ashes from burned buildings; were littered with debris and the bricks from fallen walls; were crowded with wondering Negroes, just realizing freedom.

1

Mr. Lincoln's visit to Richmond was not merely one of curiosity. Confederate armies were still in the field and fighting. The President sought prompt peace, to be followed by restoration along the lines of the plan which he had been maturing for more than a year. To bring peace quickly no influence would be more effective than that of Virginia.

A delegation of citizens left behind in Richmond called on the President at the house so recently vacated by Mr. Davis. Heading them was Judge John A. Campbell. He had been a justice of the Supreme Court of the United States. In the anxious spring days of 1861 he was one of those who attempted to negotiate peace with Secretary Seward. When war came, he became the Assistant Secretary of War of the Confederacy. Two months before Richmond fell, he was one of the Confederate commissioners to the Hampton Roads peace conference. Now, old and broken and pitifully poor, again he worked for peace for his people.

President Lincoln gave to Judge Campbell a memorandum of the terms upon which peace might be had. Three things were indispensable: full restoration of national authority, no going back on the question of slavery, no cessation of hostilities short of an end of the war and disbanding of all Confederate forces. Any proposal in accord with these indispensables would be "respectfully considered and passed upon in a spirit of sincere liberality."

For the more speedy ending of the war the President offered another suggestion, that "confiscations . . . will be remitted to the people of any State which shall now promptly, and in good faith withdraw its troops and other support from further resistance to the government."

It was suggested that Judge Campbell's group act to call together the legislature of Virginia, not the new Pierpont legislature of thirteen members, but the full legislature of the old state. The President approved. After his return to army headquarters at City Point, on April 6, he confirmed his approval by a note to Major General Godfrey Weitzel, commanding in Richmond, to permit the assembling of "the gentlemen who have acted as the legislature of Virginia . . . to take measures to withdraw Virginia troops and other support from resistance to the general government." On this authority Weitzel approved the publication of a call for such a meeting.

Back in Washington, the President was under insistent pressure from his Secretary of War, Edwin M. Stanton, to whom the approach of victory meant not so much the beginning of reconciliation as of retribution upon a South which had sinned. Under Mr. Stanton's pressure the President was prevailed upon, on April 12, to revoke the authority he had given. Reassembling of the Virginia legislature was prohibited by order from the War Department. Arrest was threatened for "any persons named in the call signed by J. A. Campbell and others, who are found in Richmond twelve hours after the publication of this notice." General Weitzel, whose wise and humane administration of affairs at Richmond was working powerfully for better feeling, was rebuked for acting on the instructions of the President, and soon removed. Even while Lincoln lived, the imperious Edwin M. Stanton proved able to win a victory for Radical Reconstruction over the President's own policy of harmonious restoration.

Perhaps, however, Stanton was the better able to carry his point by reason of the fact that military events before April 12 had made it no longer important that the legislature, or anyone else, should withdraw Virginia troops from support of the Confederacy. On Palm Sunday, April 9, at Appomattox Court House, General Lee surrendered to General Grant the last of the Army of Northern Virginia, on generous terms of which General Lee could well say that they would "have the best possible effect. It will be very gratifying and will do much toward the conciliation of our people."

Officers and men were to be paroled, under oath not to take up arms against the United States until properly exchanged; arms, artillery and public property to be turned over to proper Union officers; side-arms of officers, personal baggage and any horse of which a Confederate officer or soldier claimed ownership to be retained, with spring plowing on the farms of the South in mind; and then, "this done, each officer and man will be allowed to return to his home, not to be disturbed by United States authority so long as they observe their paroles and the laws in force where they reside."

"I tell you the Southern Confederacy has gone up the spout," said one levelheaded young Confederate immediately after Appomattox, "and I'm going home to plant corn."

General Grant's terms, and the spirit shown by the soldiers at Appomattox, constituted the first great step toward restoration and reconciliation. There was no exulting, no gloating. With rations furnished by their enemies of the day before, General Lee's veterans started for their homes. The rumor of their surrender, slowly working through the vast region of the South where ordinary means of quick communication had broken down, was met with varying emotions of disbelief, uncertainty, consternation, perhaps relief, in the scattered communities.

To the Confederate commands, still in arms, from North Carolina to the Rio Grande, the rumor meant only that the chief of Confederate armies was no longer in the fight. The government for which the armies fought was still in being, though no longer at its capital. It had become a wanderer. During the last week of the life of the Army of Northern Virginia the "capital" was at Danville. News of Appomattox reached there late in the afternoon of the day of Lee's surrender. At eleven that night the government left by train for Greensboro, in North Carolina. Finding houses there closed against them, the fugitive Cabinet and government of the Confederate States lived for the greater part of a week in a leaky passenger coach on a sidetrack, while one Negro boy cooked their rations on a fire in the open near by.

The government remained at Greensboro to consult with General Johnston. By that time, Mobile had fallen, Montgomery had been occupied, Sherman was in Raleigh. Johnston positively advised against further bloodshed in an effort to keep up a war that was over. Heavy fighting was at an end but there was fear that some Confederate leaders might attempt to make their way into the southwest, there to keep up a government in alliance with the Mexican empire of Maximilian; or that the armies might break up and take to the mountains and swamps as guerrilla bands—a danger which would have been real but for the wisdom and character of the military leaders on both sides.

News of Lee's surrender, flashed over the wires to the people of the North, meant the end of the war, the beginning of peace, immense rejoicing. On the day after Appomattox a jubilant throng visited the White House to call for a speech from President Lincoln, back from Richmond and City Point. Promising the speech the next evening, the President asked but one thing on this day of celebration, that the band play " 'Dixie,' one of the best tunes I ever heard."

The serenaders returned as appointed, on the evening of Tuesday, April 11, to hear what proved to be Abraham Lincoln's last speech. The problem of restoration was foremost in his mind, as it continued to be during the few remaining days of his life. At his last cabinet meeting, at eleven o'clock on the morning of April 14, the subject was discussed. According to the diary of Gideon Welles, Secretary of the Navy, the President "thought it providential that this great rebellion was crushed just as Congress had adjourned, and there were none of the disturbing elements of that body to hinder and embarrass us. If we were wise and discreet, we should reanimate the States and get their government in successful operation, with order prevailing and the Union established, before Congress came together in December. This he thought important. We could do better; accomplish more, without them. There were men in Congress who, if their motives were good, were nevertheless impracticable, and who possessed feelings of hate and vindictiveness in which he did not sympathize and could not participate. He hoped there would be no persecution, no bloody work, after the war was over. None need expect that he would take any part in hanging or killing those men, even the worst of them."

That night Abraham Lincoln was murdered by a madman who had read too much of Brutus.

The war President had hoped for a quick and accepted restoration of the Union before Congress came back to Washington in December. With his death began that long-drawn-out tragedy of misunderstanding, Reconstruction.

At ten o'clock in the morning of Saturday, April 15, less than three hours after the death of Lincoln, Andrew Johnson took the oath of office as President of the United States. Upon him was laid such a burden as no public servant in American history has been called upon to bear. The situation was as touchy and explosive as ever made the judicious quake—for the hardest part of war is not the fighting, but the cleaning up afterward.

While the war lasted, leaders and people were guided and sustained by a sense of purpose, of dedication to some great end—the maintenance of a nation, continent-wide, under the old flag, on the one side; fighting against invading armies for independence and individuality of the states which first formed that nation, on the other. The war had been brought on, however, in no small degree by forty years of crimination and recrimination, starting on the slavery question. Year by year the vituperation of fanatic partisans on each side had grown more bitter, broader and more inclusive until whole sections of the United States were taught distrust and contempt and hatred, one of another, such teachings as are not to be unlearned in a day. After war came the beginning of peace, but not of understanding.

Abraham Lincoln, in the commanding position which he had gradually won, with that superb politicianship which is an essential of statesmanship, sensitive as he was to currents of popular thought, master of popular expression, might have been able to restrain the vindictives of the North and reconcile the bitter-enders of the South; he might have made the South understand that while he lived there was to be no proscription and humiliation; he might have made the North understand that the true and loyal Confederate was not a wicked and willful rebel but a soldier who had battled for an interpretation of the common Constitution in which he believed, and had a right to believe; he might have been able "with malice toward none" to "bind up the wounds of the nation," to make of it a "union of hearts."

But Lincoln was dead; Seward was lying wounded, almost given up to die; the air was clamorous with rumors of Southern plots to destroy by assassination the government which war could not overthrow. A situation already desperately difficult was made immeasurably worse.

To meet it, Andrew Johnson was called. In courage, in honesty, in devotion to the Constitution and the Union of States, he was no whit below Lincoln. These qualities, fire-tested by war in Tennessee, had brought him to the Vice-Presidency, and now to the overwhelming task which Lincoln was to be spared. He lacked, however, just those qualities of Lincoln's which promised to be most useful in the work of reunion, the flexibility of mind, the wise opportunism by which that master of the hearts of men was able to lead while seeming to defer.

In public speech, more than once, Johnson referred to a former friend, then in opposition, as his "Simon Peter," and to another as his "Judas Iscariot." In his brief statement to the small group before which he was sworn into the Presidency, referring to his lot of "toil and advocacy of the great principles of free government," he added, "The duties have been mine—the consequences God's." To those who identify their aims and purposes with Deity, compromise and even wise accommodation become unthinkable.

Moreover, he was handicapped by politics and by geography. He was no Republican, but a life-long Democrat of the strict constitutional school, drafted by the National Union Convention of 1864 to strengthen the Lincoln ticket by the appeal of his record to the war Democrats of the North. He was a Southerner at outs with leaders of his own section and accepted by Radicals of the North only because they expected him to out-Herod Herod in his treatment of the South. "Johnson, we have faith in you. By the gods, there will be no trouble now in running the government!" exclaimed Senator Ben Wade, Lincoln's Radical foe, on the day after the new President took office. Support by those Radicals who, behind their mask of public grief, looked upon the death of Lincoln as a "godsend to our cause" was to last only so long as the new President, in his first natural reaction to the great crime, continued to proclaim the blood guilt of Confederate leaders and to call for punishment of treason and traitors.

CHAPTER II

"Proper Practical Relations with the Union"

From Lincoln, President Johnson inherited a definite policy, definite in its aims and objects, flexible in its ways and means. That policy, the new President undertook to carry out but in doing so he failed to take advantage of the immense strength which might have been brought to his support had he made it clear to all that the policy he pursued was that laid down by Lincoln. By adopting the policy, of course, he made it his own, but his frequent reference to it as "my policy" enabled the opposition to attack it and him in a fashion which would have been impolitic, if not impossible, had the attacks been leveled at ideas accepted and put forward as the legacy of Lincoln.

President Lincoln's idea had been to preserve the Union, and if that were not possible, to restore it as speedily as might be. It was a policy difficult to define in the midst of war hatreds, and even more difficult to carry out. As the President said in his last speech, addressing serenaders on the White House Lawn on the night of April 11:

"There is no authorized organ for us to treat with. . . . We must simply begin with and mould from disorganized and discordant elements. Nor is it a small additional embarrassment that we, the loyal people, differ among ourselves as to the mode, manner and measure of reconstruction."

These differences as to "mode, manner and measure," as he did not have to remind his hearers, had already split the dominant Republican party. As early as December 8, 1863, the President had presented a plan, based upon participation in the elections by as many as ten per cent of the former electorate of any state. Each would-be voter under the "ten-per-cent proclamation" was required to take the Lincoln amnesty oath,

"that I will henceforth faithfully support, protect and defend the Constitution of the United States and the Union of States thereunder; and that I will in like manner abide by and faithfully support all acts of Congress passed during the existing rebellion with reference to slaves, so long and so far as not repealed, modified or held void by Congress or by decision of the Supreme Court."

The Lincoln plan of state governments was not dogmatic and exclusive. It was suggested as

"a mode in and by which the national authority and loyal State governments may be re-established within said States, or any of them; and while the mode presented is the best the Executive can suggest with his present impressions, it must not be understood that no other possible mode would be acceptable."

The President himself had used another method in Tennessee and still another in Virginia, where he recognized and supported the "restored state of Virginia," a rudimentary government set up around the fringes of the old state by Francis H. Pierpont after he had successfully carried through the movement for the separation of West Virginia. Under the general presidential plan proclaimed on December 8, 1863, governments of a sort had been set up in Louisiana and Arkansas, based upon the votes of as many as ten per cent of the electorate, professing loyalty and swearing allegiance. Of these voters, some were consistent and devoted Union men who waited only the opportunity given by the passing of portions of their states under the control of Union armies. Others were disgruntled Confederates, the intensity of whose zeal was likely to be in inverse proportion to the vigor of their former protestations. Others were simply opportunists or office-seekers. But whatever their records or their motives, they formed a political people upon whom the organization of restored states might rest.

These fledgling organizations—the Murphy government in Arkansas, the Hahn in Louisiana, the Pierpont in Virginia, the Brownlow in Tennessee—had not been brought into being without most bitter opposition from within the President's own section and party. According to the theory handed down by Senator Charles Sumner, all these seceding states had committed "state suicide" and could not be restored by any such ready and simple means as the President proposed. Thaddeus Stevens, in the House of Representatives, was more practical and more bitter. The seceding states to him were nothing more than conquered provinces, to be held and governed by the will and at the pleasure of their conquerors, without any weak talk of rights of rebels, ex-rebels, or rebel states.

More troublesome to the President in his effort to reunite the nation than either of these doctrines, however, was the plan proposed in the Senate by Benjamin F. Wade of Ohio and in the House by Henry Winter Davis of Maryland, and passed by Congress on July 2, 1864, in the last hour of its session. This plan, like that of the President, recognized that the states of the South had been in a state of suspended animation so far as their relation to the Union went, and set up a machinery for re-establishing some sort of practical relation. For neither plan was there any express constitutional authority.

There were surface resemblances between the congressional plan and the one used by the President in Louisiana and Arkansas. They had, however, differences so fundamental that the adoption of the plan of Congress would have meant the destruction of whatever had been done in those states. The President's willingness to start reorganizing a state government on a basis of "loyal" voters numbering only ten per cent of the electorate was denounced by the proponents of the congressional plan as nothing less than foisting minority government upon a people by executive ukase. To launch a state government under their plan, not less than a majority of the electorate must have been registered, and have been sworn to an iron-clad oath affirming loyalty, past and future.

The most characteristic and fundamental difference between the two plans was in the matter of the oath required of would-be participants in the new state governments. The Lincoln oath of December 8, 1863, looked to the future. Its most essential word was "henceforth." The Davis-Wade oath looked backward, to the past:

"I have never voluntarily borne arms against the United States. . . . I have voluntarily given no aid, countenance, counsel or encouragement to persons engaged in armed hostility thereto; I have not yielded a voluntary support to any pretended government, authority, power, or constitution within the United States, hostile or inimical thereto."

Only those who could and would swear to these things could take part in the restored government of a state, under the plan voted by Congress. In most of the South men capable of meeting the problems of restoration who could honestly make such an oath were rare indeed, while to find a majority of the voters who could take the oath would have been a practical impossibility.

Passage of the Davis-Wade bill, with all the difficulties in the way of restoration which it imposed, was aided by the ever-wakeful jealousy of power and prerogative between the executive and legislative branches, since by its terms the process of restoration of states was committed to Congress.

Having passed its plan and put it in the hands of the President for signature, the Thirty-eighth Congress adjourned its long session and went home. Mr. Lincoln pocket-vetoed the bill, and, on July 8, 1864, promptly issued a proclamation telling why. The congressional plan was all right for any who might want to make use of it to restore a state, he said, and in that work he pledged his executive co-operation, but he would not sign the bill and so have the country "inflexibly committed to any single plan of restoration." Moreover, he did not intend to force the undoing of the start already made in Arkansas and Louisiana, under his proclamation of the previous December.

The Radicals, as the wing of the party which sought destruction of the old Southern states root and branch came to be called, were outraged. Representative Davis and Senator Wade published in the New York *Tribune* of August 5, 1864, their famous Manifesto to the country, in reply to the President's proclamation. The President was charged with a lack of candor in the reasons given for pocket-vetoing the congressional bill. The Louisiana and Arkansas organizations were denounced as "shadows of governments" and mere "creatures of the President's will," brought into being through a "farce called an election." Mr. Lincoln, they charged, was bent on holding the "electoral votes of the rebel states at the dictation of his personal ambitions." "If he wishes our support," they demanded, "he must confine himself to his executive duties . . . and leave political reorganization to Congress."

Events of the coming year were to bring about something approaching the party canonization of Abraham Lincoln, but in 1864 he was the object of bitter criticism and attack in his own party. "Lincoln has some very weak and foolish traits of character," wrote the editor of the Chicago *Tribune*, while a member of Congress declared, "There has not been a session but that our first act was to validate his infractions of the Constitution and the laws."

So early, while the war was yet on, did the Executive and the Congress come to an open break on the policy of the treatment to be accorded the seceded states. But the Executive, in 1864, was still Abraham Lincoln, commander-in-chief of an army and a navy which, between the time of the break with the Radicals in July and the election in November, were to win the battle of Mobile Bay, to capture the Southern nerve center of Atlanta, and to scourge the valley of the Shenandoah. The growing perception of his powers, and the solid fact of heartening victory at arms, won for the President the victory at the polls. The first round was lost by the Radicals—but there were to be other fights and another president.

At the beginning of February, just a week before the electoral votes for Lincoln's second term were to be counted officially, the anti-Lincoln Radicals raised a straw man of executive interference with the prerogatives of Congress by the adoption of a resolution that votes of states in rebellion were not to be included in the electoral count, nor were their representatives to be admitted to Congress. Elections had been held in some of the "Lincoln" states, and electors and representatives had been chosen, but the President had no slightest intention of attempting to force them on Congress or to try to have their votes counted. He signed the resolution passed by Congress, but with a brief and dry disclaimer of any right to control the houses in their admission of members or determination of the count of electoral votes, a primer lesson in constitutional powers and political processes. At the same time, he made it clear that his signature to an unnecessary resolution was not to be taken as an opinion on the recitals of its preamble as to the nature and state of the reorganized governments in the South.

Of real importance was the need for settlement of the question of slavery in some way more regular, final and complete than the Emancipation Proclamation, a military measure which did not touch five of the slave states at all and was only partly effective in three others. It reached only those areas where the authority of the United States was being resisted, not the states where the civil authority existed and the courts were undisturbed in the exercise of their functions.

To regularize emancipation, and to make it universal and permanent, Congress at last passed a resolution embodying a constitutional amendment forever abolishing slavery. The resolution had passed the Senate a year before but had been rejected by the House in the period of profound war discouragement early in 1864. After General Sherman had presented Savannah to the President as a "Christmas present," however, and the Confederate armies in the West had been shattered at Nashville, there was no doubt of the ultimate success of Union arms, and no need to pay particular attention to the sensibilities of the border states, or to the possibilities of a negotiated peace. The resolution, therefore, was taken from the table in the House, reconsidered, passed by the necessary two-thirds majority, and, on February 1, 1865, sent to the states for ratification.

Through the spring of 1865, states hastened to ratify the resolution which, before the year was out, was to become the Thirteenth Amendment to the Constitution. In the mathematics of ratification, the question of the status of the seceded states obtruded itself. The view of the President, which came to prevail, was that the three-fourths of the states required for ratification meant three-fourths of all states, including those which had attempted secession. Among the earliest ratifications were those of the "Lincoln states" of Arkansas, Louisiana and Tennessee, whose restored legislatures acted while Lincoln still lived and the war still went on.

And so as Lincoln talked about restoration of states to the cheering serenaders before the White House on the evening of April 11, in his last public address, he spoke from no new and sudden inspiration but from matured thought and ripened conviction. To him, the question of whether or not seceding states had ever been out of the Union was a "merely pernicious abstraction." All were agreed, he said, that the

"seceded States so-called are out of their proper practical relations with the Union. . . . Let us all join in doing the acts necessary to restoring the proper practical relations between the States and the Union, and each forever after innocently indulge his own opinion whether in doing the acts he brought the States from without into the Union, or only gave them proper assistance, they never having been out of it."

Applying this view to the criticisms of the reorganization of Louisiana, he said:

"Still, the question is not whether the Louisiana government, as it stands, is quite all that is desirable. The question is, Will it be wiser to take it as it is and help to improve it, or to reject and disperse it? . . . Can Louisiana be brought into proper practical relation with the Union sooner by sustaining, or by discrediting her new state government?"

Two days later, to Gideon Welles, Secretary of the Navy, he said again:

"Civil government must be re-established as soon as possible; there must be courts, and law, and order, or society would be broken up—the disbanded armies would turn into robber bands and guerrillas, which we must strive to prevent."

Union commanders in the field, with the willing help of responsible Confederate officers, sought just that end, to prevent the breakup of the Confederate forces into guerilla warfare. Ironically, one who was doing perhaps more than any other to bring about this desirable result, after the surrender at Appomattox, became the first conspicuous victim of official and popular outcry after the murder of Lincoln. He was not one of the Confederate "traitors" so fiercely condemned, but was William Tecumseh Sherman, whose immense achievements for the Union counted as nothing in those fevered and disordered weeks when he became suspect of leniency to rebels.

As soon as General Sherman heard of the surrender of Lee, he ordered stopped the systematic destruction of railroads and property which his men had reduced to an art. On April 13 flags of truce passed between his army and that of Joseph E. Johnston. A meeting of the two commanders was appointed for the 17th, at Durham's Station. As Sherman boarded the train to go to the meeting, the telegraph operator ran out, bare-headed, to hand him a message just received in cipher. It was the news of the death of President Lincoln.

"Keep this secret!" he ordered the operator, and went on to the appointed meeting, where he handed the dispatch to General Johnston. The General's great distress was obvious, his detestation of the crime outspoken. John H. Reagan, Postmaster General of the Confederacy, who was present, earnestly "hoped that no Confederate was in it," while to Secretary of War Breckinridge, the assassination was a "national calamity."

"I explained," wrote General Sherman, "that I had not yet revealed the news to my own personal staff or to the army, and that I dreaded the effect when it was made known." In fact, the secret was kept until after extraordinary arrangements had been made to prevent any outburst of reprisal in Raleigh, lest that capital suffer a "fate worse than Columbia." In announcing the news to his army, Sherman assured them that he considered neither the South as a whole nor its leaders responsible for the assassination. By contrast, at the same time, the Secretary of War and the Judge Advocate General, Joseph Holt, were assuring the new President that they had positive evidence that the crime of Booth had been "incited, concerted, and procured" by Jefferson Davis, Clement C. Clay, Jacob Thompson, Beverly Tucker, George N. Sanders and other Confederate leaders. On the basis of this "evidence" the President, on May 2, issued proclamations offering huge rewards for their capture—one hundred thousand dollars in the case of Mr. Davis, twenty-five thousand dollars each for the others.

While Sherman and Johnston met to discuss the surrender of nothing more than Johnston's Army of Tennessee, the discussion soon broadened to plans for an end to hostilities. A military convention to that end, entirely tentative and subject to ratification by their respective civil authorities, was agreed upon by the two commanders. The Confederate government, then pausing at Charlotte, in North Carolina, ratified immediately.

At Washington, where news of the armistice and convention arrived on April 21, a special Cabinet meeting went into a fever of discussion over it. None of the members approved. Two, Secretary Stanton and Attorney General Speed, seem to have been little less than hysterical about it. They had visions of Sherman and his western armies marching upon Washington in the manner of a victorious general of the later Roman Empire, to seize the government on behalf of rebels and traitors. Other Cabinet members, more reasoned in their disapproval, particularly objected to that part of the convention which authorized the existing Southern state governments to resume their functions upon taking the Lincoln oath of allegiance.

Such a summary scheme for civil government in the South was beyond the scope of a military convention, of course, but for it Sherman had high authority. Less than a month before, on March 27, he had met President Lincoln at Grant's headquarters to discuss the obviously approaching end of hostilities. Mr. Lincoln then authorized him to say to Governor Vance, of North Carolina, that upon surrender of the armies the people of his state "would at once be guaranteed all their rights as citizens of a common country; and that to avoid anarchy the state governments then in existence would be recognized by him as the government de facto until Congress could provide others." This was Sherman's last instruction on the subject, for to him had come no such order as that from the War Department to Grant not to "decide, discuss or confer upon any political question."

Sherman's convention was entered upon in perfect good faith but events at Appomattox and the death of Lincoln had changed everything. The effort to induce Governor Vance to lead the way toward a breakup of the Confederacy by making a separate peace for North Carolina had lost its interest and importance.

Sherman, rebuked, was ordered to resume hostilities and Grant was sent to Raleigh to see that he did so. Before Grant's arrival Sherman had notified Johnston that the armistice had been disapproved at Washington, and that fighting would begin in forty-eight hours. Johnston knew the hopelessness of more fighting. He could surrender, as he did on April 26, upon the same military terms which Grant gave to Lee's army, and with no stipulations as to government in the South. The second, and last, of the major armies of the Confederacy was no longer in being.

At Washington, Secretary Stanton's violent agitation over the Sherman-Johnston convention led him to give to the newspapers a full account of the confidential Cabinet proceedings about it, garnished with his own darkling suspicions. These newspaper accounts, colored and inflamed, brought to Sherman his first real news of how he was regarded by the government at Washington. Northern newspapers rang for days with most violent abuse of the General. He had been president of a Louisiana college when war began, it was recalled. What more natural, in the psychopathic state of the times, than the sinister implication of treachery to the North, especially when the vast "treasure" with which Jefferson Davis was widely supposed to be traveling could furnish an inducement to such conduct, and the furtherance of its escape could give a reason?

Grant, arrived in Raleigh, exercised his own good sense and did not even tell Sherman why he had been sent. The officious Halleck, Chief of Staff, who had rushed to Richmond to take charge, was not so wise in restraint. He sent instructions to certain of Sherman's subordinates to disregard his orders—a bit of meddlesome discourtesy which so outraged Sherman and infuriated the soldiers under him, that it was well for Halleck that he kept out of sight when the western army marched through Richmond on its way north. At Washington, late in May, with the whole United States looking on as the Union armies passed in their last grand review on Pennsylvania Avenue, the commander of the armies of the West had the satisfaction of publicly refusing the proffered hand of the Secretary of War. The honors rested with Sherman.

News of the final surrender of the Army of Tennessee overtook President Davis at Washington, the little town in eastern Georgia where Robert Toombs lived, on May 7. There the last meeting of the Confederate Cabinet was held. Mr. Davis clung to his fixed and illusory idea of keeping up the war in the southwest, with a few resolute men. The Secretary of War, General Breckinridge, and the commanders of the escort troops were outspoken against the idea; there was no support for it in the Cabinet. Mr. Davis, at long last, yielded his dream of Confederate nationhood.

The members did not know, of course, but as the Cabinet broke up in Georgia, General Richard Taylor had already surrendered to

General E. R. S. Canby, on the terms of Appomattox, the forty-two thousand Confederate soldiers yet scattered in small commands through the southeast. The last hope of obtaining favorable terms by further resistance was ended.

Before the end of the month of May, as rumors of surrenders to the eastward became certainty, the small commands remaining west of the Mississippi simply "broke up." Formal surrender was negotiated by their commanders on May 26 but it was largely mere recognition of an accomplished fact. The Confederacy had surrendered; its soldiers were prisoners on parole on the terms of Appomattox.

CHAPTER III

HOME TO DESOLATION

THE Confederate Cabinet dispersed, each man to go his own road home, or, as it proved, to prison or to exile. The armies were disbanding, making their way home over the scarred and ruined countryside of the South, in their ears the wise counsel of Lee, of Johnston, of Hampton, of Taylor, to return to the ways of peace.

"I have never on the field of battle sent you where I was unwilling to go myself," said Nathan Bedford Forrest to his command, last of all the troops east of the Mississippi to surrender, "nor would I now advise you to a course which I felt myself unwilling to pursue. You have been good soldiers, you can be good citizens. Obey the laws, preserve your honor, and the government to which you have surrendered can afford to be and will be magnanimous."

The wholehearted good faith with which the soldiers of such wise leaders laid down their arms was matched by the generous treatment accorded by Grant, Sherman, Canby and the men who fought under them—the "healing spirit of Appomattox," as one who surrendered there was to call it. The war was over, the soldiers ready for home.

To the Confederate soldier that meant desolation. "Never was there greater nakedness and destitution in a civilized community," wrote one Northern observer. Ruin, which came early to the fighting grounds of the first years in Virginia and Tennessee, spread through the South with the progress of the armies.

In 1864 calculated and deliberate destruction became a major war policy of the North, to break the Confederate armies by ruining the Confederate country which sustained them, using or wasting its subsistence, destroying its transportation. The devastation of a full year of war under that policy is hardly conceivable.

Sherman moved across central Mississippi, and back, and his subordinates laid waste the prairie lands of the northern part of that state. Sherman again fought and burned and ravaged his way through the length of Georgia and across the two Carolinas. Banks raided up the Red River almost across Louisiana. Arkansas was harried by smaller forces. Sheridan made good his boast in making of the valley of Vir-

18

ginia a desert. Cavalry leaders raided and destroyed in southwestern Virginia and western North Carolina. Finally, at the last end, Wilson's great cavalry expedition marked out its path of destruction through all Alabama and parts of Georgia which Sherman had missed. They were thorough in carrying out their missions of destruction.

The prostration of the South can be realized only dimly, if at all, from glimpses. Going south from Washington across the barren waste which war had made of the country between the Potomac and the Rappahannock, the traveler might have seen, though probably he did not, young Laurence Taliaferro, just back from the army, out with the ramshackle wagon and the broken-down mule which war had left him, gathering from his once fertile lands strange crops— bones of dead horses for fertilizer factories, old iron and lead bullets for junkmen.

A hundred miles away, near Lexington, four crippled Confederates on their way home together hailed a gray-headed man who turned the spring earth, while a little girl dropped corn in the furrow behind him. Asking where they might get food, they were pointed to a house near by. There a lady seated them on the porch while she prepared for them the little meat, hoecake and buttermilk which she offered with apologies because it was so little. "We have entertained others this morning, and we have not much left," she explained as she served them at table. At this moment, a neighbor lad came in to ask for General Pendleton, and was told that he was plowing. Four cripples, covered with confusion, realized that they had eaten the bread of William N. Pendleton, late rector of the Episcopal Church and still more lately brigadier general, C. S. A., and chief of artillery of the Army of Northern Virginia, prepared by his gracious wife, and given out of their own great need.

In Richmond, former officers and soldiers wearing the gray jackets which often were their only coats, with buttons decently covered with cloth—for it was now a crime to wear the Confederate button naked to the world—sat among the ruins chipping the mortar from bricks of the burned walls, preparing them for rebuilding. It was, for months, the one means of livelihood for many.

Through travel was impossible. There was no bridge at the Rappahannock, none at the James, none on the Appomattox. From trench-ringed Petersburg, railroads were out in all directions.

From Raleigh, in North Carolina, General Grant wrote to his wife in this month of May:

"The suffering that must exist in the South the next year . . . will be beyond conception. People who talk of further retaliation and punishment, except of the political leaders, either do not conceive of the suffering endured already or they are heartless and unfeeling and wish to stay at home out of danger while the punishment is being inflicted."

Columbia, "a wilderness of crumbling walls, naked chimneys and trees killed by flames," sat in the midst of a desert across which travelers and supplies had to be hauled from the ends of broken railroads pointing toward the South Carolina capital from all directions. Joseph Le Conte, distinguished geologist and chemist of the Confederate Nitrate Bureau during the war, wearing a castoff blue uniform, poled an abandoned flatboat on the Congaree River, bringing up scant supplies of food from the low country. The destitution was such, reported the mayor, that hundreds of people lived on loose grain picked up where the army horses were fed. Around the Congaree factory, near Columbia, lay the bodies of seventy-five horses shot by Sherman's men and unburied for lack of shovels. At Selma, in Alabama, carcasses of horses rotted in the streets until labor, teams and tools could be had to rid the town of their pestilential presence.

Of the railroad from Columbia to Charleston, little was left but the grade. The ties were burned, the iron ruined, the bridges and trestles destroyed. Richard H. Anderson, late lieutenant general, C. S. A., was to live for a season by his work as a day laborer in the rebuilding of the line. M. C. Butler, late major general, C. S. A., twenty-nine years old, one leg gone, was at home in upland Carolina, with a wife and three children to support, with seventy emancipated slaves on his farm, a debt of fifteen thousand dollars and in his pocket one dollar and seventy-five cents.

Charleston, once the proud and defiant leader of the movement for secession, was still proud but no longer defiant in her burned, shell-scarred ruins. The very hall where the first Ordinance of Secession was signed was gone. Henry Ward Beecher, orator when the United States flag was formally raised over Fort Sumter on April 14, the fourth anniversary of the day when it was lowered by Confederate troops, looked "upon this shattered fort and yonder dilapidated city with sad eyes, grieved that men should have committed such treason and glad that God hath set a mark upon treason, that all ages shall dread and abhor it." The people of Charleston may have differed from their distinguished visitor as to the source of the mark set upon their city, but there was no doubt that it was "dilapidated," and its people nearly destitute. Henry Timrod "goes to bed hungry every night. . . . It is the mortifying thing to all of us," wrote his novelist friend, William Gilmore Simms, "that none of us can help him." Two years later the frail young soldier and singer of the South was beyond help.

The rice fields along the Carolina and Georgia coast "had grown up in weeds or tangled shrubbery." The ingenious and elaborate system of dams, floodgates and canals by which the waters of the tidal rivers were made to irrigate the fields were "dilapidated or destroyed." The breakdown of the water-control systems had turned salt water into many of the fields, which were to return to their natural state as wild salt marsh. Thousands of square miles of rich Mississippi Delta cotton lands, with their protective levees broken by flood or cut by the armies, had gone back to brier and cane thickets.

Less irreparable than loss of water-control works, but still serious for the farmer whose labor and money had gone into the building of them, was the destruction of fences throughout the South. The fence rail was irresistibly tempting to the wood gatherers of the armies. Where they passed, fences melted.

In one way there was no great need for fences in that desolate spring of 1865, for most of the livestock was gone, taken by one army or the other, or perhaps by bands of thieves and outlaws. The grist mills to grind the corn meal which is so large a staple in the food of the South were gone, their dams broken, their wheels wrecked. Most thoroughly destroyed of all were the cotton gins—for there seemed to be men in every invading army determined to prove that Cotton was no longer King. In truth, there was little left in the wide track of the armies but dwelling houses, most of which were spared, and the bare land, now almost worthless.

Throughout the South, railroad systems were worn, wasted, broken. Better than average was the situation of the Nashville & Chattanooga Railroad, operated by the United States Military Railroads as the essential life line of Sherman's army, and returned to its corporate owners at the end of April, 1865. The report of the directors for the following year describes its condition:

"The affairs of the company were in deplorable condition, in fact, verging on bankruptcy—without rolling stock to operate it except the meagre supply saved from the ravages of war. . . . Without machine shops or machinery, the road in bad order, the bridges worn out and unsafe, station houses destroyed, and those standing unfit for use, without tools, supplies or even furniture, even to a chair or table, or a sheet of paper that the company could call its own, and, worse than all, without a dollar in the treasury to commence operations, with a floating debt from coupons due on bonds and other debts contracted previous to and during the war of between six and seven hundred thousand dollars . . . without books or stationery, we had in many instances to keep accounts on loose paper. . . . No money or credit. . . ."

Had Confederate money or Confederate bonds been worth anything that last would not have been true. The company had invested $922,000 in Confederate bonds and had, literally, barrels of Confederate money. Of United States money, however, it had none at all, and its debts were owed in that money. The directors met, considered the report of their president and the circumstances of their plight, and then, in the language of that ancient report:

"The directorate, although having a debt of five years' interest to pay [in New York], thought it best to go to work and earn the money and pay the interest and not increase the funded debt."

To physical destruction and the prostration of government was added complete disruption of the ordinary processes of living. There was no money, or at least none of any value whatever. Notes, debts, mortgages, every continuing engagement of commercial life, became worthless.

Not only must some way be found to rebuild ruins, a whole new system of labor had to be created, new channels of business and economic intercourse had to be found, a new manner of life established.

More terrible than all, perhaps, was the tragic insecurity of life and property. Bands of deserters and skulkers, guerrillas and bushwhackers infested the country, preying on all alike, white or black, Union or Confederate—for by the spring of 1865 there was no longer a government in the South which could make good its authority beyond the garrisons. Old scores were being evened up in those districts where Union men had been harried by Confederate neighbors in the days of war hysteria and persecution. Guerrilla bands, actuated by private vengeance or lust of pillage, calling itself patriotism for one side or the other, or both, as profit and convenience might dictate, made life and property in defenseless districts precarious. It was to meet this condition, in a measure, that Sherman and Johnston proposed the immediate restoration of the old state governments, upon taking the oath of future allegiance.

Across the face of this vast desolation straggled Confederate soldiers, by ones and twos, in small bands; on a few main traveled roads, almost in streams, making their way home. Where trains were operated, transportation was generously furnished, usually by the United States Military Railroads. To men going the great distances into the southwest, passage was made possible on coasting vessels putting out from ports on the Gulf of Mexico.

For most, though, the journey was a matter of horse flesh, if a man was lucky enough to have a horse; of foot work, if he did not. The short way home for great numbers of those in the armies surrendered in Virginia and North Carolina was through the mountains and down the Great Valley of East Tennessee. Bushwhackers were common on the route and Southern sympathizers not numerous—but it was the short way, and gray-jacketed men back from the armies passed down the road in squads and groups, occasionally by ones and twos, every day for weeks. Seeing their needs, one Confederate woman at the ancient town of Jonesboro, in upper East Tennessee, established at her home a sort of soldiers' canteen service, providing lodging every night for half a score or so, with meals when she had them to give, and much needed barber service by her young son, who recalls that his mother required the locks shorn from the heads of unkempt soldiers to be cast immediately upon a shovelful of hot coals to shrivel and burn, a regulation which speaks much of the distressful condition of the returning Confederate soldier.

Other groups preferred not to pass through the mountains, where violence from Union guerrillas was looked for. Young Bromfield Ridley, late lieutenant, C. S. A., member of one such group, left a record of his sixty-day homeward wanderings through the Carolinas and Georgia to Middle Tennessee. The group was large—six officers, nine soldiers, two civilian "refugees," three Negro servants who had been slaves, and one first-class fighting rooster, "Old Dick." They had wagons, being fortunate, but no money, except each man's one-dollar-and-fifteen-cent share of the last payday of Johnston's army. Somewhere they had acquired a quantity of spun thread, useful as a "circulating medium" to exchange for forage and food, as long as it lasted.

Stragglers made attempts to steal their animals, and had to be driven away by gun fire. Crossing streams with the wagons was a real problem—"bridges and ferries burned by Stoneman." The people were kind but the road was "jammed with returning soldiers" and food and forage were scarce.

This scarcity did not extend to rumors. Of them there were plenty, and none so wild or impossible as not to find some believers. On May 13 the diarist noted that

"the report is rife all along the way that Bob Lincoln has killed Andrew Johnson at Washington. A man said he had seen a gentleman who had informed him it was reported in the Knoxville *Whig* and the Augusta *Chronicle*. Don't believe it, yet am prepared now to believe anything."

Three days later, in Abbeville, South Carolina, the party "saw twelve Yankees," the first they had seen since the surrender. They heard there another rumor, that a French fleet, come to carry away President Davis, lay off Wilmington. "Don't I wish that President Davis could get on it!"

Still another rumor was met at Abbeville, that Mr. Davis had been captured. The last was true. The capture had been made six days before, in the early morning of May 10, near Irwinsville, Georgia, where he had made his way to join Mrs. Davis and the children. The former President of the Confederate States was a prisoner on his way to Augusta, whence he was to be carried by river boat to Savannah and coasting steamer to Fortress Monroe, while the two bands of soldiers that had taken part in his capture began to squabble over the payment of the huge reward offered for him.

The homeward-bound diarist, noting the rumor of the capture of the fugitive President, moved on into middle Georgia. There, on May 21, the party began to disperse. Those for New Orleans and Texas went on to Columbus, to take steamer down the Chattahoochee to Apalachicola, and coasting schooner west from there. One Kentuckian went to Florida, where his wife was "refugeeing." The other Kentuckians and the Tennesseans halted ten days, adding to themselves various civilian "refugees" and others for the movement home through the "barren waste" of Sherman's track.

The ten days' halt seems to have been a time of thorough enjoyment for young Ridley and his companions. "But for the fact of surrender, no one would dream of disaster to our people," he wrote. There were young ladies, both resident and "refugees" from Mississippi, enough altogether to make a two-horse-wagon load of "girls in low necks and short sleeves" to go to a party. The party was a candy pulling. Candy, made from homemade cane syrup, was the merest incident in the evening. Games were played: "thimble," "snap," kissing games. There was conversation about the new novels: *Les Misérables,*

Macaria. Sentimental songs were sung: "Gentle Annie," "Tipperary Town," "Massa's in the Cold, Cold Ground," "Do They Miss Me in the Trenches?" Army songs, too: "Just Before the Battle, Mother," "Joe Bowers," "Lorena," "Tramp, Tramp, Tramp," "When This Cruel War Is Over," although

> "If I ever get through this war,
> And Lincoln's chains don't bind me,
> I'll make my way to Tennessee,
> To the girl I left behind me,"

was perhaps not the happiest selection of words to be sung to the girls of Georgia.

There was a new parody of the stirring war song of the "Bonnie Blue Flag" also. The original had been first heard in a Jackson theater on the joyous evening of the day when the state of Mississippi seceded. The parody made its first appearance in *The Rebel 64-Pounder*, or *Camp Chase Ventilator* of which its author, Colonel William Hawkins of Tennessee, prisoner of war and poet, was the editor. Perhaps only a Southern poet would have sensed the rhyme in its rueful refrain:

> "Hurrah, hurrah! for peace and home, hurrah!
> Hurrah for the Bonnie White Flag, that ends this cruel war!"

"Suppose the Yankees get after you at home?" one paroled Confederate was asked.

"Oh, they ain't goin' to trouble me," was the answer. "If they do, I'll just whip 'em again."

Penniless the Confederate soldier was and ragged, and sometimes lousy, and often hungry; but he was young, for the most part, and he was going home, without vain repinings, to rebuild, to work and to live.

Whatever may have been thought of the original rights or wrongs of secession, the returning soldiers were under no illusions about the result of the war. They were able to joke about it, and to make songs at their own expense, but they knew they had been defeated and that their defeat meant the end of slavery and secession. These consequences they were willing to accept but they were oppressed with no sense of guilt. They had no intention of dishonoring their dead and debasing themselves by pretending one. They were resigned, not repentant.

CHAPTER IV

Contrasts and Contradictions

Not every Confederate soldier was willing to go to a home where all things were changed; some, threatened with proscription, dared not. Matthew Fontaine Maury, discoverer of the currents of the ocean and founder of the science of meteorology, sailed from England for home in May of 1865. In the West Indies he learned that no longer was there a Confederate States of America. He had been a Confederate naval agent in Europe, and justly feared what might await him in the stirring ferment in the South. Midsummer found him in the City of Mexico, installed as director of the Imperial Observatory there and interested in plans for settlement of ex-Confederates in the Carlotta Colony, to be established near by.

There was for a time no lack of possible settlers, especially after chaos came in Texas with the "breakup" of the armies. Confederate soldiers, dividing the supplies on hand, started working their way homeward or to Mexico. One band stopped on the way to raid the state treasury at Austin for back pay; another made a nearly successful effort to break into and rob the state prison at Huntsville. There was no longer military control, and not yet any civil government except local "home-guard" companies.

Early in June, with all possibility of resistance or control gone, Generals Kirby Smith and Magruder, commanders of troops, and Governor Murrah, of Texas, made their way to Mexico. There, among other Confederates of distinction, they might have found Lieutenant-Generals Sterling Price and Jubal A. Early, and Isham G. Harris, leader of the secession movement in Tennessee and governor of that state before and during the war, for whose arrest a reward had been offered.

Plans were made for colonies in Brazil and elsewhere for those who felt that they could not abide to live under Yankee rule. General Wade Hampton, whose fortune was wrecked and whose great mansion was a row of gaunt columns rising from a bed of ashes, when called on to lead such a movement spoke his mind:

26

"My advice . . . is . . . to devote our whole energies to the restoration of law and order, the re-establishment of agriculture and commerce, the promotion of education and the rebuilding of our cities and dwellings which have been laid in ashes."

More potent still was the counsel and example of Lee. Homeless himself—one home, on the Pamunkey, was burned; the other, on the Potomac, confiscated by the government—his constant theme was, "Stay at home. Rebuild. The South needs her sons." To his friend, Commodore Maury, in Mexico, he wrote:

"The thought of abandoning the country and all that must be left in it is abhorrent to my feelings. I prefer to struggle for its restoration and share its fate rather than to give up all as lost. . . . [Virginia] has now need for all her sons."

The need, not only in Virginia but throughout the South, was inconceivably great. That it was met at all in that first summer of 1865 was due in no small measure to the generous and friendly help of many Union garrisons in the South and of numerous agents of the newly created Bureau of Freedmen and Abandoned Lands. Rations were needed, elemental bread and meat and shelter, and these the army and the Bureau were able to furnish to destitute whites as well as to bewildered blacks.

For weeks the Union garrisons provided all there was of law and order, for on May 20 Secretary Stanton telegraphed strict instructions to all commanders that no officer of the Confederate or state governments should be allowed to function in any manner. In faraway Texas there were almost no garrisons and, practically speaking, no government. Where garrisons were more plentiful there was, of course, a certain amount of petty persecution and, as time went on, a vast lot of unneccessary compulsory oath taking. Many other garrisons, however, were like that "gentlemanly and courteous" one in South Carolina of which the Winnsboro News said that "their conduct entitles them to the good opinion of the citizens." Much depended on the state of discipline of the particular troops and the disposition and digestion of the commanding officer, and no little upon the attitude of the community itself.

One source of irritation was the constant demand for expressions of "loyalty." Of this, John T. Trowbridge, a Massachusetts observer in North Carolina, reported:

"Disloyalty is subdued. . . . They submit to the power which has mastered them, but they do not love it, nor is it reasonable to expect that they should. Many . . . are honestly convinced that secession was a great mistake. . . . They acquiesce quietly . . . and sincerely desire to make the best of their altered circumstances. Of another armed rebellion not the least apprehension need be entertained. . . . Those who are still anxious to see the old issue fought out are not themselves fighting men."

One long-range fire-eater of this class approached General Joseph E. Johnston on a Chesapeake Bay steamer not long after the close of hostilities. "The South was conquered but not subdued," insisted the bellicose young man.

"What was your command, sir?" asked the General.

"Unfortunately," he began, "circumstances made it impossible for me to be in the army," when the old General impatiently cut him off.

"Well, sir, I was. You may not be subdued, but I am."

Whether "subdued" or unreconstructed, the Confederate came to a home where all was changed. The change went deeper than mere material destruction. Men themselves were different, changed in their relations, in their minds.

Joel Chandler Harris, a red-headed boy watching the world from the side of the road in a country town in middle Georgia, wondered at the changes he saw.

"The last trump will cause no greater surprise and consternation the world over than the news of Lee's surrender caused in that region," he wrote later. "The public mind had not been prepared for such an event. . . . Almost every piece of news printed in the journals of the day was colored with the prospect of ultimate victory; and then the curtain came down and the lights went out. . . . [Our people] were confronted by conditions that had no precedent or parallel in the history of the world. It is small fault if their minds failed at first to grasp the significance and the import of these conditions, so new were they and so amazing. . . ."

So much for the whites in that rural section "remote from centers of information." Now as to the Negroes:

"Groups and gangs of negroes were passing and repassing and moving restlessly to and fro, some with bundles and some with none. . . . [Their] restless and uneasy movements were perfectly natural. They had suddenly come to the knowledge that they were free, and they were testing the nature and limits of their freedom. They desired to find out its length and its breadth. It was extraordinary, but not perilous."

Testimony is curiously mixed as to the work and movements of the Negroes in their first spring and summer weeks of freedom, probably because their conduct was as various and contradictory as the evidence. On one thing all are agreed: the pitiful poverty of the Negroes made free without land, work-stock, implements, or any of the ordinary tools of production and living.

Among the Negroes, wrote W. H. Trescott of South Carolina in *DeBow's Review* of the next year, "was no impatience, no insubordination, no violence. They have received their freedom quietly and soberly. They remained pretty steadily on the farms of their masters, a very general disposition being manifest to adjust the terms of compensation on a reasonable basis."

And yet Sidney Andrews, of Massachusetts, who visited South Carolina in the late summer of 1865, was profoundly impressed with the streams of migrant Negroes whom he met all of one moonlit night, each carrying his bundle and making his way to Charleston and the coast, where freedom was supposed to be freer, perhaps. The contradiction of which this is but one typical example probably explains itself by ordinary human differences of masters and slaves.

Various army commanders, faced with the problem of the hordes of migrant Negroes who attached themselves to the camps and garrisons even before the war ended, promulgated regulations which throw some light on happenings. General John M. Schofield, commanding in North Carolina, decreed on May 15 that able-bodied Negroes must support their families, and might not go away from home leaving aged persons helpless. Former masters were constituted guardians of minors in the absence of parents or other near relatives capable of supporting them. All able-bodied persons of suitable age were warned that they were not to be supported by the government or their former masters unless they would work. As to the terms of work, it was suggested that "for the present season they ought to expect only moderate wages" or "a fair share of the crops to be raised."

At Mobile, regulations were that those able to work who refused to do so were to be "put upon forced labor on the public works without pay." The Houston *Telegraph*, in Texas, complained that Negroes were "visiting around" while the cotton crop suffered, but urged tolerance for them on the ground that they were "not responsible for their own emancipation."

In the crop season of that year, it seems, the majority of Negroes stayed on or returned to their old plantations, after their first excursions abroad. In such cases the plantation owners furnished houses, land, stock, tools, seed, food and feed. The Negroes furnished labor. The crop was to be divided under supervision of the garrisons, or of the Freedmen's Bureau as its organization spread.

Many Negroes went away to test their freedom, or to try themselves. "I must go," said one such to a former master. "If I stay here I'll never know I'm free." "I want to move away," said another, "and feel entirely free, and see what I can do by myself"—an ambition understandable and not to be blamed.

Any generalization about a problem of labor complicated by a difference in race is more likely than not to be wrong. The belief was almost universally accepted, and asserted, in the South that Negroes would not work in freedom. The experiences of the first season of freedom should have shown the large measure of fallacy in such broad and general statements. Some Negroes worked; some did not. Some would work for one man and not for another. Some white men were just and considerate, others the reverse. Nor did the fact that a man came from the North insure any greater degree of kindness at his hands. Chaplain Conway, in charge of the Labor Bureau created by General Banks to handle such affairs in the lower Mississippi Valley, reported on July 1 that men from free states were "as ready to whip the freedman . . . as they are to condemn the same conduct on the part of the men who formerly owned the freedmen." In those early days of confusion it was all very various, very puzzling, very human.

The slavery system had always made demands for thought, planning and labor on the owner, and most of all, perhaps, on the wife of the owner, mistress of the plantation. The lifting of bondage from the black man lifted the burden from the white as well. As one Virginia mistress put it—"Freedom! It is we who are freed. We belonged to our Negroes." A lawyer-farmer in Tennessee, when displeased with the slaves on his stock farm, used to threaten to quit the labor of practicing law, stay at home on the farm, and "let all you damned trifling Negroes starve to death." The end of slavery, said Joseph Le Conte, scientist of South Carolina College, took from the white people "an intolerable burden."

With its going began the gradual extinction of the romantic legend of Southern incapacity for effort. The men and the women who restored the South from its prostration of 1865 could, and did, labor with courage and fortitude.

While Southern men made their way across desolation to homes of want and to problems for which no man could see the solution, educators of the North, gathered in the annual meeting of the National Teachers' Association, heard President S. S. Greene declare that "the old slave states are to be new missionary ground" where "we can not only teach the Negroes but can emancipate the 'poor whites' whom ignorance has so long kept in bondage."

Mr. Greene but echoed that most mischievous of all legends about the South, largely created and kept alive by romantic Southerners, that the population of the South was strictly stratified into "aristocrats," "poor white trash" and Negroes.

A people leave upon the land the marks of themselves and their way of life. Not all ante-bellum homes of the South are mansions or cabins. The land is dotted today with others, thousands of them, not large but comfortable and simple and pleasing in line, proportion and design; not the white porticoed mansion of romance, but such houses as the two-story frame in Tennessee where the heroic boy, Sam Davis, lived and is buried; or those cottages in Virginia from which came a nation's leaders; or the low, simple cottage in Kentucky where Jefferson Davis was born, or lovely "Beauvoir" in Mississippi, where he spent his last years; or plain old "Liberty Hall," in Georgia, where Alex Stephens discoursed with his friends; or any one of thousands of others, inhabited by men lost to fame.

People built those houses and lived in them—real people, neither nabobs nor "mean whites," but substantial, middle-of-the-road folk of the sort to whom it is absurd to attempt to stick such thought-saving labels as "cotton aristocracy" or "poor white trash."

At the same meeting in the North at which Mr. Greene promised emancipation for the "poor whites," President Thomas Hill of Harvard called the teachers to "the new work of spreading knowledge and intellectual culture over the regions that sat in darkness." J. P. Wickersham described slave owners as "at heart still opposed to free governments, and their crowning excellencies of free men, free thought, free speech and free schools," while the non-slaveholding whites were pictured as more ignorant than the slaves themselves. The New England Freedmen's Aid Society, in like vein, saw in the black man the force "to which the country must look in a large degree as a counteracting influence against the evil counsels and designs of white freemen."

The war had barely ended, the body of Lincoln was hardly at rest in Springfield. It would have been more than human had all those whose acquaintance with the South was a compound of abolitionist literature and war propaganda refrained from rubbing into the wounds of war the salt of patronage.

It was to be expected. It made oratory easy. It may even have been true, in instances—but it was not wise, for it made more difficult the tremendous task of those, North and South, who sought a nation truly united.

CHAPTER V

"LINCOLN" STATES

IN THE South during those perilous first weeks of peace the main business of living was somehow to live. The Confederacy which the Southern people had sought to set up had crashed into ruin; the state governments within the Confederacy, which might have carried on in an effort to maintain local law and order, were promptly squelched by orders from the War Department. Problems of government rested in Washington, upon the new President and his Cabinet.

One question underlay all others: What is a state of the United States? It is a question which the Constitution itself does not answer in terms. When that document was drawn up, states existed and were accepted as such without attempt at precise definition of their nature. Seventy-five years of national development, differently understood and interpreted by different men, led to four years of war. And still there was large room for most bitter dispute. The war had settled one thing: To use the classic summing-up phrase of Chief Justice Chase, in the case of Texas vs. White, decided in 1868, the war demonstrated that the United States was "an indestructible Union of indestructible states." But still that left open the basic question, What is a state?

Theories abounded, no one of which could be reconciled with all the facts or with the Constitution upon which all professed to be based. The two which most nearly fit into any possible legal theory of a situation which no law ever contemplated, were in every other way farthest apart—that of the Southern leaders, and that of implacable Thaddeus Stevens, to become their archenemy.

Eleven Southern states, asserting their theory of state sovereignty, said that a state could leave the Union. Twenty-two other states said they could not, and made good their saying by force of arms. "Very well," said the Southern states, in effect, "we tried to get out of the Union, and could not. The theory of the sovereignty of a state is dead; the right of secession no longer exists; but the state still exists, with its own state government in being. It is still a member of the Union,

33

and is ready to resume its place, subject to the Constitution and the laws of the United States."

Even while the remnant of the Confederate government was in southward flight, the substance of this view found expression in meetings held through the South, mostly under the leadership of "original Union men" who had opposed secession until their states "went out," and even after that event in many instances. Delegations were sent to Washington, in some cases, to present the view to the President. Meanwhile, it had already found acceptance and recognition in the Sherman-Johnston convention for the surrender of the Army of Tennessee, which recognized the existing state governments and authorized them to enter upon the work of restoration. It was recognized, also, by General Canby, to whom General Taylor surrendered the Confederate forces in Mississippi and Alabama. With the sanction of both the Union and the Confederate commanders, the governors of those two states took steps to assemble their legislatures. Every semblance of Confederate power was ended east of the Mississippi River, by that time, and there was urgent need of some form of government to take its place.

This plan for quick and ready restoration of the states found no acceptance in Washington. There was great disagreement there as to how the states of the Confederacy should be reorganized, but none whatever on the point that reorganized they must be.

To Stevens and his followers, the question was easy. The Southern states seceded. By that act they put themselves out of the Union. The war had been fought not to preserve the Union as it was but to conquer for what remained of it the territory of the South. Now, conquered, it lay in the grasp of the conquerors, to be governed at their will.

According to this relentless logic, neither states nor the Constitution of the United States existed in the South. The land was still there, subject to confiscation for the repayment to the North of the cost of the war and the pensions which would grow out of it. The people were still there, but without political organization or civil rights. These could be conferred or withheld, in the case of some or all or none, at the will of the conqueror.

Between the logical extremes of the Southern and the Stevens views fell the various programs of practical action which were adopted. To President Johnson, himself a strict constitutionalist, the state was almost a metaphysical conception. It was indeed indestructible, either by its own act or that of anyone else. It might continue to exist in a state of suspended animation, it is true, but continue to exist it must, for a Union without states was to him as unthinkable as a state without the framework of the Union.

Speaking to a delegation from Indiana, on April 21, President Johnson summed up his view, which was Lincoln's: "Their life breath [is] only suspended," he said. ". . . It was a State when it went into a rebellion, and when it comes out without the [peculiar] institution it is still a State."

The new President, however, could not accept the Southern view that the government in being at the end of hostilities should be recognized as the "state," even though it might purge itself of the "peculiar institution." To him, all such governments were tainted with treason, "the blackest of crimes." Nor could he agree with Senator Sumner that the states, by their attempted secession, had committed suicide. Still less could he accept the Stevens view that secession had succeeded and that the Southern states were out of the Union.

Among all these conflicting theories he must steer a course which, in the language of Lincoln, would restore these states to their "proper practical relations" with the Union. To work out a principle which would fit both the facts and the Constitution was difficult enough; to apply such a general principle in practice, far more so. How should the new governments of the states be organized, and by whom, and with what powers and rights, and what relations to the Union?

The thing most immediately at hand was to stop the Confederate governors in the South from assembling their legislatures for a restoration of civil government, a course to which they were encouraged by some of the Federal army commanders in the field. Such a movement was brought to an abrupt end by orders to the military to stop any exercise of governmental or legislative functions by Confederate or state officers. Only one state legislature actually got into session, that of Mississippi, and its session on May 18 lasted only one hour. Having deeply deplored the death of President Lincoln, it called a convention to consider the state of affairs, named three commissioners to go to Washington to lay the situation before the President, and adjourned in haste to avoid arrest by the Federal army.

By the end of May the old state governments were thoroughly obliterated, so much so that most of the governors were in prison, along with the civil leaders of the Confederate States. The company was distinguished. President Davis, in a Fortress Monroe gun casemate, under constant guard and surveillance, and afterward in chains, became the symbol of them all. Vice-President Stephens, a number of senators of the Confederate States, all its Cabinet except Secretaries Benjamin and Breckinridge, who made their separate escapes for Europe in open boats putting out from the lonely Florida coast, were to be found that summer of 1865 in military prisons, awaiting trial for treason.

In Washington, were a group of prisoners of different stamp—the miserable conspirators who followed John Wilkes Booth in his mad plot to kill Lincoln. Booth himself was not among them. In spite of close and immediate pursuit, he was able to stay hidden in Virginia not far from Washington for eleven days. Driven by fire from the barn in which he lay, he was shot by Sergeant Boston Corbett. The body was brought to Washington, identified, and, wrapped in an old army blanket, was buried secretly in a cellar, in an unmarked grave filled with quicklime. His diary, which might have shed light on the whole conspiracy, was turned over secretly to Secretary Stanton, and not produced at the trial of his followers. The body and the effects of the man shot by Sergeant Corbett were handled with such an air of mystery as to create in many minds the belief, persisting to this day, that the real Booth escaped.

John H. Surratt, alleged to have been second in command of the conspiracy, did escape. Others accused were rounded up quickly, including Dr. Samuel A. Mudd whose offense was that he set the broken leg of a stranger who came to his house, and Mrs. Mary E. Surratt, a Maryland lady who had come to Washington to keep a boarding-house, and whose part in the conspiracy seems to have consisted principally in being the mother of the missing John Surratt.

The conspirators, confined in heavy irons on board the monitor Saugus, anchored in the Potomac, had their heads hooded in canvas bags through which they could breathe and be fed, but from which they could see not at all. They were so held through all the rest of the month of April, in solitary confinement, each one withdrawn from the world except for the efforts of General Lafayette Baker's Secret Service to trap, wring or cajole from some one of them a statement that the plot was instigated by Confederate leaders.

On May 1, President Johnson ordered their trial by a military commission of nine officers, a precaution supposed to be necessary to secure conviction in the capital city, filled with rumors of widespread Southern plots against the government. To insure further that conviction be had, the zealous Joseph Holt was named trial Judge Advocate. The manner of organization of the court and even more the state of the times combined to deprive the accused of whatever chance of fair trial they were entitled to.

The actual trial began, with all preliminaries out of the way, on May 10, less than a week after the body of President Lincoln came at last to rest in Springfield. The commission sat in the Old Penitentiary, at first in secret session, later in the presence of a few permitted observers. There, in semi-secrecy, all were tried together on the general charge of conspiracy.

The commission completed its work, and took its first vote on sentence on June 28. David E. Herold, G. A. Atzerodt and Lewis Payne, clearly guilty, were sentenced to death by hanging on July 7. Michael O'Loughlin, Edward Spangler and Samuel Arnold, not so clearly nor so deeply involved, were sentenced to imprisonment for life, as was Dr. Mudd, for whose conviction there seems to have been no sufficient reason beyond the hysteria of the times. Sentence was executed upon these four by confinement in forbidding Fortress Jefferson, on the lonely Dry Tortugas.

The case of Mrs. Surratt presented the chief difficulty. Only four members were willing to vote the death penalty for her, and by law six votes must be had. After a night's further consideration, and upon the suggestion of the resourceful Judge Advocate, two more members were brought around to vote for death, with a recommendation of mercy to the President. The commission itself had power to vote the life imprisonment which they recommended, but preferred to pass final responsibility on to the President.

The recommendation of mercy was drawn up and inserted in the findings of the court, which went to the President for review and approval on July 5, two days before the date set for the execution.

It is known now, as it was not then, that the President did not see the recommendation of mercy for the condemned woman, and there is evidence that its concealment from him was intentional and deliberate. With the sentences before him, the President made no exception. All the condemned were to die, Mrs. Surratt along with the three conspirators undoubtedly guilty. The President shut himself away from those who came to beg for her life. On the day appointed, the four, Herold, Atzerodt, Payne and the tottering Mrs. Surratt, were hanged in the prison yard.

The shocked reaction that ran through the country at her execution warned that the time had come to end trials by military commission. The plan of so trying Confederate leaders to insure that "treason must be punished" would not do, unless it was desired to make of the prisoner in Fortress Monroe a martyr to constitutional liberty, in the North as well as the South.

More vital than the question of how to try Confederate leaders for their "treason," or whether to try them at all, was the insistent problem of restoring government in the South. On that subject, the President was bombarded with an unbelievable mass of strangely assorted advice to which he gave methodical attention during weeks of labor from early morn till late at night, with never a break in the tension.

By one ardent Union Leaguer from Tennessee he was warned against Mr. Lincoln's fault of "fattening rebels and starving those who had elevated him to power." Another zealous patriot congratulated the President and the country that "the days of criminal leniency to traitors are over; that milk and water and the oath of allegiance will not longer be relied on as sovereign remedies for treason and rebellion." One pious soul from St. Louis, after discussing Mr. Lincoln's policy and his death, came to the conclusion that "God has clearly indicated that this is not his policy."

Four days after the death of Mr. Lincoln, Gerrit Smith, long a leader of the advanced abolitionists, addressed the President as to proper terms of peace. "A peace which denies the ballot to the black man would be war," he said. The ballot to him was a matter of the heart, and not the head—a not uncommon feeling among the nineteenth-century devotees of the forms of democracy.

"The title to the soil of the whole South," Mr. Smith continued, was equitably "in the blacks and loyal poor whites, the saviors of the nation," and the lands should be divided among them. The rebel masses should be disfranchised for a dozen years, their leaders for life. However, there should be no executions, banishments or imprisonments, such punishment not being in keeping with the conception of conduct becoming to a "highly civilized people" warring against a "pre-eminently barbarous one."

Clamorous "thirst for the blood" of leading rebels changed the attitude of Mr. Smith, largely and quickly, for only five days later he wrote again, denouncing as "absurd" the charge that these men plotted the death of President Lincoln. "They had," he said, "a sincere belief in their cause. . . . The constitutional right of Secession has from the first been extensively believed in. . . . A people however great, should beware of driving to desperation a people however small. . . . The South has suffered enough."

Mr. Smith's letters are significant of the rapid return to sane balance by many in the North, President Johnson among them. Before the time came for final action on the question of Southern governments, the thought of proscriptive punishment had passed from him. He was ready to carry out the Lincoln policy of restoration.

The four "Lincoln states" were first disposed of. The Lincoln governments in Louisiana, Arkansas and Tennessee were continued without formal action. At the Cabinet meeting of May 9 formal recognition of the Alexandria government in Virginia was determined upon. This government had already been recognized for acts of the gravest importance—to register the "consent" of old Virginia to the separation and establishment of West Virginia, in 1862; to "consent" again to the transfer of Jefferson and Berkeley counties to the new state, in 1863. Governor Francis H. Pierpont, who had led the movement to set up West Virginia, was elected "governor of Virginia," or, as it was usually put, of "restored Virginia." The territory of his government consisted of a few toe-holds about the fringes of the state, under United States army protection; its legislative body numbered six senators and seven delegates, representing among them seven counties; its constitutional convention, when one came to be held, consisted of fifteen members, some without credentials; its powers were just what army officers, sometimes hostile and contemptuous, would allow it—except when it came to take its part in amending the Constitution of the United States, which it did by ratifying the proposed Thirteenth Amendment on February 18, 1865.

Recognized by presidential proclamation as the legitimate authority within the "geographical limits known as the state of Virginia," Governor Pierpont moved his government, its staff and its scant archives into Richmond, there to serve liberally and wisely under circumstances of peculiar difficulty.

The Louisiana and Arkansas governments which were tacitly continued had come into being early in 1864 under the "ten-per-cent proclamation" of President Lincoln, and had received his unfailing support until his death.

Efforts to create a new government in Louisiana were begun after the fall of New Orleans. A congressional election was held in December, 1862, under United States military control. B. F. Flanders and Michael Hahn, then chosen, were actually seated in the Thirty-seventh Congress and served until it expired on March 4, 1863. This first restoration movement got no farther, largely because of the ever-ready spirit of faction in Louisiana politics.

Another effort was made by General N. P. Banks, after Lincoln's proclamation of December 8, 1863. By that time Flanders and Hahn had split, and become the leaders of opposing wings of the "Free

State" party. In an election held on Washington's Birthday of 1864, Michael Hahn, backed by General Banks, was chosen provisional governor, with a total vote of 10,725, all cast in parishes occupied by the Union army. The new Governor was a Bavarian by birth, a graduate of the University of Louisiana, a Douglas Democrat in 1860, and editor of the New Orleans *Delta* in 1864.

In separate proclamations, civil and military, the new Governor and the army commander called a constitutional convention to meet in April. As to this, President Lincoln on March 13, 1864, gave private advice to Governor Hahn:

"Now you are about to have a convention, which, among other things, will define the elective franchise," he wrote, "I barely suggest, for your private consideration, whether some of the colored people may not be let in—as, for instance, the very intelligent. . . . But this is only a suggestion, not to the public but to you alone."

The convention, representing white citizens only, sat on the top floor of the City Hall of New Orleans, christened for the purpose, "Liberty Hall." Judge Durell, later to come to nocturnal fame, presided. Christian Roselius, German born and Louisiana's great authority on the civil law, was its most distinguished member until he withdrew because of the iron-clad oath required.

The convention abolished slavery, at the same time requesting compensation from the government for "loyal" slaveholders. It sidestepped President Lincoln's suggestion on suffrage for Negroes, authorizing the forthcoming legislature to act on the subject. It approved General Banks's order for education of both races in separate schools; authorized lotteries; moved the state capital to New Orleans; submitted the constitution to an election to be held in September of 1864; called a meeting of the new legislature for October; and finally adjourned, leaving in the hands of its chairman certain vague and indefinite powers of reconvening the body. These powers, whatever they were, were looked upon as of no importance when granted. Later their attempted exercise was to become the inciting cause of the great New Orleans riots of 1866.

As a foretaste of much more generous bodies to meet thereafter, the convention spent on itself in the 78 days of its session $125,000, which included, besides the usual items of per diem and mileage, such trimmings as $9,421.55—or $120 a day—for liquors and cigars; $4,394.25 for carriage hire; $8,111.55 for stationery, $7,000 for printing, and $4,237.50 for daily papers for the delegates; and $160 for a pen case presented to General Banks as a token of esteem.

The Hahn constitution was ratified by a vote of only 6,836, cast in twenty parishes. Under it senators and representatives in Congress were chosen and sent to Washington. The Congress then in session was the same which broke with President Lincoln's plan of restoration during the previous summer. Its ideas of what it took to constitute a restored state differed from those of Mr. Lincoln. It demanded a government based on the votes of a majority of the electorate, not merely ten per cent. It believed in a more general and rigorous disfranchisement of ex-Confederates than did the President. It claimed the right to pass on the whole set-up of the new state governments which the President was organizing. As its only effective means of asserting the claim at this time, Congress, in the exercise of its right to admit or reject members, declined to accept or seat those offering themselves from the new "Lincoln state" of Louisiana.

The "Lincoln government" in Arkansas had its beginning in a mass meeting of "loyal" men in Fort Smith, held in October, 1863. From it grew a "constitutional convention" held in Little Rock in January, 1864, to organize under the ten-per-cent plan. There were forty-five delegates, claiming to represent twenty-three of the state's fifty-seven counties, whom the Credentials Committee divided into three curiously illuminating classes—those "regularly elected," those "appointed" by parties not named, and those "entitled to seats" for reasons not mentioned.

The convention declared secession void, abolished slavery, repudiated the state's Confederate debt and chose as provisional governor, Isaac Murphy, a mountain schoolteacher and lawyer, the only member of the Secession Convention of 1861 who held out to the end for the Union. The whole new scheme of government was submitted to an election to be held in those counties within the Federal lines on March 11, 1864, when the Constitution was ratified by some twelve thousand votes out of a normal electorate of fifty-four thousand and a legislature was chosen. Two votes cast in Little Rock, one his own and the other that of a man unknown, elected the representative from Desha County, one hundred and twenty-five miles from the capital.

On April 18, 1864, the Murphy government was formally inaugurated. The legislature, with two long sessions that year, devoted much of its time to matters of revenue, mainly the matter of insuring payment of per diem and mileage to the members. They passed laws against guerrillas, bushwhackers, and jayhawkers, and a stay law for the relief of "loyal" debtors from suits at the hands of "rebel" creditors.

William Fishback, a disappointed ex-Confederate, and Elisha Baxter were elected to the Senate of the United States but, like the Louisiana offering, were rejected by Congress. However, at a third session, the legislature on April 3, 1865, ratified the proposed Thirteenth Amendment abolishing slavery—which action was accepted as entirely valid. Arkansas, it would appear, though not yet enough in the Union to elect senators, was qualified to amend the fundamental law of the United States, regardless, even, of the technical objection that no quorum was present when the legislature acted.

In Tennessee, Andrew Johnson himself, while military governor of that state, received from President Lincoln authority to organize a "republican form of government." A convention of Tennessee Unionists, of whom there were many, met in Nashville on July 1, 1863. Presiding was the aged Major William B. Lewis, long before intimate friend and member of the famous "Kitchen Cabinet" of Andrew Jackson. With their help, and by Lincoln's authority, Governor Johnson called a mass convention to meet in January, 1864, and elections to be held on March 5 of that year. The oath prescribed by the Governor was more stringent than the Lincoln amnesty oath, a fact which caused considerable confusion. Partly because of it the March elections degenerated into a "serious farce" and the first movement collapsed.

In the next month a new movement was started, this time at Knoxville in East Tennessee, where the largest part of the Union population lived. A convention, gathered there to take steps toward separating East Tennessee from the rest of the state, as West Virginia had been cut from Virginia, decided instead to organize to govern the whole state. A state convention was called to meet in Nashville on May 30, to organize the Union men and to select delegates to the National Union Convention at Baltimore, at which, as it turned out, Andrew Johnson was to be named on the ticket with Lincoln.

At a second convention, called for September 5 to act on state questions, the split began between the Radical and the Conservative wings of the Union party—to anticipate names which afterward came into common use. The credentials committee seated only Radicals, whose control was further strengthened by a proclamation of Governor

Johnson, on the holding of the presidential election in November. He required the taking of an iron-clad oath which, in its practical effect, bound the would-be voter to support the Lincoln and Johnson ticket if he wanted to cast a ballot. The McClellan electors withdrew and the votes of the state went, of course, for the National Union ticket—which, in 1864, it will be noted, was broader than the Republican party. Congress refused to receive and count the electoral vote of the state, but it recognized the election of Andrew Johnson as vice-president.

As in Louisiana, the Union party in Tennessee was badly split. A harmony convention was called to meet in the Capitol on December 9, but by that time Hood's Confederate army was back in Tennessee and sitting down before Nashville. The convention had to be postponed until January 8, a day much celebrated in Tennessee in honor of Old Hickory's victory at New Orleans. Five hundred delegates from sixty counties met on the ninth, the eighth being Sunday, with a basis of voting that assured Radical control, and, in the name of the people, assumed revolutionary powers.

Amendments to the state constitution were submitted to an election to be held on Washington's Birthday. A governor and legislature were to be elected later, on March 4, by an extraordinary arrangement of a "general ticket" on which all one hundred and nine members were to be voted on by all the voters of every county. No chances were taken this time upon the election.

The first election ratified the amendments to the state constitution, including the one abolishing slavery. Andrew Johnson resigned as military governor of the state and went to Washington to be inaugurated on March 4. On that day, William G. Brownlow was elected governor, to be inaugurated after an interregnum of a month, on April 5.

The new Governor was an extraordinary character. Born in Virginia in 1805, he became a circuit rider of the Methodist Church at the age of twenty-one, thereby earning the name of "Parson" which never left him. In 1838 he began the publication of the Knoxville Whig. Five years later he ran for Congress, to be defeated by Andrew Johnson. In his family and private life he was gentle enough. In his editorials and speeches, caustic, bitter and vituperative, he was anti-secession but not anti-slavery. Only two years before the outbreak of war he had upheld the "institution" in public debate with a Northern minister at Philadelphia.

With the coming of war, and with East Tennessee forcibly held by Confederate troops, the Parson found it necessary to escape to the North. There he remained in exile, picturesquely lecturing to huge and profitable audiences on the persecution of Unionists in East Tennessee by the "hell-born and hell-bound rebels." In the spring of 1864, with the state cleared of Confederate forces, he returned to Tennessee and now, largely by grace of his ancient enemy, Andrew Johnson, he was at the head of the government of the state.

It was Tennessee's misfortune that the new Governor, like so many of the more single-minded Reconstructionists, felt that he was called to preach and to execute the righteous judgments of a wrathful God. These judgments which aforetime had been directed at Baptists, Presbyterians, Democrats and Abolitionists, were now concentrated on "rebels," by which the Parson meant not only those who had actively or passively aided the Confederacy but also those who did not now support his own régime.

Senators and congressmen whom Tennessee sent to Washington were not seated, but the state was considered sufficiently in the Union to count the vote of its legislature, cast on April 3, 1865, as valid in the ratification of the pending Thirteenth Amendment.

Thus when the Confederacy collapsed, four of its late states had governments of a sort, seven had none. The great task of providing a machinery for restoring these the new President inherited from President Lincoln. To aid and advise him he had the same Cabinet officers who had served Lincoln, and who had heard his views and plans for the same work.

CHAPTER VI

THE RADICALS DECLARE WAR

AT President Lincoln's last Cabinet meeting, held on the day of his assassination, Secretary Stanton presented a "rough draft" of a plan for the "reconstruction of the rebel states." An amended draft of the same plan, submitted at the first meeting of the Cabinet under President Johnson, was not given detailed consideration until May 9, the day on which the Pierpont government in Virginia was formally recognized.

The draft proclamation, drawn for North Carolina but intended as a model for other states as well, called for a constitutional convention whose members were to be elected by "loyal citizens of the United States residing within the state."

"What do you mean by 'loyal citizens'?" demanded Secretary Welles.

"Blacks and whites," snapped Stanton.

Before many weeks the difficulties in determining the various grades and shades of "loyalty" among the white population of the South were to become apparent, but this first discussion turned on the political status of the Negroes. The Secretary of War, supported by Attorney-General Speed and Postmaster-General Denison, argued that the President of the United States had power to say who should vote in North Carolina or any other of the rebel states, and that this power extended to enfranchising the newly freed blacks. Other Cabinet members, except the wounded Secretary of State Seward who was still absent, stood on the old constitutional view that the Federal government had no power to enlarge the electorate of a state.

No such question could have been raised before secession. Suffrage, in those days, was still regarded in its historical light as a privilege rather than a right, to be granted or withheld by each state. Unlimited manhood suffrage was by no means universal. In sixteen of the "loyal" states Negroes did not vote at all; in most of the other six only those were allowed to vote who could meet property or educational tests more stringent than those applied to whites. The matter was one for state action in the way prescribed by the Constitution.

45

Advocates of immediate Negro suffrage in the South proposed to continue to leave the question to state action in the North, where Negroes were few and the question of small practical political importance, but to have the President of the United States by executive proclamation make voters of the great numbers of freedmen in the South.

Senator Sumner furnished a theory for such action—that the constitutional obligation upon the United States to guarantee to each state a "republican form of government" required that universal manhood suffrage be imposed in each Southern state as it resumed its political life. Senator Sumner furnished the theory, but Representative Thaddeus Stevens phrased the reason—the practical need of the votes of the slaves just freed to assure a "perpetual ascendancy to the Party of the Union."

Neither theory nor reason appealed to President Johnson. He did not oppose Negro suffrage as such, as did so many Southern Unionists, provided always that it should come about by action of the states themselves in the way prescribed by the Constitution. Constitutional short-cuts, such as Sumner's "republican government" theory, he could not tolerate, while to him Stevens' blunt and practical disregard of that instrument of government when it stood in the way of his plans was unthinkable.

On May 24 the President submitted to the Cabinet his final plan for the restoration of the states of the South, and asked of each member his individual opinion. Every man, including Secretary Stanton, approved. The plan so approved was presented to the nation in the President's two proclamations of May 29, 1865.

One proclamation, that of amnesty, applied to all states. Closely following Lincoln's proclamation of 1863, it made possible the creation of a body of "loyal" citizens. Without demanding impossible professions as to past conduct, it admitted to amnesty those who would take the oath to support "henceforth" the Constitution and the laws of the United States. To the eight classes of Confederate leaders, civil and military, excluded from amnesty by the Lincoln proclamation, President Johnson added six others. The only really significant addition was that which barred from amnesty those who combined in their persons the double offense of having supported the Confederacy and of owning property worth twenty thousand dollars or more.

This clause, an outgrowth of the new President's long and bitter fight against the Southern "aristocracy," was a feeble echo of his blasts of anathema against them during the war. "Treason must be made odious, and traitors must be seized and impoverished," he had shouted at Nashville, the year before. "Their great plantations must be seized and divided into small farms and sold to honest, industrious men."

The responsibility of power was laying upon Mr. Johnson its sobering weight. There were to be no widespread proscriptions and confiscations. Any individual in the classes excepted from general benefit of the amnesty proclamations might apply to the President for pardon. In granting such pardons when sued for, the new President continued Mr. Lincoln's spirit of liberality.

Through the operation of the amnesty proclamations and the exercise of the pardoning power by the two Presidents, the word "loyal" came to acquire a curious variety of meanings in the South. There were the "truly loyal," those who had supported the Union cause through the war, who had endured much, and who, quite naturally, felt themselves entitled to take charge of the Reconstruction. Of them there were not many outside Tennessee.

Then there were the plain "loyal," who had managed to lie low and escape actual service for the Confederacy, or for the Union either, and so were in position to claim "loyalty" to either government which might win. Of somewhat the same stripe were those who had served the Confederacy halfheartedly and now claimed benefit of "loyalty" because such service was not voluntary.

Then there were the true and genuine Confederates who, by virtue of compliance with the terms of the President's proclamation, were enabled to re-enter the body politic when "amnestied" or pardoned and to claim the rights and privileges of "loyalty."

Such individuals of these various "loyal" classes as were entitled to vote under the constitution of each state as it stood in 1861 became the political people to whom was to be entrusted the operation of the restored state government. Freedmen, not having been entitled to vote by the ante-bellum constitutions, were not of this body.

The Radicals were disappointed, outraged. They had assiduously courted Johnson since he came to the Presidency and had taken his patience under their bombardment of suggestions and advice as assent to their views. Now his proclamation left out the thing that to them was all-important, the immediate extension of the vote to the freedmen by presidential fiat. From the day of its issue they declared war on Johnson's policy, as they had warred on Lincoln's.

It was, at first, a somewhat private war. There was in the country too much of the sentiment of peace and reunion to be attacked in the open. More subtle methods were necessary, those of delay, of appeal to the ever-ready springs of prejudice, jealousy, fear and passion; of "education," which had not then come to be called propaganda. "If we cannot yet control public opinion on the direct suffrage issue, or hold a sure majority in Congress on that," wrote one Radical to another, "perhaps other topics, nearer to the popular appreciation, may serve to unite enough to prevent final action for the present. Meantime we will educate."

The lines of attack were diverse—any line at all which might lead any man to oppose the policy of speedy restoration and to vote for delay, at the least, if not for some plan to restore the Southern states only after they had been remade to the Radical pattern.

The men who planned the war, and their purposes and motives, were as diverse as the lines of attack. Charles Sumner, sincere in his enthusiasm for lofty moral purposes, from Olympian heights of superior civic virtue, often allowed his passion for equality in the abstract to obscure for him the main practical points of the political struggle. His fellow-Senator, Benjamin Wade—"Bluff Ben," his friends called him—never overlooked practical points in the fight which was to bring him to that day when the vote of but one man stood between him and the Presidency of the United States.

In the Cabinet was Edwin M. Stanton, capable, immensely energetic, despotic, nervous, irritable and irritating, convinced of his mission to stay in the Cabinet after he had broken with his chief, and from this confidential point of vantage to keep up the war to save the nation from rebels and traitors—a Messianic complex which led him into strange obliquities. Perhaps, after all, the ordinary decencies of human intercourse and obligation seemed trivial to a man bent on saving a nation from itself.

In the House was another, Thaddeus Stevens, the strongest Radical of them all. Vermont-born and raised, Pennsylvania-trained in the practicalities of politics, he was by nature in opposition. In his early political life this spirit found its expression in savage attacks on the board of commissioners in charge of Pennsylvania's program of canals and public improvements, until he was made one of the board. With the same vehemence, he opposed the Masonic order, until the anti-Masonic political movement played out. One thing he favored, protection for Pennsylvania industries, being himself interested in the manufacture of iron.

He could not long remain interested in being "for" a policy, how-

ever. With nothing to fight against, he lost interest in Congress and
retired, to come back into public life on the anti-slavery issue, at the
age of sixty-seven, and at once to find himself so far in advance of his
colleagues that he was generally in opposition, not only to the Southerners but to most of his associates and to President Lincoln himself.

The man was a born Radical. To use such powers as his to tilt
against Freemasonry was a little ridiculous; to ride the storm of the
revolution after Lincoln was more in keeping. The South he hated,
and his hatred was not assuaged by the burning of his Pennsylvania
iron works by Confederate soldiers. Hate was his driving force;
searing sarcasm, his main weapon. Goading his opponents to rash-
ness, he remained cold, relentless, implacable.

Others there were, but these four were the heart and center of
the Radical junta which was to take over the Republican party
from the Conservatives who would have continued the policy of
Lincoln; and with that powerful machinery were to take over the
government of the nation, to change profoundly its form and nature,
and all but destroy its foundations.

Yet these men were working to save the government, as they
understood it; and, regardless of their methods, it cannot be said
that their motives were entirely selfish, or even wholly partisan.
They wrought revenge upon the South but to them it was not revenge
but retribution, such retribution as might have delighted the soul of
an ancient Israelitish prophet rejoicing upon the downfall of Babylon.
The most conspicuous feature of their professed program was the
uplift of the Southern Negro, but by firing antagonisms and em-
bittering relations of the races in the South they did him immense
disservice. To the Negroes, said Beecher, the co-operation of the
"wise and good citizens of the South . . . the kindness of the white
man in the South is more important than all the policies of the
nation put together."

A major intent of the Radical policy was to make the Southern
states safely and permanently Republican, but by their political
pressure they did what four years of war did not do—fused Whigs
of the old line and Democrats into a political unit in the Democratic
party, the "Solid South."

The leading Radicals of the North, and their followers of varying
shades and degrees, were concerned that the civil rights and political
privileges of the newly freed "allies of the party of the Union" should
be secured and protected. The Radicals of the South were not interested in rights or votes for Negroes, except, in most cases, to

oppose them. Their major concern was the proper and sufficient punishment of their Confederate neighbors—some of whom had undoubtedly despitefully used Southern loyalists as long as the power of the Confederacy endured.

To these loyalists who now with the return of peace came forward to claim the places at the first table in the house of their fathers, it was no less than wormwood and gall that "amnestied" Confederates should be included among the "loyal."

That Confederates should be allowed to take the oath of amnesty was no more bitter to the "loyal," however, than was the taking of it to many a Confederate. Confederate soldiers who had surrendered with arms in their hands, and given their parole oaths binding themselves to observe the laws in force, felt that to require of them a further oath to the same effect was an indignity not to be borne.

To an officer who had not asked for presidential pardon because he could not bring himself to express regret for what he had done for the Confederacy, General Joseph E. Johnston said:

"You don't have to express any regret. Oh, yes, I did, too. I requested that His Excellency would grant me a pardon, and expressed regret that I could offer him no reason why he should."

General Lee's unceasing advice, and that of most of the military leaders of the South, was to take the oath, not to remain "unreconstructed."

When young Captain George Wise reported to his father, ex-governor of Virginia and ex-brigadier general C. S. A., that he had taken the oath, the old Governor was shocked, mortified.

"You have disgraced the family, sir!" he cried.

"But, father, General Lee advised me to do it," replied the Captain.

"That alters the case. Whatever General Lee advises is right."

General Lee not only advised; he sought by personal example to lead the way. On June 13, just two weeks after the President's proclamation of amnesty, he himself, being within the excepted classes, applied for pardon and the privilege of taking the oath. The privilege for which he asked was not then granted, although he was included, with all others, in the general proclamation of amnesty issued by President Johnson on Christmas Day of 1868. By reason of his advice and example, however, thousands of devoted young Confederates, the backbone of the future citizenship of the South, were led to make their peace with the government.

CHAPTER VII

"JOHNSON" STATES

AT THE same time that he provided for the creation of a "loyal" political people, President Johnson began to set up by separate proclamation for each state a plan for governmental machinery, and to name the men to put the machinery in motion. Between May 29 and July 13 seven such proclamations were issued, one for each of the states still without any form of civil government.

The first, issued on the same day as the general amnesty proclamation, applied to the President's native state of North Carolina. There the President chose as provisional governor, William W. Holden, editor of the Raleigh *Standard*. During the decade before 1860, the *Standard*, strongest of the organs of the Democrats, then the minority party in North Carolina, preached the right of secession. When the exercise of that right became imminent, it opposed such action until after President Lincoln called on the state for troops. Then Mr. Holden became a member of the convention of 1861, where he hurled himself into the movement with such vigor that he was reported, even, to have proposed to bequeath as a precious heirloom to posterity the pen with which he signed the Ordinance of Secession. Later, in the days of Mr. Holden's vigorous Unionism, the statement was denied but was reiterated by those present.

Mr. Holden's change of heart began early, before the first year of the war was out. At the first election during the war years, the *Standard* supported for governor young Lieutenant Colonel Zebulon B. Vance, of the county of Buncombe and the army of the Confederacy, under the mistaken impression that Colonel Vance's outspoken criticisms of the government at Richmond meant that he would favor a separate peace for North Carolina, and its return to the Union. In this mistaken estimate of Colonel Vance, Mr. Holden was not alone. In the North, Vance was called the "Northern or Federal candidate" and his election was hailed widely as the beginning of a breakup of the Confederacy, instead of the beginning of a more vigorous prosecution of the war on the part of the state of North Carolina, which it was.

51

At the second election in the war-period, held in 1863, Mr. Holden himself ran for the office of governor, which he had long coveted and had sought in 1858. His platform was peace, and his support mostly from the Heroes of America, better known as the "Red Strings," to which the North looked for a separate peace movement in North Carolina. In the election, Mr. Holden was most ingloriously defeated by Governor Vance.

The unstable Holden as a leader among the Union element showed the zeal of a convert and all the considerable ability of an experienced editor and practiced politician. In the adjoining state of Tennessee the vigorous Union military governor was Andrew Johnson, born in Raleigh. With him, Editor Holden entered into correspondence to further the cause of the Union. From this correspondence, and from the prestige of his long record of political power in North Carolina, there came to him at last the coveted governorship of his state—or, at least, a provisional governorship subject to the superior power of the military.

His instructions were to call an election for members of a constitutional convention; to hold the convention and write a new constitution; to hold elections for state and local offices for the new government to be so created—in general, to get civil government going in constitutional form, or as nearly so as the disturbed state of the times would allow. In the meanwhile, he was to appoint necessary local officials to carry on.

More fortunate than his first selection of a provisional governor, was President Johnson's second appointment, that of William L. Sharkey, named for Mississippi on June 13. As a boy of fifteen Judge Sharkey had fought with Andrew Jackson's Tennesseans at New Orleans. Eighteen distinguished years he had served as Chief Justice of the High Court of Errors and Appeals of Mississippi. In the stormy days of '60 and '61 he had been a leader of the Union party in the state. When Governor Clarke's Confederate legislature held its one-hour session on May 18, it named him as one of the commissioners to call on President Johnson about the Federal relations of the state. Penniless himself as a result of war, as was Judge William Yerger, the other commissioner, they procured a younger friend, James Hamilton, Jr., a "moneyed man," to go along as a sort of secretary and treasurer of the mission, with the privilege of paying its expenses. From their interviews with the President resulted the happy choice of Judge Sharkey as provisional governor.

As an appointee of the President, under his war power, Governor

Sharkey was entitled to draw pay for himself and support for his government from the War Department. Devoted to the Union as he was, he yet held to his old-fashioned constitutional idea of the self-reliance and independence proper to a state. Not regarding himself as an official of the United States, he declined to draw government pay. To raise in Mississippi the money to support Mississippi government was his plan, in which he succeeded so well that during the half year of his administration of affairs the state's income was more than twice its modest expenditure of $68,942.

On June 17 the President made two appointments—James Johnson for Georgia and Andrew Jackson Hamilton for Texas.

General Hamilton, "Big Injun" or "Colossal Jack" to the Texans, had been a picturesque figure in the life of that state for many years. At the outbreak of war he represented the state in Congress. As a follower of old Sam Houston he held with the Union. Early in 1862 he escaped from Texas to Mexico. From there he made his way to New Orleans, where he joined the Union Army to become a brigadier general in southwestern service.

Governor Johnson, the President's appointee in Georgia, was a lawyer of good standing in Columbus, who had served one term in Congress ten years before the war, whose Unionism was undoubted but not narrow and rabid. His appointment, in fact, was not pleasing to some of the extra-"loyal" but was well received by most of the people of the state. In the task of bringing the people to enter into the work of restoration he had the powerful help of the "war governor," Joseph E. Brown. Governor Brown, after an imprisonment of but one week following his arrest in May, returned to Georgia through Washington, where he had an interview with the President. With his strong streak of the practical, he came back to the state to urge upon its people acceptance of the situation.

On June 21 the President named Alabama's provisional governor— Lewis Eliphalet Parsons, born in New York, grandson of the Puritan divine, Jonathan Edwards, a resident of Talladega since 1840, and a lawyer who seems to have succeeded in being on both sides during the war. His appointment came only after a sharp struggle with four leading candidates, only one of whom could lay claim to the rank of "truly loyal." Two of the aspirants had deserted the Confederate service, however, which fact gave them some claim to the title of "loyal." Governor Parsons was hard to place. By some it was said that he had been head of the Peace Society, an organization of obstructionists in Alabama devoted to hamstringing the Confederacy in its war efforts. At any rate, he and two others met on May 1 with General Steele at Montgomery to inform him that two-thirds of the people of the state were willing to "take up arms" to "put down the rebels"—which was more than two members of the delegation had done for that, or any other, purpose while the fighting was on.

Peculiar interest was shown in the choice of a provisional governor for South Carolina. On the last day of June, Benjamin Franklin Perry, lawyer and editor of Greenville, was named, and the "people of South Carolina rejoiced," according to one observer. He had been a leader of Union sentiment in the state, and was among the few in South Carolina to fight secession. When secession came he "went with his state," according to the Southern conception of the duty of a citizen. A son served as a Confederate colonel. Governor Perry was a man of character and honesty. His great failing for the essentially revolutionary task to which he was called was a legalistic rigidity of mind cast in the old constitutional molds.

Last of the provisional governors to be appointed was William Marvin, named for Florida on July 13. Governor Marvin had been Judge of the United States Court at Key West for twenty-five years. When war came and other Federal officials there resigned, he stood resolutely for the Union, and so remained throughout the war. As a jurist of real distinction, particularly on matters of admiralty law, and a citizen of standing, his appointment was welcomed by the ex-Confederates—more, probably, than by some of the zealous loyalists of the state.

While the President was taking these first steps toward the organization of the seven "Johnson states," the four "Lincoln states" of Louisiana, Arkansas, Tennessee and Virginia were well away on their course of government and politics.

Even before the death of President Lincoln, Louisiana had changed governors. During the last winter of the war, Governor Hahn secured election to the United States Senate at the hands of the legislature. On March 4, 1865, he resigned as governor to go to Washington, the first of a long line of Southern Reconstruction governors who used their large and persuasive influence with their legislatures to elect themselves to the more desirable post of senator. Less fortunate than those who came after him, the Louisiana Senator-elect was to be denied the coveted seat.

To succeed Hahn as governor of Louisiana, there came to the front J. Madison Wells, whom both the Hahn and the Flanders factions had put forward the year before as their candidate for lieutenant-governor when the Free-State party split. The new Governor was a Union man, an ex-slaveholder from western Louisiana, apparently inclined to a conciliatory policy toward the Confederates returning to their homes through the spring and summer of 1865, and correspondingly mistrusted by the Radicals—a mistrust which thereafter was to extend to both parties.

In Arkansas, where conditions approaching chaos had existed for nearly two years, Governor Murphy was making some progress toward the reorganization of local government. At first, he found his efforts opposed by the Confederate part of the population, but by the end of May, when it became clear to all men that the Confederacy was no more, he received some help from that direction. The Governor tried to secure good men for the work of local government, depending upon special elections in some instances, and upon the recommendations of local mass meetings in others. More rarely, he made his own choice. Considering the difficulties of his task and his position, the progress made was considerable.

In effect, the President recognized the Brownlow government in Tennessee by his proclamation of June 13, declaring the end of the rebellion in that state. This government had been in full and zealous operation since April 2, when the legislature met.

The most important act of the legislature was a law disfranchising for a period of five years all who could not affirmatively prove their unconditional Union sentiments, and for fifteen years all who took a leading part in the Rebellion. No one was to be allowed to vote who did not hold a "certificate," to be issued only to those of proved "loyalty."

Other acts designed to keep the state safely within the Union were a libel and sedition law and a county patrol law. The first was aimed at those whose criticism of the new order might prove irritating to the authorities. The second, ostensibly aimed at guerrillas, had the effect of putting in the hands of the Governor an armed force in each county which could be used to carry out his ideas.

The spirit of the new government is indicated by the passage in the House of a bill to punish by a fine of as much as fifty dollars the wearing of the "rebel uniform" at a time when thousands of paroled Confederate soldiers were still making their way home wearing as the only clothes they had, or could get, the uniforms in which they surrendered. The Senate likewise passed a bill to prevent ministers who had sympathized with the Confederacy from performing marriages, while the House passed one to require that all who would enter into matrimony must take the oath of allegiance before the license would be issued.

The requirement of oath-taking at every turn which became such a prominent feature of Reconstruction legislation and administration reached a high point in the new Drake constitution adopted by the state of Missouri on June 6, 1865. To enumerate the various acts and attitudes of mind which would disqualify a would-be voter required a clause two printed pages long. Besides disqualification for voting, the instrument barred Confederates, certainly a most substantial minority of the population of the state, from such occupations as practicing law, teaching, preaching, or solemnizing marriages, without taking an iron-clad oath as to past, present and future conduct. These disqualifications were imposed not only for acts done but for so vague a thing as "desire" for the success of, or "sympathy" toward, the Confederate cause. To secure the right to do anything, almost, beyond breathing and paying taxes required the taking of an iron-clad oath.

So proscriptive was this constitution that outstanding Union men refused to take the oath required. Frank P. Blair, as much as any one man responsible for the fact that Missouri remained in the Union, was one of these. In his uniform of a major general of the United States Army, he presented himself before the registrars, demanded the right to vote without taking the oath, and was refused— for the new constitution contained yet another remarkable feature, that only those qualified under its terms were to be allowed to vote on its ratification. In spite of all such precautions, the proscriptive document received a majority of less than two thousand out of a total vote of nearly eighty-five thousand.

In contrast to the narrow and vindictive tone of the new Missouri constitution and the new government in Tennessee, was the message of Governor Pierpont to the restored legislature of Virginia, on June 20, when it met for the first time in Richmond for a four-day session. Recommending liberal enfranchisement laws, the Governor said:

"It is folly to suppose that a State could be governed under a republican form of government, wherein a large portion of the State, nineteen-twentieths of the people, are disfranchised and cannot hold office."

Such heresy from such a source could not be allowed to pass unchallenged. Radicals in Virginia attacked the Governor himself, with the suggestion that since his government had abandoned its hole-and-corner existence about Alexandria and moved into Richmond he had fallen under the influence of the "slave aristocracy." The Radical strategists in Washington attacked not only the Governor but his government as a mere product of presidential usurpation, without rightful warrant or validity—in spite of the fact that the only possible legal or constitutional excuse for the existence of the newly separated state of West Virginia, or for the subsequent annexation to that state of the counties of Berkeley and Jefferson, was the consent to its formation given in the name of Virginia by this same Pierpont government.

CHAPTER VIII

Government Helps and Hindrances

As THE provisional governors were appointed, the President directed the civil branches of the United States government to resume their functions in each state—the courts to sit, the Treasury to collect its customs and dues, the Post Office to extend its service.

Besides these accustomed agencies of government, a third was being installed and organized at the same time—the Bureau for Refugees, Freedmen and Abandoned Lands, under the War Department.

And behind and over all was still the military, for even the provisional governors, despite their titles, were but subordinates of the President in his capacity as commander-in-chief of the army, and their orders and policies were not seldom overruled and set aside by the generals commanding in the various states.

In its actual workings in contact with the people, government was vexatiously divided between the garrisons, the local officials appointed by the provisional governors, the Treasury Department of the United States through its cotton agents, and the Freedmen's Bureau. The army remained the real power.

Occupation of the South had raised thorny questions of policy and administration as the army in its vast sweep of conquest gathered to itself great numbers of Negroes, and considerable acreage of captured and abandoned lands, mostly along the Georgia and Carolina coast and the lower reaches of the Mississippi River.

When the problem was new and small, in the first months of the war, General Benjamin F. Butler was able to dispose of it with his off-hand ruling that slaves coming into his lines at Fortress Monroe, being capable of "giving aid and comfort to the enemy," were to be treated as captured contraband of war. "Contrabands" they became and remained to the end of the struggle, but when their numbers grew to tens of thousands, and came to include whole families, the aged, the infirm, the women and the children as well as the able-bodied men, the General's epigram broke down as a treatment of the situation.

As harassed army commanders wrestled with the unfamiliar intri-

58

cacies of uncertain African relations, a variety of organizations and methods were tried. The most extensive and the best known were the Labor Bureau of General Banks, operating on seized or abandoned plantations along the Mississippi, including the home place of Jefferson Davis below Vicksburg, and the projects of the two Shermans, first T. W. and then W. T., on the Sea Islands of the Carolina and Georgia coast, where captured and abandoned lands were divided into small plots and assigned to slave families.

Besides the army, sanitary commissions, missionary societies, freedmen's aid societies, and other benevolent agencies of the North labored in the vineyard. The Northern philanthropic organizations, in fact, were inclined to denounce General Banks's well-meant efforts to maintain a degree of order and industry and to reduce pauperism among the one hundred and fifty thousand Negroes within his command as being no better than a "re-enactment of slavery." The same charge was to be made, with more heat and persistence, against the body of acts later passed by the first legislatures of the restored states, and given the generic name of the "Black Codes."

For more than a year before the fighting ended, the need for a system better than an active competition in half-baked benevolence was glaringly apparent. Bills before Congress to centralize the control of the whole matter were debated actively through three sessions before the final passage on March 3, 1865, of the bill to establish the Freedmen's Bureau.

The next day Congress adjourned and left to President Lincoln the organization of the Bureau. He chose as its head Major General O. O. Howard, although the appointment was not actually made until May 15, and then by President Johnson, who carried out his predecessor's plan by naming the young General as commissioner of the Bureau. General Howard, a graduate of Bowdoin College and West Point, had commanded a corps in Sherman's army. He was a man of high character and good intentions, whom his friends liked to call the "Christian soldier." Those who did not agree with his views were likely to call him visionary, but it is probable that no better man was available for the immensely complex and difficult task for which he was chosen.

On May 30, the day after the President put in motion the machinery of amnesty and political restoration in the seceded states, General Howard announced the division of the former slave territory into ten districts of the Bureau, with an assistant commissioner for each district.

The first district comprised Washington, into which great numbers of freedmen flocked during and just after the war, together with all Maryland and the counties of Alexandria, Fairfax and Loudoun in Virginia. Colonel John Eaton, Jr., who had had considerable success with work among the freedmen in Tennessee and Arkansas was put in charge. Colonel Orlando Brown, with headquarters at Richmond, was in charge for Virginia. North Carolina was under Colonel Eliphalet Whittlesey, a school superintendent in Ohio before the war, with headquarters at Raleigh. South Carolina and Georgia were grouped together, with General Rufus Saxton, who was in charge of General Sherman's Sea Island experiment, as assistant commissioner, with headquarters at Beaufort, South Carolina. Colonel T. W. Osborne, with headquarters at Tallahassee, had charge of Florida, and General Wager Swayne, with headquarters at Montgomery, of Alabama.

Chaplain T. W. Conway, who had been in charge of General Banks's efforts in Louisiana, was returned to New Orleans as assistant commissioner. Colonel Samuel Thomas, from his headquarters at Vicksburg, sent forth homilies of good advice to whites and blacks in his district, the state of Mississippi. Kentucky and Tennessee were grouped together, under General Clinton B. Fisk as assistant commissioner, with headquarters at Nashville. General J. W. Sprague had charge of Missouri and Arkansas, with headquarters first at St. Louis, later at Little Rock. Texas was not included in the first division of territory but afterward General E. M. Gregory was sent to Galveston to establish the work of the Bureau in that state.

The assistant commissioners were military men of good standing, in all cases, and with considerable experience in dealing with the affairs of freedmen within the Union lines during the war, in most instances. As was to be expected, they held a distinct bias in favor of the freedmen, and in some cases a prejudice against their former owners. In the main, they were earnest, zealous, and conscientious in the work of their difficult positions. In the pre-political days of the Bureau, especially, they accomplished much of genuine benefit in adjusting the relations of the races, even though their good intentions sometimes manifested themselves in an exasperating tendency to platitudinous lecturings. "The schoolhouse, the spelling book, and the Bible will be found better preservers of peace and good order than the revolver and the bowie knife," solemnly advised Colonel Whittlesey.

The real contact between the Bureau and the people was in the local offices, however, and it was in these that the greatest difficulties appeared. The work of a local Bureau agent was trying and exacting. His powers were great and ill-defined, touching the intimacies of everyday work and life of the people, white and black. The conditions and situations which confronted him from day to day were unprecedented. Such positions required a combination of wisdom, patience, tolerance and understanding which would have been hard to find under any circumstances. To fill the places, the commissioners had to use the material at hand.

It was rather the common thing in the summer of 1865, as the organization of the Bureau was being set up over the South, to name as local agent the commander of the military garrison. In many ways this was fortunate and appropriate, although garrison commanders varied greatly in their fitness for the work, and there was a constant changing and shifting among them as the volunteer soldiers were being discharged and returned to their homes in the North.

Later there was to come a class of agents who, in many cases, fulfilled the prophetic description given in Congress during the debate on the passage of the bill creating the Bureau. "The men who are to go down there," said Representative Powell, "will be your broken-down politicians and your dilapidated preachers; that description of men who are too lazy to work and just a little too honest to steal." Under stress and strain some of them failed to live up to the last clause of the description. The agents of the Bureau, as described by Dr. W. E. D. DuBois, "varied all the way from unselfish philanthropists to narrow-minded busybodies and thieves," although, as he truly observed, the "average was far better than the worst."

In the lean and hungry time until the new crop could be made, the services of the Bureau and of the army in combatting actual starvation were worth while, particularly in the poorer hill sections where supplies, never superabundant, had been eaten and destroyed by the armies in their marches back and forth.

In harried Arkansas, according to the report of Governor Murphy, people were living in open brush shelters in the woods, begging food. Within thirty miles of Atlanta, thirty-five thousand people were reported to be destitute almost to the point of starvation. Relief came, sometimes, too late, as in the case of the grandmother who walked seventeen miles into Guntersville, in Alabama, where she had heard that she might get food for her five orphaned grandchildren. Rations were issued to her, but on the way home she died of starvation and exhaustion.

"I cannot help but remark," said one Southern reporter viewing the scene at the Atlanta depot for issuing rations, "that it must be a matter of gratitude as well as surprise for our people to see a government, which was lately fighting us with fire and sword and shell, now generously feeding our poor and distressed. . . . There is much in this that takes away the bitter sting and sorrow of the past. . . . Even crippled Confederate soldiers have their sacks filled and are fed."

Against great services of this sort on the part of the Bureau, must be set the fact that its existence and policy increased the tendency of the restless freedmen to leave the farms and flock into the towns, where society was more pleasantly varied and less monotonously regular, where government rations were to be had for the asking, where heady talk was to be heard of "forty acres and a mule" to be given to each and every man "come Chrismus."

In that trying and uncertain crop season of 1865, with a late start at the planting, with weather against them, with supplies short and the need great, anything that needlessly kept hands from the fields was unfortunate. Before the end of the year the Bureau itself was to make strenuous efforts to get "notions" out of the heads of its charges, and to induce them to return to steady work, but there was just enough plausibility in the idea of "forty acres and a mule" to keep many ignorant, credulous freedmen stirred up all through the fall and even after that.

Short of shelter and food as it was in 1865, the South was rich in one great resource—the piled-up bales for which a cotton-hungry world had been waiting four years. Cotton could be sold that year at fabulous prices, more than a dollar a pound before the end of December, and the South had cotton, even after the immense destruction by retreating Confederates and invading Union armies.

By proclamation of May 22, President Johnson opened to commerce on July 1 the long-blockaded ports of the South, except Galveston, LaSalle, Brazos de Santiago and Brownsville, in Texas, which were opened a month later. The world was eager to come and buy the cotton; the balance of trade against the United States was heavy because of the stoppage of this greatest of America's exports; the people of the South sadly needed the returns their one great cash resource could bring them—but there seems to have been something about cotton which bedeviled the minds of that generation. To some it was "King"; to others, the "root of all evil." Men, reasonably honest in other directions, seemed to feel that stealing cotton was neither crime nor sin. Instead of a free flow of cotton out and money in, this vital commerce was put at the mercy of the voracious cotton agents of the United States Treasury.

Lawful exactions on cotton under the various acts of Congress and the President's regulations of May 9, 1865, included a charge of twenty-five per cent of its value levied on all cotton raised by slave labor; a revenue tax of two and one-half cents a pound upon cotton, no matter by whom raised; and a shipping fee of four cents a pound for the privilege of moving it to market. These charges were levied on all cotton, whether of "loyal" or "disloyal" ownership, and went, or were supposed to go, to the Treasury of the United States.

"Confederate" cotton, being that sold or alleged to have been sold to the Confederate government, or paid to that government under the law of tithes or tax in kind, or set aside for such payment, or pledged to that government under its produce loan, or in any other way tainted with aid of the Confederacy, was by law forfeited to the United States. Upon it descended the locust swarm of cotton agents.

The methods of fraud upon the owners and upon the government were various. Whether any particular lot of cotton was "Confederate" or private was often a matter of doubt. Such doubts were resolved against the cotton, and its possible private owner, in the absence of "arrangements" with the agent. "Arrangements" were sometimes as simple and direct as a straight-out payment of tribute by the owner for the release of his cotton, and no questions asked. The process was apt to prove expensive to the owners, however, for other cotton agents were abroad in the land and an unrecorded seizure and release by one was no protection against a like performance by others.

Sometimes the arrangement called for some local scoundrel who was "loyal," and therefore had a status in the courts, to swear that real Confederate cotton was his private property, whereupon the co-operating agent would release it to the purported owner, the cotton would be sold on the runaway market of 1865, and the precious pair would split the proceeds.

Another method, involving less circumlocution, was to deliver the seized bales to the government, but only after "plucking" them as they passed through the agent's hands so that a bale which left the gin weighing five hundred pounds might reach the port weighing three hundred—but still a "bale" so far as records went. The toll taken from the passing bale, sold at the prices then prevailing, might yield the agent as much as one hundred dollars, or more. Slightly more complex but more profitable was the substitution of "dog-tail"

or "red-dog" cotton, worth a few cents a pound, for good cotton.
The agent got the good cotton, the government got the "dog-tail"—
but each was a "bale," and such records as there were, were kept in
bales.

"I am sure that I sent some honest cotton agents South," said
Hugh McCulloch, Secretary of the Treasury, "but it sometimes
seems very doubtful whether any of them remained honest very
long." The rewards were too great, the restrictions too slight, the
temptations too overpowering.

"So many parties, official and unofficial, were engaged in stealing
cotton," as Harvey M. Watterson phrased it, that it can never be
known how much was taken. The great munitions explosion at
Mobile, in May, 1865, which, besides killing hundreds of people and
laying in ruins twenty blocks in the center of the city, destroyed
thousands of bales of cotton, was believed by many to have been
set off by cotton agents anxious to cover up evidence of their dealings. The belief is not reasonable, however, for no one in authority
seemed to care enough about their operations at that early date to
press an investigation into their affairs. Such partial investigation
as was made afterward indicated that an alert, hard-working, and
reasonably ingenious cotton agent could earn for himself as much as
eighty thousand dollars a month—which made the twenty-five thousand dollars which one deputy agent admitted paying for his commission seem a pretty good speculation.

Cotton with the Confederate taint was supposed to be sent from
the South to two super-agents, one in New York and one in Cincinnati, who were to sell it for government account and turn in the
proceeds to the Treasury. It has been estimated that up to the middle
of 1866, when official license to steal cotton expired, as many as
two million bales were seized from the plantations and warehouses
of the South. From this cotton, worth probably as much as four or
five hundred million dollars at the prices of that day, the amount
which found its way to the United States Treasury was less than
thirty million dollars, the proceeds from some one hundred and
fifteen thousand bales which somehow ran the gauntlet of bribery,
fraud, theft and corruption.

Cotton, of course, was not the only commodity subject to what
Hugh McCulloch, Secretary of the Treasury, referred to in his
report to Congress as "general plunder; every species of intrigue and
speculation and theft." Whitelaw Reid described more particularly

"the practice of regarding everything left in the country as the legitimate prize of the first officer who discovers it." What, he asked,

"shall be thought of the officer who finding a fine law library, straightway packed it up and sent it to his office in the North? Or, what shall be said of the taste of that other officer who, finding in an old country residence a series of family portraits, imagined that they would form very pretty parlor ornaments anywhere, and sent the entire set, embracing the ancestors of the haughty old South Carolinian for generations back, to look down from the walls of his Yankee residence? . . . In general, our people seem to go upon the theory that, having conquered the country, they are entitled to the best it has, and in duty bound to use as much of it as possible."

In grateful contrast to the conduct of some of the invading authorities was the fidelity of many of the Negroes to their own "white folks." A planter in Lowndes County, Alabama, told of one of his slaves who, with pistols at his head, never flinched in his refusal to betray the hiding-place of his master's horses and mules, in the woods.

"I'm going to give that boy a little farm and stock it for him," added the planter.

The pattern of the whole great struggle to find a new way of life in the South is a patchwork of contrasts. Rascality was confined to no race or class, and neither was devotion to duty under conditions as distressing and discouraging as ever a people faced.

CHAPTER IX

The Brief Era of Good Feeling

"True, there is no war upon us," wrote a citizen of Madison, Georgia, to General Sherman in the early summer of 1865, "but then it is not peace." It was indeed not peace, what with the garrisons and provost courts and military commissions, and Bureau agents and cotton agents; and yet it is impossible not to realize that those early summer days in the South had about them a surprising tone of harmony and good feeling—more than was to be seen again for many a year.

"I have not conversed with a soldier who has returned who does not express a perfect willingness to abide the issue," continued the same correspondent. "They say they have made the fight and were overpowered, and they submit." Of this general attitude there is abundant evidence, from high and low. "I'm for the Union; we are licked but I'm glad its all over," said young Martin Gary, Confederate brigadier, on his way home from Appomattox. Eleven years later, the same Martin Gary was to be one of the organizers of the South Carolina Red Shirts, raised and inspired by a sense of intolerable injustice; but in the first summer there was "almost perfect tranquillity" in that state, as reported by the correspondent of the *Nation*, who came expecting and looking for trouble. "There certainly was no government," he wrote, "but the state of the country was not so bad as one would think."

"You may look for outbreaks in Ohio quicker than in Georgia or Mississippi," wrote General Sherman to his Senator brother. The General was back in his former home of St. Louis during the summer. There he met young Sir John H. Kennaway, Bart., Master of Arts of Balliol, making a sight-seeing tour of the United States. At the General's suggestion, he extended his tour to include the *terra incognita* of the South. The evidences of good feeling between the former soldiers of the two sides which the observant young Briton noted there astonished him.

"We were bound from Nashville to Chattanooga," he wrote, "a journey of 150 miles which the cars were advertised to accomplish in ten hours, a rather rapid rate of travel on a railroad which had been roughly handled by both sides during the late war. . . . Federals and Confederates were pretty equally represented in the cars. . . . We were immensely struck by the good feeling existing between both parties. . . . Many were the battles fought over again, many a 'whipping' on both sides admitted and accounted for; and we needed to turn our eyes outside and observe the continual traces of ruin and desolation to prevent our forgetting that it had not all been a dream."

New York correspondents reported from Florida that there were "no armed rebels" in that state, that emancipation of the slaves had been accomplished, that most ex-slaves were on the plantations working for wages, but that Southerners were not believed to be capable of securing their social and moral education—the last being a view commonly expressed in correspondence from the South.

Sidney Andrews, who came to South Carolina in the late summer to report what he saw for Radical newspapers in Boston and Chicago, found men as a rule

"owning that the South is beaten; desiring nothing so much as long years of peace, acquiescent in the overthrow of slavery and mostly disposed to make the best they can of the freedman, but utterly without faith in his capacity to labor and take care of himself."

"I have not discovered much of a sullen spirit in the State. They exult in their war record. . . . Shall we not, in other fashion though it be, also exult in the heroism of her people?"

It is "idle and foolish," he continued, "to argue that there is danger of further armed resistance to the authority of the general government in South Carolina."

Almost without exception the observations made of the state of mind of the mass of Southerners in that first early summer indicate the same spirit of acquiescence in the situation and willingness to make the best of it.

John Minor Botts, a strong and uncompromising Union man before, during, and after the war, said that "at the time of the surrender of General Lee's army and the restoration of peace there was not only a general, but an almost universal, acquiescence and congratulation among the people that the war had terminated, and a large majority of them were at least contented." This state of mind had changed by 1866, he observed, ascribing the change to the mistaken lenience of President Johnson in pardoning so many rebels that Mr. Botts began to fear a return of Democratic rule in the South. Should that come to pass, he observed, "hell would be a garden of Eden compared to the Southern states, and I should assuredly select it as a permanent place of abode if forced to choose between the two."

Mr. Botts's 1866 state of mind seems to have been not unlike that of Mr. John W. Recks, late of New York but holding Federal office at Pensacola, when he told the Committee on Reconstruction that "the only way for the government to make these people friends is just to keep them down. . . . I would pin them down at the point of the bayonet so close that they would not have room to wiggle."

The Northern mind of 1865, so far as it was expressed by those who reported conditions in the South that year, seems to have been disposed to reconciliation and restoration of the Union, with some disposition to insist that the Southern states should be received back only if they came suitably garbed in penitential sackcloth and ashes. The efforts of the garrisons and the Bureau to relieve destitution and ward off starvation were an appreciated earnest of this spirit. It was impossible, though, for Northern visitors to refrain from passing moral judgments, if, indeed, they made any effort to do so. It was an era of moral judgments.

John T. Trowbridge, more accurate than most of the visiting authors in reporting on those matters in which his moral preconceptions were not involved, found Richmond "mourning for her sins in dust and ashes—dust which every wind whirled up from the unwatered streets, and the ashes of the burnt district." Mr. Andrews described Charleston as a

"city of ruins, of desolation, of vacant houses, of widowed women, of weed-wild gardens, of miles of grass-grown streets, of acres of pitiful and voiceful barrenness—that is Charleston. . . . Here is enough of woe and want and ruin and ravage to satisfy the most insatiate heart—enough of sore humiliation and bitter overthrow to appease the desire of the most revengeful spirit."

But General Carl Schurz, traveling the South on a mission of impartial investigation for President Johnson, which was privately converted into a mission of gathering propaganda for Senator Sumner and the Radicals, thought otherwise. He laid it as a major objection to the spirit of the South that there was neither "sense of the criminality" of treason in the Southern mind, nor any "general exhibition of cordiality" to the Northern soldiers, agents and citizens who came among the Southern people.

General Schurz found what he was looking for. B. C. Truman, New England newspaperman, found a different state of mind. He did not expect the people of the South to hail him with "cordiality" and reveal to him a "sense of criminality."

"If Northern men go South," he wrote, ". . . and conduct themselves with ordinary discretion, they soon overcome these prejudices and are treated with respect. The accounts that are from time to time flooded over the country in regard to Southern cruelty and intolerance toward Northerners are mostly false. . . . There are localities in many of the Southern States where it would be dangerous for a Northern man to live but they are exceptional, and are about equally unsafe for any man who possesses attractive property."

Major H. C. Lawrence, Illinois Republican and former Bureau agent in eastern North Carolina, quoted General Abbott, a Northern man living in Wilmington, as saying

"that a Northern man is just as safe anywhere in the State of North Carolina as he is anywhere in the North. I do not say that a man cannot come here and act so without sense and discretion that he will get into difficulties with the people; he can do that anywhere. But a man who comes here and attends to his own business and does not take some pains to make himself odious, I think, is as safe here as anywhere else."

There were Northern men, however, who, often in mere thoughtless banter, did take some pains to make themselves disagreeable, if not exactly odious. Whitelaw Reid wrote that "the few Northerners on board" a train on which he rode "talked Abolitionism enough to have astonished Wendell Phillips himself." Even Rutherford B. Hayes, considerate in most relations of life, wrote home from Memphis:

"The Rebel officers are particularly interesting. I get on with them famously. I talk negro suffrage and our extremest radicalism to all of them. They dissent, but are polite and cordial."

When, however, one should be goaded into intemperate remark by some particularly provoking conversation, or when he should indulge in tall talk and bluster on his own account, the incident would be reported in the North as another illustration of sullen, smoldering Southern resentment.

From his personal acquaintance among volunteer officers of the United States Army, Major Truman mentioned numerous groups who had remained in or returned to the South to engage in business or farming, attracted by the combination of fabulously high prices of cotton and low cost of land.

"Large numbers of ex-Federal and ex-Confederate officers are engaged together in mercantile pursuits and in cotton planting," he continued, calling special attention to the number of such joint planting ventures in Florida, in southern Texas, and along the White, the Arkansas, the Red and the Mississippi Rivers. The banks of that river, he said, "are lined with plantations leased to Northern men not Federal officers."

Among the plantations along the Mississippi River was one leased and operated jointly by General Forrest and Major Diffenbach, of Minnesota. Seven other young Federals planting in that neighborhood, separated from their families, were regularly guests of the General and Mrs. Forrest at the ancient country rite of "Sunday dinner."

Nor was this sort of cordial contact confined to the country. Twelve young Union soldiers, and a like number of young Confederates, having come to the new town of Chattanooga which was beginning its growth into a city, came together in a fishing club which, through nearly seventy years, never failed to have its outings. On its last excursion, as on its first, the two sides were equally represented—the last time, one of each.

Major Truman reported that a reasonable man would have suspected that

"there was, in many sections, widespread hostility to Northern men which, however, in nine cases out of ten, is speedily dispelled by individual contact, and the exercise of a generous regard for private opinions."

General Grant, most distinguished of the investigators who traveled the South that year, said somewhat the same thing:

"My observations lead me to the conclusion . . . that they are in earnest in wishing to do what they think is required by the government, not humiliating to them as citizens, and that if such a course were pointed out they would pursue it in good faith. It is to be regretted that there cannot be a greater commingling at this time between the citizens of the two sections, and particularly of those intrusted with the law-making power."

Wide contact between the sections was impossible that year, even had there been a general desire among disinterested Northerners to go South and see for themselves. Travel in the South was thought to be dangerous, and certainly was difficult and uncomfortable, and prohibitively expensive. For the Northern traveler to pass into the South there were but four ways—by river steamer on the Mississippi, by coasting ship to the Atlantic or Gulf ports, or by one of the two rail gateways which remained, Richmond in the East and Louisville in the West.

From these gateways lines ran south; but they were broken lines, at places entirely out of commission, with bridges gone, or rails festooning the trees or telegraph poles in the fanciful twisted forms known as "Sherman's hairpins." To cross such gaps in 1865 the traveler was forced to use vehicles called by courtesy stagecoaches, at prices which seem fantastically high as expressed in the depreciated currency of the day.

Even where the railroads were in some sort of working order their rates were necessarily high. The Montgomery & West Point, one of the well equipped lines of the South before the war, was able to salvage from its wreckage but one engine, which had escaped destruction or capture because it had already been thrown aside as worn out, and fourteen condemned flat cars. With these it started hauling passengers at a charge of ten cents a mile when paid in "hard money" or twenty cents when paid in United States paper money. In the Carolinas passengers paid seven and one-half cents to ride on trains which could, with difficulty, average ten miles an hour, stopping at every sizable stream to transfer their passengers across by crude ferry, for lack of a bridge. From Petersburg to Wilmington, a distance of two hundred and twenty-five miles, was a journey of twenty-four hours; from Florence to Charleston, one hundred miles, ten hours.

Perhaps the most revealing picture of travel in the ruined railroads of the South in 1865 is found in the warning notice posted by the Georgia Railroad, which, as late as December, scheduled the one hundred and seventy miles between Atlanta and Augusta in seventeen hours. "Passengers are positively forbidden," ran the notice, "to ride upon the tops or platforms of cars. From the defective conditions of the track the cars are very likely to run off, in which case the danger to passengers is much increased in such a position."

This painful isolation of the South during the critical period of 1865 was to play its part in the misunderstandings of Reconstruction. The real story of those long and bitter years is in the minds of men. Deprived of normal contact, each section without real knowledge of the attitude or acts of the other, it was inevitable that false ideas of the South should be entertained in the North, and of the North in the South. It was even more inevitable because the two sections read the same language. Every intemperate and ill-advised utterance, duly printed and reprinted, created its own reaction of resentment.

Nothing is more real than an emotional reaction, or more powerful; nothing is more sensitive, more difficult to weigh and gauge. Inspired leadership on all sides might have preserved the early 1865 spirit of willing accommodation, and so have averted the tragedy that followed. Broad sympathy, wise forebearance, rare tact were needed all around. Such qualities are not plentiful at any time or place; it was too much to expect them between sections remote and cut off, at the end of four years of war, embittered at its closing by the murder of Lincoln.

Northern travelers who came to the South brought with them their own pattern of desirable life. Not finding that pattern in the South, they compared the worst of what they saw with the best of what they had left—as travelers will—and so condemned or patronized what they found. Mr. Trowbridge, fresh from the New England world of a day when superannuated mill labor went to the scrap heap along with worn-out machines, was duly and quite naturally indignant when he was told that some masters in Virginia were refusing to support "old wore-out niggers." Virginia, he believed, was to be "regenerated by Northern ideas and free institutions," but the Virginia of that day, with a flaming pride of state which Mr. Trowbridge noted to criticise but could not understand, did not appreciate the suggestion.

Mr. Andrews, noting that many Northern men were moving to Charleston, predicted that

"if this time five years finds here a handsome and thriving city, it will be the creation of New England. . . . To bring here the conveniences and comforts of our Northern civilization, no less than the Northern idea of right and wrong, justice and injustice, humanity and inhumanity, is the work ready for the hand of every New England man and woman who stands waiting."

Describing a particularly shiftless tavern in South Carolina and its slatternly mistress, he closed with the unctuous comment that she was "a type of woman, thank God, without counterpart in the North." Mr. Andrews was able to see some good in Southern travel, however, for in describing Greensboro, Georgia, where Mr. Seward had taught school as a youth, he gave it almost his highest praise. It has a "very Northern appearance," he said, "looking not indeed so much like a New England town as like a quiet county seat of northern New Jersey or central New York."

Reporting a trip to Lexington, Kentucky, a correspondent of the Cincinnati *Commercial* declared that the railroad going south from the Ohio River took travelers "back toward the dawn of creation at the rate of five hundred years per hour till when you reach the terminus at this end they will instinctively rub their eyes and enquire for Adam and his accomplished lady."

Provoking comments were duly reprinted in the South, of course, to the irritation of the Southerner—just as vapid, fire-eating speeches and editorials in the South were reprinted in the North, with comment, as typical and representative.

More serious was the round-trip circulation of "atrocity" stories.

"For some unknown cause a large number of persons are engaged in writing and circulating falsehoods," reported Major Truman. "Reports of an incendiary character concerning the Southern people are transmitted North."

Such reports were printed by the papers in the North, with the harsh comment that was to be expected. Story, comment and all, reprinted in the Southern press, simply added more fuel to the reviving flame of ill will.

But even the best efforts of those editors and orators who delighted to prick old wounds might have failed to embitter further the sections of the nation had it not been for the ever-present and never-solved question of the status of the Negroes.

CHAPTER X

The First Convention

Major General Carl Schurz interpreted the Southern attitude toward the freedman and his labor as a general conviction "that the Negro exists for the special object of raising cotton, rice and sugar for the whites, and that it is illegitimate for him to indulge like other people in the pursuit of his own happiness in his own way. . . . The blacks at large belonged to the whites at large."

The General's statement coincided with his own preconceptions and with those of most people in the North. Moreover, in 1865, there was a good deal of truth in his neat epigram. The Southern people at large, almost entirely without confidence that Negroes would work in freedom, were tremendously concerned about making the desperately needed crops of that year. Of course cotton, rice or sugar did not mean so much to the eloquent veteran of the German Revolution of 1848 as they did to the harassed planter who must depend on those crops to carry his family and his hands through the next year.

That the white and the black races could live and work together in the South on a basis of freedom and equality was believed, in 1865, only by advanced abolitionists and extreme advocates of "human rights" generally. Many sincere friends of the Negro, President Lincoln among them, had little or no confidence in such a solution. Colonization of the Negro population in some tropic land seemed to them a more satisfactory treatment, for the interests of both races.

Only a month before he issued the Emancipation Proclamation, President Lincoln told a delegation of free Negroes that he believed colonization was necessary because of racial differences between whites and blacks which caused them to suffer from contact with each other; that the free Negroes in a tropical colony could hope for a basis of equality such as then existed for them nowhere in the United States, not even in the North; and that the prospect of colonization after freedom would greatly lessen the objections to the emancipation of all slaves. Within the last weeks of his life, in spite of the miserable failure of colonization schemes undertaken in 1863, Mr. Lincoln talked with General Butler about further plans on a larger scale for transporting the freed Negroes back to Africa, or to tropical America.

It was widely, and correctly, believed that one of the major objections in the South to emancipation was the dread of the problem of establishing a social and economic order embracing four millions of freed slaves. In the summer of 1865 that dread was to become a reality, especially in those states where the Negro population was substantially equal to the white.

To a Northern state, with a handful of free Negroes within its borders, such a situation presented no real difficulty. It was of small consequence there what the Negroes did, or did not do, but questions which had no real meaning in the North became most pressing problems in the South. If there the Negroes failed to work in freedom the whole people, white and black, would go down in common ruin. If the Negroes were to become the political equals of their former masters they would, by sheer weight of numbers in such states as Mississippi and South Carolina, become the rulers of the state—a responsibility for which their own dependent and controlled lives had in no way fitted them. If they were to be socially commingled with the white population there was, always, the fear of racial outbreaks. In the back of the minds of men in the South were other considerations than cotton or sugar. The times were revolutionary. Hayti and Santo Domingo were almost current events then, and not remote in a shadowy historic past. The fear of an armed, idle and aroused Negro population, overwhelming in numbers, was real.

In the South that summer was an anxious searching for means and measures to meet a situation without precedent; in the North, a close and wary watchfulness of the South in all its dealings with the freedmen.

The first organized Southern bodies to consider the status of the freedmen were the constitutional conventions of the restored states, called by the provisional governors. Three subjects had to be dealt with by these conventions—proper abrogation of the Ordinances of Secession adopted in 1861; repudiation of the debts of the states incurred in aid of the Confederacy, directly or indirectly; and abolition of slavery in each state by amendment of the state constitution. These three essentials were prescribed to the conventions by President Johnson as the minimum requirement for restoration of the state governments, and the conventions did finally, after some needless debate and logic-chopping, bring themselves to follow the line of action laid down for them by the President.

As to the question of civil rights for the freed Negroes, however, neither these conventions nor the legislatures which followed them met the views of the President, of reasonable men in the North, or of their own wisest leaders. They were blind, astonishingly blind, to Northern sentiment, and to the effect of such sentiment on the acceptance or rejection of their own constitutional labors.

Both conventions and legislatures, for the most part, were made up of second-rate men, representing only part of the people. Their minds were so intent on the problem of making sure that the labor of the freedmen should continue, and that the relations of the races should be stabilized and codified, that they seem to have taken no heed of the clear warnings of Northern opinion, such as General Howard's circular of July 12 that "no substitute for slavery . . . will be tolerated."

Indications of how the North would regard the enactment of laws conceived to be discriminatory against Negroes in the South were clear enough on the surface. Beneath the surface was the skillful work of the Radical junta. Before the first constitutional convention of a "Johnson state" met to do its work, their plans were laid. They were the one group, North or South, bent and determined on a positive program. The program existed and the plans were laid before the Southern conventions and legislatures had made their mistakes. The mistakes were not responsible for the existence of the Radical plan; they were in no small measure responsible for its success. Unwittingly, these lesser men of the South, intent on their local problems, furnished to the Radicals campaign ammunition far more effective than any number of atrocity stories, or reports of zealous Bureau agents, or inflammatory correspondence to the newspapers.

Any sort of legislative action against enlarging the rights and privileges of freedmen was ascribed in the North, usually, to the persisting malevolence of the "slave power" and the unregenerate spirit of rebellion. Northern men in the South, and in actual contact with the people, usually reported otherwise. Major Truman reported:

"It is the former slave owners who are the best friends the negro has in the South—those who, heretofore, have provided for his mere physical comfort, generally with sufficient means, though entirely neglecting his best nature, while it is the 'poor whites' that are his enemies. It is from these that he suffers most."

In Texas, General J. B. Kiddoo of the United States Army believed:

"The better class of planters, who were former slaveholders, are, as a general thing, disposed to deal fairly with them . . . but there is a class of men commonly known in the States as 'adventurers,' small planters, traveling speculators, country store-keepers . . . swarming the planting regions like so many buzzards seeking for prey. . . . It is the lower class of people that have the most bitter and vulgar hatred of the negro. The more intelligent and liberal people consider the negro set free by the arbitrament of arms, and hence have no animosity towards him; while the other class hold him personally responsible and treat him accordingly."

Bureau officials in Tennessee reported the same state of affairs. One quoted a loyal Union man as saying to him, "if you take away the military from Tennessee, the buzzards can't eat up the niggers as fast as we'll kill 'em." Another reported the

"melancholy fact that among the bitterest opponents of the negro in Tennessee are the intensely radical loyalists of the mountain district, the men who have been in our armies. . . . The great opposition to the measure in the Tennessee Legislature giving the negro the right to testify and an equality before the law, has come from that section chiefly."

The defeat of the bill referred to, in May, 1865, was the first serious refusal of civil rights to the Negroes by any of the restored states. Its defeat was the act of the first "Brownlow" legislature, a body made up almost entirely of Unionists of the straitest sect. In denying to freedmen what it regarded as the white man's privilege of testifying in the courts of justice, this body of zealous Southern Unionists followed its natural bent. Mr. Trowbridge, who visited the same legislature at its next session, reported that there was "more prejudice against color among the middle and poorer classes—the 'Union' men of the South, who owned few or no slaves—than among the planters who owned them by scores and hundreds." Of them, Governor Brownlow remarked that "it is hard to tell which they hate the most, the Rebels or the Negroes."

Within less than a year, however, after the doctrine of full civil and political rights for Negroes became a major tenet of the Radical Republicans of the North, the same Tennessee legislature was to prove itself able to overcome its "prejudice against color" when party reasons demanded, and to reverse itself by passing in January, 1866, the bill defeated in 1865.

Among the "Johnson states," Mississippi was first to hold its constitutional convention. Delegates elected on August 7 gathered at Jackson on the fourteenth to remake the state's organ of government according to the new situation.

Governor Sharkey's provisional government had been in operation nearly two months when the convention met. Right from the start a conflict of jurisdiction developed between the military and the provisional civil magistrates appointed by the Governor as to most matters in which freedmen or Union sympathizers were involved. In such cases the army or the Bureau courts claimed jurisdiction and refused to recognize the civil process of the state of Mississippi.

Even before the troubles began in Mississippi a similar conflict arose in North Carolina. There Governor Holden had come to a sort of agreement with the commanding General by the terms of which the army and Bureau courts were to try those cases in which they felt an interest, the provisional state courts to try what was left. Governor Sharkey, with his background of twenty years on the bench, could not surrender so complaisantly what he considered the proper jurisdiction of civil courts. His objections were so vigorous and so long sustained that finally a War Department order came down defining the status of the provisional government of Mississippi.

"Mississippi is still to a very considerable extent under the control of the military authorities. The rebellion, though physically crushed, has not been officially announced or treated . . . as a thing of the past, the suspension of the writ of habeas corpus has not been terminated, nor has the military law ceased to be enforced in proper cases."

Being thus told just how much, and how little, of a government they were, ninety-eight delegates, "almost all gentlemen who held political opinions directly the opposite of those of Mr. Jefferson Davis," assembled in convention on August 14. Nearly all were original Union men, and all but one had "gone with the state." The one exception was the delegate from the county of which it was said that its intense Unionism led it to secede from the rest of the state to become the "Free State of Jones."

The Confederate debt was promptly repudiated, with little difficulty, but there was much discussion over the form of words in which the Ordinance of Secession should be set aside. To declare it void from the beginning, held some, would be taken as a reflection on the gentlemen who composed the Secession Convention of 1861. To repeal it, held others, would leave the implication that there had been in the ordinance some degree of validity. Finally, after much debate, the ordinance was declared "null and void." Mississippians, most of them, felt that its nullity was established only by the fortunes of war and the force of arms—a belief which was considered in the North to be evidence of a continuing rebellious spirit.

Governor Sharkey in his call for the convention outlined the situation as to slavery:

"The negroes are free—free by the fortune of war, free by the proclamation, free by common consent, free practically as well as theoretically, and it is too late to raise the technical questions as to the means by which they became so."

An element in the convention felt otherwise as to the last point, however, and did raise the question and persist in debating it for the better part of a week. To keep the record of history straight, ran their argument, the amendment abolishing slavery in Mississippi should be so drawn as to make it clear to all and for all time that the state yielded only to superior force. Moreover, they believed that an ordinance voluntary in form would cut off "loyal" slave owners from their chances to get compensation from the government for their freed slaves. Compensation was a hope which died hard—especially among those who counted themselves "loyal."

The victorious North was "not to be trifled with," warned the veteran Judge Yerger, who opposed any statement beyond the simple one that slavery was abolished in Mississippi. By a vote of eighty-seven to eleven the resolution advocated by Judge Yerger was adopted, and the argumentative resolution defeated, but not until after the protracted debate on the subject had furnished more ammunition to the Radical propagandists.

President Johnson, through the medium of a message to Governor Sharkey, laid before the convention the matter of a limited and qualified suffrage for Negroes. He wrote:

"If you would extend the elective franchise to all persons of color who can read the Constitution of the United States in English, and write their names, and to all persons of color who own real estate valued at not less than $250 and pay taxes thereon, you would completely disarm the adversary and set an example the other States will follow. This you can do with perfect safety, and you thus place the Southern States, in reference to free persons of color, upon the same basis with the free States."

This public advice was much the same as that which President Lincoln had written for the "private eye alone" of the Governor of Louisiana, two years before. The same advice was to be given again, within the same month, to the people of Texas by Judge John H. Reagan, stout Secessionist and former member of the Confederate Cabinet, from his prison cell in Fort Warren. The dangers of unlimited and immediate suffrage for unprepared Negroes, he warned the people of Texas, were to be averted only by granting to them the usual and customary rights in court, including the right to testify, and by extending to some of them the right to vote, safeguarded by intellectual, moral and, if necessary, property qualifications.

Advice of this character, no matter what its source, received no consideration at the hands of the Mississippi Convention of 1865. Negroes were given the right to hold property, by amendment to the state constitution, and the right to sue and to be sued, but all other questions as to their civil and political rights were left for the legislature, which was to meet in November. To assist the legislature in the consideration of the problem a special commission was named, to study and recommend a code of laws—the beginning of what came to be called, in the North, the "Black Code of Mississippi."

On August 24 the convention adjourned. Almost immediately the campaign for election of members of the new legislature began, with the issue nothing so advanced as suffrage for Negroes, such as the President had recommended, but the more fundamental question of whether Negroes should be allowed to testify in court. The right was advocated generally by the bench, the bar, and enlightened leaders, many of whom were still disfranchised. It was opposed with a bitterness, hard to understand in this day, by the narrower and more ignorant whites who saw in it a first step toward dreaded "equality."

CHAPTER XI

POLITICAL AMMUNITION

PRESIDENT JOHNSON was satisfied, in the main, with the work of this first convention. His three essential requirements for the recognition of the state government by the Executive of the United States had been complied with, and the President did not realize, apparently, that the things left undone, under skillful handling of the Radical strategists, were to be used for the undoing of all that was accomplished.

In midsummer of 1865 no one recognized the real strength of the Radical position, not even the Radicals themselves. Practitioners of politics had yet to learn what could be accomplished by a vigorous waving of the "bloody shirt." Even Thaddeus Stevens, whose malevolence did not take counsel of his fears, had his anxious moments, as when he wrote to Senator Sumner that "if something is not done the President will be crowned King before Congress meets." And again, "I almost despair of resisting Executive influence."

There was among the people a great weariness of war and strife that summer. As late as December of 1865 Governor Morton wrote to the President that "the great body of the people in the North will endorse your doctrine and policy." Besides Indiana's able war Governor, others who were afterward to become powers in the Radical movement were active in 1865 in support of the presidential policy of restoration—among them, John Sherman, brother of the General and Ohio's fellow-member of the Senate with "Bluff Ben" Wade, and Henry Ward Beecher, pulpit mouthpiece of a vast and substantial constituency of the North.

Nearly all the principal Union generals supported the same policy, even General Sheridan, afterward to become so vigorous a Radical, while a politician so astute in determining in advance the direction of the cat's next jump as General John A. Logan was not yet a Radical in 1865.

Even Secretary Stanton, as he afterward testified at the Johnson impeachment trial, at this time "had no doubt of the authority of the President to take measures for the organization of the rebel states on the plan proposed during the vacation of Congress and agreed in the plan specified in the proclamation in the case of North Carolina."

Such straws as were blowing indicated that the President's conservative policy of restoration was meeting popular favor. An election for congressmen was held in Tennessee on August 7. Under the strict disfranchisement laws of the state none but Union men of proved loyalty could vote, regardless of amnesty proclamations or pardons by the President, and yet six of the eight men chosen for Congress were Conservative. Using the large electoral powers granted him by the legislature, Governor Brownlow threw out the vote of twenty-nine counties, one-third of the state; but even this additional disfranchisement by wholesale changed the result in but one district, where Samuel M. Arnell, author of the law disfranchising Confederates, was declared elected in the stead of Dorsey B. Thomas, Conservative. William B. Campbell, stout old Conservative Unionist, who had led Tennessee soldiers into Mexico and had served the state as governor, was an especial target but he had four times as many votes as his combined opponents—and not even the ruthless electoral methods of 1865 could overcome such a lead as that.

The election, however, had unfortunate repercussions in the North, as indicated by the declaration that the result was "the reverse of encouraging to those expecting the Southern whites to repudiate, at the ballot box, the treason they have supported at the mouth of the cannon."

On the same day as the election in Tennessee, one more important and significant was held in Kentucky. The relation of that state to the Union was *sui generis*. At the outset of the war it was a battleground of ideas and divided loyalties, devoted to its historic mission of compromising the differences between the sections. President Lincoln's call for troops after Fort Sumter decided the issue for secession in Virginia, North Carolina, Arkansas and Tennessee, but not in Kentucky. The state continued to maintain the anxious neutrality of a would-be peacemaker through the spring and summer of 1861.

During the period of Kentucky's neutrality her support was eagerly courted by both sides. Those who placed abolition first, in fact, resented what to them seemed the President's truckling to the "slave power" in the state. "Abraham Lincoln would like to have God on his side," ran their jibe, "but he must have Kentucky." There was truth in the statement. Kentucky's support was essential to Union success, and President Lincoln, a master of negotiation and persuasion, won it. Finding peace unobtainable and neutrality impossible, the state government in September formally elected to stand with the Union.

In the Union, however, Kentucky was not admitted to full faith

The Work of the Freedmen's Bureau—Scenes in the office at Richmond.
From *Leslie's Illustrated Newspaper*.

Tennessee State Capitol, Nashville.
From Drawing by J. Wells Champney.

North Carolina State Capitol, Raleigh.
From Print in Tennessee State Library.

and fellowship in the sisterhood of loyalty. Subordinate Union military commanders, coming into the state by its own invitation, paid no attention to the fair words of their commander-in-chief, and assumed the airs and attitudes of conquerors toward a population subjected by force of their victorious arms.

Such an attitude had its natural effect. At the beginning of the war Garret Davis, zealous Unionist, sought to have his colleague, Lazarus Powell, expelled from the United States Senate because he insisted on trying to preserve to Kentuckians some of the rights of citizenship. Before the war ended, Senator Davis had become so outdone with the treatment of his state at the hands of the Union military commanders and the government at Washington, that he publicly withdrew his attack on Senator Powell, declaring that the event had proved his colleague right and himself wrong.

The incident typifies the strong opposition to the administration of the government, as distinguished from the principle of the Union itself, developed by illegal and oppressive actions in Kentucky, and even more by the lack of tact on the part of the Radical Union forces. The state was put under martial law by President Lincoln and kept there by President Johnson until October 12, 1865, six months after Appomattox. The right to sue out the writ of habeas corpus was not restored to Kentuckians for a year after the close of hostilities. Trade restrictions imposed during the war to prevent supplies from Kentucky's rich fields and pastures going South into the Confederacy were continued, and heavy garrisons kept in the state. The treatment of Kentucky by the government at Washington differed in only one particular of importance from that of the eleven states which had seceded to form the Confederacy: Kentucky was represented in the Congress of the United States.

At the August election in Kentucky, files of soldiers stood at the polls with lists, furnished by unknown and irresponsible parties, of men who were deemed not sufficiently "loyal" to vote—that is, not sufficiently in sympathy with the Radical government and the Radical military command in the state. Men named on these lists were warned away by the military if they approached the polls. Should they persist in the effort to exercise their right to vote, they were liable to arrest.

Under these conditions, with Confederates still completely disfranchised by state law, with none but Union men voting and these subjected to intimidation in the interest of Radical candidates, the Conservatives elected five of eight congressmen and a clear majority of the new legislature. That body at its first session, in December, was to repeal anti-Confederate legislation of war times, and to refuse, then or ever, to ratify the Thirteenth Amendment abolishing slavery. Kentucky was embarked on a course which was to make the state, for a generation, uncompromisingly Democratic.

In June of 1865 the Radicals barely carried Missouri on the ratification of the new constitution; in August, they failed to carry either Kentucky or Tennessee. With such results in elections where all but Union men of proved loyalty were excluded by state law, and with important Republican leaders in every state supporting the presidential policy, there was good reason for Mr. Stevens' fears for failure of the Radical plans.

Working for them, however, were two imponderable but powerful facts—in Congress, the jealousy of legislative prerogative as against the powers of the Executive, hugely grown as a result of war; in the North at large, the widespread feeling that the freed Negroes had become wards of the nation, to be protected from the designs of the "slave power." Skillful play on both states of feeling by Mr. Stevens and his associates; a certain obtuseness toward the tremendously important emotional facts of the situation on the part of President Johnson; an almost inexplicable blindness to the feelings and attitudes of the dominant North on the part of the provisional governments in the South; and a comprehensive ignorance as to things Southern on the part of the North, combined to wreck the promising plan of restoration through the provisional governments set up by Lincoln and Johnson. Major General J. H. Wilson wrote to Howell Cobb, in June:

"The whole system of slavery and slave labor must be effectually destroyed, and the Freedmen must be protected from the injustice of evil men before the people of Georgia get the State government under their own control. If . . . the original guardians of [slavery] are allowed any influence in the reorganization of the State they will resuscitate and perpetuate its iniquities, if possible."

The state of mind thus expressed, widespread in the North, only needed to be kept alive, intensified and inflamed to give the Radicals the strongest possible cards. "Atrocity reports" from Freedmen's Bureau agents, and from traveling correspondents sent to the South by Radical newspapers to find and report what was wanted, were the constant ammunition of the attack. There can be no doubt that injustices and cruelties were practiced on the freed Negroes, as there have been in all times and all societies on the weak and defenseless. Equally without doubt, there were innumerable instances of kindly and friendly relations between the races. For political purposes, these must be ignored or minimized, which was not difficult to do; the "atrocities" must be multiplied and exaggerated.

No atrocity story was too extraordinary to find credence. Listing "only a few of the murders that are committed on the helpless and unprotected freedmen," Captain W. A. Poillon, assistant superintendent of freedmen at Mobile, gave twenty-one instances of murder by shooting, hanging, drowning, and burning, alleged to have been committed in four Alabama counties within two months. Many shocking details were given (such as five bodies still hanging to the Alabama pines) and others were hinted at; but the whole vague report gives the name of no one charged with these numerous atrocities, not even of that planter who "about the last of May hung his servant (a woman) in presence of all the neighborhood."

Perhaps to supply the lack of specific corroborative facts about the twenty-one murders listed, Captain Poillon added a few general massacres. "A preacher (near Bladen Springs) states in the *pulpit* that the roads in Choctaw County stunk with the dead bodies of servants that had fled from their masters. . . . All those found on the roads or coming down the river are almost invariably *murdered*," he reported— and such a report was solemnly printed as an official document of the Senate of the United States and widely circulated through the North.

That impressionable Bureau agents in strange surroundings should believe all that was told them was natural, particularly when the stories were of such sort as would insure the continuance and enlargement of the Bureau under which they held jobs. In contrast with their lurid stories is the report of General Sherman, who, on a tour of inspection through Arkansas in 1865, found Negroes contentedly at work, with satisfactory wages and conditions, all things considered, and with protection in their rights of person and property at the hands of the civil authorities of the provisional government. Negroes could go anywhere they pleased, without any discriminatory system of "passes"; the whites were reported satisfied with their labor, and the Negroes with their work.

The belief that the people of the South and the authorities of the provisional governments were engaged in systematic persecution of their neighbors who remained loyal to the Union was so strong in the minds of some local military commanders that the claim of "loyalty" became practically a plea in bar to any criminal prosecution in their districts.

Such a conviction in the mind of General Krysyanowski, commanding at Scottsboro in north Alabama, caused him to order that the trial of fifteen men indicted for bushwhacking be stopped as a persecution of loyalists. When the court proceeded with the trial regardless of his order, he sent a detachment of Negro soldiers to Scottsboro, closed the court, released the prisoners, arrested the sheriff, and took him to Nashville to jail.

At Jefferson, in east Texas, the military forbade Judge Gray of the provisional district court to try a treasury agent indicted for swindling and cotton thievery. After two attempts to bring him to trial had been blocked by the local and district commanders, the doughty Judge took the position that if he could not try cotton thieves, even though they were treasury agents, he would try no one, and closed his court. For his contumacy he was threatened with arrest.

Texas was especially fruitful of stories of persecution of loyalists, perhaps because there was so little government and so much outlawry in the state at that time, particularly on the long Indian frontier. After the "breakup" of the Confederate armies in May, the law no longer held even a slight hold in that region. The Union garrisons, few in number, were in the interior of the state; the provisional government was not yet organized and in operation. Governor Hamilton did not reach Galveston until July 21, nor his capitol at Austin, with its offices rifled, its treasury looted, even its roof gone, until the last of that month.

For the greater part of two years no way was found to make law effective on the frontier. Deeds of violence and rapine were painfully common in that period. The outlaws responsible seem to have taken little or no interest in politics, nor to have been respecters of persons. They plundered at will, without nice discrimination as to past records of attachment to the United States or to the Confederacy, but the outrages reported in the North were those whose victims claimed sympathy and redress on the ground of loyalty.

The situation in Texas was taken as evidence of the South's vengefulness toward loyalists, its hostility toward Northern men, and its unwhipped and rebellious spirit in general. "Texas was worse than any other state because she had never been whipped," reported Major General D. S. Stanley, while the inspector general for the Freedmen's Bureau testified that "one campaign of the United States Army through eastern Texas, such as Sherman's through South Carolina, would greatly improve the temper and generosity of the people."

CHAPTER XII

CONSTITUTION WRITING

THE people of South Carolina, whose "temper and generosity" had been subjected to the improving influence of the passage of General Sherman's army, elected delegates on September 4 to a constitutional convention, which met on the thirteenth at the call of Governor Perry, in the same Grecian-porticoed Baptist Church at Columbia in which the Secession Convention of 1860 opened its sessions. Consistent Union men were scarce in the convention which, it was hoped, was to restore South Carolina's "proper practical relation" with the Union—as was to be expected in that state. Nevertheless a contumacious resolution offered by A. P. Aldrich, calling on the people of the state to "endure patiently the evils of," and "to await calmly deliverance from unconstitutional rule," received but four votes. Foremost among the sensible ex-Confederates who opposed it were Governor Pickens, the 1860 leader in secession, and Major General Samuel Mc-Gowan, who had commanded the Palmetto Regiment in the war with Mexico, and who bore wounds suffered in the Confederate service.

"It doesn't become South Carolina . . . to vapor or swell or strut or brag or bluster or threat or swagger," said Governor Pickens.

"The work South Carolina begins today she begins in good faith," said the General. "She was the first to secede, and she fought what she believed to be the good fight, with all her energies. . . . She has seen enough of war; in God's name, I demand that she shall not be made to appear as if she still coveted fire and sword."

A resolution declaring the Ordinance of Secession null and void passed promptly, without unnecessary delay, and with one hundred and five out of one hundred and eight votes. The amendment to the state constitution abolishing slavery met some opposition from a small, noisy minority which insisted on compensation for slave owners and on limiting future employment of freedmen to "manual service," but all amendments were voted down and the convention, by a vote of ninety-eight to eight, declared:

"The slaves in South Carolina having been emancipated by the action
87

of the United States authorities, neither slavery nor involuntary servitude, except as a punishment for crime whereof the party shall have been duly convicted, shall ever be reestablished in this State."

In such fashion South Carolina carried out the first two of the President's three essentials of recognition as a state. The third, repudiation of the debt incurred in aid of the Confederacy, it refused. Governor Perry, who seems never to have appreciated the fact that the provisional government of the state had no real rights or power of its own, did not recommend it, and the convention was willing enough to follow his lead.

Delegates were really more interested, it appears, in the business of remaking the ancient basis of political representation within the state so as to do away with the advantage of the low country "parishes," and to transfer the seat of power to the upcountry "districts," with their larger white populations. Parishes as political units, each entitled to a member of the Senate, were abolished. Each judicial district of the state was allotted one senator, with one additional for Charleston, but as a concession to the low country the old basis of representation was continued in the lower House, based half on property and half on population.

At once arose another question: How should freedmen be counted in the political population? The old three-fifths rule for counting slaves in the "Federal number" on which representation in Congress was based was a compromise, recognizing the status of the slave as part of the population but not part of the body of citizenship of the state. Should this compromise be continued, with each freedman counted as three-fifths of a person for purposes of representation, or should he be counted as one person, or as none?

South Carolina's local struggle over the question curiously foreshadowed the greater struggle to come in Washington. Upcountry representatives, intent on their battle with the low country for local power, had no intention of seeing free Negroes count for more than slaves, so increasing the weight of the white voters of the coastal section. Instead, they insisted, and successfully, that Negroes should not be counted at all for purposes of determining political representation, oblivious of the fact that the same reasoning could be turned against the state of South Carolina and the South as a whole by those at the North who were just as determined that the result of the war and emancipation should not be an increase of Southern strength in Congress.

The Radical alternative to this position, that freedmen should be allowed to vote if they were to be counted for representation, was not considered at the South Carolina convention, even in the form of that limited and qualified suffrage which President Johnson recommended to the Mississippi body. A few Carolinians felt, as did the President, that some form of suffrage for Negroes such as existed in most of those Northern states in which they were allowed to vote at all, would be wise. Chief among them was Wade Hampton, late lieutenant general, C. S. A., once among the largest slave owners of the South, and a true and practical friend of the Negroes of his state.

While the idea of granting political rights to the freedmen did not come before the convention, their civil status was discussed, and the whole matter referred to a commission created to draft and submit to the forthcoming legislature a body of laws on the subject—the beginning of the second of the so-called "Black Codes."

During the same fortnight in which the South Carolinians deliberated, the Alabama convention sat in Montgomery, in the chamber of the House of Representatives in which was organized the Confederate States of America.

In Alabama, after the usual debate over the form of words which should be used to accomplish the result, the Ordinance of Secession was declared "null and void." The debt in aid of the Confederacy was repudiated, almost without debate. The most interesting, and in the light of a later day the most curious, discussion took place on the other essential, the abolition of slavery.

Judge Coleman of Choctaw County insisted that the state of Alabama, before acting on the question, should await the result of a test before the Supreme Court of the United States of the validity of the Emancipation Proclamation and the legislation in furtherance of it. As for himself, he believed the Federal action unconstitutional and invalid. The state of Alabama was incapable of committing treason. That could be done only by individuals, who might be punished by confiscation of their property, it is true, but only as individuals and after trial and conviction.

"To admit the right of the Federal head by proclamation to nullify the Constitution of a State," he said, "was to concede the loss of the republic and the sovereignty of the States. The present course proposed by the majority report was one of expediency, and he was not prepared to sacrifice rights, honor, and property to it. . . . On this great principle of State rights the North was as deeply interested as the South."

Freedom of the slaves he accepted as a fact but only as one accomplished by "act of the Federal Executive and the bayonet, and not by the free and voluntary act of the people of Alabama." To adopt the proposed ordinance making it a matter of state action, he thought, would mean that those who had not participated in the rebellion but had nevertheless lost their property would be estopped from securing compensation "when the country returned to its reason."

To this interesting expression of a strict legalistic conception of the status of slavery before the adoption of the Thirteenth Amendment, with its astonishing blindness to fact, Judge Foster of Calhoun County made answer. To await a test of the Federal action by the Supreme Court was worse than useless, he said. "The war settled two questions forever, one that of secession, the other of slavery," and there was no appeal. The ordinance reported by the committee "asserted a fact, apparent to everyone, that the institution of slavery had been destroyed, not deciding when or how, whether constitutionally or unconstitutionally." The Judge added:

"We could not reduce the negroes to slavery if the United States would withdraw their forces and stand aloof. . . . The attempt would lead to the reenactment of the bloody scenes of St. Domingo. . . . The country needs repose. The people have made up their minds that slavery is gone, and are accommodating themselves to the new order of things. It is wrong to awaken delusive hopes that could never be satisfied."

By the overwhelming vote of eighty-nine to three the realistic view of accepting the situation prevailed, but the mere fact of debate on such a proposition did its small part to add to the Northern distrust of the work of the provisional conventions.

As in South Carolina, much of the intense local interest of the delegates centered in the struggle between sections of the state over the questions of including Negroes in the population of counties for the purpose of apportioning representation in future legislatures. The fight was between the "Black Counties" in the rich cotton lands of the valleys of the Tombigbee and Alabama Rivers, and the "White Counties," located largely in the mountainous belt across the northern part of the state and in the pine lands of the southeast. The doctrine of the White Counties, summarized in the statement of the Huntsville *Advocate*, that "this is a white man's government and a white man's state," became the prevailing law when the constitution was changed to base representation on white population only—once more without apparent consideration of the possibility that exclusion of non-voting Negroes from the count of population of counties for purposes of political representation within the state might point the way to a demand for reduction of Southern representation in Congress unless Negroes should be made voters.

The Alabama convention, unlike the conventions in Mississippi and South Carolina, took up in considerable detail the matter of civil rights for freed people. Slave marriages were validated, and Negroes placed for the future under the same marriage laws as whites. Inter-marriage of the races was prohibited. Negroes were given the right to acquire, hold and transfer property, to sue and be sued, and to testify in court in cases in which either party at interest was colored. Even thus limited, this ordinance aroused opposition among the more ignorant whites, while it found favor with the bar and the bench.

Neither the South Carolina nor the Alabama convention thought it necessary, or wise, in the disturbed state of the times, to submit its new constitution to popular vote for ratification. Without that, however, there were enough elections in the South that year. Except in Texas, where Governor Hamilton contented himself with merely starting the registration of "loyal" voters scattered over that vast area, the successive stages of political restoration kept the politically-minded of the South busy with elections, conventions, more elections, and legislative sessions, through the latter half of 1865.

Within a week of the closing of the conventions at Columbia and Montgomery, the North Carolina body gathered at Raleigh, on October 2. "We are going home," said the Chairman, Judge Edwin G. Reade, an original Union man who had once served in the Congress of the United States and later as a senator of the Confederate States, but the way home was to be beset with words and difficulties. There was the usual debate on the form of words wherewith the Ordinance of Secession should be formally declared dead, ending with the strongest possible declaration that the "supposed ordinance . . . is now and hath been at all times, null and void." Slavery was abolished promptly, with almost no debate. The real struggle came on the repudiation of the "rebel debt."

On the eleventh day of the convention, as it was approaching its adjournment, the resolution of repudiation was laid on the table. Governor Holden, who had said nothing on the subject in his message to the convention, telegraphed the state of affairs to the President. Prompt answer flashed back from Washington, on October 18:

"Every dollar of the State debt, created to aid the rebellion against the United States, should be repudiated, finally and forever. . . . Let those who have given their means for the obligations of the State look to that power they tried to establish in violation of law, Constitution, and the will of the people. . . ."

With the President's message before them, the members of the convention reversed the earlier decision, repudiated the debt, and adjourned. Governor Holden telegraphed the news to the President, ascribing the action taken to the "most happy effect" of his telegram.

"Please pardon no leading man unless you hear from me," he added anxiously. The Governor, it seemed, was meeting with opposition from certain ones whom he called "contumacious leaders." The old factional fights in North Carolina, in which he had taken so large and active a part, were coming to life again. One outside observer noted that much of the "Unionism" of the Raleigh convention seemed more an expression of this local factional resentment than of genuine devotion to the United States.

Laws of the Confederate period not incompatible with the new state of affairs were declared by the convention to be in force, judicial proceedings were validated and contracts declared binding. The legislature was instructed to prepare a table of depreciation of the Confederate currencies at different periods during the war, which should govern debtors, creditors and courts in settling in terms of United States money transactions originally expressed in Confederate.

Just before the constitutional convention met in the House of Delegates, a convention of freedmen gathered in the African Church at Raleigh to discuss the status of their race. Their deliberations, as reported with enthusiasm by Mr. Sidney Andrews, ended in the adoption of an address and petition to the constitutional convention and the legislature to follow. Signers of the address were James H. Harris, of Wilmington, ex-slave, upholsterer by trade, self-educated; John R. Good of New Bern, and Isham Swett of Fayetteville, barbers; J. Randolph, Jr., of Greensboro, carpenter and teacher; and George A. Ruse, of Massachusetts, late chaplain of the 32nd United States Colored Troops. Some of these men were to become leaders in the legislature in the dark days of Reconstruction, but the tone of this address, the first political act of North Carolina Negroes, is notably conservative.

"Just emerging from bondage . . . we are fully conscious that we possess no power to control legislation in our behalf, and that we must depend wholly upon moral appeal to the hearts and consciences of the people of our State. . . .

"We are fully conscious that we cannot long expect the presence of government agents, or of the troops, to secure us against evil treatment from unreasonable prejudice and unjust men. Yet we have no desire to look abroad for protection and sympathy. We know we must find both at home and among the people of our own State, and merit them by our industry, sobriety, and respectful demeanor, or suffer long and grievous ills. . . .

"Finally, praying for such encouragement to our industry as the proper regulation of the hours of labor, and the providing of means of protection against rapacious and cruel employers, and for the collection of just claims, we commit our cause into your hands. . . ."

The matter of civil rights for freedmen, so eloquently presented, was referred to a commission to be named by the Governor, which was to report to the legislature. However, during the convention and afterward, there was agitation of the question of Negro testimony, with the lawyers, in the main, favoring its admission and the laity largely against. As in Tennessee, the strength of the opposition lay among the whites of lesser standing, who found a powerful, even violent, spokesman for their point of view in Governor Holden and his newspaper, the *Standard*. Afterward, as part of the alliance with the Northern Radicals against Andrew Johnson, the Governor was to reverse his position, just as the majority of the Tennessee legislature did, and for like reasons.

Two other constitutions were done in that year of constitution writing, those of Georgia and Florida, written by conventions which met on the same day, October 25, in the village capitals of Milledgeville and Tallahassee.

The Georgia convention elected as chairman Herschel V. Johnson, one-time governor of the state, nominee of the Union Democrats for vice-president on the ticket with Stephen A. Douglas in 1860, and leader of the Union fight in the secession convention of 1861. Two others who had fought for the Union in the 1861 convention became leaders on the floor of the convention of 1865—Charles J. Jenkins of Augusta and Joshua Hill of Madison. Joseph E. Brown, though not a member, was present, occupying his old quarters in the Mansion along with his provisional successor, Governor Johnson.

At the opening of the second day's session, and almost without debate, Georgia "repealed" secession. Judge Hill raised a slight flurry the next day when he moved to reconsider and to substitute the stronger language used in North Carolina, but the flurry subsided when his motion was withdrawn in the interest of harmony.

Slavery was disposed of with even less formality. Late in the afternoon of the fourth day, in the dusk of the low-ceilinged Hall of Representatives, the reading clerk, lighting his way down a long Bill of Rights with a candle held in one hand, came to the twentieth article. Reciting that the government of the United States had, "as a war measure, proclaimed all slaves . . . emancipated," and had "carried that proclamation into full practical effect," the article declared that there should be no more slavery in Georgia,

"provided that this acquiescence in the action of the United States is not intended to operate as a relinquishment, or waiver, or estoppel of such claim for compensation of loss sustained by reason of the emancipation of his slaves as any citizen of Georgia may hereafter make upon the justice and magnanimity of that government."

In the droning monotone which reading clerks use, he lined out this astonishingly optimistic article, and paused.

"If there is no objection, and the chair hears none," said the presiding officer, "the clause will be considered as agreed to, and the clerk will read the next in order."

Except for this almost casual emancipation, and for the adoption of an ordinance prohibiting intermarriage of the races, all matters concerning the civil rights of freedmen were left to the coming session of the legislature. Relations were established with the Freedmen's Bureau by the acceptance of the offer of General Davis Tillson, the new assistant commissioner, to name provisional county officers as agents of his Bureau.

The main fight in the Georgia convention was on the repudiation of the "rebel debt." Not until the very last, and only after Governor Johnson had laid before it strong telegrams from Secretary Seward and the President, could the body bring itself to declare against paying Georgia bonds issued in aid of the Confederate war. The arguments for assumption of the debt ran from lofty pleas for Georgia's integrity as a debtor to impassioned resentment at dictation from Washington. The argument for repudiation, aside from the expediency of complying with the President's demand, was that the assumption of the debt would require the state "to tax the poor people for the benefit of the Shylocks who hold the bonds."

"No one proposed to pay for the lost slaves, for the burned houses, for the barns burnt, the fencing destroyed, the horses, cows, mules, hogs and other property taken, for the ruined fortunes of thousands," said a delegate from Bartow County. "No one proposed anything but the payment of these bonds in the hands of men who never saw the forefront of battle, and were careful to keep out of harm's way in the hour of conflict."

The debate was bitter, the result close, but finally the convention did, with certain reservations, declare the debts null and void, and adjourned.

The Florida convention "annulled" secession, abolished slavery, and, at first, referred the whole subject of debt repudiation to an election at which the people were to vote, "pay" or "no pay." Under pressure of a strong telegram from President Johnson, the last action was reversed and the debt repudiated.

The notable lack of bitterness in the proceedings of the Florida convention was largely due to the fine influence of Provisional Governor Marvin, who had demonstrated to all factions his wisdom and sense of fairness. The Confederates he had impressed with his prompt action in stopping the advertised sale by treasury agents of confiscated estates belonging to "amnestied" or pardoned owners; and by his personal petition to the President for the pardon of Senators Mallory and Yulee, and former Governor Allison, confined in Northern prisons. The entire citizenship he had impressed with wise and sensible counsel to accept the results of the war in good faith.

He did not advise social or political equality of the freedmen with the whites, but did earnestly urge equal civil rights:

"Persons of color must be admitted as witnesses in all courts of civil jurisdiction. . . . You keep the negro out of the courts and what chance has he for justice? And the North is very powerful, even after the war, and has strength to enforce its decrees."

To the Negroes thrilling with rumors of forty acres and a mule at the turn of the year, his advice was just as plainspoken:

"I want you to understand me. The President will not give you one foot of land, nor a mule, nor a hog, nor a cow, nor even a knife or fork or spoon."

To the constitutional convention he said, in his message:

"Heretofore, the negro in a condition of slavery, was to a large extent under the power and protection of his master, who felt an interest in his welfare, not only because he was a dependent . . . but also because he was his property. Now he has no such protection, and unless he finds protection in the courts of justice he becomes the victim of every wicked, depraved and bad man, whose avarice may prompt him to abuse and maltreat the helpless being placed by his freedom beyond the pale of protection of any kind. . . .

"The admission of negro testimony should not be regarded as a privilege granted to the negro, but as a right of the State . . . and of the accused, to have his testimony."

Under such promptings the convention gave to Negroes the right to sue and be sued, and to testify in all cases in which Negroes were concerned.

With the adjournment of the Georgia and Florida conventions, the work of constitution writing came to an end for the year 1865. Three more steps remained to be taken. Elections must be held under the new constitutions, to choose the men who were to run the new governments; the legislatures to be chosen must meet and complete the work started by the conventions; the new governments must be accepted by the government of the United States, in all its branches. Until these things were done, the process of political restoration of the seceded states to the Union was not to be regarded as finished.

CHAPTER XIII

MISSISSIPPI MISTAKES

MISSISSIPPI, having held the first constitutional convention, was the first of the Johnson states to elect officers under its new constitution, first to hold a session of its new legislature, and, unfortunately for the success of President Johnson's plan of restoration, the only state which acted finally on a group of statutes defining the civil and legal status of freedmen before Congress came back to Washington in December of 1865.

The legislature which enacted this first and most famous of the "Black Codes" was chosen on October 2, after a campaign largely fought over the issue of admitting Negroes into the courts as witnesses. The idea of allowing a Negro, even if he was no longer a slave, to come into court, take oath, and testify was too much for a majority of the Mississippi voters—so soon after emancipation. Leaders of better judgment were not lacking, but opponents of Negro testimony succeeded in electing a majority of the legislature upon the argument, as expressed in the Jackson News, that "if the privilege is ever granted, it will lead to greater demands, and at last end in the admission of the negro to the jury box and the ballot box."

Judge Campbell, afterward Chief Justice of the state, fairly stated and then demolished the only semblance of a basis of reason for refusing to admit Negro testimony.

"The idea that it is dangerous to admit negro testimony against whites, and that combinations among freedmen to fabricate false testimony will result in unjust convictions, will be dissipated in the mind of every sensible man who calmly reflects on the fact that it is usually difficult to convict of crime even on the testimony of whites, and that a jury of white men with all their knowledge of negro character, jealousy of caste, and prejudice against this innovation in the law of evidence, and a white judge with a court house crowded with white spectators, with white men as attorneys in both sides, will not likely be deceived and duped into improper convictions."

The importance of the subject was not in its effect upon actual administration of justice. The courts of the powerful Freedmen's Bureau, backed by the army, were freely open to Negroes whose testimony was excluded from the courts of the state. The net practical result of the obstinacy of Southern voters on the subject was that Negro testimony was accepted, not in the courts of the Southern government but in the new, strange, and usually antipathetic tribunals of the Bureau.

The importance of the action was in its effect upon the North. In a sense, the same thing is true of the whole body of Southern legislation in 1865 about freedmen. No feature of them which could be considered oppressive ever was allowed to go into effect by the Bureau or the military commanders in the various states. Moreover, even had they been enforced, it is altogether likely that the manner of enforcement would have softened the asperities of their harsh-sounding provisions.

The grave damage done by the codes arose largely from their phrasing, which, though it broadly followed that of the apprenticeship and vagrancy laws of Northern states, lent itself to half statement, innuendo, and direct untruth for Northern circulation and consumption. The Mississippi code was the only one before the country in its entirety when Congress convened. Its provisions, more stringent than those of most of the others, and particularly the circumstances and manner of its adoption, impressed upon the Northern mind a pattern of "Black Codes" which never could be dislodged or sensibly modified. And nothing was more important to the South in the years of 1865 and 1866 than the state of mind of the dominant North.

This elemental fact seems to have been totally absent from the thoughts of Mississippi's new governor, Benjamin G. Humphreys, and of the special commission which drafted the code. The Governor in his own person was something of a shock to the sensibilities of many in the North. First of the new Southern governors to be chosen, he was likewise the earliest instance of a political phenomenon to which so much Northern objection was to be raised—the "Confederate Brigadier" in office. He had not been a candidate, being "yet an unpardoned rebel," as he himself put it, "desirous of renewing my allegiance to the United States." The only candidate before the people with any sort of nomination was Judge E. S. Fisher, whom the members of the constitutional convention had offered before they adjourned in August. The Judge had been less than lukewarm toward the Confederacy; the General was looked upon as a good enough Union man because, as a Whig of the old line, he had stood for the

Union as long as there was room in the state for such a stand. The result was the spontaneous election of the "unpardoned rebel," for whom presidential pardon was secured in time for his inauguration on October 16, when the legislature convened.

The great question of the status of the freedman, Governor Humphreys laid before the legislature in a special message curiously compounded of sensible recommendations and unfortunate and unnecessary remarks.

"Under the pressure of Federal bayonets," he said, "urged on by the misdirected sympathies of the world in behalf of the enslaved African, the people of Mississippi have abolished the institution of slavery, and have solemnly declared in their State constitution that 'the Legislature should provide by law for the protection and security of person and property of the freedmen of the State, and guard them and the State against any evils that may arise from sudden emancipation'. . . . We must now meet the question as it is, and not as we would like to have it. The rule must be justice. The negro is free, whether we like it or not; we must realize that fact now and forever. To be free, however, does not make him a citizen, or entitle him to social or political equality with the white man. But the constitution and justice do entitle him to protection and security in his person and property."

Unlike the majority of his legislators, the Governor believed that Negroes should be allowed to testify and strongly urged it.

"It is an insult to the intelligence and virtue of our courts, and juries of white men, to say or suspect that they can not or will not protect the innocent, whether white or black, against . . . any perjury of black witnesses."

Questions of Negro testimony, however, were insignificant as compared with "the other great question of guarding them and the State against the evils that may arise from their sudden emancipation."

These evils, summarized as "idleness and vagrancy," were in large part ascribed to the existence and operations of the Freedmen's Bureau, by the Governor.

"Four years of cruel war conducted on principles of vandalism disgraceful to the civilization of the age," he said, "were scarcely more blighting and destructive on the homes of the white man, and impoverishing, degrading to the negro than has resulted in the last six or eight months from the administration of this black incubus. . . . How long this hideous curse, permitted of Heaven, is to be allowed to rule and ruin our unhappy people, I regret it is not in my power to give any assurance. . . ."

Having thus stigmatized as four years of disgraceful vandalism the war which, to the victors, seemed no less than a great crusade for Liberty and Union, impulsive Mississippi speech did not stop there. The special commission appointed to prepare and recommend statutes for the government of the freedmen brought in a report in the introduction of which it paid its respects to "those who are grossly ignorant in practical life and minute observation of what they speak and write, and would have us legislate."

"While some of the proposed legislation," the commission continued, "may seem rigid and stringent to the sickly modern humanitarians, they can never disturb, retard, or embarrass the good and true, useful and faithful of either race."

To those of either race who found the provisions too stringent, the suggestion was offered that they

"might flee and take sweet refuge in the more inviting bosom of the state or community who may cherish a more lively and congenial fellow-feeling and agrarian sympathy for that class and who are better able to spread them feasts and communing sacraments."

Scorning the idea of submitting to guidance by "the spirit of dictation and distempered intermeddling of those who have no place among us," the commission submitted a group of statutes which, in effect, were far less severe than would have been anticipated from the rhetorical tone of their introduction. Three principal laws were proposed—one on apprenticeship, to apply only to colored youth; a second, applicable in terms to both races, to define and punish vagrancy; and a third, establishing the civil rights of freedmen.

The justification for these and the more or less similar proposals in other states—and there was a degree of justification—lay in the disturbed conditions of the autumn of 1865. It was an anxious time. Results of the first season of free labor had left considerable dissatisfaction on both sides. Many planters and their hands had done well. With others, things had not prospered. Money with which to pay wages had been scarce, practically non-existent. Most crops had been made on share arrangements of one sort or another. The season had been poor, crops were distressingly short, there had been a good deal of vagrancy in some sections about cotton-picking time, and "shares" were reduced accordingly.

Reports about the operations of the first season of free labor, like those about every other phase of that kaleidoscopic year, are conflicting. General Fisk reported, in November, that the Bureau had supervised the making of five thousand contracts for labor in Tennessee, without complaint. By way of contrast, the Atlantic and Gulf Railroad, building through southern Georgia, reported that no man whom they hired stayed a whole month to collect his wages. General Grant reported a great deal of improvidence and incomplete work. Louisiana's crops of sugar and molasses were but a tiny fraction, hardly more than a tenth, of normal. On the Sea Islands in South Carolina and Georgia, the production of cotton was down from six thousand bales to four hundred. General Fullerton, after investigating affairs in Louisiana, reported that through the Bureau

"the idea was constantly held out to the freedmen that they were a privileged people, to be pampered and petted by the government, and the effect was most pernicious. . . . The acts of a few local agents of the Bureau were such as to destroy the confidence that should exist between these planters who were endeavoring to give free labor an impartial trial, and the freedmen who worked in their fields. These acts were done through a mistaken notion of kindness to the blacks. . . ."

From a thousand sources, some of them as irresponsible as some blue-coated private soldier with a perverted sense of humor, the blacks were being told that the great distribution of lands and mules was coming at the first Christmas of freedom. Responsible Bureau agents were doing their best to disabuse the minds of their charges of such ideas, but the glitter of the dream was too attractive not to have its serious adverse effect upon the work of the autumn—especially when plausible Northern gentlemen passed through the land selling for the reasonable sum of only five dollars per set four little red, white and blue painted pegs "from Washington," guaranteed to secure to the eager purchaser good title to any forty acres which he might select and stake out with his pretty new corner-markers.

The Southern legislative sessions fell in November and December, just before the anticipated Christmas division, while all this ferment of change was working full. The need for some sort of legal tutelage for the freedmen, designed to establish and regulate society and labor, was felt acutely. Northern men in the South recognized the gravity and difficulty of the situation. Some were frankly pessimistic, as was the disillusioned officer of the Atlanta garrison who assured Mr. Kennaway that the Negroes about the Federal camps were willing "to work a little, thieve a good deal, and then rest a while." The estimate of General Fisk was more nearly just and correct. He classified the freedmen into three general groups—those who would do well anywhere and under any circumstances; those who would work fairly well under supervision, and those who would work only under compulsion. At such a time, and under such circumstances, the Mississippians enacted their laws.

The apprenticeship law required that colored orphans under eighteen, or the children of parents unable or unwilling to support them, should be bound out by probate courts as apprentices to "some competent and suitable person," with preference to be given the former owner of the minor, if suitable. The child was to be supported, trained, and taught to read and write. Return of the apprentice to service, should he leave without cause, and judgment for the benefit of the apprentice against the master, in case of improper treatment, were provided for, as well as punishment for anyone "enticing" an apprentice away. The law did not differ greatly from the apprenticeship laws of the North, but it was immediately stamped there as a method to remand Negro children to slavery.

The vagrancy law, which applied to both races, adopted the broad and comprehensive definitions of some of the New England statutes on the subject. In addition it added two new classes—freedmen, free Negroes and mulattoes over eighteen years old found after the second Monday in January, 1866, with no lawful employment or business; and such persons

"unlawfully assembling themselves together, either in the day time or night time, and all white persons so assembling themselves with freedmen, free negroes or mulattoes, on terms of equality, or living in adultery or fornication with a freed woman."

Violations of this section were made punishable by a maximum fine of fifty dollars, or imprisonment for ten days, in the case of a Negro, or a two-hundred-dollar fine and six months' imprisonment for a white man.

Should the freedman fail to pay his fine within five days, the sheriff was directed to "hire out said freedman, free Negro, or mulatto, to any person who will, for the shortest period of service, pay said fine," with preference to be given to the vagrant's employer, if any.

The third act, regulating general civil rights, gave to Negroes the right to sue and be sued, and to testify in cases in which either party was colored, or where the crime charged was alleged to have been committed by a white person upon or against the person or property of a Negro. Negroes were authorized to acquire and dispose of personal property, except that they might not "rent or lease any land or tenements except in incorporated cities and towns, in which places the corporate authorities shall control the same." Of all the provisions of the code none excited more adverse comment than this. From any standpoint, it was an extraordinarily shortsighted blunder, especially at a time when a major complaint against the freedmen was their propensity to leave the country and gather in towns.

Every Negro was required to have a lawful home or employment by the second Monday in January, 1866, to be evidenced by a written contract of employment or by a license from designated public officials authorizing him, or her, to do irregular and job work. Contracts for labor for a period of more than one month were required to be read over to the Negro by the proper official. Should the laborer quit the service before the term of the contract was out, without good cause, he forfeited his wages for that year up to the time of quitting—a provision which recognized the essentially annual nature of making a crop. A Negro quitting service before the expiration of his contract term might be arrested and brought back, with a reward to the arresting officer to be paid by the employer and set off against the Negro's wages. In such cases there was a right of trial by justice court, with an appeal to the county court. "Enticing" labor away, knowingly employing a deserting freedman, or giving or selling him foods or supplies, was made a misdemeanor, as well as subject for a suit for damages.

Two other acts of lesser importance, but of great potency for irritation, completed the "code"—a "Jim Crow" law applying to railroad coaches, and a law prohibiting Negroes from keeping arms, engaging in riots, trespasses, malicious mischief, cruel treatment of animals, seditious speeches, insulting gestures, language or acts, exercising the functions of a minister of the Gospel without license, vending liquors, or "committing any other misdemeanor." White persons who supplied Negroes with arms or liquor were also made subject to fine and imprisonment. "By [the passage of these measures] we may secure the withdrawal of the Federal troops," said Governor Humphreys to the legislature—so little did he anticipate their effect in the North.

"We tell the white men in Mississippi that the men of the North will convert the State of Mississippi into a frog pond before they will allow such laws to disgrace one foot of soil in which the bones of our soldiers sleep and over which the flag of freedom waves," said the Chicago *Tribune* of December 1. The *Tribune's* righteous indignation might have been cooled somewhat (although probably it would not) had it examined the laws of Illinois then in effect. Illinois laws required that every free Negro within that state who did not possess a certificate of freedom and keep on file a bond of one thousand dollars with the county clerk, should be arrested and hired out to labor for a year. As to court testimony, Illinois forbade a Negro or mulatto "to give evidence in favor of or against any white person." Only in February of that same year of 1865, had Illinois repealed her law which assessed a fine of fifty dollars against free Negroes entering the state, and provided that upon failure of the Negro to pay, his services should be sold to that man who would pay the fine for the shortest period of labor—with half the fine going to the informer. Mississippi did require that all apprentices be taught to read and write. Illinois contented herself with providing that Negro or mulatto apprentices need not be "taught to write, or the knowledge of arithmetic."

Insofar as the language of the statutes went, it would seem that Mississippi was certainly no less liberal than the state in which the *Tribune* was published, and in whose political and public affairs it was so large an influence.

The *Tribune* was but one in a chorus of Northern condemnation, however; nor was Illinois the only Northern state where laws discriminating against Negroes were on the statute books. There was hardly a feature of the apprenticeship and vagrancy acts of Mississippi, and of the other Southern states, which was not substantially duplicated in some of these Northern laws, while many of the Northern provisions were more harsh in their terms than anything proposed in the South.

In the New England states, in New York, Indiana and Wisconsin the definition of vagrancy was as broad and inclusive as that in the Southern legislation; the penalty, more severe. "Servants" or "apprentices" departing from the service of the master, or neglecting their duty, were subject to fine and imprisonment at hard labor; persons "enticing" apprentices were subject to severe punishment; one without employment wandering abroad, begging, and "not giving a good account of himself," might be imprisoned as a vagrant, for periods varying from ninety days to three years, in various Northern states. In one, at least, any citizen was permitted "of his own authority and without process" to arrest such wanderers.

It is strange that even lawyers treated the Southern statutes as if they were something new in the world—and yet not so strange, for the lawyers were also politicians. James G. Blaine grew eloquently sarcastic at the use of the words "master" and "servant" in the Southern acts, as if it were an innovation designed to establish a system of caste, when as a lawyer he must have known that the words came down from the English common law to describe well-understood legal relations, and were in full and frequent use in the laws and decisions of every state, his own included.

Not all the condemnation of the Mississippi action was Northern, however, or even outside the state. The Jackson *Clarion* declared the action "unfortunate" and hoped that the legislature would correct its mistake. The Vicksburg *Herald* held similar views and urged that the constitutional convention be reassembled to treat the situation. The Columbus *Sentinel's* caustic comment, reprinted in other state papers, was that those responsible were a "shallow-headed majority more anxious to make capital at home than to propitiate the powers at Washington. . . . They are as complete a set of political Goths as were ever turned loose to work destruction upon a State. The fortunes of the whole South have been injured by their folly."

CHAPTER XIV

LEGISLATIVE IRRITANTS

THE "folly" of the Mississippi legislature was to go even further. In spite of repeated urgings from President Johnson that the pending Thirteenth Amendment be ratified, lest a "failure to act create the belief that the act of your convention abolishing slavery will hereafter be revoked," the legislature on December 4 rejected the Federal amendment abolishing slavery.

"The argument is," telegraphed the President to Governor Sharkey, "if the convention abolished slavery in good faith, why then should the legislature hesitate to make it a part of the Constitution of the United States?"

The argument of the President was pertinent but the Mississippians had a counter-argument. They had already adopted a state constitutional amendment abolishing slavery within their own borders. They intended to abide by that in good faith so that ratification of the Federal amendment would be of no practical effect, so far as Mississippi was concerned. They had no real objection to abolishing slavery again, they said, but the proposed Thirteenth Amendment contained a second clause giving Congress power to enforce the article by appropriate legislation, and to that they were unalterably opposed. It was, they held, dangerous to grant more power of any sort to the Federal government, and especially to open up a subject which would be used by Radicals and demagogues against the peace and quiet of the country. Slavery had already been abolished by state action everywhere except in Kentucky and Delaware, said the legislature, and therefore the public mind should be withdrawn from the subject which had been "so irritating in the past, and the door as effectively closed against all future agitation as it was possible for human wisdom to do."

Wherefore, the legislature of Mississippi, in the exercise of its wisdom, pointedly refused to ratify the amendment, and thereby did no little to keep the agitation going.

In this action Mississippi was alone among the former Confederate States. The four states whose restoration had been started in the time of President Lincoln—Louisiana, Tennessee, Arkansas, and Virginia—were early in the ratification column. The other states added their ratifications promptly, as each legislature met. The ratifications of South Carolina, Alabama, North Carolina, and Georgia became the last four of the twenty-seven needed to complete the amendment of the Constitution, and were so counted by Secretary Seward in his proclamation of December 18, 1865. These ratifications of an amendment to the Constitution of the United States were almost the only actions of the restored Southern states which were accepted by the Congress at Washington.

South Carolina's ratification was given by a legislature chosen on October 18. At the same election James L. Orr, whose long career of office-holding had included a term as speaker of the House of Representatives at Washington, and one as senator of the Confederacy at Richmond, was chosen governor. He was the only candidate formally before the people holding a nomination from the members of the constitutional convention, but as in Mississippi there was a spontaneous movement among the voters to select for the place a Confederate soldier, in this case Wade Hampton. In spite of his own strenuous efforts to prevent it, General Hampton came near to being elected. A majority of the votes in the state outside his home district were cast for him but the General's personal influence at home was enough to secure there a practically unanimous vote for Orr, and so to elect him by a narrow majority.

On October 25 the legislature convened for a preliminary session at Columbia. The old capitol was burned, the new one still standing but roofless, fire-scarred walls in an enclosure littered with unplaced building stone. South Carolina College, however, had survived the fire, and there the legislature gathered, the Senate in the library and the House in the chapel.

On November 13 the legislature ratified the Thirteenth Amendment, with a reservation that the second section should not be construed as giving to Congress any power to legislate on the political status or civil relations of former slaves. Before adjournment they received the report of the commission named by Governor Perry to prepare a system of laws for the freedmen; passed an act "preliminary to the legislation induced by the emancipation of slaves," in which the policy of the state was declared to be that those of less than seven-eighths Caucasian blood were "not entitled to social or political equality with white persons," but should "have the right to acquire, own and dispose of property, to make contracts, to enjoy the fruits of their labor, to sue and be sued, and to receive protection under the laws in their persons and property."

Having elected Governor Perry and John L. Manning to the United States Senate, hopefully, the legislature recessed until November 27, when it convened to inaugurate Governor Orr and to set up a complete body of law, minutely regulating the civil, political, economic and domestic place of the freedmen in the life of the state. The intended effect of the code, it would seem, was to restrict the opportunities of freedmen largely to agricultural labor and domestic service. To engage in other callings required a special license with a high fee—one hundred dollars for a "merchant or peddler"; ten dollars for an "artisan."

In the ninety-seven sections of the act on domestic relations of the Negroes, there are minute "Regulations of Labor on Farms," including the hours of labor "from sunrise to sunset, with a reasonable interval for breakfast and dinner." "Servants shall rise at the dawn in the morning," said the law, "feed, water and care for the animals on the farm, do the usual and needful work about the premises, prepare their meals for the day, if required by the master, and begin the farm work or other work by sunrise."

Servants were required to be "quiet and orderly in their quarters, at their work, and on the premises," and to "extinguish their lights and fires, and retire to rest at reasonable hours." Keeping servants at home on Sunday, except for work of daily necessity to be done in turn, was prohibited. "Absentees on Sunday shall return to their homes by sunset," ran the law, while none might be "absent from the premises without the permission of the master."

For willful disobedience, habitual indolence, "want of respect and civility to himself, his family, guests or agents," or for absence on two or more occasions without permission, a master might discharge a servant; or, upon complaint to the district judge or magistrate, and proof of such misconduct, he might have inflicted upon the servant "suitable corporal punishment" or a "pecuniary fine," at the same time remanding the servant to his work. "Enticing away" a servant was made a misdemeanor, and also a subject for civil action for damages.

The code laid upon the master certain obligations as well, the violation of which would justify a servant in quitting the service. Masters were required to furnish a sufficient supply of "wholesome food," as well as to pay the stipulated wages for one "rated as full hand, three-fourths hand, half hand, or one-fourth hand, as the case may be." Battery upon the person of the servant was prohibited, and invasion by the master of his conjugal rights.

Besides the general regulations for "servants in husbandry," special regulations were made which throw light on the South Carolina conception of the perfect house servant in 1865:

"Servants and apprentices employed as house servants in the various duties of the household, and in all the domestic duties of the family, shall, at all hours of the day and night, and on all days of the week, promptly answer all calls and obey and execute all lawful orders and commands of the family in whose service they are employed.

"It is the duty of this class of servants to be especially civil and polite to their masters, their families and guests, and they shall receive gentle and kind treatment."

General rights and relations of persons of color received attention, also. The first thirteen sections of the act dealt with the relations of husband and wife, parent and child. Persons living with more than one husband or wife were required to select a permanent spouse by April 1, 1866. Other slave marriages were validated and children legitimated.

Fifteen sections of the code deal, in great detail, with the relations of master and apprentice, requiring, among other duties of the master, that the apprenticed child be sent to a school for colored children at least six weeks in every year.

Eviction of aged and helpless ex-slaves from their quarters was prohibited before January 1, 1867, except for cause and upon court order. Elaborate provisions were made for clearing the quarters of other Negroes not employed on the place. The proceeds of a special poll tax on freedmen were to be expended by the Board of Relief of Indigent Persons of Color.

"Vagrancy and idleness" were declared to be "public grievances," to be punished as crimes. The list of those to be considered as vagrants is long and inclusive, going back to some of the Puritan New England statutes, and perhaps to old England, through the regulations made for ex-slaves in the British West Indies, upon which the Carolina enactment is said to have been based. Vagrants included all persons without regular homes, reputable employment and visible livelihood; those peddling without license; all common prostitutes and gamblers; and even "those who are engaged in representing, publicly or privately, for fee or reward, without license, any tragedy, interlude, comedy, farce, play or other similar entertainment, exhibition of the circus, sleight-of-hand, wax works, or the like; those who, for private gain, without license, give any concert or musical entertainment of any description."

Having thus protected the people of Carolina from the wiles of unlicensed entertainment, whether by white or black, the list of vagrants tails off through fortune-tellers, sturdy beggars, common drunkards, and poachers to those who "frequent the premises of others, contrary to the will of the occupants."

Freedmen were forbidden the liquor trade in all its branches, or the possession of arms suitable for "military use." "Servants in husbandry" were forbidden to sell farm produce without written permission from the master—an ordinance passed in recognition of the offense, then common in the South, of stealing loose cotton to be sold after night at a "dead-fall," a type of low dive, store and doggery springing up around the towns.

Stealing of cotton baled for market was considered a much more serious crime, being made one of a long list of offenses to be punished by death when committed by a person of color, along with house-breaking, horse- or mule-stealing, rape or attempted assault with intent, having sexual intercourse with a white woman by "personating her husband," and raising an insurrection or furnishing arms, ammunition, or a place of assembly for that purpose.

Even if we make all allowance for the troubled times and the unprecedented chaos, and recall that the freedmen for whom they were legislating had been slaves but a few months before, it is hard to understand how the lawyers who laid the foundation of the code, or the legislators who enacted it, could have been so insensible to the current of thought and opinion. The reaction to the Mississippi enactments had already begun before South Carolina came to act on her code, but South Carolina, relentlessly logical in following out her theories, went on her course, sublimely blind to consequences. In fact, Governor Perry recommended that the code be passed "to remove all pretense for military rule in the state, as well as facilitate its speedy restoration to the Union"!

Not every Carolinian, however, was quite so blind to the facts of the case and the times. "Many believe," wrote a correspondent of the Charleston Courier under the pseudonym of "Juhl," "that it would have been better to have made no such ostentatious legal and judicial distinction between the races. . . . This would have been . . . certainly less offensive to those whose renewed antagonism it were folly to invoke."

At best, the "way home" for a restored Southern state government was not smooth and easy. North Carolina, unlike Mississippi and South Carolina, undertook no general legislation as to freedmen, and when her legislature came together it ratified the Thirteenth Amendment, promptly on December 1, and without reservation. Yet events in that state took such a turn that opponents of Southern restoration were able to hold it up as an example of persisting rebellious spirit.

Unlike so many of the provisional governors, the immediate ambition of Governor Holden was not election by the legislature to the Senate of the United States, but election by the people as governor of North Carolina. To this end a minority of the members of the constitutional convention were procured to call on him to run for election as governor, to continue the work he had begun as provisional governor. Reluctantly, Jonathan Worth, provisional treasurer of the state, an old-line Whig, of Quaker descent, and one whose Unionism was of more stable character than that of Governor Holden, was brought into the race in opposition.

Neither candidate made an active canvass. The Holden press strove to make the issue one of readmission of the state. "W. W. Holden and Go Back to the Union, or Jonathan Worth and Stay Out of the Union," was the way the *Standard* defined the situation. The opposition viewpoint was sharply stated by the Charlotte *Times*. "Vote for Holden and be loyal, and vote against him and be a traitor. That is the English of it. And if that is to be the test, then we are a traitor and glory in the treason."

Mr. Worth was elected handsomely—a result which the Holden press at home tried to represent as an expression of anti-Unionism. Unfortunately, their estimate of the situation, colored up for home consumption, was accepted at the North, even by the President. In thanking Governor Holden for the "noble and efficient manner" in which he had served, Mr. Johnson added:

"The results of the recent elections in North Carolina have greatly damaged the prospects of the State in the restoration of its governmental relations. Should the action and spirit of the legislature be in the same direction, it will greatly increase the mischief already done and might be fatal."

This message referred not only to the result in the gubernatorial election but also to the fact that only one of the seven successful candidates for Congress could take the iron-clad test oath of 1862 required for holding that office. This fact was much commented on and criticized by the Holden press, which itself had supported five defeated candidates who, if elected, could not have taken the same oath. Even in North Carolina, with its comparatively large proportion of Union men, it was difficult to find men of standing and ability who could honestly make oath that they had given no form of comfort and support to the Confederate cause at any time.

Under the leadership of such men as Governor Worth and former Governor William A. Graham, the legislature of North Carolina showed a fine degree of wisdom and judgment in dealing with its problems when it came to meet in February, 1866, but so completely did Governor Holden control the channels of information to the northward that no attention seems to have been paid to the significant fact that the people ratified the anti-secession and anti-slavery amendments to the state constitution by an almost unanimous vote.

The people of Virginia found a difficulty similar to that of North Carolina when they came to choose congressmen on October 12. Several of those elected, including A. H. H. Stuart, whose work for reconciliation was outstanding, could not take the iron-clad oath.

As a further step in the restoration of harmonious government in Virginia, the people overwhelmingly ratified the amendment which repealed those clauses in the Alexandria constitution disfranchising Confederates. This action, taken under the wise leadership of Governor Pierpont, angered the small group which was growing into the Republican party in Virginia. Lewis McKenzie, defeated candidate for Congress in the Alexandria district, declared that the "loyal men of the state were to be totally sacrificed and turned over to the power of the secessionists." The wholesome results of Governor Pierpont's leadership toward complete reconciliation were thus to be used, when Congress met, as one more of the many arguments against allowing the South to govern itself.

Early in its session, in December, the Virginia legislature repealed the disfranchising clauses of the Alexandria constitution, as it had been authorized to do by the October election. It also attempted to undo one other act of the Alexandria government by revoking its consent, on behalf of Virginia, to the annexation of Berkeley and Jefferson Counties to West Virginia in 1863. When Congress came to act on this question in March, 1866, however, it accepted as valid

the consent given by the shadowy Alexandria government and disregarded as null and void the revocation of that consent by the first
legislature which was in any way representative of the entire state.
This position the Supreme Court of the United States sustained,
by a divided vote, in 1870.

By the time Congress met in December, the new legislatures
of Georgia and Alabama were in session, and both had ratified the
Thirteenth Amendment before the first week in December ended,
becoming the twenty-sixth and twenty-seventh states in the list. New
governors were elected in both states, as well as legislatures and
members of Congress. United States senators were elected by the
legislature, too, but of all this political action the only part to be
recognized by the United States government was the ratification of
the amendment. The same anomaly is presented in the case of all
the Southern governments which ratified the amendment—that is,
all except Mississippi—of being in the Union for purposes of amending the fundamental Constitution, and out of it for such transient
purposes as the election of representatives and senators.

The new governor in Alabama, who was not allowed by Washington
to take office until after the amendment had been ratified, was
R. M. Patton, of Lauderdale County, a Union man of good character and ability, and leader of the movement to base political representation in Alabama on white population. The new senators, elected
in December, were Provisional Governor Parsons and George S.
Houston. Of the six representatives elected in November, five had
been original Union men and opposed secession, the sixth had been
a major general of the Confederate Army. Neither of the senators,
and none of the congressmen, could take the iron-clad test oath,
nor is it likely that any man who could have done so would have
been able to secure election.

In Georgia, the new governor was Charles J. Jenkins, judge of the
State Supreme Court and an old-line Union Whig. At the same
election, on November 15, seven congressmen were chosen, no one
of whom could take the iron-clad oath, although five of the seven
were original Union men and only two had been active Secessionists.

On December 6 the new legislature completed the ratification of
the Thirteenth Amendment, without reservations as to the enforcement section such as those made by the Alabama and South Carolina legislatures. Howell Cobb, in a letter written the next day,
summed up this final action on slavery: "I think they will get the
'peculiar institution' thoroughly disposed of after a while. It has

now been abolished by Congress, the President, war, state convention, legislatures, etc. If all that don't kill it, I would like to know
what would?"

The institution was killed, but one more Southern state, Florida,
had yet to drive in its ratification that month, on December 28. The
Florida legislature was not elected until November 29. Its members
were, in the main, lately of Confederate sympathies. The new
governor, elected at the same time, was David S. Walker, a quiet,
unassuming country gentleman from central Florida, an original
anti-secession man who had gone with the state. The new congressman—Florida was then entitled to but one—could not take the iron-
clad oath.

The whole political situation in the state was such that Senator
Sumner was moved to read to the Senate the outburst of one of his
numerous anonymous Southern correspondents:

"The election has been held and, as you may expect, rebels elected.
The legislators are four-fifths rebel officers, from Brig. Gen. Joseph
Finegan down to a corporal. . . . The people of Florida are more hostile
than they have ever been. They were surrendered too soon."

Governor Marvin, in his estimate, was more just and wise than
Senator Sumner's unknown informant:

"What is very remarkable is that as a general rule the most zealous
original secessionists accept the results of the war in a better spirit than
the original Union men who got dragged into it against their will."

The Governor was but noting what struck so many observers of
the South in that anxious time—that the former Confederate soldier,
"the backbone and sinew of the South," was the "real basis of reconstruction." "I know of very few more potent influences at work
in promoting real and lasting reconciliation and reconstruction than
the influence of the returned Southern soldier," reported Mr. Truman to the President.

Purblind and misguided as was so much of the political activity
of the half year between the beginning of the Johnson restoration
and the convening of Congress—those months in which President
Lincoln had hoped to see much accomplished while Congress was
away from Washington—it cannot be said that it showed any spirit
of sullen rebellion.

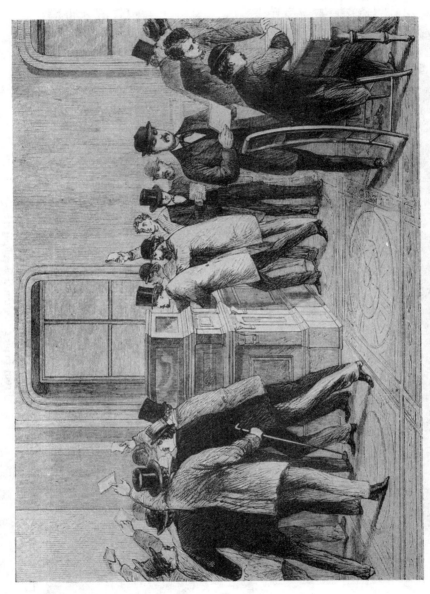

Gentlemen of the Press Filing their Despatches at the Opening of Congress.
From Leslie's Illustrated Newspaper.

The Mardi Gras Parade of the Krewe of Comus, New Orleans, 1867—"The Triumph of Epicure."
From Leslie's Illustrated Newspaper.

Men who had supported the Confederacy were elected to office, not to flaunt their gray uniforms in the face of the country but because, by and large, the better men of the South had been active in the Confederate cause. Codes of law to govern the freedmen were passed because of the desire to make freedom "work." The Southern people had a genuine misgiving in regard to the system, a distrust which was shared by those officers of the United States Army who had had experience in the management of the government's plantations along the Mississippi River during 1863 and 1864, as is abundantly indicated by the tone and details of their labor regulations then promulgated.

By the autumn the South had come to put its faith in its well-founded belief that President Johnson sincerely wished to restore the constitutional relations of the Union, and in its delusive confidence that he would be able to carry through his policy.

The skill and power of the opposition neither the President nor the Southern leaders gauged correctly. The President's own defects of temperament, and the South's strange blindness to the interpretations put upon acts of whose necessity and rectitude it was convinced, combined to put it in the power of this opposition to wreck the President's plan—a result accomplished the more easily by reason of Lincoln's death and its manner.

Governor Madison Wells of Louisiana had been an active Unionist, a participant in the plans for restoration of that state to the Union as far back as 1862. He had served as lieutenant governor and as governor under the Lincoln organization of the state. On November 6, the nominee of both factions, he was elected governor for a full term. From a Union standpoint his sentiments were "sound"; he had voluntarily emancipated his own slaves. Certainly if any Southern politician should have sensed the effect upon the North of the Southern labor legislation, it would seem that Governor Wells would have been the man. Yet, as part of the attempt to rid Louisiana of what the Constitutional Union party called "that incubus, the Freedmen's Bureau," he approved and signed a vagrancy bill not greatly different from that of Mississippi.

This became one of the laws concerning which Mr. Blaine and Senator Henry Wilson were to grow so righteously indignant. Perhaps, though, what Southern political bodies did, really made little difference, for Mr. Blaine later devoted two pages of his powerful rhetoric in *Twenty Years* to denunciation of Louisiana laws which never became laws, while Senator Wilson, in a bill in Congress to nullify Southern peonage measures, cited the same acts which never were enacted.

The political minds of the South, working in a maze of legal, social and political complications in 1865, tried earnestly, according to the lights and conditions of the time, to bring about order and stability—and the results of their efforts became important almost solely as furnishing the irritants which Radical writing and speaking were to use to inflame the victorious and controlling North.

CHAPTER XV

THE BUSINESS OF LIVING

ELECTIONS, conventions and legislative sessions there were in plenty in the South in the late months of 1865 but neither politics nor public affairs were the real preoccupation of the population.

The people had to bring back into productivity fields which had become "forests of weeds." They had to restore shelter destroyed by war or dilapidated after years of makeshift and neglect. Under new conditions, and strange, they had to put in motion once more the whole machinery of producing things and putting them into the hands of those who would use them.

To do all these things, they needed cash and credit. Cash in the South was entirely insufficient for the needs. Credit had to be had, and on almost any terms. One Mississippi planter, a Confederate general officer, returned from war to rescue his place from ruin, made his 1865 cotton crop with money borrowed in the North at sixty per cent interest, the loan to be repaid in cotton.

Usurious as the rate seems, it is to be remembered that the risks were great. There were risks of government action—confiscation talk was still in the air in the summer of 1865—and above all there were risks of labor, for no one knew yet whether or not the field Negroes would really work in freedom, subject only to the ordinary compulsions of making a living.

One reason for the reluctance of many freedmen to contract their labor at that season was expressed in an Alabama Negro's remark that "they say if we make contracts now, we'll be branded and made slaves again." So common was this belief that Colonel Thomas, assistant commissioner of the Freedmen's Bureau for Mississippi, found it necessary to make public proclamation that while signing contracts of employment would not enslave Negroes, vagrancy would result in their being put to labor "in the public works." General Davis Tillson, in Georgia, issued orders in October that all Negroes should be aided to get work, and that the able-bodied who refused it when offered should no longer draw government rations.

The soil and the season were ripe for mischief makers, Northern

117

and Southern, intentional and unintentional. Many Northern friends of the Negroes were fired with missionary zeal and an impatient fever for progress; many Southerners, learning little and forgetting less, were temperamentally unfitted for the new order of things. The first class agitated demands impossible of fulfillment. The second class, by their intemperate speech about freedom and freedmen, not only created difficulties locally but furnished the ammunition most needed by those who, for their own political profit, did not want to see peaceful and harmonious restoration of the Southern states.

A time was to come when many, if not most, of the officers of the Freedmen's Bureau were to use their positions and power for political purposes, but in the first months of freedom the political future of the Negroes was not yet apparent. In those months, prior to the quiet and almost unnoted spread of chapters of the secret political order of the Union League of America in the towns and villages and at the crossroads, which began in the autumn of 1865, most of the officers of the Bureau were zealous, according to their lights, to make freedom "work."

In their endeavors, as the Christmas season approached, they were increasingly plagued by the persistence of the belief on the part of their charges that the great "division" of land and mules was to take place at the holiday. In Texas, General E. M. Gregory, the assistant commissioner, warned the freedmen, in November, that they would get nothing from the government at Christmas or any other time but, to judge from Governor Hamilton's reports, the warning had slight effect on many of the freedmen. General Rufus Saxton, assistant commissioner in South Carolina, reported before Christmas that "the impression is universal among the freedmen" that they were to have forty acres each in January, and that the utmost endeavors of the Bureau agents had been unable to eradicate "so deep-seated a conviction."

Not even the personal appearance and advice of General Howard himself could accomplish it. He was listened to respectfully, because he wore the blue uniform and was the representative of the paternal government from which all blessings were to flow—and from which the unbelievable blessing of freedom had already flowed. Incorrigibly hopeful believers in the coming division dismissed his words, however, with the explanation that he probably had been seduced by the former slave owners into an attempt to persuade them to execute contracts to labor.

Even one so unfailing in his criticism of the widespread Southern belief that Negroes would not work in freedom as Mr. Trowbridge, gives implied support to that view by noting at Vicksburg and Natchez, just after the Christmas holidays had passed, that "the freedmen who, before Christmas, had refused to make contracts, vaguely hoping that lands would be given them by the government . . . now came forward to make the best terms they could."

To the same effect testified Stephen Powers, traveling correspondent of the Cincinnati *Commercial*, that the Negroes up to Christmas "had been thriftless, gay, improvident, and relying on what they confidently expected, the division of their old masters' property at that time."

The state of the Negroes, as the first Christmas of freedom approached, was as varied as any man not devoted to the establishment of a preconceived thesis would reasonably expect. A Northern planter on the Sea Islands complained that it was costing him nearly a dollar a pound to make his cotton because of the impossibility of getting the work done promptly and properly under the new conditions of labor—a view which, it was reported in the *Nation*, "would be expressed perhaps in less temperate language by the greater number of Northern planters in Port Royal." On the other hand, a Southern planter in Monroe County, Alabama, reported that his work was going on well, with good prospects for a profitable crop. And there were experiences and opinions of all shades in between.

A major difficulty of the Bureau in its attempts to help, not only in its early days but throughout its span of operations, was that of securing men who could handle the difficult and delicate tasks of a Bureau agent. General J. S. Fullerton, assistant commissioner in Louisiana, who was not a Radical in his sympathies, reported that some agents had shown such a "want of tact, conciliation and sound judgment," and had been so blinded by their prejudices, that they had created and fostered enmity between blacks and whites, an enmity which, so far as the whites were concerned, was to be found principally among that class which feared Negro competition and dreaded Negro equality.

General Fullerton's predecessor in office in Louisiana, Chaplain T. W. Conway, was in the North making speeches about Southern conditions. The Chaplain, who was of the Radical persuasion, felt that only the Bureau kept Louisiana from a "condition of anarchy and bloodshed" in which the Negroes would be "murdered by wholesale. . . . It will not be persecution merely; it will be slaughter; and I doubt whether the world has ever known the like. These southern rebels, when once the power is in their hands, will stop at nothing short of extermination. . . ."

General Fullerton's story, however, was different. "It is not true," he said, "that there are great numbers of freedmen being murdered by the whites in Louisiana. . . . By telling only the bad acts that have been committed, and giving them as an index of society, any large community could be pictured as barbarous." That, most unfortunately, was about how Southern conditions were being reported in the North.

"These reports of outrages upon the colored people, of ill-treatment of the northern settlers, are quite exceptional cases and exaggerated, if not altogether false," testified John Tarbell, brigadier general in the United States Army, and after the war a plantation owner in Mississippi. He felt strongly that

"all these statements in the newspapers did the educated people of the South very great injustice. There are, no doubt, disloyal and disorderly persons in the South, but it is an entire mistake to apply these terms to a whole people. I would as soon travel alone, unarmed, through the South as through the North. The South I left is not at all the South I hear and read about in the North."

The tale of the routine of the ordinary relationships of life lacks interest, and tends to be overlooked even by the impartial observer, while there were plenty of acts and expressions of aversion to the new order to make good copy for those on the lookout for evidences of unrepentant animosity. Few who reported to the North these loose and violent expressions were observant enough to note, as did Mr. Trowbridge on his tour of the South, that "every man who curses the black race and prays for its removal or extermination, makes exceptions in favor of negroes he has raised or owned, until I am beginning to think that these exceptions constitute a majority of the colored population."

The New England reporter put his finger on what John R. Lynch, a colored leader of Reconstruction in Mississippi, long afterward described as the "bond of sympathy between the two races at the South—a bond that the institution of slavery with all its horrors could not destroy, the Rebellion could not wipe out, Reconstruction could not efface, and subsequent events have been unable to change."

The resumption of ordinary economic life in 1865 was made more difficult by the camps or colonies of freed people which sprang up around some of the army posts and Bureau offices. Crowded conditions and the lack of work in such camps bred distress and disease, only partially compensated for by the opening of hospitals and the issue of rations. Mr. Trowbridge, who visited as much of the South as any one traveler in the first year of freedom, found one such colony, Camp Contraband near Chattanooga, where the officer in charge reported that he was issuing no rations to three thousand men, women and children living in cheerful, self-supporting contentment. The presence in Chattanooga of a garrison of a thousand colored troops, however, may have furnished at least part of the economic base of life at the camp.

One intelligent freedwoman explained to the visitor that "a heap was workin' and a heap is lazin' round." She laid her own inability to raise chickens to the fact that "the neighbors just pick 'em up and steal 'em in a minute," to which she added the illuminating comment, "I never stole in my life but from them that owned me."

The helpless, the aged and the very young in many cases were left behind in the old home quarters to be supported by former masters. To this was due, largely, the fact that the Bureau had only about a thousand colored paupers to support in the state of Georgia, Mr. Truman reported to the New York *Times*. In practice the former masters were rarely so sternly logical as the editor of the *Southern Cultivator*, who declared:

"The law which freed the negro, at the same time freed the master. . . . If any officer can make the master support the old and infirm slave, he can also make the slave continue under and support the old and infirm master."

As might have been expected after the great upheaval of 1865, the coming of winter found many Negroes still wandering, homeless and unplaced. Colonies of ex-slaves in squalid huts clustered along the railroad tracks near Gallatin, Tennessee, struck Sir John Kennaway as he entered the territory of the former Confederate States, while, on the line between Corinth and Memphis, Mr. Trowbridge was impressed by little outdoor fires, each the center of a group of homeless Negro families. On the same journey, however, he was even more impressed by the happy throngs of comfortably clad freed people crowding on the train to go to Memphis to "buy Christmas" with their share of their first season's earnings.

Memphis, in that December season, was on a boom. Nineteen hundred new dwellings were under construction or contracted for. In the forests of the South, by that time, were to be found hundreds of small portable sawmills, brought down from the North, all busy getting out the lumber to supply the demands of cities such as Memphis, which the war had brought to the front.

Memphis, which had suffered hardly at all physically, was thriving on the world's demand for cotton. On its levee, crowded with a "superb array of steamers" and covered with acres of bales and casks, streams of drays were loading and unloading all day and into the night, when the roustabouts worked on by the lurid illumination of "great smoking and flaring flambeaux," wood and bituminous coal burning in iron baskets hung from the ends of spars.

Atlanta, which, to refugees returning from North or South in the spring, had seemed "nothing but piles of brick and ruins" which could never be cleared, was in a perfect fever of building before the winter set in. Its streets, ankle-deep in mud at the crossings, were not lighted. "Everywhere were ruins and rubbish, mud and mortar and misery," even as late as December, with hundreds of inhabitants living in wretched hovels made of scraps of tin roofing and other materials salvaged from the burnt district, but everywhere was rebuilding and hustling activity. Lots on Peachtree Street were selling at forty dollars a front foot; rents were enormous; hotels, in spite of a raging epidemic of smallpox, were crowded with travelers of all sorts, particularly drummers—for the wholesale houses of Baltimore and New York, of Louisville and Cincinnati, met there to compete for the reviving Southern trade. Sir John Kennaway hardly knew "whether to wonder most at the completeness of the ruin which had swept over Atlanta, or at the rapidity with which its restoration was being effected."

Chattanooga, which owed "half its eight thousand inhabitants and all its notoriety to the war," impressed the traveler approaching by the railroad between Lookout Mountain and the Tennessee River, toward nightfall, with the "lurid glare upon the black waters of sparks and flame sent out from the chimneys of a rolling mill busy day and night in turning out railroad iron to replace the waste of war."

The need for railroad iron and railroad power and rolling stock was great as winter approached. Most of the railroad lines had been returned by the government to their owners, after much taking of oaths and proving of loyalty on the part of directors and officers. All of the lines were burdened with interest due on bonds held mostly in the North, on which no payments had been made for the five years of separation, and with heavy floating debts as well. Many of them were burdened with the obligation to pay to the United States large sums for benefits and improvements alleged to have been made to their lines during their use by the Military Railroads. All of them were in physical condition verging on wreck and ruin.

Like the farmers of the South, the railroads needed credit which was to be had only on the most onerous terms. The South Carolina Railroad, a strong line before the war, was offered loans in the North to purchase rail and equipment, at a discount of thirty-five per cent. The owners, having little left of their principal lines between Charleston and Columbia and Augusta, except the bare grade, met the situation by robbing the "upper lines" of the company, above Columbia, of their iron, and using the iron to re-lay the more important lines below Columbia. In this way, the railroad reached Columbia again in October, with iron taken from the Camden Branch. Camden had to wait until late in the spring of 1867 before iron was available to restore the line there.

Between Charleston and Augusta a gap of fifty miles of complete destruction was still to be crossed in the winter of 1865-1866, while between Charleston and Savannah the wreck of the railroad was so complete and the difficulties of its rebuilding were so great that during the first two years after the war it was not even attempted. Not until 1870 was the service restored, and even then important bridges such as that over the Ashley at Charleston were missing.

In North Carolina, where the railroads had not been subjected to the same systematic destruction, their dilapidation was more the result of the wear and tear of war; their financial burdens, more the result of a misplaced confidence in Confederate currency. The North Carolina Railroad, between Goldsboro and Charlotte, in which the state had a large interest, had put part of its faith in cotton, with eight hundred bales stored in South Carolina, nearly enough at 1865 prices to have met all its current liabilities at the end of the war—but most of the eight hundred bales were lost or stolen in the days of licensed and unlicensed cotton theft.

In Georgia, the coming of winter still found unspanned the gap in the main line of the Central Railroad, between Savannah and Macon, where one hundred miles of bent rails and burnt bridges testified to the "conscientious thoroughness with which Sherman's army had done its work of destruction."

The rolling stock of the railroad between Meridian and Selma, cut off on the Meridian end of the line by the destruction of bridges, could not be used for the work of rebuilding the ruined line about Selma. With seventy-eight bridges to be rebuilt between New Orleans and Canton, Mississippi, General Beauregard tackled the job of rehabilitating the New Orleans, Jackson & Great Northern with such zeal and energy that trains were running through before the end of October, while the other principal railroad of that region, the Mobile & Ohio, which had suffered less, was open as far as Corinth in late July.

More than opening of railroads, however, was required to restore the mail service in Mississippi. Lack of "loyal" men who could take the iron-clad oath required of postmasters kept most of the post offices closed. As late as midsummer of 1866 but eighty-nine offices had been opened in the state, while in Alabama there were only one hundred and seven, and in Georgia, one hundred and seventy-two out of a total of eight hundred forty-four in that state in 1859. In Arkansas, difficulty of transportation and scarcity of loyal personnel for postmasters combined to limit the mails, even at important points, to three times a week. In towns over the South it was not unusual for citizens to club together and send each week to the nearest open post office for their mail.

CHAPTER XVI

Churches and Schools

In this critical time the South suffered from its prolonged isolation. Local newspapers, scanty and insufficient at best, largely depended for news of other than strictly local affairs on "exchanges," often brought to them casually through the kindness of some "gentlemanly conductor" or an obliging traveler on the trains.

The result, in some cases, was an undue emphasis on political discussion, frequently without sufficient information; but most of the country papers devoted themselves more to local affairs—the reopening for business of the local blacksmith shop; the opening of a "Select School" or a "Female Seminary" by some local gentlewoman; the erection of a new mercantile house, or the arrival of new stocks of goods; perhaps a report of smallpox in or near the town; the announcement of church services or lodge meetings; the occasional news of local shootings or affrays; the innumerable and unremarkable small affairs of everyday living.

There was, however, enough of political comment of the more provoking sort to bring from Governor Walker, of Florida, a warning that "every intemperate paragraph in a newspaper is particularly adapted to being reported to the North and magnified and made to play an important part in the war upon the President." The Governor continued:

"The custom which has so long prevailed among our people and newspapers both South and North, and with such disastrous results, of speaking evil of each other, should be desisted from. . . . The only object of certain journals would seem to be to prejudice one section of the country against the other. . . . The Northern papers of this class reject as odious all notice of anything good that is done in the South, and collect with care every instance of lawlessness, great or small, real or imaginary, and parade it in their columns until the minds of their readers are poisoned against us, and they mistake the act of one lawless individual for the uniform conduct of the whole community.

"On the other hand, some of our Southern papers notice nothing good in the North but cull with care every instance of elopement, murder, theft, robbery, arson, burglary . . . until their readers are taught to believe that the North is utterly corrupt."

Perhaps the correspondent of the New York *Times* had these latter papers in mind when he reported, toward the close of 1865, that "the editors of the South are almost as disloyal and contemptible and almost as malign and mean as the ministers of the Gospel."

The Southern ministers and their congregations were, indeed, the cause of much disappointment and animadversion at the North, in the months after the surrender. They not only seemed to show no contrition and repentance for their sins of disloyalty and rebellion, but they showed little disposition to return to the fold. The Episcopal Church of the Confederate States, meeting at Augusta in November, voted to reunite with the church in the United States, but the other principal denominations of the South, which had a longer history and experience of separate existence, seemed to prefer to continue their separate ways, and to recover for their own use the church property which the military had turned over to the representatives of corresponding Northern denominations, or of the missionary societies, who had followed the army to the South. These representatives, in most instances, seem to have looked upon military conquest as a sufficient grant of ecclesiastical authority.

The policy toward the Southern churches, described by one as that of "disintegration and absorption," met fierce resistance on the part of those whose church connections and associations were to be subjected to the process, resistance so fierce that the policy failed utterly. The Northern church connections, insofar as the whites of most of the South were concerned, remained on a missionary footing, while, within a year of the peace conferences, synods and conventions of the Northern churches in the border states of Maryland and Kentucky began to break away and enter the Southern church bodies.

The great field for Northern missionary effort, of course, was among the freed people. The two colored Methodist bodies, which began their work among the people of the coastal islands held by Union arms from 1862 on, spread rapidly under the guidance, in some sections, of able colored ministers who had come to the South as chaplains of Negro regiments. The Methodist Church, South, which had nearly four hundred thousand colored members before the war, lost more than three-fourths of them during the first year of freedom, after which the seventy-eight thousand remaining communicants organized the Colored Methodist Episcopal Church. Because of its relationship to the white church from which it sprang, the colored Methodist body came to be called, by the more aggressively political members of the other colored churches, the "Rebel Church," the "Democratic Church," or even the "Old Slavery Church."

Adjustments were to be made not only between Northern and Southern church bodies of the same dogma and faith but also between the white and colored members of local congregations throughout the South. Fairly typical of how this was accomplished was the experience of the First Baptist Church at Montgomery, with three hundred white and six hundred colored members before and during the war. When it was felt wise to separate the congregations, both co-operated in the erection of a new church house for the colored body, which continued to use the old church while the new was being built. When all was ready, the colored congregation was launched with its organization and machinery fully established and working, with the blessing and support of the whites.

Education of the freed people presented both problems and opportunity. That they should be educated was never doubted at the North. Immediately after the close of the war the Southern churches declared that freedmen must be educated to fit them for their changed condition of life. Moreover, there was no objection of consequence to this view in the early months of freedom. The problem was not whether they should be educated, but how they should be educated, and by whom and to what end.

The case for education at the hands of Southerners was strongly put by the Selma *Times*, in discussing measures proposed by citizens of Oxford, Mississippi. Its line of reasoning was that the Negroes were, to a certain extent, unprepared for freedom; that both interest and duty required their education; that "if it ever was good policy to keep them ignorant it certainly is no longer so, but the very reverse"; that they would, in all probability, hereafter be granted the right of suffrage; that "ignorant voters are the curse of our country"; that "if we do not teach them someone else will, and whoever thus benefits them will win an influence over them which will control their votes . . . so much for policy and interest—the least elevated form of the argument."

On grounds of both policy and moral obligation, the same argument was pressed by many others. The Methodist Church in the South, under the leadership of Holland N. McTyeire, afterward bishop, made itself felt in the work. The Episcopal bishop of Mississippi, former Senator Brown of the same state, former Governor Moore of Alabama, and J. L. M. Curry, former representative from that state in both the United States and the Confederate Congresses, Governor Orr in South Carolina, and numerous others were outspoken in their advocacy of immediate education of the Negroes by their Southern neighbors. In Georgia and elsewhere many owners of large plantations established schools for the children of their hands.

As to one thing all observers of the time are agreed—the pathetic eagerness of the freed Negroes, old and young, to learn. In Selma, leading Negroes published an appeal to their "dear friends and former masters," urging that well-educated widows and crippled men establish schools for the colored people, to which they guaranteed their undivided support. "We prefer you to any other to have the money derived from our daily labor for teaching our children," they said. "If you all stand back, strangers will come in and take the money. . . . They are not ashamed to take money from any class of men."

To this appeal the *Times* responded:

"The negroes are among us, for good or evil; they must be taught to support themselves and contribute to the commonwealth; they must be made useful members of society; or failing in this they will become an insupportable tax upon the property, enterprise, and productive industry of the country, and the whites will be dragged down with them to a lower depth of poverty and woe than we have yet reached. . . ."

Despite such views, the Southern people did not, perhaps could not, take advantage in any large way of the opportunity offered by the eagerness of the freed people for education. In fact, in the early years after the war, "the poverty of his father and the impotence of the state let the white child abide in ignorance." To the reasons for lack of educational opportunity so aptly put by Miss Thompson, should be added at least one other, widespread indifference to education. The support given to the whisky shops—there were four hundred and eighteen in Nashville, according to General Fisk's count—and the liberal use of tobacco and snuff give point to the remark of one New England traveler that education suffered because, unlike tobacco, it was not regarded as a necessity of life.

But however hesitant the Southern whites may have been in regard to colored education, or for whatever reason, there was no hesitation on the part of the Northern missionary or freedmen's aid organizations in entering the field. To their efforts was due the fact that in the early years after the war Negro children, on the whole, had better opportunities for schooling than the poorer white children. Nor were the efforts of the Bureau or the missionary groups confined to children. "In the same room, and pursuing the same studies, the child and the parent—youth and gray hairs—all eagerly grasp for that by which, obtained, they are intellectually regenerated," reported a Bureau official, noting that in one school in North Carolina there sat side by side four generations, daughter, mother, grandmother, great-grandmother. "All are full of enthusiasm with the new knowledge," said another report.

As with so many other parts of the process of remaking the South after the war, the failure of the freedmen's schools to attain the results so eagerly looked for was due largely to the human element. The road to learning proved to be rough and stony, the immediate rewards meager. Teachers of competence and tact and genuine devotion, of whom there were never too many, found their difficult problem of adjustment made far more difficult by the excessive zeal and the mania for minor martyrdoms exhibited by some of their co-laborers in the vineyard.

Some even labored in such a spirit as to create the belief, among their Southern neighbors, that they felt that "an educated Negro was even more obnoxious to the slave-holding Southerner than a free Negro, hence educated Negroes should be multiplied." That the work of really competent and useful teachers should have been handicapped and all but destroyed by the sowing of such impressions is another of the tragedies of that bitter and vengeful time.

But not all the zeal and sacrifice of the teachers who came down from the North was lost. In spite of the antagonism to colored education aroused by the less judicious among them, the wiser founded institutions and started processes whose influence continues.

Such institutions included the Penn School at St. Helena, South Carolina, which Miss Laura M. Towne founded in 1862 and continued to direct for nearly forty years, and the Avery Institute, founded at Charleston in 1865. Such teachers as Miss Towne, Miss Martha Schofield and Miss Abby D. Monroe, who gave long lives of intelligent devotion to Negro education in South Carolina, mixed with their book education a strong streak of the practical. Another

teacher of the same fine sort, Miss Elizabeth Hyde Botume, stated
something of their program:

"We are convinced that plenty to eat would harmonize and Christian-
ize them faster than hymns and sermons; and that needle and thread
and soap and decent clothing were the best educators and could
civilize them sooner than book learning."

There was among many of the Negroes an eagerness for learning
which belied the widespread belief among Southern people that the
race could not be educated. Booker T. Washington, the slave boy
who became great as all-around educator, recalled the early days of
Negro education in the South. He said:

"Few people who were not right in the midst of the scenes can form
any exact idea of the intense desire which the people of my race showed
for education. It was a whole race trying to go to school. Few were
too young, and none too old, to make the attempt to learn."

Even in 1865, a start was made toward the education of the Southern
Negroes to be teachers of their own race. Twenty-three abandoned
government-hospital buildings located on sixteen acres of ground at
Nashville were purchased in the autumn of that year by the American
Missionary Society and the Western Freedmen's Aid, to become the
nucleus of Erastus Cravath's Fisk University, whose Jubilee Singers
were to save for posterity and present to the world the fast disappearing
beauties of the Negro spirituals. Within less than ten years, this handful of men and women, most of them out of slavery, had earned with
their songs enough to replace the abandoned temporary hospitals in
which their college started with the elaborate brick and stone Jubilee
Hall.

Without aid, as yet, of private philanthropy or government bureau,
a way was to be found to carry on the education of the whites. The
sparse and scattered population of the rural districts of the South
always had been an obstacle to rural education. In many of the
cities and larger towns public-school systems were in operation before
the war, while most of the states lent some aid to common schools
from the proceeds of invested school funds. When the war ended,
those funds were lost or greatly depleted, through the vicissitudes of
war or too great confidence in Confederate obligations. Disorganization and insecurity, impoverishment, a certain indifference to ele-
mentary education when the problem of daily subsistence was so

pressing, combined to slow down the reopening of the schools, and their wider spread, particularly in the country districts.

The seats of higher learning in the South, almost without exception, came to the end of the war worn and wasted to the last degree. Governor Brownlow, zealous Unionist that he was, reported to the legislature of Tennessee, with indignation, that the "library, equipment and apparatus" of the State University at Knoxville had been "burned by the Federal army." The Universities of Mississippi and Alabama had suffered far greater losses, as had the Virginia Military Institute. The University of Georgia was able to reopen in the autumn of 1865, with seventy-eight students, mostly grown men and ex-soldiers, occupying a campus overgrown with weeds and buildings defaced by garrisons. The University of North Carolina, struggling along with still fewer students, finally was forced to close its doors for four years.

In all the South the most persuasive and potent influence for peace and accommodation was Robert E. Lee. At Appomattox, in the spring, he had insured that there was to be no dragging agony of guerrilla resistance; that there was to be a quick and clean-cut peace, as quick and as clean-cut as the victors would allow. And now, in the fall, he found and accepted his opportunity to work, through education of its young manhood, for the reconciliation and regeneration of the South. The opportunity was brought to him by Judge Brockenbrough, representing the trustees of Washington College, a small institution and obscure, in the remote mountain village of Lexington. Wearing a borrowed suit of clothes, having none of his own presentable, and with borrowed money, he journeyed to the farm in Powhatan County where General Lee was, to offer to him the presidency of the school, founded upon gifts of George Washington, which war had not spared in its passage. The offer, extended with timidity and trepidation at its presumption, was eagerly embraced, subject only to General Lee's fear that a president who was excluded from amnesty might "draw upon the college a feeling of hostility." That he could not consent to do, with his conviction that it was "the duty of every citizen to do all in his power to aid in the restoration of peace and harmony, and in no way to oppose the policy of the state or general government directed to that object."

His doubts removed and his objections overruled by the board of the college, the General rode to Lexington, to be installed on October 2, with a minimum of ceremony, as president of Washington College, and there, in the first autumn of the peace, to enter upon the last great work of his great life.

CHAPTER XVII

The Joint Committee of Fifteen

PRESIDENT LINCOLN, it will be recalled, on the last day of his life, expressed his gratification that Congress was not to meet again until December, thus allowing almost two-thirds of a year to establish his policy of restoration of the Southern states. That policy President Johnson inherited and carried forward with increasing success until, by the time that Congress was to meet, there remained to restore the Southern states to the "practical relations" with the Union which Lincoln had sought but one more step—the admission of their representatives and senators into the Congress of the United States.

The first session of the Thirty-ninth Congress was to convene on Monday, December 4, 1865. In anticipation of the session, the sprawling, unfinished city of Washington filled up with all manner of characters in political life or on its fringes—men with a grievance, men with a claim, men with a hope, "placemen, would-be placemen and postmasters in expectancy" who might be seen "to liquor up in the crowded bars." To a more dubious class of gentry Willard's Hotel addressed its

"NOTICE TO THIEVES

Every thief seen about the house will be *shown up to all the guests* by the detectives employed by the proprietors, and then locked up in prison for further hearing."

Underneath the surface confusion one determined group knew what it wanted—and had a plan to get it. The members of this group wanted to turn the country aside from the path toward reconciliation, to keep the Southern states out of practical relations with the Union and to keep the wounds of war open and running until they could so remake the form and frame of the government as to "secure perpetual ascendency to the party of the Union," as Thaddeus Stevens phrased it.

By "the party of the Union" that great Radical did not mean the Republican party which had elected Lincoln in 1860, nor the Na-

132

tional Union party composed of Republicans and war Democrats which had elected Lincoln and Johnson in 1864. He meant the extremist faction which had become too advanced for Lincoln, even before 1864, and which now, in the prevailing welter of conflicting parties, factions, policies and purposes, saw its opportunity to combine the pleasurable project of humiliating the South with the profitable establishment of government by and for the more highly industrialized states of the North—all in a righteous glow of saving the Union and advancing human rights, according to ideas sincerely entertained.

"Do you really think," asked Secretary Welles of Senator Sumner, "that Massachusetts could govern Georgia better than Georgia could govern herself?"

"That," was the unhesitating reply, "is Massachusetts' mission."

To bring about the desired result the inner circle of this determined group had a positive plan—a plan that, first, would appeal to the jealousy of prerogative by "asserting the jurisdiction of Congress"; that, second, would halt all positive action toward Southern recognition except with the consent of the most Radical elements in Congress; that, third, would "delay, delay, delay, on one ground or another," to give the Radicals time and opportunity to "educate," discuss, agitate, exasperate, inflame.

The first essential step was to capture the machinery of the caucus in Congress of the party which had elected Lincoln, and by so doing to render impotent those Moderate leaders in the Union party who otherwise might join with Democrats in carrying out Lincoln's policy of restoration.

At a secret council of war of the Radical high command, some thirty strong, held on Friday, December 1, the plan of action was explained and adopted. At the regular caucus of the members of the National Union party, held on the Saturday, Thaddeus Stevens presented the resolution agreed upon by the inner circle the day before, a resolution so simple on its face, so innocuous in appearance, that Henry J. Raymond, chairman of the National Union party committee and a supporter of the President's policy, let it slip by to adoption without objection.

The resolution bound the caucus members, Moderates and Conservatives as well as Radicals, to vote to admit no members from the Southern states to either House unless both Houses should agree; to refer the credentials of applicants for admission to either House, and all other matters connected with the status of the Southern states, without debate or action, to a joint committee representing both Houses; and to take no action on such subjects until the joint committee should report.

From each of the Southern states except Texas, where the process of reorganizing the government was not yet complete, claimants were ready to offer themselves for admission to Senate and House. The Southern claimants—"impudent claimants," Stevens called them— were men of standing, in most cases, holding certificates of election from state governments already recognized by the executive branch of the government, and by Congress itself, in the acceptance of their ratifications of the Thirteenth Amendment, abolishing slavery. Not all of them could take the iron-clad oath, having held civil or military office under the Confederacy, but some of them had been staunch Unionists at times and places when to be a Unionist required no small measure of courage and steadfastness. Even those who had served the Confederacy were, for the most part, "old Union men," whose selection promised the beginning of a fusion of conservative political elements in the South with like-minded men in the North. Such a party in the South, had it been allowed to develop, surely would have been worth infinitely more to the Union, and even to the Republicans as a partisan organization, than the strange mixture which was to grow from the action of the Radicals taken with intent to make the South safely and perpetually Republican.

The test of the Radical plan came on Monday, December 4, when the House of Representatives convened before galleries crowded with those who had come to see and hear what many fondly anticipated would be the final act in the reuniting of the nation. The session, as usual, opened with the calling by the Clerk of the House of the temporary roll, ordinarily made up of those holding certificates of election. On the roll as made up and called by Edward McPherson, the Clerk, appeared the name of no Southern representative, not even that of Horace Maynard, member-at-large from Tennessee, who, the President believed, could not be denied admission. Maynard, a native of Massachusetts and graduate of Amherst, was an uncompromising Unionist before, during and after the war. He had served in the first Congress during Lincoln's administration, by election from the same state, then engaged in active resistance to the general government. Maynard's was the test case. If he were not to be seated, no member from the South might expect to be received.

As the Clerk passed over his name, the Tennessee member-elect demanded, and demanded again, the right to be heard. The Clerk did not answer. James Brooks, of New York, minority leader, took up the fight. "I wish to know when the matter of admitting Southern members will be taken up," he demanded of McPherson. The Clerk glanced to Stevens for instructions.

"I have no objections to answering the gentleman," said Stevens. "I will press the matter at the proper time."

The House accepted the dictum of the masterful old Radical and proceeded to its work of organization. Schuyler Colfax was re-elected speaker, responded to his election, and declared the House open for business. The first business was the introduction, by Stevens, of the joint resolution agreed to by the caucus, committing all matters in connection with admission of Southern members or Reconstruction to the Joint Committee of Fifteen. Under suspension of the rules, and as a party measure, the resolution was passed at once and transmitted to the Senate, where Sumner had introduced the same proposal. In the Senate, William Pitt Fessenden, senator from Maine and a good lawyer, objected on constitutional grounds to that part of the resolution which required action by both Houses to admit members to either, and made good his objection. Amended to exclude that feature, the resolution was passed and sent back to the House, which accepted the amendment—for, after all, as a practical matter the Radical end of halting the restoration of the Southern states was equally well gained by the committing of the whole subject to the Joint Committee on Reconstruction.

As James G. Blaine wrote afterward, "it was foreseen that in an especial degree the fortunes of the Republican party would be in the keeping of the fifteen men who might be chosen," wherefore the appointing powers in House and Senate were careful to assure an overwhelming majority of Republicans—twelve out of fifteen— and a working majority of reliable Radicals.

Perfectly well aware that they had won no more than the chance to win their battle, the Radical junto undertook, with fierce energy and ingenious cunning, to find or manufacture issues, to develop discords and promote strife, to use their powerful Committee of Fifteen to produce propaganda, and the Congress of the United States as a sounding board to get it to the country. Andrew Johnson, whom they had expected to use, had revealed a disappointing, old-fashioned devotion to his own conception of the Constitution with a definite division of powers between state and nation—but Andrew Johnson, they believed, could be blackened, rendered impotent, or destroyed, while the Constitution, which barred hasty and radical change, could itself be changed or subverted.

Against them, the Radical leaders had the genuine desire for peace and reconciliation of a people weary of strife. In their favor they had that trait of human nature which makes it easier to aggravate differences than to promote accord. And at that sort of thing the directors of the Radical program were men of far more than ordinary skill and experience. Among them were many of the old Abolition agitators, whose fanatic powers had been proved, and who were genuinely convinced that if the freedmen were "left to the legislation of their late masters, we had better have left them in bondage."

But even so, the fight was to be hard and the issue close. At the outset, many who later came to be among the high priests in the Radical movement, supported the presidential policy—Oliver Morton, Indiana's forceful war Governor; John Sherman and John A. Bingham, of Ohio, and Lyman Trumbull, of Illinois; even John A. Logan, who was later to become a Radical of Radicals, but who in 1865 was vociferating his support of the presidential policy.

No one thing turned these men, nor the others who went with the Radicals before the end of the campaign. Failure to agree with the President on detailed issues, or changes in their way of viewing them, affected some. More important, and more effectual, was the conviction which grew during the campaign that the President's policy could not win, and that those who went down with him to defeat would find themselves outcasts in the political wilderness.

Inability to weld together into a compact political organization the diverse and sometimes conflicting elements that supported the President foreshadowed failure. The President's unwillingness, or inability, to use the executive patronage to further his fight gave another indication. Ineptitudes in the management of his campaign and the success of the Radical propaganda in presenting Johnson to the country as an uncouth inebriate, "the successor of Jefferson Davis as the leader of the Confederacy," determined to wreck on the rock of his stubborn ambition the Union which Lincoln had saved, gave warning that the man who would be on the winning side had best not be with the President at the end. The "bloody shirt" was waved in denunciation of the President as the leader and friend of those "who carved the bones of your unburied dead into ornaments and drank from goblets made of their skulls." The net result was a steady drift away from Johnson of strong political personalities and forces which, properly aligned, might have saved the day.

The President suffered from isolation. He had inherited Lincoln's policy but not the machinery of his party, which he needed to make the policy effective. He had inherited Lincoln's Cabinet also, and in the Cabinet one member, the Secretary of War, who not only did not and would not resign when he found himself out of sympathy with his chief's policy, but who constituted himself a spy upon his chief. Secretary Stanton went even beyond this, establishing through his control of the War Department telegraph line, the only one which was available to the White House, a censorship on the messages received and dispatched by the President.

Johnson's very unwillingness to force the resignation of Stanton became the basis of part of the propaganda against him. He did not remove the Secretary, it was whispered, because Stanton had "proof" of his complicity in the murder of President Lincoln.

Even among those Cabinet members who adhered steadfastly and loyally to his policy, the President found a distrust and dislike of one another which, at times, paralyzed the action of the chief who listened to all of them. Meeting streams of callers, as the custom of the day required, reading and carefully answering a mountainous mail, the President was yet out of touch with the effective political sentiment of the dominant North.

For campaign purposes he had to be, and was, painted as the "drunken tailor," surly and ill-mannered when sober, violent and abusive when not. In spite of the rehabilitation of President Johnson by modern students, the picture remains in the popular mind as one of the best illustrations of the persistence of an untruth repeated often enough.

Coming to Washington to see the opening of Congress and to hear the message of the President, Sir John Kennaway, who with his companions called at the White House to meet the President, wrote:

"His manners were those of a perfect gentleman and his appearance certainly prepossessed us in his favor. . . . It was marvelous that a man who only learnt to write after he was married, should now be able to control the destinies of so great a people; nor was it less to be wondered at that one, part of whose early life had been spent on the tailor's shopboard, should be able to receive us with the ease and frankness of an English gentleman."

Assuredly this was no light praise from such a source, entirely without partiality in the political campaign then beginning.

The reading of the President's message to Congress was postponed until after the Committee of Fifteen had been created and entrusted with all matters connected with further restoration. The thoughts in this first message were the President's; the drafting had received the able help of the historian and politician George Bancroft.

The message outlined the principles which had guided the President's policy—that "so long as the Constitution of the United States endures, the state will endure"; that the region lately in rebellion should not be held as territory conquered by military force, since that would imply that those states had "ceased to exist"; that the acts of secession, void from the beginning, had "impaired but not extinguished" the states whose inhabitants had tried to secede; that the functions of those states had been "suspended but not destroyed"; that he had, therefore, by gradual steps which were outlined, restored those functions to vigor; and that the restored states, regarding the "return of the general government only as a beneficence," had given good augury for the future by the ratification of the Thirteenth Amendment. Its adoption, he said, "reunites us beyond all power of disruption; it heals the wound. . . . It makes us once more a united people."

The next step was to be the admission of Southern representatives to the two houses of Congress, each of which, as the President pointed out, was the exclusive judge of the "elections, returns and qualifications" of its own members.

As to the political status of the freedmen, the President declared that it was not permitted to make them "electors by the proclamation of the executive." Under the Constitution, that was a responsibility of the several states, which could, "each for itself, decide on the measure, and whether it is to be adopted at once and absolutely, or introduced gradually and with conditions." He urged that Negroes be secured in their freedom and property and their right to work and enjoy the fruits of their labors. He avowed his belief that the races could "live side by side in a state of mutual benefit and good will" but cautioned against too great haste. "I know that sincere philanthropy is earnest for the immediate realization of its remotest aims," he said, "but time is always an element in reform."

His position and his message received high praise. Morton, Andrew, the old Roman Thomas Ewing, the great Northern generals—Grant, Sherman, Thomas, Meade, Schofield, even Sheridan—praised it. "I know of nothing better in the annals even when Washington was chief and Hamilton his financier," wrote Charles Francis Adams. Henry Ward Beecher gave thanks that "God has raised him up . . . to serve Nation rather than self or party."

To all of which the sardonic Stevens and the Olympian Sumner and their allies could afford to pay small heed. They had their resolution and their committee. They could afford to wait and were able to agitate and inflame.

On December 18, the President sent to Congress his special message on the insurrectionary states. With the partial exceptions of Texas and Florida, they were reorganized, he said, and "yielding obedience to the laws and government of the United States with more willingness and greater promptitude than under all the circumstances could reasonably have been anticipated." The Thirteenth Amendment had been ratified by all the reorganized states except Mississippi; the people were going back to work; disorder was dying down; the sense of nationality was growing.

To the message he attached a special report by General Grant, whom he had sent to the South on a tour of investigation. The General reported that the "mass of thinking men of the South accept the present situation of affairs in good faith . . . that they not only accepted the decision arrived at as final but . . . that this decision has been a fortunate one" as to both slavery and the right of secession.

After "four years of war, during which law was executed only at the point of the bayonet," General Grant found that only small garrisons were needed in the South but recommended that they be composed of white troops, rather than colored. He found the citizens of the Southern states "anxious to return to self-government within the Union as soon as possible . . . in earnest in wishing to do what they think is required by the government, not humiliating to them as citizens, and that if such a course was pointed out, they would pursue it in good faith."

Senator Sumner probably did not feel it politic to refer to General Grant's report as a "white-washing affair," but he did apply the epithet to the President's message transmitting it, and countered with a report of another general, Carl Schurz, also sent south by the President to investigate. General Schurz, advising privily with the Senator, had set out to find support for the Radical position, and naturally had found what he sought. His findings, presented with all his fervor and considerable literary skill, were by their very nature more sensationally readable than the matter-of-fact conclusions of General Grant. That "treason did not appear odious" in the South; that "submission" was accepted merely "as the only means by which they could rid themselves of the Federal soldiers and obtain once more control of their own affairs"; that such control would be exercised for the virtual enslavement of the black wards of the nation; and that the freedmen needed a measure of political power to protect themselves against "oppressive class legislation and private persecution," were his conclusions.

Mr. Stevens expounded to the House his own theory of the situation at this time. Appealing to the law of nations, he declared that the late war between acknowledged belligerents severed the original compact between them, and "broke all ties that bound them together. The future condition of the conquered powers depends upon the will of the conqueror. They must come in as new states or remain as conquered provinces. Congress . . . is the only power that can act in the matter." His recommendation was territorial governments in the South, for some years to come, under which the "people of these provinces . . . can learn the principles of freedom and eat the fruits of foul rebellion."

To "secure perpetual ascendency to the party of the Union" he proposed that none of these "outside or defunct states" should be admitted until the basis of representation was changed in those states to actual voters, rather than the Federal number made up of all free persons plus three-fifths of the slaves. Otherwise, he warned, the Southern members, "with the Democrats that will in the best of times be elected from the North, will always give a majority in Congress and in the Electoral College. . . . I need not predict the ruin that would follow."

Besides reduction in Southern representation he urged that lands be confiscated wholesale in the South, to pay part of the war debt of the nation and to furnish homesteads for the freedmen. Around them, he wanted to throw Federal legislation to protect them from their former masters.

Not urged at this time, because sentiment in the North was not yet judged to be ready, but an integral part of the Radical plan, was the vote for the ex-slaves of the South. It was no part of the plan to impose it on the Northern states, or even to agitate the issue there where it was not popular at that time. As Senator Howard wrote to Sumner, in November, colored suffrage was wanted for the South as security for the future, "whatever the *northern* people may do to their own *blacks.*" Connecticut had held an election on a Negro-suffrage constitutional amendment that year, and defeated it by a strong majority. Illinois had defeated a similar proposal, in 1863, by a vote of six to one, and still had a provision in its constitution severely limiting the right of free Negroes to enter the state, as did Indiana. Within the year both Wisconsin and Ohio were to defeat Negro-suffrage proposals by heavy majorities. Mr. Sumner attempted to impose Negro suffrage upon "the States lately declared to be in rebellion" by act of Congress, knowing that he could not muster the two-thirds majority needed to pass a resolution to amend the Constitution. His bill received only seven votes in the Senate besides his own. Other Radical leaders, more practical than Mr. Sumner sometimes was, were wise to keep the issue as far out of sight as possible in the congressional campaign of 1866.

One intent of the Radical program was to make of the Southern states permanent vassal-allies of a Republican party of the Radical persuasion. This was to be accomplished through the creation, in the South, of a new electorate, by requiring those states to grant to the ex-slaves the right to vote. To some of the Radicals such a step was no more than just retribution. "It is curious," confided Gideon Welles to his diary," to note the bitterness and intolerance of the philanthropists in this matter."

To others, it was a great step in the march of progress toward the Rights of Man. The *Atlantic Monthly* declared that the "safety of the republican form of government we desire to insure in the Southern states has more safeguards in the *instincts* of the *ignorant* than in the *intelligence* of the *educated.*"

To still others, no doubt, it was what General Sherman said it was, a scheme "whereby politicians may manufacture just so much more pliable electioneering material." Governor Brownlow said to a New York audience, "I find here at the North you do not need, and many of you do not want, Negro suffrage. We are not so. We want the loyal Negroes to help us vote down the disloyal traitors and white people"—a position to which the once violent Negrophobe had been driven by the necessities of practical politics.

But whatever the motive, or the mixture of motives, the Radical plan for a new political people in the South overlooked the element essential for permanent success. New voters could be created; new leaders could not. Because of the lack of such leaders the whole scheme imposed upon the South from without was to collapse when the support of Federal bayonets was withdrawn.

"Leadership is a gift, not a device," said Governor Andrew in his valedictory address to the Massachusetts legislature. The Radical plan was based upon a rejection of the natural leaders of the South. Among those holding certificates of election to the Thirty-ninth

Congress were men who could have worked powerfully for sound restoration and a genuine two-party system of government in the South. Alexander H. Stephens and Herschel V. Johnson, for example, were not sent to the Senate from Georgia as a gesture of defiance. They were sent because, on their records, they were the best men available around whom a true party of reunion could have been formed in the state. But they, and all men like them, were to be rejected; to be forced into a party called Democratic which, in the lower South, was to become the white race politically organized. The Radical policy left nowhere else for such men to go.

It was a result not unforeseen by wiser men of the North. John A. Andrew urging in January, 1866, "a vigorous prosecution of the Peace—just as vigorous as our recent prosecution of the War," truly stated the situation:

"The Southern people . . . fought, toiled, endured and persevered, with a courage, a unanimity and a persistency, not outdone by any people in any Revolution. . . . They whose courage, talents and will entitle them to lead, will lead. . . . We ought to demand, and to secure, the co-operation of the strongest and ablest minds and the natural leaders of opinion in the South. If we cannot gain their support of the just measures needful for the work of safe re-organization, re-organization will be delusive and full of danger. . . ."

The able war Governor of Massachusetts saw clearly the need "to extend our hands with cordial good will to meet the proffered hands of the South." But between them, and in control of the political machinery through which the peace had to be prosecuted, stood a group who instead wrought root-and-branch Reconstruction "to secure perpetual ascendency" to the Republican party whose machinery they had captured—and who, so doing, created the solidly Democratic South.

CHAPTER XVIII

Race Relations in Law and Living

Paying small heed to affairs in Washington, the cotton South began with the new year of 1866 its great annual gamble of making a crop. The Christmas holidays had passed without the great division and distribution of homesteads expected by so many of the Negroes, and without the outbreaks and uprisings feared by some of the whites. Hope was in the air. The price of cotton was high, even after the unexpectedly large quantities of old cotton hidden away in the South came on the market. The cotton farmers were eager for hands, the cotton hands willing to work. The new relationship of labor, land and capital was to receive its first full year's test.

Throughout the cotton belt, and elsewhere in the South also, hiring and contracting were going on, in various forms and under various arrangements. As the Winnsboro *Tri-Weekly News*, in South Carolina, reported, the Negroes were "in a state of anxious locomotion, changing homes, moving luggage, hunting places, and making arrangements for the coming year." There was ground for their anxiety, which was shared by the planters eager to establish a stable basis of employment, and by the military and the Bureau officials, anxious in most cases to get proper contracts made and to see that they were kept.

During the short season of 1865, many Negroes were unwilling to contract their labor except on a month-to-month basis, according to the rule of the then inexperienced Bureau, which did not recognize the essentially annual nature of cotton raising. In 1866, however, most contracts were made on an annual basis, on some sort of share system. Plans were almost as various as individual employers and workers, at the outset, but generally they fell into one of three classes—fixed money rent for the use of the land, to be paid by the tenant; a fixed share of the crop to be paid as rent, perhaps one-third; or farming "on the shares," with the landowner furnishing land, seed, implements, work stock, and food, feed and supplies for the year for the tenant, his family and his stock, usually made available by means of a credit at "the store" against which supplies were

143

charged as drawn. Depending on whether the landowner furnished all or only some of these necessary elements in the making of a crop, his share usually varied from one-half to two-thirds of the crop, with the half-and-half division most general. The general assumption was that the landowner was entitled to one-third of the proceeds and the laborer to one-third, the balance to be divided according to the relative "furnishings" of the two parties.

The Negroes showed, in 1866, a strong desire to obtain land, by lease, "on the shares," or, best of all, by purchase, but there were large numbers who preferred to work for money wages. The high price of cotton at hiring time led to the offer of good wages, for the time and place, ranging up or down from one hundred and fifty dollars per annum, besides food and shelter, for a first-class field hand. In the lumbering and turpentine industries money wages usually ran to twice farm wages, but no food was furnished.

A week's allowance of food for one person, as prescribed by the Bureau in Florida, was four pounds of bacon, one peck of meal, one pint of syrup or its equivalent. In addition, in farm work, there was usually an allowance of a garden patch and opportunity to work it.

On some such terms, in general, the people of the South, white and black, undertook the work of supplying themselves with a living, and the United States with two-thirds of all its exports—essential, as the Secretary of the Treasury reported in the following year, "to save the country from ruinous indebtedness to Europe."

From a Texas black-belt county came the report that two-thirds of the freed population were at work at good wages, that seven thousand labor contracts had been filed with the Bureau officials, and that unemployed freedmen were becoming scarce. From Mississippi, Colonel Thomas, of the Bureau, reported that, on the whole, conditions were satisfactory and the freedmen better treated than might have been expected—although in another connection, he stated that two-thirds of them had been swindled out of part of their wages in 1865.

However, General Tillson, assistant commissioner in Georgia, reported that the Negroes were being treated fairly in business, while one of Stevens' correspondents in the South wrote him that "all people of good character are inclined to do them justice" and that "those who wish to defraud them are persons who have, for years, been regarded as *tricky* in their relations with neighbors of their own color."

In dealing with the ignorant and helpless freedmen, of course, there was great opportunity for successful frauds, but it is possible also that not all the trouble was due to trickiness on the part of the landlords. There was always the possibility of misunderstanding of arithmetic on the part of the tenant, as in the case of the hands on a plantation in Wilkes County, Georgia, working for a one-fourth share, who quit work when they found that the hands on a neighboring plantation were to receive one-fifth.

In another case, in Georgia, a tenant who was to pay one-fourth of the crop of corn raised as rent for the land, hauled three loads— all there was in the field—to his own house. When the landlord asked for his share, the tenant replied, in genuine astonishment and perfect good faith, "You ain't got none, sah!" "Why, wasn't I to have the fourth of all you made?" "Yes, sah; but hit never made no fourth; dere wa'n't but just my three loads made."

Usually, however, if anyone suffered from ignorance of arithmetic, it was the Negro tenant, as in the case of one who, failing to get the one-half of the crop to which he was entitled by agreement, was put off by his employer with the explanation that the season had been bad and only half a crop was made.

Henry D. Clayton, former major general in the Confederate Army, sitting as judge of the restored state of Alabama, charged the grand jury of Pike County that two things were necessary to remedy the evils growing out of the abolition of slavery: "First, a recognition of the freedom of the race as a fact, the enactment of just and humane laws, and the willing enforcement of them. Secondly, by treating them with perfect fairness and justice in our contracts and in every way in which we may be brought in contact with them. . . ."

Judge Clayton undoubtedly stated the aspiration of Southerners of his own sort but there was, just as truly, a need to protect the Negroes from Southerners of the meaner sort, and from that sort of Northerners as well, for by 1866 thousands of the latter had come South, attracted by the low price of lands and the high price of cotton.

At the beginning of the year, General Swayne, assistant commissioner in Alabama, reported that five thousand Northern men had settled in that state, mostly planting and trading. Others were to be found in the active lumber business in Louisiana, and on plantations along the Georgia and Carolina Sea Islands, and in the up country, as well. In the Carolinas, many plantations were sold at low prices to Northern operators—some of them competent and able planters; some adventurers who later became "carpetbaggers"; some high-minded and philanthropic theorists, many of whom were to suffer disillusionment akin to that of the Northern planter, a thorough-going Abolitionist, who came to the conclusion, after a season's experience, that farming could not be carried on profitably in Georgia since the cost of producing cotton was about doubled.

As to that, J. D. B. DeBow, editor of *DeBow's Review*, the leading commercial publication of the South, was not ready to commit himself in January. The great enigma was whether or not the efficiency of labor could be kept up to the standard before the war. "They are working now very well on the plantations," he said, but it was too early yet to know. If the efficiency could be kept up, however, Mr. DeBow had no doubt that, on the mere money question, the South would be better off than under slavery, "because it is cheaper to hire the Negro than to own him. Now a plantation can be worked without any outlay of capital by hiring the Negro and hiring the plantation."

That was just what many Northern men were doing, with high hope of profit. So many acres of land, producing so many bales of cotton, sold at such and such a price, less expenses of so much—thus ran their roseate calculations, which failed to take into account the unpredictables of weather, markets and labor, resulting in grievous disappointment in many cases.

The story of one such venture is told in a letter, written after the end of the year by a landowner in Perry County, Alabama, who in January, 1866, rented all his lands to a "real codfish Yankee officer." The Southern planter had made no cotton in 1865 but had "raised corn enough to do my place bountifully" in 1866. The lease for that year specifies and appraises the stock and equipment of a considerable plantation of that time—eleven mules, valued at from seventy-five to two hundred and fifty dollars each; four turning plows, six sweeps, two bull tongues, five double-plows, one four-horse plow, one grindstone, ten singletrees, two doubletrees, one large and one small wagon, two chopping axes, one broadaxe, one well bucket, one hand-saw, two augers, one drawing knife and thirteen clevises, all together valued at $2226.50. Furnished with the place, to be returned at the end of the season in kind or in value, were three thousand pounds of bacon, slaughtered and cured on the place, and hams, shoulders and middlings; corn sufficient to feed the mules and "bread the hands" engaged in cultivating the place, and fodder for the stock. Down and dead timber was allowed to be used for firewood—for all of which, with the use of fifteen hundred acres of land, the tenant was to pay $3,000 in rent at the end of the season.

The tenant, according to the letter of the landlord in April, 1867,

"made a grand and total failure, killed many of mules, broke down the balance, destroyed and made away with all my corn, killed all my pork hogs, shoats, sheep, goats, etc. Made no crop, then pulled up stakes and run away and never paid me a cent . . . now I have nothing but my land and two ponies—do not own a hog. I am trying to buy a sow and pigs now. I was throwed so flat I have not the means to cultivate my own land, therefore was forced to rent out my land again this year."

Such results were not entirely unforeseen by the more experienced planters and cotton men. Warning those "who are madly bending all their energies to the production of the staple, to the almost entire exclusion of all others," the Memphis *Bulletin*, early in March of 1866, expressed doubt as to future high prices of cotton.

"The production has been and continues to be greatly stimulated throughout all the ends of the earth. . . ." it said. "When the crop of the world for 1866 is estimated by some of the shrewdest cotton merchants both in England and America at 6,000,000 bales . . . it is time for the planters of the South to revise their calculations of 'four or five acres of cotton to one of corn,' and 'pitch' their crops on a different and more grain-growing scale.

"That the hard lessons of economy and industrial dependence which the last three years of the war were supposed to have so deeply inculcated should have been so soon forgotten is almost incredible. Could the planters be entirely certain of fifty cents per pound for their cotton every year for the next five, it would still be their true policy to raise a full crop of grain. And it would still be their true policy to invest their every surplus dollar in the establishment of manufactures of all kinds in their midst."

But at the beginning of the planting season of 1866 cotton was still selling at fifty cents a pound, and to Southern landowners and Northern lessees alike that seemed the way to riches. Traveling by steamboat from Memphis to Vicksburg and Natchez, at the time of the Christmas and New Year's holidays, Mr. Trowbridge found both classes of planters seeking labor. To him, the Southern planters appeared to be "an anxious, panic-stricken set . . . going down to

hire freedmen," querulously complaining because the freedmen preferred to hire to Northern men.

As to their preferences in employment there is conflict of testimony, but regardless of to whom the Negro hired, the prime work
of the Bureau at the time was to see that he was not imposed upon
in his contracts, or in his treatment. This trying task the Bureau
performed, in its early and comparatively non-political days, with a
considerable degree of satisfaction to blacks and whites alike, in many
localities and sections.

In Georgia, by an arrangement worked out between General Tillson
and Herschel V. Johnson, president of the constitutional convention, two hundred and forty-four civil agents of the Bureau were
appointed from among the residents of the state. The General reported at the end of the year that "they did not encounter the prejudice felt against officers of the army, or agents from the North, and
were thereby enabled more readily to secure justice to the freedmen,
and to build up and foster a healthy public opinion. . . ." A large
majority of them, he said, proved competent and faithful in meeting
their difficult responsibilities, "in not a few instances gaining a
temporary unpopularity by their fearlessness in announcing and defending the rights of the freedmen,"—an earnest of what might have
been the results of a policy of confidence in and toward the South.

In Louisiana, General Fullerton abolished the freedmen's courts
and transferred pending cases to the courts of the restored state, because of equality of treatment there, while Colonel Thomas took
like action in Mississippi. In Florida, the Bureau set up a labor system which the state authorities later adopted into their labor laws—
for which they were roundly criticised by the Radical orators and
press of the North. General Sickles commended the courts of South
Carolina "upon the manner in which the civil authorities, and especially the superior tribunals, have fulfilled their novel functions to the
freedmen as citizens," while Charleston newspapers commended
General R. K. Scott's administration of the Bureau for its "judgment and sound discretion." The Arkansas *Gazette* believed that
the Bureau had advised the Negroes well in that state, and that contracts would be observed—a belief shared by General Howard.

Generals Steedman and Fullerton, sent South by the President on
an investigation tour, reported in June that "faithful agents have
been aided by the goodwill of the citizens; incompetent and meddlesome ones have aroused bitterness and opposition." Bureau officers

"who can act from facts and not always be guided by prejudice in favor of color" were recommended by General Grant, but, as the possibilities in using the Bureau to further the Radical position in the congressional campaign developed, the time came when, according to the Fullerton-Steedman report, "nearly all the Bureau officers are in correspondence with Radical senators and Radical newspapers."

Relieved of the dread of the Christmas uprising, and reassured as to the willingness of Negroes to work in freedom, the governments of the restored Southern states began to show a broader and more realistic spirit in dealing with those questions in which the Bureau had its particular interest. Addressing the Georgia legislature by invitation, Alexander Stephens expressed the growing conviction that to the Negroes, "poor, untutored, uninformed, liable to be imposed upon," there should be secured "ample and full protection . . . so that they may stand equal before the law in the possession and enjoyment of all the rights of person, liberty and property."

But despite such wise advice from enlightened leaders; despite what Governor Orr of South Carolina referred to in his message to the legislature as the surprisingly large "amount of voluntary labor" put forth by the blacks during the first season of freedom; despite the rising evidences of the effect upon Northern sentiment of anything which was, or which could be made to look like, discrimination in law between the races, the legislatures of the restored states meeting early in 1866 persisted in the passage of codes of law and conduct for the Negroes, reasonable enough from their own point of view but highly inflammatory material for outside consumption.

To constitute damaging campaign material it was not even necessary that the discrimination alleged should appear in the law itself. Virginia passed a vagrant law, in its terms applying to all alike without distinction of color, which provided that convicted vagrants might be hired out for terms of three months, and that a vagrant so hired out who should run away might be worked an additional month, wearing ball-and-chain if the hirer so desired. Ordering that the statute be not enforced in any way against colored persons, Major General A. H. Terry, military commander in the state, declared that its "ultimate effect will be to reduce the freedmen to a condition of servitude worse than that from which they have been emancipated—a condition which will be slavery in all but its name."

Commenting on General Terry's order, a Richmond paper observed:

"It is the misfortune, rather than the fault, of the Virginia agriculturist that he cannot offer higher wages to the negro. The want of capital, the exhausted condition of the state and the unsettled state of the country, forbid that he should compete with farmers of more prosperous states."

The net effect, on the outside mind, was the impression that Virginia legislators and newspapers considered a vagrancy statute, with ball-and-chain trimmings, a substitute for wages. Whether as a result of this experience or of general observation of the workings of freedom, in February the legislature repealed all laws dealing with slaves and slavery; legalized slave marriages and legitimized their offspring; and abolished all distinctions in law between the colors, in contrast to the elaborate regulations of the colored race of some of the more southerly states. Finally, over the intense opposition of the lower classes of whites, it granted to the freedmen the right to testify in cases in which they or their rights were involved.

In a special session beginning on January 18, 1866, the legislators of North Carolina received, considered, and, in general, adopted the report of a special commission appointed by Governor Holden to recommend legislation for freedmen. The civil status of the freed people was to be the same as that of the considerable body of free persons of color in the state before emancipation. In suits at law and in equity their rights were the same as those of white persons. Crimes and punishments were to be the same for both races, except for the death penalty for attempted rape of a white woman by a colored man. Slave marriages were validated and registered; mixed marriages, forbidden. Dealings between white and colored persons were protected when the amount involved was more than ten dollars by a statute of frauds which required a contract in writing to be signed and witnessed by a white person who could read and write.

The proposal that colored testimony be admitted as a matter of right in all cases in which colored persons or their rights were involved, and by consent in all other cases, brought on a four-day debate. There was the usual opposition among the usual class of whites, in this case led by Provisional Governor Holden, who had gone out of office in December, when Jonathan Worth, the elected governor, took over the chair. Differences in treatment between the two races were relatively slight in the North Carolina code but they met objection among the officers of the Freedmen's Bureau. When the constitutional convention reassembled in May, the code was amended to abolish all discriminations—but, in the meanwhile, North Carolina had done its part toward furnishing ammunition for the Radical campaign.

Governor Holden's opposition to granting to Negroes the right to testify in court was ascribed by the Raleigh *Sentinel,* in fact, to a desire to irritate and infuriate Radical sentiment in the North so as to bring about congressional interference with the restored government in North Carolina. Governor Holden himself lent some color to the charge by his declaration of "war on traitors," particularly warning that if the press of the state did not cease their praise of the Confederate Governor Zebulon Vance, accompanied by disparagement of his successor Holden, the President would be called on to have Vance put back in prison, where he was just after the war, and brought to trial for treason.

In Tennessee, with a legislature strongly Radical in sentiment, the bill to admit Negro testimony did not pass until January 26, 1866, after three months of heated consideration and angry debate. At the beginning of the following week, Samuel M. Arnell, Radical leader, presented in the House of Representatives a new franchise bill, designed to make impossible any such results as those of August, 1865, when the Conservatives carried the election for congressmen. The new bill denied the right of suffrage to everyone who had not constantly and at all times opposed secession and the Confederate cause; created a system of registration under control of the Governor, through power of appointment and removal; and reduced the electorate of the state to the white Unionists, three-fourths of whom lived in the strongly Union section of East Tennessee.

With the bill up for final reading in the House of Representatives, on February 23, twenty-one members declared that they would not form part of a quorum to pass such a measure, resigned and left the House in an uproar. Angry Radicals charged the speaker with complicity in a conspiracy to break the quorum, which accusation the Speaker rebutted by hurling a handy inkstand at the head of his accuser, as well as calling him several different profane sorts of a lying scoundrel.

In calling special elections to be held on March 31, to fill vacancies, Governor Brownlow warned the voters not to send back the men who had resigned to break the quorum. The voters overwhelmingly disregarded the warnings and sent back sixteen of the resigning members, and three others of like mind. Presenting themselves to the House, nineteen of the twenty-two new members elected were refused seats on the ground that they were publicly pledged to filibuster again, if necessary, in opposition to the franchise bill. At the same time, by seating the three Radicals chosen at the special elections to fill vacancies, a quorum was secured and the franchise bill was passed, promptly, on April 12. Under pressure from the Governor and threats from Radical members to have East Tennessee secede from the state as West Virginia had done from the Old Dominion, the bill was forced to passage in the Senate on May 3, and Tennessee was, presumably, made safe for the Radical cause.

"Any means must be resorted to, if necessary," said one speaker at the Radical jollification in celebration of the event, "to keep rebels from the polls and out of office." The Nashville *Union & American*, however, warned that the passage of the bill would lead to ill will and trouble. "Tennessee wants peace, on the basis of liberty and constitutional forms. This, sooner or later, the people of the state will have," it said.

The new Florida legislature, at its first sessions beginning in December, devoted itself largely to consideration of another of the futile "Black Codes" recommended by a special commission appointed by Provisional Governor Marvin, who had been succeeded in office by his elected successor, Governor Walker. The code, which embraced the principle of different laws for the races, was never in wide operation, and much of it, probably, was never intended to be enforced, for reasons explained by John Wallace.

Wallace, born a slave in North Carolina, discharged from the United States Army at Key West, settled in Tallahassee. Self-educated, he served in both houses of the Florida legislature after 1868. After the close of the Reconstruction period, he published his book *Carpet-Bag Rule in Florida*, showing that the errors and excesses of that period were due not to the newly enfranchised colored citizens but to the contamination and contrivance of strange white men who came among them persuasively representing themselves as saviors of the race. Wallace wrote:

"Many of these laws (of 1865-66), we know, of our own knowledge, were passed only to deter the freedmen from committing crime. For instance, the law prohibiting colored people handling arms without a license was a dead letter, except in some cases where some of the freedmen would go around plantations hunting, with apparently no other occupation, such a person would be suspected of hunting something that did not belong to him and his arms would be taken from him. We have often passed through the streets of Tallahassee with our gun upon our shoulder, without a license, and were never disturbed. . . ."

While some freedmen did not get justice in their contracts, he said, "the great majority of whites carried out their contracts to the letter, and the freedmen did as well as could be expected under the changed condition of things. These laws were taken advantage of by the carpetbaggers to marshal the freedmen to their support after the freedmen had been given the right to vote."

The right to vote, freely and unrestrained, in the mass, came to the Negroes as a policy imposed on the South through Radical Reconstruction but in 1865 and 1866 numerous Southerners of high position urged that the right to vote be given to properly qualified members of the race. In South Carolina, where the Negroes were a majority of the population, so wise a leader as Wade Hampton urged such a step. In Georgia, Alexander H. Stephens, at the time that he was being held up to the scorn of Congress as the sort of unrepentant rebel whom the South sought to place in the halls of national legislation, urged upon the Georgia legislature that "such members of the black race as could come up to some proper standard of mental and moral culture, with the possession of a specified amount of property" should be allowed to vote.

A bill proposing Negro suffrage, with educational and property qualifications, presented to the Alabama legislature early in 1866 by a member from a Black Belt county, was tabled, largely because of the strong opposition of the white Counties in North Alabama. General Swayne, head of the Bureau in the state, was positive in his opinion that, in time, the whites of Alabama would have extended suffrage to the Negroes had it not been for the alienation of the races by the Reconstruction Acts and other legislation. In fact, unofficially and informally, Negroes voted in minor elections in the state in 1866.

Acting at the end of February, with the advice and approval of General Swayne, and after the veto of earlier legislation by Governor Patton, the legislature of Alabama put the races upon a practical equality in civil rights, insofar as the terms of the law were concerned, with minor exceptions. As to this legislation, General George H. Thomas testified that "Alabama has attempted to pass laws as judicious as they could at the time to regulate the affairs of the freedmen."

Last of the former states of the Confederacy to attempt legislation on the status of the freedmen, Texas reflected somewhat the experiences of the other states, and followed the trend toward a more equal treatment of freedmen in the law developing in 1866. Meeting on February 7 for a session that lasted until April 2, the constitutional convention of the restored state accepted the abolition of slavery by act of the United States government; granted to Negroes the right to property, and rights in court, including the right of testimony in cases where Negroes were involved, and authorized the legislature to grant full rights of testimony "as to facts hereafter occurring."

Shortly before the adjournment of the convention, a caucus of the Radical element tendered to Provisional Governor Hamilton their nomination for governor in the election to be held in May. When he declined the nomination, former Governor E. M. Pease was nominated. Opposing elements nominated J. W. Throckmorton, president of the convention, an original Unionist who voted against secession in the 1861 convention, but who "went with the state," entered Confederate service as commissioner to the Indians, and became a Confederate brigadier.

Regardless of the ideas of Southern legislators as to the sort of legislation suitable for the colored population, the Union military commanders had the last word—and that word, under War Department General Orders No. 3, of January 12, 1866, was that there should be no prosecution of colored persons "charged with offences for which white persons are not prosecuted or punished in the same manner and degree." Congress, moreover, in the language of Mr. Stevens, was taking "no account of the aggregation of whitewashed rebels who, without any legal authority, have assembled in the capitals of the late rebel states, and simulated legislative bodies."

The net effect, therefore, of all the deliberations and discussions, the labors and the strivings, of the legislatures of the states lately in the Confederacy was to furnish to the Radical propagandists the material which they so well knew how to use.

The acts of the legislature of West Virginia, which Congress had created, however, were given full faith and credit. Meeting in January, that body submitted to an election to be held in May a constitutional amendment disfranchising all those who had given "voluntary aid or assistance to the rebellion," and then, to make quite sure that the election should go right, prohibited voting in the election by those who were to be disfranchised if the amendment should be ratified. Even then, and with all the care that could be taken through control of the machinery of registration and election, the majority for the proscriptive amendment was only seven thousand out of a total vote of more than thirty-seven thousand.

Nor could Congress refuse to deal with Kentucky as a state, regardless of Radical resentment at its rapid conversion to "rebel principles." Kentucky, never having seceded, was not under a provisional or restored government, but it was included under military command, just as the states to the south, and was included in the operations of the Freedmen's Bureau, after Kentucky slaves were officially freed by the proclamation of the ratification of the Thirteenth Amendment on December 18, 1865.

The Bureau undertook its work in Kentucky, under General Fisk, with good intentions, poor judgment and unfortunate results, to furnish many of the irritants to Kentucky pride which helped create the resentment that made the state "go Confederate," in the eyes of the Radicals.

In its sessions early in 1866, the Kentucky legislature went right to work to remove Confederate disabilities imposed during war times. The expatriation act was repealed, without any embarrassing requirements as to oath-taking because, as one member put it, the legislature was opposed to "promiscuous swearing." The oaths required of ministers, jurors and schoolteachers were abolished in January, 1866, while in the following month military interference in an election was declared to render it void. Four Radicals were unseated in the Senate, eight in the House, and new elections ordered held. Almost all the vacancies were filled by Conservatives—among them young John G. Carlisle, beginning his public career.

To the Louisville Courier, the policy followed by Kentucky was one of broad and healing reconciliation. To the Radicals it was "renewed rebellion." The legislature at Frankfort, said the Cincinnati Gazette, was "as disloyal in spirit as any that ever met in Richmond or South Carolina." The popularity of returned Confederates was resented. "If anyone wishes to see a rebel city let him come to Louisville," wrote the Gazette's Kentucky correspondent. Pictures of Lee and Jackson were to be seen everywhere, but none of Lincoln, Grant or Thomas, he complained.

Radical resentment at Kentucky's apostasy from "loyalty" was to produce even less temperate comment. General Palmer's attitude and speech were such as to draw from General Sherman the comment that he was "all right for a monarchy or consolidation; all wrong for our old form of government." Speaking in Lexington in January, according to the *Observer & Reporter*, General Fisk declared that

"only the day before yesterday, in Lexington, thirteen discharged colored soldiers stood in the streets, in full sight of the Henry Clay monument, with their bodies lacerated, their backs bleeding from the cruel lash, their heads cut to the scalp, and one or two of them with their eyes put out! And what for, do you suppose? Simply for going to their former masters and asking for their wives and children."

An investigating committee of the legislature, sent to Lexington, reported on February 3 that it had invited the General to prove his charges; that he did not appear; and that the charges, "false and slanderous," were "but a continuation of the system of misrepresentation to which the people of this state have been exposed for several years at the hands of office-holders of the general government."

General Fisk brought the immediate controversy to a close with the heated reply that he had suggested the names of witnesses for a broad investigation, which the committee did not make because of the "vindictive, pro-slavery, rebellious" attitude of the majority of the Kentucky legislature—a declaration afterward broadened, when certain local courts declined to recognize the authority of the Bureau, to include certain Kentuckians as "the meanest, unsubjugated and unreconstructed rascally rebellious revolutionists that curse the soil of the country."

CHAPTER XIX

The Great Amendment

WHATEVER may have been the exact state of affairs in the South at any particular time, the tendency toward sensible adjustment of the relations of races so recently master and slave is evident. Neither conditions nor tendency, however, had any real meaning to the Radical group that had captured the machinery of Congress, except as they might be used to demonstrate to the Northern electorate the enormity of Southern designs—designs against the freedmen, against the loyal bondholders who held the war debt, against the Northern war veterans, against Northern business, against the government itself. To a generation which had been reared in a belief in the innate depravity of the "slavocracy," it was no great trick to parade the isolated acts of individuals, or the well-intentioned but ill-advised efforts of legislative bodies, as conclusive proof of the unrepentant state of provinces conquered, it is true, but not yet sufficiently whipped of justice.

Secure in its control of the situation, the Committee of Fifteen began the great inquisition into the state of the South. Its four subcommittees, sitting in Washington during the winter and early spring, heard a total of one hundred and forty-four witnesses. Of that number, at least one hundred and fourteen were of groups which might have been expected to be biased against the policy of speedy Southern restoration and home rule. Ten of these were Northern officeholders in the South; fifteen, Northern officers of the Freedmen's Bureau; thirty-eight, Northern army officers; ten, Northern travelers; three, Northern men living in the South—two of whom failed to give the kind of condemnatory responses to questions sought by the committee.

Twenty-one who testified were Southern white loyalists, whose hope of future political preferment hung on the success of the Radical policy. Eight were Negro loyalists. Two provisional governors and one restoration governor were examined; and four members-elect of Congress, seven officeholders under the Southern state governments, and sixteen non-officeholding citizens of the South.

The twelve witnesses from North Carolina who appeared in Washington embraced one native of the state; two ministers and Bureau agents who had lived in North Carolina before 1860; eight officers or ex-officers of the army, including six who were then officers of the Bureau; and one newspaper editor who had been in the state as a war correspondent before the fall of Wilmington in 1865.

Among the Virginia witnesses who appeared before the same sub-committee was Robert E. Lee, who assured them that "so far as I know the feeling of the people of Virginia they want peace." Other witnesses from the state, however, mostly native loyalists or Republicans who had come in from the North after the war, testified to the rebellious attitude of the Virginians, and their hostility to freedmen and white Unionists, who, it was alleged, required protection of United States troops for their safety.

Even less representative were the witnesses who described affairs in the states more distant from Washington. Of the sixteen witnesses who appeared in Washington to describe affairs in Arkansas, five were government officeholders; six had made only short visits to the state, with small opportunity to learn much about it; only three were qualified by residence or long contact to give real evidence. No former Confederates testified. Of ten witnesses from Mississippi, there were no Democrats and only two citizens of the state. The others were army officers, a treasury agent, and a witness who described himself as being "engaged in ascertaining the amount of cotton in the Southern states for an association of New England manufacturers."

All the witnesses were required to answer questions, often leading and suggestive. These answers were later classified and summarized in such fashion as to give the strongest possible coloring in support of the predetermined position that there was little loyalty in the South, and that little merely a submission to continuing force; that Confederates had no regrets except for their failure; that the "rebellion was being reorganized," as one witness put it; that Northern men were not cordially received in the South; and that freedmen were worse off under the legislation and impositions of their old masters than they were in slavery. One hundred thousand copies of the eight-hundred-page report of the committee, containing the summaries and conclusions, as well as the testimony, were printed and circulated at government expense to become a campaign document of the highest importance.

On February 6, Congress completed the passage of a bill enlarging and extending the operations of the Freedmen's Bureau, and sent it to the President for his approval. Lyman Trumbull, Moderate Senator from Illinois, chairman of the judiciary committee. and author of the bill, felt that it should, and would, be approved. This feeling was strengthened by the fact that at the time the Moderates were undertaking to secure the admission of the state of Tennessee to Congress and the Union, a project dear to the Tennessean President whom Mr. Stevens enjoyed describing as "an alien enemy, a citizen of a foreign state . . . not legally President."

The sub-committee which had inquired into affairs in Tennessee recommended its admission on February 15. Favorable action on this recommendation by the Committee of Fifteen, it was felt, would furnish a basis for an accommodation of differences on the Freedmen's Bureau bill, and perhaps other matters in dispute.

The Radicals could have no objection to the Tennessee government of the time, in fiercely loyal hands of their own persuasion, but it did not suit their plans to compose differences with the President in any degree. When the committee met, therefore, on February 17, Mr. Williams of Oregon moved that the whole Tennessee question be taken from the Moderate sub-committee which had made its report, and be re-referred to a new sub-committee. By the margin of one vote, eight to seven, the committee approved the plan, and set up a new all-Radical sub-committee—Williams, Conkling and Boutwell—which recommended that Tennessee be not readmitted until the state furnished "guarantees" for repayment of the Union war debt and against enfranchisement or admission to office for a period of at least five years of all who had participated in rebellion.

Convinced by the success of this Radical maneuver that no basis of accommodation was possible with a Congress which they controlled, President Johnson vetoed the extended Freedmen's Bureau bill, on February 19, on the grounds that there was no present necessity for such a law, since the old law had yet more than a year to run; that the new bill enlarged and extended military jurisdiction; that it provided arbitrary punishments for crimes vaguely defined, without presentment or indictment, trial by jury, or right of appeal; that its relief and educational features, not properly functions of the Federal government, would double present expenses of the Bureau; that the bill transferred the care, and also the control, of four millions of people to the Executive, who might use them for political purposes; and, finally, that the bill was passed by only a part of a Congress, with eleven states not represented.

The veto message was mild in tone, cogent in reasoning and almost archaic in its devotion to a Constitution of limited and defined powers, but about its author the storm broke. On February 20, amid excitement and under the crack of the party whip, both houses passed a concurrent resolution, offered by Mr. Stevens, that no senator or representative should be admitted from any of the insurrectionary states until both houses of Congress should have declared the state entitled to representation—in effect, the same resolution which the Senate had refused to accept from the House at the opening of Congress in December.

On the following day, after a debate of which Republicans would be "ashamed . . . ten years hence," according to General Sherman, the Senate sustained the veto of the President, with thirty votes for passing the bill over the veto and eighteen against—less than the two-thirds majority required.

Mass meetings supporting the President's veto were held on Washington's Birthday, in Northern cities, while in Kentucky salutes were fired at Frankfort, and resolutions commending the President's policy and course were passed at Louisville, Lexington, Danville and other towns. Even the Radicals in Kentucky, as part of a move to increase their waning popularity in the state, sought to claim Johnson as their leader, and asked for the removal of the Bureau and the Federal troops from the state. At a mass meeting of citizens of New York, David Dudley Field commented on "the curious feature of the Freedmen's bill . . . that it took the blacks under the protection of the Federal government, as if they were not able to take care of themselves, while the same persons who urged . . . the measure are the most clamorous to give this same dependent population a large share in the government of the country."

On the night of Washington's Birthday, a great crowd of serenaders calling at the White House to congratulate the President, demanded of him a speech. William H. Crook, whose service at the White House began with Lincoln and extended through five administrations, says that the President "began to speak to the crowd calmly and dispassionately." "Of two extreme elements in the nation," said the President, "one would destroy the government to preserve slavery; the other would break up the government to destroy slavery." As the crowd responded to the telling power of his oratory—for, as Colonel Crook says, he was an orator—"the President began to speak more warmly." As the speech was reported:

"I said in the Senate in the very inception of this rebellion, that the states had no right to secede. That question has been settled. Thus determined, I cannot turn round and give the lie direct to all that I profess to have done during the last four years. I say that when the states that attempted to secede comply with the Constitution, and give sufficient evidence of loyalty, I shall extend to them the right hand of fellowship, and let peace and union be restored. I am opposed to the Davises, the Toombses, the Slidells and the long list of such. But when I perceive on the other hand, men . . . I care not by what name you call them . . . still opposed to the Union, I am free to say to you that I am still with the people. I am still for the preservation of these states, for the preservation of this Union, and in favor of this great government accomplishing its destiny."

From the crowd voices called, "Name them! Name them!"

"The gentleman calls for names . . ." said the President. "I say Thaddeus Stevens of Pennsylvania. I say Charles Sumner of Massachusetts. I say Wendell Phillips of Massachusetts."

Another voice from the crowd: "Forney!" referring to the Pennsylvania politician who was secretary of the Senate and editor of the Radical Washington *Chronicle*.

"I do not waste my fire on dead ducks."

A humiliation to the nation, the maudlin incoherencies of an inebriate, disgusting to all right-minded citizens, cried the Radicals in Congress and in the press. That it was none of these things, except as it was made so to appear in the accounts, is certain. As Colonel Crook says,

"Mr. Johnson's manner in delivering public speeches was one which could not be translated into newspaper language. . . . He had a calm, assured way of talking. . . . His bearing was quiet and dignified, his voice low and sympathetic. . . . I have been startled myself to read the same speech in the paper that I had heard the day before. One would think, from what was written, that a violent demagogue was brandishing his arms and shrieking at the top of his lungs. . . . Had he been sympathetically reported, the country would have had a different impression of him."

To abandon the protection of the dignity of the presidential office to swap words with unknown voices from a crowd in the darkness was unwise, but the provocation was great. In Congress and out, in the press and through the visits of inspired delegations, he had been badgered for months, his utterances distorted, his acts misconstrued. To a president without the usual support of the partisan press of that time, and without the channels of a communication with the nation open to a president today, the temptation to express himself must have been unbearably great. He had shown exemplary patience under months of provocative nagging. "Can you ask him," said John Sherman in the Senate on February 26, "because he is president to submit to insult? . . . a man who never turned his back upon a foe, personal or political. . . . I see him yet, surrounded by the Cabinet of Abraham Lincoln, pursuing his policy . . . one of the real heroes of this war."

Failure to repass the new Freedmen's Bureau bill over the veto stimulated the Radicals to extreme efforts and measures to secure a reliable two-thirds majority in the Senate. In the search for the additional vote needed, they took note of the fact that a protest had been filed the year before against the seating of John P. Stockton, Democratic Senator from New Jersey, on the ground that he had received the votes of a majority of those present and not a majority of the entire membership of the legislature which elected him. There was so little merit in the protest that no member of the predominantly Republican Judiciary Committee, to which it was referred for investigation, took it seriously enough to vote to sustain it. Senator Daniel Clark of New Hampshire, however, did not sign the report recommending that the new Senator from New Jersey be confirmed in the seat where, in fact, he had been sitting for two months before the unnoted report was filed. No further action was considered necessary.

By March, however, when it became a matter of moment to find or make another Radical vote in the Senate, there was a new legislature in New Jersey, Republican on joint ballot. To unseat Stockton, therefore, meant another Republican vote in the Senate. Senator Clark offered a resolution to oust him, at a time when one Conservative Senator, the venerable Solomon Foot of Vermont, lay dying; another, Dixon of Connecticut, was seriously ill in Washington; and a third, William Wright, Stockton's colleague, had returned to his New Jersey home because of illness. Before leaving Washington, however, in anticipation of action in the Stockton case, Senator Wright had arranged a pair on that particular question with Senator Lot Morrill of Maine.

The Clark resolution to unseat Stockton was defeated on March 23, by two votes. The report of the Judiciary Committee, that Stockton was entitled to his seat, was voted on next, and carried, by a vote of twenty-one to twenty. Senator Morrill had respected his pair with Wright so far and had not voted on either question. At the end of the second roll call, however, when it became apparent that his one vote could block affirmative adoption of the report which would have confirmed Stockton in his seat, the pressure upon him from his Radical colleagues became too great to be withstood. The chamber rang with calls for his vote. "Vote! Vote! Vote!" was Sumner's cry, reinforcing his previous private advice that Morrill owed it to his colleagues and his country to break the pledge given in his pair with Wright. Under the stress of excitement and the drive of party necessity, Morrill voted "No," and tied the vote, justifying himself on the claim that the time limit of his pair had expired.

Outraged at the bad faith shown to his absent colleague, Stockton made the mistake of voting in his own case. His vote carried the resolution, twenty-two to twenty-one, but it gave an opportunity, at the beginning of the next week, for Senator Sumner to denounce him for the impropriety, the disrespect to the Senate, involved in voting in his own case. Stockton agreed to withdraw his vote, the Senate reconsidered its action, and set the Stockton case for voting on another day, March 27. By that time, another Conservative Senator, E. D. Morgan of New York, was sick, while neither Dixon nor Wright were able to be back in the Senate. Pleas for delay of forty-eight hours to give them a chance to come in were disregarded with scant consideration, and Stockton was unseated by a majority of one vote. Even James G. Blaine of Maine, rock-ribbed in his Republicanism and practical in his political views, felt that the haste in unseating Stockton was "hardly justifiable," and that he was not treated with "magnanimity or generosity." On legal grounds, however, following the argument of Maine's Senator Fessenden, he believed the Senate had the right to unseat him.

On March 27, the very day on which the Radicals cleared the way to get the additional vote they needed in the Senate, the President returned to Congress, with his veto, Senator Trumbull's Civil Rights Bill. During the nearly two weeks which the bill had been in his hands, he had been urged by his Moderate friends to sign it as a move of conciliation, regardless of its imperfections as a piece of legislation. General Jacob D. Cox, Governor of Ohio, wrote him:

"Few people have read it through. They judge it by synopses of its provisions which have been published very briefly in the country papers. They fasten their minds upon the fact that the bill declares that the freedman shall have the same rights of property and person, the same remedies for injuries received and the same penalties for wrongs committed, as other men. . . . They do not look to the means employed to enforce the provisions of the bill . . . they do not care much about or very well understand them. . . ."

The Ohio Governor felt that it would be "well to *strain a point* in order to meet the popular spirit and impulse rather than to make a strict construction of duty the other way."

Whatever he thought of this advice, the President, convinced by this time that no peace could be gained by yielding his convictions to the Radicals, vetoed the bill on strong constitutional grounds—objecting not to the ends sought so much as to the means provided and the powers assumed. The bill, he said, attempted to create citizenship by Federal action, without action of the states. It made freedmen citizens with no preparation; created a whole new catalogue of undefined crimes; impaired the judicial power of the states by giving exclusive cognizance of cases to the United States courts; and, in general, was such an "absorption and assumption of power by the General Government" as would, if acquiesced in, "break down the barriers which preserve the rights of the States."

Immediately, the Radicals went to work to pass the bill over the veto. Stockton was already unseated. His colleague, Wright, was still ill at home. On April 5, George F. Edmunds was appointed to the Senate from Vermont, vice Solomon Foot, deceased. On the next day, the Moderate Dixon, of Connecticut, was at home sick. That day, having their two-thirds vote, the Radicals repassed the bill in the Senate, thirty-three to fifteen. Three days later, the House repassed it, one hundred twenty-two to forty-one. For the first time in American history, a presidential veto of a major measure had been overridden by Congress.

The same skillful political management which, in little more than four months, had given the Radicals power to override a presidential veto in Congress, was to continue, through the months of the campaign for the election of the next Congress, accumulating strength from many and diverse sources, through arguments and appeals, sometimes more effective than scrupulous or consistent.

There was no haste on the part of the Radicals to define and present the issues of the campaign. Delay and opportunism were of the essence of their plan of operations but, finally, the all-powerful Committee on Reconstruction was prodded into recommending, on April 30, the four proposals which were lumped together as the Fourteenth Amendment.

The first proposal in the amendment was national citizenship, created and protected by the national government. No state, it was declared, shall "make or enforce any law which shall abridge the privileges and immunities of citizens of the United States," nor shall "deprive any person of life, liberty or property, without due process of law," or "deny to any person within its jurisdiction the equal protection of the laws."

Secondly, it was proposed to apportion representatives among the states in accordance with the whole number of inhabitants, reducing the representation of any state which denied the "elective franchise" to males over twenty-one years of age "except for participation in rebellion or other crime."

As it came from the committee and passed the House, the third section of the proposed amendment excluded from the right to vote for electors and members of Congress until July 4, 1870, "all persons who voluntarily adhered to the late insurrection, giving it aid and comfort." As amended in the Senate, and afterward accepted by the House, the section omitted reference to voting but instead disqualified from holding public office all those who, having held a state or Federal office which required an oath of allegiance to the United States, had subsequently engaged in or given aid and comfort to the rebellion. This constitutional disqualification from holding any office, civil or military, state or Federal, legislative, judicial or executive, was for all time to come, unless removed by a two-thirds vote of both Houses of Congress.

The fourth section prohibited forever any compensation for the loss of slave property and insured the repudiation of debts "incurred in aid of insurrection or of war against the United States."

To carry out the fifth, or enforcement, clause there were offered two bills—one declaring high military and civil officers of the Confederacy ineligible for Federal office; and a second, cunningly contrived, which proposed the restoration of a state to the Union as soon as the new Fourteenth Amendment should become part of the Constitution, provided that the state itself had ratified the amendment and incorporated it into its own constitution and laws.

The latter bill, having been introduced and used to create the desired impression that Congress was offering definite terms of admission to the Southern states, was quietly tabled without a vote on the merits. There was no intention that Southern states, other than Tennessee, which already had a government regarded as reliably Radical, should be admitted on any terms short of those finally required—the creation by granting the vote for the freed slaves of a new and presumably Radical electorate.

The majority of the committee, twelve of the fifteen, claimed for the Congress all power to fix future political relations. "Within the limits prescribed by humanity, the conquered rebels were at the mercy of the conquerors," their report read. Election of "notorious and unpardoned rebels" was cited to show that it was not safe to rely on the loyalty of the rebel states. Even President Johnson, it was pointed out, in his official proclamation of April 2, terminating the state of war, had not shown enough confidence in his own work of restoration to "remove the military force, to suspend martial law, or to restore the writ of habeas corpus, but still thought it necessary to exercise over the people of the rebellious states his military power and jurisdiction."

Implying that Congress should be no less careful of future loyalty and safety, the majority report described the feeling of the Southern people, at the collapse of the Confederacy, as "abject submission," without hope "except that by the magnanimity of their conquerors their lives, and possibly their property, might be preserved." Unwise use of the pardoning power, and the general conciliatory attitude of the North, had bred a change. "In return for our leniency we receive only an insulting denial of our authority."

The people of the seceded states, in the view of the majority, were entitled only to "such rights, privileges and conditions as might be vouchsafed by the conquerors"—a point of view more pungently phrased by Senator Zachariah Chandler, who limited the rights of a rebel to "the constitutional right to be hanged and the divine right to be damned." Before granting anything, the majority concluded, "adequate guarantees against future treason and rebellion" must be given, in the shape of amendment of the fundamental law to determine the rights of all citizens everywhere in the nation, regulate representation equitably, fix a stigma on treason, and protect loyal people from war claims or repudiation of war obligations.

The minority of three on the committee stood on the theory that "A state once in the Union must abide in it forever. She can never withdraw or be expelled from it. A different principle would subject the Union to dissolution at any moment." If the seceded states were not still in the Union, to submit to them amendments to the constitution was an absurdity. The national power to suppress insurrections had been properly used, not to destroy the state but to subdue rebellious individuals and preserve the state; the congressional duty to guarantee a republican form of government should be exercised upon the organs of government submitted by the people of the states.

The Southern states, it was pointed out, were in a minority. They had already agreed to repudiate the rebel debt, waive all claims for compensation for slave property, and sustain the inviolability of the obligations representing the Northern war debt. The majority now demanded, it was said, that these states disfranchise their own citizens, and also reduce their representation unless they were willing to admit to the ballot colored males over twenty-one, "a class now in a condition of almost utter ignorance." This method of indirection was proposed, it was insisted, because direct action for Negro suffrage in all states would have been obnoxious to most of the North.

"The effect, then, if not the purpose of the measure," said the minority, "is forever to deny representation to such states, or, if they consent to the condition, to weaken their representative power and thus, probably, secure a continuance of such a party in power as now controls the legislation of the government. The measure, in its terms and in its effect, whether designed or not, is to degrade the Southern states. To consent to it will be to consent to their own dishonor."

The Fourteenth Amendment was actually four amendments in one, bound together into an indivisible whole. To two of these, the first section, defining and guaranteeing the rights of the citizen, and the fourth section, dealing with the Union and Confederate debts and the claim for compensation for emancipated slaves, there could have been no serious objection in either North or South. Another, the second section, proposing to cut down Southern representation if Negroes were not allowed to vote, might also have been accepted by the Southern legislatures to which it was submitted, had there not been bound into the amendment the third section. That section, in the language of Senator Trumbull, required the people of the South "to put some sort of stigma, some sort of odium, upon the leaders of the rebellion." In fact, it went far beyond the "few leaders" mentioned by its proponents, and extended its disqualification to practically all men who had, in any substantial way, been trusted as public leaders of the Southern communities before the war, a total of many thousands.

Without the third section, wrote General J. Z. George of Mississippi, afterward, "it is highly probable that the Southern people would have accepted the Fourteenth Amendment as the final terms of Reconstruction, if it had been so proposed." But it was not so proposed.

Indeed, the astute authors of the amendment did not expect the Southern states to consent to it, and would have been disconcerted if they had. The Fourteenth Amendment, as offered, was not a statement to the South of terms and conditions of admission. It was a statement to the voters of the North of a campaign platform on which to carry the election—after which, any implied promise in the amendment could be disregarded and the Southern states made over to the right measure.

The bill making a direct promise of readmission upon ratification had been quietly stifled in Congress on July 20, before the campaign was well under way. In the campaign, leading Radicals carefully and consistently refused to commit themselves to any such promises, while General Butler assured the Soldiers' & Sailors' Convention in Pittsburgh that there would be requirements for readmission other than mere ratification. Theodore Tilton's *Independent* was even more indiscreetly frank in its statement that:

"We know personally every prominent member of Congress, and we know that the leaders do not mean to admit the unadmitted States on the mere adoption of the amendment. Moreover, we know personally the leading radicals . . . outside of Congress, and we know that they have no intention of making the amendment the final measure of admission."

For Northern consumption, there was no suggestion of forced Negro suffrage. In most states, that was too explosive a subject to handle during the campaign. The whole impression there, cleverly created, was that the South was being offered peace and readmission on terms which included no more than a reduction in representation if suffrage were not granted to the Negro by state action.

At the same time, there was every reason to believe that the third section, disqualifying from public office great numbers of those who had been active in Southern public life, would insure the rejection of the amendment by the Southern states, other than Tennessee. Henry J. Raymond charged at the time that the third section was "inserted for the express purpose of preventing the adoption . . . of any of the amendments," while such careful later studies as those of Benjamin B. Kendrick and David M. DeWitt came to the same conclusion, that there was no intention that the Southern states should ratify the amendment in 1866, nor to admit them as states of the Union had they done so. Rejection, regardless of the section on which it was based or the reasons for it, would be yet one more proof of the stiff-necked contumacy of the South, one more reason for a thoroughgoing, root-and-branch Reconstruction.

Even in Tennessee difficulties developed in ratification of the amendment, which had to be swallowed whole or not at all. When Secretary Seward submitted the amendment to the states, including those whose legal existence and competence the Radicals denied, on June 20, Governor Brownlow immediately called a special session of the legislature to ratify. Recalcitrant members were slow in responding, so slow that officers had to be sent out to arrest them, bring them into the House, and physically hold them there, in defiance of a writ of habeas corpus, in order to secure a quorum. A majority of the quorum so secured, but a minority of the whole membership of the House, gleefully ratified on July 19, whereupon (the Senate having acted already on July 11) Governor Brownlow wired the results to Washington:

"We have ratified the constitutional amendment in the House, 43 for it, 11 against it, two of Andrew Johnson's tools not voting. Give my respects to the dead dog of the White House."

Accepting as official this uniquely informal communication, Congress very promptly admitted Tennessee to the Union, on July 24, 1866—an act which was calculated to confirm the carefully fostered popular impression that any Southern state not too stubborn to ratify would be welcomed back into Congress.

The campaign was to be fought, in heat and violence, on surface issues—the Boys in Blue, the Bloody Shirt, the Constitution and the Flag. The real issues were those of practical politics. There was the not totally unreasonable fear that some future combination of Southerners with the Repudiationists in the North might impair the obligation of the national debt. There was the constant threat of abandoning the high-tariff policies adopted during the war as revenue measures, with a return to the low-tariff policies of preceding decades. David Wells, special internal revenue commissioner, strongly criticised the tariff in his monumental fiscal report, made at this session of Congress. The tariff laws, he reported, were "only equivalent to legislating a bounty into the pockets of the producers," while Federal taxation in general he found to be "neither definite in amount, equal in application, nor convenient in collection," leading to higher prices, decreased consumption and trade.

The Radicals predominantly represented those sections and groups that believed they benefited by the situation and wished to preserve it. To allow the economic issues to be presented to the Northern electorate on their merits was no part of the Radical plan. Their task was to bring to their aid others who, with different economic interests, could yet be persuaded by the surface issues of the fight with the President to support their program. War bitterness, tenderness for the protection of the Negro, a general conviction of Southern wickedness, these were to be the real emotional appeals in a campaign designed to keep power in the hands of the Radical group.

The intent, said Mr. Stevens, was "to work a radical reorganization in Southern institutions, habits and manners," to break up the "foundations of their institutions." The "American people," wrote James Russell Lowell, "are resolved, by God's name, to Americanize" the South.

That invincible conviction of moral superiority was to convert the campaign, before its end, into a holy war—a war to "preserve to the party of the Union a perpetual ascendency."

CHAPTER XX

MEMORIES AND HOPES

THE Southern people, in that spring of 1866, went about their business, their politics and their daily living with a new hope. When they, or the most of them, thought about politics at all they were apt to think of the power of the President and of his determination to secure as rapidly as possible a complete restoration of civil government in their states. And there were so many other things to think of, and to work at, besides politics.

With the coming of the spring flowers—early, in the lower South— spontaneously there appeared at the first anniversary of the surrender a movement for memorial observances in the cemeteries. In many places, the Federal cemeteries were included in the kindly office of remembrance. One such impartial decoration, at Columbus, Mississippi, inspired the poem of Francis Miles Finch, "The Blue and the Gray," published in the *Atlantic Monthly* in the spring of the following year. Reprinted and recited thousands of times at Memorial Day observances of later years, the poem passed into common speech and common thought as one of the earnests of future reunion.

Just as the United States government was creating its beautiful national cemeteries on battlefields and at army centers, so the citizens of the South began to assemble their scattered dead in Confederate cemeteries. At Richmond, with its Hollywood, where so many Confederate soldiers and leaders had been buried during the war, a Memorial Association was formed to preserve and beautify the Confederate burying places. At Franklin, Tennessee, Randall McGavock created on his farm such a cemetery for the fifteen hundred Confederates who fell in that brief and bloody battle. The ladies of Winchester, Virginia, started a movement to gather the dead of the numerous engagements about that place into a suitable cemetery. In Memphis, a tournament was held, on May 22, to raise funds for a Confederate monument in Elmwood. Money was being raised in Augusta, in Noxubee County and in the university town of Oxford, in Mississippi, and in many another Southern town and county for like purposes. Miss Augusta Evans, author of *Macaria* and *Beulah*, who had just published

171

the phenomenally popular *St. Elmo*, was refused permission to erect a Confederate monument in Bienville Square, at Mobile.

These memorial movements, and particularly the spread of historical societies in the South, were distinctly displeasing to some in the North, who looked upon all such doings as evidences of continued disloyalty, at the least, or even, as one testified, as camouflage for reorganizing rebellion.

Relief for the living began to be organized, as well as memorials for the dead. A Benevolent Society, organized among the ladies of Nashville, used the fund raised by collection of dues of one dollar a month to provide artificial limbs for maimed ex-Confederates. Newspaper reports indicate that the idea spread widely over the South. An informal "shoe exchange" was established, in at least one case, by one-legged men who had no use for one shoe out of each pair they bought, because they were without means to secure anything better than an ordinary peg leg.

What political activity there was in the South during the spring, outside the comparatively small group of Southern loyalists, was intended to help President Johnson, although most of the activity probably did more harm than good. In Arkansas, the ex-Confederate element, readmitted to the electorate and to a part in public affairs when the "restorers'" Supreme Court held invalid the test oath in the post-war constitution of the state, began the organization of Johnson or National Union Clubs. Knowing that they would be able to capture it at the next election, they became zealous for the continuance of the Murphy government which they had opposed and derided, while Governor Murphy and the original "restorers" turned against the government they had created, and recommended to the Radicals at Washington that this result of Abraham Lincoln's efforts at restoration be obliterated.

This earnest of what would happen in the South whenever the Confederate or Conservative element was given full voting rights was not lost on the Radical strategists at Washington, nor was the fact that the same element carried the first election held in Texas under the new constitution, in May, 1866, by a majority of four to one. The restoration governor of Texas was to be General Throckmorton, nominated by the Conservatives, and not former Governor Pease, whom the Radicals supported.

The transfer of power from the provisional Hamilton government could not be made, however, until the President approved. The provisional Attorney-General wrote Radical leaders in Washington urging delay, as much delay as possible, in making the change. The correspondence, finding its way into the newspapers, raised a political storm in Texas, whereupon Provisional Governor Hamilton turned over affairs to his Secretary of State, Judge Bell, and hurried away north to join the campaign against the President.

Kentucky continued to pursue her course of independence, turning more and more away from the Radical policy which dominated the state at the close of the war. On May 1, at a convention in Louisville called by the *Courier* of that city, with eighty-five counties represented, the Democratic party in the state was reorganized. Union Conservatives, remaining out of this convention, met at the call of George D. Prentice of the Louisville *Journal*, on May 30. The Radicals, left alone, sought an alliance with this body but were rejected. "Loyal men in Kentucky," wrote one Radical, "will have to ask an amnesty from the rebels"—a state of affairs which was to be turned against the President, in the North.

In June, Provisional Governor Holden, with all the vehemence that usually accompanied one of his political about-faces, came out for congressional Reconstruction, and against the President's policy of restoration under which he had accepted appointment in North Carolina. Governor Holden's support of the congressional program was but one indication of the drift of groups in the South, many of them disappointed of their desires in the restoration, or Johnson, governments.

On May 18, in Alexandria, the Union Republican party was organized in Virginia, with John Minor Botts as chairman, a place which he was to hold until after congressional Reconstruction became an accomplished fact, when he was to be ousted as too conservative.

In South Carolina, colored political organization began as early as November, 1865, with a convention in Zion Church, Charleston, at which there first appeared delegates whose names were to become well known in the later Reconstruction days of the state. The convention forwarded to Congress a well-prepared address, appealing against the Carolina "Black Code" and urging equal suffrage for Negroes.

The Negroes of Florida, with smaller chance for education than those of South Carolina, went further in their first adventure into politics. Understanding that they had been enfranchised, a group met at Tallahassee; elected Joseph Oats, formerly a slave of Governor Walker, to represent them in Congress; raised several hundred dollars for his expenses, and sent him to Washington. Oats, staying in parts unknown until the money was spent, returned to Tallahassee, according to the account given by John Wallace, on May 20, 1866, with marvelous stories of the things he had accomplished for his constituents while in Congress. His accomplishments had been so great, in fact, that he insisted that he must be protected from the jealous whites who would assuredly kill him if they knew of all that he had done for the colored people. Protected by a committee armed with pistols and old cavalry sabers, therefore, the "Congressman" appeared before a mass meeting of two or three thousand persons, and made his report.

But to most of the people of the South, white and black, political events had small immediate interest that spring. There still was so much to do, not only to put in and cultivate and gather the crops, but to repair and reopen mills and shops and stores. Beset as they were, the Southern people were making, that spring, the small beginnings of new crops and new industries, also. The raising of vegetables and garden truck for distant markets was begun about Charleston, from which steamers carried eighteen hundred crates and baskets of early vegetables to New York that season, and about Crystal Springs, Mississippi, which started by raising vegetables for the New Orleans market and expanded to ship to the markets of the North. Commercial production of peanuts had its small beginnings in southeastern Virginia, about the same time.

It was to be discovered, also, that something could be done with the cottonseed left in piles about the gin houses, besides burning it or throwing it into the creek. Earlier attempts to start the business of crushing the cottonseed for its oil and meal had been interrupted by the war, but to crush the 1866 crop there were in operation in the South four small mills. By 1870 there were twenty-seven mills, and a great conservation industry was well on its way.

The business of spinning cotton began to revive, also. The cotton mills at Columbus, Georgia, which had been destroyed in General Wilson's last great raid of the war, were rebuilt by the spring of 1866, and new machinery was being sought to provide work for five hundred hands. Seven small cotton mills were being put in repair in up-country South Carolina, the beginning of an industry which within another year was to have some thirty-two thousand spindles in operation.

In Alabama, General Josiah Gorgas, who had been the Confederacy's able chief of ordinance, and his associates, undertook the development of iron works in Bibb County. As yet, the Southern works were makers of charcoal iron but in the next year General John T. Wilder, who had commanded an Indiana brigade in the fighting about

Chattanooga, came back to Tennessee to start making iron with coke. The Roane Iron Company, which he and his associates founded, operated coal mines, coke ovens and pig-iron furnaces at Rockwood, a new town named for one of the Indiana developers of the enterprise, and a rolling mill at Chattanooga, making the light iron rails which were then standard on the railroads.

Newspaper reports showed that the work of replacing broken bridges over major streams was going on, all over the South. The new railroad bridge over the Cumberland at Clarksville was finished in May. The iron railroad bridge over the Tennessee at Decatur, to cost one hundred and eighty thousand dollars, was under way, and the new highway suspension bridge at Nashville was to be finished early in the summer.

Transportation continued to be a great difficulty. High rates charged by the steamboats for taking cotton from Augusta to Savannah—eight dollars a bale downstream, with upstream freight at eight dollars a hundred pounds—were the subject of complaint. There was no help for it, however, as the railroad connecting the two places was still out of commission, and would be until well into the summer. The Western & Atlantic Railroad, owned by the state of Georgia, was using its earnings to make repairs, under the efficient management of Major Campbell Wallace. Other roads in the section through which the great Union raids passed were doing likewise, to the best of their ability, but the state of transportation in that section is indicated by the newspaper report of the robbing of the wagons of the Southern Express Company between Blackville and Augusta, where there had been a railroad before Sherman passed.

The railroad between Columbia and Charlotte, it was hoped, would be in running order by midsummer, as would the line between Meridian and Vicksburg, over which no through train had passed since the summer of 1863. Work was in progress, too, on new railroads. Fifty miles of the Macon & Brunswick were to be built, and seventy more graded, before the end of the year, with the aid of endorsement of its bonds by the state of Georgia in the amount of ten thousand dollars for each mile completed. As security for the loan of its credit, the state held a lien on the road. Between Atlanta and Charlotte, on the new Georgia Air Line, and between Macon and Augusta, the graders were at work.

In the late spring of 1866, the company of Pullman, Ramsay & Kimball was incorporated in Tennessee, to operate sleeping cars on the railroads in the South. Hannibal I. Kimball, who was associated with George M. Pullman in the venture, had been a New England carriage manufacturer, with a considerable Southern trade served through warehouses in Charleston and New Orleans. Strolling out Peachtree Street, on his first visit to Atlanta, Mr. Kimball came across a crowd surrounding a young auctioneer, George W. Adair, who had "come out of the Confederate army with absolutely nothing" and was "selling anything at auction from a billy goat to a corner lot." The object at sale that day was a corner lot. Mr. Kimball stopped, listened, became interested, and bid it in for six thousand dollars. He telegraphed Mr. Pullman for the money, which was promptly sent. The sleeping cars went into service in the South bearing the name, Pullman, Ramsay & Kimball, as travelers of that day recall, but Mr. Kimball soon withdrew from the venture, to devote himself to the booming real-estate and political business of Reconstruction Atlanta.

Cotton and construction created a demand for mules. "Aged broke mules are in good demand in the Southern market," reported the Citizen of Paris, Kentucky, at the opening of the planting season. Nine head sold on that market for an average of two hundred and seventy-five dollars each, in greenback currency, of course; seventy-five head, on the same day, sold for an average of one hundred and sixty dollars.

Efforts to attract immigration to the South were begun with considerable hopes and disappointing results. Two immigration companies operating in Georgia quit before the fall, when they found that white laborers from Europe or the North were not only hard to get but unsatisfactory when got. The state of South Carolina sent John A. Wagener, founder of the successful Walhalla colony at the foot of the Blue Ridge, back to Europe as immigration commissioner. Toward the end of the following year he returned to Charleston, bringing the first shipload of immigrants on the German bark, Gauss.

While the South was trying to bring in white immigrants, the African Colonization Society was continuing its efforts to colonize the freed Negroes in Liberia. Free passage was offered from Charleston and Baltimore, and more than two thousand went to Africa in 1866 and 1867. Their accounts of life in Liberia, and of its people and climate, and their longing to get back, discouraged others from following.

Attempts were on foot, also, to colonize Southern whites in the countries of Latin America, especially Brazil, where the Emperor Dom Pedro's government was reported to stand ready to extend its warmest welcome. Parties from South Carolina and Mississippi were met at

Rio with bands playing "Dixie," and with offers of land at twenty-two cents an acre, but the movement never developed into a success, partly because of the opposition of such leaders as Wade Hampton.

But the great movement of population, both white and black, was not across the waters. It was to the west, and particularly to the southwest. Families, with their stock and their dogs, their wagons and their gear, took up the trail, making camp by the road, "going to Texas," or beyond, in a mass migration which continued with yearly fluctuations throughout the years of Reconstruction and afterward.

Neither politics nor business dampened the social life of the people in the first years of peace. "I never knew so much real social enjoyment in Columbia as in the years 1866 and 1867," wrote Joseph LeConte, of the University. "Society was really gay, the necessary result of the rebound from the agony and repression of the war. . . . As everybody was poor, the gatherings were almost wholly without expense, and therefore frequent. The hostess simply furnished lemonade and cake, and the young men a Negro fiddler."

Elizabeth W. Alston Pringle recalled "the young ladies, nicely dressed, in the simplest muslin, sweet and fresh," not such as would be seen at the ball in the great world but creations, nevertheless, which "filled with admiration." Millinery styles, fresh from Paris and much discussed, bore the name of the Empress Eugénie, or of Charlotte Corday. Others were known as the Versailles, the Benoîton, the Promenade and the Chaperon.

At the carnival season of 1866, the very first after the war, the Mistick Krewe of Comus took possession of New Orleans once more. Through the throngs on Canal Street there moved a torch-lit Mardi Gras procession of floats depicting, in fanciful form, the Transformations of Comus.

Making calls in a country cart instead of a carriage, a lady of Hernando, Mississippi, smilingly referred to it as her "carte de visite," according to the People's Press. The same paper, week after week, contained such pleasant announcements as the "Basket Pic-Nic to be given by the young men of our village in Owen's Grove next Saturday"; or the concert by the young ladies of Mrs. Moseley's Select School— where it appears that the scholars were required to furnish their own lights, with coal oil advertised in the papers at one dollar a gallon.

In the South that spring were held scores of "Grand Tournaments" wherein knights, with long and slender lances, entered the lists before the court of the Queen of Love and Beauty and the spectators assembled. The competition consisted in riding three times around a circle of some three or four hundred yards, at top speed, tilting at rings two and one-half inches in diameter, suspended above the course at intervals of forty or fifty yards. The knight who plucked the largest number of rings upon his lance won the honor of naming and crowning the Queen. In a typical tournament at Hernando, this honor was won by the Knight of the Raven Tresses, a visitor from Memphis. The Knight of the Broken Lance, the Star of Hope and the Blue Knight, local horsemen, won the right to name and crown three of the Maids of Honor, while a fifteen-year-old Texan, Master Johnny Oliver, amid great applause, won the right to crown the fourth. The tournament was graced with knights of plumes of various colors, a Knight of Chance, a Knight of Despair, a Knight Rob Roy, one Knight of Tennessee, two Confederate Knights, and one other, evidently of a humorous turn, who dubbed himself the Trundle-Bed Ranger.

"Gentlemen so unfortunate as to have visited the state of matrimony," said the rules, were barred, regardless of their grace and prowess in horsemanship. After a picnic lunch "bountifully provided" in a near-by grove, and the crowning of the Queen, the gathering adjourned to the little town to hear a concert by the visiting Philharmonic Society of Memphis, assisted by vocal ladies and gentlemen.

Tournaments, concerts, "tableaux vivants," and other set entertainments did not furnish the only diversions of the time, even in the smaller towns, for in Hernando the opening of a novel "Ice Cream Saloon & Soda Water Fountain" was announced in the summer of 1866, while one enterprising local merchant advertised that he had "on hand and for sale several hundred pounds of ice."

By the publication of numerous bits of personal information, the Southern newspapers of the time show the natural and human interest taken by the Southern people in what their leaders in the late war were doing. So it was noted that Admiral Raphael Semmes had been elected probate judge at Mobile, an office which his unpardoned condition prevented him from holding; that General Henry A. Wise had resumed the practice of law at Richmond; that General John B. Magruder was a leader-writer for the Times of Mexico City, where the empire of Maximilian still held precarious possession; that Colonel L. Q. C. Lamar had returned to the chair of ethics and metaphysics at the University of Mississippi, which had one hundred and seventy-two students at the close of the school year; that General Beauregard, who had gone to Europe to seek funds for the restoration of the Great Northern Railroad from New Orleans, had been offered command of the new Rumanian Army by the Hospodar of Wallachia-Moldavia, and had refused; that General W. W. Loring had accepted a similar offer to command the armies of the Khedive of Egypt; that General A. P. Stewart was at Cumberland University, teaching mathematics; and that General D. H. Hill had launched, at Charlotte, North Carolina, a new Southern magazine, *The Land We Love*.

There was a great outpouring of Southern periodicals each more or less devoted to the promotion of Southern letters and the rehearsing of Southern glories. There were the *Southern Metropolitan*; the *Ladies' Home*, of Atlanta, edited by Miss L. Virginia French, and *Scott's Monthly Magazine*, also of Atlanta; the *Southern Family Visitor*, published at Grenada, Mississippi; and the *Nineteenth Century*, founded by the Reverend Mr. Hicks at Charleston. William Gilmore Simms wrote for it, not because it paid but because he wanted the South to have an organ. So, too, did Sidney Lanier, and Alexander Stephens, and the aging Judge Augustus Baldwin Longstreet. There were literary articles and articles on current affairs—"The Status and Prospects of the Negro," "The Morality of Round Dancing," "The Morality of Second Marriages," "The Morality of Attending Theatrical Performances." There were poems, "Keep Heart, Brave Southrons," and long vindications of the Southern position and course in the late war. It was, indeed, an organ of the South but like so many earlier organs, published in happier days, it was to die of inanition.

Published outside the territory of the late Confederacy but widely read by Southerners, were the *Old Guard Magazine*, published in New York, and, most widely read of all, A. T. Bledsoe's *intransigeant Southern Review*, which was to be founded in Baltimore during the following year of 1867, and to expound Southern opinions with an unreconstructed vigor beyond that of any publication issued in the insurrectionary states.

To all this activity in the resumption of a peaceful life in the South, however, the outside world paid small heed. Attention, as is usual, focused upon the disorders which might have been expected to accompany so great a social revolution. President Johnson, whose peace proclamation on April 2 brought the state of war to an official end, except in Texas, continued the garrisons. The military commanders retained their authority over the processes of government where they chose to exercise it, and affairs went on much as before, except that new points of jurisdiction might be raised in trials before military commissions. The raising of such questions, however interesting they may have been to the lawyers, had small practical effect in preventing the military from carrying on their trials to the appointed end.

President Johnson expected disorders in the South but he told a reporter for the Boston *Evening Commercial* that he felt that "there will be no more than there would be at the North were the number of black laborers sufficiently numerous to enter into rivalry with the white laborers"—a prediction that was to be tragically borne out within half a century by great race riots in Chicago, Omaha, East St. Louis, Springfield and elsewhere in the North.

The race riot began its appearance as a Southern phenomenon, however, in the spring of 1866, in time to have its effect upon the congressional campaign. At Norfolk, on April 16, a procession of freedmen celebrating the passage of the Civil Rights bill by Congress was enveloped in a confused and scuffling riot, in which two whites and two Negroes were killed. Investigation by the military showed fault on both sides.

Less political in its beginnings but far more serious and of far greater political consequence in the end, was the riot in Memphis, which began on April 30 in a quarrel between Negro soldiers and Irish policemen, developed into general race rioting, and continued for three days of insensate ferocity, with more than forty Negroes killed.

Garrisons of Negro soldiers, according to observers from General Grant down, were focal points for disturbance and possible violence. "The only disturbance we have is from the garrisons," wrote Governor Perry to the President. "They are behaving badly, both to whites and blacks." Governor Sharkey reported that "the great amount of complaint originates from the localities where the Negro soldiers are," a complaint which resulted in withdrawal of the last of the Negro garrisons from the state before the end of May.

In Texas, Brenham was burned that spring by its Negro garrison, infuriated by a fight with white residents to whom local Negroes had fled for protection after a party of drunken soldiers had broken up a colored ball to which they were refused admission. After the first brush, in which two of the soldiers were wounded, the entire garrison, with its commander, marched on the town, broke into stores under the guise of searching for arms, and fired them by accident or design. Indictment of the commanding officer for burglary and arson never could be brought to trial by the civil authorities because of the position assumed by the military, that the acts were committed in discharge of duty while the prosecutions arose from malice, vindictiveness and disloyalty.

Victoria, Texas, was terrorized by its garrison, according to the report of Governor Throckmorton, while in North Carolina a party of Negro soldiers from Fort Macon, arrested in Beaufort on the charge of rape and attempted rape, were rescued by the garrison upon threat of turning the guns of the fort upon the town. At Wilmington, also, there were threats of trouble with the large Negro garrison but at Elizabeth City and Edenton the conduct of similar garrisons was reported as good.

More depended upon the capacity of the military officer in command, however, and upon the discipline of his troops, than upon their color. Ill-disciplined white troops at Asheville, North Carolina, caused as much trouble as any of the colored garrisons, while at other stations well-disciplined garrisons, led by capable officers, were looked upon as valued friends of peace and good order. As General Tarbell stated to the Reconstruction Committee, in those districts where the officers of the Bureau were "upright, intelligent and impartial" and the garrisons were "under good discipline," they were welcomed by the people, who were glad of their presence and protection.

Thoughts of protection from disorder, or even of the need of protection, were far from the minds of six young men—John B. Kennedy, James R. Crowe, Frank O. McCord, Richard R. Reed, John C. Lester and Calvin Jones—who, in the village of Pulaski, Giles County, Tennessee, relieved the tedium of life that spring by the nocturnal initiations of a new secret society. Their ghostly mummeries began to spread a superstitious awe through the neighborhood, especially after the Den of the Klan was established in the ruins of a house wrecked by a cyclone on the day after Christmas, 1865, eerie and mysterious in a tangle of trees blown down by the storm, looped and twined with great creeping vines.

And so, just for fun and apparently by accident, was born the Ku Klux Klan, to spread widely through the South and to give its name to a movement even more widespread—a movement which, in various forms and guises, was to oppose to the overwhelming power of the government the secret, uncontrollable, desperately dangerous terror of the unknown.

The movement, wrote William Garrot Brown, "was neither an accident nor a mere scheme. It was no man's contrivance, but an historical development" from the condition of a "disordered society and a bewildered people."

CHAPTER XXI

A Policy in Search of a Party

THE restoration policy initiated by Lincoln and inherited by Johnson was, in the spring of 1866, a policy in search of a party. It had supporters in the North, where the voting was to be done, in large and important numbers; but the supporters, perhaps a majority of the voters, were divided and separated among parties and factions within parties. The Democratic party in the North would have been glad to take possession of the Lincoln-Johnson policy as its own—but in 1866 and for years thereafter there were too many in the North to whom "Democrat" meant "Copperhead," and both meant "traitor." The war Democrats, many of whom had joined with the Republicans under the leadership of Lincoln to form the Union party, were anxious to make restoration their policy, as were many of the Republicans in the Union party. The organization and machinery of the Union party, however, was fast going into the strong and shrewd hands of the Radicals. The Southern majority, insofar as it was organized and active, was zealous in support of President Johnson and his policy— a fact which was to be used to damn what the Radicals called "My Policy" as pleasing to rebels and, therefore, to be despised of all loyal men.

That there must be a new organization in which men who believed in a nation reconciled and reunited might work together regardless of party was plain, but how such an organization should be brought into being, by whom it should be created and controlled, what should be its precise policy and procedure, even the name by which it should be known, were questions of the greatest delicacy and difficulty.

The beginning was taken on June 25, with the issue of a call for a convention of National Union men to meet in Philadelphia on August 14, to organize for the election to Congress of men favorable to the admission of loyal representatives from the Southern states. The call, largely drafted by Senator James R. Doolittle, after weeks of consideration and consultation with congressional and Cabinet leaders of Conservative leanings, declared that there was "no right anywhere to dissolve the Union . . . neither by secession nor exclusion," and de-

182

manded that "war measures should cease" but did not attack directly and by name the Fourteenth Amendment—an omission viewed with misgiving by some of the supporters of the movement.

That amendment, adopted by the House on June 8 and by the Senate on June 13, had just been submitted for ratification to the state legislatures, including those bodies in the South which, according to the Radical doctrine, were illegal but not too illegal to ratify. The provisions of the amendment had become the Radical platform for the campaign; its disposition, the paramount issue—on the surface.

The issue extended into the President's Cabinet. Four members, opposed to the policy of their chief, favored ratification. When the issue was brought into the open by publication of the call for the Philadelphia convention, three of the four—Attorney General Speed, Postmaster General Dennison and Secretary Harlan—resigned and went into the Radical camp. The fourth, Secretary Stanton, remained in the Cabinet, a Radical lookout within the innermost councils. Outside the Cabinet, there was a steady drift of leading political figures from the policy of the President to the position of the Radicals.

The idea of the National Union convention, however, received wide and strong endorsement. Henry J. Raymond, chairman of the Union party which had elected Lincoln and Johnson in 1864, expressed the hope that the August convention would lay the foundation for a national party, including all the Union party except the Radicals, all the Democrats of the North, and the majority of the people of the South. Prominent war Democrats, such men as Garret Davis and James Guthrie of Kentucky, who in time of trial had been steadfast in Union support, General John A. Dix of New York, General Lovell H. Rousseau of the Union Army, and Senator Reverdy Johnson of Maryland, came out in strong support. But, unfortunately for the success of the effort, other Democrats whose support of the war was reckoned as something less than lukewarm showed a disposition to climb aboard what they hoped would be a band-wagon.

The Radical charge that the President's intent was to turn the government over to the "traitors" was given color by the use of the names of every prominent anti-war Democrat of the North who openly aligned himself behind the Johnson policy. The true Conservative position, as stated in a resolution offered to the Senate by James Dixon, was that every state should be admitted "to its share in public legislation whenever it presents itself, not only in an attitude of loyalty and harmony, but in the persons of representatives whose loyalty cannot be questioned under any constitutional or legal test."

Interposing themselves as defenders of the country against the alleged designs of the President, the Radical high command proposed a government centered in an omnipotent Congress which could register, immediately and without delay, the "popular will" of the moment. Stevens, Sumner, and their associates were impatient of the conception of the Constitution of the United States as a fundamental law, restraining citizen, executive and legislator alike. The Congress, in their theory of government, was empowered to act for "the best interests of society" as interpreted by the majority at any particular time, unrestrained by the specific restrictions of the Constitution, and regardless of the powers reserved to the states and the rights guaranteed to the individual. Such provisions of the fundamental law, they held, had no application to the Congress, "the sovereign power because the people spoke through them." For provisions of the Constitution which stood in the way of unrestrained action for the general welfare as the majority in Congress conceived it, Stevens and Sumner had complete contempt.

Against this view Johnson opposed the older conception of government and the Constitution. "Ours is a government of limited powers," he told a delegation of Union soldiers during the campaign, "with a written constitution, with boundaries both national and State, and these limitations and boundaries must be observed and strictly respected if free government is to exist; and, coming out of a rebellion, we ought to demonstrate to mankind that a free government cannot live on hate and distrust."

However right the President may have been in his belief that a free government could not live on hate and distrust, the Radical command was to prove, beyond a doubt, the campaign value of the skillful employment of those emotions. President Johnson, on the other hand, absorbed in his struggle to preserve the principle of constitutional government, failed to dramatize and present to the country collateral issues upon which he might have stirred up emotional reaction against the Radicals.

The President appealed to law and reason. He pressed his views to their logical conclusion, unwilling or unable to compromise and adjust. The Radicals, on the other hand, allowed no issue which might split their own ranks to be pressed to a finish. Eastern Radicals wanted high-tariff protection for their manufacturers. Western Radicals did not want it voted just before election; wherefore, just before Congress adjourned, the high protectionists themselves tabled a bill levying the highest duties known up to that time. That question could wait until after the election.

The President failed, even, to dramatize the issue presented to his hand by a Congress which, as one unfriendly critic put it, "at its first session voted Four Thousand Dollars extra pay to its members but failed to make any provision for the payment of bounties to the soldiers."

At long last, on July 28, Congress adjourned. Two days after its adjournment, and two weeks before the National Union convention was to meet in Philadelphia, there flared up in New Orleans, to obscure any issue which might have been raised on economic or fiscal questions, a political race riot. In its last stages, the riot was an outburst of bloodthirsty brutality; but neither in its extent, duration or destructiveness, in the baseness of the motives which brought it on, nor in widespread and unprovoked attacks upon innocent Negroes, did it compare with the great draft riots in New York City only three years before. The New Orleans riot, however, occurred at a critical time in a campaign, and in a city half-Southern, half-foreign, and therefore, to the provincial-minded Northerner of the time, wholly, even if seductively, wicked. Its political causes were lost in obscure charge and counter-charge; its events were the subject of partisan investigation and report. It was, in short, perfect material for a campaign of hate and distrust.

Louisiana, in the summer of 1866, was governed under the constitution of 1864, written and adopted by loyalists under President Lincoln's ten-per-cent plan. With the end of the war and the return and pardon of the Confederate soldier and sympathizer, the government of the state and of the city of New Orleans had passed into the control of that element. This shift of power caused the Radicals who had written the constitution, and set up the original government under it, to come to regard the whole thing as null and void. After the rejection of Louisiana's representatives in Congress, J. Madison Wells, who had been elected governor of the state as the unopposed nominee of both Radical and Conservative elements, came around to the same view.

The first plan of the Radicals was to ignore their own handiwork as constitution makers, call a new convention to frame a government for the "territory of Louisiana," and apply to Congress for admission to the Union as a new state. Anticipating that a bill to admit such a state would most certainly meet a presidential veto, and fearing that the necessary two-thirds majority to repass it could not be secured, the Radicals sought some way to get a new constitution for the existing state so framed that power might safely be held in their hands.

As a sort of afterthought, the convention of 1864 had adopted a resolution authorizing its president to "reconvoke the Convention for any causes, or in case the Constitution should not be ratified, for the purpose of taking such measures as may be necessary for the formation of a civil government in the State of Louisiana." But the constitution had been ratified; elections had been held under it; and the civil government so created was in operation even though not in Radical hands. The reconvening resolution was not part of the constitution, nor had it been submitted to popular vote for ratification, but it was hoped that the vague language of the resolution might give some color of legality on which the Radical majority in Congress could base recognition of a new government and constitution for the old state, without having to run the risk of presidential veto.

Whatever power of reconvocation the resolution created lay in the president of the convention. The president did not act, but the secretary, in the name of "Several members of the Convention, as well as the Executive," issued a call for a meeting of the body on June 26— the first open step in the course of events leading up to the riot. Thirty or forty members, a quorum being seventy-six, gathered in New Orleans that day. Judge Durell, the former president, was not there. R. K. Howell, who had been a member of the convention but had resigned, was elected president, with no quorum present. The last faint shade of legality left the proceedings.

The new "president" called the convention to meet on July 30 to "revise and amend the Constitution and to consider the adoption of the XIV Amendment." Governor Wells gave his practical, though private, support to what was essentially a bare-faced attempt at a coup d' état in Louisiana. Judge Howell went to Washington to secure congressional and military support for the coup, including indirect assurances from Thaddeus Stevens himself. General Gordon Granger, on the ground in Louisiana, wrote to the President early in June, outlining the scheme and predicting its end in revolution and anarchy.

No secret was made, after the call was issued, that the plan was to amend the constitution so as to enfranchise the Negro and disfranchise the Confederate; to declare all elections held under the constitution of 1864 void, and call new elections; and to present to the Congress such a government as would be accepted by the majority as the true and legal government of the state of Louisiana.

Negro mass meetings held in New Orleans before the convention were addressed by men described by General Sheridan, in a report to General Grant, as "political agitators and revolutionary men." How revolutionary the agitation was appears in the speech of Dr. A. P. Dostie, a Northern dentist settled in New Orleans, delivered on the Friday night before the Monday on which the convention was to assemble, and recorded in the *Annual Cyclopedia* for that year:

"I want the negroes to have the right of suffrage and we will give them this right to vote. There will be another meeting here tomorrow night, and on Monday I want you to come in your power. I want no cowards to come. I want only brave men to come, who will stand by us and we will stand by them. Come, then, in your power to that meeting, or never go to another political meeting in this State. We have three hundred thousand black men with white hearts. Also one hundred thousand good and true Union white men, who will fight for and beside the black race against the hell-bound rebels, for now there are but two parties here. There are no copperheads now. Colonel Field, now making a speech inside, is heart and soul with us. He and others who would not a year ago speak to me, now take me by the hand. We are four hundred thousand to three hundred thousand, and cannot only whip but exterminate the other party. Judge Abell with his grand jury may indict us. Harry Hayes, with his *posse comitatus*, may be expected there, and the police, with more than a thousand men sworn in, may interfere with the convention; therefore, let all brave men, and not cowards, come here on Monday. There will be no such puerile affair as at Memphis, but, if we are interfered with, the streets of New Orleans will run with blood. . . ."

Two days before Doctor Dostie's speech, Judge Edmond Abell, himself a member of the convention of 1864, had charged the grand jury that the proposed reassembly was illegal and revolutionary, while Mayor John T. Monroe had notified General Absalom Baird, commanding in the absence of General Sheridan, that its members would be arrested "unless the Convention was sanctioned by the Military."

General Baird, without instructions, advised that the convention not be molested on the ground that if it were legal it had a right to meet, while if not legal, its acts would be null and void and would be so declared by the United States courts. The fear of the Louisiana Conservatives, however, was that Congress, by accepting the results of the contemplated *coup d' état*, would conclude action of the courts on what was, after all, a political and not a judicial question.

On the day after Doctor Dostie's speech, and the Saturday before the convention was to meet, Governor Wells did not show up at the temporary capitol in New Orleans. Lieutenant-Governor Voorhies and Mayor Monroe informed General Baird that they intended to ask for the indictment of members of the convention and their arrest by the sheriff, if the meeting were persisted in, to which the General replied that the military would release members if arrested and possibly arrest the sheriff. Anxious, Baird telegraphed the War Department for instructions, which never came, because, as was afterward developed, Secretary Stanton had withheld the wire from consideration by the President or the Cabinet.

And so the stage was set for the events of Monday, the thirtieth—with every element timed for the explosion. In an early morning proclamation, the Mayor urged the preservation of peace and order. Between ten and eleven o'clock, the Lieutenant-Governor asked General Baird for troops to preserve order in the city. The General, intending to furnish the troops, conceived the idea that the convention was called to meet at six o'clock, instead of noon, and held the troops at Jackson Barracks until the critical hour was past and the damage done.

Meanwhile, relying on the protection of the military if there should be trouble, the convention met at the Mechanics Institute at noon, found that hardly more than one-third of a quorum were present, and adjourned until one o'clock. During the hour's recess, a procession of Negroes, with flag flying and drum beating, marched across Canal Street toward the Institute. An inflamed mob opened sullenly to let them pass. There was shoving and jostling, a shot was fired, but the procession held on its way. Regular and special police arrived. As one of them arrested a newsboy for stirring up trouble, he was fired at, presumably by one of the Negroes in the procession. Mob spirit flamed. The Negroes were driven into the hall of the Institute; the mob, infuriated and drunk, surrounded and stormed the building. Some of the police joined the mob; some struggled against them. Former Governor Hahn owed his life to rescue by a detail of the police, as did others, while there were policemen who refused to take prisoners. At least one of them was knocked down, for his brutality to a prisoner, by the chief of police, Thomas E. Adams. Doctor Dostie was killed, and Doctor Horton, the minister who offered prayer at the opening of the meeting. Deaths, as reported by Dr. A. Hartsuff of the United States Army, included, besides these, thirty-four colored citizens and "one disloyal white." Eight members of the convention were wounded, according to the same report, and nine loyal whites, one hundred and nineteen colored, and ten policemen. Mayor Monroe and Lieutenant-Governor Voorhies, on the other hand, reported that the police had suffered forty-two casualties, killed and wounded, besides others among citizens of the sort whom Dr. Hartsuff classified as disloyal.

To the Radicals, it was the "St. Bartholomew's Day of New Orleans," and as such was fully exploited in the usual partisan investigation by Congress. The exact truth of such an affair never can be known. The minority report alleged that the purpose of the Radicals was to provoke a riot, an attack on the colored population which could be suppressed by the military before the white leaders of the movement were seriously endangered but which would furnish an excuse for congressional intervention in Louisiana. If that were the plan, it miscarried through the misunderstanding that kept General Baird's troops out of the city until 2:40 P. M., by which time the active riot was over and a sort of uneasy order was restored by the police.

To General Sheridan, who investigated upon his return to Louisiana, the affair of the thirtieth "was no riot. It was an absolute massacre." But wherever the truth lies, the stark fact of loyal men, white and black, shot down while engaged in what seemed to the outside world a mere political gathering, innocent enough regardless of its legality, was of the first importance in the campaign just beginning.

CHAPTER XXII

CONGRESS GOES RADICAL

ON AUGUST 14, 1866, in a vast two-storied auditorium erected for the purpose in the city of Philadelphia, packed to the walls with more than ten thousand cheering citizens, resounding with the airs of "The Star Spangled Banner" and "Dixie," decorated with the flag of the Union and the emblems of each one of its thirty-six states, Postmaster General Randall called to order the National Union Convention—the first political gathering since 1860 truly national in its composition.

Into the hall, at the call to order, marched arm-in-arm Major General Darius Couch, of Massachusetts, who had commanded a corps in the Army of the Potomac, and Governor James L. Orr, of South Carolina. Behind them, arm-in-arm, dramatizing the re-union of states, marched the delegates from the two states.

As the delegates took their seats, the convention chose as its temporary chairman General John A. Dix, of New York, the same who, as Secretary of War in 1861, had issued orders to shoot the first man who attempted to pull down the United States flag. Senator James R. Doolittle, of Wisconsin, staunch Unionist and supporter of Lincoln, elected as permanent chairman, took note of the scene before him:

"If the people . . . could have seen—as we saw—Massachusetts and South Carolina, by their full delegations, coming arm-in-arm into this great convention; if they could have seen this body, greater in numbers, and in weight of character and brain, than ever yet assembled on this continent under one roof, melting to tears of joy and gratitude to witness this commingling, there could be no struggle at the polls in the coming elections. . . . Unfortunately, the whole people of the Northern States do not witness what is now transpiring here; therefore the greater work still rests upon us from this time until the election of the next Congress."

That the convention could be seen by the people of the North only through the eyes of a press almost wholly partisan and antagonistic was indeed unfortunate. Even such statements of those friendly to the purpose of the convention as that "every eye was suffused with tears of joy" gave the opposition opportunities for ridicule. Tears of joy were a more common and acceptable literary device in 1866 than they would be today, no doubt, but even in 1866 there was something incongruous in the idea as applied to a political convention, an incongruity which led to the satirical description of a gathering genuinely important and promising as "The Tearful Convention." So, the dramatic device of a joint entry by the delegations from the two states which, to the popular mind, represented the extremes of feeling caused the convention to be caricatured, in word and picture, as "The Arm-in-Arm Convention"—the name by which it is best known even now.

In spite of opposition, jibes and sneers, however, the convention was a gathering of distinction, and its work gave promise of a better basis of union. It represented elements in the North which had supported the war for union from conviction, and elements in the South which offered the most hopeful basis for the development of a truly national party. In the background, however, seeking to become prominent in its deliberations, were Northern politicians of the school of Fernando Wood, of New York, and Clement L. Vallandigham, of Ohio, men whose attitude toward the prosecution of the war had brought upon themselves the hatred and distrust of the great mass of Northern people. By infinite tact and persuasion, these two were dissuaded from thrusting themselves forward in the convention and claiming seats and the right to vote. Through the weeks of the campaign, however, it was not to be possible to keep others of like record from publicly and noisily attaching themselves to the cause of those who sought the election of congressmen favorable to readmission of the ten Southern states yet out of the Union.

The convention declared for the "Constitution and Union unaltered," and against secession and exclusion, alike. It held that qualifications for suffrage were a matter for the states; that rebel debts were invalid and national debt inviolate; and that freedmen should be protected in person and property. Except for the proscriptive clause, and the clause which sought to force Negro suffrage or a reduction in representation upon the Southern states, the Fourteenth Amendment was approved.

On August 17 the convention adjourned. The following day, in Washington, an official copy of its proceedings was presented to the President by a committee of two delegates from each state, with

Senator Reverdy Johnson, of Maryland, as chairman. The President, with General Grant standing by his side in the East Room of the White House, responded to the presentation "happily and well." The campaign to elect a Congress friendly to the Lincoln-Johnson policy of restoration was formally launched.

The Radicals, in spite of the strength of their position in many ways, were greatly concerned. The Philadelphia convention, which had been managed wisely and well, had made its impression, and must be discredited. Ridicule was one weapon—even the great James Russell Lowell stooped to sorry punning upon the name of Chairman Doolittle—while abuse of "King Andy" and "My Policy," reports of "Southern outrages," and continued appeals to war animosities furnished the rest. That the President himself had "inspired" the New Orleans riot, even, and "aided and abetted" the mob was charged by leading Radical publications.

Meanwhile, the President went ahead, as far as was within his power, in the work of restoration. On August 20, proclaiming the end of the state of insurrection in Texas, which had not been included in the proclamation of April 2, he declared that "peace, order, tranquillity, and civil authority exist throughout the whole of the United States." The restored government of Texas, last of the former Confederate states to complete its reorganization, was complete. The new Governor, Throckmorton, had been inaugurated. New senators—one of them the aged David G. Burnet, once president of the Republic of Texas—were to be elected, although, as the event proved, election did not mean admission to the Congress.

The executive declaration of the end of insurrection in the South attracted small attention, however. Interest was centered on the campaign, with a counter-convention, assembling upon the call of Southern loyalists, yet to be held at Philadelphia, and conventions of Union soldiers and sailors favorable to Johnson's program to be held in Cleveland, and those opposed to be held in Pittsburgh. Never before had there been such a furore of political activity in a year in which no president was to be elected.

The Southern loyalist convention, meeting on September 3, was planned as a counter-demonstration. While the meeting was called, ostensibly at least, by the persecuted loyalists of the South, it was more largely attended by Radicals and recent converts to Radical doctrines from the North. In virulent opposition to the President and all his works, they were alike, but as practical politicians they were far apart on the question of Negro suffrage, and the prominence to be given Negroes in the proceedings and the campaign. Because of that and other differences, the convention met not as one but as two separate bodies. Said Governor Samuel Cony, of Maine:

"I believe that the negro at the South is better fitted to vote than the most accomplished rebel from the Potomac to the Rio Grande; but I don't believe in making negro suffrage an issue now. Our great object is to secure the next Congress. If we don't get that, then all is lost; if we do get it, then all is safe."

Governor Brownlow, of Tennessee, however, spoke as a Southern loyalist politician, strong in the new-found faith, when he shouted:

"I would rather be elected by loyal Negroes than by disloyal white men. I would rather associate with loyal Negroes than with disloyal white men. I would rather be buried in a Negro graveyard than in a Rebel graveyard; and after death, I would sooner go to a Negro heaven than a White Rebel's hell."

The Parson's violence, however, went beyond mere questions of suffrage. He professed to see a renewal of rebellion in the making, and proposed to prepare for the war which he believed was imminent. This war, he thought, should be fought by an army organized and armed in three divisions—the first, armed with guns and rifles "to do the killing"; the second, "armed with pine torches and spirits of turpentine" to "do the burning"; the third, carrying surveyor's chains and compasses "to survey the land into small parcels and give it to those who are loyal to the North." The idea was greeted with tumultuous applause.

On the fourth day of the meeting of the Southern delegates, the Committee on Unreconstructed States brought in a report which included a recommendation of Negro suffrage. The border state delegates tried to adjourn without action. Former Provisional Governor Hamilton, of Texas, representing the position of men whose political future depended upon granting the ballot to the large number of Negroes in their states, excitedly denounced such a move. James Speed, of Kentucky, chairman of the convention, withdrew and took with him all but fifteen of the delegates from the border states. Whereupon, on the next day, the Southern delegates adopted the Negro-suffrage recommendation, and the Northern delegates, who had been awaiting their action, quietly folded up and went home without action, hoping that they could keep the issue quiet in their own states where, as one of them put it, it "would ruin us."

When the loyalist convention met, President Johnson was already embarked on his swing around the circle, in an attempt to reach the people of the United States face-to-face with his own conception of the situation and the reasons for his policy. The occasion for his trip was the dedication of a monument to Stephen A. Douglas, at Chicago. The route selected was to take him through almost all the Northern and border states, except New England, and the arrangements were such that he was to have opportunity to meet and address audiences at important cities on the way. The party included, besides the President, his daughter, Mrs. Patterson, and her husband, one of the senators from recently admitted Tennessee; Secretary Seward; Secretary Gideon Welles and his family; Admiral Farragut, another Tennessean who had shown his devotion to the Union, and Mrs. Farragut; General Grant and his chief of staff, General Rawlins; an entourage of other officers and secretaries, and a group of newspaper correspondents, most of them representing hostile papers. The trip, the party and the program were of a sort which has become familiar since but which then was new.

Traveling by special train, the party left Washington at 7:30 on the morning of August 28. At Baltimore, one hundred thousand people greeted the presidential party, which was driven through the streets to Fort McHenry. At the speaking, Seward acted as master of ceremonies, while Grant and Farragut shared honors and enthusiasm with the President. Similar scenes were repeated at Philadelphia, where the party spent the night. At 11:30 in the morning of August 29, they arrived at Jersey City, were ferried across to the Battery, and driven up Broadway, where "every window was white with cambric waved by fair hands," to the City Hall. Half a million persons participated in the reception which, in the opinion of General Rawlins, never had been excelled. Dinner at Delmonico's that evening was followed by speeches, with the President appealing for fair treatment:

"I fought those in the South who commenced the Rebellion and now I oppose those in the North who are trying to break up the Union. I am for the Union. I am against all those who are opposed to the Union. I am for the Union, the whole Union, and nothing but the Union."

On the following day the party proceeded up the Hudson by boat, stopping at West Point to review the corps of cadets. From Albany, the movement was across New York State to Buffalo. Everything was going well, and enthusiasm ran high, both among the presidential party and the populace.

Trouble began at Cleveland. A great crowd gathered in front of the hotel, calling for a speech. The President finally was prevailed upon to appear upon a balcony, to thank them for their welcome. Scattered through the crowd were groups of hired hecklers, placed there to play upon Johnson's weakness. The President had been warned against such a situation by wise advisers, who urged that he say nothing extemporaneously beyond the mere courtesies of response to welcomes. Disregarding such warnings, however, the President plunged into an exposition and defense of his policies. The opportunity for which the hecklers waited had come. The President of the United States once more had allowed himself to be drawn into exchanges with provocative voices in the darkness. What he said was not wrong in itself, but it was most unwise in that it lent itself to every form and degree of misrepresentation, including the innuendo, or even the charge, that the whole party was on a drunken orgy.

On September 6, the President dedicated the Douglas monument at Chicago, and went on, by train, to Springfield and Alton. From Alton the party proceeded to St. Louis on thirty-six steamboats, one for each state in the Union. At St. Louis a great crowd called for the President, who was waiting for a civic banquet to begin at the Southern Hotel. Against his own judgment, but at the urging of the local committee, he stepped out on a balcony to say a few words, and stayed to say many, under the intoxication of his own oratory, and the provocation of voices from the crowd. Again, what Johnson said was not in itself so unwise as it was to say anything at all under circumstances which lent themselves so strongly to misrepresentation.

From St. Louis the party proceeded to Indianapolis, where a first-class riot was staged about the hotel where the President was lodged. At Louisville there was a splendid reception and demonstration, but rowdyism marked the receptions at Cincinnati and Pittsburgh. At Washington, which the party reached on September 15, there was the unusual spectacle of a popular and official demonstration for a president returning to the capital city, and the swing around the circle was over.

The Radical newspapers, that is, most of the newspapers of the North, exhausted themselves in their derision and denunciation of the swing around the circle. It was described as a continual drunken orgy—although the evidence is clear that, with the exception of General Grant, none of the party drank to excess. The words of the President were not only twisted out of context and meaning but were directly misquoted, a practice made easy by his habit of extemporaneous remark. His tendency to make himself the central figure of his remarks, also, gave an opening for derision. Forney's paper, the Philadelphia *Press*, headlined all accounts of the tour with variants of one word—"I", "Me", "My" and "Mine."

The tour gave opportunity, also, for Copperhead politicians to thrust themselves forward into public notice—a danger from which the President's campaign suffered much. One such politician, a congressman who insisted upon a prominent position on the St. Louis program, aroused the anger of General Grant. "I can stand a Rebel," said the General, "but a Copperhead like Hogan I cannot forgive." Every such incident was reported and magnified, to the disgust of those in the North whose feelings toward Copperheads was about the same as that of Confederates toward the class known during the war as "homemade Yankees."

Immediately after the return of the presidential party to Washington, a convention of Union soldiers supporting the Johnson policy met in Cleveland on September 17. Major General Wool, who had commanded an American division at Buena Vista, presided. Prominent in the meeting were Generals Gordon Granger, George A. Custer, Thomas Ewing, Jr., and Lovell H. Rousseau, all with distinguished records in the great conflict. From the meeting came a joint letter to the President urging the removal of Stanton as Secretary of War.

Finally, on September 26, at Pittsburgh, was held the last of the political conventions of the year, a demonstrative gathering of soldiers and sailors opposed to the presidential policy, with Major General Benjamin F. Butler as its leading figure, and chairman of the resolutions committee.

The great drawback from which the President's campaign suffered, and the one which in the end was to prove fatal, was the lack of an effective organization in each state through which the voter of moderate sentiments could express his wishes. In most Northern states, one party was controlled by the Radicals, while anti-war Democrats were so prominent in the councils, or even the control, of the other party as to repel Conservative Republicans and war Democrats who might otherwise have voted with the President.

This situation and its result were foreshadowed at the first of the 1866 elections, that in Connecticut in April. There the Johnson forces were divided between English, the Democratic nominee for governor, and Hawley, the Republican nominee, a Radical running on a platform which commended Johnson personally but condemned his policy of restoration. With no clear leadership on the Conservative side, and with no place for an out-and-out Conservative to cast his vote comfortably and without mental reservation, the Radical carried the state by a majority of only 541 out of a total vote of 87,407.

Kentucky, voting in August, went Democratic, or rather against the Radicals, in a landslide, hailed at the North as an omen of what would happen were the Southern states to be allowed to participate in government. The result, according to Kentucky observers, was due to the indignities put upon the state by its Radical rulers after the war, but to the Cincinnati *Gazette* it appeared that "the rebel gray has whipped the Union blue at the polls."

Arkansas, also voting in August, at the first election after the Supreme Court of the restorers' government had declared unconstitutional the clause in the state constitution which disfranchised ex-Confederates, elected almost a complete slate of Conservative Union men—all congressmen but one, almost all members of the legislature, and a new State Supreme Court, composed of ante-bellum justices. Since Arkansas representatives were not yet admitted to Congress, the election was without direct effect. It was used, however, particularly with Governor Murphy's statement that "Union men were being hunted down and shot by rebels," as material for the Radical campaign.

Maine voted in September. As in so many other states, the moderate Republican or war Democrat was forced to a choice between a Radical and an anti-war Democrat, whose managers even went to the length of bringing into the state such outside speakers as Fernando Wood, of New York. Maine, naturally, went for the Radical cause by heavy majorities.

In New York, which did not vote until November, there was a joint convention of Democrats and Conservative Republicans on September 11, to make nominations and agree on an organization for an effective fight. Dean Richmond, one Democrat wise enough and strong enough to have kept down factionalism among his fellows, died just before the meeting. For governor, the war Democrats favored General Dix, who was likewise preferred by the President. By a sharp convention trick, however, the Tammany organization managed to give a nomination to their candidate, H. W. Hoffman, and so lost the election on both state and national issues—although even then, the Radicals won by a majority of only 22,092 out of a total vote of 713,018.

Pennsylvania voted in October. Again, the choice was between Radical and anti-war Democrat, with no channel through which men of moderate views could make themselves felt. Even then, the Radical majority in the race for governor was but 11,439 out of a total vote of 596,141, although eighteen of twenty-four congressmen elected owed Radical allegiance.

In Ohio, also voting in October, the chairman of the Democratic party was a Vallandigham follower who would support none but "regular Democratic nominees." Again, the choice had to be between such Democrats and out-and-out Radicals. The Radicals won sixteen of the nineteen congressmen, but even then the Democrats cast nearly forty-six per cent of the total vote. What might have happened in 1866 with a sensible combination of Democrats and Conservative Republicans is indicated by the results of the next year, when such a combination elected the Governor and a majority of both houses of the legislature.

In Indiana, also an October state, the same lineup was forced upon the Conservative who sought a way to express his views. The issue of the election was Copperheadism, with Morton developing his technique of the bloody shirt and Schuyler Colfax declaring that Mrs. Robert E. Lee had vowed that as soon as Arlington was restored to her by President Johnson, "not a Yankee bone should stay in the ground." And yet the state went Radical by a majority of only 12,445 out of a total vote of 323,959.

Results in the states which voted early foreshadowed the results of the elections in November—an overwhelming victory for the Radicals. The new House of Representatives, to be seated in March, 1867, was to be made up of one hundred and forty-three Republicans and only forty-nine Democrats. The complexion of the state legislatures determined that the next Senate was to number forty-two Republicans and eleven Democrats. Against such majorities executive veto could avail nothing. The course of events in the nation, and the treatment to be accorded the conquered South, was to be in the hands of the Radical junta. Old Thomas Ewing wrote to his son Tom:

"States and Nations have been conquered by force, but never so governed. . . . People may be driven to desperation by what they conceive cruelty, insult and injustice, but no degree of forbearance, kindness and oblivion of past errors can ever make rebellion again acceptable to the crushed and ruined South."

In the jubilation of Radical victory there was no room for such thoughts.

CHAPTER XXIII

"The Sinful Ten"

ELECTIONS and their results continued to be of less immediate interest to most of the people of the South than crops and their prices. The cotton crop of 1866 was short, a result commonly laid to the failings of the new system of labor by contract. Nevertheless, the price fell from the high levels of the year before, partly because of stimulated production elsewhere in the world, partly because of the coming into the market of much old cotton produced and stored, or hidden, during the war.

Cotton suffered, moreover, the burden of the special Federal tax of two and one-half cents per pound. Imposed upon a commodity so largely raised for export as was cotton, this tax became "practically an export duty," as the New York Chamber of Commerce described it in a strong protest. Such a tax, said the Chamber, was

"practically equivalent to charging the Southern farmer with that amount for the purpose of paying it over to the cultivators of India, Egypt and Brazil. And still he is expected to compete successfully with those growers. . . .

". . . the imposition of a discriminating tax which tends to make the rich of the north richer and the poor of the south poorer operates as a discouragement to those who, with heavy hearts but honest endeavor, strive to regain their lost fortunes."

The heaviest burden of the tax, in its practical workings, fell not on the rich "rebels" against whom it was especially aimed, but on the cotton tenants, black and white, in large part the "loyal" who were the supposed objects of congressional solicitude.

Not only money crops, but food and feed crops, were short in the South in 1866. Governor Patton of Alabama had estimated, in the spring, that three-fourths of the twenty thousand widows and sixty thousand orphans in that state lacked the necessities of life. Many were close to actual starvation, while thousands, he said, had not tasted meat for months. With fifteen thousand dollars raised by citizens of Nashville, ten thousand dollars raised in Montgomery, and other funds, the Governor had gone to the West and purchased supplies to tide the people over until the new crop could be made.

The new crop, however, proved disappointing, not only in Alabama but elsewhere in the South. The South Carolina legislature, on the recommendation of Governor Orr, authorized the issue of three hundred thousand dollars in state bonds for the purchase of three hundred thousand bushels of corn for the destitute. The bonds could not be sold at par, as provided in the act, nor could corn be purchased at a dollar a bushel if the bonds had been sold.

More effective than this abortive attempt at relief were the efforts of private citizens in Kentucky. Ten thousand bushels of corn were sent from that state for the relief of the poor in Georgia alone, with large quantities of food, clothing and supplies going to other Southern states as well. Money for relief purposes was raised by subscription, by fairs, horse races and entertainments of all sorts, while the Louisville & Nashville Railroad contributed free transportation of relief supplies on which the regular freight charges would have amounted to many thousands of dollars.

Cholera scourged the South in the summer of 1866, and smallpox in the autumn, but neither epidemics, short crops, low prices, nor the political disaster of which they were as yet but half aware kept the people of the South from their work of rebuilding those things which had to be restored—homes, farm buildings, fences, ways of transportation, churches.

In the fall of 1866 a bell rang in the steeple of the Baptist Church at Jackson, Mississippi, the first heard there in more than three years. New bridges across the Cumberland and the Tennessee replaced those destroyed in the Fort Donelson-Shiloh campaign of 1862, and trains once more ran between Louisville and Memphis. In October, the Louisville & Nashville Railroad decided to extend its lines into the coal fields of southeastern Kentucky, to "develop the resources of the state," and so to end its dependence upon Pittsburgh for coal.

The South Carolina Railroad reported that by the end of the year it had acquired locomotives and rolling stock "quite sufficient for any possible demand," while in Charleston a street railway was opened for service in December, with a celebration which included wines, liquors and oratory by the mayor and by William Gilmore Simms.

In North Carolina and East Tennessee, the French Broad River Railroad was being graded between Morganton and Morristown, with fifteen miles of track laid at the western end before the end of the year. Work was started, in Alabama, on a line from Montgomery through the undeveloped mountain mineral regions to the limestone valley of the Tennessee, in the northern part of the state. Mississippians were busying themselves with the project of a railroad from Memphis to Selma, while construction crews were being lined up between Mobile and New Orleans, and between New Orleans and Donaldsonville, to start work on a railroad projected from Chattanooga through New Orleans to Houston, with a branch to connect with the Texas & Pacific, then starting out to build from Shreveport to the western ocean. The day was one of expansion, as well as rebuilding.

Cotton manufacturing, started before the war in a small way, was revived and extended in 1866. From the Piedmont of the Carolinas to the water-power sites on the Chattahoochee, a dozen small mills were in operation by the end of the year, with machinery secured from the North or from England. In spite of their inventory loss because of the sharp drop in cotton prices, they managed to keep going and to lay the foundation for the great cotton-manufacturing industry of the Southern states.

In all this fever of restoration and expansion, Northern men and Northern capital had no small part. Many Northern immigrants became highly respected and well liked citizens of their new states. Others, who plunged into Southern planting with no slightest doubt that their own superior management and the gratitude of the Negroes to one of their liberators would insure success, found bitter disappointment. Of those who failed, some returned to their homes in the North; others remained in the South, to find politics more profitable than planting.

Lack of success in planting, whether by Northern immigrant or native Southerner, was not always to be attributed to the fault or failing of the Negro labor. Benjamin H. Hill, late senator of Georgia in the Senate of the Confederate States, declared:

"How to make the negro observe his contract on the one hand, and how to make the bad white man fulfill his contract on the other, is just now the pons asinorum of our labor system."

Impressed with the difficulties of that problem, the legislatures of Southern states which met during the autumn and winter of 1866 continued to tinker with codes and regulations, without regard to the effect of their actions on the sensibilities of the Northern electorate, or the all-powerful majority in Congress; without regard, even, to the fact that the laws over which they so earnestly debated were, in large part, set aside in practice by the authority of the military commanders or Bureau officers.

Governors of restored states who regarded the President's proclamation of peace as legally and definitely ending the war, strove mightily to secure recognition of the supremacy of the civil authority over the military, but commanders and Bureau officers, zealous to protect freedmen and Union men, or men who claimed that status, rarely accepted such an idea in matters affecting those classes. It became the fashion in the South for those charged with criminal offenses to lay their troubles to "loyalty" during the war.

An extreme case of the sort, in all its aspects, is shown in the prolonged correspondence between Governor Throckmorton and successive military commanders in Texas about the alleged martyrdom for his Union sentiments of one Lindley, known by his neighbors to have been a violent Secessionist. Having been active in the business of horse-stealing, being threatened with arrest, and fearing the testimony against him of a certain Duncan and Daws, the ingenious Lindley imposed upon the local military commander with a story of his unwavering loyalty to the Union, and of savage persecution by his rebel neighbors, culminating in the hanging of his son by Duncan and Daws, who were forthwith arrested upon that charge. While they were under military arrest, and without interference by the officers in charge, Lindley removed all danger of their testimony by shooting and killing both of them.

Indicted by the grand jury of Bell County for the double murder, Lindley advanced his claim of persecution as a Union man to secure his trial and acquittal by military court. Later, being again under arrest, he demanded a guard of troops. Relying on the promise of citizens, Governor Throckmorton assured the commander that the prisoner would be safe—an assurance violated when a mob seized and hanged Lindley, who for outside consumption became another martyr because of his " Union sentiments."

When Governor Throckmorton urged upon General Sheridan that United States troops might better be employed in protecting the long and defenseless frontier against outlaws and hostile Indians than in heavily garrisoned interior towns, the General replied with the charge that outrages upon Union men and freedmen, due to the "old rebellious sentiment" of the people of the state, exceeded Indian depredations on the frontier. Governor Throckmorton, better acquainted with the state, knew what General Sheridan was unwilling to believe—that many of the reputed Union men had been "brawling, blatant Secessionists" of notoriously bad character. "I know some of the veriest rogues and scoundrels," said the Governor, "who . . . have applied to the military and asserted that they were in danger because of their Unionism, when in truth their Unionism was never heard of until after the surrender."

Trials of non-military persons by military commission, rather than in the civil courts, continued regardless of the President's proclamation of the end of hostilities and the restoration of peace. As late as December, 1866, a military court at Richmond refused to surrender to the civil courts, on writ of habeas corpus, Dr. J. L. Watson, who previously had been tried and acquitted by the state courts for killing a Negro in Rockbridge County.

The conflict of jurisdiction as to the affairs of freedmen produced curious results, in some cases. In Georgia, finding that the Bureau would not recognize apprenticeship contracts made according to the state statute, the legislature enacted a law making the Bureau's contracts valid, just as if they had been made according to the terms of the Georgia statute. In North Carolina, which was without a penitentiary, the military prohibited corporal punishment by whipping for crime and then found it necessary to evade its own order by hanging culprits by the thumbs to the lampposts in Raleigh.

In the main, however, relations between the well-disposed, white or colored, were working toward a more stable basis of peace and accommodation in 1866. At a time when Mr. Stevens was demanding of the House of Representatives that the United States "at once do something to protect these people from the barbarians who are daily murdering them; who are murdering the loyal whites daily, and daily putting into secret graves not only hundreds but thousands of the colored people," General T. J. Wood, commander at Vicksburg, was reporting:

"I think it is not going too far to say that substantial justice is now administered throughout the state by local judicial tribunals to all classes of persons, irrespective of race or color, or antecedent political opinions. . . .

"It should not, perhaps, be a matter of surprise that so many outrages and crimes occur and go unpunished, but rather a matter of marvel that so few occur."

Negro relations were not the only subjects considered by Southern legislatures in their fall and winter sessions, of course. The new legislature in Arkansas, in control of the ante-bellum Democrats, spent most of its time undoing what the 1864 and 1865 legislatures had done. A new tax law, with sharp reductions in the rates, was enacted. By a bill passed over the veto of Governor Murphy, ten per cent of the state's annual revenue was appropriated for "the relief of the destitute, wounded, or disabled soldiers not otherwise provided for by the United States"—a description which could apply only to Arkansans who had soldiered for the Confederacy. Another appropriation of ten thousand dollars was made to buy artificial limbs for soldiers who were so described in the act that only Arkansas ex-Confederates were eligible to its benefits.

Like the other Southern legislatures, Arkansas went through the solemn formality of electing senators who never would get beyond the outer doors of the Senate of the United States. It went further, however, and sent an official commission to Washington to confer with the "Federal government" about the status of Arkansas. They saw the President, met the Cabinet, and returned to Arkansas with a warning to the people as to "the importance, the absolute necessity of remaining quiet, of preserving good order, and a quiet submission to a rigid enforcement of the law." It is apparent that the great majority of the people of Arkansas at this time acquiesced in their restored government as it existed. The ex-Confederate legislature enacted a code for the regulation of freedmen more liberal than that of any other state, establishing equality in all rights except voting, jury service, and militia duty, while prohibiting mixed marriages and mixed schools. The same legislature passed a general amnesty law, applying to the acts done during the war by jayhawkers and bushwhackers on both sides. A delegation of Radicals, representing a convention held at Fort Smith, did go to Washington to interview sympathetic congressional leaders in an effort to have the "Confederate" government overthrown, but another convention of moderate Unionists, meeting at Van Buren, expressed the more general sentiment in its demand for "security for the future rather than indemnity for the past."

The farmers of Arkansas were more interested in making their crops than they were in politics. The state was reasonably peaceful, for a community which still was on the frontier. Taxes were being paid in amount sufficient to create an actual surplus in the treasury, according to Governor Murphy's report to the legislature, recommending a reduction in the rate. The state was actually restored, except for its lack of representation in Congress and the presence of military garrisons—a forerunner of the type of restoration which the natural course of events might have been expected to produce in other Southern states had time and circumstance allowed.

In Georgia, the legislature enacted, in December, a law to set up a carefully planned educational system; authorized the establishment of an Agricultural & Mechanical College for the state; and provided for free tuition at the state university for each indigent maimed ex-soldier who would agree to teach in the schools of Georgia as many years as he received college aid. Under this act, ninety-three former Confederate soldiers enrolled at the university.

The critical question before Southern legislatures, however, was the Fourteenth Amendment. Tennessee, controlled by the Brownlow anti-Johnson forces, ratified promptly, almost as soon as the amendment was submitted. Texas rejected the amendment in October; Georgia, in November; Florida, at the beginning of December. The House of Representatives of Florida expressed the general sentiment in its comment:

"Our present relations with the general government are certainly of a strange character. Beyond the postal service, our people derive no benefit from our existence as a State in the Union. We are denied representation even when we elect a man who has never in fact sympathized with armed resistance to the United States, and who can in good faith take the oath. We are at the same time subject to the most onerous taxation; the civil law of the State is enforced and obeyed only when it meets the approval of the local commanders of the troops of the United States; the Congress of the United States enacts laws making certain lands subject to entry at a small cost by the colored portion of our population and denies the like privilege to the white man by restrictions amounting to a prohibition. We are, in fact, recognized as a State for the single and sole purpose of working out our destruction and dishonor."

As to that, Governor Walker of Florida had his own views:

"We will bear any ill before we will pronounce our own dishonor. We will be taxed without representation; we will quietly endure the government of the bayonet . . . but we will not bring as a peace offering the conclusive evidence of our own self-created degradation."

Moved by like sentiment, one after another, the Southern states rejected the proffered Fourteenth Amendment, not because they objected to all its provisions but because there could be no separate action on the disqualifying clauses to which they did object. Alabama followed Florida, in spite of the earnest recommendation of Governor Patton that the legislature "look the matter squarely in the face" and recognize that Congress would ruin the state if they were not willing to consent to the proscription of a few thousand men.

North Carolina, Arkansas and South Carolina followed, before the Christmas holidays; Virginia and Mississippi in January, 1867; Kentucky, too, rejected the amendment in January, overwhelmingly, during the same session in which an appropriation was made to reinter in the soil of the state of Kentucky Confederate dead lying in other states. Alabama considered the amendment again in January, and again rejected it. Mississippi rejected it the same month; Louisiana, early in February, 1867.

"The last one of the sinful ten," declaimed James A. Garfield in the House of Representatives, "has at last with contempt and scorn flung back into our teeth the magnanimous offer of a generous nation. It is now our turn to act."

Mr. Garfield's intimation that action was to be taken as the result of the contumacy of the "sinful ten" was merest rhetoric. Action, long planned, had been under way since the first Monday in December, 1866, when the Thirty-ninth Congress opened its second session.

CHAPTER XXIV

"Congress Is the People"

When the Thirty-ninth Congress assembled for its second session, on the first Monday in December, the surface scene of confusion was not unlike that of the year before, when the same members came together for their first session after the surrender. Washington, its hotels, its boarding-houses, and its bars were jammed. The Capitol, its cloakrooms and its lobbies, swarmed as before, with the difference that claimants holding certificates of election to Congress from Southern states were not there. The futility of presenting themselves for admission was too apparent.

Before the actual assembling of Congress the inner group of determined root-and-branch Reconstructionists met in private caucus, as they had done the year before—but, again, with a difference. In December, 1865, there had been apprehensions among them as to the power and effect of executive influence; there was need for winning converts from among the great body of congressmen of moderate inclinations, disposed to let the work of restoration proceed; there were the exigencies and uncertainties of an impending campaign and election.

In December, 1866, however, these anxieties had passed. Congressional converts had been won, the congressional elections carried. The determined group which, in 1864, had fought Lincoln with so little success, and which, in 1865, had "trembled" with apprehension as to what the executive might do, in 1866 confronted an executive already weakened, soon to be stripped of power, with his influence, even, all but destroyed. To that great height of power in government, power almost supreme and unchecked, had they advanced in two years of almost fanatic concentration on a positive and aggressive policy, aided by the drift of events.

In the campaign and election of 1866 it had been necessary to keep some issues in the background; to dissemble as to others. Many voters, if not most of them, had cast their ballots with the idea implicit that the Southern states were to be brought back into the Union on the terms of the Fourteenth Amendment. No such direct

208

commitment had been made, but John A. Bingham of Ohio insisted that "the people of the United States so understood and accepted" the issue of the election of 1866, and that "not a few gentlemen here" owed their re-election to the Fortieth Congress to that understanding. Mr. Stevens stoutly denied that there was any understanding, "expressed or implied," as to admission on the terms of the Fourteenth Amendment. The directing group in Congress, therefore, felt free to interpret the popular will as to the South as seemed best to them. They were not bound to vote to readmit the insurrectionary states even if they should proceed to ratify the amendment—which no one expected them to do. Since, with complete and enthusiastic unanimity, the states not yet admitted were rejecting the amendment, the way was now open for the Radical leaders to let the country know that more than mere ratification of the Fourteenth Amendment would be demanded before the admission of the conquered states to the Congress. Mr. Cullom said to the House of Representatives:

"During the last session of this Congress we sent to the country a proposed amendment to the Constitution. . . . The people of the rebel States by their pretended legislatures are treating it with scorn and contempt. . . . It is time, sir, that the people of the states were informed in language not to be misunderstood that the people who saved this country are going to reconstruct it in their own way, the opposition of rebels to the contrary notwithstanding."

Additional conditions of Reconstruction, beyond those in the Fourteenth Amendment, were discussed from the first week of the session. To admit the Southern states to representation, even to the reduced representation contemplated by the amendment, was not safe, from a Radical point of view, so long as the governments of those states were in the hands of those whom Senator Sumner described as "hostile populations which have just been engaged in armed rebellion."

The Southern states, therefore, must be remade in a pattern reliably Radical. That could be done only by Federal action, extending the vote to freedmen, wholesale and at once. Against such a project stood the Constitution, wherein regulation of the suffrage was explicitly reserved to the states.

There were processes for amendment of the Constitution, of course, but in 1867 not even the most convinced and ardent advocate of the step believed that there was the slightest chance that an amendment to extend the vote to Negroes would be ratified, even by the Northern states. In only six states were they allowed to vote at all, and in one of these, New York, the right was restricted by property qualifications which did not apply to whites. In fourteen other non-slaveholding states, in the four slave states which did not secede, and in Tennessee, which already had been readmitted to Congress, Negroes were not allowed the vote.

Only in the territories of the United States and in the District of Columbia could Congress say who might vote and upon what terms and conditions. There an immediate start could be made, and an example set. In January of 1867, therefore, bills were passed, and repassed over the veto of the President, granting to Negroes in the District and in all territories the right to vote, without qualification or restriction other than those which applied equally to whites.

President Johnson's veto was not an expression of hostility to Negro suffrage in and of itself. In common with most of the more enlightened Southerners of the time, he felt that it was coming, and should come through action of the states, gradually and with preparation. In that way, he felt, the "new order of things will work harmoniously," while to force it before a community was ready for it, he believed, would "result in the injury of both races."

The President's point was especially pertinent to the situation in the District of Columbia. In an election held in December, the District voted—7,337 to 36—against extending the suffrage to the colored population, greatly swollen by the influx of war refugees and others seeking there the promised land. Such election results meant nothing to Mr. Stevens, however. To grant suffrage to the Negroes of the District of Columbia was a first step toward securing it in the South, and that, as he said in his speech of January 3, would

"insure the ascendency of the Union party. . . . I believe . . . that on the continued ascendency of that party depends the safety of this great nation. . . . I am for negro suffrage in every rebel state. If it be just, it should not be denied; if it be necessary, it should be adopted; if it be a punishment to traitors, they deserve it."

The knowledge that Negro suffrage would be a bitter dose for the South added a certain spice of pleasure to the program, no doubt, but Mr. Stevens' sentiments are not to be attributed to mere malice toward a beaten foe. The Radical leader of the House had a passion for Negro equality as intense as that of Senator Charles Sumner himself.

He would have liked to see Negro suffrage in all states, but that he knew to be impossible at the time. Northern states which could vote for themselves were voting it down wherever the question was presented. Connecticut, Wisconsin and Minnesota had rejected it in 1865. Kansas was to do so in 1867; Michigan and Missouri in the following year, and New York in 1869.

Mr. Stevens, intensely realistic in his view of things political, proposed to leave the question to state action in the North, for the time being, but to impose the suffrage on the rebel states, at that time almost the only states which had a Negro population large enough to make their votes of practical political importance. There, too, Congress itself had or could assume a degree of authority. It could not act directly to establish suffrage qualifications within a state, it was conceded, but, through its power over the ten insurrectionary states still out of the Union, it could coerce them into doing for themselves "voluntarily" what could not be imposed directly.

Upon the reconvening of Congress after the Christmas holidays, Mr. Stevens called up on January 3, 1867, his bill to sweep away the Lincoln-Johnson restoration governments in the South, and to set up in their places new governments based on an electorate made up of the "loyal," that is, Negroes and the comparatively few whites who could bring themselves in that class. Mr. Stevens' bill and others were before the Committee on Reconstruction for a month, emerging on February 6 as the Reconstruction bill—a preamble reciting that there were no legal state governments and no adequate protection for life and property in the late rebel states; four sections which grouped the states into five military districts and established, in detail, the military organization and rules for their government until new and legal state governments could be set up; and a fifth section, instructing the military rulers as to the steps to be taken to reconstruct the governments on the new pattern, and to present them to Congress, suitably garbed for readmission to the sisterhood of states.

To this bill Mr. Blaine and Mr. Bingham offered a moderating amendment, to allow such whites as would be able to qualify under the Fourteenth Amendment to vote along with the "truly loyal" in the Reconstruction process. With scorn and contempt for such a "step toward universal amnesty and universal Andy-Johnsonism," Mr. Stevens drove the bill through the House in a week. Most of the Moderates, hearing themselves denounced by Mr. Stevens as "hugging and caressing those whose hands are red and whose garments are dripping with the blood of our and their murdered kindred," proved unable to stand up under the assault, and at the last were found voting with the Radical majority.

From the House, the bill went to the Senate on February 13. For four days of almost continuous session, day and night, the Senate debated the measure and then, at six o'clock on the morning of Sunday, February 17, passed it—but with amendments. One of these restored to the President, as constitutional commander-in-chief, the power to appoint the military governors, a power which the House had sought to take from him and confer upon the General of the Armies, General Grant. Another was substantially the Blaine-Bingham amendment which the House had rejected.

In the great need for haste to get the bill to the President in such time that he could not pocket-veto it, as Lincoln had pocket-vetoed the Radical Reconstruction bill in 1864, the House accepted the amendments of the Senate, and, on February 20, sent the bill to the President for his action.

That he would veto it, no one doubted. That it would be passed over his veto, was equally certain. That under it there would be created ten new state governments was foregone. Of these ten state governments Senator Henry Wilson could say truly:

"With the exercise of practical judgment, with good organization, scattering the great truth and the facts before the people, a majority of these States will within a twelve month, send here Senators and Representatives who think as we think, speak as we speak, and vote as we vote, and will give their electoral votes for whoever we nominate for President in 1868."

Against this dazzling prospect of success in concentrating the whole power of government, the very "will of the people," in the congressional majority there appeared but two obstacles, a stubborn President with old-fashioned constitutional ideas, and a Supreme Court which insisted upon testing acts of Congress against the rights reserved and the guarantees established in the Constitution of the United States.

As to the President, the Radicals of his own state, gathered in convention to nominate Governor Brownlow for re-election, had pointed the way when they resolved that the people were "ashamed of the unprincipled adopted son of Tennessee, now President of the United States, for his deception and degeneracy, and will endorse any action of Congress that will legitimately deprive him of his continued power."

Both suggested lines of attack were followed. To weaken the President by defaming him, the House created a committee, under the chairmanship of Ashley of Ohio, to dig up some sort of grounds for his impeachment. To limit his power over civil appointees, the Tenure of Office bill was passed. By rider to the Army Appropriation bill, his authority as military commander-in-chief was transferred largely to the General of the Armies, who was required to maintain his headquarters at Washington, under the immediate eye of Congress.

"Though the President is Commander-in-Chief," said Mr. Stevens, "Congress is his commander, and, God willing, he shall obey. He and his minions shall learn that this is not a Government of kings and satraps, but a Government of the people, and that Congress is the people."

With the President reduced to practical impotence, there remained against this last startling proposition of the supremacy of a majority in Congress but one obstacle—the Constitution originally ordained by "the people of the United States," wherein certain powers carefully were reserved from the Congress and certain rights were guaranteed to the states or to the people. Even these powers, it appeared, were to be gathered into the hands of the triumphant majority, representing the will of the people as expressed in the most recent election, when once more the Supreme Court intervened as the protector of the guaranteed rights of individuals and minorities.

Two weeks after the opening of Congress, on December 17, 1866, the Court published its opinion in *Ex Parte Milligan*—one of the landmark cases in the thousand-year struggle for the rights of the individual.

Early in the war, by executive order and congressional act, the government of the United States suspended the right of habeas corpus, and authorized military arrest and trial of citizens, even outside the field of military operations. Under these acts and orders, there came about a situation well described by the Secretary of State, in a war-time conversation with Lord Lyons, the British ambassador. Said Mr. Seward,

"My Lord, I can touch a bell on my right hand, and order the arrest of a citizen of Ohio. I can touch a bell again, and order the imprisonment of a citizen of New York; and no power on earth, except that of the President, can release them. Can the Queen of England do as much?"

One of the citizens whose arrest was ordered under this state of affairs was Lambdin P. Milligan, long-time resident of Indiana, not a member of the military forces, who was arrested on October 5, 1864 by order of the military commander in the state, and charged with conspiracy against the government, affording aid and comfort to the enemy, inciting insurrection, disloyal practices and violations of the laws of war, all growing out of membership in the Order of American Knights or Sons of Liberty.

On October 21, Milligan was tried by military commission, found guilty and sentenced to death by hanging. At the regular term of the United States Court in Indianapolis, no effort was made by the government to secure the trial of Milligan by jury, in the ordinary way. No indictment was returned against him—in itself a circumstance which entitled him, under a statute of March 3, 1863, to be brought before the civil court on writ of habeas corpus, and either placed upon trial according to the law of the land or discharged from custody altogether. Insisting that, in the state of disaffection toward the war in Indiana, Milligan could not be convicted by a civil jury, the government stood upon his conviction and sentence by the military commission.

That sentence having been approved by the President, Mr. Milligan was fairly on his way toward execution when his attorneys went before the United States Circuit Court in Indiana with a petition for a writ of habeas corpus. The Circuit Court, dividing in its opinion, certified the case to the Supreme Court for decision.

In the opinion of the majority of the court, neither president nor Congress had the power under the Constitution to require that a citizen be put upon trial before a military commission in a state which was neither invaded nor engaged in rebellion, and in which Federal courts were open and in the unobstructed exercise of their judicial functions.

"By the protection of the law," said the majority, "human rights are secured; withdraw that protection and they are at the mercy of wicked rulers, or the clamor of an excited people."

The announcement of this high doctrine provoked an outburst of rage against the court, denounced for thwarting the will of the people as expressed in an act of Congress. Under such a decision, declared Mr. Stevens, the lives and liberties of loyal men everywhere were in grave danger. The decision, he said, "places the knife of the rebel at the throat of every man who dares proclaim himself to be now, or to have been heretofore, a loyal Union man." Impeachment of Justice David Davis, the friend and appointee of Lincoln, who wrote the opinion, and of the justices who concurred with him, was mooted.

Into this storm of congressional rage, the Supreme Court plumped two more five-to-four decisions in the Test Oath Cases, on January 14, 1867. In *Cummings v. Missouri*, the court held that a state constitution which undertook to require a retroactive test oath from ministers of the Gospel and schoolteachers was contrary to the Bill of Rights of the Constitution of the United States. In *Ex Parte Garland*, the court held that an act of Congress, and a rule of the court itself, requiring that lawyers take the iron-clad oath of 1862 before being admitted to practice, was likewise contrary to the Bill of Rights. In the one case, the court found in the Constitution protection of the rights of unpopular minorities against the action of a state; in the other, against the action of Congress and the Federal government.

In the Missouri case, brought up on appeal by the Reverend Father John A. Cummings, before and after the war a priest of the Catholic Church, the majority of the court held that the attempt to prohibit preaching or teaching by those who did not take the all-inclusive and drastic test oath of the "Drake Constitution" of 1865 was, in effect, an attempt to punish whole classes of persons for acts which were not criminal when committed. By its terms, they said, the oath was "aimed at past acts, not future acts," and that as to those acts the state sought to change the usual presumption of innocence unless proved guilty, to guilty unless proved innocent.

The Cummings case enraged those whose interest in punishment for the past exceeded that in restoration for the future. The Garland case infuriated them—for the Augustus H. Garland whom the Supreme Court allowed to resume the practice of his profession before the courts of the United States had been a representative and a senator in the Congress of the Confederate States, from the state of Arkansas. Pardoned by the President in July, 1865, he found the doors of the courts effectively closed to him as an attorney because he could not swear to the iron-clad oath of 1862, that he had never supported the Confederacy.

The decision of the court did not rest alone on the pardon by the President. It went to the broader ground, that the requirement of such an oath as a condition to practicing law was a deprivation of the means of livelihood; was, in effect, a punishment other than, and in addition to, the punishments in effect at the time the imputed crime was committed; and so was an *ex post facto* law such as was prohibited by the Bill of Rights. Young Garland—he was thirty-six years of age at the time—arguing his own case before the Supreme Court, secured the decision which opened the doors of the courts to thousands of ex-Confederate lawyers, whose future value as loyal citizens of a restored nation was to be of value incalculable.

At the time, however, the declaration that the Constitution and its Bill of Rights extended their protection to ex-rebels, who had rights which not even acts of Congress could violate, brought upon the court a storm of congressional rage and abuse. Immediately there appeared in the House a bill to require nothing less than a unanimous decision of the court to hold invalid an act of Congress claimed to be violative of the Constitution. Threats were made to use the power of Congress to take away the appellate jurisdiction of the court, or even to abolish the court altogether by amendment to the Constitution. Nothing, it was felt, should be allowed to balk the immediate exercise of the will of the people as expressed by their elected representatives in Congress.

But rage against the court could wait. The immediate business in hand at this session of the Congress was to complete the job of creating in the South ten vassal states, reliably Radical.

On March 2, the President returned to the House, with his veto, the bill for military Reconstruction of these states according to the desired pattern. The House immediately passed the bill over his veto, and transmitted it to the Senate, which, on the same day, did likewise. Said Mr. Garfield in vivid phrase:

"This bill sets out by laying its hands on the rebel governments and taking the very life out of them; in the next place, it puts the bayonet at the breast of every rebel in the South; in the next place, it leaves in the hands of Congress, utterly and absolutely, the work of reconstruction."

With ten states of the South "utterly and absolutely" in its hands, with the executive reduced to practical impotence, an impatient Congress, convinced of its mandate from the people, was all but the supreme law of the land. There remained only the restraints and prohibitions of a Constitution interpreted by a judiciary which, itself, could be, and in due time would be, put in its place.

BOOK TWO

''Reconstruction''

CHAPTER XXV

Synthetic States

ABRAHAM LINCOLN waged, for four years, a war which, in July, 1861, just after the disaster at Bull Run, the Thirty-seventh Congress declared was "to preserve the Union with all the dignity, equality and rights of the several States unimpaired; and that as soon as these objects are accomplished the war ought to cease."

The war, or at least organized hostilities, came to an end. Andrew Johnson, one of the authors of the 1861 statement of its purposes, took up where Lincoln laid down the struggle "to preserve the Union," or to restore it, as nearly as might be, to a Union of states with "dignity, equality and rights unimpaired."

And now, with the passage over the President's veto of the Reconstruction Act of March 2, 1867, that attempt ended in failure. The Union was not to be preserved; the states were not to be restored. The Union was to be remade; the states were to be "reconstructed."

To insure against lapse or pause in the execution of this purpose, its interpretation of the popular will, the expiring Congress resolved that its successor, the Fortieth, should come into session at once, rather than wait for its first regular session in December, 1867, nine months hence. No chances were to be taken on the action of Southern state governments and peoples, looked upon as resentful, even rebellious, against the new order of government set up in the act of March 2. Nor were chances to be taken with the President in Washington, suspected by congressional leaders of dark designs to use his executive authority, perhaps his military power, to overturn their plan of Reconstruction.

Suspicions as to the good faith of the President in the execution of the duties of his office as laid down by acts of Congress were unfounded. Promptly he named general officers to command the five military districts into which the South had been divided—John M. Schofield for District No. 1, which had been the state of Virginia; Daniel E. Sickles for District No. 2, the Carolinas; John Pope for District No. 3, Georgia, Alabama and Florida; E. O. C. Ord for District

No. 4, Mississippi and Arkansas; and Philip Sheridan for District No. 5, Louisiana and Texas.

To govern the territories assigned to them, the new commanders took over the existing state governments and their local agencies. These governments ceased to have even the shadowy half-independence they had enjoyed under the Lincoln-Johnson plan of restoration, and became, under the congressional plan, merely convenient agencies of administration, subject in all respects to the military power, and liable at any time to be abolished, modified or superseded. In general, this paramount authority of direction, removal and appointment was exercised sparingly and with restraint by the military commanders, most of whom were practical army men given a job to do and bent on doing it with as little disturbance as possible.

Under the terms of the Reconstruction Act, military government was to continue until the states were remade and readmitted to the Congress. The process of remaking required, in each state, an election, open to all males twenty-one years of age and more, of whatever race, color, or previous condition, except those "disfranchised for participation in rebellion or for felony at common law" and those who would be disfranchised by the pending Fourteenth Amendment when it should be adopted; the holding of a constitutional convention; the adoption of a new constitution which would grant the vote to Negroes and whites alike, and would deny it to the excepted classes of ex-Confederates; the approval of this new constitution by Congress; the election of a legislature and a governor under the new constitution; the ratification by the legislature of the Fourteenth Amendment to the Federal Constitution; and finally, the ratification of that amendment by enough legislatures to secure its adoption as part of the Constitution of the United States. With all that done, properly and in order, the new-born states might be readmitted to fellowship in the Union.

Immediately, however, there appeared a defect in the plan for remaking states. The states didn't want to be remade. They didn't like military government, it is true, but they preferred it to the sort of government which they saw ahead of them under the plan of Reconstruction. Under the rule of the generals, it was rightly expected that a few civil officers, here and there, would be removed and replaced with "loyal" men; a few criminal cases would be tried before military commission rather than civil courts; a few acts of the legislature would be superseded by military general orders setting up a different rule of law—but those things, distressing as they might be to what the Charleston *News* described as "a brave, a sensitive and a suffering people," were to be accepted rather than the prospects of Reconstruction as they appeared. The lure of regaining representation in Congress was not enough, in most states, to cause them to initiate the steps necessary to that end.

The plan of Congress, however, was not to be balked so easily. The new Congress, in session by virtue of the foresight of its predecessor, promptly passed on March 23 the first Supplemental Reconstruction Act, which put upon the commanders the responsibility for initiating and carrying through the steps of Reconstruction, without regard to recalcitrant state governments or reluctant peoples.

A great registration in each state was to be held by the generals commanding; elections were to be called; dates to be set and arrangements made for constitutional conventions; deliberations of those conventions were to be guided and supervised; new legislatures were to be elected, and their sessions organized and carried through; the Fourteenth Amendment was to be ratified; and the whole process and its results reported to Congress. The first step, the general registration of voters, was ordered to be completed by September 1.

The policy of inaction which so promptly failed, however, was not the only defense tried by the Southern states. Almost immediately after the passage of the Reconstruction Act, the restored state government of Mississippi applied to the Supreme Court of the United States for an injunction to restrain President Johnson from performing what the petition described as the "ministerial duty" of putting the act into effect. On broad grounds of policy, the Supreme Court denied the application.

Finding that the President could not be enjoined in such fashion, in April the state of Georgia, through Governor Jenkins, went before the court with its suit for an injunction restraining subordinate officers—Secretary of War Stanton, General Grant, District Commander Pope—from carrying out the act. The court declined to entertain the suit, in May, for lack of jurisdiction of the subject matter. The judicial power which could protect civil rights when assailed was not to be extended to prevent the carrying out of the political process ordered by the Congress.

By orders of the district commanders, registration machinery was set up in each of the ten states to be reconstructed. The task to be accomplished was not easy, under any circumstances. It was doubly difficult because of the scarcity of competent "loyal" material for registrars, in many sections. The usual setup, from which there were many departures, was a three-man county board, composed often of one army officer, ex-army officer or bureau sub-agent in the vicinity, one local "loyal" white, and one freedman. Registrations were held at different dates and places, beginning with the spring and continuing into the fall. Registrars carried the books about to the different precincts, inviting all qualified to present themselves for enrollment. Compensation to the registrars was on a per capita basis, ranging up to as much as forty cents per name listed in thinly settled country districts. Every effort was made to secure the most complete listing possible of the recently freed population, a task of no small difficulty in the disturbed state of the times.

Coincident with the registration, through the summer of 1867, went the organization of the prospective new voters. In this work, native white Unionists who had become Republicans vied for leadership with imported Republicans from the North. Less conspicuous in the early stages of the movement were the shrewder and more intelligent of the Negroes, both native and Northern, who emerged into positions of leadership among their less favored fellows.

The native element of the white Radical leadership came to be known among their Conservative neighbors as "scalawags"—a name of uncertain etymology which came to have, in the popular mind, the connotation of "renegade."

The imported element acquired after a time the designation of "carpetbaggers." The first suggestion of the name is credited to A. J. Fletcher, native white Reconstruction Secretary of State in Tennessee, who said:

"No one more gladly welcomes the Northern man who comes in all sincerity to make a home here, and to become one of our people, than I, but for the adventurer and office-seeker who comes among us with one dirty shirt and a pair of dirty socks, in an old rusty carpetbag, and before his washing is done becomes a candidate for office, I have no welcome."

Neither name was entirely just. Many of the so-called "carpetbaggers" came south before there was any prospect of political plunder of the Southern states through the organization and manipulation of the ignorant mass of new voters. Many of them were men of substance and standing whose first Southern ventures were in planting or other business, and who gravitated, naturally, into positions of political leadership when the organization of the party to which they belonged began to be extended into the South. There were enough of the other kind, however, to make the name stick, and to give it general application.

In like fashion, there was great diversity among those who came to be lumped in popular speech under the derisive term of "scalawag." Particularly in the early stages of Reconstruction under the military acts, there were men of character and standing in the South, mostly among those who had opposed secession from the beginning, who felt that the course of wisdom called for co-operation by the Southern people, through the organization of the Republican party. Many of these men abandoned the attempt after the early stages; others, more deeply committed, remained in the Republican or Radical ranks to the end. Most of the so-called "scalawags," however, had shown no great attachment to the Union when such an attachment meant difficulty and danger. Some of them had been what the Governor of Texas described as "blatant, brawling Secessionists," so long as that was the popular side. Many of such men earned the deep detestation in which they came to be held by the majority of the Southern people.

In the upper South, where a large element of the population had been actively and sincerely attached to the Union, native whites played a larger part in the leadership of the newly organized Republican or Radical party than they did in the lower South. In those states, lacking such an element in the older resident population, the leadership naturally fell into the hands of the new residents who had come in during and after the war.

In Virginia, at the outset, the contest for leadership of the new Republican organization was between John Minor Botts, staunch old Virginia Whig and Unionist, who sought to lead along Conservative lines, and the Reverend James W. Hunnicutt, native of South Carolina and later publisher of a religious newspaper at Fredericksburg. As was true of so many of the more violent Southern Radicals, the Reverend Hunnicutt had been a slaveholder and an active Secessionist. In Reconstruction days in Virginia, he became the editor of the Richmond *New Nation*, the leading Radical organ of the state.

In the first test of power between these two, the Reverend Hunnicutt succeeded in carrying with him, along the Radical path, the convention held on April 17 to organize the Republican party in Virginia. Of two hundred and ten delegates, one hundred and sixty were colored. To them Hunnicutt appealed in such fashion and tone as to disturb many Republican leaders in the North. Of him, the

New York *Times* said—and it might have been said with equal justice of others of the new leaders beginning to come to the front in the South—that "he and such as he are unceasing in their endeavors to organize the blacks as a party which shall hereafter control Southern affairs."

In discussing the same convention, the New York *Tribune* voiced the opinion that "to organize a campaign on the Hunnicutt plan is to abandon any hope of a permanent Union party in the South. We cannot afford to array the white against the black or the black against the white."

Such expressions by one of the great pundits of the Republican party in the North, wise as they were, meant nothing to the practical politicians in the South busily organizing to take full advantage of the opportunities presented to them by the vindictives of Congress. Their chance of profitable preferment depended upon doing precisely the thing against which the *Tribune* thundered its warning—and that thing they proposed to do.

For some of the native Southerners among them, it required still another switch in attitude, another swap of convictions. In North Carolina, for example, former Provisional Governor Holden, in ready anticipation of the effect of the new dispensation, came out for Negro suffrage with all the violence with which he had formerly opposed it. "Traitors," he said, by which he meant former rebel leaders who might seek to take any part in the process of Reconstruction, "traitors must take back seats and keep silent. . . . The issue is Union or Disunion. He who is not for the Union deserves to have his property confiscated and to suffer death by the law."

At the convention held on March 27 to organize the Republican party in North Carolina, Governor Holden, R. P. Dick and Thomas Settle, all former active Democrats, took command of the movement. The one native North Carolinian present with a clear Republican and non-Confederate record was the courageous old pre-war Abolitionist, Daniel R. Goodloe. Counseling against the radical steps urged by the Holden group, he urged moderation and co-operation. To the Negroes he said:

"Listen to no man who whispers the word confiscation in your ears or disfranchisement, or injury in any form, to your law-abiding white neighbors. . . . Ask them how long they have been champions of your rights. In ninety-nine cases out of a hundred you will find that such men would have sold you to the sugar and cotton planters of the far South at any time before you were set free."

Such advice, however, could prevail hardly at all against the bright promises of politics and the attractive mysteries of the secret political societies of the time.

Most effective of these instruments for organizing the prospective voters were the Union Leagues, or Loyal Leagues as they were more commonly called. Founded in Northern cities, the organization was at first purely patriotic, to sustain the war spirit of the North flagging under the reverses of 1862. As territory in the South was occupied by the Union forces, the League came south, too. In the North, after 1865, the organization evolved into a group of social clubs, with a degree of political purpose. In the South, between 1865 and the new dispensation of 1867, the organization included mostly Union men who had come south with or behind the armies, and native whites who had sided with the Union. Of the latter, there were not enough to form a really potent political force, outside three or four states of the upper South.

As Negro suffrage approached, however, the character of the order began to change. The loose federation between local Leagues which had prevailed in the Northern cities was replaced with a close-knit organization in each state, under a common head. Negroes were initiated in such large numbers as to become the majority in most of the local Leagues, while as the Negroes came in, many of the original native white members, especially in the highland regions of the upper South, dropped out.

In the lower South, the membership of the Leagues came to be almost entirely among the newly enfranchised colored people; its leadership, among the class locally referred to as "imported Yankees," to distinguish them from the "homemade" product. The proclaimed object of the Leagues was

"to preserve liberty and the Union . . . to protect, strengthen and defend all loyal men, without regard to sect, condition or race; to elect honest and reliable Union men to all offices of profit or trust in National, State and local government; to secure equal civil and political rights to all men."

The League, in the South, as explained by its grand deputy for the state of Virginia, General Edgar Allan, "was organized as an aid to the effective carrying out of the humane objects and purposes of those in the North who believed that the ballot in the hands of the negro would be preferable to bullets in the muskets of a standing army, which would have been necessary for an indefinite period in many sections of the South."

Meeting at night, the Leagues formed "a system of night school in which the negroes were instructed in the privileges of citizenship and the duties they owed to the party which had made them free and given them the exercise of suffrage."

This instruction was given after elaborate services and ceremonies, carried out in darkness, with much clanking of chains and shuffling about of hooded figures. The heart of the organization was its fearsome oath, binding the members to uniform action in accordance with the instruction of its leaders, instruction usually designed to separate the freedmen politically from the local whites, and to attach them to the Radical leadership, whether native or imported. Said Abraham Smith addressing a Radical convention for Negroes held in Nashville on April 14:

"If it had not been for the radicals we would be slaves today. . . . The radicals fought four years to free you, and the rebels fought four years to enslave you. All the radicals in the Tennessee legislature voted to give you the right of suffrage, and the rebels voted against it. To vote for a conservative is to vote for the chains of slavery to be riveted to your necks."

Such appeals, difficult enough for Conservatives to counter under any conditions, were reinforced and made fully effective by the organization of the Leagues. Everyone initiated, according to S. B. Hall, a South Carolina member, was obligated by oath to support those nominated by the order. Should an ignorant member show a disposition to do otherwise, he might be

"threatened to be reported to the President of the United States, and that, after freeing them, he would take back their freedom and place them in slavery again. Others would tell them that you swear to do this, and that if you do not carry out your obligations, you will be liable for perjury and perhaps sent to the penitentiary."

Office-seekers, he said, would make inflammatory speeches at the meetings, "telling the colored man who was his friend and who was not; at the same time giving their (former) owners a general raking, and instructing them that their former owner merely wanted their votes to place them back in slavery as soon as the Democratic ticket was elected. . . . They were told that the Yankee was their only friend—he had fought and bled on the battle field for their liberation."

The rapid spread of the Loyal Leagues through the South aroused great and genuine apprehension among the whites. "There is no disputing the fact that the fears of the whites with reference to these leagues were well founded," wrote the ex-slave John Wallace, afterward, "for the men who controlled them had really nothing in view but public plunder. . . . But for the influence of the more sensible of the colored people, the property of the country would have in many instances been destroyed by the midnight torch."

Violence, open or furtive, was not a purpose of the Leagues, however, even though it may have been an effect in particularly tense and inflamed situations. The purpose of the Leagues in the South was political. As the League at Montgomery put it, the organization was "the right arm of the Republican party." The Leagues furnished the local instrumentalities necessary to carry out the new scheme of government of the Southern states by remote control from Washington. The new electorate in process of creation in the South was trained already to look to the government at Washington as the source and supply of all good—including this new and but vaguely comprehended boon of suffrage. This gratitude needed only organization and direction to make it effective in carrying out the central will at Washington through the forms of democracy in the states. That necessary organization and direction, the Loyal Leagues were to give.

Through ritual and through precept, the freedmen's gratitude for benefits conferred by government was to be made the main force of political action. A catechism containing a "dialogue between a newly enfranchised freedman and a sound Radical Republican" neatly capitalized gratitude to Abraham Lincoln for emancipation, and to the congressional Radicals for enfranchisement, with ingenious indirect threats that Democratic or Conservative victory at future elections would mean not only the loss of the franchise but actual re-enslavement. Colored men were warned that they should "shun the Democratic party as they would the overseer's lash and the auction block," whether they found it under that name or under the names of "Conservative, Copperhead or rebel" party.

When such Southern leaders as Wade Hampton in South Carolina and Nathan Bedford Forrest in Tennessee sought a basis of co-operation and accommodation with the new voters, at barbecues and other gatherings addressed by white and colored speakers, the effective Radical reply was that the very votes which were being solicited had been given the Negroes by the Radicals, who now stood ready to offer them opportunities to hold public office, and to practice political and social equality. So effective was the answer that men of General Hampton's type were forced regretfully to the same conclusion to which he came, before the end of the summer of 1867, that "there is no longer a possibility of that entire harmony of action among our people for which you and I have heretofore hoped and strived."

The Radical program had in it all the elements of temporary political success. To the new voters, it appealed on the potent grounds of gratitude for benefits past and expectation of benefits to come. It attracted them by its novelty, and by the mystery which the Leagues lent. It was maintained by the power of a victorious central government and opposed, in the South at least, only by a people defeated, divided, disheartened; to a considerable extent, disarmed.

Effective political resistance to the program, within the South, was hardly possible, even had there not been such serious division in the counsels of the old white electorate. Open physical resistance was still less possible, particularly since the Loyal Leagues began to develop into a sort of partisan militia, armed and drilling, while militia organizations of the states were prohibited, except in Tennessee, where Governor Brownlow's newly organized state guards were maintained in aid of the Radical program. To the people of the North, the idea of Southern militia organizations savored too strongly of the old system of slave "paterollers," while there were alarmists who professed to see even in such innocuous organizations as historical societies dark plots to renew the rebellion as soon as the Northern armies completed their demobilization. Even in Texas, with its long and turbulent frontier insufficiently garrisoned for protection against either the plains Indians or marauding desperadoes, Governor Throckmorton was not allowed to organize a protective force.

But there did arise in the South an opposition—terrible because it moved in darkness and secrecy to accomplish ends that could not be reached openly; dangerous to friend as well as enemy, because, in the very nature of things, its membership must be secret and disguised, impossible to control and exposed to vicious imitation; bearing in itself the seeds of its own destruction; and yet, for all that, in the words of

Albion Tourgee, Union officer, Reconstruction Judge in North Carolina, and author of a partially autobiographical novel of the period:

"It was a daring conception for a conquered people. Only a race of warlike instincts and regal pride could have conceived or executed it. . . .

"It differed from all other attempts at revolution—for revolution it was in effect—in the caution and skill with which it required to be conducted. It was a movement made in the face of the enemy, and an enemy, too, of overwhelming strength. . . . Should it succeed it would be the most brilliant revolution ever accomplished. Should it fail—well, those who engaged in it felt that they had nothing more to lose."

CHAPTER XXVI

The Lasting Evil

IN THE spring of 1867, there met in Nashville, most secretly, delegates from the scattered Dens of the Ku Klux Klan which had sprung up in Tennessee and nearby states during the year or more since the formation of the first Den at Pulaski.

Of the Nashville meeting almost nothing is known, definitely, beyond the fact that when its members came together they represented local bodies separate in their organization and operations, except for the common recognition of a vague primacy in the original Pulaski Den; and that when they adjourned, they had set up the framework for a general organization extending from a common head down to the last Ghoul in each local Den.

Everything else about the meeting—as is true of so much of the traditional information about the Ku Klux movement—must be conjectured. Its date is uncertain, not earlier than April, probably not later than the first Monday in May. Its gathering went unnoted, either by the newspapers of the day or by the agents of the Radical state government or its allied Federal garrison. Its membership is unknown; its proceedings, even its name, unwritten except for the "Prescript of the Order of the *** "

It may have met in Room 10, one of the high-corniced, marble-manteled, parlor bedrooms of the then new Maxwell House. In that room, at any rate, according to the story published forty years later, Nathan Bedford Forrest, late Lieutenant General, C. S. A., was initiated into the order by the stripling John W. Morton, late Chief of Artillery in Forrest's Cavalry, and then Grand Cyclops of the Nashville Den.

The meeting itself is vague in the shadow of secrecy which necessity imposed, but from it the Klan emerged not as a mere idea but as a purposeful organization as compact and unified as the times and circumstances allowed.

Its creed, as stated in the Revised and Amended Prescript, later adopted, recognized its members' "relation to the United States

230

Government, the supremacy of the Constitutional Laws thereof, and the Union of the States thereunder"; its "peculiar objects" being

"First: To protect the weak, the innocent, and the defenceless, from the indignities, wrongs and outrages of the lawless, the violent and the brutal; to relieve the injured and oppressed; to succor the suffering and unfortunate, and especially the widows and orphans of Confederate soldiers.

"Second: To protect and defend the Constitution of the United States, and all laws passed in conformity thereto; and to protect the States and the people thereof from all invasion from any source whatever.

"Third: To aid and assist in the execution of all constitutional laws, and to protect the people from unlawful seizure, and from trial except by their peers in conformity to the laws of the land."

The territory of the Invisible Empire established in the prescript was declared to be that of the thirteen states claimed by the Confederacy, and Maryland. Its authority was centered in the Grand Wizard of the Empire—universally believed to have been General Forrest, whom Southerners, in the fashion of the time which liberally bestowed allusive nicknames, knew as the "Wizard of the Saddle."

The Grand Wizard, in addition to his own staff of ten Genii, had power to appoint for each of the Empire's Realms, coterminous with the states, a Grand Dragon. Each Grand Dragon, besides his own staff of eight Hydras, named for each of the Dominions of his Realm, corresponding roughly to congressional districts, a Grand Titan. Each Grand Titan, with a staff of six Furies, named for each of the Provinces of his Dominion, corresponding to a county, a Grand Giant. The Grand Giant, whose staff consisted of four Goblins, named for each Den of the Province a Grand Cyclops, who had as his staff two Night-Hawks. Appointments in each territorial gradation of the order were subject to approval by the chief officer of the next larger unit. Each of the units had, also, staff officers bearing the titles of Magi, Monk, Scribe, Exchequer, Turk and Sentinel. The "body politic" of the order were "known and designated as Ghouls."

What is known of the organization, as distinguished from what is surmised, is to be found largely in the Revised and Amended Prescript, which itself forbade the keeping of identifiable rosters or records. This prescript, taken from Nashville to Pulaski, was thrust by a hand unknown through a convenient hole in the wall of the printing office of the Pulaski *Citizen*, and there was set up in type and printed by Laps D. McCord and J. H. Kirk. No copy of this, or of the earlier prescript, ever fell into the hands of hostile authorities. But three copies of the documents are known to have survived the destruction of records, ritual and regalia by the Klan itself when dissolution was decreed by the Grand Wizard.

The Klan worked, at first, through terror of the ghostly unknown—robed riders, taller than life, speaking in tones of the sepulcher, demanding and drinking buckets of water to assuage the thirst which had been burning since death at Shiloh or Chickamauga; detachable heads, skeleton hands, muffled hoofbeats.

Nor were these demonstrations confined to lonely plantation cabins. To strike awe into whole populations, well-advertised parades were held, many of them on the night of July 4, 1867, when hooded riders and sheeted horses marched and counter-marched, to the signals of rockets and whistles, in perfect order and awesome silence, through the dim tree-shadowed streets and around the dusty courthouse squares of Southern towns.

In local newspapers there began to appear notices which to the initiated might have conveyed nothing more than information as to the next meeting of the local Den, but which were so phrased as to add to the general impression of dreadful mystery which the Klan sought to build about itself and its operations. Only men of education and imagination could have written notices such as this one, quoted by Mrs. Myrta Lockett Avary:

K K K

The Raven Croaked
And we are come to Look on the Moon.
The Lion Tracks the Jackal
The Bear the Wolf
Our Shrouds are Bloody
But the Midnight is Black.

The Serpent and Scorpion are Ready.
Some Shall Weep and Some Shall Pray.
Meet at Skull
For Feast of the Wolf and
Dance of the Muffled Skeletons.

The Death Watch is Set
The Last Hour Cometh
The Moon is Full.

Burst your cerements Asunder
Meet at the Den of the Glow-Worm
The Guilty Shall be Punished.

Quite obviously, however, general awe and vague terror could not long remain effective, by themselves, in meeting the particular situations which Klan members felt required attention. When vague and general warnings failed of effect, direct and individual threats of force and violence followed, sometimes to be executed, if execution should become necessary, by the Den which passed judgment and imposed sentence after trial by Ku Klux forms; sometimes to be executed by a neighboring Den which might be requested to come in and carry out the decree.

By no means all these warnings or visits were directed to Negroes. The first purpose of the Klan was protection, particularly the protection of the ex-Confederate element of the population, whether from the depredations or threats of over-zealous Loyal Leaguers, or from the dreaded visits of outlaw bands made up principally of skulkers and deserters from both armies. To carry out such a purpose, quite as often as not, involved Ku Klux attention to white men of one sort or another.

Such was the Klan in its organization and methods in its earlier and more responsible days. Even then, in spite of its array of horrendous titles and its seemingly strong chain of authority, the course of the local Den was largely beyond effective control from headquarters, and depended more upon the character of its own membership and leadership than it did upon any general rule of the order.

Worse still, for the permanent success of the movement, its success bred imitators who adopted Ku Klux disguise and adapted Ku Klux methods to the base uses of plunder or private vengeance. From the acts of these vicious imitators, whether white or black, Radical or "rebel," not even the most conscientious Den could protect its good name. Judging from the tone of the warning orders which Klans published in Southern newspapers—before such publications came under the ban of the anti-Ku Klux laws—the organization came to be greatly troubled by these uncontrollable bands of outside imitators.

The Ku Klux Klan was not the only white secret society in the

South with purposes more or less similar, nor was it the largest. Almost contemporaneous with it in organization, and larger in membership, was the order of the Knights of the White Camellia, founded in Louisiana at Franklin, St. Mary's Parish, by Judge Alcibiade de Blanc. Combining with other local protective societies, the new organization established headquarters on May 23, 1867, in New Orleans, from which point it spread over the Gulf states as the Ku Klux spread over the territory farther north. Spies got into the order of the Camellia in New Orleans, early in its career, and pretty well paralyzed it as an effective agency of direct action toward its professed objective of the supremacy of the white race.

No direct connection between the Ku Klux and the Camellias has been established, nor between either of them and other and smaller organizations of like general purpose, such as the Constitutional Union Guards, the White Brotherhood, the Pale Faces, or the Knights of the White Rose, active in various states and sections during this period. Without such a connection, however, they all may be considered as part of one movement. Judge Tourgee, whose novels on Reconstruction were hailed by admirers in the North as the *Uncle Tom's Cabin* of a new crusade, believed that the various orders were, in fact, separate and lower degrees of the same order, held together by a mystic and higher inner circle, the dread Invisible Empire.

It was, as Thomas W. Gregory, afterward attorney-general of the United States, described it, "the most thoroughly organized, extensive and effective vigilance committee the world has ever seen, or is likely to see"—but it was, after all, a vigilance committee, with the fatal defect of a membership necessarily secret and disguised.

The evil wrought upon Southern society by the movement is obvious. Private and secret violence and vengeance, uncontrolled and in the nature of things uncontrollable, was condoned as a substitute for public law. And yet it is equally apparent that some such movement was inevitable and necessary. Lawless itself, it did establish, for a critical time, law of a sort to protect a people and their institutions from disintegration and degeneration. It could not hold to the note of high purpose for long, and, dissolving, it left the South plagued with vicious successors and imitators. Its justification must rest upon the ultimate law of self-preservation. "Northerners and Southerners who did not live in that day and in black belts," wrote Mrs. Avary, "can form no conception of the conditions which gave rise to the white secret societies of which the most widely celebrated is the Ku Klux."

That mature and responsible men took charge of the movement

which grew out of the prankishness and tomfoolery of the original
meeting in Pulaski is, in itself, a recognition of those conditions, a
reflection of the loss of confidence of the Southern whites in the
intent and the power of their local governments under Reconstruction
to afford protection and security. These, not politics, were the original
purposes of the order, for which its ghostly terrors were first brought
into play. It is significant that a later congressional committee, seeking to gather and to magnify every instance of activity by the Klan
movement, or its imitators, which could in any way be construed as political violence or pressure, reported nearly all its cases of "outrages"
as having taken place in the years after 1867.

In that first year of the new dispensation, in fact, many responsible
white leaders of the South sought earnestly to find a basis of co-operation with their former slaves, to avoid letting the color line become
the line of cleavage between political parties in the South. These men,
who had grown up in the old belief that voting was not a natural
right but a responsible privilege, did not object to the sudden enfranchisement of the freedmen because they were Negroes. They objected to dumping into the electorate an undigested mass of voters,
in the main necessarily ignorant and irresponsible, whose only training
for participation in government was a conviction, based on experience
and precept, that therein lay the bountiful source of benefits. The objection, as events proved, was not unreasonable.

Holding such views, and recognizing that Negro suffrage was inevitable after the passage of the Reconstruction Act, men of this
way of thought sought to make the best of it by strengthening the
ties of common interest between the local whites and the prospective
new voters. Even before the passage of the first Supplemental Reconstruction Act, the legislature of Virginia, acting upon the advice
of Governor Pierpont, had decided to initiate the steps necessary for
the Reconstruction of that state under the original act—a decision
which became of no moment when the new act transferred the entire
authority in the matter to the district military commanders.

Among themselves, however, Virginians and Southerners of all
other states continued to debate what their course should be—
whether they should participate in the elections and conventions to
be held, and should seek to align with themselves the responsible
individuals among the new voters; or whether they should stand apart
and aloof, scornful of the whole proceeding. The newly established
Richmond *Times* was so intemperate in its diatribes against any join-
ing of hands with the "bloodstained hands" of its late enemies, that

General Schofield ordered its suspension because of its "insult to United States and Confederate soldiers" who had "long since extended to each other the cordial hand of friendship," coupled with a stern warning against "efforts . . . to foster enmity, create disorder and lead to violence."

General Lee, on the other hand, though scrupulously refraining from any public part in political discussion, privately advised that those entitled to vote under the act should participate and "endeavor to elect the best available men to represent them in the convention, to whose decisions everyone should submit."

Throughout the South ran the same sort of division in opinion and diversity in conduct, in the early days of the process of making a new electorate. In Arkansas, as an example, two of the most popular military leaders gave opposite advice. General T. C. Hindman advised registration and voting under the act; General Albert Pike advised continued passive acquiesence in military rule, rather than co-operation under the terms of Negro suffrage. In Louisiana, the great name of Beauregard was added to those counseling co-operation, while in Mobile a public meeting, in April, came out strongly for "harmonious relations" with the new Negro voters, both because of "gratitude for their fidelity in the past, in war as well as in peace, and because our interests in the future are inseparably connected with their well-being."

General Wade Hampton, in a speech in South Carolina, urged Negro suffrage by state action.

"The negroes . . . have behaved admirably . . . and are in no wise responsible for the present condition of affairs. Should they in the future, be misled . . . let us consider how ignorant they necessarily are, and let us, only the more, try to convince them that we are their best friends. Deal with them with perfect justice, and thus show them that you wish to promote their advancement and enlightenment."

Negro suffrage had already come by state action in Tennessee, enacted in February, 1867, by the Brownlow legislature, which had overcome its original hostility to the idea. Meanwhile, the exclusion of "rebels and rebel sympathizers" in Tennessee had been made still more stringent by requiring the testimony of two witnesses to "loyalty," as well as the taking of the iron-clad oath as to past conduct, as a prerequisite to registration. Since no one might vote without a certificate of registration, and since the commissioners of registration who made up the eligible lists and selected the judges and clerks of election were appointees of Governor Brownlow, there was small opportunity for the ex-Confederate element in the population to make itself felt politically.

The attempt was made, however. An attack on the constitutionality of the new disfranchisement law, on the ground that it was passed by a legislature from which members were wrongfully excluded, failed when the Supreme Court of the state sustained the statute on March 21, 1867.

Both ex-Confederates and Conservative white Unionists, of whom there were many in Tennessee, joined in efforts to persuade the freedmen to align themselves with that element. Conservatives in Nashville invited the Negroes to participate in their county convention on April 1, and some did so. The great difficulty in making such a movement successful, however, was recognized by Albert S. Colyar, who had been a Confederate congressman and who, in a life which lasted nearly a century, was to be lawyer, editor and a leader in the industrial revival of the South. He said in a public address at Winchester:

"Any appliance will be used and every conceivable device resorted to to prejudice the freedmen against their former masters. Fortunately, notwithstanding the late war, in which it was confidently predicted there would be a war of races, there is the best possible feeling between the two races."

That there were ties of interest and of affection between individuals of the races no one can doubt. The "old master," in many instances, remained the resource of the former slave in sickness and in distress, his refuge in trouble, his reliance in all the relations of life— except political. There, barring pleas for rational co-operation between responsible whites and blacks, stood the bright and glittering promises of those who, in the freedman's mind, represented the "government," and who stood to profit from political distrust and antagonism between the races; the reiterated threats of disfranchisement and re-enslavement if the Negro voters failed to support these Radical friends; the ostracism, even the violence, of the zealous Loyal Leagues toward the Negro who had the temerity to vote "against his color."

Therein lies the great and lasting evil which Reconstruction wrought upon the public and political life of the Southern states—antagonism of the races, carefully cultivated for political profit. From that sprang the extravagance, the corruption, the mountainous public debts of the Reconstruction régime; the violence, the trickery necessary to combat and overthrow that régime; and, finally, the forcing of most of the whites into a single party—a South solidly Democratic, the answer to the attempt, temporarily successful, to make a South solidly Republican.

CHAPTER XXVII

RECONCILIATION AND REHABILITATION

But even in that summer of 1867, when responsible men of the South, almost in despair, watched the overturn of the ancient foundations of order and government in their states, all was not strife and contention. Neither vindictives in Congress, nor agitators at the South, could completely stop the processes of healing and rebuilding.

On the afternoon of Saturday, May 11, Jefferson Davis, prisoner of state, stepped ashore from the James River steamer, *John Sylvester*, at the Rocketts Wharf, in Richmond. He was not free, for with him was General Burton, commandant of Fortress Monroe, where the President of the Confederacy had been imprisoned, but he was on his way to arraignment before a Circuit Court of the United States, as the first step in the trial for which he had so desperately longed.

For two years and two days Mr. Davis had been held a military prisoner. His captivity, at first needlessly harsh and humiliating, had become in time less rigorous. In truth, there never was any necessity for the elaborate precautions with which he was long surrounded—sentries multiplied; an officer and soldiers constantly in the room with him, or, afterward, constantly watching him through gratings on three sides of his room; the withholding of a knife and fork with which to eat his meals, lest his sense of guilt and dread might drive him to suicide. In his proud soul was no sense of guilt, no dread of consequences. His greatest anxiety was for trial before the courts—a trial in which there might be exhibited to the world the Confederate conception of the treason with which he was charged; the responsibility for the refusal to exchange prisoners which led to the sufferings and deaths of Northern soldiers in overcrowded Southern military prison camps; and the absurdity of the charge of Confederate complicity in the assassination of President Lincoln, conceived by Judge Advocate General Holt, put forward by Secretary Stanton, accepted by President Johnson, and published in the proclamation offering rewards for the arrest of Mr. Davis and others.

On any charge which might be brought against him, the President of the Confederate States eagerly sought trial; but upon just what charge he might be tried, and before what tribunal, and in what jurisdiction, had been questions of great perplexity to the government of the United States ever since his capture. Foreseeing some such situation, Mr. Lincoln had expressed the hope that the fugitive President of the dissolving Confederacy might escape, but Mr. Lincoln's murder had changed all that. Public and officials alike had clamored for his capture, his trial by summary process, and his prompt execution. "Hang Jeff Davis!" passed into popular song and speech. The quickest and the simplest way to that end, it seemed, was trial by such a military commission as had condemned the Booth conspirators and Mrs. Surratt.

But by autumn of 1865, Attorney General Speed, Chief Justice Chase and President Johnson had all come to the conclusion that there could be no trial of Mr. Davis on the main charge against him—high treason—before such a body. For a while longer, Secretary Stanton continued to urge that he be tried before military commission on charges of inciting the murder of President Lincoln, and responsibility for the deaths of Union prisoners of war by starvation and cruelty, while the Judge Advocate General continued to deal with, and to reward, one Conover, a perjurer, who professed to have proofs of the assassination charge. By May, 1867, however, no one believed longer in the tissue of suborned lies spun by Conover, or felt that Mr. Davis was behind the mad deed of Booth; nor did any responsible official believe that Mr. Davis could be convicted upon the "Andersonville" charges, as the obscure Major Wirz had been. He must be tried, if at all, on the charge of high treason, and before the courts of the United States, not a mere military commission—particularly after the decision of the Supreme Court in the Milligan case.

Accordingly, Mr. Davis was brought up the river to the Richmond which he had last quitted as the president of the Confederacy abandoning its capital, to stand before the court as the symbol of the Southern people. His trial had become, in their eyes, their trial; his guilt their guilt, his treatment their treatment.

Harshness in treatment of the prisoner had ended months before. On his return to Richmond he was technically in custody of General Burton, but was unguarded. He was accompanied by Mrs. Davis, by Burton Harrison, his former private secretary, who had done much to bring about this arraignment before the civil courts, and by one or two other old friends. At the wharf and all along the streets to the Spotswood Hotel, where he was to lodge, he was greeted by crowds whose joy was no less sincere because subdued. Saturday night and all day Sunday, throngs of old friends called, in what was almost a triumphal levee.

Monday morning, May 13, the prisoner of state went before the court. The district judge of the United States presiding was John C. Underwood, a wartime appointee who had held court in the restored state of Virginia, when Alexandria was the capital. In the exercise of his judicial office there he had confiscated the handsome home of a Confederate, ordered it sold, and had it bought in for himself, at a fraction of its value—a proceeding which the Supreme Court of the United States was afterward to reverse, and to declare "a blot upon our jurisprudence and civilization."

But in May, 1867, Judge Underwood was a power in Virginia. Before this judge, hated, feared and despised by the Conservatives of Virginia, Mr. Davis was to be brought. There was genuine apprehension that the judge might simply transfer him from the military confinement of the Fortress, which in time had been made comfortable in all but restraint of liberty, to confinement by the civil power in a felon's cell in the local jail. The courtroom was tense when General Burton, soldierly in full uniform, marched in with his tall, thin, erect prisoner and surrendered him into the custody of the United States marshal.

The district attorney, proceeding according to Attorney General Stanbery's instructions given in accordance with an agreement with Charles O'Conor of New York, chief of counsel for Mr. Davis, announced that the government was not ready to go to trial—as, indeed, it was not and never would be—whereupon motion was made that the prisoner be admitted to bail.

The decision of Judge Underwood was not predictable, but, after a moment of tense and painful anxiety, it came down:

"The case is undoubtedly bailable, and as the Government is not ready to proceed with the trial, and the prisoner is and for a long time has been ready and demanding trial—it seems eminently proper that bail should be allowed."

And then came a great moment of reconciliation of North and South, when there stepped forward, as first to sign the bond of one hundred thousand dollars, Horace Greeley, militant editor of the New York *Tribune*; followed by Augustus Schell, of New York, for himself and for his friend Cornelius Vanderbilt; Gerrit Smith, the devoted Abolitionist, friend and financial backer of John Brown of Ossawatomie; Benjamin Wood, of New York; A. Welsh and D. K. Jackson, of Philadelphia; and a dozen Southern sureties, including the redoubtable Virginia Unionist leader, John Minor Botts.

The wish of Abraham Lincoln, that in the peace there be no bloody work of hanging for treason, was to be fulfilled. The treason case against the President of the Confederacy was continued from time to time until December, 1868, when it came again before the Circuit Court of the United States, composed of Chief Justice Chase, in whose circuit Virginia lay, and District Judge Underwood, on motion to quash the indictment. The Chief Justice favored the motion to quash; Judge Underwood opposed it. The division of opinion was certified to the Supreme Court for decision, but, before action could be taken, the general amnesty proclamation of President Johnson, on Christmas Day, 1868, put an end to the prosecution. The case was nol-prossed in the court at Richmond in February, 1869; the prisoner was discharged; and the sureties on the famous bond which had been a binding tie of reunion between the sections were released from their obligations.

The release of Jefferson Davis was the most conspicuous, but by no means the only, evidence of Northern helpfulness toward the people of the "conquered provinces" whose government and institutions were being remade to order of the vindictives in Congress.

In February, 1867, while Congress was preparing to pass the Reconstruction Act, George F. Peabody, Massachusetts-born merchant of England, established the Peabody Fund, with a munificent gift of one million dollars, which was doubled two years later. The fund was to be used for "the educational needs of those portions of our beloved and common country which have suffered from the destructive ravages, and the not less disastrous consequences, of civil war."

The Peabody Fund, in the spirit in which it was established and administered, became a powerful agency for reconciliation. Its trustees included men of both the North and the South, among them General Grant, Admiral Farragut, Hamilton Fish of New York, William Aiken of South Carolina, William A. Graham of North Carolina and A. H. H. Stuart of Virginia. Its first agent and manager, Dr. Barnas Sears of Boston, one-time president of Brown University, followed the wise policy of using its resources for the advancement of the education of both races, through aid to the public-school systems in hundreds of towns and cities. Doctor Sears incurred the wrath of some of his more zealous Abolitionist neighbors by recognizing and supporting separate schools for white and colored children, rather than insisting upon mixed schools. He realized, however, that to insist upon mixed public schools in the South would have meant, in all probability, no public schools supported by local taxes.

Mixed schools never were countenanced by the whites in the South, nor by most of the blacks. In the first years after the war, however, there was far less of antagonism to Negro schools than there was to be later. Besides the plantation schools established by enlightened landowners for the children of their hands, there were regularly organized schools in the cities, privately supported, for Negro children, such as the Franklin Street School in Charleston, supported financially by the Episcopal Church, and recruiting its teaching staff among the white ladies of the city. Throughout the black belt states the same sort of thing was going on, in one fashion or another, while the public school boards in Southern cities, or such of them as had survived the war, began to make special provision for colored children. Many of these schools were taught by native whites. In South Carolina, in this period, about one-half of all the native whites who taught in the public schools were in schools for Negroes.

What with the small beginnings of public-school education for Negroes, the development of the Freedmen's Bureau schools, and the outpouring of Northern missionary effort in private schools, the Negro child promised to fare better, educationally, than the white. Not a few of the many schools established by private Northern generosity in the South were in every way worth while, and have served and survived until this day. Much of the effort, however, well-intentioned as it was, took no account of the realities of race relations or economic conditions in the South. Both in the aims and methods of the education which it sought to impart to the freedmen, and in its attitude toward the freedmen's white neighbors, it was misdirected.

All sorts of schoolteachers came south—some good and wise, moved by a genuine missionary zeal; others, impractical, opinionated zealots, blind to the truths of the life about them, or hunting for the satisfaction of the martyrdom which some obscure complex in them demanded. "Some very good people can be very trying," dryly observed Mrs. Avary.

The attitude of teachers of this sort toward their work and toward the peoples with whom they dealt was of a piece with that expressed by General John Pope, commanding the third district in the summer of 1867, to General Grant:

"It may safely be said that the marvelous progress made in the education of these people (the freedmen), aided by the noble charitable contributions of Northern societies and individuals, finds no parallel in the history of mankind. If continued, it must be by the same means, and if the masses of the white people exhibit the same indisposition to be educated that they do now, five years will have transferred intelligence and education, so far as the masses are concerned, to the colored people of this District."

While much of the education brought south to the freedmen was totally impractical, and some of it was positively harmful, a beginning was made in that form of education which the immediate circumstances of the freedmen seemed most to require. In the economy of a large slave plantation there was opportunity for the training and development of various industrial and agricultural skills. With the break up of the old plantation life, there was bound to develop an acute need for some other form of training in these skills. Talladega College, the first school for Negroes where industrial training was combined with general education, was founded by De Forrest in Alabama in 1867, to be followed by General Samuel Chapman Armstrong's Institute at Hampton, in Virginia, founded the following year. "An imitation of Northern models will not do," said General Armstrong. "Right methods of work in the South must be created, not copied." From Hampton, the ex-slave boy Booker T. Washington went to Alabama to found the most widely known of all schools of the type, Tuskegee Institute.

Howard University, at Washington, was established in 1867 by the Freedmen's Bureau, for whose chief it was named, while Atlanta University was founded by Edmund Ware, in the same year, as a co-educational school for Negroes. During the same period, still other schools which have continued to do valuable work in the training of Negro leaders were established, principally through the American Missionary Association. There were Tougaloo in Mississippi, Straight in New Orleans, Biddle at Charlotte, and others.

While new schools and colleges were being founded for the Negroes, and while the old colleges continued to struggle to re-establish themselves and their work for the white youth, one important Southern university was closed by military order. When a hot-headed student devoted his commencement address at the University of Georgia, in 1867, to an attack on the policy of Reconstruction in general, and the co-operative course of former Governor Joseph E. Brown in particular,

General Pope promptly closed the university and kept it closed until the following year.

Regardless of the trials of the present or the dark riddle of the future, the Confederate past was not to be forsworn or forgotten. The Memorial Days for decoration of the graves of soldier dead, Confederate and Union, which had been inaugurated spontaneously over the South in the first spring after the surrender, were observed generally in the second spring. During the year between, memorial associations had been at work, caring for Confederate graves in local cemeteries, or family burying grounds. Ladies' memorial associations, such as the ones formed at Vicksburg and Spotsylvania Courthouse, undertook the heavier duty of caring for the graves of all buried on or near the greater battlefields. In aid of such services of remembrance, legislatures of some of the former Confederate states made small appropriations for the care of the graves of soldiers of those states buried on the Virginia fields, while the legislature of Kentucky appropriated funds to bring home the bodies of its Confederate dead buried elsewhere.

In these evidences of continuing devotion to the heroisms of the war, some Southerners saw a chance to profit in pride or pocket. Of one such post-war patriot who offered a public lecture on "The Chivalry of the South as Illustrated in the War," the Hernando *People's Press* acidly observed that he "had exhibited it by keeping out of it."

But regardless of memories, regardless of the developing political situation, regardless of everything, there was work to do if the people would live—the plowing and the planting, the building and rebuilding that must have seemed endless and all but hopeless; the completion and extension of works interrupted by war; the founding of the new industries whose development was to play a part in the final recovery.

That the energies of the Southern people should be applied to develop Southern industries was the recommendation of General Lee, beginning to expand the curriculum of Washington College from the old conception of a strictly classical education to include such vocational training as law, engineering and even journalism.

General Richard Ewell, one of General Lee's corps commanders in the Army of Northern Virginia, farming at Spring Hill, in Tennessee, laid the small foundation of the chief dairy breed in the South, through the importation of two cows and a bull from the Island of Jersey in April, 1867. Landing in Baltimore, the animals traveled by rail to Pittsburgh, by steamboat to Cincinnati and thence to Nashville, and by rail again from Nashville to the Ewell farm.

The fertilizer industry in the South also had its small beginnings in the same year of 1867, with the discovery and first development of phosphate rock deposits of South Carolina. Three scientific men shared in the discovery of the fields—Dr. St. Julien Ravenel, who found the first specimens; Dr. N. A. Pratt, of Georgia, who analyzed the samples; and Professor F. S. Holmes, who suggested the site on the banks of the Ashley River where the first large deposits were found. Through their efforts, capital was enlisted and work started on what was to become a major Southern industry.

Before the end of the year, the Wando Manufacturing Company, formed by Carolina capital, and the larger Charleston Mining & Manufacturing Company, financed in Philadelphia, had made experimental shipments to the North. In the first year's operations a total of six tons of rock was mined, the first of the many millions of tons to be mined in South Carolina, Florida and Tennessee. Within another year, solid schooner-loads were being shipped North for treatment with sulphuric acid, and prospectors were locating the workable beds, which lay in a belt ten to twenty miles inshore, extending some seventy miles from the Wando River on the north to the Broad on the south.

Deposits lay not only under the land but also under the beds of navigable coastal rivers, which were the property of the state of South Carolina. Various companies were granted the right, by the state, to engage in "river mining" in the stream beds, upon the payment of royalty of one dollar a ton. "Land mining" did not call for payment of royalty to the state, but it required the removal of several feet of earth above the phosphate rock with the primitive tools of the time, an operation decidedly more difficult and expensive than dredging the rock from the beds of the rivers.

Shipment of the raw rock to the North for treatment with sulphuric acid to make it usable as fertilizer was soon replaced by treatment in Charleston with acid brought down from the North, and later with acid manufactured there from raw sulphur imported from Sicily.

Reviving trade between the South and the rest of the world called for the restoration of steamship services from Southern ports. Before the end of 1867, such connections had been established between Savannah and Charleston, on the one hand, and New York, Philadelphia, Baltimore and Liverpool, on the other.

From Louisville and St. Louis, also, "fast freight" lines were established early in 1867 to handle freight into the South in through cars, moving over several railroads without breaking bulk. One such line, known as the "Green Line" because of the stripe of paint of that color on the cars assigned to its service, reached the South Atlantic states by way of Nashville and Atlanta. In the first year of its operation it carried 8,874 barrels of "provisions," beef, pork and lard; in the second year, 16,265 barrels. Another such line, from Louisville to Mississippi, New Orleans and Mobile, by way of Humboldt, Tennessee, announced a schedule of three-and-one-half days, without breaking bulk, from the Ohio River to the Gulf of Mexico. From Louisville, too, ran a daily line of through sleeping cars to New Orleans, by way of Humboldt, Jackson, Tennessee, and Jackson, Mississippi.

Grouping of separate small railroad lines into larger systems was beginning also. In North Carolina, strenuous but unsuccessful efforts were under way to bring into one system the four railroads in which the state had a large interest. In Virginia, in April, 1867, four small railroads in southside and southwest Virginia were brought together, under the leadership of General William Mahone, and with the aid of Governor Pierpont, into the Atlantic, Mississippi & Ohio Railroad, a through line from Norfolk to Bristol.

The process of rebuilding ruined railroads and completing those which war had left unfinished was still far from complete. The Mobile & Ohio, which had stopped at Columbus, Kentucky, at the time of the war, was being built on, in 1867, to its original goal of the Ohio River. The Memphis & Little Rock, halted by war at the White River, was being built from both ends toward the middle, slowly, because of lack of capital. The Selma & Dalton, started during the war and built as far as Blue Mountain, Alabama, was under construction toward Rome and Dalton, in Georgia.

In Alabama, also, the South & North Alabama was being built from Montgomery into the mountainous and mineral regions to the north. Through acts passed by the restoration legislatures, both Alabama and Georgia were offering state aid to encourage the building of railroads which all agreed were a prime necessity for revival of industry and agriculture. Usually this aid was to be accomplished by lending the credit of the state, through issue of its bonds to the extent of some specified sum for each mile of road completed—twelve thousand dollars in the case of Alabama. The state's investment was to be protected, usually, by a first lien on the property of the railroads built with its aid. The plan itself was sound and workable when properly administered, but laxities and frauds in its execution during the days that were to come led to some of the worst abuses of Reconstruction.

In all this work of starting new industries and salvaging old, and of

raising the crops on which all alike depended, increasing labor difficulties were to be met, as well as the obstacles of lack of finance.
Progress had been made since 1865 in the work of building a new
labor system for the South, even though employers continued to
complain of the gadding about of their help, or of the frequent all-
night religious revivals, which, as one provoked planter remarked, "impaired industry to an alarming extent without improving morality."
But in the summer of 1867, the excitements and diversions of the new
dispensation created new distractions.

The business of getting registered, and of getting organized politically, was so great a hindrance to the needs of industry that General
Sickles, commanding in the Carolinas, ordered registration activities
suspended until after the crops were "laid by" in August. In Tennessee, the new assistant commissioner of the Freedmen's Bureau,
General W. P. Carlin, came to the conclusion, in May, that much
unnecessary idleness and excitement among his charges was due to the
incitement of Radical political agitators, and issued an order to the
personnel of the Bureau that they should not use their official positions to secure the nomination and election of candidates to office, an
order to which the local Radicals objected violently. In August he
found it necessary to order that those who had been offered work
and had refused it should no longer be carried on the Bureau's relief
rolls.

At the August elections in Tennessee, the Negroes voted for the first
time in the South, in any major or general election, as a result of the
action of the state legislature taken in February. The campaign,
carried on while only the preliminaries of registration were under
way in the other former Confederate States, was between Governor
Brownlow, candidate for re-election, and Emerson Etheridge, an
outspoken West Tennessee Unionist leader, nominated by the Conservative Republicans. Etheridge received almost as many votes as
Brownlow had received in the election of 1865, but the Brownlow
vote shot up from the 1865 figure of 23,353 to 74,484.

Such a result the Conservatives ascribed to the enlargement of the
electorate through the Negro-Suffrage Act, and to the completeness
of the Radical control of the machinery of election—both portents of
what was to be expected, said the Conservatives, when freedmen in
other of the former Confederate States should receive full rights of
suffrage as the gift of the government, through its Reconstruction
Act.

CHAPTER XXVIII

"Loyalty Must Govern"

CONGRESS was in session, off and on, through the whole year of 1867, determined to see that all went well in the process of political revolution which it had decreed.

The first hitch in the process, the inaction of the civil governments of the Johnson states, was overcome by the prompt passage, on March 23, during the first extra session of the Fortieth Congress, of the first Supplemental Reconstruction Act, transferring the initiative to the hands of the district commanders.

But as the district commanders got into their work they found perplexing problems in the interpretation and administration of the law. Not many of these problems related to the status of the freedmen. All of suitable age, or appearing to be so, were admitted to the registration rolls as a matter of course. They were, as Professor Fleming put it, looked upon as "voters ex *colore*," while collateral questions, such as the right to sit on juries during the period of transition, were usually solved by some such orders as those of General Pope in the third district, General Canby in the second, or General Mower in the fifth, that the fact of registration made freedmen eligible for such service, regardless of what the existing constitutions of the states might say on the subject.

The really difficult questions had to do with the political status of whites of varying shades and degrees of "loyalty," and with the powers of administration and government of the district commanders, in the interim before the new reconstructed state governments should be set up and in operation. On these questions, the generals in charge asked instructions. The President referred the matter to the chief law officer of the government, Attorney General Henry Stanbery, for an interpretation of the acts.

Two opinions were rendered by the Attorney General. The first, on May 24, held that an applicant was entitled to registration as a voter upon taking the oath prescribed in the act, and that the board of registration had no power to go behind the oath and inquire as to its truth or falsity.

The second opinion, on June 12, held that the acts did not make the existing civil governments in the states entirely subservient to the military, and that the generals commanding did not have the power to remove and replace civil officers at will.

Before making either opinion public, the President submitted both to the judgment of his Cabinet at a meeting on June 18, and asked their advice on the main questions involved. The entire Cabinet, except Secretary Stanton, agreed that under the two acts then on the books, taking the oath was conclusive as to the right of an applicant to be registered; that the registrars could not take testimony to go behind the applicant's oath; that the right to register and vote was not forfeited by "participation in rebellion alone"; that disfranchisement was to be imposed only upon those who, having held an office which required the taking of an oath to support the Constitution of the United States, had thereafter participated in rebellion; that the offices whose holding would work disfranchisement did not include mere ministerial government positions; and that aid to the rebellion which was conscripted or involuntary did not work disfranchisement.

The effect of the opinion of the Attorney General and the Cabinet, of course, was to lessen greatly the extent of white disfranchisement in the South, as compared with what the Radicals thought they had written into the law. Instructions in accord with this strict, but sound, interpretation of the language of the Reconstruction Acts were issued to all district commanders on June 20, to remain in force only until Congress had a chance to revise its acts again, at its second extra session of the year, which convened on July 3.

On July 19, the Congress completed the work of passing, and repassing over the President's veto, its second Supplemental Reconstruction Act, intended to establish clearly and to make more rigid the Radical interpretation of the preceding legislation. The new act gave the registration officers express power to go behind the oath of an applicant for registration; denied registration to those who claimed the right solely because of presidential pardon or amnesty; required all who would be registered to take the iron-clad oath covering conduct in the past, rather than the oath of future loyalty which was all that Lincoln required; and directed a thoroughgoing purge of the registration lists to remove all those already registered who could not comply with these new and more restrictive requirements.

On the administrative side, the new act undertook to put all power in the War Department, free of control by the civil arm of the government. It confirmed the power of administration in the general of the Armies, rather than the president; gave express power to the district commanders to remove civil officers, subject to the approval of the general of the Armies; confirmed all removals previously made; and provided that no military officer engaged in the work of Reconstruction should be bound by the opinion of any civil officer of the government.

After the passage of the act of July 19, there was no longer any doubt as to the congressional intent, the sufficiency of the language used to express that intent, or the spirit in which it was to be executed. Congress claimed the power, and proposed to exercise it, to reduce the executive arm of the government to impotence in the work of erecting new states in the territories of the old. "Rebel" participation in that process, moreover, was to be held to the narrowest limits. "Loyalty," said Schuyler Colfax, speaker of the House of Representatives, "must govern what loyalty has preserved."

There was even the possibility that Congress might undertake to extend its Reconstruction operations to states which never had been out of the Union. Of the four former slaveholding states which did not secede, only Missouri had fallen in with the Radical program. Delaware, Maryland and Kentucky overwhelmingly rejected the Fourteenth Amendment in the early months of 1867. Maryland in May added the further offense, in Radical eyes, of adopting a new state constitution which restored the vote to ex-Confederates, an earnest of the overwhelming Democratic victory in the state which was to come the next year.

But it was Kentucky which really aroused the rage of the Radicals, when, on May 4, the state overwhelmingly elected a straight Democratic ticket of nine representatives to sit in the Fortieth Congress. Kentucky, said the Cincinnati Commercial, had "gone overwhelmingly for the rebels. . . . Kentucky is today as effectively in the hands of the rebels as if they had every town and city garrisoned by their troops."

Like protests from local Radicals, and those on the borders who had an interest in Kentucky affairs, led to two immediate results. On July 3, when Congress reconvened, the House of Representatives refused to seat the nine Democrats elected by Kentucky, on the ground that the "loyal voters . . . had been overawed and prevented from a true expression of their will and choice at the polls by those who have sympathized with or actually participated in the late rebellion." General

John A. Logan, whose early doubts on his course had resolved themselves into a most intense form of Radicalism, expressed the attitude of the House:

"The only reason Kentucky was not in the rebellion was because it was too close to the border and was afraid to be, for in the hearts of a majority of its people treason rankled as it did in the hearts of the people of South Carolina."

Senator Sumner, feeling that "nothing can be more certain than that Kentucky, at this time, is without a republican form of government," proposed in a speech in the Senate, on July 5, to remedy that lack by applying the process of Reconstruction to a state fully and undeniably in the Union.

'Kentucky needs reconstruction, and it is our duty to provide it. Put her on an equality with the Rebel States. Let her colored citizens enjoy the full-blown rights of citizens, and let the white Unionists there have the protection of their votes. You sent muskets once; send votes now."

Senator Sumner's speech was but part of the movement to make Kentucky the "Sixth Military District," as the Cincinnati *Gazette* put it. The movement went so far that the House of Representatives, on July 15, instructed its Judiciary Committee to inquire whether the states of Kentucky, Maryland and Delaware had a republican form of government of the sort which the United States is required to guarantee in each state.

Kentucky, at the time, was in the midst of a campaign to name a governor and other state officials at the regular election in August. The effect of the refusal to admit the state's duly elected representatives to Congress, the threats to put the state under military rule, and the slurs upon the patriotism and courage of a people which had put more soldiers in the Union army than had many of the states in the North, was to confirm and intensify the people in the sentiments engendered by their mistreatment at the hands of the central government.

The state's answer to what the Kentucky *Yeoman* called the "outrage perpetrated upon the right of representation" was not submission to threats, but the triumphant election of the Democratic candidate for governor, John L. Helm, with a vote which more than doubled that of his Radical and Conservative Republican opponents combined. Governor Helm, who had served in the same office before the war, was an original secessionist and the father of General Ben Hardin Helm, who had met death at the head of the Orphan Brigade of Kentucky Confederates. Every candidate on the successful Democratic ticket, except the nominee for governor and one other, had served in the Confederate forces.

Such a result in a state where Radicals had been supreme as long as the army controlled, could not fail to bring renewed and still more vigorous demands for military Reconstruction of the state which the Cincinnati Commercial described as "reliable, rebel old Kentucky, the pride and joy of every traitor from the Ohio to the Gulf." Local Radicals circulated petitions to Congress, praying that the state be put under military rule, while Joseph Holt, the Judge Advocate General and a Kentuckian, tried to get the Judiciary Committee of the House to come to the state, hold hearings and recommend Reconstruction. "Why should Congress treat Kentucky different from any rebel state?" demanded Sam McKee, one of the candidates for Congress defeated at the May election, who was afterward to be seated by the Radicals.

Garret Davis, United States senator from Kentucky, whose staunch Unionism during the trying days of the war did not prevent him from outspoken objection to the policy pursued toward the state, denounced the local politicians fostering the proposed Reconstruction of Kentucky as "treasury rats," chronic office-seekers who "have not the ability, character and popularity to obtain office and salary by popular suffrage, who hovered upon the skirts of the army during the war, and wish that army to be organized again so that they may still feed and fatten upon its offal."

The complaints of these local politicians, and the pressure of Radical demands, had enough influence with the House of Representatives to keep Kentucky unrepresented in the summer session of 1867, except for the admission, two days before the end of the session, of Major G. M. Adams, who had served during the war with the Union Army. Not until December were six other Democrats—Proctor Knott, James B. Beck, Asa P. Grover, Thomas L. Jones, J. S. Golladay and L. S. Trimble—admitted. Sam McKee, Radical, shown to have been defeated by fifteen hundred votes on the face of the returns, was seated also. John Young Brown, Democrat, whom the returns showed to have been elected by six thousand majority, and who was conceded to be the choice of the voters of his district, was denied his seat on the ground that he had given aid and countenance to the Confederacy. Governor Stevenson denied the right of Congress to exclude representatives on such grounds, refused to call another election to fill the vacancy and left the sixth district unrepresented throughout the life of the Congress.

Kentucky's final word on the subject—unless the later election of John Young Brown to Congress and as governor might be so called— was expressed in the resolution of the state legislature, at its next session, that

"If this Congress may apply, through an oath of office, a test of present or past political sentiments, another Congress, controlled by the devotees of the Grand Army of the Republic, may require that each member shall swear to having actually served a specified term in the army or the navy . . . We do most solemnly and earnestly protest against such action, which if persisted in, and established as the policy of the government, will render the elective franchise a farce and what we have been taught to regard a constitutional liberty but a solemn mockery."

While the Radicals might denounce Kentucky as much as they wished, and might arbitrarily keep out her elected representatives, the elections in that state were, in truth, but one indication of reaction in the loyal states against the vindictive policy pursued by the majority in Congress. Northern states which had voted with the Radicals in the general election of 1866 began to go Democratic in the off-year elections of 1867. The popular General Rutherford B. Hayes, Republican, was elected governor of Ohio by less than three thousand majority, but with a Democratic legislature, and a majority of more than fifty thousand against the proposed amendment for Negro suffrage by state action. Kansas and Minnesota likewise voted against Negro suffrage in their state constitutions. Pennsylvania and California went Democratic, by small majorities, and New York by nearly fifty thousand. Conservative victory in Connecticut caused one intensely Radical editor to dub the state, "Backsliding Connecticut."

But in the off-year election results of 1867, there was a clear indication of a practical way to meet this threat of future Democratic success which, to convinced Radicals, meant no less than the triumph of treason. The contrast between the results in Kentucky and Tennessee was illuminating. The two states were generally similar in topography, economics and population. Even in the days when Henry Clay, in the one state, and Andrew Jackson, in the other, led opposing parties, the states had shown a striking tendency to vote alike. At the elections in August, however, the Radicals won in Tennessee, by two votes to one, while in Kentucky they were defeated by about the same ratio. In Kentucky, Negroes did not vote; in Tennessee, they did. Tennessee was the only state in the Union, with any considerable colored population, which had Negro suffrage in 1867. But there were ten other states in the South, most of them with a larger proportion of colored population than Tennessee, which could, with proper haste and attention to detail, be restored to representation in Congress and the Electoral College before the 1868 elections—and restored with Negro suffrage. No lesson of politics could have been clearer. The South was the place to find the new voters needed to overbalance threatened defections elsewhere; and completion of the process of Reconstruction was the way to find them. Even those, such as Thaddeus Stevens, who had originally favored a long period of military government as a punishment for the South, saw the practical advantages, even the necessity, of haste.

The process of making these new voters was turned over completely to the War Department, free of interference by civil officers, by the act of July 19. The head of that department, Secretary Stanton, was the representative of the Radicals of Congress in the inner councils of the President. Congress had sought to protect him in that position by the passage, on March 2, of the Tenure of Office Act, which provided that the Secretary of War and other Cabinet officers should "hold their offices respectively for and during the term of the President by whom they may have been appointed, and for one month thereafter, subject to removal by and with the advice and consent of the Senate."

For more than a year the President's wisest and most disinterested advisers had urged upon him the necessity of getting Stanton out of the confidential relationship of a Cabinet minister. Many suspected, but no one knew then, what is now known of the tortuous course of double-dealing upon which Stanton embarked after the assassination of Lincoln. The President hesitated to act. Just after Congress adjourned its summer session, however, on July 20, the President learned that his own Secretary of War had drafted for the Radicals the second Supplemental Reconstruction Act, which had for its purpose the impairment of the proper constitutional powers of the Chief Executive of the United States, and the personal humiliation of the man who held the office.

The President's patience was almost at the breaking point. On

August 1 he prepared, but did not send, a letter to the Secretary of War, calling for his resignation because of "public considerations of a high character." At a Cabinet meeting that day, after Stanton had taken his departure, the President discussed the matter with the remaining members. There was division of opinion, not as to the desirability of being rid of Stanton, but as to the policy of removing him at that late date. Action was reserved.

On the same day, however, a chance question of a lawyer arguing for the defense in the trial of John H. Surratt, then in progress in Washington, brought on the final provocation of the President to action.

John Surratt, escaping from Washington on the night of the murder of Lincoln, had made his way to Rome, to seek refuge by enlistment, under an assumed name, in the Papal Guard. There he had been recognized, had escaped again to Egypt, whence, after a long delay due to the seeming reluctance of the American authorities to seek his extradition, he had been brought back to the United States to stand trial for complicity in the plot to murder President Lincoln. John Surratt was not to be tried before a military commission, as his mother had been, for in the meanwhile the Supreme Court had decided the Milligan case. After six weeks of trial in a court of the District of Columbia, the case reached the stage of argument at the end of July.

In argument, lawyers for the defense taunted the prosecution for its failure to put in evidence the record of conviction of those alleged to be Surratt's fellow conspirators. "Why didn't you bring it in?" ran the question. "Did you find at the end . . . a recommendation of mercy . . . that the President never saw?" It was a shot in the dark, but it struck true. On August 3, the chief counsel for the government, having consulted with Judge Advocate General Holt, produced the record and accused the President of having signed the warrant for Mrs. Surratt's death with the recommendation of the commission for mercy "right before his eyes." "And there it is," he concluded dramatically.

The newspaper accounts of this development, coming to the President on the morning of Sunday, August 4, were the first intimation he had had of the duplicity practiced upon him two years before by the Judge Advocate General, undoubtedly with the knowledge and approval of his chief, the Secretary of War. On Monday morning, the fifth, the outraged President acted at last, and sent the note demanding Stanton's resignation.

To most of the Cabinet group it was inconceivable that a minister should refuse such a request; but Stanton, convinced of his mission to save the nation, had no slightest intention of resigning. On the following day he wrote the President: "Public considerations of a high character, which alone have induced me to continue at the head of this department, constrain me not to resign the office of Secretary of War before the next meeting of Congress."

There the matter stood for a week, while the President consulted with his advisers, and particularly with General Grant, whom he wished to have act as Secretary of War *ad interim*. On Sunday, August 11, the General of the Armies agreed to hold the position until the President should make a permanent appointment. On Monday morning, the President notified Stanton of his suspension from office, and directed that the business of the department be transferred to General Grant, as *ad interim* Secretary. At the same time, he advised Grant of his appointment, after which Grant notified Stanton that he had accepted the "assignment." Stanton notified both his successor and the President that he yielded the office only because he had "no alternative but to submit to superior force."

Stanton's suspension in no wise impeded the execution of the Reconstruction Acts, nor was it intended to do so. General Grant, already in direct charge of the process, simply took on additional and larger duties as acting Secretary of War, and the process of registration and election went on without interference.

After Stanton's removal, however, the President did exercise his constitutional power as commander-in-chief of the army by transferring the generals in charge of the fifth and second military districts to other commands, and replacing them with men in whom he had greater confidence.

The first of the generals to be removed was Philip Sheridan, Grant's particular friend and protégé, in charge of the fifth district. The course of Reconstruction in that district, Louisiana and Texas, had been turbulent from the beginning. The fiery and impetuous Sheridan, in command, was suspected by many, North and South, of intent to make a bid for Radical support for the Presidency by the vigor and dramatic dash of his administration of affairs. His removals from office began in April, almost as soon as his administration. Before his own removal from command, the list of civil officials displaced by him included the aldermen and levee commissioners of New Orleans, the Mayor of that city, the Attorney General of the state, and, finally, on June 3, the Governor of the state, Madison Wells, whose course in office General Sheridan described as being "as sinuous as the marks left in the dust by the movement of a snake." So many of the Conservatives of Louisiana had come by that time to entertain the same sort of opinion of Governor Wells that his removal did not excite the indignation which might otherwise have followed. "All's well that ends Wells," quipped the New Orleans *Times*. To be governor, in name at least, the General chose first Thomas J. Durant, who declined, and then Benjamin F. Flanders, at that time a treasury agent in New Orleans. To some of the other places vacated, he named capable business men; to others, local Radical hacks and representatives of the rising class of Negro politicians in the state.

General Sheridan's impetuous methods of removal were applied to the Texas portion of his domain as well. On July 30, alleging that the elected Governor Throckmorton was an "impediment" to Reconstruction, he removed him from office and put in his stead former Governor E. M. Pease, the man whom Throckmorton had defeated in the restoration election of 1866. Retiring with dignity, Throckmorton issued an address reciting his difficulties with the military, which had been considerable and almost continuous, but urging the people to register, vote for a convention, and elect as delegates to it good sound Union men, as the surest road to peace and eventual true Reconstruction.

General Sheridan was one of the popular heroes of the North, the subject of school-boy declamation. To remove him was doubtless impolitic, but the President, exasperated by his indiscretion, if not insubordination, in the publication of inflammatory dispatches to the War Department, and by the general tenor of his administration, relieved him of command on August 17, and ordered him to command of the department of the Missouri. On September 5, General Sheridan left New Orleans for a triumphal progress up the river to St. Louis, while Radical organs continued to berate the President for his removal.

To succeed him in command of the fifth district, the President first named General George H. Thomas. When it developed that Thomas was unable to serve on account of his health, the President named General Winfield S. Hancock, who did not arrive at his post in New Orleans until November 29. In the meanwhile, General Charles Griffin held the command until September 15, when he died of yellow fever at Galveston, and was succeeded by General Joseph A. Mower.

The removal of General Daniel E. Sickles, in command of the second district, composed of North and South Carolina, was principally due to conflict with the Federal judiciary. General Sickles, who had been a lawyer, was active in intervention in matters of legal process throughout his administration. Among other steps, in his General Order No. 10, he had established a "stay law" in both states under his command for certain classes of debtors. At that time only the state courts were open and functioning in the Carolinas. In June, 1867, however, Chief Justice Chase joined with the Federal judge in North Carolina in holding a term of the United States Circuit Court at Raleigh. At that term of court an execution issued, in favor of a creditor residing in another state, against a North Carolina debtor. The United States marshal, acting under the execution, sought to sell property at Wilmington to satisfy the debt. The local commander there, acting under General Sickles' general stay order, refused to allow the sale, and was sustained by his commander.

There was, then, a direct conflict not between state and Reconstruction powers but between the process of a United States court and the orders of a United States military commander. The Attorney General of the United States moved to protect the judicial process by obtaining an indictment against General Sickles for obstructing its execution. In the midst of angry correspondence, the President settled the matter, on August 26, by ordering General Sickles to be transferred, and replaced by General E. R. S. Canby, who took command on February 5.

The President's action in the case of General Sickles was not due to his general administration of affairs in the states in his charge, which had been satisfactory in the main, but to his conflict with other departments of the United States government. Regardless of that, it added another count to the Radical indictment of the President. Their view of the whole process of Reconstruction was correctly expressed by General Sickles, when he wrote General Grant that he did not "believe that processes of the courts of the United States should override the orders Congress has empowered me to make for the execution of its measures." To that view, that even casual military orders issued in furtherance of the congressional policy of Reconstruction should prevail against the civil executive or judicial arms of the government, the Radicals heartily subscribed.

The course of President Johnson, on the other hand, throughout Reconstruction, was to execute laws passed by Congress according to his rigid sense of duty, but, at the same time, to seek proper means of bringing these laws before the courts of the land for judicial review of their constitutionality. The means must, however, be proper. When the state of Mississippi, in April, sought to enjoin the President of the United States from executing the Reconstruction Acts, he directed his Attorney General to appear before the court in opposition, on the ground, which the court later adopted in its decision, that the President of the United States could not be enjoined where only political questions were involved directly, and not rights of person and property.

Before Congress reconvened on November 21, however, a new case arose in Mississippi, which promised to bring before the Supreme Court the constitutionality of the whole scheme of Reconstruction, through judicial determination of the right to liberty of W. H. McCardle, former Confederate colonel and then editor of the Vicksburg *Times*. Colonel McCardle, free and unrestrained in his criticism of military Reconstruction in Mississippi, was arrested by order of General Ord on November 13, and imprisoned for trial by a military commission on charges of impeding Reconstruction and inciting the whites to resistance. The prisoner appealed to Judge Robert A. Hill for a writ of habeas corpus to bring himself and his case before the United States Circuit Court. The writ was granted, the case heard, the conviction sustained, and the prisoner remanded to the military. From the action of the Circuit Court, under the statute then in force, appeals in such cases lay directly to the Supreme Court of the United States.

Here, it seemed, was to be a clean-cut issue of the liberty of a citizen, not an abstract question of political administration. If the Reconstruction Acts were in accord with the Constitution and valid, editor McCardle belonged in jail. If the Acts were contrary to the Constitution, and invalid, editor McCardle belonged at large. It was, clearly, such a case as comes within the judicial province, and as such it was to become most perturbing to the Radicals whose confidence in the practical advantage of their course was greater than their confidence in its constitutionality.

CHAPTER XXIX

A Season of Politics

NEITHER removals of officers nor doubts as to the constitutionality checked the progress of Reconstruction in the South. Registration was completed in all states by October, and the first election on the question of holding a constitutional convention had been held, in Louisiana, on September 27 and 28. Before Congress reassembled, on November 21, 1867, elections had been held in every state but Texas, and the first of the constitutional conventions, that in Alabama, was already in session, while dates had been set for the others in that month and in December and January.

To the new voters, the whole period of registration, campaigns and elections was a season of eager excitement and wonder. The Conservative whites, however, were of many minds on the subject. Many were disfranchised; others, who could vote, were hopeless of the result or scornful of the whole business; others were for obstruction of the process by every means permitted; still others were for making the best of the thing by co-operating with sensible white Republicans, or with the new colored voters.

Perhaps the most persistent and promising efforts toward co-operation were made in Virginia, where such Republicans as Governor Pierpont and John Minor Botts, incensed at the Hunnicutt leadership and tactics, called a convention at Charlottesville to form a Conservative Republican party in the state. Northern leaders who feared the results of the threatened split in the newly organized party, intervened through the Union Leagues of Philadelphia, New York and Boston, and secured a conference which arranged for a new convention of all factions, to meet in Richmond on August 1. A "co-operators" convention at Charlottesville selected delegates to the Richmond meeting, as part of the movement for common action among Conservatives of all parties, principally sponsored by the Richmond Whig.

The convention called to reorganize the Virginia Republicans assembled on August 1, at the African Church in Richmond. Freedmen gathered about the church in the early morning hours, poured in as soon as the doors were opened at eleven o'clock, took possession,

261

effectively blocked the entrance of the Botts element and the co-operators' delegates, and, along with some fifty white delegates to the April meeting held a tumultuous mass convention, which refused to hear Mr. Botts and listened to incendiary harangues by the Reverend Hunnicutt—scenes which were more or less repeated outside the church, in near-by Capitol Square, where John Hawxhurst addressed a milling mass of freedmen. "Co-operation" in Virginia was over. The Richmond *Whig* sorrowfully noted that there were but two tickets now, "the run-mad radical and the conservative."

In South Carolina, where there was no such large element of responsible Republicans as were to be found in Virginia, the attempted co-operation took a different turn. Supported by the great name and influence of Hampton, strenuous efforts were made by Conservative whites for an alliance with the new electors, through joint political rallies, with processions and free barbecues, and speeches on the true interest of the freedmen in the coming election, all to no real avail.

Even while the movement lasted, there were white leaders who denounced it and urged a straight-out fight to defeat the constitutional convention, and remain under military rule. Finally, a week before the election in October, the "co-operators" movement came to its end when Moderate whites, meeting at Columbia, with General James Chesnut, Jr., as president, and Governor Perry and General Hampton as vice-presidents, resolved that the Reconstruction Acts and all things done under them were illegal, and urged the white people of the state to stay out of the election entirely.

According to the Reconstruction Acts, any state in which a majority of the registered voters did not participate in the election on the question of holding a constitutional convention was to remain under military rule. This clause in the act, apparently intended to be in some fashion a punishment for recalcitrants, was seized upon in the South as a way to escape the Reconstruction governments. Benjamin H. Hill, one-time Whig congressman from Georgia and later one of the youngest of the senators of the Confederacy, outlined the plan and policy in his "Notes on the Situation," the publication of which began in the Augusta *Chronicle* on June 19. Every white man who could do so, it was urged, should register, since registration involved no commitments, no implication of consent to Reconstruction, but no white man should vote, in the hope that the total vote cast would be less than half the number registered.

This device became the reliance, in all states, of those who counseled united action to obstruct Reconstruction. "Who cares for such repre sentation as will be foisted upon the people under its operation?" queried Herschel V. Johnson, who had joined with Alexander Stephens in leading the fight against secession in 1861. Like many others, Mr. Johnson felt that the whole scheme of Reconstruction was without warrant or authority in the Constitution, and would be so declared if ever it could be placed properly before the Supreme Court. The elections to be held, he believed, were mere catches to get the people to give some sort of consent, with the idea that such an appearance of consent, no matter how obtained, could be used to cure the constitutional defects of the whole scheme.

Most of the efforts of the whites in the Southern states to obstruct or mitigate Reconstruction, at least during the preliminary period of military rule, were carried out under the designation of "Conservative," which seems to have been first used in that sense, in the call of General James H. Clanton, of Alabama, on July 23, for the "Conservatives" of that state to meet in convention in Montgomery on September 4. General Clanton, an original anti-secession Whig who had fought for the Confederacy, used the name as one broad enough to include all men, Democrat or Whig, black or white.

When the convention met on September 4, it included all those elements. There were even Negro Conservatives, subject as they were to proscriptive pressure from the more radical of their own race. One of these Negroes, Wade Potter, had to be rescued from a Negro Radical mob by the boldness of General Clanton himself. The convention heard J. L. Williams, chairman of a colored "Special Committee on the Situation," before adopting resolutions which called for peace, education of the Negro, and local control of the suffrage.

In Mississippi there was more than the usual division of sentiment as to the policy to be adopted by the whites. A convention of "Constitutional Union men," meeting in Jackson on October 15, urged that the whites abstain from electing delegates to the convention. Another, and probably stronger party, backed by Senator Albert G. Brown, Judge John C. W. Watson, Judge William Yerger, General Barksdale and others, advised that the whites should take part and do the best they could. General J. L. Alcorn, a former Whig who had opposed secession but had "gone with the state" after it was an accomplished fact, went even further. He proposed that the whites of Mississippi should "open negotiations" with the national Republican party, since the national Democratic party, as he believed, could do nothing for Mississippi.

While the Conservatives might differ as to their proper course toward registration and voting under the Reconstruction Acts, there was no such division among the new voters and their Radical political friends. They might disagree as to whom they were to vote for, but there was no disagreement that all should register and all should vote. Organization to that end began early, and continued throughout the season of the campaign.

The "Union" convention of Arkansas met in Little Rock, as early as April 2, to organize what was to become the regular Republican party in that state. Besides resolutions of the sort calculated to stir political animosity, a regular state committee of fourteen members was set up, and organization of Loyal or Union Leagues in every voting precinct in the state was urged as the best means of bringing out the full strength of the party.

On May 7, the Republican Union party organized at Charleston, in South Carolina, and called a convention to meet in Columbia on July 25. Seventy delegates, representing nineteen counties, appeared at that convention. Among the leaders was Thomas J. Robertson, a South Carolinian of prominence who favored a platform "broad enough to accommodate the human race." The other leaders were Northern men, of both races. One of them, R. H. Gleaves, an intelligent mulatto who had come to South Carolina from Pennsylvania in 1866, was president of the gathering, which set up a central committee and, likewise, confided to the Union Leagues most of the real work of organization.

In North Carolina, also, Northern men took the lead in the organization of the state Republican party. General Abbott, of Wilmington, was president of the convention in September; Governor Holden, chairman of the state executive committee which it created. There was no effort to attract to the party the old leaders of the state but, instead, a discernible intent to keep the affair in the hands of those in control. Old Daniel Goodloe declared that the new organization was a "preposterous abortion" for the purpose of parceling out offices among the controlling "Ring." For that, and for his opposition in general, he was read out of the party by Holden. Declarations looking toward confiscation and division of lands, were found to be so far ahead of even Radical sentiment in the state that a special meeting of the state executive committee, later in the month, had to tone them down.

Among the Radical Republicans in Louisiana, however, there was not even that much of a disposition to regard prevailing white local sentiment. At their convention, in August, they declared for "perfect equality" between the races, division of offices on an equal basis, no limit to the enfranchisement of the loyal and complete disfranchisement of rebels; division of lands; and equality in schools. This convention, representing the extreme faction in Louisiana, was a symptom of the split in the Radical ranks which already was developing.

In Mississippi, the Republican party was organized on September 10, at Jackson, by a convention in which one-third of the delegates were freedmen and another third Bureau agents, registrars and others appointed to carry out the preliminaries of Reconstruction.

In Texas, in October, a sharp factional fight broke out among the Republicans right from the start. One faction, the *ab initio* Radicals, who stuck to the doctrinaire position that everything done in the name of government in Texas since March, 1861, was void, were led by Morgan Hamilton, brother of Andrew Jackson Hamilton, whom Andrew Johnson had made provisional governor in 1865. "Colossal Jack" himself, who also had become a Radical, led the wing which supported the more moderate course of Governor Pease.

The first summer of Reconstruction in Florida, according to report of the assistant commissioner of the Freedmen's Bureau, was a period of "politics and public meetings," during which measures were taken for the "quiet instruction of the freedmen in their rights and duties under the Reconstruction Acts." The quietness was somewhat flawed, however, by the early development of a three-way factional split among the Republicans, who had a handsome majority of the total registration. Colonel O. B. Hart, a native Union man, led the more conservative faction. Colonel T. W. Osborn, of New Jersey and the Freedmen's Bureau, led a second wing, based largely on the Lincoln Brotherhood, of which he was state master. The "Mule Team" faction, most radical of all, was led by Liberty Billings, late of New Hampshire and possessor of a fervid style of Old Testament invective, who had come south as an officer of a Negro regiment during the war. Associated with him were Daniel Richards, of Illinois, and William U. Saunders, Negro, of Maryland.

But regardless of organizations of parties or factions, the elections held in the autumn of 1867 all came to about the same result. In every case, a majority of the registered electorate voted, although in some cases, it was a very narrow majority; a huge majority of the votes cast were for "The Convention," as the question was put; and heavy Radical majorities were elected to membership in the conventions. That the results of Reconstruction would be pleasing to the congressional majority, and that there was little or nothing the

Conservatives could do about it, was abundantly indicated by the elections.

The first was held in Louisiana, on September 27 and 28. In that state nearly 83,000 Negroes were registered, less than 45,000 whites. The election was almost unanimous for holding a convention— 75,000 for, 4,000 against. Alabama, with a registration of 104,518 colored to 61,295 whites, voted on the first three days of October, with a huge majority for holding a convention. In Virginia, where the election lasted four days, October 18-21, the registered colored voters went almost solidly for holding a convention, while the whites divided, about one-fifth of them voting for a convention and the others against. The combined result was a vote of almost two to one for a convention. In Georgia, where a five-day election began on October 29, the Reconstructionists had a runaway victory, 102,283 for the convention, 4,127 against, most of the Conservative whites not voting.

Arkansas' election began on the first Tuesday in November and continued, with election officials moving the polls about, until everyone had his chance to vote. Conservatives charged that it was only by grace of this activity of the registrars in drumming up Radical votes that it was possible to muster a majority of the electorate, but regardless of how it was done the reports showed 27,416 votes for a convention and 13,558 against, out of a total of 66,805 registered voters.

Mississippi, in an election held at the same time, with a registration of 60,107 Negroes and 46,636 whites, voted for a convention by 69,799 to 6,277. Levi, colored servant of General Samuel G. French, New Jersey-born soldier who in the war with Mexico had served the United States and in the Civil War had served the Confederacy, reported to the General how the election was conducted in the Mississippi Delta. At his polling place there were some two hundred men when he went to vote, only two of them white, and those two "inside the house." Levi, who cast his ballot for what he called "the invention," handed his "paper," which was his certificate of registration, to the "two white men inside the room, through a window. They looked at it, handed it back to me, and said 'open your hand'; I did so and one of the men then put a little folded paper in my hand, then took it out and put it in a box and said 'Move on.'" It will be observed that in at least one particular the forms of democracy were observed. Levi was allowed to touch his ballot before it was deposited for him.

Florida, with a total registration of 15,434 colored and 11,148 white voters, cast 14,503 votes, or only 501 more than a majority, at the three-day election held in the middle of November. About 1,000 whites and 13,000 Negroes voted, all but 203 of them for the convention. While most whites did not vote, one who did endorsed upon his ballot a sentiment fairly general—"I don't give a damn whether the convention is held or not."

In the Carolinas, the elections were held on November 19 and 20. North Carolina, with a total registration of 179,653, and with a white majority, cast its vote for a convention, 93,006 to 32,961. South Carolina, where almost two-thirds of the registered voters were Negroes, went for the convention by 68,768 to 2,278, most of the whites not voting. The correspondent of the New York Herald who observed this first general exercise of the franchise by the freedmen of South Carolina, wrote that some brought their baskets "to put it in," and that others, on election days, could not remember the names they had given at the time of registration, which is understandable enough when the newness of some of the names is recalled.

The Carolinas were the last of the Southern states, except Texas, to vote on the question of holding a constitutional convention. Texas, which did not vote until February 14-18, 1868, followed the pattern of the other elections. Just a few more than one half of the voters registered cast their ballots, 44,689 of them voting to hold a convention, 11,440 against.

By the time the vote was taken in the Carolinas, the Alabama convention, which met on November 3, was more than half way through its work of writing a new constitution for the state along Radical Reconstruction lines; the Louisiana convention was preparing to open its sessions on November 23; and calls had been issued for meetings of the conventions in Virginia and Georgia in December, and for those in other states early in the coming year.

On November 21, the day after the election in the Carolinas, the Fortieth Congress reconvened for its third special session of the year, to survey the progress and state of its work of Reconstruction.

CHAPTER XXX

CLIPPING THE COURT'S WINGS

TEN constitutional conventions were held in the South—eight going on at the same time—to construct states of a new sort, to be fitted into the general framework of government in a new way, in the winter and spring of 1867-68.

The Fourteenth Amendment, enlarging the domain of the Federal power, was not yet ratified, but there was no doubt that it would be as soon as the votes of the new Southern states should be made available. Without waiting for that, however, the convinced Radicals of the Fortieth Congress proposed to bring about a redistribution of the powers of government among the three co-ordinate branches established in the Constitution, without the formality of a constitutional amendment.

The supreme power of government, they believed and asserted, lay in the Congress, which they declared to be the repository and interpreter of the popular will. This concentrated power, free of executive, judicial, or even constitutional restraint, was to be exercised upon persons, states, or the other branches of the Federal government, always for the good of the nation and its wards, the freedmen, but the good of the nation as the majority in Congress saw it.

The times, ran the thought, were at a crisis, and restrictions in a Constitution written long before, whether they were guaranties of the rights of individuals or of minorities, or reservations of rights in the states, or checks and balances within the general government, were not to be allowed to block, or even to balk, the immediate execution of the "will of the people."

The President, according to this doctrine of government, was a subordinate of Congress, and responsible to the majority in that body, not independently responsible to the people from whom he held his office by independent election. The Supreme Court, in the same view of things, acted at its peril in holding that bills passed by Congress were not laws such as the Constitution authorized.

Declarations of such theories of government had not been lacking among the more extreme members of Congress, but before the session of 1867-68 the majority in Congress were not ready to follow such an idea. Perhaps they never would have been, had it been stated baldly, but, during that long and bitterly impassioned session, the time came when resentments, fears and hopes combined to bring them to act upon a theory which most of them did not expressly espouse. When that time came, fortunately for the future of America, there were to be found in the ranks of the majority enough men—just enough—to block that action and to save the American idea of government under a written constitution, subject to change upon the expression of a deliberate popular will but not subject to the vagaries of the results of each election.

On November 25, four days after the winter sessions of Congress opened, the Judiciary Committee recommended to the House of Representatives that Andrew Johnson be impeached for high crimes and misdemeanors.

The committee's recommendation was made by a five-to-four vote. The majority rested its report upon the record of an investigation as arbitrary, irrelevant and flimsy as any committee of Congress ever indulged in. The investigation began in the hate-warped brain of James M. Ashley, of Ohio, who, in the frenzy of the debate over the President's veto of the District of Columbia Negro-suffrage bill, on January 7, 1867, dramatically but vaguely charged the President with usurpation of power and violation of law, and offered a resolution of impeachment.

To investigate these vague and general charges, the House named the Judiciary Committee. The investigation being unfinished when the Thirty-ninth Congress came to an end, it was continued by order of the new Congress. For months, the committee heard all manner of testimony, from sources of all sorts, hundreds of pages of it. Upon the record, in June, the committee voted, five to four, that no grounds of impeachment had been shown.

Extremists, however, urged that no such report should be made to the House, and insisted that further opportunity be given to procure the necessary evidence to sustain their charges. The committee accordingly kept the matter open and the parade of witnesses went on, in the attempt to prove complicity of the President in the murder of Abraham Lincoln; corrupt misuse of the pardoning power and the appointing power; corrupt disposal of government property; or some other, any other, impeachable offense.

Behind the scenes, while the witnesses were paraded before the committee, the self-appointed prosecutors were busy in their search for evidence, or its manufacture if nothing suitable could be found. Jails and penitentiaries were scoured. One Sanford Conover, alias Dunham, whose earlier testimony before the committee had been so patently false that it had resulted in his conviction and sentence for perjury, had a new revelation under promise that a pardon would be forthcoming, but recanted when he became convinced that the promisers could not deliver. Attempts were made to procure evidence of treason in non-existent letters alleged to have been written to Jefferson Davis by Johnson, when military governor of Tennessee during the war. Attempts were made to persuade the imprisoned John Surratt to save his neck by implicating the President in the Booth plot to murder Lincoln—all to no avail.

No lack of evidence, however, abated Ashley's obsession on that subject. On November 23 he was called before the committee, on the demand of the two Democratic members, to explain why he had not presented to the committee or to some competent court the evidence which he continually claimed to have that Johnson was party to the plot to kill Lincoln. His explanation was that the evidence he had was

"not that kind of evidence which would satisfy a great mass of men, especially the men who do not concur with me in my theory about this matter. I have had a theory about it. I have always believed that President Harrison and President Taylor and President Buchanan were poisoned, and poisoned for the express purpose of putting the vice-presidents in the presidential office. . . . Then Mr. Lincoln was assassinated, and from my standpoint I could come to the conclusion which impartial men, holding different views, could not come to. It would not amount to legal evidence."

The committee did not accept Mr. Ashley's strange conclusions as to the President's guilt in the murder of his predecessor, but sometime between June and November, a majority did come to the conclusion that the Constitution did not mean what it said in the section which declared that "The President . . . shall be removed from office on impeachment for, and conviction of, treason, bribery, or other high crimes and misdemeanors."

The majority report, prepared by George S. Boutwell and signed by himself and four other Radical members, argued that impeachment was "not necessarily a trial for a crime" but was a political process for settling political differences between Congress and the Executive. This extraordinary argument was based on laborious citation of precedents for political impeachment, from the days of the Germanic tribes down through Anglo-Saxon history, completely ignoring the new idea of constitutional government developed in the United States.

The conclusion of the majority was that the acts of the President cited in the report constituted "high crimes and misdemeanors within the meaning of the Constitution," wherefore they did

"accordingly, in behalf of the loyal people of the United States, whose rights and interests he has betrayed, and whose government he has attempted to subvert; in vindication of the law that he has violated, and the justice that he has condemned, and in the name of the thousands who have died that the Republic might live, recommend and respectfully insist that he be impeached, and held to answer therefor before the Senate of the United States."

The concluding sentences of the report of the majority give evidence of the emotional state which could lead men in the Nineteenth Century to believe that the cause of government by law would be advanced by turning back to Plantagenet ideas of impeachment for political acts.

But while five of the seven Radical members of the committee might surrender their judgment to the personal and political passions of the time, two other Republicans kept their balance. The chairman, James F. Wilson, of Iowa, later to serve as the first Secretary of Agriculture, prepared, and Frederick E. Woodbridge of Vermont joined in, a report that impeachment "must be for some offense known to the law, and not created by the fancy of the members of the House." Such an offense, they continued, had not been shown in the testimony before the committee, much of which was "of no value whatever . . . mere hearsay, opinions of witnesses . . . utterly irrelevant to the case." Their only possible conclusion, on "the real evidence in the case," was that it was a

"political contest and that . . . the day of political impeachments would be a sad one for this country. Political unfitness and incapacity must be tried at the ballot box, not in the high court of impeachment."

To this conclusion of the Wilson report, the two Democrats on the committee subscribed. They did not, however, accept its statements as to the political course of the President, and they went even further in their condemnation of the methods used by the com-

mittee in its investigation. Much of the testimony they characterized as "malicious whispers"; some of the witnesses as "vile vermin
who had gossip or slander to retail . . . permitted to appear and place
it upon record for the delectation of mankind." Had the committee
members known then as much as was afterward developed about
the scavenging activities of Mr. Ashley and some of his associates they
might have been even stronger in their condemnation.

In spite of the methods of inquiry, and the tense emotions of
thousands of persons in the country who believed "that it would
be a righteous act to get him out of the way by any means, fair or
foul," the Democratic minority reported that "it is really wonderful
that so little has been elicited that tends in the slightest degree to
tarnish the fair name of the President."

The House of Representatives was not yet ready to engage in impeachment on purely political grounds. On December 7, after two
days' debate, the majority report was rejected, and the House refused
to impeach, by a vote of one hundred and eight to fifty-seven. For
impeachment, the vote was fifty-seven Republicans, no Democrats;
against impeachment, sixty-seven Republicans, forty-one Democrats.
Six of the Republican representatives from Tennessee voted to impeach; one, Alvin Hawkins, against. Against impeachment, also, were
such Republican leaders as Blaine, Bingham and Garfield. The House
of Representatives did not like Andrew Johnson, but it was not yet
ready to subscribe to the idea that to get rid of him it was necessary
to do away with the constitutional distribution of powers in the
government. And there for the time, the matter of impeachment
of the President rested.

Five days later, on December 12, the President reported to the
Senate his suspension of Secretary Stanton and the appointment of
General Grant as Secretary of War *ad interim*. Referred to the Military Affairs Committee, the report did not come before the Senate
for action until after the Christmas recess, when, on January 10, 1868,
the committee recommended that the Senate not concur in the suspension. The recommendation of the committee was based on a
right claimed under the Tenure of Office Act, passed in the closing
days of the Thirty-ninth Congress. The President did not recognize
such a right, and in making his report to the Senate had not acted
under the requirements of an act which he believed unconstitutional
but in accordance with his understanding of his general constitutional
powers and duties.

The purpose of the President, in fact, was to get the matter before the courts, where he was confident of the outcome—a confidence justified by events long afterward, when a case under such an act finally did come before the Supreme Court for decision. In pursuance of his purpose, the President had secured, or thought that he had secured, a promise from General Grant to hold the office himself, if the Senate did not concur in the suspension of Stanton; or, if he did not feel that he could resist the action of the Senate, to resign the office back into the hands of the President from whom he had received it, so that "he would at least leave the office . . . in the condition in which it was when he was appointed."

Both as to the meaning of the law and as to what the agreement between them was, either at the time of his appointment or at the time of their conference during the days while the question was under debate in the Senate, General Grant disagreed with the President. There was much confusion in the negotiation and the President may have taken General Grant's well-known silence at more than its actual meaning, but the weight of the evidence of those in touch with both of them at the time seems to sustain the President's recollection of events and conversations. There was not, however, a clean-cut meeting of minds between the President and the General.

On January 13, after a Saturday and a Monday of debate, with a Sunday of conferences in between, the Senate voted, late in the afternoon, to reinstate Stanton as Secretary of War, a member of the President's Cabinet ex officio. Under the agreement between them, as the President recalled it, General Grant should have resigned that night and replaced the office within presidential control. Instead, he went to the office of the Secretary early Tuesday morning, locked the doors, turned over the key to an assistant adjutant-general, went on to his office as general of the Armies, and left the assistant adjutant-general to hand over the key to Mr. Stanton, who was already in the building and waiting. To the President, General Grant sent an aide with notice that his "functions as Secretary of War ad interim ceased from the moment of the receipt" of official notice of the Senate's action.

At the Cabinet meeting that day, the President taxed General Grant with his failure to live up to their agreement as to the disposition of the office of Secretary of War, and there was afterward an exchange of controversial letters between them. There, again, matters rested for more than a month, with Mr. Stanton again in possession of an executive department, this time not as the secret spy of the Radicals in Congress, but as their open representative, holding office by their will and against the wishes of the Chief Executive; and with General Grant, and all his great popularity in definite and positive alliance with the Radicals, against the President.

But one more step remained to complete the subordination of the Presidency to the will of Congress—successful impeachment and conviction of the President for the "high crime and misdemeanor" of differing politically with the majority in Congress.

The Executive Department, it seemed, was about to be put in its proper place of subordination, but there remained the disturbing possibility that, as it had done in the Milligan and Test Oath cases, the Supreme Court might find that there was no warrant in the Constitution for the course of Congress in Reconstruction.

On January 10, the same day on which the Senate took up the matter of reinstating Secretary Stanton, that possibility began to become acutely disturbing. On that day, there appeared before the Supreme Court Jeremiah Sullivan Black, the same whose argument had proved so potent in the Milligan case, to move that the court advance for early hearing the appeal of Colonel W. H. McCardle, the Vicksburg editor in jail for his too free criticisms of Reconstruction.

One of the acts passed by Congress in 1867, intended to protect the "loyal" from process of Southern state courts, had confirmed the right to apply to the Circuit Courts of the United States for the writ of habeas corpus and established the right of direct appeal from those courts to the Supreme Court of the United States in such cases. The McCardle case was before the Supreme Court under the provisions of this act, on appeal from the United States Circuit Court of Mississippi. That court had held the Reconstruction Acts valid and the imprisonment of the Vicksburg editor, therefore, legal.

A week after Mr. Black moved the advancement of the case, the Supreme Court granted the motion and set it for argument on the merits on the first Monday in March. The matter was indeed becoming serious in its threat to the plans of the Radicals. Once more, the storm of abuse began to break about the bench. "The Supreme Court," said the fanatically Radical *Independent*, "is at this hour the guilty confederate of Andrew Johnson." Mr. Stevens introduced in the House a bill to deprive the court absolutely of jurisdiction over cases arising in connection with the Reconstruction Acts. The House was not ready to follow him in so bald a dodge as that, but it did pass, hastily and by a party vote of one hundred and sixteen to thirty-nine, a bill to require a two-thirds majority of the Supreme Court to declare a bill passed by Congress inconsistent with the Constitution. Even the most apprehensive of the Radicals—and most of them seem to have been apprehensive as to the constitutional fate of their measures—felt that one-third of the court would sustain them.

The Senate, less overwhelmingly Radical than the House, refused to pass the two-thirds bill. Proceedings went on before the court, with preliminary argument as to jurisdiction, on the last day of January and the first of February. The government was represented not by the Attorney General, who had given an official and public opinion that the acts were not constitutional, which precluded him from defending them before the court, but by Senator Lyman Trumbull, engaged by the War Department as special counsel to defend the acts of the General commanding the fourth military district. The court, having heard the argument, held that it did have jurisdiction, and let the case go on to hearing on March 2.

Argument was had before the court, ending on March 9. Then, indeed, a way had to be found to prevent the case from going to the decision which the Radicals so greatly feared. Such a way was found when, three days after argument ended, Mr. Schenck of Ohio asked leave of the House to call up and pass a Senate bill which enlarged the jurisdiction of the Supreme Court by allowing the court to review judgments against internal revenue officers in the same way in which it already had jurisdiction to review cases against customs officers. Mr. Schenck explained the bill correctly enough and asked unanimous consent for its consideration. Mr. Stevens went through the show of objecting, but withdrew his objections. Mr. Schenck, again explaining that the "whole effect of it is to place officers of internal revenue on the same footing with officers of customs," moved the passage of the bill. While Mr. Schenck still held the floor, Mr. Wilson of Iowa asked his leave to offer an amendment to the bill, adding a section:

"And be it further enacted, That so much of the act of February 5, 1867, entitled 'An act to amend an Act to Establish the Judicial Courts of the United States, approved September 24th, 1789,' as authorizes an appeal from the judgment of a Circuit Court of the United States to the Supreme Court of the United States, or the exercise of any such jurisdiction by said Supreme Court on appeals which have been or may hereafter be taken, be and the same is hereby, repealed."

Mr. Schenck, still holding the floor, accepted the amendment and called the previous question on the bill and amendment, thereby effectively cutting off demands for explanation or discussion. The bill passed, with no more than the handful of members who engineered it knowing what it was about. Mr. Schenck moved to reconsider and immediately moved that the motion to reconsider be laid on the table, which was done *pro forma*. The House had done its part toward cutting off jurisdiction of the Supreme Court in the dreaded McCardle case.

On the same day, the bill as amended was rushed back to the Senate for its concurrence. Senator Buckalew asked that someone explain what the amendment meant. Senator Williams declared that the amendment explained itself. Senator Buckalew, not satisfied, moved that the matter be postponed a day. "I should like to have time to read the law which it is proposed to repeal," he added, plaintively. Mr. Buckalew's motion was defeated, and the amendment accepted. By such shabby parliamentary maneuvers, the Supreme Court was deprived of jurisdiction of the only case which had come before it squarely raising the question of the constitutionality of the scheme of Reconstruction. The purpose, as expressed by General Schenck, when the trick was uncovered, was "to clip the wings of that Court."

President Johnson, on March 25, vetoed the bill as establishing a precedent which might "eventually sweep aside every check on arbitrary and unconstitutional legislation." On the following day, after the first real debate which was held on the measure, the Senate passed the bill over the veto of the President, to be followed, on March 27, by the House in like action—an action which the Supreme Court accepted, by dismissing the McCardle case even after it had been argued, for lack of jurisdiction.

The Congress had moved one step nearer to supreme power in the government.

CHAPTER XXXI

More Writing of Constitutions

While the Congress, in its own practical way, was going ahead in its job of remaking the government of the United States, the constitutional conventions which it had called into being were reconstructing the states of the South.

Between November 3, 1867, and May 18, 1868, nine such conventions met, deliberated, drafted new and sometimes strange constitutions, and adjourned. The convention in Alabama met first and adjourned first, on December 10, 1867. Before it adjourned, the conventions in Louisiana, Virginia and Georgia were in session. Those in Mississippi, Arkansas, North Carolina, South Carolina and Florida met in January. Of these eight conventions in session at the same time, the first to complete its work was that in Arkansas, which adjourned on February 14, 1868; the last, in Mississippi, which adjourned on May 18, after a session of 115 days. On June 1, two weeks after the Mississippi convention closed, the last of the state conventions, that in Texas, began a session which, with its recesses and intermissions, was to continue until the last month of the year, to complete twelve months and more of constitution writing in the South.

No two conventions were the same in racial or political complexion, in the distribution of influence and leadership among a majority made up of "carpetbaggers," "scalawags" and Negroes, or in the caliber and course of the small delegations of conservatives which furnished the party of opposition in each convention.

But while no two conventions were exactly the same in makeup or program, they all had to deal with somewhat the same questions. Just what should be the relations to the general government of this new sort of state which was being constructed? What should be the status of the freedmen, legal, civil and political, and what should be the relations between them and their white neighbors? How should "rebels" be disfranchised and disqualified to the desired degree, without at the same time removing from the scene of active politics considerable and important groups of rabid "radicals" who beforetime had been no less rabidly "rebel"?

There were other questions, too, not necessarily political in character, questions of education, of administrative organization, of the nature and form of government and its institutions, as distinguished from the processes of politics. With such questions, some of the conventions dealt in their various fashions, but the emphasis everywhere was on the political process of creating reliably Radical states, content to accept a subordinate place in the national councils, but capable of providing votes, congressional and electoral, when needed.

In Alabama, only four of the one hundred delegates elected to the convention were listed as Conservatives, while ninety-six were Radicals of various shades and degrees, including eighteen agents of the Freedmen's Bureau, thirty-seven other newcomers to Alabama from Northern states, and eighteen Negroes. Neither the number of Negroes in the convention, however, nor their general conduct, justified the derisive name of the "Black Crook Convention," given by the New York *Herald's* special correspondent, even though nine of the Negro delegates were reported to be entirely illiterate, seven to be able to do no more than sign their names, and only two capable of really writing.

Of the white delegates, thirteen held and certified to their own elections, while seven others never had seen the counties they were presumed to be representing. Samuel A. Hale, Alabama Unionist, and brother of Senator John P. Hale, of New Hampshire, thus described the three delegates from his county, two whites and one black:

"The two whites were strangers here. . . . One of them, called Rolfe, is said to be a vagrant from the State of New York, where it is said he has a wife and family living, whom he has not seen in four or five years. . . . He had been here some three or four months prior to his election as a delegate, sometimes working as a carriage trimmer, sometimes drinking whisky and making drunken exhibitions of himself upon our streets. . . . Of the other white delegate, called Yordy, . . . I had never heard until the day of his nomination. . . . Yordy claims to have been a captain in the Federal Army."

That such men were elected in Alabama, Mr. Hale ascribed to the votes of Negroes who "knew nothing of what was on their bits of paper," and who were controlled by Bureau agents, most of whom were themselves candidates.

The Alabama convention, under the helpful influence of General

Wager Swayne, who combined the duties of Bureau head and military command, went to work promptly after it had disposed of the troublesome question of its own compensation. That was fixed, without great debate, at eight dollars per day plus forty cents per mile of travel to and from the convention. The real difficulty was in determining how the compensation was to be paid. The scrip, or "state money" of the restoration government, headed by Governor Patton, was refused, even when it was explained to the members that the scrip was receivable for taxes in Alabama. Of what use, asked one delegate, was money which was good for nothing but to pay taxes, since neither he nor most of his fellow members had any taxes to pay? General Pope, to whom the matter was submitted, settled it by ordering local taxation to raise the money to pay the convention.

"The great object which ought to govern the action of the convention," declared E. W. Peck, the chairman, "is to keep the State out of the control of disloyal men." Mr. Peck was a New Yorker by birth, but had been a Whig and Unionist lawyer in Tuscaloosa before the war. His experience in the South led him to support a proposed suffrage article in the Constitution which, of course, affirmed the disfranchisements and disqualifications required by Congress in the Reconstruction Acts and the Fourteenth Amendment, but would allow others to vote upon a showing that they had aided in the Reconstruction, and upon the taking of an oath renouncing the right of secession, accepting the political equality of all men, and agreeing never to attempt to injure any man or class of men because of loyalty or affiliation with any particular party. To those who objected to allowing ex-rebels to vote even under these conditions, Mr. Peck replied:

"Most of the men who entered into the scheme of secession, I believe, have been honest, honorable, Christian men, and if they consented to take this oath they would keep it. . . . Under this oath, the Republican party would gain two votes where their enemies would get one. There were many good men who participated in the rebellion who are now in favor of reconstruction, and would gladly take this oath."

Validation of slave marriages by the convention of 1865 had raised such matrimonial complications and difficulties for some of the members or their friends that the action of 1865 was revoked, the old marriages declared invalid, and the marital status as of November 30,

1867, validated and made binding. Local white members sought to prohibit mixed marriages but the newcomers from the North, as part of their appeal for the support of the Negro delegates, resisted so vigorously that the whole question was left open, as was the question of mixed schools.

These and other points of difference and disagreement among the various elements in the convention had so split the almost solidly Radical majority, before the end of the convention, that only sixty-six delegates voted for the constitution as drafted, eight voted against it, and twenty-six did not vote at all. Thirteen of the delegates, on December 10, 1867, the day the convention adjourned, signed and issued an address to the people, protesting against the "degradation and abasement of the white population" involved in the new scheme of government.

This protest from among the members of the convention itself was indicative of the feelings which came to a head in what came to be known as the White Man's Movement. The movement started, at the beginning of the new year, at a Conservative convention in Dallas County, with resolutions offered by former Governor Parsons. General Clanton was its manager. Its policy was "Register if you can, but do not, under any circumstances, vote"—for the Reconstruction laws required that a majority of those registered must vote if the handiwork of the constitutional conventions were to be ratified.

The constitutional convention of Louisiana met at the Mechanics Institute, in New Orleans, on November 23, 1867, to remain in session until March 9, 1868. The convention included an equal number of white and colored delegates, forty-nine of each, with ninety-six Republicans out of the total of ninety-eight. Many of the Negroes were men of education, chosen from among the distinct class of free persons of color which had existed in Louisiana before the war. From this group came Pinckney Benton Stewart Pinchback, ablest of the colored delegates and perhaps the ablest man in the convention, a man who was to go far in Louisiana Reconstruction politics and to hold high office. He signalized his entry into the field by ably opposing, and defeating, Dr. G. M. Wickliffe, a dentist from Clinton, once editor of an anti-abolition journal but in 1867 burning with the zeal of a convert, in his demand that all offices of the convention be divided equally between the two races. Pinchback stood out for the principle that offices should be bestowed on the basis of general fitness, not of race.

As in the case of other conventions, there was early difficulty about financing the delegates in their deliberations, met by the levy of a special tax of one mill on the dollar on all property, with a stringent penalty of twenty-five per cent for default in payment.

During the first week of the convention, General Winfield S. Hancock, the new military commander of the fifth district, arrived in New Orleans and promptly issued his General Order No. 40. "Peace and quiet reigned" in the department, he announced, and

"the great principles of American liberty still are the lawful inheritance of this people, and ever should be. The right of trial by jury, the *habeas corpus*, the liberty of the press, the freedom of speech, and the natural rights of persons and the rights of property must be preserved."

Except where there was forcible resistance to the law, he declared,

"the administration of civil justice appertains to the civil courts. The rights of litigants do not depend on the views of the general commanding this district; they are to be adjudged and settled according to the laws. . . . Arbitrary power such as I have been urged to assume has no existence here. It is not found in the laws of Louisiana or of Texas; it cannot be derived from any acts of Congress; it is restrained by a Constitution. . . ."

That a commanding general who expressed such ideas might interpose to prevent the collection of the special tax for the expenses of the convention was a disturbing, but groundless, fear of many of the members. The tax was collected, the expenses paid, and the deliberations of the convention carried to their completion in a new constitution which provided that the paramount allegiance of Louisianans was to the United States, not to the state; that all persons should enjoy equal rights on public conveyances, and in all places of business or public entertainment; and that all public schools, and particularly the University of Louisiana, should be open to both races on equal terms.

The privilege of voting was to be denied to those, among others, who had held office in the Confederate States, led guerrilla bands, written or published newspaper articles or preached sermons advocating treason, or voted for or signed ordinances of secession—except that one with a convenient conscience could be purged of these offenses by signing a certificate acknowledging the moral and political wrong of secession, and expressing regret for having given aid or comfort thereto. The would-be voter, in fact, might be excused from furnishing this certificate of regret if, prior to January 1, 1868, he had shown himself a good Reconstructionist. Some such provision was made necessary by the considerable number of zealous Radicals in Louisiana who, in Confederate days, had likewise been zealous, or at least vocal, in that cause.

Anticipating the results of the convention, the Republicans of Louisiana held their state convention in New Orleans on January 14, 1868. Right from the start there was a split between the "Pure Radical" faction led by the colored Roudanez brothers, one-time residents of Santo Domingo and publishers of the New Orleans *Tribune*, and the "Compromising" or "White Republicans." The Roudanez faction offered as their candidate for the nomination for governor, Major F. E. Dumas, a free man of color, who had commanded a battalion of Louisiana colored troops in the Union Army. The "Compromising" faction offered a young man who had come south with the Federal army; had been dismissed by order of General Sherman, after actively siding with General McClernand in the dispute between that officer and General Sherman; had been reinstated by the authorities at Washington; had again come south, to New Orleans, to engage in the practice of law and politics; and who now, still less than twenty-six years of age, was well into a notable and stormy career in Reconstruction politics.

Young Henry Clay Warmoth, by all accounts, was a splendid figure of a man, strikingly handsome, concededly able, bold and determined, adroit—unscrupulous, his enemies said—the sort of figure which inevitably comes to the top in the whirlpool of revolutionary politics. Cordially hated by the Conservatives, he came finally into an alliance with elements of that party, which brought upon him the violent dislike of the more radical elements of his own party. He survived it all, however, politically and personally, to live to a great age, and to become one of the few Radical Reconstruction governors to write for posterity his own story and view of events.

In the convention of January, 1868, he won his first great party victory—nomination for governor of Louisiana, by a vote of forty-five to forty-three. Major Dumas, the defeated candidate, was offered a place on the ticket as lieutenant-governor, but declined, and O. J. Dunn was named for the place as representative of the colored element. The whole state ticket named included two Negroes and five whites, one of whom was Chaplain T. W. Conway, who had come south with the army and remained with the Bureau, who was nominated for superintendent of education.

The Pure Radicals, resentful, held their own convention and made nominations—for governor, Judge Taliaferro, a native Radical white; for lieutenant-governor, the same Major Dumas whom Warmoth had defeated for the nomination.

On December 3, the same day on which the first regular session of the Fortieth Congress opened, the Virginia constitutional convention, derisively known as the "Black-and-Tan Convention," met in Richmond. Of its one hundred and five members, seventy-two were elected as Radicals, thirty-three as Conservatives. The Radical majority consisted of twenty-five Negroes and forty-five whites, of whom fourteen were native Virginians and the others from a variety of states and foreign countries. Having elected Judge John C. Underwood as president, and received ceremonial visits from Governor Pierpont and District Commander Schofield, the convention recessed until January 2, 1868, when it reconvened to remain in session until April 17.

Perhaps because it was so close to Washington and the North, perhaps because of the dramatic contrast of such a convention sitting in the halls which Jefferson had designed and in which the Congress of the Confederacy had sat, the Virginia convention received unusually full treatment from the Northern press. To the correspondents, the solemn and owl-like gravity of misdirected parliamentary procedure; the interminable speeches and motions and points of order; the lack of deliberative dignity; the earnest aping of more experienced members; the whole atmosphere of unintended comedy relief, afforded infinite amusement.

The work of the convention, however, was no worse, and in some respects better, than that of the other Reconstruction gatherings. None of the old political leaders on either side was active, leaving the proceedings largely in the hands of untried and, in some cases, illiterate men, some of whom became intolerably verbose. On March 24, a fellow-delegate offered a resolution limiting Dr. Thomas Bayne, of Norfolk, to five speeches a day.

The constitution, adopted by a vote of fifty-one to thirty-six and signed on April 17, established a system of free education but did not attempt to impose mixed schools. It placed a larger proportion of the burden of taxation on local landed property, partly to encourage the breakup of large holdings. It went further than the Reconstruction Acts in the disfranchisement of ex-rebels and their disqualification from holding public office, in spite of the efforts of General Schofield, who appeared before the convention in person to say:

"You cannot find in Virginia a full number of men capable of filling office who can take the oath you have prescribed. County offices pay limited salary; even a common laborer could not afford to come from abroad for the purpose of filling them. I have no hesitation in saying that I do not believe it possible to inaugurate a government upon that basis."

General Schofield spoke from experience and with wisdom, but to no avail. Disfranchisement and disqualification remained in the constitution promulgated by the convention, to become the central rallying point of the Conservative party of opposition in Virginia.

This party, the outgrowth of a notable convention in Richmond on December 11, 1867, organized with A. H. H. Stuart as chairman, and with such leaders as John B. Baldwin, John Letcher, Thomas S. Bocock, J. R. Branch, and R. M. T. Hunter. Its call to the people of Virginia was for "vigorous and united effort to save ourselves from ruin and disgrace." "Our rights may be wrested from us," they declared, "but we will never submit to the rule of an alien and inferior race. We prefer the rule of the bayonet."

The constitutional convention in Georgia, assembling on December 9 in Atlanta instead of the old capital at Milledgeville, unwittingly gave expression to the true aspect of all the Reconstruction conventions in its very first resolution, addressed to General Pope.

"In obedience to your orders," the resolution read, "this convention is now assembled and organized and invites your presence in the convention at your pleasure."

The convention so assembled included one hundred and sixty-nine delegates, of whom twelve were white Conservatives, nine were whites from outside the state, thirty-seven were Negroes, and the balance whites of the "scalawag" persuasion. There were, in the Georgia convention, a group of leaders such as Rufus B. Bullock, a native of New York, who had come to Georgia in 1859, and who was to become governor; Benjamin Conley, of Augusta, who succeeded to the Governorship after Bullock's flight from the state, and Amos T. Akerman, originally of New Hampshire, who had come to Georgia in 1854, practiced law in Elbert County, opposed secession but served in the Confederate Army, and who was to become attorney general in the Cabinet of President Grant.

The Negroes in the convention included characters as varied as Henry M. Turner, who came south as chaplain of a Negro regiment, was afterward postmaster at Macon, and finally a respected bishop in the African Methodist Church; and Aaron Alpeoria Bradley, afterward a member of the legislature, from which he was expelled on the charge that he had served a sentence in state's prison in New York for felony.

The Georgia convention, too, had difficulty about getting itself paid. Governor Jenkins and John Jones, treasurer, refused to pay out forty thousand dollars of the state's funds for per diem and ex- penses of the convention. General George G. Meade, who had been appointed to the command of the third military district when the President removed General Pope on December 28, ordered the state officials to honor the warrants of the convention. When the officials again refused, the General removed them from office, on January 13, 1868. Later in the month, the Comptroller and the Secretary of State were removed, and all the offices filled by the appointment of junior officers of the army. Military government in Georgia was complete during the sessions of the convention, which lasted until March 11, 1868.

The convention did not limit white suffrage beyond the restric- tions imposed by Congress, and it granted Negro suffrage, of course, but only after urging by the war Governor, Joseph E. Brown, who addressed them on invitation on January 9. Through evasion or oversight the section dealing with the right of Negroes to hold pub- lic office was left in a most ambiguous condition—a fact which later led to much delay and confusion in the readmission of the state.

Georgia Conservatives met in state convention at Macon on De- cember 5, 1867, to organize for the election which was to come after the convention had finished its work and submitted the constitution to a vote of the people. Since officers were to be voted for at the same election, the Conservatives nominated as their candidate for governor, John B. Gordon, late lieutenant general in the Army of Northern Virginia, whose eligibility rested on the fact that before the war he never had taken an oath of allegiance, since he had held no office, civil or military, which required it.

In the two states of the fourth military district, Arkansas and

Mississippi, the constitutional conventions opened on January 7, 1868. In Arkansas, the convention consisted of fifty-one delegates—forty-three whites, none of whom were native to the state; and eight Negroes, three of whom were natives. Twenty-three of the delegates were known as "carpetbaggers," having come into the state with or after the Federal armies, but these twenty-three controlled the politics of the convention, under the leadership of Joseph Brooks, a preacher from Iowa, and James Hinds, a lawyer from New York, both of whom had come to the state in 1865. Thomas M. Bowen, the president, the four vice-presidents and the chairmen of nineteen out of twenty-six committees came from the group. The Conservative delegation numbered only six, with John B. Bradley and J. N. Cypert, both of whom had remained active in their support of the Confederacy to the last, as the principal spokesmen.

As in other states, the Arkansas convention had trouble with getting its pay. It voted itself seventy-five thousand dollars out of any funds accumulated by the former government, or any new funds coming in, and sent a special messenger to Vicksburg, to get General Alvan C. Gillem, who had succeeded General Ord in command, to let them have the money. When the messenger got back to Little Rock with the news that General Gillem would allow fifty thousand dollars, there was a rush on the treasurer to draw pay, which was calculated at eight dollars per day, with travel expense at twenty cents per mile each way, plus eight dollars per day for travel time. Each member, among other perquisites, was allowed ten newspapers each day, or the equivalent in weeklies. As in most of the conventions of the time, the printing business, which in that day and time was an adjunct of the newspaper business, gave excellent opportunities for deals and jobs profitable alike to papers, printers and members.

Though in session only a little more than five weeks, the convention managed to spend altogether one hundred and eighty-seven thousand dollars before completing, on February 14, a constitution which fifteen of its members refused to sign. The constitution provided for Negro suffrage, of course, and disfranchised large classes of whites, except that anyone not barred by Congress might vote upon a showing that he had openly advocated or voted for Reconstruction, and accepted the equality of all men before the law. The appointing power of the Governor was greatly enlarged; the terms of all officers made to run until January 1, 1873; and the forthcoming election on constitution and officers was turned over, in all its details, to an election commission of three, Joseph Brooks, Thomas Bowen and James L. Hodges.

The state was gerrymandered, charged the Conservatives, so as to create the largest possible number of reliably Radical districts—a practice not confined to Reconstruction conventions in Arkansas, but common enough in the politics of all times and places. A system of universal education was set up, on paper, with mixed schools provided for in the constitution.

While the constitutional convention was in session, both Democrats and Republicans held their party conventions in Little Rock. For governor, the Republicans, meeting on January 15, named General Powell Clayton, of the Federal army, who had married in Arkansas and remained there after the war, as a planter. General Clayton, who was to remain a dominant figure in Arkansas Republican affairs for a generation, lacked neither ability nor force. So much of the latter did he have, in fact, that his nomination started an exodus of the more pacific spirits from the party. General Clayton, too, long survived Reconstruction, and published his own memoirs of events in Arkansas and his part in them.

The Democratic convention, meeting on January 27, announced that it would do nothing which could be construed as a recognition of the validity of anything done by the constitutional convention; declared for a "white man's government in a white man's country"; and organized to "vote down the constitution."

So high was the partisan feeling in Arkansas that special protection was prescribed by the convention for Unionists, while the chaplain, in his closing prayer, besought that the forthcoming campaign should be carried on by the use of reason, logic and love, unless, he added significantly, the Radicals should be "compelled to resort to other means in self-defense."

In contrast to the Arkansas session of thirty-eight days, the Mississippi convention remained in session for one hundred and fifteen days, ending on May 18, 1868. The restoration convention of 1865, on the other hand, did its work in just eleven days. The one hundred delegates to the convention included nineteen Conservatives, something more than twenty "carpetbaggers," and twenty-nine "scalawags." Among the colored delegates were eight preachers. General Beroth B. Eggleston, an Ohio soldier, was president; Thad P. Sears, another ex-Union soldier, secretary. Among the leaders were Colonel A. T. Morgan, of Wisconsin; General W. S. Barry, former commander of a Kentucky Negro regiment; and General George C. McKee, an Illinois lawyer and a graduate of Knox College.

The convention voted itself ten dollars per diem, and forty cents a mile travel money, levying a special tax which bore lightly on the "loyal" people, of course. Besides $116,150 in delegates' pay, the convention spent about $50,000 on its attachés and running expenses; more than $28,000 for the printing of its proceedings in various Republican papers springing up in the state; and more than $30,000 to General James Duggan, who had established such a paper in Vicksburg the year before, and to General E. Stafford, of the Jackson *Mississippi Pilot*, for their services as public printers.

The convention asked General Gillem to levy another special tax for refugees and the destitute, which Gillem declined to do, on the ground that there was plenty of work in Mississippi for everyone who wanted it. The convention, in its zeal for the dispossessed, likewise "canceled" all debts incurred prior to April 28, 1865, but the level-headed Gillem disallowed any such constitutional innovations. Judge Watson, Conservative, sought to introduce another innovation by his motion that no member of the convention should be eligible to hold any public office created by it, but that one was promptly voted down by the membership, and never got to General Gillem.

In April, the convention adopted a stringent disfranchising clause, proscribing all who had aided the Confederacy except private soldiers and such others as had also "aided Reconstruction" by supporting and continuing to support the convention. When this clause was adopted, by a vote of forty-four to twenty-five, fourteen of the white delegates to the convention resigned, but enough remained to offer, as their contribution to the final draft to the constitution, a preamble which began: "We, the carpetbaggers and scalawags of Ohio, Vermont, Connecticut, Maine, Africa, . . ."

In North Carolina, where the convention opened on January 14, 1868, and continued until March 17, there were Conservative delegates who developed exceptional proficiency in gadfly tactics of opposition, stinging and annoying with the play of their wit the huge majorities before which they were helpless. The North Carolina convention contained one hundred and seven Radicals, thirteen Negroes, sixteen "carpetbaggers," the balance natives, and only thirteen Conservatives. Among the Reconstructionist leaders were General Joseph C. Abbott, of New Hampshire, editor and lawyer; Lieutenant Albion W. Tourgee, of Ohio, lawyer, and afterward judge and novelist; General Byron Laflin, of Massachusetts and New York, all ex-army officers, and G. W. Welker, of Pennsylvania, preacher. Three of the colored delegates, James H. Harris, J. W. Hood and A. H. Galloway, showed gifts of leadership. In the Conservative corner, barbed thorns in the side of the convention, were Captain Plato Durham and Major John W. Graham, ex-Confederates.

The North Carolina convention, financed by a special tax levy, cost $86,356.89, besides about $5,000 in printing. As compared with other Reconstruction conventions, the cost was moderate, although it was high as compared with previous conventions in North Carolina. Chairmen of most of the important committees were delegates from other states, who prescribed for North Carolina the governmental ideas to which they were accustomed. Not all the changes were bad, by any means, but the number and extent of changes to be assimilated at one time were confusing. A new public school system, with no requirement for separate schools, was created; the counties were divided into townships, on the New England model; judges were to be elected by popular vote, instead of by the assembly, and for terms of eight years, instead of for life; qualifications for office-holding were made less restrictive. Plato Durham, on this point, solemnly moved that the qualifications for governor and lieutenant-governor should be the ability to read and write.

The suffrage clauses were broad, allowing the vote to all men except those who denied the existence of a Supreme Being, or who had been convicted of felony or treason. The Conservatives objected to lowering the old voting standards so as to "confide the power of making laws to those who have no property to protect, and to bestow the right to levy taxes upon those who have no taxes to pay."

For the relief of debtors, the convention passed a stay law, effective until January 1, 1869, and applying to all civil proceedings founded on causes of action arising before May 1, 1865, which was made effective at once by General Canby. An element in the convention, led by Tourgee and Welker, representing Guilford County, urged that the state debt be repudiated, on the ground that the new state being created under the Reconstruction Acts was under no obligation to pay the debts of the old.

Before the convention ended, organization of both parties for action under the new order of things got under way, with conventions in Raleigh on the same day, February 6.

For governor, the Republicans nominated former Provisional Governor Holden, with a full ticket of imported white Republicans for the other offices. The nominees for seats in Congress included four natives and three of the "carpetbag" element.

Most of the delegates to the Democratic convention were Whigs of the old line who, as everywhere in the South, were being driven into a single party. Former Governor and Senator Graham was chairman; former Governors Vance, Bragg and Manly, among the delegates. Regardless of past differences, the convention organized as the Democratic party and chose delegates to the forthcoming Democratic National Convention. Later in the month, the state executive committee made nominations, including Zebulon Vance, Confederate war governor, for governor. When Vance wisely declined, the nomination was laid upon Thomas S. Ashe, who had been a Confederate congressman and still was under political disabilities on that account.

South Carolina, in Reconstruction times, exercised a most undeniable fascination upon the national mind. It was not as other states, either in itself or in its ways. And, more than that, it bore the distinction, the wicked distinction as it appeared to most in the North and to some in the South as well, of having started all the trouble by its leadership in secession. In Charleston, the very city where the Secession Ordinance was adopted and signed, the constitutional convention which was to remake the defiantly different little state into the pattern of conformity, met on January 14, 1868, and the press of the nation watched.

The convention, in its setting, its membership and its proceedings justified the interest it inspired. It was the first governmental body in which an overwhelming majority of the members, seventy-six out of one hundred and twenty-four, were colored—and two-thirds of the colored members had been slaves less than three years before. The convention was the embodied fulfillment of the prophecies of retribution.

Of the forty-eight white delegates, twenty-three were natives of South Carolina, twenty-five natives of other states and of foreign countries, a division which is not to be wondered at when the extreme scarcity of active white Unionists in South Carolina is recalled. Many of the native whites in the convention, in fact, had discovered the virtues of Unionism only after the defeat of the Confederacy. J. M. Rutland, "scalawag," had once been so violent in his sentiments the other way that he made up a purse to purchase a new cane for Preston Brooks, after that Congressman had broken his over the shoulders of Charles Sumner. Franklin J. Moses, Jr., as secretary to Governor Pickens, had hauled down the Union flag at Fort Sumter.

He had favored the Johnson plan of restoration until the political power of the state had definitely been put in the hands of the Negroes, by Congress, whereupon he started on a new political career which was to make him speaker of the House, adjutant general, a trustee of the state's university, governor, and, finally, a wandering, penniless outcast. Still another was C. C. Bowen, of Rhode Island and Georgia, faro bank dealer, dismissed from the Confederate Army and discharged from various jails, whose new career of politics was to take him into the halls of Congress.

Not all the native whites in the convention were of this sorry stripe, however. The chairman was Doctor Albert G. Mackey, a writer of works on Masonry and a consistent Unionist. Thomas J. Robertson was a respectable businessman, whose willingness to work with the Reconstructionists secured for him a seat in the United States Senate, which he occupied throughout the period.

Not less startling in their variety were the twenty-five white delegates from other states and countries. Most distinguished among them, in education and character, was Daniel H. Chamberlain, of Massachusetts, scholarly graduate of ancient schools and universities of the East, who came to South Carolina with the army, remained as a planter in the Berkeley District, and entered upon a career of politics which took him to the governor's chair—where he narrowly missed earning great and genuine distinction. In contrast to Chamberlain, was the Reverend Frank B. Whittemore, also of Massachusetts, a minister who came south to organize schools for the Freedmen's Bureau, and remained to enter politics. The Reverend Whittemore's commanding ability to sing and to speak louder than most carried him into the halls of Congress, whence he was expelled upon conviction of selling appointments to West Point and Annapolis. Triumphantly re-elected by his trusting and admiring constituents, he was refused admission, even to a Reconstruction Congress, with General John A. Logan leading the fight to keep him out and General Benjamin F. Butler fighting for his admission.

Another Massachusetts member of the convention was Justus K. Jillson, who was to serve as state superintendent of instruction for nine trying years. An honest, energetic superintendent, he was powerless to do more than complain and protest at the diversion of the public moneys from the schools. In spite of his efforts, Superintendent Jillson was to see illiteracy increase in South Carolina under the actual workings of the elaborate paper system of public education set up by the convention and succeeding legislatures.

South Carolina experienced also a phenomenon rare in the other Southern states—"carpetbaggers" of color. Robert Brown Elliott, lawyer, editor of the Charleston *Leader*, who was to become speaker of the House and twice a member of Congress, offered the striking contrast of educated Massachusetts speech and a coal-black skin. The Reverend Richard Harvey Cain, commonly known as "Daddy" Cain, came South in 1865 as a missionary, became the publisher of a missionary paper, served in the legislature and in Congress, for two terms, made his reputation in standing up for the colored race politically, as against whites of all sorts, including "carpetbaggers," and closed his career as a bishop of the African Methodist Church.

W. J. Whipper, of Ohio, who was to become a judge, by election at least, was in advance of his day by urging votes for women, as well as for men. Jonathan Jasper Wright, colored lawyer of Pennsylvania, who came south as a Bureau agent, was to become a different sort of judge, serving as associate justice of the Supreme Court of the state until the end of the period, in 1877.

Most of the fifty-odd native South Carolina Negroes in the convention had had small opportunity to develop the qualifications desirable in writers of a constitution, but it was of them that F. W. Dawson's Charleston *Daily News* was able to say:

"The best men in the convention are the colored members. Considering the influences under which they were called together, and their imperfect acquaintance with parliamentary law, they have displayed, for the most part, remarkable moderation and dignity. . . . They have assembled neither to pull wires like some, nor to make money like others; but to legislate for the welfare of the race to which they belong."

Among the native Negro leaders, however, were men of education and ability. Francis L. Cardozo, Charleston-born, educated at a Scottish University, experienced in teaching in New England, returned to South Carolina after the war to teach in Charleston, and later to become the leader among the native-born Negroes in Reconstruction politics. Beverly Nash, former slave, a barber in Columbia, and said to have been a good one; Robert C. DeLarge, a tailor in Charleston who, by way of the Bureau and the legislature, was to become a member of Congress; Alonzo J. Ransier, nearly white, who was to go to Congress and become lieutenant-governor, were representative among the native colored leaders. One of the most interesting and substantial of the group was Robert Smalls, the Charleston harbor pilot who, during the war, sailed the *Planter* out to join the blockading fleet. He was to become a member of Congress, where he remained for several terms after the overthrow of the Reconstruction régime.

The convention lasted fifty-three days, with compensation at eleven dollars a day, payable in warrants when the state was without funds. All the members of the convention together paid less than one thousand dollars in taxes, more than half of which was paid by one white Conservative. The other whites averaged less than six dollars each. One colored delegate paid eighty-three dollars and thirty-five cents in taxes, while the other seventy-five averaged less than fifty cents each. Almost half the members of the convention paid no taxes whatever.

In spite of the manifest incapacity of so many of its members, however, the actual work of the convention, on paper and in theory, at least, was not bad. The constitution produced accorded with what Chairman Mackey denominated as a "progressive age." It was more liberal than most of the Reconstruction constitutions in its disfranchisements and disqualifications. It stressed national unity; reorganized local administration; established the principle of equality of all men before the law and set up a system of public education, in theory though not in fact; liberalized the homestead and exemption laws; and, in general, was theoretically well framed, rather on the New England model with a dash of Ohio and other states thrown in.

The constitution recognized mixed schools, on the optimistic theory that "the most natural method of removing race distinctions would be to allow children, when five or six years of age, to mingle in school together. . . . Under such training prejudices will eventually die out." The recognition was more theoretical than practical, however, since there was no attempt to mix the races in the schools.

At the beginning of March, a week before the adjournment of the constitutional convention, the Republican party convention was held, composed largely of the same delegates. Plans were made and an organization formed to secure the adoption of the constitution at the elections to be held in mid-April. Nominees were chosen for the fourteen state offices to be chosen under the constitution if adopted, twelve of the fourteen nominees being members of the convention.

A month later, on April 2, representatives of Democratic clubs in many towns held a state convention, unanimous in its intense opposition to the new constitution and all its works, but divided as to ways and means of combating them. One element would have nothing to do with the business, fearing that to make nominations for offices would be looked upon as a tacit acceptance of the validity of the constitution itself. Another group, which favored nominating a ticket and making a canvass, carried the day and named a candidate for governor, who, thereupon, announced his agreement with the first point of view. So divided, and with the election completely in the hands of the friends of the constitution, the opposition movement was hopeless from the start.

Most tumultuous of all the conventions was the one which convened in Tallahassee, on January 20, 1868, to write a new constitution for Florida. Forty-six delegates were elected, of whom two were Conservative whites, eighteen were Negroes, and the balance about evenly divided between "carpetbaggers" and "scalawags." Jonathan Gibbs, Philadelphia-born Negro, educated at Dartmouth and the Princeton Theological Seminary, a Presbyterian divine and a man of character and ability, was the outstanding colored member of the convention, although he was eclipsed during its noisy sessions by the more vocal and more radical William U. Saunders, Baltimore barber, and the Reverend Charles H. Pearce, of Canada. Most of the "carpetbagger" members had come to Florida shortly after the war. Many of them were ex-army officers, and few properly could be called "carpetbaggers" who had come down merely for political office and public plunder. Of the "scalawag" members, several were deserters from the Confederate Army, and not ashamed of it.

Upon the opening day of the convention, with less than two-thirds of the elected delegates present, Liberty Billings' "Mule Team" faction of Radicals took command. Daniel Richards, of Illinois, whom John Wallace afterward described as a "carpetbagger of moderate ability and elastic conscience," was elected chairman, by a coalition of most of the Negroes and a few of the whites. The organization of the convention and its committees passed into the hands of the most radical of the Republican factions. Before the week was out, there was open conflict between them and the more moderate element, made up of a few of the Negroes and most of the whites.

The fight centered on the question of eligibility of Billings, Richards and other leading Radicals for the seats to which they were declared elected. On February 1, the controlling faction successfully defeated any effort to inquire into their own eligibity, whereupon eighteen of the "Opposition" withdrew in a body and proceeded to the near-by town of Monticello, there to set up in business as an independent constitutional convention. Twenty-two delegates remained in Tallahassee; three others joined the Monticello convention, to give it twenty-one members. Neither convention had a majority of the forty-six elected. Both conventions wrote constitutions. The Tallahassee group, having finished a draft of its constitution and sent it to Atlanta for approval by General Meade, recessed for a week on February 8.

Two nights later, the Monticello convention returned in a body to Tallahassee, quietly took possession of the convention chamber in the State House at midnight, arrested two members of the other faction found in the city, dragged them into the hall to make a quorum, and proceeded to organize by deposing Richards as president, and electing in his stead Horatio Jenkins, Jr. Amid excitement, but under the protection and tacit approval of the army commander at Tallahassee, the revamped convention adopted the constitution written at Monticello.

General Meade, the district commander, hurried to Tallahassee to settle the situation. Arriving on February 17, he found the Jenkins convention in possession of the capitol, the Richards convention holding indignation meetings in churches, lodge rooms and on the public square. The General persuaded both chairmen to resign, and brought the two groups together again in the convention hall, on February 18, with Colonel John T. Sprague, army commander in Florida, in the chair. On the reorganization of the convention the Monticello group dominated. Jenkins was re-elected president, by a vote of thirty-two to eight, while Billings, Saunders, Richards and Pearce, whose doubtful eligibility had caused the split, were declared not citizens of Florida and therefore ineligible.

By February 25, the convention had completed its work, again adopting the Monticello constitution, which enfranchised the Negroes but went no further in disfranchisement of the whites than the acts of Congress required. It contained, also, an arrangement limiting the representation of any one county which, the Radicals charged with truth, made it possible for "less than one-fourth of the registered voters to elect a majority of the state senate, and less than one-third to elect a majority in the assembly." The purpose of the limitation, obviously, was to reduce the representative strength of the eight counties in which there were heavy colored majorities, where most of the population of the state was then concentrated.

Texas moved through the processes of Reconstruction always one step behind the other states, because of the difficulties imposed by its size, remoteness and lack of communication and transportation. While new constitutions were being written elsewhere, the Texans were voting on February 10-14, 1868, on the question of holding a constitutional convention, and electing the delegates to compose it if held. A conference of Conservatives in Houston, in a last minute effort to carry out the scheme of voting *against* holding a convention, and voting *for* Conservative delegates to sit in it if held, managed to bring out just enough votes to make the total cast more than half the registration. Votes for a convention numbered 44,689; against, 11,440.

Of the ninety delegates elected, there were only nine Negroes, of whom the acknowledged leader was G. T. Ruby, an educated man from New England, who had settled in Galveston. Of the whites, twelve were Conservatives, many of whom had been Unionists during the war. The Republicans, dividing into moderate and ultra-Radical factions, included nearly a score who had served in the Union Army, and half a dozen who had been in the Confederate. Nearly all the members of the convention were Texans by birth or adoption before the war, however, with only six or eight true "carpetbaggers."

The convention did not begin its sessions until June 1, 1868. In the first test of strength, E. J. Davis, the candidate of the Morgan Hamilton ultra-Radicals, was elected president over Judge Colbert Caldwell, the candidate of the Andrew Jackson Hamilton moderates. The first session of the convention, which lasted until August 31, and spent more than one hundred thousand dollars, devoted comparatively little time to the business of actually writing a constitution, but expended a vast lot of time and developed intense factional heat over the question of whether or not all public acts since 1861, including those of the Hamilton provisional government and the Throckmorton restored government, were void *ab initio*, or merely voidable; over various propositions for the state to divide itself into three, or perhaps four, states as authorized under the terms of the annexation of 1845; and over the extent of lawlessness in the state, of which there certainly was more than enough, and the responsibility for it.

On the ninety-second day of the session, having spent all the money the military commander would let them have; with their work far from completed, and almost deadlocked by factional quarrels, the convention recessed until December 1. In the meanwhile, new taxes would come in to pay for their further deliberations, and, it was confidently and rightly believed, a new president of the United States would have been chosen at the November elections.

CHAPTER XXXII

Seven Senators Save the Constitution

While lesser Reconstructionists worked away at remaking the states of the South to the new pattern, the leaders in Congress kept on with their part in the grand design of making the government immediately responsive to the will of the people as understood, interpreted and applied by themselves.

The whole way of thought of the Reconstructionists was to identify the welfare of their party and the success of its every policy with the welfare of the nation. Quite sincerely, for the most part, they believed that the safety of the nation depended upon the continuance in power not only of the Republican party but of their particular sect of Republicans. The majority of the Reconstructionists in Congress were men convinced of the purity of their motives and the righteousness of their mission, and impressed with the idea that from the electorate, if not from Deity itself, they had received a mandate for their course. It is an exalted state of mind not unknown in public life in times of stress and crisis.

Impressed as they were with their mandate, however, and convinced as they were of the correctness of their course, they were more than a little concerned about what the Supreme Court would have to say about the constitutionality of their measure, and they were thoroughly outdone with the continued, and to them contumacious and obstructive attitude of the President.

Through the first months of the winter session, Southern affairs received comparatively little active attention on the floors of Congress, unless the abortive attempt in the House to impeach the President, and the successful attempt in the Senate to get Secretary Stanton back into the war office, could be so considered. In truth there was plenty else in the affairs of the government to which the Congress might have given its attention, to judge from the statement of David A. Wells, the very able special commissioner of Internal Revenue, made in January, 1868, that "fraud and incompetency in official position" was depriving the government of a large part of its legitimate revenues. Wells asserted "that nearly $266,000,000 due to the Government has in one year either not been collected through the incompetency of its agents, or has been collected by them and either stolen by them or divided between them and the persons owing it."

The internal revenue taxes had a special bearing on the South, through the tax of two and one-half cents a pound on cotton, imposed in 1865 and kept on, at varying rates, ever since. The tax had been the subject of unheeded protest from commercial men and bodies, Northern as well as Southern, and of restoration legislatures in the South, as being burdensome, unjust, and, in effect, a tax on exports. Its administration had been criticised as a source of fraud and oppression. Finally, during January, certain of the Reconstruction constitutional conventions in the cotton states made representations to Congress as to the oppressive bearing upon the "loyal" of a tax originally designed to bear upon the "rebel" population. Action followed, on February 3, when Congress at last repealed the tax.

The Supreme Court's announcement that it had accepted jurisdiction in the habeas corpus appeal of Colonel McCardle, which squarely involved the constitutionality of the Reconstruction Acts, coincided disconcertingly with the news that Alabama, in the first election held on one of the new Reconstruction constitutions, had failed to ratify it. The constitution received an overwhelming majority of the votes cast in the election, of course—70,812 for ratification and only 1,005 against—but the total vote for it was nearly 15,000 short of a majority of the state's registered voters, although the polls had been kept open five days, February 4-8, 1868.

The correspondent of the Cincinnati Commercial at Montgomery noted the great "Negro interest and enthusiasm" for the constitution, but the results of the election showed a distinct loss in Reconstruction sentiment among that part of the white population which was allowed to vote. Eighteen thousand whites had voted to hold a convention, but only five thousand voted to ratify the document which the convention drafted. Congress was faced with the defeat of the handiwork of the first of its satellite conventions.

Attempts were made in the House of Representatives, in February and March, to admit Alabama, rejected constitution and all, without success. Alabama, therefore, remained in a sort of status quo of suspense, while various plans were offered and debated, and partially passed, to set up some kind of provisional government on the basis of the rejected constitution. Against all such plans, the Conservative executive committee thus memorialized Congress:

"We are beset by secret oath-bound political societies, our character and conduct are systematically misrepresented to you and in the newspapers of the North. . . . Continue over us, if you will, your own rule by the sword. Send down among us honorable and upright men of your own people, of the race to which you and we belong, and . . . no hand will be raised among us to resist by force their authority. But do not, we implore you, abdicate your rule over us, by transferring us to the blighting brutality and unnatural domination of an alien and inferior race."

In anticipation of the ratification of the constitution in Alabama, officers to serve under it were voted for at the same election. The Radical nominees, with huge majorities of the votes cast, although less than a majority of the registered electorate, naturally looked upon themselves as elected and entitled to serve, despite General Meade's official report that the constitution had failed of adoption.

The Radicals claiming election, consequently, met at Montgomery on February 17, organized themselves as a legislature, and for some time attempted to transact legislative business, including the election of two United States senators "to sit upon the trial of that renegade and traitor, Andrew Johnson."

For Andrew Johnson had at last been impeached of "high crimes and misdemeanors" by the House of Representatives. The high crimes and misdemeanors were not specified—that was to come later—but the impeachment had been voted, on February 24. The immediately inciting cause was the President's attempt, on February 21, to remove Secretary Stanton from the War Department, with intent to get the Tenure of Office Act into the courts for judicial determination of its constitutionality. To the inflamed imaginations of the time, however, this second abortive attempt to oust Stanton was an attempt to reverse the policy of Congress and undo the work of Reconstruction, even, some believed, to overthrow the government by force.

The immediate result of the attempt to remove the Secretary of War was a bit of almost pure farce. As Secretary ad interim, the President named the Adjutant General of the Army, Lorenzo Thomas, to whom he gave two papers, his own commission and a notice to quit, to be served on Mr. Stanton. General Thomas, elated at his new dignity but a little shaky in his resolution and considerably in doubt as to his procedure, went to the War Department, served the notice to quit on Mr. Stanton and claimed the office of Secretary.

Refusing to yield, Stanton ordered him back to the Adjutant General's office, whereupon the General returned to the White House, made a partial report of the affair, and was sent back to the War Department to "take charge of the office and perform the duties."

Meanwhile, both the President and Mr. Stanton reported the actions of the day to the Senate, which, in executive session, resolved by a vote of twenty-eight to six that the President was without constitutional or legal power to remove the Secretary of War and designate any other officer to perform his duties.

Copies of the Senate's resolution were sent that night to the President, to Mr. Stanton and to General Thomas. The General was enjoying his evening. At Willard's Hotel, the great convivial gathering-place of Washington in that day, and later at his own home, he announced that he intended to take possession of the Secretary's office in the morning, by force if necessary. Still later in the evening, at a masquerade ball at Marini's, the General was found by the messenger of the Senate and served with a copy of the Senate's resolution.

During the same evening, hearing of the General's declarations, Secretary Stanton secured a warrant for his arrest. The arrest was made, at General Thomas' home, before breakfast on February 22. Under custody of the marshal, the General went by the White House and reported his predicament to the President. "Very well," said the President, "that is the place I want it in—the courts."

Unfortunately for the President's plans, however, when the General was taken before the Justice who had issued the warrant, bail was offered him. The General made bond; secured his own release from custody; took the case right out of the hands of the courts where the President wanted it; and proceeded again to the War Department.

There he found Mr. Stanton in full and fortified possession, surrounded by a zealous group of congressmen and others, determined to resist by force any attempt to remove him. Another long colloquy between the rival claimants to the office, wherein each attempted to order the other about, ended with General Thomas' plaintive request of the Secretary that "the next time you have me arrested, please do not do it before I get something to eat." It being then after twelve o'clock, the General complained that he had had nothing to eat or drink that day. The Secretary remedied at least part of that lack by dividing fairly and equally the contents of a small vial of whisky in the office, followed by carefully measured equal drinks from a regular bottle brought in by a messenger. So ended the General's short dream of acting as Secretary of War, with Mr. Stanton in full possession, eating and sleeping in the office to avoid any possibility of losing the advantage of that possession, and guarded, day and night, by forces in and about the building. So began, too, in an air of anxious excitement, the final and successful attempt to secure the impeachment of the President by the House of Representatives.

On the morning of February 22, the President sent to the Senate as his nominee for Secretary of War the name of Thomas Ewing of Ohio, father-in-law of General Sherman, and a man against whose character, attainments and patriotism no one could offer criticism. The Senate, not being in session on account of the Washington's Birthday holiday, did not receive the nomination until the following Monday, February 24, a day of such excitement that the nomination was simply ignored and never acted upon.

For on that day, the House voted its impeachment of the President. The resolution of impeachment, brought into the House on the afternoon of Saturday, the twenty-second, by the Committee on Reconstruction, read simply "That Andrew Johnson, President of the United States, be impeached of high crimes and misdemeanors in office." Charges and specifications could be developed later. The immediate thing was to get the resolution through in the excitement being whipped up throughout the country over the President's alleged attempt to violate the Tenure of Office Act and subvert the government itself by the removal of the Secretary of War.

Debate went on through Saturday and all day Monday, to end, late that afternoon, with the adoption of the resolution by a strict party vote—one hundred twenty-six Republicans for, forty-seven Democrats against. The House had done the unprecedented thing of adopting a blanket impeachment, before investigation and without the allegation of any specific impeachable act. But Washington was filled and the country resounded with wild rumors of the plots of the President, once he should succeed in getting Stanton out of the way as the sentinel of Reconstruction.

Having adopted its resolution without specific articles of impeachment, the House created a committee of seven to devise and draft them, and another committee, of two, Thaddeus Stevens and John A. Bingham, to notify the Senate of the impeachment of the President and of the fact that the House would "in due time exhibit particular articles of impeachment against him and make good the same."

This confident declaration was followed, on March 4, by the appearance at the bar of the Senate of the House's committee of managers—John A. Bingham, George S. Boutwell, Benjamin F. Butler, John A. Logan, Thaddeus Stevens, Thomas Williams, and James F. Wilson—to present the eleven articles of impeachment which had been devised, not so much to present facts or do justice as "to make good" the impeachment already voted, by offering as varied a line of vote-catching charges as could be assembled.

Eight articles, with variations in emphasis and legal phraseology, charged the President with unlawfully attempting to remove Stanton in violation of the Tenure of Office Act and of the Constitution, and with conspiring with General Thomas, in violation of the war-time act of 1861 against conspiracies to hinder officers from performing their duties. The ninth article, based on rumors that the President had tried, through General Emory, to engineer a coup by use of the Washington garrison, charged the President with attempt to violate the Army Act of March 2, 1867.

The tenth article, adopted on March 3, a day later than the others, was the especial concoction of General Butler. It did not charge the President with violation of specific law, as did the first nine, but merely with having attempted to bring Congress into "disgrace, ridicule, hatred, contempt and reproach" through "inflammatory and scandalous harangues," and with having degraded the Presidency, "to the great scandal of all good citizens."

The eleventh article, also adopted as an afterthought, was Mr. Stevens' special contribution. It was justly known as the "Omnibus Article," a vague and wordy re-hash of all the others, with a few additional details, designed to afford somewhere within its bulk of language something upon which any and every doubtful senator might hang a vote for conviction. Senator Buckalew described it as

"nondescript and a curiosity in pleading. As an article on which to convict its strength consists in its weakness—in the obscurity of its charges and the intricacy of its form. . . . Considered in parts it is nothing—the propositions into which it is divisible cannot stand separately as charge of criminal conduct or intention; and considered as a whole it eludes the understanding and baffles conjecture."

The most striking thing about all these eleven voluminous articles of impeachment is that no one of them charged a corrupt act or, indeed, any act which was impeachable. The whole burden of the charges was a matter of political differences with the Congress, which were alleged to be "unlawful."

Having received the charges on March 4, the Senate adjourned until the next day, when Chief Justice Chase joined the senators in "form ing a court of impeachment for the trial of the President of the United States." The Chief Justice was sworn, and in turn swore each of the members of the Senate sitting as a court of impeachment to "do impartial justice according to the Constitution and the laws." One of the senators so sworn was Benjamin F. Wade, of Ohio, president pro tem of the Senate, who would succeed to the Presidency in the event of the conviction and removal of Johnson. The Constitution forbids the vice-president to take part in the impeachment trial of a president, but objection to the swearing of Senator Wade, whose position as the political beneficiary of the conviction of a president was analogous to that of a vice-president, was overruled and the Senator was sworn to "do impartial justice" in a case in which he had a strong personal interest. On March 6, the Senate adopted rules for its governance as a court of impeachment, and adjourned, in that capacity, for a week.

A week earlier, on the night of February 28, Senator Wade had made a surprise attempt to add two reliably Radical members to the two-thirds majority in the Senate, by securing the passage, over the veto of the President, of the bill admitting Colorado to statehood. The bill, with the veto, had been lying on the table of the Senate, without action, for nearly a year. A year before, when Congress had passed bills to admit the territories of Nebraska and Colorado as states, the President vetoed them, on the ground, as to both territories, that they had but a tiny fraction of the population necessary to justify one member of the House of Representatives; and further, as to Colorado, that there had been fatal irregularities in the proceedings leading up to the act of admission, including failure of a majority of the voters of the territory to ratify the proposed new state constitution.

The veto of the Nebraska bill had been overruled, promptly, and the state had been admitted, with two strongly Radical senators, Thayer and Tipton, but the Colorado veto had not been acted upon. Just before midnight on February 28, Senator Wade saw, or thought he saw, an opportunity to muster the two-thirds necessary to pass the Colorado bill over the veto and so to add two more Radicals to the majority in the Senate which was expected to vote him into the Presidency. Without notice, he had the bill and veto called off the table, and demanded a vote. Unable to carry the thing through that night, because of objections of senators who were less rough and ready in their methods than "Bluff Ben," the vote had to be deferred until the next day, when the bill received less than the necessary two-thirds majority. The Senate thus declined to enlarge its membership in advance of the impeachment trial—just as later, in May, and just before the vote on the impeachment articles was to be taken, it declined to join the House in rushing the admission of new senators from the states undergoing Reconstruction.

On March 13, the Senate, sitting as a court of impeachment, with the Chief Justice of the United States presiding, opened the trial of the President. Andrew Johnson appeared, not in person, but through able and distinguished counsel—Henry Stanbery, who had resigned as attorney general to be free to engage in the case without embarrassment; Benjamin R. Curtis, one-time member of the Supreme Court, where he was one of the dissenters in the Dred Scott decision, and a leader of the bar of Massachusetts; and Thomas A. R. Nelson, of Tennessee, long-time friend and associate of Andrew Johnson, chairman of the Greeneville convention which had tried to keep Tennessee from secession, and one of the representatives which East Tennessee had sent to the national House of Representatives during the first year of the war. To these were added William M. Evarts, a leader of the bar of New York, and William S. Groesbeck, of Cincinnati, who as a young man had read law in the office of Salmon P. Chase, now the chief justice.

Counsel for the President asked forty days' time in which to study the voluminous and involved articles of impeachment, prepare their defense and file their answer. The Senate granted ten days. On March 23, therefore, the President's attorneys made answer. On the next day, the managers of the impeachment for the House of Representatives filed their replication to the answer, and the issues were before the Senate for hearing and action. Over the opposition of counsel for the President, the trial was set for March 30, six days later.

The real issue of the case, in spite of irrelevant testimony and wordy debate, was drawn right at the beginning. The Chief Justice took the position that in matters of impeachment the Senate was a court. General Butler, opening for the impeachment managers, argued that it was not a court in the judicial sense but a political body empowered to try and to determine the political fitness of the President. The point was neatly put by Senator Sumner, one of the "judges," if the Chief Justice were right in his view that impeachment was a judicial process and the Senate a court. To the Senator, however, the proceeding was "political in character—before a political body—and with a political object."

The political crimes charged against the President were disagreement with Congress, which he freely admitted; and an unlawful attempt to violate the Tenure of Office Act, which he denied, on the ground that the act itself was invalid, being contrary to the fundamental law of the Constitution. Evidence that the President's intent in his attempt to remove Stanton was to secure a test of the law was held admissible by the Chief Justice, but, on appeal, was refused by a majority of the Senate.

In fact, if the prosecution was to have a chance to convict on the evidence and the law, such testimony had to be ruled out, for members of the Cabinet were ready to go before the Senate and testify that every member of the Cabinet considered the act unconstitutional when it was passed; that Stanton had been especially emphatic in his objections, had furnished several of the ideas incorporated in the President's veto message, and had asked to be excused from preparing a draft of the message only because of a rheumatic arm; and that Stanton, along with every other member of the Cabinet, had agreed that the act, as drawn, did not apply to the hold-over members of the Cabinet, appointed by Lincoln and continued in office under Johnson.

The act read, in effect, that Cabinet officers should hold office "for and during the term of the President by whom they may have been appointed and for one month thereafter," subject to removal by and with the advice and consent of the Senate. No doubt the Congress which passed the law intended that members of the Lincoln Cabinet remaining in office under President Johnson could not be removed except with Senate approval. Through clumsy draftsmanship, they said exactly the opposite. The protection from removal intended to apply to the Lincoln holdovers uncovered them, and covered the Johnson original appointees, in whom the Congress had not the slightest interest.

Opened with an argument of invective and epithets by General Butler, the prosecution continued with five days of testimony, hardly more than the pro forma business of making a sworn record of facts as to which there was no real dispute.

On April 9, the defense opened with a presentation of the law in the case by former Justice Curtis, followed by evidence as to the President's acts. With much argument as to the admissibility of evidence, and an evident disposition on the part of a majority of the Senate to restrict the testimony for the President to the narrowest limits, attorneys for the defense were able to show, by General Emory himself, that the ninth article was groundless; and by General Sherman and others, that the purpose of trying to remove Stanton was not to obstruct or overturn the government but to test the acts of Congress involved.

Taking of testimony closed on April 20. Two days later, final argument opened, with four speeches on a side, continuing until May 6. In these arguments, the defense lawyers, with the facts, the law, and a distinctly higher level of legal ability on their side, clearly had the best of it. It was apparent, before the end of the trial, that the outcome probably would depend upon a small group of Republican senators who insisted upon regarding themselves as impartial judges, rather than as political prosecutors.

On April 23, the day after argument opened, the President sent to the Senate the nomination of General John M. Schofield to be Secretary of War. While the nomination was not acted upon until after the trial, it had its bearing on the outcome, as an indication of the high type of man whom the President desired to have as Secretary of War.

Monday, May 11, the Senate deliberated behind the closed doors of executive session. Voting on the articles of impeachment was to begin the next day, but the sudden illness of Senator Jacob M. Howard caused the taking of the first vote to be postponed until Saturday, May 16.

Meanwhile, the drift of the discussions in the executive session of Monday had leaked out and had indicated that there was doubt of mustering the thirty-six votes, two-thirds of the Senate, necessary for conviction. Immediately, the Senate, and particularly those members whose votes for conviction were regarded as doubtful, were exposed to every manner of pressure from back home. Mass meetings and political bodies telegraphed resolutions; individuals used the most abusive tactics on doubtful senators; even the churches took a hand. From Kansas came a telegram to Senator Edmund G. Ross, signed by "D. R. Anthony and a thousand others," demanding his vote for conviction. When Senator Ross replied that he would vote according to his oath and his conscience, Mr. Anthony and his thousand unnamed associates expanded themselves into the whole state and wired, "Kansas repudiates you as she does all perjurers and skunks."

From North Carolina, Governor Holden wired his prayer that "the usurper in the White House" be found guilty. "In the name of humanity, liberty and justice," he asked, "can it be possible that Andrew Johnson will be acquitted?" The Union Leagues in Tennessee denounced Senator Joseph S. Fowler and the "seven recreants" for their "perfidy." The West Virginia legislature addressed resolutions to its senators, while the Methodist General Conference, in session at Chicago, offered prayer that senators might be saved from error—meaning in particular that Senator Waitman T. Willey, of West Virginia, a devout member of the denomination, might vote for conviction. A conference of one of the Negro Methodist Churches, in session in Washington, short-cut the circumlocution of referring the matter to Deity, and prayed to the Senate direct that it convict. As the Chief Justice wrote, privately, at the time, ". . . All the appliances to force a measure through Congress are in use here to force a conviction through the Court of Impeachment."

At the end of the week of pressure, on Saturday, May 16, came the first vote, taken on the eleventh, or Omnibus Article, the one which seemed most likely to attract the largest number of wavering senators. On the call of the roll, the first of the doubtful Republican senators to be reached was William Pitt Fessenden, of Maine, a senator of high caliber. "Not Guilty," he voted, to be followed, in turn, by Joseph S. Fowler, of Tennessee; by James W. Grimes, of Iowa; by John B. Henderson, of Missouri; by Edmund G. Ross, of Kansas, upon whom the most merciless pressure had been applied; by Lyman Trumbull, of Illinois; and, finally, right at the end of the roll call, by Peter G. Van Winkle, of West Virginia, all voting "Not Guilty." The vote stood, Guilty, thirty-five; Not Guilty, nineteen—and impeachment had failed by one vote.

The Senate adjourned until May 26, to give ten days more in which to bring pressure to bear on the seven senators who had balked the Radical majority. The managers of impeachment, under the leadership of General Butler, put through the House a resolution of investigation of the alleged "improper or corrupt means used to influence the determination of the Senate." The investigating committee seized private messages from the telegraph offices; it forced banks to exhibit the private accounts of their customers; it employed spies to sneak out and search the contents of wastebaskets; it indulged in innuendo, when it found no evidence to sustain its charges; and, altogether, it managed to create at home, and especially abroad, the impression that at least some of the seven senators had acted through improper and corrupt motives.

That such outrageous innuendoes, which never attained to the dignity of charges, should have had wide acceptance is evidence of the pathological state of mind of the times. The nature of the charges against the President were vaguely apprehended by the partisan mass of the public, and not at all understood. They had been taught to look upon the President as a "traitor" and a "rebel," such a one as no senator might conceivably vote to acquit for any good and proper reason. They, and most of their representatives in Congress, were strong for conviction on general principles. The Radical press raged and clamored, the pulpit thundered, while the practical politicians put on the pressure, preparatory to trying to vote on some other of the articles of impeachment.

To such lengths was this process of intimidation carried, that the impeachment managers even sought to have Senator Henderson called before the House to be interrogated on his vote for acquittal. About that vote, John Sherman, who voted "Guilty," was to say to Henderson two years later, "You were right and I was wrong."

After ten days of such tactics, on May 26, the question of guilt or innocence was again put, first on the second and then on the third article. Again the vote was thirty-five for conviction, nineteen for acquittal—one less than the two-thirds necessary to convict—and the great Impeachment Trial was over.

President Johnson had been so traduced and vilified, so blackened in his reputation, that a whole generation of Americans was to grow up in the belief that a wicked ruler, or at the best one unfit for his office, had escaped conviction by the narrowest possible margin, but he remained in office, surrounded by restrictions of every sort, but still President and still in his own sphere an independent representative of the people who elected him.

The seven senators, when they refused to vote that the President had committed a crime in differing with the Congress, did two things. They did justice, at great cost to themselves, and in the face of almost overwhelming popular pressure and hysteria. That most certainly was no small thing to do but they did more. They preserved the distinctive American plan of government—a government of co-equal branches, each independent in the sphere assigned to it by the Constitution which established and governed them all.

CHAPTER XXXIII

Six New States

To COMPLETE the creation of the new synthetic states in the South, according to the formula of the Reconstruction Acts, required still other steps to be taken, both in the states and at Washington—ratification of the new constitutions by the voters; election of new officials and legislators; approval of the new constitutions by Congress; ratification of the Fourteenth Amendment by each of the new state legislatures; and then, finally, admission of new senators and representatives to the houses of Congress, with such other fundamental conditions as Congress might prescribe in each case. The rebirth of a state was a political process neither short nor easy.

Alabama's failure to ratify, in the first of the elections on the new constitutions, showed up glaringly another defect in the already twice-amended Reconstruction Act. The conservative white populations had found a way to defeat Reconstruction, or at least delay it, and remain under military rule, by registering and refusing to vote. That prospect would not have disturbed greatly the Reconstructionist leaders a year before, but events in 1867 and the election prospects of 1868 warned that their best hope of continued power lay not in keeping the Southern states out of the Union but in bringing them in, as speedily as possible, to secure additional electoral votes and congressional strength.

Late in February, 1868, therefore, Congress passed its third Supplemental Reconstruction Bill, to govern the constitutional elections yet to be held. This bill, which became law over the veto of the President on March 11, provided that a majority of the votes cast, not a majority of the total registration, was necessary for ratification; that only ten days' residence in a state would be required before voting, regardless of any state law to the contrary; and that the new officials to be chosen in each state were to be elected at the same time and by the same voters who were to pass on the constitutions. The way to readmission was to be speeded and smoothed.

Two days after the bill became law, General Grant notified General Gillem, commanding in Arkansas, of its provisions. On the same day,

310

the voters in Arkansas began to cast their ballots in an election which lasted two weeks, until March 27. The Conservatives charged that the election was a remarkable piece of political trickery and fraud: that the registrars holding the election (themselves candidates) changed the polling places arbitrarily and secretly, carted the registration books and ballot boxes around to the new and unaccustomed places of voting, erased registrations and substituted others, made false certifications, switched ballots, tolerated repeating and encouraged ballot-box stuffing. In spite of these practices, many of which were tacitly admitted, the constitution received a majority of only 1,316 votes out of more than 54,000 cast, and, of course, much less than a majority of registration. Under the amended law of March 11, 1868, however, it was enough.

Just after this election, and before the inauguration of the Clayton government, Ku Klux warnings began to appear in Arkansas. One such, posted on a tree near Pine Bluff, General Clayton's home, called on

"Spirit Brothers; Shadows of Martyrs; Phantoms from gory fields; Followers of Brutus. . . . When shadows gather, moons grow dim, and stars tremble, glide to the Council Hall and wash your hands in tyrants' blood; and gaze upon the list of condemned traitors. The time has arrived. Blood must flow. The true must be saved.

> Work in darkness.
> Bury in waters.
> Make no sound.
> Trust not the air.
> Strike high and sure.
> Vengeance! Vengeance! Vengeance!

Tried, condemned. Execute well. Fear is dead. Every man is a Judge and this Executes. . . . Fail not!"

Whatever that may have meant to the initiated, it was taken by Governor Clayton as a threat against the new administration of affairs in Arkansas which was to come into power when the Congress should give its permission.

On May 7, Mr. Stevens brought up in the House a bill to admit the state of Arkansas to the Union, upon the further fundamental condition, not expressed in the original Reconstruction Acts, that there should thereafter be no change in its new constitution to deprive any citizen of the right to vote granted in that instrument. Within a week, the bill was through the House and sent to the Senate, then engaged in the latter stages of the impeachment trial. Although the Senate interspersed its sittings as a court of impeachment with legislative sessions, it did not act upon the Arkansas bill until after the final vote was taken in the case of the President. Then, on June 6, it passed the bill to admit Arkansas to representation as a state of the Union, and sent it to the White House. Vetoed by the President on June 20, it was repassed through both Houses by June 22, and Arkansas, following Tennessee by an interval of almost exactly two years, became the second of the former Confederate States to be brought back as a recognized state of the Union, and the first to come in under the Reconstruction Acts.

Anticipating this action, the newly elected legislature of the state had gathered in Little Rock on April 2, and opened its sessions, although outside the legislative halls the Murphy government continued to function. The first action of the new legislature was to ratify the Fourteenth Amendment on April 3, by coincidence the same day on which Iowa, last of the Northern states to ratify, took like action. The Arkansas legislature promptly chose United States senators, also, in anticipation of their admission. These senators, Benjamin F. Rice and Alexander McDonald, together with L. H. Roots, James Hinds and Thomas Boles, the new Representatives, were in Washington ready to be sworn in as soon as the state was admitted.

On July 2, after Congress had acted to admit the state, the new governor, Powell Clayton, was sworn in before a crowd occupying a bank of seats placed under the oaks in front of Arkansas' Doric-columned capitol. After the ceremony, the retiring Governor led his successor into the executive office, furnished with a long pine table, an open case of pigeonholes, homemade split-bottomed chairs, a print of George Washington and a barrel. From the straw in the barrel, Governor Murphy fished a stone jug of moonshine whisky, extended its hospitality to his successor, and committed the government of Arkansas into the strong hands of young Clayton, then but thirty-five years old.

The Arkansas government was dominated by the Governor, with powers greatly enlarged in the new constitution, with his associates of the group commonly known as "carpetbaggers." The name was a misnomer in many cases, in Arkansas, but using it as the common description of men who had come into the state during or after the war, it appears that in the initial government, that element in political life held the Governorship, both United States Senatorships, two of the three seats in Congress, and most of the state administrative and judicial offices.

On May 11, that being the day on which the Senate in executive session began its deliberations on the impeachment trial, the Committee on Reconstruction reported out to the House the measure which came to be known as the "Omnibus Bill" for the readmission of six states—the two Carolinas, Georgia, Florida, Louisiana and Alabama. Readmission was conditioned upon the ratification of the Fourteenth Amendment by the legislatures, and upon the further "fundamental condition" that the new state constitutions should never be amended to disfranchise any class of citizens then declared voters.

While the bill was following its usual course through the two houses, including repassage over the President's veto, the new states were holding their local elections, where they had not already been held, and some were ratifying the Fourteenth Amendment, so as to be ready to resume their statehood upon the final passage of the bill, which came on June 25, 1868.

Alabama was included in the Omnibus Bill, despite the failure of its voters in February to ratify the new constitution under the law as it then stood. Congress, which made that law, had, and did not hesitate to use, the power to set it aside and make one new and different. The other five states were included as a result of a series of elections on the new constitutions, held in April and the early days of May, under the law as revised.

South Carolina's ratification election, held on April 14-16, resulted in the adoption of the new constitution by a vote of 70,758 to 27,228. The Conservative whites failed to agree on a policy, while whites of the Radical persuasion, both native and imported, controlled the great new Negro vote which carried the election. State and local officers were chosen at a later election, on June 2 and 3. The new Governor was to be Robert K. Scott, of Ohio, brevet major general, and assistant commissioner of the Freedmen's Bureau for the state; the Lieutenant-Governor, Lemuel Boozer, "scalawag." The Attorney General elected was Daniel H. Chamberlain, scholar, Union soldier, Low-Country planter, before he entered Carolina politics. The financial officers were Treasurer Niles G. Parker of Massachusetts, who came south as captain of colored troops, and Comptroller-General John L. Neagle, a native of North Carolina, who had been in the Confederate service. The new Adjutant- and Inspector-General was F. J. Moses,

Jr., a native white whose father was chief justice of the state. In this first group of state officers there was but one colored man, Francis L. Cardozo, secretary of state, and head of the Union League in South Carolina.

Of the entire group, Chamberlain and Cardozo were easily outstanding in education and ability. The caliber of most of the officials, or at least the local and contemporary estimate of them, is indicated in a story told of Timothy Hurley, the only Irish-born member of the legislature. Mr. Hurley, who came to Charleston from Connecticut, was publisher of the *Leader*, a Negro newspaper. One of his white newspaper contemporaries said of him that he was "respected by nobody, liked by everybody." He was invited to a stag dinner given by Governor Scott, in celebration of his election, so the story runs. Others invited, besides state officials, included a dozen of the leading citizens of Columbia, none of whom came to the party.

"Mr. Hurley," said the Governor, "I think we have here a beautiful entertainment, delicious foods, good wines, tasty decorations, a fine orchestra—but are you not surprised that so few of the gentlemen of Columbia have responded to our invitation?"

To which Mr. Hurley made smiling reply: "Governor, I think if I were a gentleman I wouldn't be here myself."

In the new legislature, the Senate had twenty-four white and nine colored members; the House, forty-eight white and seventy-six colored. Only seven senators and sixteen representatives were Conservatives, the rest Radicals. The legislature was called into special session on July 6, at Janney's Hall, in Columbia, for the purpose of ratifying the Fourteenth Amendment, which it did, almost unanimously, on July 7 and 8. On the next day, July 9, South Carolina was declared again in the Union, entitled to four seats in the House of Representatives and two senators.

Like most of the state officers, the first congressmen under Reconstruction were white. Two were natives, Manuel S. Corley and James H. Goss; two were imported, the Reverend B. Frank Whittemore, of Massachusetts, and Christopher Columbus Bowen, of Rhode Island and Georgia. The two United States senators elected by the first legislature were Thomas J. Robertson, a native businessman of wealth and position, and Frederick A. Sawyer, a fine type of Massachusetts schoolteacher who had come to Charleston in 1859 to head the Normal School.

South Carolina, it seemed, was quietly accepting a result which it could not avoid. There were some small attempts at Ku Klux operations, which the Charleston *News* dismissed as the "fancy of a few hairbrained youths." Governor Orr, whose provisional administration was to be succeeded by that of General Scott, sincerely believed that the part of wisdom for the substantial white people of South Carolina was to conciliate and lead the Negroes toward good government for the state. It was a high and difficult ideal but, as one acute contemporary observer noted, would have had small chance of success in practice, not because of any innate depravity of the Negroes but because of the seemingly inescapable laws of political action.

"Had all the white politicians been men of Orr's standards and practices," said the observer quoted by Dr. William Watts Ball, "he would have been right. . . . Judge Orr's mistake was in not perceiving that he and others like him would be helpless to withstand the white demagogues in a mixed party . . . experts in buying the Negroes with money, flattery and whisky."

Louisiana voted on April 16 and 17, in a quiet election, in which the new constitution was ratified by a vote of 51,737 to 39,076, and new state officers were elected. The new Governor was to be that "remarkable young man" from Illinois and Missouri, twenty-six-year-old Henry Clay Warmoth, who ran well ahead of the constitution and handsomely defeated the nominee of the Pure Radical faction, Judge Taliaferro. Oscar J. Dunn, a Louisiana colored house-painter, was chosen lieutenant-governor, along with the rest of the Warmoth, or "Compromising Radical," ticket.

The new Governor, who was formally inaugurated at New Orleans on July 13, surprised friends and opponents by an address which, said the New Orleans *Times*, was of "a tone far more moderate and conciliatory than had been expected." Young Warmoth had gone from Illinois to Missouri at the age of eighteen; had been admitted to the bar within a year; had raised more than seven hundred men for the Union army before he was twenty; was lieutenant colonel on the staff of General McClernand before he was twenty-one; was dishonorably dismissed from the service on charges of absence without leave and spreading prejudicial reports about the Vicksburg expedition; proceeded to Washington, and laid before the President and the War Department evidence to show that injustice had been done him and he had been improperly discharged; was reinstated in the service in time to command a regiment in the fighting about Chattanooga before he was twenty-two years old. Now, at twenty-six, he was to become governor of one of the most important and most difficult of the Reconstruction states.

The state whose government was being entrusted to him had seen its property values cut almost in half in four years of war and three of restoration. Taxes were in arrears for the years from 1860 to 1867. The state was being financed with scrip, with a circulating medium of shinplasters. Both the state debt, and that of the city of New Orleans, were unknown, while their securities were selling at twenty-five cents on the dollar. The levees were still broken, for the most part. There were no roads in the state worthy of the name, and but four paved streets in the city of New Orleans. Top wages for skilled labor ran from two dollars to two dollars and a half a day; for field hands, fifty to seventy-five cents a day. New Orleans had no wharves, few warehouses, only two lines of one-mule street railways. For drainage, it had open ditches; for water supply, cisterns on the roofs or the muddy Mississippi, with the slaughterhouses on the river bank just above the main water intake. The young Governor, whom Senator Carpenter described in the Senate as "embodying in himself the elements of revolution, and delighting in the exercise of his natural gifts in the midst of political excitement," surely had need of all his resource and daring.

Four days after Congress passed the Omnibus Bill, the new Louisiana legislature met in New Orleans, on June 29, 1868, to remain in session until October 20. Out of a Senate of thirty-six members, seven were colored, including the Lieutenant-Governor presiding. The one hundred one members of the House were about equally divided between the races. In both chambers the Republicans had majorities, but by no means the overwhelming majorities found in most of the other Southern states. These majorities the Republicans proposed to increase by unseating many Democratic members through the requirement of the iron-clad oath of 1862, rather than the milder oath of the 1868 constitution. Once more the New Orleans mob began to gather about the Mechanics' Institute, while police forces and a regiment of artillery were called out. General Grant settled the matter by positive instructions that the oath to be administered should be that of 1868, which left the Democrats in possession of their seats.

On July 9, the legislature ratified the Fourteenth Amendment and proceeded to the election of William Pitt Kellogg and John S. Harris as United States senators. The new senators, the first admitted from Louisiana since 1861, took their seats in Washington on July 18, 1868.

North Carolina voted on its new constitution, and elected new state officials, on April 21-23. The vote for the constitution was 93,086; against it, 74,016. By substantially the same vote, W. W. Holden defeated Thomas S. Ashe, the Conservative nominee, and, at last, realized his consuming ambition to be elected governor of North Carolina. The Radicals elected all but one congressman and overwhelming majorities in both houses of the legislature—thirty-eight to twelve in the Senate, eighty to forty in the House.

Reconstruction governments in the South are usually thought and spoken of as Carpetbagger-Negro governments. The makeup of the first North Carolina Reconstruction legislature indicates how far from the fact this conception is, in some cases. There were Negroes in the legislature, three in the Senate and sixteen in the House; and there were "carpetbaggers," seven in the Senate and about twenty in the House. But the great majority of the Radical strength in both houses was made up of native white North Carolinians.

On July 1, 1868, the new government was installed in Raleigh. On the day before, Governor Worth, in a dignified though futile protest, had written the new Governor:

"You have no evidence of your election, save the certificate of a major-general of the United States Army. I regard all of you as in effect appointees of the military power of the United States, and not as deriving your powers from the consent of those you claim to govern.

"Knowing, however, that you are backed by military force here which I could not resist, if I would, I do not deem it necessary to offer a futile opposition, but vacate the office without the ceremony of actual eviction, offering no further opposition than this my protest. . . .

"I surrender the office to you under what I deem military duress, without stopping, as the occasion would well justify, to comment upon the singular coincidence that the present State government is surrendered as without legality to him whose own official sanction, but three years ago, proclaimed it valid."

On July 2, the legislature ratified the Fourteenth Amendment by an overwhelming majority. Two days later, on Independence Day, Governor Holden delivered his inaugural address before a huge throng. Within the week, John Pool, native white, and General J. C. Abbott, originally of New Hampshire but then resident in Wilmington, were elected to the United States Senate, to be sworn in on July 13. A week later, on the 20th, the last of the representatives in Congress was seated, and North Carolina was restored to the roll of states.

While the steps of admission to the national government were being completed, Governor Holden busied himself with the exercise of his local appointing powers. The first large group of officers to be named were the justices of the peace. A sample of local opinion of the Governor's appointees is found in the story of one such magistrate who told the county clerk in Pitt County that he wished to "qualify." When the clerk asked him what he meant, he explained that he wanted to be sworn in to his new office.

"All right," said the clerk, "I can swear you in but all hell couldn't qualify you."

Florida voted on May 6-8, both on the constitution and the election of new officials, after a campaign in which the sharp factional differences which developed in the constitutional convention continued to plague the Republicans. In spite of this, however, and in spite of a listless sort of campaign by the Democrats, the constitution was ratified by a vote of 14,561 to 9,511, and the "regular" Republican ticket was elected by a somewhat larger majority. Heading that ticket as candidate for governor was Harrison Reed, one-time newspaper publisher in Wisconsin, who had come to Florida just after the war as United States mail agent for the state. The new Governor was described by his friends, and conceded by most of his opponents to be, "a high-minded, honest and honorable man," whose intentions were to make the best of a difficult problem of government. His Lieutenant-Governor, likewise from Wisconsin, was William M. Gleason, lumberman and speculator in the pine and turpentine resources of Florida.

The new legislature included, in the Senate, sixteen Republicans and eight Democrats; in the House, thirty-seven Republicans and fifteen Democrats. There were, in the two houses, only nineteen Negroes and thirteen "carpetbaggers."

On June 8, before the joint assembly of the legislature, Governor Reed was sworn in and delivered his inaugural address. On the next day, the legislature ratified the Fourteenth Amendment and then recessed until June 15, having been notified by the local commander of troops at Tallahassee that his orders from the district commander at Atlanta were not to acknowledge the new government in any way until Congress approved.

Reconvening, the legislature went into joint assembly to elect new United States senators. By June 19 it had chosen Adonijah S. Welch, a white schoolteacher from Michigan then engaged in teaching in a Negro school; and Thomas W. Osborn, of New Jersey, who had been the Freedmen's Bureau commissioner for the state. The new senators, and Charles M. Hamilton, of Pennsylvania, ex-army officer and Bureau agent, the state's new congressman, were all seated in Washington by July 2, and the stage was set for the formal relinquishment of government in Florida from the hands of Colonel Sprague, the military commander, into those of the new civil government, with due celebration, on July 4, 1868. Another state was reconstructed.

Governor Reed, under the new constitution, had large powers of appointment to local offices which he did his best to exercise wisely and temperately. His great difficulty was in finding qualified men who were also politically acceptable. As John Wallace afterward wrote:

"The Governor was forced to appoint men as county judges and solicitors, some of whom it was very doubtful as to whether they had ever seen the inside of a law book. Many of the carpetbag office-holders, anterior to their advent in the South, had been blatant Democrats at the North, but not even respectable cross-roads politicians, yet who now claimed to be great men and proper leaders of the colored people of the State."

State and local officials, chosen at the elections in early February, stood ready and waiting to take over the government of Alabama when Congress finally decided to include their state in the Omnibus Bill of June 25.

The Conservative plan of registering and refusing to vote, as it turned out, had not blocked the final recognition of the new government by Congress. By keeping Conservative voters away from the polls, it had merely insured that the new government should be almost one hundred per cent Radical in its personnel. It had, however, done one other thing not then noted. It had, as a practical matter, made it impolitic, if not impossible, for Congress so to change its own laws as to admit senators from the state of Alabama at a time when they would have added two Radical votes for the conviction of Andrew Johnson in the impeachment trial.

Upon passage of the Omnibus Bill, General Grant ordered the district commander at Atlanta to remove Provisional Governor Patton from office and replace him with the Governor elected in February, William M. Smith. The new Governor was a native white Alabamian, an original opponent of secession but one who had been so far converted to the doctrine as to offer himself, without success, as a candidate for the Confederate Congress.

Associated with him in the government were A. J. Applegate, lieutenant-governor, late of Ohio, Wisconsin and the Federal Army, and other state officers from Maine, New York and Wisconsin. The state Senate was made up of thirty-two Republicans, of whom one was a Negro and nine were from the North, with an opposition consisting of one lonesome Democrat. In the House, there were ninety-seven Republicans, of whom twenty-six were Negroes, and three Democrats. Freedmen's Bureau agents were prominent in the legislature and in county offices throughout the state as well.

Six congressmen, elected in February, included a Federal official at Mobile who once had been a congressman from Michigan; four Freedmen's Bureau agents, with varying backgrounds and histories; and one local white who, after acting as a recruiting or conscript officer for the Confederate Army, had become a sergeant in the Union forces.

On July 13, on the call of Governor Smith, the legislature met at Montgomery, promptly ratified the Fourteenth Amendment, and sent to Washington, as senators from Alabama, Willard Warner, a man of good character and ability, who had entered the Union Army from Ohio; and George E. Spencer, a New Englander who had been in politics in Iowa and Nebraska before he came to Alabama as a sutler with Federal troops, and finally joined an Alabama Union cavalry regiment.

On July 21, the senators and congressmen representing Alabama were seated at Washington, in both houses. Five of the six states included in the Omnibus Bill, and six of the ten states still out of the Union, had completed the required steps for admission, and were received into both houses of Congress, before the long sessions which had started in November, 1867, ended on July 27, 1868. In form, they were states all complete, with governors and legislatures and constitutions, and with senators and representatives in Washington, but neither the General of the Armies nor the Radical leaders in Congress were yet willing to withdraw the leading strings and leave them on their own. The "military districts" were regrouped into "departments"—but the garrisons remained.

CHAPTER XXXIV

Four States Still Out

In Georgia, Mississippi, Virginia and Texas the course of Reconstruction was more troubled, and the final readmission of the states, for various reasons, was further delayed.

Georgia's election on a new constitution and new state offices was held on April 20-23. The constitution was ratified by the comparatively small majority of 17,972 votes. Rufus B. Bullock was elected governor over General John B. Gordon by the even smaller majority of 7,171 votes. The strength of the Conservatives and the Republicans in the legislature was not far from equal.

Both sides charged, with vehemence, that the other had used fraud and violence. Both the Ku Klux and the Union Leagues took an active part in the campaign. A Klan notice, with cabalistic introduction, greeting and signature, and vague and general threats of a suspended "terrible retributive vengeance," appeared in the Atlanta *Intelligencer* on March 14.

On April 2, on the other hand, there appeared in the Savannah papers a counter notice, addressed to

"KKK and all BADMEN of the city of Savannah, who now threaten the lives of all the Leaders and Nominees of the Republican Party, and the President and Members of the Union League of America. If you Strike a Blow, the Man or Men will be followed, and the house in which he or they takes shelter will be burned to the ground.
TAKE HEED! MARK WELL!
Members of the Union.
For God, Life and Liberty!!!"

The warning, at the time, was attributed to A. A. Bradley, one of the Northern Negro leaders who, as Frances Butler Leigh wrote, "began pouring in, and were really worse than the whites, for their Southern brethren looked upon their advent quite as proof of a new order of things, in which the Negroes were to rule and possess the land." In 1868 and 1869, wrote Mrs. Leigh, when the Loyal Leagues were strong in the coastal counties of Georgia and when large-scale vagabondage reached a "climax of lawless independence," she slept with a pistol by her bed.

In middle Georgia, at Macon, there was displayed at a campaign mass meeting of Negroes a crude banner with picture and inscription: "Every man that don't vote the Radical ticket this is the way we want to serve him—hang him by the neck." Intimidation, it seems, was part of the campaign practice on both sides, not just one.

The case of violence most noted, both within and without the state, was the murder of G. W. Ashburn, in Columbus, on the night of March 31. Ashburn, slave overseer of brutal reputation before the war, became a leader of the Negroes in Radical politics after enfranchisement, and a member of the constitutional convention. Presumably because of his course of conduct and alleged incendiary activities, he was shot to death by a band of men. Nine young men, arrested on suspicion, were taken to Atlanta for trial before a military commission, beginning in June. The trial became a legal battle, with former Governor Joseph E. Brown retained to assist in the prosecution, and Alexander H. Stephens and six others of the ablest lawyers in the state representing the defense. Finally, on July 21, the case was suspended and remanded to the civil courts, where it never was brought to trial again.

The Ashburn assassination and most other cases of violence were attributed to the Ku Klux Klan, which, in 1868, was spreading over Georgia. The course of events and the state of mind which led to the spread of "an organization, a brotherhood of the property-holders, the peaceable, law-abiding citizens of the state, for self-protection," was afterward described before a committee of Congress by General Gordon—who did not, of course, identify the organization with the Ku Klux Klan. He testified:

"The instinct of self-protection prompted that organization, the sense of insecurity and danger, particularly in those neighborhoods where the negro population largely predominated. The reasons which led up to this organization were three or four. The first and main reason was the organization of the Union League, as they called it, about which we knew nothing more than this: that the negroes would desert the plantations and go off at night in large numbers; on being asked where they had been would reply, sometimes, 'We have been to the muster'; sometimes, 'We have been to the lodge'; sometimes, 'We have been to the meeting.' We knew that the 'carpetbaggers,' as the people called those who came from a distance and had no interest at all with us, who were unknown to us entirely; who from all we could learn about them did not have any very exalted position at their homes—these men were organizing the colored people. . . .

"Apprehension took possession of the entire public mind of the State. Men were in many instances afraid to go away from their homes and leave their wives and children, for fear of outrage. Rapes were already being committed in the country. There was this general organization of the black race on the one hand, and an entire disorganization of the white race on the other hand.

"We were afraid to have a public organization; because we supposed it would be construed at once, by the authorities at Washington, as an organization antagonistic to the government of the United States. It was therefore necessary, in order to protect our families from outrage and to preserve our own lives, to have something that we could regard as a brotherhood—a combination of the best men in the country, to act purely in self-defense, to repel the attack in case we should be attacked by these people. That was the whole object of this organization. I never heard of any disguise connected with it; we had none, very certainly. This organization, I think, extended nearly all over the State. . . . It had no more politics in it than the organization of the Masons."

In that statement General Gordon expressed the state of mind of the Georgians of the time, whether justified or not, and the aims and intent of those responsible for the organization and spread of the Ku Klux Klan, of which he himself was popularly supposed to have been the chief in Georgia.

In the Omnibus Bill readmitting six states, a special condition was attached to the admission of Georgia. The state was not to be granted representation in Congress until it had expunged from its new constitution the clause which outlawed the collection of debts due prior to January 1, 1865. This special demand the legislature acceded to on July 21. On the same day it ratified the Fourteenth Amendment. On the twenty-second, Bullock, who had been serving as provisional governor by military appointment for a month, changed his status by being inaugurated as governor of the state, and the legislature proceeded to the election of United States senators.

For the long term, Governor Bullock and the Republicans supported former Governor Joseph E. Brown, while the Conservatives again brought forward Alexander H. Stephens. There being no majority on the first ballot, the Conservatives and certain moderate Republicans united on July 29, to elect Judge Joshua Hill, with one hundred and ten votes to Governor Brown's ninety-four. In the short-term race, the Conservatives and Moderates elected H. V. M. Miller, over Foster Blodgett, supported by Governor Bullock.

Georgia's new senators were not chosen until two days after Congress adjourned, and so were not seated, but on July 25 her seven congressmen-elect were sworn in and seated in the House of Representatives in Washington. Five days later military rule in the state was declared at an end.

On the same day on which the Georgia congressmen were admitted, however, there began a movement in the legislature which was to undo the work of Reconstruction and to throw Georgia back into the class of the unrepresented states. On July 25, Conservatives in the Senate launched an attack upon the eligibility of Negroes to hold office under the somewhat vague wording of the new constitution. The resolution offered that day was defeated but was brought up again and passed, on September 7, when factional fights had begun to develop between the Bullock and the anti-Bullock Republicans. Three Negro senators were expelled—Tunis Campbell and George Wallace, solely because they were persons of color; A. A. Bradley, because of that fact and an alleged previous conviction of a felony in New York. Two weeks later, on September 23, the House followed the lead of the Senate by expelling twenty-eight of its members because they were persons of color.

In June of the following year, the Supreme Court of the state held that Negroes were eligible to hold office under the new constitution; but regardless of local constitutional questions, the legislature of Georgia, if it desired to keep the state under civil government, was most unwise in purging itself of its Negro members. The net effect of their action was to throw the state once more out of the Union, into which it had to be readmitted a second time, with additional restrictions and fundamental conditions.

Texas continued under military rule throughout 1868 because the constitutional convention did not complete its work until the last month of the year, but Mississippi, alone among the states undergoing Reconstruction, was able to make good its preference for remaining under military rule by mustering an actual majority of votes against its proposed constitution, at an election held on June 22.

The constitution submitted on May 18, after a one-hundred-fifteen-day session of the convention, was far more proscriptive than the requirements of the Reconstruction Act and Fourteenth Amendment. It was figured, in fact, that if the constitution should be ratified, not more than one thousand whites in the state would have the voting privilege, while not even Congress could remove the disabilities imposed without the concurrence of the Mississippi legislature. Because of these rigorous disfranchising and disqualifying clauses; because of the requirements of mixed schools; and because the constitution placed autocratic powers in the hands of the next governor, with eight thousand offices to fill, the Conservative whites, after early indecision, put forth tremendous efforts, under the leadership of the vigorous and forthright General J. Z. George.

The elections called for June 22 were not only on the question of ratifying the constitution, but also to choose state officials, legislators and congressmen. For governor, the Radicals nominated General Beroth B. Eggleston, president of the constitutional convention. He and nominees for all other offices were Northern white men. Neither Negroes nor "scalawags" appeared on the first Republican ticket in Mississippi.

In an election conducted by the military, and accompanied with a minimum of disorder, the Eggleston constitution was defeated by a vote of 56,231 for and 63,860 against, while General Eggleston himself was defeated by Governor Humphreys by a somewhat larger majority. Four of the five congressmen elected were Democrats, the one Republican being George C. McKee, living in the Vicksburg district. Nearly half the legislators who received a majority of the votes were Democrats. Only twelve were Negroes.

Ku Klux threats against Negroes who might vote with the Radicals were opposed by threats that Negroes who voted with the Democrats would be sold back into slavery in Cuba, as a fitting reward for their ingratitude. The bewildered and bedeviled Negroes, naturally enough, did not vote, in about half the cases. Outcries of fraud and intimidation were raised by the supporters of the constitution, after which an elaborate ex parte investigation was had by a committee of the convention. On July 8, an address and appeal was sent to Congress, urging that the election be set aside. On July 24, the House of Representatives took such action, and passed a bill to reassemble the convention, rewrite the constitution, and have another election. The Senate, however, declined to pass the bill, and the whole matter went over to the next session. Mississippi was to remain under military government.

In fact, a week before the election, Mississippi passed into a new and more direct phase of military government when General Irwin Mc-

Dowell, commanding the United States forces in the state, removed from office Governor Humphreys and his Attorney General, on the ground of obstruction to the process of Reconstruction, and replaced the Governor with General Adelbert Ames, of Massachusetts and the regular army. General Ames, an engaging young man of good ability, and a son-in-law of General Benjamin F. Butler, exchanged a promising career in the army for a stormy and finally disastrous course in Mississippi politics.

Governor Humphreys, upholding his claim as the elected representative of the people of Mississippi, declared that he would yield neither his office nor the governor's mansion to anything short of the superior force of "stern, unrelenting military tyranny."

"If you want military pantomime," replied General Ames, "it shall be carried out with all the appearance of reality without actual indignity." A file of soldiers, therefore, escorted the Governor from his quarters and cleared the way for the entry of his successor.

Former Senator Albert G. Brown was sent to Washington by the Democrats to make it clear to the Congress that the rejection of the constitution was due not to fraud and violence, but to dislike of its proscriptive tone which was general among the whites, and was shared by many of the blacks; and that the defeat of General Eggleston and his ticket was due to the fact that they represented this proscriptive and intolerant spirit. If the people of Mississippi had a chance to vote on a constitution without such stringent disfranchising and disqualifying clauses, he promised that it would be adopted with unparalled unanimity—as in fact it was, in the following year.

In Virginia, even before the adjournment of the constitutional convention, a new governor was appointed by the military authorities, to replace Governor Pierpont, whose independent and conservative course had lost its influence in a day when men of the Hunnicutt and Hawxhurst type were rising to leadership. The restoration Governor had even been refused the honor of election as a delegate to the constitutional convention by a Richmond constituency made up largely of Negroes under the influence of Judge Underwood and Mr. Hunnicutt, both of whom were elected delegates, along with two Negroes and one James Morrissey, Irish, who had come to Richmond during the upheaval.

General Schofield, in announcing the removal of Governor Pierpont on April 4, 1868, gave no reason other than the fact that the term for which he originally was elected had expired, as it had some months before, and that he was ineligible for re-election to a second term under the Alexandria constitution. To replace him, the military commander named General Henry H. Wells, late of New York and Michigan, who had come to Virginia early in the war and served as provost-marshal at Alexandria. There was irony in the nativity of General Wells, in the light of Governor Pierpont's statement just a month before, in a letter to Senator Willey, that all the offices in Virginia were about to be filled by New Yorkers. "There is not a valuable office in the state but half a dozen New Yorkers are after it," he wrote. The appointment of General Wells was disappointing to Messrs. Hunnicutt and Hawxhurst, both of whom hoped to be elected governor under the new constitution when completed and ratified.

The constitution was completed on April 17, 1868, with stringent clauses of disfranchisement and disqualification. General Schofield wrote to General Grant that the ignorant majority in the convention "could only hope to obtain office by disqualifying everybody in the state who is capable of discharging official duties and all else to them was of comparatively slight importance." In adopting the constitution, the convention proposed to submit it for ratification to an election to be held on June 2.

Preparatory to that election, the Republican state convention met in Richmond on May 6, to make its nominations. Governor Wells, already in office, was nominated for governor, with one hundred and twenty-five votes against forty-five for Hawxhurst and eleven for Hunnicutt. Six votes were cast for the deposed Pierpont. Seven of the eight congressional nominees were chosen from the "carpetbag" element of the party. On the following day the Democrats likewise nominated a state ticket, headed by Colonel R. E. Withers for governor, and a congressional ticket as well.

The stage was set for an election which was not to be held. Governor Wells, already in office by military appointment, was not anxious for one, nor was General Schofield, feeling as he did about the sort of government which would be organized under the proscriptions of the new constitution. Since the election could be held only on authority of General Schofield, and he declined to order one, the whole subject of the further Reconstruction of Virginia went over to the next session of Congress. Virginia remained under military rule, with General Wells as governor, and as military commander, General George Stoneman, who succeeded Schofield as military commander, when the latter on June 1 became Secretary of War in the stead of

Stanton, who resigned after the Senate failed to convict the President in the impeachment trial.

The civil government in Tennessee, which had been recognized by Congress as a full-fledged state two years before, made its appeal for help to the military during the summer of 1868, also. On the night of June 13, Congressman Samuel M. Arnell was sought on a train near Columbia by a band of Ku Klux "with pistols and rope in hand," according to his telegram to Governor Brownlow. Governor Brownlow, who had disbanded the Tennessee state guard, organized to help carry the August, 1867, election against Emerson Etheridge, telegraphed General Thomas, the army commander at Louisville, for Federal troops to take over six counties in the state where, the Governor declared, "the civil laws cannot be enforced, nor loyal men allowed to exercise their rights and liberties."

General Thomas had been importuned before for troops to support the Governor in various enterprises, including the putting down of an "insurrection" in Nashville so that the Radicals might seat as mayor one A. E. Alden, the "carpetbagger" commissioner of registration. Tennessee, the General said in substance to its Governor, was a state and should attend to its own policing, whereupon the Governor called a special session of the legislature, to open on July 27.

At that session, a second anti-Ku-Klux law was passed. The first, passed in February, had authorized the sheriffs to recruit posses to hunt down the Ku Klux. It had failed of its purpose because, Governor Brownlow thought, many of the sheriffs were themselves members of the Klan. The second law was accompanied by a measure for the revival of the Tennessee state guards and their strengthening for the second war which the Parson continued to preach.

"We want another war to put down the rebellion," he wrote a week after the Arnell incident. "After that is fought, reconstruction will be easy in the Confederacy. We will only want a surveyor-general and a land office, with a deputy in each county, and a large amount of hanging."

Affairs in Tennessee were drifting toward open hostilities when, on August 1, a group of thirteen former Confederate general officers, including General Forrest, met in Nashville and issued a declaration to the legislature on the situation. There was no intent to overthrow the government, they said, but,

"inasmuch as the supposed danger to the peace of the State is apprehended from that class of the community with which we are considered identified, as inducement and reason to your honorable body not to organize such military force, we pledge ourselves to maintain the order and peace of the State with whatever of influence we possess."

The offer, of course, was not accepted. It was, in fact, rejected as an impertinence, while the legislature proceeded to pass its state guard law, authorizing the Governor to organize such a force, to send it into any county upon the request of public officials or of "ten Union men of good moral character," to declare martial law, quarter the troops on the county, and assess the cost against it. Membership, activity, aid or sympathy to the Ku Klux, or anyone else who should "prowl through the country or towns, by day or by night, disguised or otherwise" to disturb the peace or alarm the citizens, was made punishable by a fine of not less than five hundred dollars and imprisonment for a term of not less than five years.

Armed with his new law, Governor Brownlow issued, on September 16, a proclamation remarkable both for its matter and the manner of its issue. It was issued through the parson's newspaper, the Knoxville Whig, with requests of all loyal papers to reprint, without going through the usual formality of entering it in the state's proclamation book, under the great seal. It called on all "good people," white and colored, to "raise companies of loyal and able-bodied men" and bring them to Nashville, while the Governor would decide later whether to call them into action. Naturally, no companies were raised or transported to the capital under such vague and general orders, but the threat of arming and using them was enough to shock the people of the state into a willingness, and even more than a willingness, to have General Thomas send troops into Tennessee, as an alternative preferable to another undisciplined Brownlow "army."

In their various ways, and with varying results, the controlling powers were getting the reconstructed states ready to take their prescribed part in the presidential election of November, 1868.

CHAPTER XXXV

The Campaign and Election of 1868

The campaign of 1868 was to be fought out principally on the "Southern question." There were other issues, of course, mostly economic and financial, but events and sentiments conspired to make the status and condition of the Southern states and their colored citizens the dominant emotional issues of the campaign—and campaigns are won and lost on emotional issues more than economic.

The National Union Republican nominee for president was the popular war hero of the North, General Grant, chosen unanimously on the first ballot at the convention held in Chicago on May 20-21. Two years before, in the campaign of 1866, even General Grant himself would have been hard put to it to say whether he was Democratic or Republican. The result of the 1866 elections pointed to the Republicans as the party for one who would be elected president in 1868. The General's quarrel with President Johnson, over his *ad interim* appointment as Secretary of War, was the final break that determined the Republicanism of General Grant.

For vice-president, Schuyler Colfax of Indiana, speaker of the House of Representatives, was nominated on the sixth ballot, blasting again the aspirations of Senator Ben Wade, who, just the week before, had seen the Presidency of the United States elude him by one vote, when the Senate failed to convict Andrew Johnson.

The platform adopted in Chicago took note of the impeachment trial, in a long plank which recited as fact all the charges, official and unofficial, against the President and concluded that he had been "justly impeached for high crimes and misdemeanors, and properly pronounced guilty thereof by the vote of thirty-five Senators. . . ."

Congressional Reconstruction was approved, as was the

"spirit of magnanimity and forebearance with which men who have served in the rebellion, but who now frankly and honestly co-operate with us in restoring the peace of the country and reconstructing the Southern State governments upon the basis of impartial justice and equal rights, are received back into the communion of the loyal people."

The thorny question of Negro suffrage, to which the party was committed in the South where it was important, but for which the North was not considered to be ready, was dealt with in an ingenious plank:

"The guaranty by Congress of equal suffrage to all the loyal men of the South was demanded by every consideration of public safety, of gratitude, and of justice, and must be maintained; while the question of suffrage in all the loyal States properly belongs to the people of those States. . . ."

To an appealing candidate and an effective platform, the Republicans added the supreme touch of a perfect campaign slogan in the famous phrase of General Grant's letter of acceptance—"Let us have peace." Just as "back to normalcy" was to do in another post-war campaign, it crystallized into a phrase a common longing—which was as delusively unobtainable in one case as in the other.

The Democrats, meeting in New York on July 4, battled for five days to a deadlock over a formidable list of candidates—Chief Justice Chase, who was not a candidate but would take a Democratic nomination for the Presidency, since he could not get one from the Republicans; George H. Pendleton, of Ohio; Thomas A. Hendricks, of Indiana; General Winfield Scott Hancock of the United States Army, and others. The deadlock ended on the fifth day and the twenty-second ballot, with the nomination of Governor Horatio Seymour, of New York, permanent chairman of the convention, who had forbidden the use of his name as a candidate but was forced to accept the nomination. Governor Seymour, by abilities, training and character, was undoubtedly better qualified for the Presidency than the great soldier whom the Republicans had chosen, but against him was brought the fact that he had been critical of what he held to be the usurpations of the Lincoln government during the war. The Democratic nominee for the Vice-Presidency, however, Major-General Frank P. Blair of Missouri, had a record of war achievement which, in the minds of many, balanced any supposed lack of sympathy toward the prosecution of the war on the part of the head of the ticket.

The Democratic platform countered the Republican on almost every issue. As to Reconstruction, the platform demanded immediate restoration of all states, amnesty for past political offenses, and the "regulation of the elective franchise in the States by their citizens. . . ." Against Republican pride in the congressional policy, the Democrats pictured it as an act of bad faith, in view of the professed war declarations of the Union; an exercise of military despotism in time of peace; a threat to the continued existence of coequal states in the government; and, in general, "unconstitutional, revolutionary and void." The congressional policy, "instead of restoring the Union . . . has dissolved it," the platform declared.

Neither platform devoted attention to the tariff but there was a conflict of position on the question of how the war bonds should be paid. The Republicans denounced any form of repudiation as a "national crime" and declared for the payment of the war debts according to the spirit as well as the letter of the law. The Democrats urged that such bonds as did not specify that they were to be paid "in coin" should be paid in "lawful money" by which was meant the depreciated greenback currency of the times. The Democratic position was that this was the money which had been paid for the bonds, and that now to pay them off in the more valuable gold would give the bondholders an unwarranted advantage. "One currency for the Government and the people," ran their position, "for the laborer and the officeholder, the pensioner and the soldier, the producer and the bondholder."

Part of the Republican strategy of the campaign was to strengthen the party in the South, both by bringing as many as possible of the states back into voting relations with the Union, and by making eligible to vote and hold office in those states as many former Confederates and Confederate sympathizers as might be expected to co-operate with the newly organized local Republican parties. Besides bills to admit states, therefore, Congress passed, in June and July, a series of bills granting amnesty and full political rights to more than thirteen hundred individuals in the Southern states. Not all of them, by any means, were those who had pitched their political tents in the camp of the Republicans, but most were. Among those thus "amnestied" and made eligible to hold office by congressional act were General James Longstreet in Louisiana, General J. L. Alcorn in Mississippi, Franklin J. Moses, Jr., in South Carolina, Governor Holden in North Carolina, and Governors Bullock and Brown in Georgia.

While Congress was winding up its affairs, to go home for the campaign, the rush of ratifications of the Fourteenth Amendment by the legislatures of readmitted states created a constitutional conundrum for Secretary of State Seward, the officer charged by law with the duty of certifying the adoption of constitutional amendments.

On July 20, by official proclamation, the Secretary of State undertook not to answer the questions raised but to state the facts as to ratifications and let Congress and the country draw their own conclusions. He announced that he had received ratifications from the legislatures of twenty-three states and from newly constituted bodies "avowing themselves to be and acting as" the legislatures of six more states in the South, but that the legislatures of Ohio and New Jersey had, after ratifying, withdrawn their consent by resolutions and so notified him. If the ratifications of those states were to be considered irrevocable, notwithstanding their subsequent withdrawal, then, said Secretary Seward's proclamation, the amendment had been ratified by three-fourths of all the states and was valid.

Such a conditional proclamation, of course, was not satisfactory to the majority of Congress, which, on the following day, passed in great haste a concurrent resolution reciting by name twenty-seven ratifying states; declaring that these were three-fourths of all the states, which mathematically they were not, since the Union then consisted of thirty-seven states, counting those in the South; declaring the Fourteenth Amendment to be part of the Constitution; and directing that "it be duly promulgated as such by the Secretary of State."

A week later, on July 28, Secretary Seward did so promulgate the amendment in another proclamation, giving a list of ratifications and withdrawals which again differed from that in the congressional resolution, but included the ratification by Georgia, which had been had in the interim. Georgia, as it afterward developed, was only temporarily in the Union, but its ratification was deemed sufficient. It was all very irregular and very confusing, and it introduced some troublesome precedents in dealing with ratifications and withdrawals of ratification of constitutional amendments, but the Fourteenth Amendment, regardless of irregularities, was at last in the Constitution.

Two weeks later, on August 11, Thaddeus Stevens died. His work was done. He had seen slavery destroyed and the "slave power" which he hated, humbled. He had seen the spirit of caste in the South, as he considered it, abased. He had seen his "Great Amendment" adopted as part of the Constitution, and government taken out of the hands of those who, to him, were irreconcilable rebels. He had seen a whole group of states made safe for what he looked upon, sincerely, as the "party of the Union," through the medium of the votes of the blacks for whose equality he had fought. And so, worn with age and labors, he died, and was buried, at his own insistence, in a colored graveyard in Lancaster, Pennsylvania, beneath a stone which bears this inscription of his own writing:

"I repose in this quiet and secluded spot, not from any natural preference for solitude, but finding other cemeteries limited as to race by charter rules, I have chosen this, that I might illustrate in my death the principles which I advocated through a long life,
           Equality of Man before his Creator."

To most of the white people of the South, Stevens was the archenemy. Not all of them would have said it but many of them must have felt a certain sympathy with the editorial expression of the *Planter's Banner*, published at Franklin, Louisiana, by Daniel Dennett, who had been a New Hampshire schoolteacher. Under the heading, "Old Thad Stevens Dead," Editor Dennett wrote:

"The prayers of the righteous have at last removed the Congressional curse! May old Brownlow, Butler and all such political monsters soon follow the example of their illustrious predecessor! . . . The Devil will go on a big bender now. With Thad Stevens in his Cabinet, and Butler in Washington, he can manage things in both Kingdoms to his liking. . . ."

Bitterness was the tone of the campaign, in spite of the studied moderation of Governor Seymour's own declarations and the appeal for peace by General Grant.

To the partisan Republican of the time—and most men were partisans in that day—the Democracy was a compound of treasons, rebellion in the South, Copperheadism in the North.

To the partisan Democrat, particularly the Democrat from the Southern or border states, the Republican purpose was to destroy free and constitutional government and to erect a despotism in the South.

General Blair, the Democratic nominee for vice-president, was impolitic in his expressions but he said frankly and vigorously what many another less pungently articulate Democrat thought. General Grant, he said,

"exclaims: 'Let us have peace.' 'Peace reigns in Warsaw' was the announcement which heralded the doom of the liberties of the nation. 'The empire is peace,' exclaimed Bonaparte, when freedom and its defenders expired under the sharp edge of his sword. The peace to which Grant invites us is the peace of despotism and death."

It would have been hard for the people of the North who read the Republican journals and heard the Republican orators to have believed that there was even that sort of peace in the South in the summer and autumn of 1868. Disorder and violence, of which there was, in all conscience, more than enough, was magnified, exaggerated and distorted into a veritable "reign of terror," instigated and carried out by the mysterious Ku Klux for political purposes.

The roll of authenticated occurrences of the sort commonly denominated "Southern outrages" in the Radical press is long enough and distressing enough, but when considered against the background of the situation, of the vast area of the South, the size of its population, and the disordered and unsettled state of the times, they appear more as sporadic and occasional than as general and epidemic.

General Howard, head of the Freedmen's Bureau, went through the South from Virginia to Texas, in August and September. His opportunities for information were excellent, from Radical sources as well as Conservative. He attended sessions of the new legislatures, and liked what he saw there. Of the South Carolina legislature, which had the largest proportion of Negroes, he reported that

"these men were in earnest. They were educating themselves to legislation by legislating. Every pulse of the heart of the majority beats for the flag, for the Union. And who would substitute for such a legislature even extraordinary ability and learning, coupled with disloyal sentiments and intense conviction of the righteousness of State supremacy?"

The General was in thorough sympathy with the congressional policy of Reconstruction, including equal voting and office-holding rights for Negroes. He talked freely, with his subordinates in the Freedmen's Bureau, which, by that time, had come to be looked upon in the South as a government-supported arm of the Republican party. He talked, too, with white Conservatives, who told him that

"all the Republicans want of the negro is just to lift themselves into power and they care not what becomes of him. They are trying to degrade us beneath the negro from sheer malice."

From the account of his two-months' trip, which he gave upon his return to Washington, judging both from what he said and what he did not say, the General saw no "reign of terror" in the South. There were outbreaks and outrages, as was to be expected, but there was no general and systematic violence such as the campaign stories depicted.

The question of the Southern attitude toward the Negro, or rather what the Northern electorate might believe about that attitude, was a matter of real concern to the managers of the Seymour campaign. One of the managers, General W. S. Rosecrans, who had commanded Union armies at Corinth, Stone River and Chickamauga, went from New York to the White Sulphur Springs, where leading Southerners were accustomed to be in the heated season. From all of them, General Rosecrans sought expressions as to the South's loyalty to the Union and its kindly intent toward the Negro population. Finally, he asked and secured a formal statement of the views expressed to him informally in conversation by his one-time Confederate enemies.

This statement, drafted by Alexander H. H. Stuart, at the request of General Rosecrans made through General Lee, was signed by General Lee and thirty other leading Southerners at the resort. It recited that the Southern people had accepted the results of the war, abolished slavery, renounced secession and returned to peaceful pursuits. It regretted that their action had not "been met in a spirit of frankness and cordiality" such as would have healed "the wounds inflicted by the war." It expressed kindly feelings toward the Negroes, based on long association and on mutual self-interest, but expressed, also, opposition to "any system of laws that would place the political power of the country in the hands of the negro race," not because of any feeling of enmity toward them but because the Negroes, "at present," were regarded as without the intelligence or other qualifications necessary "to make them safe depositories of political power. They would inevitably become the victims of demagogues, who, for selfish purposes, would mislead them to the serious injury of the public."

The "White Sulphur Letter," in spite of the eminence of its signers and the wide endorsement which it received from other leading Southerners, attracted in the North but a fraction of the attention bestowed upon the current reports of "Southern out-rages," actual and imputed.

Much was made, in North Carolina particularly, of what was alleged to be a plot of those who owned and directed most of the property in the South, to force colored voters into support of the Democrats by threats of eviction and starvation. Eighty-eight Republican members of the legislature, in an address to the people issued late in August, asked with a fine rhetorical flourish:

"Did it never occur to you, ye gentlemen of property, education and character—to you, ye men, and especially ye women, who never received anything from these colored people but services, kindness and protection—did it never occur to you that . . . they may not be willing to starve, while they are willing to work for bread? . . . that if you kill their children with hunger they will kill your children with fear? . . . that if you good people maliciously determine that they shall have no shelter, they may determine that you shall have no shelter?"

To such incendiary pronouncements from the legislators, the Raleigh *Standard*, which Governor Holden had sold privately to General Milton S. Littlefield, head of the ring of speculators who had marked out North Carolina for theirs, added a series of still more inflammatory editorials. The first, appearing on September 2, under the heading "Retaliation," posed the question of what might be done, under the forms of law, to defeat "this wholesale crusade of oppression carried on against the colored race to starve him into voting against his choice."

"Of course it is not to be supposed that men and women and chil-dren will starve to death while corn is standing in the fields and while hogs and cattle are not kept under lock and key! But these are matters of minor importance and are to be expected, however much the necessity may be deplored."

Having thus suggested the propriety of plain theft, the *Standard* continued with an outline of a program for redistribution of the wealth of the state through tax-supported housing and public works:

"Whenever the Republicans have control of a county, let a meeting of the commissioners be called at once. Let them make out a list of all the colored stonemasons, bricklayers, plasterers, painters and carpenters. Then let them select a site of sufficient dimensions for a village of from five to fifteen hundred colored paupers, as the case may be. The work itself will give employment to a considerable number of persons, and some time will be required to complete it. Then let the county paupers be moved in and be provided with houses and food at the expense of those who have made them paupers. Let the tax be so laid as to affect only the large landowners. Not one in twenty owns any land at all, and the large landowners are much rarer."

To its economic arguments the *Standard* added appeals for vigorous political work. One such editorial, appearing on September 18, roused such feeling in Raleigh that the nominal owner and editor of the paper, one N. Paige, escaped lynching by hurried departure under cover of the night. The editorial advised the Republican party canvassers:

"But whatever else you work, don't forget to work among the women. The Confederacy wouldn't have lasted a year if it hadn't been for them. One good rebel woman is worth a dozen rebel men. Go after the women, then. They will make their husbands and lovers shout for Grant and Colfax until they are hoarse, if you will manage to replace some of the diamond rings and laces Frank Blair stole from them when he was here. And don't hesitate to throw your arms around their necks now and then, when their husbands are not around, and give them a good ————. They all like it, and the Yankeer you are the better it takes. Our experience with female rebs is, that with all their sins they have a vast amount of human nature, and only want to have it appreciated to be the most loving creatures imaginable. . . . Don't read Judge Pearson's letter to them, but give them Byron and Shelley in volumes, and you will have them in your arms, if not in your party, in less than a week."

The political depravity which could have led to publication of such an editorial in the midst of a situation so explosive as the Radicals professed to believe existed in North Carolina, is hard to conceive.

Violence was not a notable feature of the campaign in North Carolina, however, although the Governor frequently threatened to call out the North Carolina State Militia, derisively dubbed by the Democrats, the "Nigger Carpetbagger Scalawag Militia."

Of actual outbreaks of violence in the South as a whole, however, there was a shocking plenty. That they were all political in their nature, or entirely one-sided in their origin, is not so clear.

In the eastern cotton belt of Georgia, where there was a considerable excess of colored population, the Ku Klux was said to have been in active operation, under the direction of General Dudley M. DuBose, son-in-law of General Robert Toombs. The Klan in that section was long afterward described in the *Uncle Remus Magazine* by John Calvin Reed, its chief in Oglethorpe County, as an "underground and nocturnal constabulary, detective, interclusive, interceptive, repressive, preventive—in the main—punitive only now and then." Whether because of the activities so described, or for some other reason, the Republican vote in Oglethorpe County was to fall from the 1,144 which Bullock received in April to 116 for Grant in November. In the seven counties of the area the Republican vote fell from 8,019 to 2,924, while the Democratic rose from 4,003 to 6,202, a result which was ascribed to a combination of intimidation of some voters, direct purchase of others, and general ballot-box fraud.

Whatever of trouble there may have been in eastern Georgia was overshadowed by the Camilla riots, in southwestern Georgia. As usual, there were differing accounts of the cause and course of events. Both accounts agreed that a body of some three hundred Negroes, led by N. P. Pierce and John Murphy, Republican candidates, started on a march from Albany to Camilla; that the sheriff at Camilla, hearing of their approach, met them a few miles out of town and attempted to persuade them to disarm and disband; that when the attempt failed he returned to Camilla, raised a posse and marched out to meet the advancing column; that the parties met, the usual party unknown fired a shot, and a general melee ensued, in which eight or nine Negroes were killed, besides a score or more wounded, with no whites killed, and only a few wounded.

The Bureau agent at Albany sent to the North stories which were palpable exaggerations, and upon which General Meade did not rely. Governor Bullock, however, did and urgently asked for troops to maintain order in Mitchell County, where, he alleged, there was a general Democratic plot to prevent Republican meetings by violence. A legislative committee appointed to investigate declared that there was no such situation, and that Pierce, Murphy and other Republican office-seekers were the instigators of trouble. General Meade, on the ground, sustained the report of the committee but the papers in the North accepted the Bureau agent's version. The *Nation*, one of the fairest of the Northern weekly journals, which sought to give as accurate a picture as might be of affairs Southern, described the riot as a "shocking massacre. The murders continued to be committed through the afternoon and night, the woods being scoured by hunters with dogs, and negroes shot without mercy. Their offense was Radicalism."

The pattern of affairs in Louisiana was one that was to become distressingly familiar. Outbreaks there were, as Professor John R. Ficklen says, more "race wars" than the "political massacres" which were reported in the North, for when the armed bands of whites and blacks faced each other in the little courthouse towns, or on the roads leading into them, Southern white Republicans were quite likely to be found lined up with Democrats in putting down what, to them, was a "Negro uprising."

In New Orleans affairs were somewhat different. There was more or less rioting, in a small way, in that turbulent city, which the Republicans charged was part of the program of political intimidation. The intimidation was not all on one side, however, as even Governor Warmoth was forced, upon one occasion, to rescue from lynching at the hands of an angry mob of Republican Negroes one Willis Rollins, a loud and incoherent Negro Democratic orator from Mississippi, who had been chased from the stump in Canal Street to take refuge in a Democratic club room near by.

The really savage affairs, however, took place in the parishes of Bossier, St. Landry and St. Bernard. As to each of these affairs there are the usual irreconcilable stories, all set forth in much detail in the testimony later taken in contested election cases, but from the conflict of testimony some idea of events may be gained.

In Bossier Parish, in the far northwest corner of the state, trouble started in the summer, with a disturbance alleged to have been the result of an effort by armed Negroes to seize and divide lands. Eighteen of the leaders were tried for inciting a riot, convicted and sent to prison by a jury made up of both whites and blacks. Into the tense situation engendered by this affair, there was interjected in October a series of incidents which started with an unprovoked assault upon a Negro by a white stranger, said to have been from Arkansas, and which led through various steps to the murder, by a band of Negroes, of two local white citizens whom they were holding prisoners. The affair culminated in a general "race riot," which might more properly be called a "Negro hunt." Armed bands of whites pursued the Negroes, who scattered into the woods and swamps, and shot a number which varies from forty to one hundred and twenty, according to whether the Democratic or the Republican estimates are accepted.

The affair in St. Landry Parish seems to have started in an effort by excited Republican Negroes in the town of Opelousas to prevent other Negroes in the near-by town of Washington from putting into effect a rumored intention to join forces with the Democrats. Emerson Bentley, late of Ohio and the Federal Army, wrote an account of the affair in the Opelousas paper which was resented by the Seymour Knights, a Democratic campaign organization. They visited and severely whipped editor Bentley, who thereupon left Opelousas— or "escaped," as the Republicans put it—and made his way to New Orleans. Upon the spreading of a rumor that he had been killed, a march of the Negroes upon Opelousas began. Most of the marching bands were persuaded to turn back but one small group persisted. After the usual squabble about the first shot, firing broke out, resulting in the wounding of three whites, the killing of four Negroes. Eight Negroes were arrested, jailed, and that night taken from the jail and murdered. The shooting and killing which then started continued for two weeks. Negroes killed in the Parish numbered, according to Republican estimates, from two to three hundred; according to the Democrats, from twenty-five to thirty.

The St. Bernard riots seem to have been more the result of liquor and race feeling between the Negroes and the large Italian population of New Orleans than of politics. When Pablo Filio, proprietor of a grocery which, as the fashion then was, was also a saloon, refused to admit a band of drunken Negroes on the night of October 25, they riddled his store and house with a fusillade of shots, one of which struck and killed Filio. As his wife and daughters fled, the store was pillaged for its liquor. From near-by New Orleans swarmed The Innocents, an organized band of a reputation which made their name seem ironic, to avenge the death of their compatriot. A number of Negroes were killed in the fighting, as usual. Sixty were jailed but later released, on order of the Freedmen's Bureau, for lack of specific charges. By order of the parish judge they were again arrested. There is no record of their final disposition.

In Arkansas, according to charges by Governor Clayton, a "secret organization, military in its character, styled 'Knights of the White Camellia' but more popularly known as the 'Ku Klux Klan,'" had inaugurated a veritable "reign of terror," with the murder of "hundreds of quiet and law-abiding citizens," without any effort being made to bring them to punishment. The Conservatives, on the other hand, denied responsibility for the undeniable violence in Arkansas, and charged that it was either campaign thunder manufactured for local and Northern consumption, or that, in some cases, the murders were committed by Radicals upon other Radicals suspected of leaning to the Conservative side.

The Conservatives insisted that they were pursuing the political course of registering, in those cases in which they could take the prescribed oath, and preparing to vote. There was, however, a distinct division of opinion among them on the question of whether men disfranchised by the new constitution should register and take the oath. One opinion was that anyone was justified, in the existing state of affairs, in taking any oath which he had to take to do what he could to rescue the state. General Albert Pike, on the other hand, warned against taking oaths with mental reservations. Still a third group seems to have felt that the gains which might be expected from registering and voting were simply "not worth the perjury," as one put it.

Arkansas assassination, regardless of by whom it was committed, was not confined to the lowly in station. Late in September, Major-General T. C. Hindman, of the Confederate Army, seated in a room in his home in Helena, was killed by a shot fired through the window from the darkness outside. James Hind, one of the Reconstruction congressmen, was killed in Monroe County in October, while Joseph Brooks, later to be governor, was wounded. Radicals charged the Conservatives with the crimes, while Conservatives laid them to factional differences among the Radicals.

The most revolting crime recorded from Arkansas, however, was the murder of William Dallas, a deputy sheriff, and "Fed" Reeves, a Negro whose offense seems to have been no more than that he was standing near by and some dead Negro was needed for the ghastly joke of tying the white and the Negro together, embracing, in the public road. For this double murder, one Stokeley Morgan, desperado pure and simple, was afterward tried and executed.

Governor Clayton, in anticipation of the declaration of martial law in Arkansas, which was not to come about until after the election in November, as early as August 27 ordered the militia officers in certain counties to enroll their men, with the "utmost secrecy and dispatch." The matter of arming the forces to be called into the field presented difficulties, however. The War Department declined to supply arms and ammunition, as did some of the governors of Northern states to whom Governor Clayton made application. Finally, through an agent sent North, he bought for the state four thousand stands of arms, with powder and cartridges, and had them shipped to Arkansas by way of Memphis.

From Memphis the shipment was to move on the chartered steamer *Hesper* by way of the Mississippi and Arkansas Rivers, to Little Rock. The *Hesper* got away from the Memphis landing on the morning of October 15, 1868. Hardly had it reached the head of President's Island, downstream, when a band of pseudo-river pirates, disguised, appeared at the wharf, seized the steam-tug *Nettie Jones*; gave chase to the *Hesper*, overhauled and boarded her; broke open the cases of muskets and dropped them into the Mississippi; cast off and returned to Memphis, to doff their disguises and resume their usual occupations. The capture and "liquidation" of Governor Clayton's arms were alleged at the time, with probable truth, to have been acts of friendly assistance by the Memphis Den of the Klan for their fellows in Arkansas. One member of the party, according to oral tradition, at least, was long afterward to become a member of the Cabinet of a Republican president of the United States.

The Klan in Tennessee was threatened with troubles of its own, at this time, with Governor Brownlow adding to the list of proclamations, which earned him the nickname "Old Proc," new and vivid official denunciations of it and all its ways and works. When General Thomas sent Federal troops into twenty-one counties in the state, in advance of the election, everyone breathed easier.

In Virginia, Mississippi and Texas, where there was to be no voting for presidential electors in 1868, there was less of disturbance than in some of the other states. The contrast between the quiet in Mississippi and the turbulence in its neighboring states where political excitement was at heat, in fact, was pointed to by Conservatives as another argument against the folly and wrong of the process of Radical Reconstruction. Many white Mississippians, and no doubt some black, congratulated themselves that they were spared the turmoils of politics in those trying days.

While Texas was not voting for presidential electors, it was recognized that Texas "outrages" were just as good for campaign purposes as those in states which already had their reconstructed state governments. Perhaps they were even better, since they could be laid to the policy of moderation pursued by the district commander, General Hancock, and supported by President Johnson. There were feuds amounting almost to local wars on the frontiers of the state, carried on by outlaw bands strong enough to defy the troops and even to plunder their supply trains, all of which could be attributed to the continuing spirit of rebellion, and charged against the Democratic party.

An official committee of the Texas constitutional convention, near the beginning of the campaign, issued a report on lawlessness and violence, which charged that in the three and one-half years since the war, five hundred and nine whites and four hundred and eighty-six freedmen had been murdered in Texas, most of them because of "the hostility entertained by ex-rebels toward loyal men of both races." Pressed by the Conservatives for more specific information on murdered loyalists, a list of thirty-seven instances was produced, twenty-three whites and fourteen Negroes, but with names given in only eight cases, and four of those wrong. That there had been many homicides in Texas during the period all admitted, but the conclusions of the report, either as to the number or their causes, are hard to accept. The report, however, went North as a campaign document, while Morgan Hamilton and Judge Caldwell were sent to Washington to press upon Congress the necessity of filling all local and state offices with loyal men, the organization of a loyal militia, and the placing of the control of the coming election on the new constitution in the hands of the convention itself, rather than those of the military commander.

Distressing as even a partial recital of the violent outbreaks of the campaign period is, it is apparent that the reports for Northern consumption were exaggerated and embroidered, as is to be expected, and that the actual situation, bad as it was in spots, was not one of general terror. The election, in spite of General Grant's great popularity, bade fair to be close, and the "Southern outrage" story was worked for its full political value. That the stories were accepted and implicitly believed by most of the Northern people is obvious.

State elections began to be held in August. In that month Kentucky, as had become her habit, elected a Democrat, J. W. Stevenson, governor, by a majority of more than four to one. With the exception of one judge, the Radicals lost every race. To Radical newspaper denunciation in the North, young Henry Watterson, who was not yet known as "Marse Henry," made answer. Of all the states which remained in the Union, he said, Kentucky alone was

"true to herself and to the professions with which the war was begun. She proscribed no one. She gave welcome to all. . . . In Kentucky . . .

public opinion is the only arbiter of public questions, and every man is allowed to hold office who obtains votes enough. . . ."

Comparing the one-sided election results in Kentucky with those in Massachusetts, he declared that for doing her own thinking and voting, as Massachusetts did hers, Kentuckians

"are denounced as traitors to our country and a despotism is sought to be placed over us by those who claim that we ought to be forced to vote for Republican candidates and Republican measures, and who declare that if we do not we are guilty of rebellion and should be punished therefor."

Maine went Republican in September. In the October state elections, the Republicans carried Indiana by a majority of less than a thousand; Pennsylvania by less than ten thousand; and Ohio by only seventeen thousand.

The November presidential election, however, resulted in an electoral landslide for Grant—twenty-six states with a total of two hundred and fourteen electors to eight states, with a total of eighty for Seymour, three states not voting. Of the late Confederate States which took part, the Republicans carried Alabama, Arkansas, Florida, North Carolina, South Carolina, and Tennessee; the Democrats, Georgia and Louisiana. Florida was carried by the simple device of dispensing with a popular election, ostensibly to save expenses, and having the legislature name three Grant-Colfax electors for the state. Of the former slave states which did not leave the Union, the Republicans carried Missouri and West Virginia; the Democrats, Delaware, Maryland and Kentucky.

That Louisiana and Georgia went Democratic was charged, by the Republicans, to violence, fraud and intimidation. That these were factors in the election there can be no real doubt, although they were by no means the only causes that led to the reversal of the results of the spring elections, when Bullock defeated Gordon and Warmoth defeated Taliaferro. In Louisiana there was a most thorough Democratic organization, which made its special appeal to colored Democrats, who, too, suffered from intimidation and abuse. At least one was killed, while driving a carriage in a Democratic procession, in spite of strenuous efforts on the part of the white Democrats to protect those Negroes who were voting with them. The Warmoth-Taliaferro results, in the spring elections, moreover, are not properly to be compared with the Grant-Seymour results in the fall. The latter was a contest between the two parties; the former, a contest between two factions of Republicans in which many Democrats voted for Warmoth as what they considered the lesser of two evils, to defeat Judge Taliaferro and his Roudanez backing.

The proportions of the electoral landslide for General Grant are deceptive as a test of the relative strength of the two candidates. In popular vote, Grant received a majority of only 309,000 in the country as a whole—a majority which would have been a minority but for the votes of the nearly half a million Negroes which were cast for him.

John R. Lynch, one of the colored statesmen of Reconstruction in Mississippi, and an acute observer, points out that

"The Republicans were successful, but not by such a decisive majority as in the Congressional election of 1866. In fact, if all the Southern States that took part in that election had gone Democratic, the hero of Appomattox would have been defeated. It was the Southern States giving Republican majorities through the votes of their colored men that saved that important national election to the Republican party."

CHAPTER XXXVI

SUFFRAGE AND AMNESTY

WITH General Grant safely elected, the Fortieth Congress, whose sessions, regular and extraordinary, had been almost continuous since it took office on March 4, 1867, came back to Washington on the first Monday in December, 1868, to open its last session.

Twelve senators from six Southern states, admitted to their seats just at the close of the previous session, were on hand, as were thirty-two representatives from seven states. All of the senators were Republicans. Two—Pool of North Carolina and Robertson of South Carolina—were native Southern whites; ten were recent residents of the states they represented. Of the ten, two—Warner of Alabama and Sawyer of South Carolina—were outstanding among their fellows in character, ability and dignity. Among the representatives, thirty were Republicans, of whom sixteen were of the group of newcomers in their states to which the term "carpetbagger" was usually applied.

In the lobbies, were Joshua Hill and Dr. H. V. M. Miller, the senators chosen by the legislature of Georgia, awaiting admission, and a committee from the Mississippi convention, urging that the defeat of the constitution in that state be ignored and the new government inaugurated without the consent of the voters.

Credentials of the Georgia senators-elect, when presented, were referred to the Judiciary Committee, along with a letter from Governor Bullock protesting the illegality of the action of the legislature, taken in September, in expelling its Negro members and replacing them with the white candidates who had received the next highest vote. The Judiciary Committee's report, made on January 25, 1869, recommended against the seating of the senators, on the ground that Georgia had not complied with the terms of the Omnibus Act of readmission. In the view of the majority of the committee, the expulsion of the Negro members showed "rebel control" of Georgia and a "purpose to resist the authority of the United States." Chairman Lyman Trumbull disagreed, and filed a minority report.

There the matter rested, for the remainder of the session, with no action by the Senate other than the negative one of not accepting the

347

credentials of the Georgia senators and admitting them to their seats. A like question was also before the Committee on Reconstruction of the House of Representatives, without action being taken. There, however, failure to act meant that the seven representatives, who had been accepted and seated in July before the expulsion of the Negro members, were to continue to hold their seats until the end of the Congress.

Governor Bullock's message to the Georgia legislature, when it met in January, 1869, strongly urged the expulsion of all members who could not take the test oath, and the reseating of the colored members expelled in September. The legislature would have none of the plan, which was substantially the same, however, as the one to be imposed on Georgia, with still other conditions, by an act of Congress in December of that year. The immediate result of the legislature's inaction was that, when the electoral votes were canvassed in Congress, on February 10, the House of Representatives voted against counting the nine votes of Georgia, the Senate voted in favor of counting them. The ballots were counted, therefore, both with and without the vote of Georgia and the result announced both ways—two hundred and fourteen for Grant in either case; eighty for Seymour, counting Georgia; seventy-one not counting Georgia.

From Mississippi three committees appeared before Congress. A Committee of Sixteen, representing the Eggleston constitutional convention, presented the results of an ex parte investigation of the elections in June, which declared that the constitution had been ratified, regardless of the official report of the general commanding; and urged Congress "for the speedy and permanent relief" of the loyal to declare the rejected constitution adopted, to readmit the state, and to declare the Eggleston ticket elected to office.

In opposition appeared a committee of Conservatives, and another committee of "Conservative Republicans," of whom all but one were Northern men. They presented evidence to Congress of the fairness of the election in June, and the acceptance of its results by the people of Mississippi. General Gillem, the army commander, testified as to the precautions he had taken to secure a fair election. As indicating the general opposition to the constitution among the white people of the state, including Northern newcomers, he cited Union soldiers who voted and worked against the adoption of the constitution.

Judge J. W. C. Watson, a Whig of the old line who had spoken against secession in 1860 and 1861, but who "went with the state" and was a member of the Confederate Senate after 1863, was probably the most striking and effective witness. He had been a member of both the 1865 and 1868 constitutional conventions, but had resigned from the latter after the adoption of the proscriptive disfranchising and disqualifying clauses and canvassed the state against the adoption of the constitution. The people of the state, he assured the committee of Congress, would ratify a constitution without such proscriptions. In default of action by Congress, Mississippi continued under the rule of the army, with General Adelbert Ames as provisional governor by military appointment.

Toward the end of December, writing under the name "Senex," Alexander H. H. Stuart, who had served in the Cabinet of President Fillmore, published simultaneously in the Richmond *Dispatch* and the Richmond *Whig* an analysis of the Virginia situation. It was useless, he declared, to resist Negro suffrage, which had solid Northern support behind it. On that point, he suggested yielding, as a possible way to get rid of the disfranchising and disqualifying articles in the constitution:

"Is it not better to surrender half than lose all? The Southern people have already made concessions such as passing the constitutional amendment abolishing slavery, and granting the blacks the right to testify in the courts, and neither of these measures has been followed by disastrous consequences. It would probably be likewise in the case of negro suffrage. The intelligence and the wealth of the South would continue to govern as before."

The effect of such a communication was sensational. The ultraconservative press, led by the *Enquirer* and *Examiner* of Richmond, were bitter against such a suggestion, even when it came from a man of the standing of Mr. Stuart. The movement which "Senex" had instituted, however, was more than a communication to the papers. It was followed by a call to forty Conservative leaders to meet in conference in Richmond, on the last day of the year. Twenty-eight of those invited attended. The meeting declared, as its policy toward Negro suffrage, that they "were prepared, and they believed the majority of the people of Virginia are prepared, to surrender their opposition to its incorporation into their fundamental law as an offering on the altar of peace, and in the hope that union and harmony may be restored on the basis of universal suffrage and universal amnesty."

From the conference, there was selected a Committee of Nine to go to Washington, confer with Congress, and work out the best arrangement possible for the complete restoration of Virginia. Besides Mr. Stuart as chairman, the Committee of Nine consisted of John L. Marye, Jr., James T. Johnston, W. T. Sutherlin, Wyndham Robertson, William L. Owen, John B. Baldwin, James Neeson and J. F. Slaughter. This committee, with the endorsement of General Stoneman upon their enterprise, went to Washington, established close relations with such Northern Democrats as the able Thomas A. Hendricks, of Indiana, and prepared to present their cause to the committees of Congress.

Three delegations from Virginia appeared, when hearings began on the state's constitutional status on January 21, 1869—an official Radical delegation, whites and blacks, headed by Governor Wells; an official delegation of the more moderate Republicans, headed by Franklin L. Stearns; and the Committee of Nine, for whom John B. Baldwin spoke. The "Nine" did not favor Negro suffrage, he stated, looking upon the sudden admission of four hundred and fifty thousand blacks to the electorate as a "fearful experiment" but they were willing to accept the policy of the Federal government in the matter. The editor of the *Virginia State Journal*, the chief Radical organ, testified as to outrages upon Radicals, while Governor Wells assured the committee that the only hope for justice in Virginia lay in the Republican party.

No action was taken at the session, and Virginia continued as Military District No. 1, with a "carpetbag" governor by military appointment. Beneath the surface, however, the forces were at work which were to spare Virginia the experiences ahead of her more southerly sisters. The Committee of Nine had aroused the sympathetic interest of General Grant in the situation. Meanwhile, Governor Wells had alienated the support of some of the more conservative Republicans. Late in October, 1868, Richard T. Wilson, representing the Baltimore & Ohio Railroad, arrived in Richmond to propose the sale of the state's interest in the Virginia & Tennessee Railroad to the Baltimore line. Governor Wells was favorably impressed with the proposition, and wished to accept. General Stoneman disapproved, which insured that the step would not be taken at that time, while General Mahone was incensed at a plan which would definitely have blocked his proposed consolidation of all the railroads in the southern part of the state into a through east-and-west line based on the port of Norfolk. With William Mahone behind the movement, the Republican state executive committee met in January, 1869; set aside the nominations made in May in anticipation of the election on June 2, which was never held; and called another nominating convention to meet at Petersburg in March.

When Congress assembled in December, Texas, the third of the states not yet admitted, was not represented by a committee in Washington. Before the end of the congressional session it was represented by two committees, one for each factional wing of the Republican party in the state. The battleground between the two factions was the constitutional convention, which had recessed in the summer until December, when it met presumably to finish its work of writing a new constitution. Actually, the session developed its greatest fight over the insistence of the extreme Radical faction, led by E. J. Davis and Morgan Hamilton, that the state of Texas divide itself into three, or perhaps four, states. By high-handed parliamentary tactics, Chairman Davis was able to carry this proposition through the convention on January 20, 1869, after a parliamentary fight which included resignations, expulsions and wholesale quorum-breaking. Every newspaper in the state, Republican and Democratic, except the San Antonio *Express*, the organ of the Davis faction, opposed the division. Even in San Antonio, which was to become the capital of the proposed "West Texas," a mass meeting of citizens resolved against the division of the Texas of their pride.

The divisionist element in the convention created an official commission of six to present their views to Congress, while the anti-divisionist opposition sent an unofficial commission to oppose them. Meanwhile, the convention, more than eight months after it had first convened, got down to serious constitution-writing. The Davis-Morgan Hamilton faction fought to force into the constitution a rigidly proscriptive test oath which would have disfranchised the great majority of the whites of the state. Against such a policy stood Andrew Jackson Hamilton, fighting almost alone among his fellow Republicans at first, for the wiser and more generous course of making the disfranchising clauses no more restrictive than the Fourteenth Amendment and the Reconstruction Acts required. By courage, persistence and parliamentary skill, "Colossal Jack" managed to carry his ideas through, by the narrow margin of thirty to twenty-six, and so to save Texas from what he foresaw would be a heritage of hatred.

The Houston *Telegraph*, reflecting upon the fact that Jack Hamilton had "labored to give the ballot to those who had bitterly opposed him . . . at the risk of having it used against himself," and that to do this he had broken with his own party to aid a "people who he believed had wronged him," was moved to commend him as a "patriot, firm, tried and true, deserving the gratitude of our whole people of all parties."

The convention wrangled on to its end. So bitter became the feeling between the factions—more bitter, said Chairman Davis, than the hatred of either side for rebels or Democrats—that the convention, at the last, split itself into two bodies, one of which adjourned on February sixth and the other on the eighth. On the last day in which the two factions sat together, however, it was resolved to submit the constitution to a popular election in July, at which officials should also be elected.

With a constitution written and submitted, the commissions representing both factions hurried away to Washington, where they arrived about the middle of February, to call on General Grant and to present their views to Congress. In a memorial dated March 2, 1869, the Davis-Morgan Hamilton "divisionist" faction presented a gloomy picture of affairs and of Radical prospects in Texas. If the new constitution should be allowed to be voted on, they believed, the government would pass into the hands of "ex-Confederates and so-called Republicans." Their suggestion was that there be no election but that Congress intervene, call another constitutional convention, and give an opportunity to write another constitution for Texas; or, better still, for the several Texases which were in contemplation. If that could not be done, they proposed that the state be divided into three territories, to be held under territorial government until such time as it was safe to establish state governments.

The Jack Hamilton "Moderates" delegation presented their memorial on March 16 to the first session of the Forty-first Congress. The memorial defended conditions in Texas, opposed the idea of dividing the state, and, in a particularly fine passage, remarked that there was "too strong a temptation to punish their opponents, and to preserve power to themselves," to allow those "temporarily clothed with power" to be, in the heat of conflict, the best judges of what should be done about suffrage. They urged, therefore, a broad and generous policy.

"We wish to sit down by our hearthstones once more in peace. We do not wish to prolong a contest which, if prolonged, can produce only the bitter fruit of settled and implacable hate."

Congress did not undertake to settle the questions at issue in the three states not yet admitted to representation; but it did, by a joint resolution passed on February 16, undertake to insure that the civil administration in those states should be in the hands of the loyal and none other. The military commanders were required to remove from office all who could not take the famous iron-clad test oath of 1862. As a result of this resolution, General Stoneman reported, in March, that out of 2,504 persons appointed to office in the state of Virginia by himself and his predecessor, General Schofield, only 329 could take the oath required. In Mississippi, the effect of the resolution was practically a clean sweep of state and local offices. General Ames, who became military commander as well as provisional civil governor on March 5, in the course of a few weeks, replaced the "rebels" with about 2,000 appointees—60 sheriffs, 75 county and other judges, 16 prosecuting attorneys, 120 court clerks, 70 county treasurers, 60 county assessors, 50 mayors, 220 aldermen and a long list of other offices. To fill these offices, it was hard to get respectable native whites, so that, perforce, the offices had to be filled with imported whites and Negroes. General Ames, moreover, even removed many of the "loyal" appointees of Generals Ord and Gillem, and replaced them with "loyal" men of his own following.

Another step taken by Congress in this short session, the submittal to the states of the proposed Fifteenth Amendment by resolution of February 26, 1869, had less direct and immediate bearing on the South than it did upon the Northern states. Negro suffrage was already established in most of the Southern states, and soon would be in others, by state action. It still was rare in the North, however, and was being refused in most cases when voted upon, regardless of the Republican platform pledge to leave suffrage to the states in the North. The new amendment was felt to be necessary, both as an act of political justice to the Negroes everywhere and to insure further that there should be no backsliding upon the part of the Southern states.

And, besides, as Mr. Boutwell of Massachusetts pointed out in the discussion, there were 1700 Negro male adults in Connecticut, 10,000 in New York, 5,000 in New Jersey, 14,000 in Pennsylvania, 7,000 in Ohio, 24,000 in Missouri, 4,000 in Delaware, and 35,-000 in Maryland, all potential voters who might be expected to rally to the cause. "Are we to decline the services of 150,000 men who are ready to do battle for us at the ballot box in favor of human rights?" he asked.

Mr. Boutwell was urging one of Senator Sumner's favorite theses, that Congress had the power to establish "universal suffrage to all adult male citizens," without submitting an amendment to the Constitution. He was partly moved to that position by the fact that "there are but twenty-five States to which we at the present time could look for the ratification of this amendment," and that "three other States" would have to be secured to ratify. The majority, however, having in mind the fact that Virginia, Texas and Mississippi were still out of the Union, and that ratification of the proposed amendment could easily be made one of the conditions precedent to their return, were less concerned about the problem of finding twenty-eight ratifying states. A resolution proposing a Fifteenth Amendment, therefore, was submitted in the usual way.

The amendment provided that "the right of citizens of the United States to vote shall not be denied or abridged by the United States or by any state on account of race, color, or previous condition of servitude," and expressly gave to Congress the power of enforcement.

In the debate upon its passage, Senator Oliver P. Morton, who wanted a stronger amendment, offered prophetic remarks. The amendment, he said, prohibited disfranchisement for only three reasons:

"Colored men . . . may be disfranchised for want of education or for want of intelligence. . . . Those States . . . may perhaps require property or educational tests, and that would cut off the great majority of the colored men from voting in those States, and thus this amendment would be practically defeated in all those States where the great body of the colored people live. Sir, if the power should pass into the hands of the Conservative or Democratic population of those States, if they could not debar the colored people of the right of suffrage in any other way they would do it by an educational or property qualification."

Ratification of the Fifteenth Amendment went forward with a rush. Within a month ratifications had been received from eight legislatures; within little more than a year, ratifications had been received from the necessary three-fourths of the legislatures and, on March 30, 1870, the amendment was proclaimed as part of the Constitution.

While Congress was giving its attention to the three states in which the processes of Reconstruction were incomplete, and the state of Georgia in which they had gone awry, problems were developing in others of the state governments of the South, already reconstructed and presumably launched on their own careers, some of which threatened to force themselves upon congressional attention.

Governor Clayton, of Arkansas, however, was not one to take his troubles to Washington by calling for Federal troops, as so many of the Reconstruction governors did so often. He had been organizing his own army through the months of the campaign, and on November 4, 1868, the day after the election, had declared martial law in ten counties. Three days later the state was divided into four military districts, each under command of a militia brigadier-general or colonel, with a force of militia, rallied principally from the mountainous regions in the northwestern part of the state and from the plantation Negroes in the East.

In the southwestern district, the militia rendezvoused at Murfreesboro on November 13, under command of General Robert F. Catterson. On the following day the First Arkansas Cavalry, white troops from the Ozarks, met the "enemy" in the Battle of Centre Point, a victory for the Clayton forces. The "enemy" professed to be no more than citizens of a quiet village, whose crime was voting the Democratic ticket, and who had not been informed of the declaration of martial law in their vicinity. When the columns of the Catterson command converged upon them from three directions they resisted, they said, because they thought it was a mass invasion by guerrillas. Sixty prisoners were taken, as a result of the engagement.

To judge from the record of military trials and executions during the period of martial law in southwest Arkansas, there was no lack of violence in that region, although it has slight appearance of having been political in its causes. One "Bud" Griffith, alleged desperado, was hanged for the murders of Major Andrews, Lieutenant Willis and an unknown Negro in the previous October. A Negro was executed for the rape of a white woman. The military sought, also, to capture the notorious guerrilla leader Cullen Baker, but were anticipated by Thomas Orr, Baker's brother-in-law, who shot him on private account. Four weeks earlier, it seems, Baker had hanged Orr, but evidently had done the job unskillfully or insufficiently.

The military operations in the southeast, carried on by Negro troops enlisted principally in the region about Pine Bluff, centered in Drew and Ashley Counties. At Monticello, an agreement was reached between the citizens and the military for a non-partisan "County Guard" to preserve order. Carried out in good faith, the agreement resulted in the lifting of martial law in mid-December.

In the northeast, Brigadier General Upham, a Freedmen's Bureau agent in Woodruff County, assembled his forces in a stockade at Augusta, seized fourteen citizens of the town as hostages, to be killed if the stockade were attacked, and spread his operations over a considerable area. Complaints by citizens of plunder, blackmail and occasional murder, were investigated by Keys Danforth, the adjutant general of the state, upon whose report Governor Clayton exonerated Upham's troops of blame.

At the Christmas season the war front moved to Crittenden County, on the Mississippi River opposite Memphis, where, Governor Clayton stated, "desperadoes held complete possession." From Helena, Colonel J. T. Watson marched toward the north with a force of Negro infantry, to establish a stockade at Marion. From Augusta, Colonel William Monks, of Missouri, marched south with six companies of white cavalry to join him. During the military occupation of Crittenden County, according to Governor Clayton, four confessed Negro rapists were executed, four other prisoners were shot while trying to escape, and one Moffard was hanged for various murders and for shooting Captain E. G. Barker, Bureau agent at Marion.

Following his first proclamation of martial law, the Governor, on December 8, added Conway County to the list of those where the law could not be enforced. The trouble in Conway County started as far back as August, when a band of armed Negroes attended court at Lewisburg, where one Negro was to be tried for killing another's dog. White citizens undertook forcibly to disarm all in attendance, which started a series of fights. Governor Clayton, on a chartered steamboat, hastened up the Arkansas to Lewisburg, accompanied by a delegation of representative men, Democratic and Republican. After addresses by the Governor and by Augustus H. Garland, it was agreed that the arms should be restored to the Negroes, who, on the other hand, agreed that there should be a cessation of disturbance.

The agreement not being carried out fully, trouble smoldered on through the autumn, to culminate in December in a series of murders and incendiary fires in Lewisburg, which did not abate when martial law was proclaimed and the town was occupied by four companies of militia. The Democrats charged the violence to the militia; the Republicans to the Ku Klux—and both may have been right. After nearly three weeks of the disturbance, peace was restored again, by agreement.

Before the end of the martial law period in Arkansas, which

lasted about four months, and in Crittenden County continued until March 21, 1869, opposition to the Governor's policy developed within his own party, as well as among the Democrats. The legislature, which came into session on November 17, supported the Governor and after a debate of eight days, tendered their thanks to General Catterson and his command, by resolution. John G. Price, speaker of the House of Representatives, and editor of the Radical party organ, the *Daily Republican*, was deposed from his office and deprived of the public printing because of his paper's opposition to the Governor's military activities. Mr. Price saved his editorship of the party organ, however, by recanting and belatedly coming to the defense of the party of martial law. That policy, according to one member of the legislature, was "to make Arkansas Republican or a waste howling wilderness."

The reward of Mr. Price, for getting back into line, was not only the retention of his editorship, but also the restoration of a share of the state printing, which once had been his own monopoly. Bills for the state's printing were running nearly one hundred thousand dollars a year, as much as the whole cost of running the state government in the pre-war days, partly because of the great lists of tax notices and other legal printing.

Government by martial law in Arkansas, which Governor Clayton felt was necessary to tranquilize the state, proved to be a costly affair. The immediate bills amounted to more than two hundred thousand dollars, while claims for property wrongfully taken or destroyed, allowed and paid in 1871, mostly to the militiamen themselves, came to another one hundred and twenty thousand dollars.

Governor Reed, of Florida, was having difficulties, too, due principally to the persistence of intense factionalism among the handful of white Republicans in the state who sought to make use of the voting strength of the Negro majority. Chief leaders in the fight were Governor Reed, with the state patronage, and Senator Osborn, with the more profitable patronage of the Federal government. Governor Reed seems to have started out to give the state as good a government as the conditions permitted, but he was hampered from the beginning.

His Lieutenant-Governor, he charged, had attempted, as early as the summer of 1868, to induce him to buy a new issue of Florida State bonds with depreciated scrip, which could be picked up at from thirty to fifty cents on the dollar, and then to sell the bonds in the

North, at seventy cents on the dollar, with a split of the profits between them. Differences developed with other leaders, and were
accentuated when the Governor, acting under a doubtful claim of
constitutional power, undertook to declare vacant the seats of a
number of members of the legislature who, in defiance of a plain constitutional provision, were holding other state offices as well.

On November 3, 1868, the legislature convened to name presidential
electors who would cast the vote of the state for Grant. Impeachment of the Governor was in the air, as well as a demand for the
passage of a bill for extra legislative salaries for the day's work of
relieving the voters of the state of the trouble of naming their own
electors. The Governor, ready to bring the fight out in the open,
called the legislature to meet in special session that night.

The legislature voted itself additional salary; the Governor vetoed
the bill; the legislature promptly repassed it. Then, upon the afternoon of November 6, Horatio Jenkins, Jr., a member of the Senate,
crossed to the House of Representatives and, as a "private citizen,"
brought charges against the Governor of lying, incompetence, lawless declaration of vacancies in the legislature, embezzlement of state
funds, and corruption in making appointments to office. Immediately,
a member of the House moved that the Governor be impeached of
"high crimes and misdemeanors," which was thereupon done, by a
vote of twenty-five to six. With the precedents of the Johnson impeachment fresh in mind, the House appointed managers who at
once proceeded to the Senate and preferred charges. The Senate took
the charges under consideration. Upon the following day, both
houses adjourned until January, when the trial was to be had.

Governor Reed's official family split. The Lieutenant-Governor,
Gleason, issued a proclamation deposing the Governor pending trial,
and assuming the office himself. To this proclamation, the Secretary of State, Alden, affixed the great seal of Florida. The Adjutant-
General, Carse, stood with his chief. He swore out warrants for
Gleason and Alden for "conspiring" against the government; had
them arrested and bound over to court; and insured against a counter-
stroke by raising a volunteer guard which patrolled and picketed the
capitol for six weeks. A new great seal was bought and a new Secretary of State, the able Jonathan Gibbs, appointed as its custodian.
"Governor" Gleason, not being able to get into the capitol, established his seat of government at McGuffin's Hotel, in Tallahassee.
The war went so far that the Reed adherents charged the Gleason
men with bringing to Tallahassee one Luke Lott, notorious desperado,

for the purpose of assassinating Reed under such circumstances that the crime could be laid to the "Southern Ku Klux."

Under a law which allowed the governor to call upon the Supreme Court of the state for declaratory judgments on doubtful questions of law, Governor Reed presented the situation to that tribunal. On November 24, 1868, the court ruled that Reed had not been impeached lawfully because the Senate before which the charges were preferred was without a quorum at the time. A bare quorum of the Senate, it was shown, had been in the room, but one-third of that quorum had taken other offices in the state government and so, held the court, had vacated their seats in the Senate. Governor Reed, taking the offensive, now sued out a writ of *quo warranto* against the Lieutenant-Governor and had him ousted from office because he had not been a citizen of Florida the required three years before his election.

When the legislature came back to Tallahassee to try the Governor, in January, 1869, it found the tide running too strongly in his favor. The whole tempest of November and December was ignored, by tacit consent; all records of impeachment expunged from the journals; and a new committee of the House of Representatives appointed to investigate the affairs of the Governor's office. This committee, reporting on January 26, recommended that there be no impeachment, a recommendation which the House accepted by a vote of forty-three to five.

Florida's disorders, however, did not all arise from Republican factional rows, by any means. The state was cursed with a rising tide of violence, descending in many cases to the depths of barbarity. Much of the violence was the work of bands of white "regulators," whose methods went from warnings to whippings, to banishment, to murder, and even to torture and the mutilation of corpses. The disorder was curiously "spotty," with peace and apparent content prevailing in one county while in its neighbor there was violence which, upon a few occasions, amounted to practical anarchy. Like so many other contradictions of the whole disturbed period, this diversity is probably explainable on the ground of the differences in the quality of leadership, Democratic and Republican, white and black, in the various communities.

In the early days of the new government, the legislature had authorized Governor Reed to request Federal troops to preserve order. The Governor, however, preferred to have Florida do its own governing and proposed to organize and arm a force of state militia. Like Governor Clayton, he bought arms in the North, two thousand rifles. On the way to Tallahassee, on the night of November 6, 1868, the rifles were thrown from the railroad cars, as the train ran between Lake City and Madison, and were broken up. At the time there was some uncertainty as to whether the act was the work of white "regulators" or of an anti-Reed faction of Republicans. Long afterward, in an address before the Texas and Arkansas Bar Associations, T. W. Gregory of Austin, who was to be attorney general in the Cabinet of Woodrow Wilson, gave the story as he had it from the lips of "an honorable member of our profession" living in Austin, Texas:

"Every telegraph operator, brakeman, engineer and conductor on the road over which these arms entered the State was a Ku Klux; the shipment was watched at every point, and between Lake City and Madison the entire two carloads of guns were thrown from the moving train at night by a select band . . . who had quietly boarded the train at its last stop. The Ku Klux left the train at the next station and destroyed the shipment before it was missed, and this notwithstanding the fact that two coaches filled with United States soldiers, sent to guard the arms, were attached to the same train."

In still another Southern state, the ruling Radicals professed to find it necessary to raise a local army in this period. On January 20, 1869, Governor Brownlow of Tennessee called out his state guards, to use them against "those masked villains, called Ku-Klux" and "certain ambitious men . . . advising the overthrow of the State government." A month later, with his army of sixteen hundred troops assembled in Nashville under the command of Brigadier General Joseph A. Cooper, the Governor issued a second proclamation, declaring martial law in the county of Giles, where the original Ku Klux Klan had been born, and in eight other counties in Middle and West Tennessee, to each of which garrisons of the state guards were dispatched. He announced that he expected, in a short while, to make those sections of the state "as orderly and quiet as East Tennessee is today."

Five days later, on February 25, the Parson resigned his seat as governor to proceed to Washington to take the seat in the Senate to which his legislature had elected him a year and a half before. D. W. C. Senter, of Grainger County, speaker of the Senate and a man of far more temperate views and expressions than the Parson, became governor, by succession, while the old Governor journeyed through East Tennessee and Virginia to the capital, on the doubly pleasurable mission of taking over the seat occupied by Senator Robert Patterson, the President's son-in-law, and of seeing Andrew Johnson himself come to the end of his term as president.

The President soon to retire had small part in the proceedings of Congress during its last session, or even in the government of the country. He did, however, to the disgust of the more radical and proscriptive, make one great and wise use of his pardoning power in his proclamation of general amnesty, on Christmas Day, 1868, granting full and complete pardon to all Confederates. Political disabilities imposed by the Fourteenth Amendment he could not remove; but as far as his power of pardon extended, he exercised it to the full.

"Treason," he had once said, "must be made odious, and traitors punished." That was in the fiery latter days of the war, and in the time of bitter grief following the murder of Lincoln. Time, experience, and the responsibility for the reunion of a separated nation had brought Andrew Johnson to see, quickly and in advance of many of his fellow-countrymen, that a whole people might not be proscribed forever.

CHAPTER XXXVII

"Stealing by Statute"

On March 4, 1869, General Grant began his eight years in the White House. His sincere wish, without any slightest doubt, was to bring to the country the peace which he had invoked in the outset of his campaign for the Presidency, but peace he could not command. It was not to come until another president sat in Washington.

The nation of which General Grant became president was in one of its periods of exuberant expansion. Population was gaining, immigration increasing, the public lands of the West filling up with settlers. Agricultural production and industrial output were rising. New processes and new products were being introduced. Cheap ways to make steel were beginning another industrial revolution. The railroad air brake, just invented, was to make possible, for the first time, mass transportation at high speeds, on the land. Petroleum refining and the integration of the oil industry, besides making its millionaires, was making it possible to lubricate all the new machinery which came crowding to the service of mankind. Strong men, restless men, some of them ruthless men, were turning their energies and their powers to organizing, developing, "exploiting" if you please, the new things and the new ways—to make money for themselves, of course, but in the doing of it to multiply vastly, to improve immeasurably, and to distribute far more widely the goods and services obtainable by the average family.

When General Grant was inaugurated, the whole nation was watching, as if it were some great sporting event, the ends-of-track of the two Pacific Railroad companies, which had crossed plain and mountain and desert, race toward each other to connect, on May 10, at Promontory Point in Utah. So great an achievement of vision and courage and creative organization, so great an enterprise of peace, the world of its day had not seen, nor had the touch of scandal come to cloud the greatness of the thing which, incredibly, had been done—and America thrilled to its accomplishment.

Even in the South, with all its physical prostration and its prob lems of government and labor and social organization, the touch of enthusiasm was felt. The cotton crop of the 1867-68 season had been the largest since the phenomenal crop of the year when war broke out, and the 1868-69 crop was not far behind. "The all-absorbing question," as one Georgian wrote, in the midst of all the political excitement of 1868, "is not impeachment, nor reconstruction, nor repudiation, nor the next President, but *labor*."

And black labor, in spite of threats and disturbances here and there, was doing well. The old plantation system was breaking up by economic pressure. Negroes were eagerly acquiring small farms for themselves, with a passion for landowning which has, among many, persisted to this day. Farm laborers did not want to work in the old gang system of slavery days. They wanted to buy, if they could; or, if they could not, to work land on some form of independent contract, either by direct rent or "on the shares."

The South was making the great discovery that Negroes would work in freedom. Three years of experience with free labor, in the opinion of the Charleston *Daily News*, had convinced the planters that

"To hire the negro at reasonable wages . . . is cheaper for the planter in the long run than to run the risk of his cost when owned, and to assume responsibility of his clothing, doctor's bill and support when disabled by disease and old age."

J. H. Christy, elected to Congress but not seated, testified that in northeastern Georgia the Negroes

"behaved better than I had any idea they would. . . . There are some of them who gather about the towns and tell these cock-and-bull stories about being run off by Ku Klux. The truth is, they come to town because they do not want to work. Generally the Negroes work better than I supposed they would. A great many of them acquire property. I suppose there are from sixty to seventy-five in my town who have houses and lots. They are industrious Negroes. . . ."

Like views were given by other observers. The Helena *Monitor* spoke of the extent to which thrifty Negroes were buying land in Arkansas. In Tennessee, the Columbia *Herald* commented upon the success of free Negro labor in its county, while the Nashville *Press and Times* declared that the "moral and industrial habits" of the freedmen "do not fall below the expectations of their best friends." Since the first year after the close of the war, it noted, the number of landowners among them had perhaps doubled. Many who were farming on a sound basis had ended the year 1868 able to discharge their obligations, improve their places and equipment, and "add numerous comforts to their households." As an example of one such farmer, the Nashville paper described the operations of a Negro in Tipton County who, on a rented farm of thirty acres, had raised fifty barrels of corn, eighty bushels of wheat, two thousand pounds of tobacco, and five bales of cotton, the total being worth about seven hundred and eighty dollars. In addition to these crops, this practitioner of the art of diversified farming had raised hay, oats, turnips and potatoes for his stock, two mules, a horse and a cow, and for his family.

To those not so thrifty or so fortunate as to be able to begin independent farming operations on land owned or rented, there was open the opportunity of field work, for wages. To the modern eye the wages seem low, but to the planters of the time they seemed extraordinarily high. "The wages paid to Negro laborers in the cotton fields of Arkansas," said the Little Rock *Gazette*, "far exceed the wages ever before paid to labor anywhere, except in California during the few years after the first discovery of gold." In Arkansas, in Kentucky, and in the lower South ineffectual efforts were made to bring in Chinese coolies, by contract, as had been done in California. A Chinese Immigration Convention held at Memphis, in 1869, sent an agent to China, who contracted for and shipped one hundred and eighty-nine coolies, practically none of whom remained on the farms. In Kentucky, prospects of an influx of Chinese led the Lexington *Observer & Reporter* to remark, exultantly, "The tune then will not be 'forty acres and a mule,' but it will be 'work nigger or starve.'" Kentucky Negroes objected to the introduction of the Chinese, of course, but they went further and contributed a real help to the problem of labor through an exchange, operated by Negro ex-soldiers, which placed more than three thousand Negroes in jobs in the first half of 1869. Of this labor office it was said that it "sent a laborer into every cornfield and almost every occupation of trust in Kentucky."

Not all Negroes, by any means, were farmers or field hands. There were men of the skilled trades, blacksmiths, carpenters, stonemasons, bricklayers and the like, many of them plantation-trained under the old economy which made of each large plantation almost a self-contained unit in matters of labor. To the growing towns, where such a man might follow his trade, they inevitably went. In construction, in lumbering, in the general run of industries requiring heavy work, the Negroes were to be found, working, for the most part, in reasonable co-operation and harmony with the whites.

Only in politics, and in affairs touched with politics, did there seem to be an impassable barrier between the mass of Negroes and the mass of whites. Edward King, who really saw the South and its people during the years of travel which went into his *Southern States of North America*, was struck with the fact that "the same negro who will bitterly oppose his old master politically, will implicitly follow his advice in matters of labor and investment."

Therein lay another of the tragedies of the period known as Reconstruction, the inability of the better Southern whites of the time to conceive of the Negroes as political beings, until after the chance to guide and work with them had passed into alien or inferior hands. Politics, moreover, became increasingly important in the daily life of the South as public authority and activity were extended into widening fields of endeavor.

Education, for instance, had been a matter of comparatively slight public concern in the South. There were public schools in the South before the war, but there had been no strong and general system, and no recognized principle of general support through state and local taxation. During the period of Reconstruction, public education was made, on paper and in theory at least, a definite major activity of each state government. Results did not always measure up to the theory but the Reconstruction legislatures established a principle of the definite responsibility of the state for public education which endured beyond the period of their control.

In transportation the Reconstruction governments acted upon a theory which had been established and accepted long before the war, and had been recognized and continued by the restoration governments of 1865 and 1866. The theory of encouragement of the building of necessary railroad facilities by the loan of the state's credit, or by direct participation by the state, had merit. It long antedated railroads, in fact, and had been used to encourage the development of turnpikes and navigation improvements, before the railroad established its definite superiority as a transportation medium.

The theory was sound, and where soundly carried out it had produced immense benefits. The state of Tennessee, to take but one example, before the war aided the building of a railroad between Nashville and Chattanooga, to connect the interior with the seaboard through the system of railroads in Georgia. The state's aid was given through endorsement of the bonds of the railroad, with a lien retained on the property to protect the state's loan of its credit. The bonds were paid by the railroad, the state was out not a cent, and the building of the line multiplied many times the productive possibilities, the value and the tax returns of the region through which it passed.

The failure of the transportation policy of the Reconstruction governments was in the carrying out of the theory. The theory was one difficult enough to carry out in the best of times, which the period of Reconstruction certainly was not. The whole country, North perhaps more than South, was in the grip of boom psychology. The standards of political morality and commercial conduct were low. To those difficulties was to be added, in the South, an electorate without education, susceptible to manipulation by appeals to class and race consciousness, without the steadying effect of widespread ownership of property. The representatives of such an electorate, themselves usually without a true stake in the long-range welfare of their communities, provided pliable material for those with schemes to get rich quick through the use of the public resources.

It happens that in most of the states where such public plunder prevailed a large proportion of the voters were newly enfranchised freedmen, but the phenomenon was not necessarily one of government based on Negro votes. It developed in other states where the Negro vote was slight, almost negligible. The great Tweed Ring stealings in Democratic New York, at the same period proved that rascality was neither Republican nor racial, necessarily.

The Negroes, in fact, beyond furnishing the mass of voters upon which some of the plundering governments in the Southern states were sustained, had less to do with the pillage, and got less out of it, than their white leaders and manipulators. Generally speaking, no more than petty graft was the portion of the Negro official and legislator. One observer of a legislative session in Alabama reported that votes were bought at "prices that would have disgraced a Negro in slavery times." The big gains went to the "carpetbagger" and the "scalawag" in public office, and to the promoter and the financier who, in turn, manipulated them. Of these, not all were Northern. There were Southern whites, non-office-holding, who helped pull the strings and pocket the proceeds.

It happened, too, that most of the promotions and plunder, on the grand scale, had to do with the projection and building of railroads, because railroads were, at the time, the only form of business enterprise which had generally developed to proportions which made promotion worth while. Of railroads, too, there was the greatest need.

Most of the South still depended, at the opening of the period, upon the slow, uncertain and expensive service of steamboats fighting floods or dodging sandbars in the rivers which so interlace the Southern country. New Orleans, seated at the nexus of a network of navigable rivers, found, after the railroads were opened into Mississippi and Alabama, that cotton which once had come out of the country in May of the year after it was picked and ginned, began to come out in December of the year of its growth, or in January of the following year. In Arkansas, with steamboats on the Mississippi, the Arkansas, the White and the Ouachita, and with seven steamers in service, in the winter, between Memphis and Little Rock alone, there was much fretting and complaint at the uncertainties of navigation. When another steamboat was added to the Little Rock service, the *Gazette* announced that "even with that, merchants naturally and justly complain at the delay in the delivery of their freight." Behind many of the railroad schemes before the various Reconstruction legislatures there was real reason and a genuine need for the improvement. Not all of them were the products of rascality—though the financial results of some of the well-intentioned schemes did not greatly differ from those designed primarily as a vehicle of plunder. It was not given to men, in government or in business, either then or now, to foresee infallibly the outcome of enterprise.

When President Grant was inaugurated, the first Southern state to be turned over to Radical government, Tennessee, was nearing the end of this phase of Reconstruction. Besides increasing the state's activities and raising state salaries, the Brownlow government embarked upon a broad program of improvement. New railroads, and old ones in their rehabilitation after the war, were to be aided from the proceeds of state bond issues. The state debt, which consisted largely of liabilities incurred in aid of the development of turnpike and railroad companies before the war, began to mount—nearly five million dollars added in 1866, as much more in 1867, a total of more than sixteen million dollars of new debt by the end of the administration. Meanwhile, inability to repair the ravages of war and meet the expenses of the post-war period with the revenues they could earn, forced most of the turnpike companies and railroads of the state to default on the interest on the bonds which the state had endorsed in their aid. The state enforced its lien on the turnpikes, in most cases, and gave them to newly organized private companies to maintain and operate. It enforced its lien on some of the railroads, also, took them over, and attempted to operate them on a self-supporting basis, without success. Later, in another administration, the lien was again enforced on behalf of the state by foreclosing on the defaulting railroads, through court process, selling them for several million dollars, and applying the proceeds to the public debt.

The new bonds offered by Tennessee to support its Reconstruction plans of progress in transportation were sold with difficulty. Speculators secured some of them at prices as low as seventeen cents on the dollar. Forty cents on the dollar was not an unusually low figure, while Governor Brownlow congratulated the state upon its sound financial condition when a temporary rise in the value of its bonds carried them up to seventy-five cents on the dollar. Even the Governor's physical affliction of an increasing palsy, which made it impossible for him to sign the numerous issues of state bonds, helped to depreciate their value. In answer to rumors that bonds were being signed and sold in New York by unauthorized persons, and the proceeds never coming to Tennessee at all, the Governor, in 1868, sought to reassure bondholders and prospective purchasers that such signatures on the bonds as did not appear to be genuine were the work of secretaries who had not learned to imitate his signature sufficiently well. Such an announcement, an open invitation to forgery and counterfeiting, finished the destruction of the state's credit, insofar as the post-bellum bonds were concerned.

The Brownlow government in Tennessee was neither a Negro government nor a carpetbag government. Negroes played small part in it, and "carpetbaggers" were not prominent. It was a Radical government, based on disfranchisement and proscription, and carried on by leaders of a fanatic vindictiveness which blinded them to the failings of one who could present a plausible record of a Unionism sufficiently strong.

In North Carolina, as in Tennessee, Negroes were not prominent in the new government, except as voters, nor were "carpetbaggers" numerous in office. Opportunities in extra-official manipulation and speculation in the bonds of the state were more attractive. North Carolina had fair credit, for a state which had passed through a war and was undergoing the uncertainties of Reconstruction, when the Holden government took over. Bonds representing the debt of some thirteen and three-quarter million dollars were selling at around seventy-five cents on the dollar. Of the bonds, nearly a million dollars represented debt incurred before the war to aid plank roads and navigation projects; nearly nine millions, debt incurred in the development and post-war rehabilitation of the railroad system of the state; and the balance for miscellaneous purposes. The state owned a controlling interest in several of the principal railroads—as it does today, in some cases—and was secured by a lien on other lines. Some of the lines in which the state was directly interested were left unfinished at the outbreak of war; others were in need of rehabilitation and improvement. There was, in all quarters, a strong and genuine demand for much needed railroad extension and development.

To take advantage of that situation and that demand, there appeared plausible and persuasive gentlemen with schemes and ideas. To them the legislature, which opened its sessions in July of 1868 and continued, with slight intermissions, through that year and the next, listened and was persuaded. As was developed afterward in two fraud investigations, some of the persuasion was very direct indeed. Twenty-two members were listed in the fraud reports as having received more than two hundred thousand dollars during the little more than a year that the pickings lasted. For these and other favors, they voted to issue bonds, to trade bonds, to donate bonds, to perform a variety of operations with state bonds, mostly in violation of the constitution of the state. By early 1869 the state was unable to pay the interest on its bonds, and the price was sliding downward. By the autumn of that year, the legislature had authorized a total of $27,850,000 of bonds, nominally in aid of railroads, of which $17,640,000 had been actually issued and sold for what they would bring. The "sale" of one lot of bonds was accomplished by the president of the railroad to whom they had been turned over, cashing them in a New York gambling house for chips, which he very promptly lost at games of chance. The case is extreme but illustrative. Not much of the money realized on the bonds ever found its way to the railroads.

Right from the beginning of the year of bond frauds in North Carolina there were honest and sagacious Republicans in the legislature who saw the drift of things and suspected what they could not then prove of the methods by which the business was being carried through. The Republicans in opposition, led by E. W. Pou, received little more attention than the disregarded handful of Conservatives in the legislature. The day of the opposition was to come, but when General Grant took office as president these aspects of Radical Reconstruction had not begun to press for public attention except in the states where, as one mordant wit put it, "loyalty" was coming to mean "stealing by statute."

Legislatures of most of the readmitted states were in session when the new President was inaugurated, or had completed their sessions but a short while before. It was recognized by those who had seen the legislatures at their work that their proceedings lacked parliamentary finish but that was to be expected, under all the circumstances. What was not recognized, as yet, was that the surface disorder and inattention to business, which characterizes most legislative bodies at their routine work, covered, if it did not conceal, a fundamental ignorance of or indifference to good government which was to lead to political and financial disaster.

By coincidence, on the very day of the inauguration of President Grant in Washington, the legislature in Columbia took a recess to enjoy the running of a match race between horses backed by Speaker Franklin J. Moses, Jr., and Representative W. J. Whipper, on a bet of one thousand dollars. The Speaker's horse lost, whereupon, three days later, the winner graciously moved and carried through the House of Representatives of the state of South Carolina an appropriation of one thousand dollars as a gratuity to the Speaker for the urbane and competent manner in which he had presided through the long session of the House, then coming to a close.

This first session of the first Reconstruction legislature in South Carolina devoted much attention to financial matters. Governor Orr reported that when he turned over affairs to Governor Scott, in July, 1868, he left more than $95,000 in the treasury. Governor Scott reported that he had to start his administration with only $45 in the treasury. Whatever the true situation, the new Governor and legislature undertook to improve it by borrowing first $125,000, then $500,000, then $1,000,000, apparently for floating debt and current expenses; another $1,000,000 to pay the interest on the state debt; and $200,000, later increased to $500,000, to buy lands to be managed by a land commissioner, subdivided and sold to settlers. Other bonds were authorized to be issued for the "conversion of state securities," in an amount not specified, an arrangement which resulted, it was charged, in an overissue of bonds of some six million dollars in two years. Still another bond issue of indeterminate amount authorized was that to retire the circulating notes of the state's Bank of South Carolina, which was to be closed out. Diligent advertising for holders of such bills to turn them in for redemption, it was charged, produced only about half a million dollars in bills. To redeem these, the legislative committee appointed to carry out the transaction issued $1,259,000 of bonds, while one member of the sub-committee appointed to count and destroy the bills redeemed was charged with depositing $30,000 of them in a Columbia bank.

South Carolina fiscal affairs were further complicated through the employment of a financial agent in New York, H. H. Kimpton, a college classmate of Attorney General Chamberlain. Mr. Kimpton was surety on his own bond in the amount of fifty thousand dollars, to safeguard the state in his handling of millions. He was given and used wide discretionary powers in disposing of the state's bonds through various channels and at various prices, and in attempting to bolster up the state's failing credit by hypothecating bonds as collateral on other obligations of the state, on a basis of about forty cents on the dollar. Upon default, when Mr. Kimpton could put up no more collateral, the hypothecated bonds would be sold by the purchaser, with a further increase in the state debt. Altogether, there is small wonder that a London banker wrote the president of the South Carolina Railroad that English investors feared that the disordered state of credit in the South might continue so long as the "State governments were under the control of uneducated persons."

South Carolina was not alone in her growing fiscal troubles, however. In Louisiana, the taxes could not be collected; interest on the state's debts could not be paid; and expenses were rising. Short-term notes had to be sold to pay the interest on other bonds, with the new notes yielding more than thirty per cent per annum, besides commissions paid. General obligations of the state sank as low as forty-seven cents on the dollar; special levee bonds as low as twenty-five cents. As a means of supporting the state's credit, it was moved in the legislature that no bonds be sold at less than fifty cents on the dollar. And, finally, to make the financial collapse more complete, current expenses of the state were paid in depreciated warrants, or "scrip."

In spite of the state's critical state of finance, the Louisiana legislature was eager to lend aid to public improvements, principally levees, canals and railroads. In aid of the Mississippi and Mexican Gulf Canal, six hundred thousand dollars of state bonds were voted. A more ambitious plan was the New Orleans and Ship Island Canal Company, chartered to construct a canal which was supposed not only to bring transportation advantages but to drain the surrounding swamp areas. In aid of it, the legislature voted two million dollars and four hundred thousand acres of land and all the other resources of the drainage commissioners of the metropolitan district. Governor Warmoth vetoed the bill, but it passed through both houses over his veto, on March 2, 1869. Aid to railroads, principally in the form of state endorsement of the company's bonds in the amount of twelve thousand five hundred dollars a mile, with a second mortgage given to the state as security, met general approval, even among the Conservative Democratic leaders and press, in those cases where the proposed railroad seemed to serve a need and to have a chance for successful operation. The levee bills, also generally approved in principle, fell down in practice because of the impossibility of disposing of the large amount of state bonds necessary to do the work.

Other business engaged the attention of the Louisiana legislature, also—civil rights and equal accommodations for Negroes in theaters, railroad trains, streetcars and other public places; an enlargement of Governor Warmoth's powers over the New Orleans metropolitan police; and the creation of a monopoly of butchering in New Orleans in the hands of the Crescent City Live Stock Landing & Slaughter House Company, the same concern which afterward figured in the Slaughter House Cases before the Supreme Court of the United States.

In March, 1869, Governor Warmoth accused his state auditor, Dr. Wickliffe, of reselling the scrip received by him in payment of taxes; secured his indictment on fourteen counts; and undertook to remove him from office, pending trial, and replace him with L. T. Delassize, a wealthy Negro. Dr. Wickliffe moved his office across Conti Street, warned the people to transact no business with the new auditor, and entered into a lengthy war of court process, injunctions and trials, with the Governor. The war, which lasted for a year, with Wickliffe in and out of the office, and with charges and counter-charges flying fast, ended with the impeachment and conviction of the auditor and his flight from the state.

In one form or another, and under various names, scrip was common to most of the Reconstruction states and was subject to the same sort of abuses wherever it was found.

Arkansas went on a scrip basis in the summer of 1868, with public assurance that not more than two hundred thousand dollars of the paper would be issued, to be redeemed by July 1, 1869, out of the incoming taxes. Extraordinary expenses of the military operations of the winter, and other costly developments, had caused an issue of three hundred and fifty thousand dollars in scrip by March, 1869, and the market was down to sixty cents on the dollar. Besides the state's general scrip there were outstanding, also, "swamp land warrants" issued by the commissioner of public works, who, in October,

1868, had announced with a flourish that "grand enterprises of importance will be commenced, and rapidly pushed to a successful completion." For the "swamp land warrants" there was no market.

In March, Arkansas general scrip was made receivable for state taxes of all sorts, whereupon, much to the benefit of the scrip dealers in Little Rock, its value jumped up thirty cents on the dollar in one day. For the next five years there was to be, in Arkansas, an active market for speculation in scrip, every manner of scrip—state, county, city, improvement district. Its principal, and almost its only use, was to pay taxes. Its value fluctuated widely, and sometimes wildly, accordingly as it was made good, or made not good, for taxes of different sorts and in different jurisdictions. It offered a fertile field for profitable speculation by tax collectors and other public officials, who might collect the taxes or draw their pay and emoluments in money, and settle their public obligations with scrip, purchased sometimes for as little as twenty cents on the dollar, until, in the final collapse, it became of no value at all.

In Florida, in the spring and summer of 1869, promoters from the North, by way of North Carolina, exhibited a simple but effective way to make profitable use of depreciated corporate securities. Before the war, the Pensacola & Georgia Railroad and the Tallahassee Railroad had received aid from the counties through which they ran. As security for the aid advanced, the counties took the bonds of the railroad companies. War devastation and subsequent confusion had made it impossible for the two lines to meet their obligations. On February 6, 1869, therefore, they were advertised to be sold at auction by the trustees of the Florida Internal Improvement Fund, for the benefit of the holders of the bonds. When the sale was cried off, there stepped up George W. Swepson, promoter, "with more than a million dollars first-mortgage bonds stuffed in his breeches pockets, which had been purchased by him at thirty to thirty-five cents on the dollar," from the county governments which owned them. For the balance of the purchase price, nearly half a million dollars, he gave a check which, as the Supreme Court of the United States afterward found, was worthless. Even the money which was used to buy up the bonds, the court held, had been embezzled from the railroad in North Carolina of which Mr. Swepson and Milton S. Littlefield had obtained control, through the aid and complaisance of that state's Radical legislature at its 1868 session.

In June, 1869, the two railroads so acquired were consolidated into the Jacksonville, Pensacola & Mobile Railroad, which solicited and secured state aid, in the amount of sixteen thousand dollars a mile, in state bonds to be exchanged for a like amount of bonds of the railroad company as security, the proceeds to be spent "to complete, equip and maintain the road."

With the eight-per-cent state bonds so secured, in the total amount of $4,000,000, General Littlefield went to New York, London and Amsterdam, where the bonds were sold to innocent Dutch investors, at about seventy cents on the dollar. Of the proceeds, nearly $2,800,000, only $309,000 ever reached the railroads of Florida. The balance was consumed in commissions and "expenses" of various sorts. Governor Reed, who himself was charged with having been the recipient of $223,750 of the amount, finally reported to the legislature:

"It appears that the bonds of the company were entrusted to one of the firms of swindlers who abound in New York, who by fraud and villainy have diverted the proceeds from the work for which issued."

Other railroads, also, received state aid, as did various organizations for the improvement and navigation of inland waterways. Governors, senators and other public officials served on the boards of directors of most of these corporations, along with the promoters of the enterprises.

A people, white and black, desperately poor, needing above all things peace and readjustment and the opportunity to work and rebuild, had been turned over to organized plunder under the forms of law. It was not done with malicious intent. The mass of the people of the North wanted no more than a just peace. Even the men directly responsible for the policy did not foresee for the most part the consequences of the thing they did. With an obtuse "pietistic humanitarianism," a general confidence in unlimited democracy, and an unshakable conviction of the superiority of Northern ways, they had undertaken to telescope into a few short months generations of development and experience in self-government, to carry out a most delicate and difficult social adjustment by the rough expedient of "putting the bottom rail on top."

CHAPTER XXXVIII

From Virginia to Texas

RECONSTRUCTION was complete in seven of the former Confederate States, insofar as compliance with the steps laid down by Congress and its acceptance of their results could make it, when General Grant came to the Presidency in March, 1869. In Georgia the required steps had been taken, but the results had not been accepted because of the refusal of the legislature to agree that the new constitution meant that Negroes could hold office as well as vote. In Mississippi, Virginia and Texas the steps required for a state in process of Reconstruction had not been completed.

Two weeks after the new administration began, the Georgia legislature removed their state one step farther from final admission into the Union by rejecting the Fifteenth Amendment. The legislature itself divided on the subject, with the Conservative-controlled House voting for ratification, and the Radical Senate voting against it, by virtue of the deciding vote of its president, B. F. Conley. The fact that so important a Bullock lieutenant cast the final and deciding vote against the amendment gave the Conservatives ground to charge that the Governor engineered the movement as part of a plan to have Georgia kept out of the Union and under military tutelage, until the legislature could be reshaped and brought under his control. Refusal to ratify, however, had no immediate effect upon the status of Georgia. In default of further action by Congress, the state remained until 1870 half in and half out of the Union, with an elected civil government at home but without representation in Washington.

While Georgia was removing itself farther from final admission, there were in Washington in March, 1869, three committees from Virginia, three from Mississippi and two from Texas, representing different factions or points of view, and each seeking in its own way the final Reconstruction of its state. All elements besieged the new President with their varying versions of what had happened, and their proposals as to what should be brought about. Regular hearings were arranged at which spokesmen of the different committees stated their

375

cases before the President was ready to make his recommendations to Congress.

Under the workings of the resolution which had been passed to keep the Fortieth Congress in session to watch President Johnson, the new Forty-first Congress began its first session in March, instead of waiting until the regular date in December. General Benjamin F. Butler, who aspired to the leadership in Reconstruction affairs left vacant by the death of Thaddeus Stevens, introduced a bill into the House, on March 19, to reconstruct Mississippi, where his son-in-law, General Ames, was serving as military commander, provisional governor and, in fact, just about the whole government. General Butler's bill called for a reassembling of the Eggleston convention, whose handiwork had been rejected by the voters; the creation, by that convention, of a new provisional government; the setting up of new election machinery; and the submittal of the constitution to another election to be held by the new officials. Commenting upon the plan of his Massachusetts colleague, Henry L. Dawes observed that he would as soon leave to the prisoners the selection of a penitentiary warden, as he would leave to the reassembled convention in Mississippi the choice of a provisional governor for the state.

The point at issue, in both Mississippi and Virginia, was on the proscriptive clauses of disfranchisement and disqualification, whether they might be voted on separate and apart from the rest of the constitutions, or whether the documents must be swallowed or rejected as a whole. In Texas, where the proposed constitution had no such clauses, the point was simply one of political maneuver whether the elections should be held early, as the Andrew Jackson Hamilton faction of Republicans wanted them, or late, as the Davis-Morgan Hamilton faction wished.

On April 7, in his first message to Congress, the new President recommended an act permitting a separate vote on those clauses which limited the right of ex-rebels and rebel sympathizers to vote and hold office. The House, on the next day, went further than the President had asked by authorizing him to call elections in Virginia, Texas and Mississippi at such times as he thought best, with the privilege of voting separately on such clauses as the President might choose. Under the aggressive leadership of Oliver P. Morton, the Senate added ratification of the Fifteenth Amendment as another requirement for the readmission of a state. The House accepted the amendment and the bill became law on April 10.

A month later, the President called an election in Virginia to be held on July 6, and in Mississippi to be held on November 30, with separate votes to be taken on the proscriptive clauses in both cases. Before the elections were announced, and even before the passage of the act, organization, negotiation and combinations were under way among the various parties and factions.

The Virginia Republicans reassembled their state convention in Petersburg on March 9 to reconsider the nominations for state offices made the year before, in anticipation of the election which was not held. "The farmers of Virginia are too much occupied with their own immediate concerns to give great attention to state politics," wrote Edward King, observant Northern reporter who happened to be present. The delegates in attendance, however, whom Mr. King described as a "disreputable and lawless rabble," took the subject of the choice of a temporary chairman seriously enough to stage a first-class riot, which the local police could not control. By the second day of the convention, however, Governor Wells was able to control affairs enough to have his nomination of the year before renewed. Changes were made in other places on the ticket, however, including the naming of Dr. J. H. Harris, colored, for lieutenant-governor. Privately, friends of Wells declared that the nomination was maneuvered by the Governor's enemies to weaken the ticket. The platform reaffirmed approval of the Underwood constitution, opposed its amendment in any way, and especially opposed universal amnesty.

Having failed to get Governor Wells off the ticket, or to make more moderate the platform, nine anti-Wells leaders caucused in a Petersburg hotel, to lay plans for a moderate movement. In the group was Edgar Allan, a member of the Underwood constitutional convention, who had opposed the imposition of conditions harsher than those required by the acts of Congress, and had warned the Negro delegates that, under the constitution proposed, designing white men would use Negro votes to secure office for themselves for a few years, and a few years only. Then, warned Allan, the whole thing would be swept away, leaving to the Negroes and their children a legacy of the hatred of the white population of Virginia. Another of the group, and the dominant spirit in it, was General William Mahone, who was not to become the head of the Readjuster movement for yet another dozen years.

As a result of the plans of the Petersburg caucus, a moderate ticket was put in the field under the name of "True Republican," with a nominating address, signed by one hundred and fifty responsible Republican citizens. Head of the ticket so nominated was Gilbert C.

Walker, Virginian and Republican, who had opposed proscription and had aided the Committee of Nine in its efforts toward restoration and reconciliation.

This put three tickets in the field, since the Conservatives, nearly a year before, had nominated Colonel R. E. Withers, late of the Confederate Army, for governor, with a full ticket, on a platform condemning the Underwood constitution *in toto* and Negro suffrage in any form. The Committee of Nine and the group led by General Mahone, working separately, persuaded the Conservatives to hold a second convention, on April 28, at which the Withers ticket gave up their nominations and left the race. Acceptance of the resignations by the Conservative convention, against the vigorous opposition of important members, left the race to the two Republican tickets—one favoring the Underwood constitution unamended; the other, accepting it but for its proscriptions against former Confederates and Confederate sympathizers.

The constitution, even without its disfranchisements and disqualifications, but with Negro suffrage and Negro rights to hold office, was bitter medicine for many of the strict Conservatives. They were brought to accept it in June, however, by the logic of the situation and the persuasions of the men who had been working since December to unite all of the Conservative way of thought behind one ticket. Several Negro nominees for the legislature received Conservative backing, while a considerable number of Negroes supported the Walker ticket, forming colored clubs to promote his candidacy and oppose proscription of their white neighbors.

The "regular" Republican Negroes, meeting in convention in May to renew their support of the Wells ticket and platform, urged General Canby, who replaced General Stoneman as military commander in April, to appoint Negroes to fill some of the 2,613 offices in the state which his predecessor had reported as vacant because of the lack of qualified persons who could take the test oath required by Congress. Negroes were urged not to throw away their votes by casting them for men who had opposed their aspirations and had called them "apes and cornfield niggers."

The election was a sweeping victory for the moderate Republicans. The test oath and disfranchising clauses were beaten by votes of about 84,000 for, to 124,000 against them, while the constitution without these clauses was ratified, 210,585 for, to 9,136 against. Walker was elected governor, with 119,535 votes to 101,204 for Wells, with slightly smaller majorities for other members of the Moderate ticket. The new legislature was overwhelmingly Conservative and Moderate in its make-up. There were twenty-seven Negroes in the two houses, including three Negro Conservatives. Virginia, exulted the Norfolk *Journal*, was "redeemed, regenerated and disenthralled."

More remained to be done, however. The heads of the Moderate ticket could take the test oath, which General Canby ruled would be required before the new government could enter upon its functions, but many of the newly-elected legislators could not. Ratification of such an oath had been defeated in the election, but General Canby was proceeding under the old law, which was still in force, and would remain in force until the new legislature should ratify the Fifteenth Amendment and Congress should accept and approve the new Virginia constitution. But, under the General's ruling, the new legislature could not meet and take such action unless its members took the old oath, which many of them could not do.

The knot was cut by the Attorney General of the United States, Amos T. Akerman, to whom the matter was referred. He ruled, on August 28, that the legislature might meet without taking the oath, and might do the things needful to secure Federal recognition, but could not embark upon a general legislative program until the Federal authorities had approved the new constitution without the test-oath requirement. Mr. Akerman's common-sense opinion cleared the way for the return of Virginia to the Union.

On September 21, General Wells resigned as governor, to be replaced immediately by Governor Walker, through military appointment by General Canby. Two weeks later, on October 5, the new Virginia legislature met. On the fourth day of the session, and by almost unanimous votes, it completed the ratification of the Fourteenth and the Fifteenth Amendments, reported its action to Washington, and awaited acceptance by Congress.

It was to be Virginia's good fortune to come back into the Union under a civil government committed to a policy of reconciliation. It had been the ill fortune of Tennessee, first of the former Confederate States to be restored to full representation in the Union, to come back under a government of a different sort. While Parson Brownlow was governor, the administration of affairs in Tennessee was carried on in a spirit of righteous retribution for the sin of treason, and revenge for past wrongs suffered by the Unionists of East Tennessee. With the resignation of Governor Brownlow to go to the Senate, and the accession of De Witt Clinton Senter, there came into government in Tennessee a new spirit of reconciliation, and of retrenchment as well.

A new governor was to be chosen at the elections in August, 1869. The Republican nominating convention, held on May 30, split wide open, with the result that there were two Republican candidates—Governor Senter, representing the Moderate wing; Colonel William B. Stokes, representing the Radical wing. Wisely, the Democrats made no nominations and threw their strength to Senter. Andrew Johnson, returned home from Washington, likewise supported Senter as, curiously, did Senator Brownlow, in a feeble fashion not characteristic of him.

At the outset of the campaign, on June 1, control of the government of the capital city was lost to the Radicals, when Chancellor Charles Smith, holding court in the near-by county of Sumner, granted the petition of four hundred and sixty-six citizens that the city of Nashville be placed in the hands of a receiver, to save it from further spoliation by its Reconstruction rulers, headed by Mayor Alden, a carpetbagger of recent arrival and obscure antecedents. Mayor Alden objected, without avail, and ran for election in August, to meet defeat, while the city accepted, and rejoiced at, rule by the court receiver, John M. Bass—a portent of the growing weariness of the people, even the Union people, of the continued violence, abuse and extravagance which had marked the Reconstruction period.

In the state election, on August 5, 1869, Governor Senter won handsomely by a vote of 120,333 to 55,036. The result was not a partisan or factional victory. It was an overwhelming expression of the longing for peace in Tennessee, and convincing evidence that the state had regained the power of self-government. The new legislature chosen at the same election, strongly Conservative in sentiment, met in October, inaugurated Governor Senter for a full two-year term, and called a constitutional convention, to meet on January 10, 1870.

Tennessee did not undergo Reconstruction in the technical sense of coming under the operation of the act of March 2, 1867, but it did pass through a long and difficult process of restoration, beginning with the appointment of Andrew Johnson as military governor in 1862. That process passed into a new and final phase with the demonstration, in August, 1869, that a majority in both parties preferred peace to punishment.

On July 13, a week after the election in Virginia, the President set November 30 as the date for the election in which Mississippians were to be given their opportunity to vote separately on the objectionable clauses of the constitution which they had rejected the year before.

In an effort to take advantage of what was believed to be a strong leaning of the new President toward favoring his family and other connections with public office, the Moderate wing of the Republicans in Mississippi launched the "Dent movement," to make Judge Louis Dent, brother of Mrs. Grant, governor of Mississippi. His attenuated standing as a Mississippian was based on the fact that he had come to Coahoma County after the army, as a lessee and operator of an "abandoned" plantation; that he had married in the state; and that he had, while residing at the White House, helped the Conservative Mississippians to block the schemes of the Committee of Sixteen which sought to establish the regime of the Eggleston convention rejected by the voters in 1868.

In the middle of August, however, the President demonstrated that his bent toward nepotism did not extend so far as backing his brother-in-law for election as governor of Mississippi, when he made public a letter to Judge Dent declining support, regardless of relationship. The Dent movement, by that time, had gone so far that its promoters could not afford to stop it, nor was Judge Dent willing to withdraw, even after the expression of his distinguished brother-in-law's political disapproval. The Conservative Republicans, consequently, at a convention held on September 8, formally nominated a Dent ticket, made up of Democrats and Republicans, including former Union soldiers and one colored man, named for secretary of state as an appeal to the Negro vote. The Democrats made no nominations, and turned what support they could to the Dent movement.

The Radical Republicans, meeting on September 30, shelved General Eggleston as their nominee for governor, and his fellow-nominees for other offices, and named as the head of their ticket J. L. Alcorn, a native of Illinois but a long-time resident of Mississippi, who had served the Confederacy for a few weeks as brigadier general of local defense forces. A man of substance and of oratorical power, he had been elected to the United States Senate by the restoration government of Mississippi but had been refused his seat, along with other like claimants. He had early come to the conclusion that the course of wisdom for the South was to cut loose from the national Democracy which could do nothing for the section, and put itself under the wing of the ruling Republicans. He had, therefore, urged acceptance of the congressional plan of Reconstruction.

On the Alcorn ticket were Captain R. C. Powers, a former Union soldier, for lieutenant-governor; the Rev. James Lynch, colored, of Indiana, for secretary of state; Captain H. R. Pease, late of Connecticut, for superintendent of education; and Henry Musgrove, an ex-Union soldier from Illinois, for auditor. The ticket thus had the support of the three elements of Reconstruction sentiment—native, imported and colored. It had, also, the support of the President in Washington and of General Ames.

Against such a combination of forces, the Dent movement never had a chance, and was defeated by two votes to one. The legislature elected at the same time had thirty-six Republicans and seven Democrats in the Senate, and eighty-two Republicans and twenty-five Democrats in the House.

More important in its final effect, however, was the action of the voters of the state on the constitution. The disfranchisement and disqualification clauses were defeated by votes of more than forty to one; and the constitution without these clauses was ratified, almost unanimously, in justification of Judge Watson's prophecy. A clause prohibiting the loan of the state's credit for any purpose, also submitted separately, was ratified, a fact which was to save Mississippi from some of the heavier burdens of Reconstruction which fell upon other Southern states.

The Texas campaign was under way, with its accustomed vigor, before the President determined the date upon which the elections were to be held. On June 7, the more Radical faction of Republicans held a convention of some seventy-five delegates and alternates at Houston, decided to support the constitution even though it contained a liberal re-enfranchisement clause, nominated a partial ticket headed by E. J. Davis, for governor, and left the work of completing the nominations to the chairman of the new State Executive Committee, J. G. Tracy. Mr. Tracy, an ex-Confederate who the year before had been publisher of the violently Democratic Houston *Telegraph*, was postmaster at Houston and publisher of the newspaper organs of the Radical Republicans.

The more moderate element of the Republicans held no formal convention, but backed Andrew Jackson Hamilton for governor on the strength of his candidacy announced by telegram from Washington, on March 18, and informally endorsed by the old State Executive Committee at a meeting in Austin on April 20. The Hamilton faction urged upon the President an early election; the Davis faction sought delay.

The deciding factor between them was Major General John F. Reynolds, West Point classmate and close friend of the President's, who came back to Texas as military commander in April, when General Canby went to Virginia. General Reynolds developed an ambition to become United States senator, as representative of the state which he commanded and for the Reconstruction of which he was responsible. The way to realize that ambition appeared to lie in alliance with the Davis faction. On July 7, the prestige of "regularity" was put behind that faction by its recognition at the hands of the Republican National Committee, the earliest recorded instance of what was to come to be the common phenomenon of an award of regularity to one or the other of contending Southern Republican factions by the national authorities. The Davis faction's desire for a late election prevailed, also, with the dates set for November 30- December 3.

On September 25, in the midst of a fiercely fought campaign, General Reynolds published a letter supporting the Davis ticket. Provisional Governor Pease, resenting statements in the letter as to his administration of affairs, resigned his office, which was not filled by the General, and went into the A. J. Hamilton camp. A small Democratic faction, violently hostile to Hamilton under any circumstances, put out a ticket on September 29, to make a hopeless race whose only effect was to draw off enough Conservative votes from Hamilton to help elect Davis.

The power of the commanding general was thrown against Hamilton because, said General Reynolds, his backing consisted of a coalition of Democrats and ex-rebels; because, said Hamilton, he would not agree to support the General's aspirations for a seat in the Senate. Regardless of the reason, the General removed many Hamilton men from offices in the provisional government during October and November; and, on November 10, ordered a ten-day supplemental registration, conducted by Davis registrars, many of whom felt that only pure Radicals were not "rebels." The registration resulted in striking from the lists numerous whites of Moderate persuasion.

With all the prestige of "regularity," the support of the military, and the control of the machinery of registration and election, General Davis was elected governor by a majority of but eight hundred in a total vote of eighty thousand. In the Senate the Radicals had seventeen members to thirteen Moderates, and in the House of Representatives fifty members to forty.

This strong spirit of faction in Texas was not unique among the Reconstructionists. In every state, divisions of the same sort appeared, almost as soon as the governments passed into the new hands. Within a year of his inauguration, the vigorous Governor Clayton of

Arkansas was faced with a move among his Republican associates to seize the capitol during his absence from the state, and hold it against him upon his return. Governor Reed, before his first year of office in Florida was out, was facing a second attempt at impeachment at the hands of an overwhelmingly Republican House of Representatives. Governor Holden, in office little more than a year as an elected governor of North Carolina, was fighting in the third session of his legislature to stave off an investigation of some of the frauds and corruptions of the first two sessions, with frantic appeals from his old organ, the Raleigh *Standard*, for Republicans to "act with Republicans and not enemies." The proposed investigations were denounced as a "stab at the Republican party," the work of a "snarling minority." Republicans who supported that minority were characterized as "Judases who seek to betray those who have trusted them."

In Louisiana, the feud between Governor Warmoth and Auditor Wickliffe and the pure Radicals went merrily on with charge and countercharge, while in Alabama, Governor Smith was resisting demands of the extreme wing of his party that troops be called out and the state put under military rule.

In the factional fights, already so prevalent in 1869 in the Republican state governments set up only the year before, the Democrats found opportunity. Both factions of Republicans in Arkansas, as early as October, 1869, were bidding for Democratic support and pledging themselves to the removal of ex-rebel disabilities. A Liberal Republican party, newly formed at Little Rock, first declared for this action, while Governor Clayton, in a speech on the following day, described disfranchisement as a "temporary expedient," the need for which had passed.

At the close of the legislative session, in April, 1869, the Lieutenant-Governor and seventeen members of the legislature of the "scalawag" element, issued an appeal to the people against the Governor and the "ring of penniless adventurers" into whose hands, they charged, the state government had fallen. Counts in the indictment against them were the "criminal abuse of power" in the use of the militia; the unfair distribution of state aid to railroads; the illegality of accepting the Holford bond claims at face value; and the general extravagance of the state government.

Thirty years before, in its efforts to aid the establishment of banks in Little Rock and Van Buren, the state of Arkansas issued bonds which could not be sold at the time, but which had been pledged as collateral for loans in New York. Upon failure of the banks, and nonpayment of the loans, the bonds put up as collateral were sold, and passed into the hands of James Holford of London, whose heirs sought, vainly, to collect interest and principal. In April, 1869, the legislature of Arkansas, at the instance of the Governor, recognized the claim filed by the Holford heirs in 1860, with interest, and directed the issue of refunding bonds to pay it. Upon rumors of fraud and corruption in the whole transaction, the Governor afterward held up the exchange of new bonds for the Holford bonds, an act for which he was charged, by some, with exceeding his authority for the purpose of impairing the credit of the state.

In July Governor Clayton went to New York on business connected with the Holford bonds. Catching the Governor out of the state, his opponents procured Lieutenant-Governor James M. Johnson to come from his mountain home at Huntsville to claim the Governorship. Physical possession of offices in dispute had great importance throughout the Reconstruction period, and there was more than one race or midnight raid to seize and hold a capitol. In this first race of the sort, the anti-Clayton plans leaked, and the Governor hurried back from New York, beat the Lieutenant-Governor to the office, and left him only the opportunity to express violent anti-Clayton sentiments to a serenading crowd. The Clayton forces retaliated with quo warranto proceedings challenging the right of the Lieutenant-Governor to his office. The proceedings were dropped, however, for a straight-out factional fight in the political campaign and at the polls, after the Liberal Republicans organized an opposition faction, on October 14, appealed to Democrats and former Whigs to join them, and challenged the Clayton forces on the issues of autocratic power, fraud, favoritism and extravagance in government. The lines were being drawn for the election fights of 1870.

There was still, however, a reliable issue with which to combat the development of such schisms in the ruling Republican ranks—violence and "outrages." Governor Smith, of Alabama, declared that one of his carpetbag associates in government

"did not want the law executed, because that would put down crime, and crime is his life's blood. He would like very much to have a Ku Klux outrage every week to assist him in keeping up strife between the whites and the blacks, that he might be more certain of the votes of the latter. He would like to have a few colored men killed every week to furnish semblance of truth to Spencer's libels."

To those who sought, in the summer of 1869, to have him call out the militia, Governor Smith replied: "Nowhere have the courts been interrupted. No resistance has been encountered by officers of court in their efforts to discharge the duties imposed upon them by law." The Governor of Alabama, however, did not have the acute appreciation of the political value of "atrocities," and the possibilities in their exploitation, developed by some of his associates—particularly when the atrocities could be related to the mysterious and dread Ku Klux Klan.

With new state governments based on Negro suffrage in full operation, under protection of the army, and with early ratification of the Fifteenth Amendment assured in the summer of 1869, it was supposed that the need for the special services and protection of the Freedmen's Bureau had passed. Its work was discontinued on July 1, except for educational activities which were to be carried on for three years longer.

The Bureau was born of necessity, to meet a desperate situation under unprecedented and almost impossible conditions. Its record was better than its reputation, in the fields of direct relief, where the Bureau distributed twenty-one million rations to destitute whites and blacks; of adjustment of labor relations; and of education, where its achievements were considerable. Even in the bitterly controverted field of the administration of justice, the Bureau courts were useful in preventing individual cases of injustice and oppression. There is truth as well as exaggeration in Dr. W. E. B. DuBois's description of the effects and reactions of the two different sorts of courts in the South:

"Bureau courts tended to become centers simply for punishing whites; while regular civil courts tended to become solely institutions for perpetuating the slavery of the blacks."

The great obstacle to the success of the work of the Bureau, particularly after it became apparent that its charges were to be made voters, was the demoralization of politics. That the patronage of Bureau positions, and the prestige which they gave among the new voters, should be used to further ambitions and designs was natural and inevitable—and the inevitable happened, very promptly. When the Bureau's work came to an end, many of its agents were to be found holding state or local office in the new governments which they had helped to create.

CHAPTER XXXIX

The Last State Admitted

At some time during the first half-year of the administration of President Grant, in the spring or summer of 1869, the Grand Wizard of the Invisible Empire of the ❋❋ ordered that body to dissolve, to disband its Dens, to burn or bury its regalia, to destroy its ritual and records.

Mysterious in its death as in its birth, the reasons for the Ku Klux Klan ordering its own disbandment are the subject of conjecture. The circumstances under which the order was issued, even the time of its issue, are unknown. The order was issued—that is certain—and was obeyed by regularly organized Dens to which it came through the established channels of Dragons, Titans and Giants. The order did not reach all Dens; or was not obeyed by all; or new Dens were organized by men who had gone to other sections of the South carrying with them imperfect memories of the prescripts and rule of the order; or secret and disguised activities were carried on by persons totally unauthorized, for purposes of their own. At any rate, what passed for and was spoken of as Klan activity continued for several years after 1869, when, as all agree, the authentic order of the Ku Klux was officially disbanded by the man to whom authority had been granted, two years before, to issue such an order whenever, in his opinion, it was justified.

Exactly when the order was issued is not of record, nor why. It is agreed that it was after General Grant had become president, and perhaps after he had evinced a willingness to allow a separate vote on the proscriptions in the Virginia and Mississippi constitutions. The order may not have been issued, however, until after the August elections in Tennessee when the era of better feeling in that state was confirmed by the overwhelming Conservative vote.

No records were kept, and men of that time who held office in the workings of the authentic Klan retained their reticence about it, even to the end of their lives. J. C. Lester, one of the six of the original kuklos in Pulaski, in his history of the Klan published in 1884, which, in the edition edited by Professor Walter L. Fleming, remains the most complete record of the organization from the inside, sets the time of disbandment as the spring of 1869. The late Judge James P. Young of Memphis recalled, however, that he received from Nashville the order to disband the Memphis Den after the definite news had come of the results of the Senter-Stokes election, and the further fact that those results were to be accepted without contest. That, of course, would fix the date of the order of disbandment early in August, 1869.

There is no more agreement as to the reasons for the disbandment than there is as to the less important question of its date. One reason advanced is the passage of anti-Ku Klux laws by the newly-reconstructed states, and, in particular, the anti-Klan activities of Governor Brownlow and his Tennessee State Guards. The reason seems almost no reason at all for an organization which was born to defy and set at naught what it looked upon as unjust and unholy laws. As to Governor Brownlow, he had ceased to be governor of Tennessee and had gone to the Senate before the earliest date suggested as the time of disbandment.

Another suggested reason is that the work of the Klan was done, with civil government restored in all but three of the Southern states and the promise of early restoration there. The fact is, however, that the civil governments in operation in most of the Southern states at that time were not such as would have seemed desirable to those who directed the affairs of the Klan, and that their existence and operation would not have been taken as a fulfillment of the purposes for which the Klan was organized.

The more likely reason for dissolving the order was that its responsible chiefs came to the conclusion not that the work of the order was done but that its usefulness was ended.

In correspondence of the New York World, from Wilkes County, Georgia, published on January 9, 1870, unsigned but written by Miss Eliza Frances Andrews, the situation is clearly put:

"When the Ku Klux Klan was first introduced into Georgia, it seemed more like a sort of organized practical joke upon the negroes than any serious enterprise. . . . But before long the low-downers took to 'Ku-Klucking' as they call it, and then cruelties began to be practiced, and decent men withdrew from the organization altogether. . . . Whenever a set of low, disorderly fellows feel inclined to commit a rascality, they put on masks and call themselves Ku Klux. A true statement of the case is not that the Ku Klux are an organized band of licensed criminals, but that men who commit crimes call themselves Ku Klux."

And there was nothing the heads of the authentic Klan could do about it. It is difficult to get even an inkling of what went on in the latter months of the existence of the authentic Klan, after the practice of publishing Klan notices and warnings in the newspapers came under the ban of the laws, but a trend can be discerned in the tone of the later messages published. These messages were quite as much concerned with threatening imitators of the Klan's name and disguises, and outside users of secret methods, as they were with the original business of warning and "regulating." Thus, even before the Klan was driven completely underground, evidently it was finding that its secret membership and disguised operations laid it open to imitation by others who could use its name and methods for the basest and most cruel ends.

The real reason for the end of the original and authentic Klan, most probably, lay in the forced realization among its leaders that a machine had been created which, by its very nature, could not be controlled and directed to its professed ends, and which could not be protected from imitation even by the very elements of the population against which its terrors were sought to be directed.

That the Invisible Empire had been dissolved by its Grand Wizard was not known publicly at the time, or indeed for long years afterward. There were farewell parades of hooded riders and sheeted horses, as a gesture of defiance, but outside the ranks of the Klan itself no one knew that they were preludes to the destruction of regalia and records. To the outside world, activities of the sort ascribed to the Ku Klux continued, sporadically, while the very words and all that they conjured remained as part of the stock in trade of the Radical politician, in Congress and out.

In the long session of the Forty-first Congress, which began in December, 1869, there was discussion of Ku Klux activities, and action against them, but less of both than there was to be in later sessions, when a more intensive cultivation of the "Southern question" became necessary. The major business of the winter session of Congress had to do with the completion of the process of Reconstruction in the South. In his annual message to Congress, the President called attention to the fact that Virginia was ready and waiting for acceptance, a fact made further evident by the presence in Washington of a committee of the new Virginia legislature. While the President recommended the admission of the state, General Butler, who had succeeded to the chairmanship of the Committee on Reconstruction, refused to countenance it except upon still further fundamental conditions.

By a close vote in both Senate and House the state was finally admitted to representation, on January 26, 1870, upon the following fundamental conditions: that the suffrage clauses in the constitution should never be changed to deprive any class of citizens of the right to vote therein granted; that there should be no change in the requirements as to time and place of residence of voters; that there should be no change in the right to hold office because of race, color, or previous condition of servitude; and that there should be no change to deprive any citizen or class of citizens of school rights secured by the new constitution of the state. To these fundamental conditions affecting the state was added one other requirement: that only those who could take oath that they were not subject to the disabilities of the Fourteenth Amendment, or that their disabilities had been removed by act of Congress, could be seated as members of the Virginia legislature.

Under the authority of this act, which became a law on January 26, 1870, Governor Canby announced, on the next day, that Military District No. 1 had ceased to exist, and that the state of Virginia had resumed her powers of government. Four days later, on February 1, Virginia's representatives in Congress were seated, and the Reconstruction of the state was complete.

When Congress met in December, the elections had been held in Mississippi and Texas, but their new legislatures had not yet met to perform the required acts of ratifying the Fourteenth and Fifteenth Amendments. The Mississippi body met in its provisional status, on January 11, 1870, and proceeded to the ratification of the amendments, with only eight votes cast against the Fourteenth and but one against the Fifteenth Amendment. With five Democrats out of thirty-three members in the Senate, and twenty-five out of one hundred and seven members in the House, it is striking that only one vote was cast against the Negro suffrage amendment. The explanation lies in the state of feeling of the Democratic members. Negro suffrage they already had in Mississippi, by state action forced upon them by a Congress representing only Northern states, most of which were rejecting the same rule for themselves whenever they voted on it. The proposed amendment, when ratified, would force the same rule upon the Northern states which they had already forced upon Mississippi and the Southern states, a prospect which gave the Mississippi Democratic legislators a certain sardonic satisfaction.

The legislature proceeded, likewise, to the election of United States senators, so that they might be ready to take their seats promptly upon acceptance of the state into the Union by Congress. Three were to be chosen, one for a full term of six years, beginning on March 4, 1871; one for an unexpired term of five years, ending on March 4, 1875; and one for the short term of one year, ending on March 4, 1871. For the full term, the legislature chose General Alcorn, the new governor. For the long unexpired term, the choice was General Ames.

By agreement, the locum tenens of the short term, to fill the gap until Governor Alcorn should take office, was to be a colored man. The Rev. James Lynch, of Indiana, elected secretary of state, was looked upon with favor for the place, but his election would have vacated an important state office. The Republican caucus, therefore, decided upon the Rev. Hiram Revels, also of Indiana, and one of the fifteen colored preachers who were members of the legislature, partly because of a powerful and eloquent prayer with which he had opened the Senate upon its convening.

The choice of Hiram Revels as the first Negro to sit in the Congress of the United States was fortunate. Born in North Carolina, raised in Indiana, he had become a Methodist minister and teacher at Baltimore. During the war he had assisted in raising Negro regiments, and had come to the South with the Bureau, to settle in Natchez as a preacher. He was able and conservative in his course, sensible of the historic distinction which had come to him, but more interested in honestly serving the interests of his race.

On February 3, debate began in Congress upon the admission of Mississippi as a state. Three plans were under consideration—admission of the state without conditions other than those already required; admission on the further fundamental conditions which had been required of Virginia; and admission with power reserved to Congress to deal further with the state even after it was readmitted.

The points of view were well expressed, in a two-weeks' debate in the Senate, by Senators Morton and Trumbull. Morton declared that the experience of the past eighteen months with the other reconstructed states had shown the necessity of continued congressional control:

"I know the common idea was, without consideration, that when these states were once restored to representation they passed entirely from under the jurisdiction of Congress and we were done with them. That was illogical as experience has now shown. We must follow the doctrine of Reconstruction to its consequences, and if necessary we must deal with these states after they have been readmitted."

The opposite point of view was expressed by Senator Trumbull, chairman of the Judiciary Committee:

"The committee believed Congress had no power to impose such conditions; that they have no binding force; that their effect is evil and evil only; that it is keeping up a distinction in regard to the states which could do no good and may do much harm. I believe that when a state is entitled to representation in this Union it becomes one of the states of the Union, and is a full and complete state with all in all respects."

The more moderate view prevailed, partly, suggested Representative S. S. Cox, because of the waiting presence of a colored senator to be inducted into the seat of Jefferson Davis. At any rate, on February 23, 1870, Mississippi was admitted to Congress as a state, upon the same further fundamental conditions required of Virginia. Two days later, on a certificate of election issued by Adelbert Ames, brevet major general, U. S. A., provisional governor of Mississippi, Hiram Revels was sworn in as a senator of the United States.

Besides issuing a certificate of election to Senator Revels, General Ames, in his capacity as military commander, issued, on February 26, a general order terminating military rule in Mississippi, and in his capacity as provisional governor issued to himself a certificate of election as senator. The latter was not so potent in effecting speedy entrance as had been the certificate issued to his new colleague. Not until April 1, 1870, and then only after a debate in which he was charged with ineligibility because he was not a bona fide resident of the state, and impropriety in using his official position to further his own election, was he finally seated and sworn in.

Before that time, on March 8, the legislature had reassembled in Mississippi, no longer in a provisional status, in a session which continued until July 21. On March 10, the third day of the session, General Alcorn was inaugurated as governor, with a fulsome oratorical effort in which he referred to the states returning to the Union as "pardoned children" who had been "restored by grace." Secession he termed a "fallacy," "treason" and "revolutionary." His former support of it he explained on the ground that then "I spoke not as a sophist, after the fashion of Calhoun, but as a rebel, after the fashion of Caesar." To which the Jackson *Clarion* added the comment that he had been, likewise, a "soldier after the manner of Falstaff."

On February 8, while Congress was debating the terms of admission of Mississippi, the Texas legislature met in a provisional status to perform the acts necessary to secure congressional recognition, and to elect United States senators—a political act which was of extreme importance in all the Reconstruction states. General Reynolds exercised a strict supervision of the organization of the two houses, extending to the determination of questions of contested elections and the appointment of temporary officers. Subsequent cases of election contest were decided by unseating the A. J. Hamilton Moderates, and seating the representatives of the Davis faction, to give the Radicals a secure control of the legislature.

The Fourteenth and Fifteenth Amendments were ratified on February 14, by a vote almost as nearly unanimous as that in Mississippi. Between that date and the end of the session, on February 24, the legislature struggled with the election of senators. Unexpectedly strong opposition developing to his candidacy, Governor Reynolds withdrew his name from consideration in a dignified public announcement that he was not a candidate, and had not authorized the use of his name, because of his conviction that he should not accept civil office at the hands of a legislature of Texas which was so largely the creature of his own political acts done as the directing head of Reconstruction in the state. He raised the further question that his residence of three years in the state as military commander was not such as constituted him an inhabitant of the state in the sense in which that phrase is used in the constitution.

With General Reynolds out of the way and Governor Davis pledged to retain the Governorship, the Radical caucus chose Morgan Hamilton as senator for the short term, to expire March 4, 1871, and for the six-year term to follow; and J. W. Flannagan, lieutenant-governor, for the unexpired term ending March 4, 1875.

On March 30, 1870, a bill to admit Texas as a state upon the same conditions imposed on Virginia and Mississippi became law. The senators and representatives from the state were seated in Congress; the new state government shed its "provisional" character; and, on April 16, 1870, General Reynolds completed the process of Reconstruction by a general order bringing military authority to an end and turning over all power to the civil government.

But one state, Georgia, now remained unrepresented in Congress. The disposition of Georgia was before Congress, off and on, from the very beginning of the session, in December, 1869, when the President recommended a second reconstruction of the state in his annual message, until July 15, 1870, when the bill for its admission was finally passed.

On December 22, 1869, Congress passed a bill which, in effect, remanded Georgia to the status of a military district, pending the imposition of further conditions of admission. The new act required the reassembling of the legislature; the restoration of the Negro members expelled in the autumn of 1868; the taking of the oath of the Fourteenth Amendment or congressional relief from its disabilities by all members; and the ratification of the Fifteenth Amendment.

On January 4, 1870, the Third Military District was reconstituted, by orders of the General of the Army, to include only the state of Georgia, with General Alfred H. Terry as district commander. On January 10, the legislature reconvened under the conditions of the act of December 22. General Terry convened a military board to pass upon the election and qualifications of all members. As a result of what came to be called "Terry's Purge," the expelled Negro members were reseated, and, in addition, twenty Democratic members were ousted and replaced by their opponents who had had the next highest vote. With strong Radical majorities established in both houses by the turbulent two weeks of the "purge," Benjamin F. Conley was re-elected president of the Senate, and R. L. McWhorter speaker of the House. Governor Bullock, at last, had a close-knit and harmonious regime. "The Government has determined," said President Conley in his inaugural address, ". . . that in this republic Republicans shall rule."

The purged legislature ratified the Fifteenth Amendment, as required, and also reratified the Fourteenth, on the theory that the legislature of 1868 which had previously done so was illegal, although that ratification had already been accepted in Washington as valid. On February 16, Foster Blodgett was elected to the United States Senate, for the term to begin in 1871 and end in 1877; H. P. Farrow was elected for the term ending in 1873, to which the previous legislature had chosen Joshua Hill; and R. H. Whitely for the short term ending in 1871, to which Dr. H. V. M. Miller had been elected. With these essentials attended to, the legislature adjourned until April, while debate as to the status of Georgia went on in Congress.

On February 25, Chairman Butler introduced into the House a bill to readmit Georgia on the same terms as Virginia and Mississippi, but with the further condition that the Bullock regime should be

legislated into power by Congress for an additional two years, beyond
its normal expiration in November, 1870. This extension, said the
chairman of the Committee on Reconstruction, was within the powers
of Congress over the reconstructed states. "If the judgment of the
House goes with mine," he said further, "I trust we shall also exhibit
to Tennessee the power that Congress had to protect all its citizens . . .
against wrong, rapine and murder."

The judgment of the House, however, did not go with that of the
chairman. Instead, it adopted an amendment by Mr. Bingham, of
Ohio, to readmit Georgia on the "Virginia conditions" without extending the term for the Bullock government, and sent the bill to the
Senate.

There, strenuous efforts by Senators Morton, Sumner and Wilson
to restore the Butler plan of extending the Radical term of office in
Georgia, were met by as strenuous and more successful opposition on
the part of Senators Trumbull, Schurz and Edmunds. Upon the
Butler plan, Senator Edmunds turned the withering weapon of sarcasm:

"We ought to extend this invention to the other Southern States;
and I would suggest to extend it to the Democrats of the Northern
States too, because it will save us possibly a good many doubtful States.
Let us provide by a general act, in the interest of human rights, that
not only this legislature, which we have now got into a condition of
loyalty, and Republicanism too, I will add, by the introduction of
fifteen or twenty good Republicans who would have been in before
if they had got votes enough, but that in all doubtful States . . . the
existing legislatures when Republican, shall hold over for two years
more; and it might be wise, as we have an election for members of
Congress this fall, to apply it to the present House of Representatives
at the other end of the Capitol."

The readmission of Georgia was further complicated by proposed
anti-Ku Klux amendments, foreshadowing the acts on the subject.
Debate continued through March and April, with the first speech of
Senator Revels, on March 16, as one of its dramatic high lights.
Naturally, the first Negro Senator favored the proposal of the Radical
leaders that the Bullock government be prolonged two years.

A major argument for the prolongation scheme was the stock story
of Southern atrocities. Senator Trumbull paid his respects to the
argument in the Senate with the statement of his belief that many of
the newspaper stories were inspired by "telegrams emanating from

this city. The telegraph is used to create a public sentiment to operate upon Congress." In Georgia the newly established Atlanta *Constitution* published on its editorial page an ironic advertisement:

"Wanted—Ku Klux Outrages.

"Wanted, a liberal supply of Ku Klux outrages in Georgia. They may be as ferocious and bloodthirsty as possible. No regard need be paid to the truth. Parties furnishing must be precise and circumstantial. They must be supplied during the next ten days, to influence the Georgia bill in the House. Accounts of Democrats giving the devil to Republicans are preferred. A hash of negroes murdered by the Ku Klux will be acceptable. A deuce of bobbery is necessary. Raw head and bloody bones, in every style can be served up to profit.

"The highest price paid. Apply to R. B. Bullock, or the Slander Mill, Atlanta, Ga., and to Forney's *Chronicle*, Benjamin F. Butler, or to the Reconstruction Committee, Washington, D. C.

"Georgia Railroad Bonds traded for this commodity."

The last thrust was aimed at the persistent report that bonds issued by the state were being used to influence favorable consideration by Congress of the prolongation scheme. These reports led to an investigation by the Judiciary Committee of the Senate, which found by a majority vote of five to two that the Bullock lobby in Washington had used corrupt and improper means to influence votes in the Senate.

On April 19, the Senate refused to accept the House bill and adopted one of its own. The House refused to accept the Senate bill, and the matter hung, a subject for conference and negotiation, until July 15, 1870, when finally the Georgia bill became law, without the scheme to prolong the Bullock government for two years more.

The persistent desire of Governor Bullock for continued office at Federal hands was not yet quenched, however. On July 18, he reported to the legislature that the Federal soldiers would remain in the state until its representatives were actually seated in Congress, which could not be before the next regular session in December. In the meanwhile, he announced, the legislature could go ahead with its legislating by permission of General Terry. On July 26, the Bullock Senate passed a resolution to forbid the holding of an election in Georgia in November, 1870, on the theory that statehood was not fully recognized until Congress actually received and seated representatives from Georgia. This final attempt to extend the Bullock regime until November, 1872, by default in electing successors, was barely defeated in the

House when twelve Republican members acted with the Democrats after the Attorney General of the United States, A. T. Akerman, himself a resident of Georgia, wrote to leading legislators of the state urging that an election be held in 1870.

And so, more than five years after the last armed resistance of the Confederate States had come to an end, the last of the seceding states was restored to the Union as a state entitled to representation in Congress.

Reconstruction was complete, in theory at least, not only in the states of the South but in the framework of the national government, for on March 30, 1870, the President had sent to Congress a message notifying them that the Secretary of State had issued his proclamation of the ratification of the Fifteenth Amendment by three-fourths of the states. The message, which the President declared a justifiable "departure from the usual custom," hailed as an act of the grandest importance in the history of free government the enfranchisement of four million persons so recently declared by the Supreme Court to have "had no rights which the white man was bound to respect"— thereby giving wider currency and permanence to the mischievous misconception of what Chief Justice Taney actually said in the Dred Scott decision:

"It is difficult at this day to realize the state of public opinion in relation to that unfortunate race, which prevailed in the civilized and enlightened portions of the world at the time of the Declaration of Independence and when the Constitution of the United States was framed and adopted. . . . They had for more than a century been regarded as beings of an inferior order; . . . and so far inferior, that they had no rights which the white man was bound to respect. . . . This opinion was at that time fixed and universal in the civilized portion of the white race."

Before the last of the Southern states was finally allowed representation in Congress, legislation had already been enacted under the enforcement clauses of the Fourteenth and the newly ratified Fifteenth Amendment, to extend Federal control into what once had been regarded as the peculiar province of the states. This First Enforcement Act of May 31, 1870, was, in part, a reaction to the success of the Conservatives in Tennessee and Virginia and their threat of success in other states, notably North Carolina. Senator John Pool, of that state, arguing that lawlessness in the South demanded that the Federal government take action to enforce the new amendments, urged its passage as the ground upon which "the Republican party must stand in carrying into effect the Reconstruction policy, or the whole fabric of Reconstruction, with all the principles connected with it, amounts to nothing at all; and in the end it will topple and fall unless it can be enforced by appropriate legislation."

Republicans of all shades of opinion, Moderate and Radical, joined in the passage of such legislation in the First Enforcement Act, an elaborate affair of twenty-three sections, some of which were borrowed from the Fugitive Slave Act of 1850, with reversed application—an historic irony which did not escape attention.

The law created some eighty-seven new and different Federal crimes which might be committed by those who sought to obstruct or restrain the free exercise of civil or political rights by the newly enfranchised citizens. It sought to protect the right of citizens of the United States as citizens in each of the states, against discrimination because of race, color, or previous condition; and to protect equal opportunity to qualify and to vote, by severe penalties for any hindrance or obstruction to that right, whether by threats, violence, intimidation, discharge from employment, or ejectment from lands or houses. It prohibited going disguised upon the highway, with a penalty of a five-thousand-dollar fine, ten years' imprisonment and disqualification for holding office, plus punishment for any other crime that might be committed incidentally.

Exclusive jurisdiction was conferred upon the Federal courts in such cases, and special Federal officers and commissioners, besides the use of the army and the navy of the United States, were authorized. The prohibitions of the act were directed not at the states but at individuals in the states, or at groups of individuals conspiring together.

It was, in fact, to be the final step in Reconstruction—new states, in new relations to a new sort of national government. With its passage at the end of May, and the final admission of Georgia in mid-July, 1870, the work of Reconstruction, inaugurated by the act of March 2, 1867, was complete.

BOOK THREE

REDEMPTION

CHAPTER XL

The Elections of 1870

Secession and four years of war destroyed the governments of the Southern states. Two years of presidential effort failed to restore them. Three years of congressional Reconstruction brought into being, by the summer of 1870, governments at last acceptable to national authority in all its branches.

But before the last of the Southern states was reconstructed to the satisfaction of the ruling powers, the elaborate new governments set up began to crumble. In truth, there was in them small strength of their own—a few men, white and black, who saw in them the hope of a new day; many men who saw in them fairer opportunities than they had known before of political preferment or public plunder; a vast mass of ignorant voters, grateful to "the government" for what it had done for them, and disposed to follow those who could connect themselves with that great dispenser of good gifts. What strength the new states had was from without, not from within, and that, at the end, proved unavailing to protect them from the desperate determination of the old rulers to rule again in the states which they and their fathers had founded and builded.

The story of the last six years of the period of Reconstruction is one of counter-revolution—a counter-revolution effected under the forms of law where that was possible; effected by secrecy and by guile, where that would serve; effected openly, regardless of the forms of law, with violence or the threat of violence, where that had to be. But the counter-revolution was effected, at a cost to the South and its future incalculably great, justified only by the still greater cost of not effecting it.

In the early months of 1870, while Congress and the states, belated in Reconstruction, were working on the final steps of that process, the inherent weakness of the new governments was being made apparent in the sessions of the legislatures in most of the states.

In Tennessee, however, decisive steps to end the abuses complained of in the Brownlow government were taken by the strongly conservative legislature elected in August, 1869. On November 15, the legis-

401

lature called a constitutional convention to assemble in Nashville on January 10, 1870. Definitely Democratic in its membership, the convention organized by electing as chairman John C. Brown, late commander of a division in the Confederate Army of Tennessee, and proceeded to write a new constitution for the state. In the main, the new constitution was a redraft of that of 1834, with changes suggested by recent experience. "Freemen" and "free white men" became, in the new draft, "persons" or "citizens." Protection was provided against the state's becoming a partner or stockholder in banks; against the issuance of charters of incorporation except under the terms of general law; and against issuing state bonds to aid railroads in default.

Power to declare martial law "in the sense of unrestricted powers of military officers or others to dispose of the person, liberties or property of the citizen" was denied to any department of the state government, while the militia could be called out only in case of rebellion or invasion, and upon the declaration of the general assembly that the public safety required it. Recollections of the Brownlow military proclamations and operations were still fresh in 1870.

The constitution, completed on February 23, 1870, was ratified at a special election held on March 30. In November, new Democratic state officers, headed by General Brown as governor, were elected to take office a year later, in October, 1871, when the term for which Governor Senter was elected in 1869 was to expire. With the election of Governor Brown and his associates, under the new constitution, the restoration of Tennessee to the full measure of statehood was complete.

Frequent legislative sessions, in some cases so long as to be almost continuous, and in all cases so costly as to be in and of themselves a real burden on an impoverished people, were characteristic of the period, and at no time more so than in the year 1870. The informality, not to say frivolity, of the sessions impressed all observers. Dissension and squabbling among factions were of more real significance than members with feet on their desks, reading newspapers, or other members cracking peanut shells, or the palpable ignorance of law and parliamentary procedure, which was to be expected. Such splits exposed devious trails of bargain and sale, fraud and corruption, running through many of the Reconstruction projects for the amelioration of the common lot by public borrowing and spending.

Much of the work of the 1870 legislative sessions was directed to the political campaign of that year and to control of the elections to be held in most of the states. Throughout the period of Reconstruc-

Fair of the Washington Light Infantry in Hibernian Hall, Charleston, for the Regimental Fund for Widows and Orphans.

From Leslie's Illustrated Newspaper.

Hiram Revels, first Negro to Sit in Congress, Taking the Oath As United States Senator from Mississippi.

From *Leslie's Illustrated Newspaper.*

tion, there was a constant tendency for the "ins" to pass laws, concentrating in their own hands the entire machinery of holding elections and determining the results. Laws granting such extraordinary power to the officials who happened to be in office were necessary, it was explained, to have fair and peaceable elections, and to protect the results of Reconstruction from the machinations and violence of the common enemy, the "rebels."

The climax of this sort of legislation was reached in Louisiana, where, in February and March, 1870, the legislature passed a group of bills which concentrated in the hands of the governor powers unparalleled up to that time. The governor had power to decide who might cast a ballot, when, where and how it should be cast, and how it should be counted and returned. Parish registrars, appointed by and responsible to the governor, made up the lists of voters and conducted the elections in every detail. Returns of the elections were to be made by them directly to the governor. The governor, the lieutenant-governor, the secretary of state and two senators named in the law were constituted a Returning Board, with power to scrutinize the returns made by the registrars; to throw out any poll, precinct or parish which appeared to have been carried by fraud or violence; and to determine and declare the result of the elections.

Of this law, Governor Warmoth afterward wrote in his memoir, *War, Politics and Reconstruction*:

"This was an extraordinary law—it was a dangerous law; for if the Governor and Returning Board should abuse their powers and act in a partisan spirit they could control absolutely any election held in the State.

"But the violence and outrages of the Presidential election of 1868 were pointed to as the reason—or the excuse, at least—for this legislation."

Ostensibly to curb violence and intimidation in future elections the governor was given yet other extraordinary powers. On election day, the entire peace machinery of the state was put under his control, while judicial officers were forbidden to issue writs of mandamus or injunction to interfere with the conduct of the election by the governor's appointees according to his orders. A special state constabulary was created, with a chief constable in each parish to be appointed by the governor, and a new militia law, authorizing the creation of five regiments. The police force of New Orleans was put completely under the control of the governor rather than the local authorities. At the same session a special court was created, to be known as the Eighth District Court, with a judge appointed by the governor, and with exclusive jurisdiction in all cases which involved public and political questions.

These extraordinary powers, in addition to the other extraordinary powers of removal and appointment of local and parish officials, already granted to or assumed by the governor, seemed to cement his authority beyond all possibility of successful attack. One more step remained to be taken, to amend the constitution of 1868 so as to remove the prohibition against the governor's re-election. The same legislature, by unanimous vote of both houses, submitted to the people such an amendment, to be voted on at the election in November, 1870, when congressmen, legislators and local officials were to be chosen.

Upon the recommendation of Governor Warmoth, the legislature submitted three other amendments, also: to restore the right to vote to all ex-Confederates disfranchised by the state constitution of 1868; to limit the state debt to twenty-five million dollars; and to make any defaulting tax collector ineligible for public office until all of his defalcations should be made good.

In some other directions, however, the wishes of the Governor were not so potent. The legislature went in for "progress" on the grand scale and not always in ways and directions which met His Excellency's approval, as shown by his veto of the law to subscribe to the stock of the Mississippi Valley Navigation Company, for example, or of the law to pave St. Charles Avenue in New Orleans with patent blocks, at the expense of the state.

The Governor expressed concern over the finances and credit of the state, in his message at the opening of the session in January. The legislature promptly voted itself pay and mileage in the amount of five hundred thousand dollars, payable in a special sort of scrip which was to have preference over other state warrants. It increased the printing appropriation from one hundred and forty thousand dollars to two hundred thousand dollars, so that all the faithful newspapers in the parishes might be taken care of, and passed on to other financial schemes.

On January 31, a great mass meeting of citizens gathered in Lafayette Square in New Orleans to protest against "the financial schemes now pending . . . calculated to increase the burdens of the people, depreciate the bonds, and ruin the credit of the people. . . ." A delegation of one hundred was named to call upon the Governor and both houses of the legislature and present the resolutions, supported by the signatures of citizens in the parishes.

The Governor's reception of the delegation was unexpectedly cordial. He agreed with them that something should be done to check the extravagance but, said he, "nearly every prominent broker in the city was engaged in lobbying" the five-million-dollar improvement bond bill through the Senate. "It was only by exposing the fact that one of their emissaries had come into this very chamber and laid upon the desk of my secretary an order for fifty thousand dollars that I was able to defeat it," he added as he went on to mention names.

Of those whom the Governor accused of an attempt to bribe him, some indignantly denied the charge; others admitted the attempt, but declared that it failed only because they did not offer enough. Auditor Wickliffe, whom the House had impeached on charges brought by the Governor, and whom the Senate convicted unanimously, made countercharges during his trial, of blackmail, bribery and fraud by the Governor. "It can be proved," he charged, "that he never signed a bill of pecuniary benefit to anyone that he did not demand and receive money or other consideration for his signature."

More embarrassing to the Governor politically than charges of this sort was the passage by the legislature of a second civil rights bill, making it a criminal offense, punishable by fine and imprisonment, to refuse equal accommodations to colored persons on public conveyances and in licensed places of business. A civil rights bill without criminal penalties, which the 1869 session of the legislature had passed after hearing Senator Pinchback's bitter complaint that he had been refused "a drink of common whisky in a common grogshop," was signed by the Governor. The new bill, far more drastic, had been passed, the Governor charged, with deliberate intent to "put him in a hole" with the colored voters, when he should refuse to sign it. Exercising a curious constitutional authority to hold a bill without action until the beginning of the next session of the legislature, the Governor neither signed nor vetoed it at the time of its passage.

The effect of the various factional irritants began to be visible at the state Republican convention held in New Orleans on August 9, 1870. The convention was made up, overwhelmingly, of Negro delegates, who proceeded to elect the colored Lieutenant-Governor Dunn as chairman over Warmoth himself. The pure Radical faction, controlling the convention completely, created a new State Central Committee, in opposition to Governor Warmoth and to his plans for having himself made eligible for re-election.

The resourceful Warmoth, with the collaboration of the Collector of the Port of New Orleans, J. F. Casey, another brother-in-law of President Grant's, organized an auxiliary committee, to support Republican nominees in the coming campaign but also to support the constitutional amendment in which they were particularly interested. The opposing faction, headed by United States Marshal S. B. Packard, and Lieutenant-Governor Dunn, denounced the separate campaign committee as a bolt from the regular Republican party.

In the November election, however, the Governor, with his extraordinary powers of election control, and with his ability to raise campaign funds among his appointees, proved more than a match for the opposition. His constitutional amendments were adopted; his friends returned to the legislature, in some cases from counties in which they did not even reside. "Warmothism," as his enemies dubbed the political system in force in Louisiana, came through its first factional test with apparent success, but with what proved to be fatal cracks in its foundation.

In Florida, another governor with extraordinary powers of appointment to state and local offices faced a split in his party in 1870. For the third time, but not the last, the House of Representatives considered impeachment of Governor Reed when the legislature met for its regular session in January. The charges, this time, were having accepted a bribe of seven thousand five hundred dollars in connection with legislation to aid the Littlefield-Swepson railroad promotions; having substituted depreciated scrip for money actually received, in settlement of accounts with the state; and having embezzled money of the Internal Improvement Fund. A committee recommendation that he be impeached was defeated, however, by a vote of twenty-seven to twenty-two, a vote much closer than the forty-three to five by which the second attempt to impeach him, during the previous year, had been defeated.

A new legislature was to be elected in 1870, a new lieutenant-governor to replace the deposed Gleason, and a representative in Congress. The Republican state convention, in Gainesville on August 17, developed a sharp cleavage between "carpetbaggers" and the aggressive Negro political leaders, complicated by the crosslines of the Reed-Osborn factional fight. The fight ended with the nomination of Samuel T. Day, carpetbagger, of Senator Osborn's faction,

for lieutenant-governor, and Josiah T. Walls, Negro, for congressman, in the place of Charles M. Hamilton, the carpetbagger who had
been elected two years before.

Meeting two weeks later, in Tallahassee, as the "Reform Conservative" party, the Democrats made a distinct bid for the support of
property-owning, taxpaying Republicans who might be dissatisfied
with the way the government was run. Silas Niblack, a former Union
man, was nominated for Congress, while for lieutenant-governor the
party put forward William D. Bloxham, energetic, able, attractive
young planter, who had served as a Confederate officer. He had demonstrated his practical sympathy with the aspirations of the freed
people by establishing and supporting a school for them on his
plantation, immediately after the war.

In the election, in November, with its usual share of violence,
riot and intimidation, the Reform Conservative party made its best
showing since the beginning of Reconstruction. They increased the
Democratic strength in the House of Representatives, and named
most of the senators chosen that year. The two races, for lieutenant-
governor and congressman, resulted in apparent Democratic vic-
tories.

Authority to canvass the returns and declare the result, however,
was in a Returning Board of state officials, two Republicans and one
Democrat. Before the board could proceed with their canvass, at the
end of November, they were served with an injunction to restrain
them from doing so, issued by a circuit judge of the state. The United
States District Court thereupon ordered the arrest of the state judge,
on a charge of violating the new Federal Enforcement Act by his
"interference" with an election. When the state judge was arrested
and carried off to Jacksonville in custody of the United States marshal, the Republican majority of the Returning Board considered the
injunction dissolved; proceeded to canvass the returns in the absence
of their Democratic colleague; rejected the returns from nine Democratic counties; and declared the Republicans elected by a majority
of about six hundred.

Their certificate of election, however, was but the beginning of the
struggle. Josiah Walls became the first Negro representative of the
state in Congress, but the question of who was lieutenant-governor
was dragged through nearly two years more of court procedure and
legislative juggling, to play no small part in the fourth and final
attempt to impeach Governor Reed.

The new government in Texas followed the lead of the older reconstructed states in centralizing authority in the hands of its governor. By act of the legislature, at its session beginning on April 26, 1870, Governor Davis was given power to conduct registration of voters; to fill vacancies in office, including many supposedly elective under the constitution; and to appoint local officials in all municipalities chartered by the legislature. When citizens of Galveston protested against the character of appointments made there in July, a Radical journal pointed out that the town was "at the mercy of the Governor" and threatened them with worse if attacks on the Governor did not cease.

Fifteen Davis Republicans in the Senate battled long and strenuously with eleven Democrats and three moderate Republicans over a new state-militia bill. The objection was not to the formation of a militia but to placing the entire control of it and the uses to which it was to be put in the hands of the Governor. On June 21, twelve of the opposition left the chamber and broke the quorum. All were arrested immediately. Four were brought back into the Senate chamber and kept there, to make a quorum. Eight were kept under arrest for three weeks, while the triumphant majority went ahead to pass the militia bill and others desired by Governor Davis, including one for legal advertising and public printing by a "loyal" newspaper in each judicial district.

Finally, the legislature relieved the voters of Texas of trouble by postponing the election of representatives in Congress, due to be held in the fall of 1870, and that of state officers in the fall of 1871. The purpose, frankly stated by the Governor's official organ, the State Journal, was to see that the offices were kept out of the hands of the enemies of the administration. The justification for such a course, in the eyes of the Governor, was his knowledge that his administration represented a minority of the voters of the state and his conviction that his continuance in power was necessary for the good of Texas and particularly for the preservation of the rights of its Negro citizens.

Other Republicans, however, did not share this conviction, and by the summer of 1870 had begun to meet and agitate for a change. In this they were encouraged by some of the Democrats, with an eye to a fusion. Bitter-end Democrats, however, opposed any sort of fusion with any sort of Republicans.

Special elections held in November, 1870, to fill vacancies in the legislature, showed a strong drift against the Radical Republicans. There could be no general election for two years more, however, during which time Governor Davis and the twelfth legislature of

Texas continued to accumulate the resentments which were to overwhelm them.

Since there were to be no elections in recently reconstructed Mississippi in 1870, there was no occasion for the intense factionalism shown in some of the other states. At the spring and summer session of the legislature, Governor Alcorn was given a strong militia law, while an anti-Ku Klux law was passed for future use. The only serious disturbance of harmony among the Republicans was the question of state printing and legal advertising—always an important question, both because of the volume of printed matter and stationery which Reconstruction governments seemed to require, and because of the close connection between the job printing and newspaper business in those days. The printing question was settled by leaving the contract in the hands of the same firms which had enjoyed it under Provisional Governor Ames. The Governor, however, insisted upon vetoing the measure to require publication of all legal and official notices in one "loyal" paper in each judicial circuit. The Governor's veto saved money for the public, but, since most of these papers were promoted by members of the legislature or other important politicians, it cost him dearly in political support in later factional fights.

On one thing the new government was agreed. Names of counties and cities given in honor of leaders of rebellion should not continue to contaminate the map of Mississippi. Leesburg became Ellisville; Lee County became Lincoln. In this they were but following the example of the legislature in Confederate days, which bestowed the name of Davis upon the county known as the "Free State of Jones." Jones County got its original name back, at the hands of the 1870 legislature, while new counties created bore such patriotic names as Union, Sumner and Colfax—names which did not survive the restoration of Democratic rule in the state.

With the 1870 session of their reconstructed legislature, Mississippi taxpayers began to find out that government of the sort to which they were to grow accustomed came high. Pay and expenses of the legislature that year were $258,400, considerably more than three times the highest figure recorded by any ante-bellum legislature.

Arkansas, though without a session of its legislature in 1870, was torn by a factional and party campaign, which began with the formation of the Liberal Republican party in the autumn of 1869 and continued until the election in November, 1870. Republicans divided into Clayton "Regulars," who had control of the machinery of election; Liberal Republicans, under the leadership of Joseph Brooks, formerly an Iowa preacher but more lately an anti-Clayton aspirant for office in Arkansas; and a third faction, who gave their unorganized support to the Democratic-Conservative party. The burning issue was the candidacy of Governor Clayton for the United States Senate, before the legislature which was to be elected in 1870 and to meet in 1871.

Two of the three congressmen elected in November were Democratic-Conservatives, while in the legislature the party increased its strength to eight senators and twenty-nine representatives. These, with the eight representatives elected by the Brooks Liberals, were not enough to take control of the legislature away from the masterful Clayton; but the struggle to maintain that control bred a bitterness between the Republican factions which paved the way for the final overthrow of Radical government in Arkansas.

In North Carolina, the beginnings of the break in the ranks of Reconstructionists were made clearly apparent in the legislative session of the winter and spring of 1870. In January, over the opposition of Governor Holden's friends, the Senate created another committee to investigate the rings and lobbies which, in the picturesquely violent language of editor Josiah Turner of the Raleigh *Sentinel*, had made the state "the 'hog trough' of the Union" where "such swine" as various "carpetbaggers" named "come to wallow with native hogs like Holden, Victor and Greasy Sam."

The legislators were much concerned, also, over the expiration of their own terms of office. By reason of an ambiguity in the constitution, it was possible to take the position that the first Reconstruction legislature was intended to hold office until after the election of 1872, instead of that of 1870. A considerable faction of the Radicals did take such a position, "trying to persuade Cuffee Mayo," said the *Sentinel*, "that bi-ennial meant once in four years and four months." The position was too weak to maintain in the face of determined opposition, however, and elections were ordered to be held in August, 1870.

Another strenuous fight developed over the passage in January of a stringent anti-Ku Klux law, introduced by Senator T. M. Shoffner, of Alamance. The new law, more rigorous than the one passed in the preceding April, gave the governor power to declare counties in a state of insurrection, practically superseding all ordinary processes of government.

In spite of the new law, the activities of those who called themselves or were called Ku Klux, increased. The official head of the Klan in

Alamance County had disbanded its Dens during the preceding year, when he had found it impossible to maintain the sort of discipline such an organization needed. On February 26, Wyatt Outlaw, Negro head of the Union League in the county, who had fired upon the Klan upon the occasion of its first and only "official" parade, was found hanged on a tree in the yard of the courthouse at Graham. A semi-idiotic Negro, who saw some of the band that did the deed, disappeared and was not heard of again until his body was found in a pond.

The hanging of Outlaw was but the most conspicuous of a series of assaults, and not a few murders, in Orange, Alamance, Chatham and neighboring counties. Not all the outrages were the work of the secret societies. At least one was prevented by the head of the local unit of the Constitutional Union Guard in Alamance County when a group of alleged Ku Klux from Orange County planned to hang Senator Shoffner, nominal author of the law against them, and send his body to Governor Holden. One who was privy to the plan remarked to a responsible citizen that they were coming to Alamance County that night "to suspend Shoffner's writ of habeas corpus." Prompt action turned back the visiting "regulators," while the threatened Senator was escorted to Greensboro for safety.

Not many of the acts done appeared to have so definite a political connection as this one threatened, however. Some, no doubt, were justified in the minds of the perpetrators by the idea that the state of the times demanded extra-legal protection for persons otherwise defenseless. Many seem to have been merely the result of the passion for anonymous "regulating." Regardless of the source or the motives, the acts of violence created a state of desperate terror for a considerable part of the population in central North Carolina. While the disturbance attributed to the Ku Klux still went on, the legislature adjourned on March 28, 1870, to the unrestrained satisfaction of the Conservative population.

As Byron Laflin, one of the original carpetbaggers and a leader in the various rings and lobbies, started for the train to leave Raleigh on the last day of the session, according to the Wilmington Journal, a friendly bystander called out:

"You are coming back, General?"

"Is there anything to come back for?" he replied.

His remark was a practical man's recognition of the obvious fact that Radical prospects were not good for the election of the new legislature in August. Besides revelations of rascalities at Raleigh, they were having to carry the load of odium accumulated by some of their representatives in Congress. John T. Deweese, expelled from Congress for selling appointments to the Military Academy, insisted that his punishment was not for selling cadetships but for selling them so cheaply as to break down the established market.

Besides a new legislature, and an attorney-general for the state, new congressmen were to be chosen in August. For the Democrats, the principal issues were corruption and inefficiency in office; for the Republicans, violence and "Ku Kluxism." That issue received its most dramatic demonstration right at the outset of the campaign. Senator John W. Stephens, a political detective of Governor Holden, came into Caswell County seeking evidence to be used in prosecutions under the Ku Klux law. While there, the local Conservatives charged, he improved his opportunities by attending a meeting of the Union League where he handed to each of twenty Negro members a box of matches which then were a novelty with the suggestion that they might be put to good use in burning barns. Nine barns were burned in the county in one night. While Stephens was still there, local people learned of his connection with the burnings in such a way that they believed him responsible.

A few days later, Stephens attended a mass meeting at the courthouse in Yanceyville, for the presumed purpose of making notes of the speeches. While in the crowded courtroom, he received a whispered message. The detective arose, followed the messenger out through corridors thronged with citizens, white and black, and disappeared. The next morning his body, bound, gagged, stabbed, strangled, throat cut, was found in an unoccupied office on the ground floor with windows opening upon a courthouse yard which, at the time of the murder, was crowded with people.

The fact of the death of the powerful Senator Stephens, and the mysterious manner of his death, were a sensation. It was attributed to Ku Klux, although there were some who believed at the time that it was the work of enemies of Stephens among the Republicans. Evidence which became available long afterward, some as late as the deposition of Captain John G. Lea, last survivor of the band, published after his death in September, 1936, makes it certain that the affair was deliberately planned and carefully executed by picked men of the local Klan. Stephens, lured into a vacant room, was there quickly and quietly murdered, while other Klansmen stood outside, prepared to start a noisy sham fight among themselves to cover any sounds which might escape and attract attention.

The gruesome mystery of the death of Senator Stephens precipitated, in the minds of the Governor and his advisers, the idea of a military movement against the Ku Klux, as part of the campaign. Senator John Pool, down from Washington, pressed the idea upon a council held by the Governor in Raleigh on June 7, and carried it through over opposition. The plan was to raise two regiments of troops, white mountaineers in the western part of the state, colored troops in the east, to declare the "Ku Klux counties" in a state of insurrection, and march in the troops to make arrests, bringing with them their own military commission for the trial of those arrested. Arms and equipment were to be secured from the government at Washington, whither Senator Pool was to return to keep up the flow of atrocity and outrage stories in the Northern press in sufficient variety and abundance to justify the military operations.

So began the "Kirk-Holden War" in North Carolina, taking its popular name from the Governor and from George W. Kirk, who during the war had commanded a regiment of North Carolina Union troops with ferocious vigor. Colonel Kirk, by proclamation called on his old soldiers and others to "rally to the standard of your old commander," for service of six months, with the pay, clothing and rations of United States troops, to aid in enforcing the laws against acts "committed by the rebel K.K.K. and 'southern chivalry.'"

From Morganton, the concentration point, his nine companies marched eastward through the state on July 6. As the troops reached Alamance and Caswell Counties, the Governor declared them in a state of insurrection. Wholesale arrests of Ku Klux suspects began. In Alamance County alone, eight-two were arrested, and at least three were hanged by the neck until unconscious, in an effort to extort confessions. Governor Holden, according to his *Memoirs*, afterward personally discharged and ordered punished Lieutenant Colonel Bergen, late of New Jersey, responsible for this particular bit of persuasion.

Arrests were followed by applications to Chief Justice Richmond Pearson for writs of habeas corpus, which Colonel Kirk promptly refused to honor. Such things, he said, had "played out" and he took orders only from the Governor. The Governor sustained his military commander and refused to recognize the writ of his Chief Justice until the "insurrection" should be quelled. The Chief Justice acquiesced, and the making of arrests continued.

"Kirk's Lambs," according to the report of Captain George B. Rodney, United States Army, stationed at Yanceyville, were "nothing more than an armed mob" roaming the country, pillaging at will, insulting citizens with impunity, and even threatening to attack the United States troops. Governor Holden, however, being assured of the support of President Grant, if needed, could afford to disregard such reports.

On July 30, just before the election, James E. Boyd, Conservative candidate for representative from Alamance County, with fifteen others whom he had induced to join him, signed a confession of membership and activity in the Ku Klux. His confession added little to what was known of the workings of the Klan, but since no one knew just how much he did know, and it was known that he had accepted a fee from the Governor to work up evidence against his fellow members, there was a sudden exodus from North Carolina of several hundred young men.

The state election, at the bottom of the excitement, took place on August 4, while Colonel Kirk's prisoners were still in jail, awaiting trial. The Democrats carried the state in the race for attorney-general by a close margin; elected five of the seven congressmen chosen for full terms, and one of the two to fill out unexpired terms; and, most important of all, returned a majority of more than two-thirds in both houses of the new legislature.

Arrests continued in the Kirk-Ku Klux War on the day after the election; but on the second day, August 6, Judge George W. Brooks, of the United States District Court, who had come to the conclusion that he had jurisdiction, issued writs of habeas corpus to have the prisoners brought before him.

Governor Holden wired President Grant for support. To his chagrin, a reply came back from the Secretary of War, acting upon the advice of Attorney General Akerman, advising the Governor to yield. After an unsuccessful attempt to get the case back into the state courts, whose jurisdiction had been flouted, even to the extent of tearing up writs served on Colonel Kirk, the cases of the prisoners were brought before Judge Brooks, on August 18. When the only evidence presented against them by the state was the Governor's order for their arrest, the Federal judge discharged all prisoners from custody.

A month later, on September 21, amid a flurry of court orders and opinions, bench warrants, indictments and civil summonses, state and Federal, the Kirk army was discharged from the service of the state, to return to its native mountains, while its commanding officer and his second-in-command surrendered themselves to the custody of the

United States Circuit Court, to escape some of the various suits and prosecutions brought against them in the state courts. When Judge Hugh L. Bond, of the Federal Circuit Court, discharged the cases against Kirk and Bergen, they managed to evade the waiting officers of the state and make their way back to Washington, to be rewarded with minor positions in government service.

On November 10, five months after the beginning of his military adventure, Governor Holden proclaimed the end of the state of insurrection in Caswell and Alamance Counties, and congratulated the people upon the "peace and good order throughout the state." The Kirk-Holden War was over, and unrestrained rule of North Carolina by Radical Reconstructionists was nearing its end.

In South Carolina, upon the first day of the new year 1870, the Charleston *News* proposed that the people get together upon a broad platform of conciliation and regeneration, to make 1870 the "Year of Happy Deliverance" for the state.

In March, during the session of the legislature, editors of anti-Radical newspapers met in convention in Columbia and called a state nominating convention, to meet on June 15. The convention of June 15 adopted the name of the "Union Reform party," intended to appeal to old Whigs, Democrats and moderate Republicans alike. For governor, it nominated Richard B. Carpenter, originally from Kentucky, a Republican who as such had been elected a judge by the first Reconstruction legislature. For lieutenant-governor, it named Matthew C. Butler, late major general, C. S. A. The platform adopted was broad enough in its recognition of the results of Reconstruction, it was thought, to appeal to honest Republicans opposed to the Scott regime. With those candidates and on that platform the campaign was launched for "happy deliverance."

The "ins" in South Carolina fortified themselves with the usual airtight election laws at the 1870 session of the legislature, with complete control of registration, election and returns in the hands of the governor. The law, said some members of a congressional committee which investigated South Carolina affairs the next year, "could not be better calculated to produce frauds by affording the facilities to commit and conceal them."

The Radicals, holding their convention in July, nominated Governor Scott for re-election, with fulsome praise of his administration, and strengthened the appeal to colored voters by nominating for lieutenant-governor, Alonzo J. Ransier, a forceful and intelligent Negro of Charleston, free before the war.

The Reform party charged that the Scott administration had trebled the public debt, multiplied the taxes, and arrested development. The Radicals retorted that the Reformers were but Democrats in disguise—about as bad a name as they could have been called in the eyes of many South Carolina voters of that time.

The reply of the Radicals took the form of appeals to race and class prejudice, also, according to testimony of Judge Carpenter before the Ku Klux committee the next year. The Judge testified that Beverly Nash, colored senator, said in a public speech:

"The reformers complain of taxes being too high. I tell you they are not high enough. I want them taxed until they put these lands back where they belong, into the hands of those who worked for them. You toiled for them, you labored for them, and were sold to pay for them, and you ought to have them."

There was some Ku Klux work in the campaign, though not a great deal. The Union Leagues were moderately active, also, but the real activity along that line was supplied by the "hep men," fourteen regiments of Negro militia organized and armed by the Governor, at an admitted cost to the taxpayers of $374,000. Captain John B. Hubbard, chief constable of the state under Governor Scott, afterward testified that the purpose was political, partly for the effect of intimidation which it was supposed to have, partly to sustain the interest and enthusiasm of "organizers" with regular pay from the state treasury. The political-military operations of the militia regiments, he stated, had created an increase of crime and bloodshed. The most serious outbreak of the time was at Laurens, on the day after the election, where a fight between a white man and a white state constable spread into a riot, first in the town and then in the county, resulting in the death of from seven to eleven Negroes, and one white, Volney Powell of Ohio, "carpetbagger."

The election, on October 19, was a smashing victory for the Radicals, 85,071 to 51,537. All four of the representatives in Congress elected were Radicals, and three of the four, Joseph H. Rainey, R. C. DeLarge and Robert B. Elliott, were Negroes.

Fraud and violence were charged by both sides, and apparently with good reason in each case. But even making allowance for the Governor's control of the election machinery and of the public treasury, it appears that the Union Reform movement was defeated not so much by ballot-box frauds or Returning Board figuring as it was by an inability to draw to itself enough Republican votes, white or black. The "straight-out" Democrats who had been cool to the movement and critical of even such Confederate figures as General Butler and General Kershaw for their part in it, had their opportunity to reiterate their opinion that there was nothing to be gained by appealing to Negro voters against the blandishments of the Radicals. The "happy deliverance" sought in 1870 was not to be found for yet another seven years.

In Alabama, the Conservatives had allowed the first election under the Reconstruction Acts to go by default when they refrained from voting in an effort to defeat the ratification of the constitution. In consequence, the state had enjoyed, from the time of its admission, an all-Radical government—a governor of the "scalawag" persuasion, a state Senate with but one Conservative member, and a House of Representatives with only three. The constitution of 1868 provided that the first Senate elected should classify itself into those with two-year terms and those with four, so that thereafter one-half of the Senate should be chosen at each election. This the first Senate consistently refused to do, so that all members were sitting for four-year terms, to end in 1872. The Conservatives made a determined drive in 1870 for the governor's office and the control of the House of Representatives.

For governor, they put up Robert Burns Lindsay, Scottish by birth, a graduate of the University of St. Andrews, and a lawyer in Alabama since 1845. The Republicans nominated Governor Smith. The race was hard and close, with all the usual arguments and appeals. There were riots, considerably exaggerated for Northern consumption, at Eutaw and at Tuskegee. The latter was unusual in that three whites were killed and no Negroes. James Alston, a Negro member of the legislature, shot by a rival, put himself under white protection. Other Negroes, thinking that he had been wounded and captured by the whites, raised the alarm and called for Negro volunteers to rescue him. Besides local aid, a volunteer company started to go from Montgomery, but was turned back by the strenuous persuasion of General Clanton.

The election was held under a new law described by the Republican reporter, Charles Nordhoff, as "one of the most perfect machines for political fraud that I have ever heard of," rendered still more perfect by an amendment at the 1870 session of the legislature making it a misdemeanor for "any person to attempt to interfere in any manner with any other person who may desire to vote."

In actual practice, the polling places were so arranged, according to the statement of General E. W. Pettus, that to reach the ballot box voters must pass through a narrow gateway at which one of the election officials stood to inspect the ticket about to be deposited by each Negro. If the ticket was satisfactory, the Negro was allowed to deposit it without question. If not, the inspector changed it for one that was, or attempted to do so.

Lindsay, the Democratic nominee, received 76,997 votes to Governor Smith's 75,568. The Senate, of course, remained Radical, while the Democrats secured a shadowy majority of the House of Representatives. Governor Smith denounced the results of the election, held on to his office, and secured an injunction forbidding the official canvassing of the returns for governor, and the inauguration of his successor.

The injunction, however, did not run against E. H. Moren, Democrat, just elected lieutenant-governor. By quick action, and with the co-operation of the new House majority, and the unwilling acquiescence of certain senators who were caught in the chamber and held there, the new Lieutenant-Governor had the votes canvassed in joint session of the legislature and declared Lindsay elected governor.

For more than two weeks, two governors tried to rule in Montgomery, one recognized by the Radical Senate and the other by the Conservative House. By a process of attrition, however, enough of the senators abandoned their hopeless position to get the government going, within three weeks, with both houses recognizing Governor Lindsay.

In joint session, the legislature elected a Democratic senator, George Goldthwaite, to succeed Willard Warner. Of the representatives in the Forty-first Congress, three were returned to the new Congress—one Democrat, one "carpetbagger" and one "scalawag." The three members elected for the first time included one Democrat, one Independent, and one Negro.

Much of the state administration and most of the county and local governments remained in Radical hands. The Democratic hold on the government, in fact, was painfully precarious—but it was a hold. The unbreakable grip of the Radicals in Alabama, gained in the defaulted election of 1868, was at least loosened.

That war rancors and resentments in the border states, where they had been most virulent, were dying out was indicated by the results of the 1870 elections, also. The Radical hold on West Virginia and Missouri, gained during and just after the war, and confirmed and maintained since that time by constitutional proscriptions against ex-Confederates and their sympathizers to the most remote degree, and by complete control of the machinery of registration and election, was definitely broken.

In West Virginia, after the ratification of the Fifteenth Amendment, an influential element in the Republican party advocated a more liberal "let up" policy toward the Democrats whom they had so successfully held down since the founding of the state. The Flick amendment to the constitution, removing the disfranchisement and political disabilities of ex-Confederates and their sympathizers, was submitted by the legislature in 1870 and ratified by the voters in the following year. The same legislature which submitted the Flick amendment voted to remove the capital city of the state from Wheeling to Charleston, to which place the government and its records were transported on the steamboat *Mountain Boy* in March, 1870. The capital of the state remained on the banks of the Kanwha until May, 1875, when it was loaded on steamboats, two this time, and taken back to wheeling, to remain there for another ten years before floating to Charleston again, to come to rest.

In the fall election of 1870, even before the Flick amendment was ratified, a coalition of Liberal Republicans and Democrats carried the state against the Radical Republicans who had ruled it. The Radical majority in the House of Delegates was reversed, the Democrats controlled the state Senate by one vote, and two of the three representatives sent to Congress were Democrats. A constitutional convention was called and a new constitution written on the basis of "universal amnesty and universal suffrage." With the ratification of that constitution at the next election, in August, 1872, Reconstruction was at an end in the war-born state of West Virginia.

The coalition of Liberal Republicans and Democrats which carried Missouri in 1870 was destined to have still greater importance as the genesis of a national movement. The men who originated it were, almost without exception, onetime Radicals who had wearied of the narrow and intolerant policies of those in charge of the government of Missouri under the rigidly proscriptive constitution of 1865. They included such men as Carl Schurz, then United States senator from Missouri; B. Gratz Brown, a "Charcoal" Republican, in the wartime vernacular; and William M. Grosvenor, editor of the St. Louis *Democrat*, which, in spite of its name, was the principal Republican newspaper of the state and had displayed strong Radical leanings. The movement was supported by other Republicans who had not been

"Charcoals" but "Claybanks," as the more moderately inclined were called during the war—such men, for example, as Samuel T. Glover, staunch Unionist lawyer of St. Louis, who was fined five hundred dollars for practicing his profession without taking the ironclad test oath of the Drake constitution. It was backed, too, by the Union Democrats, under the leadership of General Frank P. Blair.

In the 1870 election the coalition made a clean sweep of Missouri. Six amendments to the Drake constitution, doing away with the objectionable test oaths and proscriptions of that document, were adopted by overwhelming majorities. B. Gratz Brown was elected governor, handsomely, with a coalition legislature, which, at the first opportunity, sent General Blair to the United States Senate, to replace Charles D. Drake, whose rabidly Radical leadership in 1865 had been rewarded with a seat in Washington in 1867. In Missouri the elections of 1870 brought an end to the period of Reconstruction.

CHAPTER XLI

GAINS IN AGRICULTURE, EDUCATION AND TRANSPORTATION

THE ELECTIONS of 1870, the first in which Negroes voted in all states under the terms of the Fifteenth Amendment, resulted in a reduction of the Republican majority in the House of Representatives of the new Forty-second Congress to a meager thirty-five votes. The Congress which met in December, 1870, however, to give further attention to the "Southern question," was the old Forty-first Congress, with its hundred-vote Republican majority in the House.

A survey of the political results of its Reconstruction efforts and those of its predecessors, at that time, would have shown firm Radical control of the executive and legislative branches of government in the states of South Carolina, Florida, Mississippi, Louisiana, Arkansas and Texas, even though in several of those states its downfall was foreshadowed by factional splits; Conservative control of the legislatures, with moderate Republican governors in Tennessee and Virginia, and with a Radical governor in North Carolina; divided control of the legislature in Alabama, with a Democratic governor precariously in office; and a Radical government in Georgia, facing the unwelcome test of an election to be held December 20-22, 1870.

The survey would have shown a South which, for five years since the close of the war, had been kept in an almost continuous turmoil of politics, necessarily to the detriment of work and production. Political campaigns, as Miss Eliza Frances Andrews of Georgia wrote to the New York World, were being "reduced to authorized systems of bribery" by wholesale, with the prospect that "venal electors" would "auction themselves in a body" to the party or candidate which promised them the most.

It would have shown a staggering rise in the cost of government in the South. The increase was partly necessary because of the increased prices of everything resulting from a depreciated currency and because of the inescapable costs of restoration and rebuilding. It was due, partly, to an increase in the services offered by government to a larger body of citizens. It was due, still more, to the waste and inefficiency, and to the downright corruption and peculation, incident

421

to the revolution in government. There was no incentive for economy in governments where a majority of the voters looked upon taxes not as a burden to be borne but as an unlimited source of benefits to be received.

And yet, in spite of the crushing burden of the heavy taxation necessary to finance the eagerly sought "progress" which was the rallying cry of Reconstruction, somehow, through it all and in spite of it all, rebuilding of Southern life went on.

For one thing, not all the money collected for new transportation facilities and new schools was diverted into channels of personal gain, nor was it all spent unwisely. The whole country, including the South, was in the boom state which necessarily accompanies a tremendously rapid expansion of production, and especially transportation facilities, financed with borrowed money. There was bad judgment, in plenty, and downright fraud and peculation to an amazing degree, but of the money that actually got into the works of production and transportation, much was spent for things which the South needed and which, in the long run, were economically and socially worth while. In Alabama, for example, the state endorsed the bonds of the Alabama & Chattanooga Railroad, for one million three hundred thousand dollars more than an exceedingly liberal law provided, and then issued direct to the company state bonds in the amount of two million dollars. The bill to grant this additional aid was at first defeated at the 1870 session of the legislature, until a sufficient number of its opponents could be brought to reconsider and pass it, at a cost said to have been thirty-five thousand dollars. Much of the money so secured was not spent on the railroad at all but in the erection of an opera house and a hotel in Chattanooga, by the promoters, J. C. and D. N. Stanton, of Boston. In the endorsement and issue of the bonds, and in keeping the accounts of the state with the promoters, Governor Smith was almost unbelievably slipshod and careless.

Such an enterprise, of course, failed miserably, early in 1871, with its affairs so complicated that, during the depression which soon followed, no one seemed to know or to care much who owned the road or who was to operate it. When Edward King sought to buy a ticket, he could find no one to sell it. A bystander advised him, however, to go ahead and get on the train which "the captain," meaning the conductor, was just "running and making what he can out of it." Employees of that part of the road in Mississippi seized and operated the line to pay their wages, while the part in Georgia was operated by that state under a receivership separate from that of the part in Alabama. It would be hard in all the fantastic annals of Reconstruction finance to find a more hopeless-looking affair.

As part of its long effort to connect the rich agricultural regions in the northern and southern parts of the state with a railroad across the mountainous section between, the state of Alabama also endorsed bonds of the South & North Alabama Railroad, under an act passed in 1870. Again, the endorsements actually made were more generous than the law provided, although the consequences were not disastrous as in the case of the Alabama & Chattanooga. In 1871, the South & North Alabama was leased to the Louisville & Nashville, under an agreement to complete it through to the Tennessee Valley.

In October of that year, the line crossed that of the struggling Alabama & Chattanooga at the mountain village of Elyton, in a region where earlier attempts at ironworking had failed for lack of transportation—and the city of Birmingham, destined to become the center of Alabama's greatest riches, was born.

By the beginning of the decade of the 'seventies, the last of the railroads which had been so throughly destroyed during the war were being restored to full service. Lines which had been left unfinished, because of the war, were being restored and completed at last. New lines of transportation were being opened to meet new needs. In the spring of 1870, for the first time since the war, trains ran from Savannah to Charleston, or at least to the south bank of the Ashley River, opposite that city. In the same year, the line from Vicksburg west to Monroe was restored by a new company, and the road from Pensacola to the Alabama line, which had been robbed of its rails for use elsewhere at the beginning of the war, was restored to operation. The Montgomery-Mobile line, which war had stopped twenty miles from its goal, was bridging the broad rivers about the head of Mobile Bay, to reach the city on the west shore.

On February 18, 1870, a railroad bridge was opened across the Ohio River at Louisville. The bridge, designed and built under the direction of Albert Fink, was remarkable as containing channel spans of three hundred and seventy feet and four hundred feet, the longest which then had been built on the American continent. Still more significant, it was, according to the Courier-Journal, "the first and only connecting link between the great railway systems of the North and South."

When war broke out, in 1861, there was indeed not a single connection between the railroads of the two sections. In 1862, as a military measure, the government laid railroad tracks on the Long Bridge across the Potomac at Washington, and operated trains over it to reach the Southern lines at Alexandria, but the bridge at Louisville, completed five years after the war, was the first regular railroad connection between the sections. Before it was finished, however, another was being built across the Ohio between Cincinnati and Newport, to be opened to traffic in the spring of 1872.

Besides making new connections with other sections, there was great activity in improving transportation routes within the South. From Louisville on the west and from Norfolk on the east, railroad lines were reaching for the coal fields in southeastern Kentucky and southwestern Virginia, about Cumberland Gap. From that region, other lines were being built to the Carolinas. Between Mobile and New Orleans, a new line along the Gulf coast was opened in the spring of 1870. Southward from the Ohio River, a new railroad was opened from Henderson to Nashville, about the same time, and one was being built from the south bank opposite Cairo, where there was not to be a bridge for nearly twenty years more, to Jackson, Tennessee, there to connect with lines into Mississippi.

In Georgia, whose railroad network was the most extensive of any Southern state before the war, the legislature authorized the loan of the state's credit, at the rate of twelve thousand dollars to fifteen thousand dollars a mile, to thirty-seven railroads during the administration of Governor Bullock. Only seven of the roads actually received endorsement of their bonds, however, and two of these, the Richmond Air Line and the Macon & Augusta & Atlantic, declined the state's aid and returned the endorsed bonds when they discovered that they could make better arrangements in the private money markets.

Some of the new railroad lines, especially among those hastily organized to take advantage of the liberal state-aid laws, were mere devices to siphon money into the pockets of promoters, through disposing of bonds made salable by the endorsement of the states. Others were attempts to meet a real transportation need, sometimes with success, sometimes with unfortunate results. Roads built ahead of the traffic anticipated, or excessively financed, or not too well managed failed during the panic of the 'seventies, or before, and were foreclosed and bought in by creditors. Several such lines were acquired by the states which had a lien on them by reason of having endorsed their bonds; were operated for a season by the states, and afterward sold for what they would bring to stop the losses of continued operation under the conditions of the times.

"One wonders where all the money is to come from to carry out so many public works at once . . . ," wrote Robert Somers, an intelligently observant Scotsman who traveled through the South in 1870 and 1871, "but there can be no doubt of the immense utility of railways to the agricultural population." Mr. Somers discovered also, on his visit to Atlanta, their importance in the birth and phenomenal growth of Georgia's new capital city. Through "the debris of newly-built houses and the ruins of old ones," his train reached the center of the city, where, as he wrote:

"The various railroads which meet at this crowded point do not go to the town; the town is gathering thick and hot haste about the railways. A general depot is being built, but, like everything else in Atlanta, it is unfinished; and on the arrival of a train under rain the passengers are put down in the mud, to be there screamed at by steam-engines and high-pressure negroes, scared by the tolling of bells, and barricaded on every side by trains of cars, bales of cotton, boxes of merchandise, . . . and all sorts of building materials."

Inquiring for a hotel in "this city of Babel," the Scottish traveler "was immediately told Atlanta had the biggest thing of the kind in creation . . . the H. I. Kimball House, sir. Have you nary heered of the H. I.?"

The "H. I.," wrote Mr. Somers, was a "really magnificent edifice," with a "steam-power elevator," a hall "as big as a church," and suspended above it a "gaselier . . . of such magnitude and brightness as might grace any opera house in the largest cities of the world." Mr. Kimball, the traveler was told, conceived the design of a grand hotel, so successfully carried out, after a fortunate speculation in which he purchased an unfinished opera house, for a reputed price of eighty-five thousand dollars, and "sold it immediately to the 'reconstructed' state at three hundred and fifty thousand dollars for a state house, to serve in room of the deserted building at Milledgeville." Mr. Somers added:

"Mr. Kimball has naturally become a man of great influence in Atlanta. He is a munificent patron of state fairs, horse-races, and every good work. His political influence is even thought, with probably a little dash of popular superstition, to be supreme in the state. A common saying in Georgia is that Blodgett, senator, controls the Governor, but that Mr. H. I. Kimball controls Blodgett."

"Blodgett, senator," referred to Foster Blodgett, elected by the reconstructed legislature to the United States Senate for a term to begin on March 4, 1871. Meanwhile, since January 1, 1870, he had been superintendent of the Western & Atlantic Railroad, built and owned by the state of Georgia and operated by it directly before, during, and after the war. The line was strategically located as a connecting link between the upper central South and the railroad systems of Georgia and the Carolinas. Before the war it had proved itself a valuable asset to the state. During the war, it had furnished the essential life line, first, of the Confederate armies about and above Chattanooga, and then of the Federal armies fighting southward to Atlanta. After the war, the road, which had been systematically ruined when General Sherman cut loose from his supply line for his March to the Sea, was restored to profitable operation under the capable and economical management of Major Campbell Wallace, appointed by the restoration government.

Under the Bullock government, according to the facts developed by an investigating committee in 1872, the road became a political adjunct of the administration. Ed Hurlbut, the Republican superintendent of registration, became the first superintendent, with "Fatty" Harris, a New England carpetbagger who had been particularly useful in organizing the legislature, as "supervisor," and Mr. Blodgett as treasurer. Superintendent Hurlbut was removed when he broke with the Governor in 1869, and Mr. Blodgett, who neither had nor claimed experience in railroading, was appointed to the place to run the road's "public and political policy," as he expressed it afterward.

The road was operated on the principle that none but "patriots" might so much as "pull a coupling pin" on the state's line. It was the vehicle, too, for a variety of frauds in pay rolls, purchases, claims, lawyers' fees and the like, as well as simpler and more direct appropriation of revenues to private purposes. N. P. Hotchkiss, an auditor, explained to the investigating committee that he had managed to save twenty thousand dollars out of his two-thousand-dollar salary in less than two years, "by the exercise of the most rigid economy." McWhorter Hungerford, Radical, and business agent for the road under Blodgett, told the investigating committee that none of the Radical politicians on the pay roll were fortunate enough to secure a place as a passenger conductor. Those places, he said, were reserved largely for sons of members of the legislature.

With all its mismanagement the line remained an essential link in the interior communications of the South. By the summer of 1870, the roads connecting with it, north and south, were complaining of the unsafe condition of its track and equipment, and the uncertainty of its settlements. A great demand that the road be taken out of politics led to the passage of an act by the legislature, in October, 1870, to lease the road for private operation, to the company which offered the highest rental, with acceptable security. Two companies contended for the lease which, on December 27, 1870, was awarded for twenty years to one headed by former Governor Joseph E. Brown and including among its stockholders leading political figures of all parties, Democratic as well as Republican.

Through water and rail services, connecting Northern seaports with interior points in the South, were developed by the coastwise steamship lines, in co-operation with the railroads of the South in this period. In 1870, for example, the Great Southern Freight Line advertised through services from New York, Boston, Baltimore and Philadelphia, connecting at Charleston with the through cars of "fast freight lines," operating without transfer and over a "uniform and unbroken gauge" to points in the southwest as far as Memphis and St. Louis. To meet Charleston competition, the Central of Georgia Railroad, based on Savannah, acquired lines in 1871 which extended its operations north to Atlanta and west to Alabama, and in 1872 purchased a steamship line to New York and Boston. Five steamship lines operated from New Orleans, three of them direct to Liverpool, principally for the carriage of cotton. Norfolk also had direct liner service to England, besides that to the North Atlantic ports. An interesting feature of the steamer service out of Norfolk were the "truck steamers," carrying to eastern markets the vegetables raised in the rapidly developing trucking section about that port. The business grew to require, by 1874, daily boats to Baltimore, New York, and Boston, in the season, and tri-weekly service to Philadelphia.

The passenger packets on the Mississippi, in the same period, reached the peak of their glory before passing into their final decline. On June 30, 1870, the South forgot its politics and its troubles to watch the last of the great steamboat races, and the greatest—that of the *Natchez* and the *Robert E. Lee*, from New Orleans to St. Louis, for a side-bet of ten thousand dollars, suggested and arranged by Johnny Hawkins, proprietor of New Orleans' finest barroom. From the start at New Orleans, before the greatest crowd that city had ever seen, the boats raced past towns where bells rang and cannon boomed, past plantations where bonfires lighted the banks and little knots of cheering spectators waved them ahead, with the *Lee* leading the whole way, to cover 1218 miles in three days, eighteen hours and fourteen minutes—three hours and a half ahead of the *Natchez*.

"Here comes the *Natchez*, and the *Robert Lee*" passed into folk song, along with "I've been workin' on the railroad," to embalm two phases of life in the South at the beginning of the 'seventies.

There were phases of that life other than politics and production, also. There was a deal of pleasure, such as that of the "bevy of young ladies and gentlemen whirling on 'parlour skates' " whom Mr. Somers observed in a large hall upstairs in a new building at Cartersville, Georgia. There was amateur baseball, too, engaged in half-apologeti-cally to judge from the defensive references to it in local newspapers, but engaged in with enthusiasm, nevertheless, to judge from the size of some of the scores. There were new drinks, such as the "cold-tea lemonade, iced," declared by the few in New Orleans who had tried it to be superior to soda waters and fizzes. Iced drinks were coming into wider use following the development, at New Orleans and else-where, of the new industry of manufacturing ice. This gift of applied science was taken from the laboratory to the field of commercial pro-duction. Abstract science received recognition, of a sort, in the New Orleans Mardi Gras festivities of 1872, with a parade devoted to depicting, in carnival fashion, the "Darwinian Descent of Species."

Back of the activity and development in transportation, of course, there was production. The period was one of changing methods and shifting locale. The breakup of the plantation system is shown in the census figures. The number of farms of one thousand acres or more in Alabama was reduced from six hundred and ninety-six in 1860 to three hundred and six in 1870. In Georgia, the decline was from nine hundred and two to four hundred and nineteen; in Vir-ginia, from six hundred and forty-one to three hundred and seventeen, and so, to greater or less degree, throughout the South. The total number of farms in Mississippi increased in the decade from forty-three thousand to sixty-eight thousand; in Louisiana, from seventeen thousand to twenty-eight thousand; and in South Carolina, from thirty-three thousand to fifty-two thousand. Even in Tennessee, which before the war had been a state of relatively small farms rather than great plantations, the number increased from eighty-two thou-sand to one hundred and eighteen thousand. The increase in the number of farms did not mean so much an increase in the farm area, as a decrease in average size. In North Carolina, another state of relatively small farms before the war, the average size of farms declined between 1860 and 1870 from three hundred and sixteen to two hundred and twelve acres.

"A great revolution in agriculture is going forward," wrote Robert Somers in his book, *The Southern States Since the War*. This particular observation was made of the district about Augusta, but it might have been applied with equal force to almost any part of the South. In the old large plantation areas, Mr. Somers was assured by one competent observer that

"the negroes are working better and stealing less every year, and would be well enough if the political agitators would only let them alone."

To that conclusion, however, at least one exasperated planter of the black belt of Alabama, William F. Samford, would not have agreed. He wrote:

"We are poorer today than we were on the day of the surrender of the Southern armies. Our carpetbaggers and negro scalawags have imposed intolerable taxation. . . . Why don't we raise hogs and make our own bacon? Why, a hog has no more chance to live among these thieving negro farmers than a Juney bug in a gang of puddle ducks. . . . All this great staple producing region is essentially upon the sheriff's block."

On the other hand, the people in the mountain regions of Alabama, according to a statement of the new governor, Lindsay, were "better off than they ever were at any time before." They were raising cotton, with their own labor, which yielded from one hundred dollars to one hundred and fifty dollars a bale on the 1869 crop. They did not have to buy bacon, selling at twenty-two cents a pound, more than double the prewar price, because they could raise their own meat.

Everywhere in the South, Mr. Somers found the production of cotton by small, family-operated farms on the increase; that of the large plantations on the decrease. "Speculators," said Mr. Somers, "looking only at the diminution of negro labour, and at the state of the large plantations, the disorganization and diminished productiveness of which are very apparent, have formed erroneous conclusions" about the production of cotton.

Another mistaken opinion, said Mr. Somers, was that held in the North that "the southern cotton-growers are an inert, unskillful race." The Scottish observer was greatly impressed by the energy, care and diligence of those who operated plantations, particularly on the almost universal share system. As he saw the system,

"The planter gives the land, his stock and implements, working capital and credit, his skill and plodding care and watchfulness from day to day for the chance of half the cotton which his hands may be induced to plant and till, or may think it worth their while to gather when it is ripe."

In spite of all the difficulties, wrote Mr. Somers,

"Planters have declared to me that they could not do without the 'darkies' in the field, so superior are they to any white labour that has yet been tried."

Summing up a year's observations, he concluded:

"The system of free labour has been attended with a degree of success to which the planters themselves are the most forward of all in the southern community to bear testimony. . . . Apart from this vexed question of politics, on which there are substantial grounds of griev-ance, I can scarcely recall an instance in which any planter or other employer of negro labour has not said that the result of emancipation, in its industrial bearings, has been much more favourable than could have been anticipated, or who has not added an expression of satis-faction that slavery, however roughly, has been finally effaced."

In spite of these unexpectedly favorable results of the revolution in labor and production, however, Mr. Somers noted that the burden of taxation in the South was "much more onerous" than in any other part of the United States, both because of the "immense collapse" of property values and the new demands for expenditure for railways and other public works, including the "building and endowment of free schools for the whole population." Such a titanic program of rebuilding and progress, he thought, "required all prudent and care-ful consideration." Instead of such consideration, he noted, "taxation in the South had been grossly abused by a corrupt and reckless admin-istration which . . . is now receiving a check likely to be permanent and effective."

The public school systems in the South, most of which were newly established as state activities and all of which were in great need of wise and prudent administration and support, suffered not only from the character of the state governments but also from the shortsighted opposition of many of the white citizens.

The state governments, with most enlightened provisions for public education in their constitutions and on their statute books, had a most unenlightened way of failing to collect the school revenues, or of diverting them to other and presumably more pressing purposes when collected. Only a little more than one-fourth of the revenues collected by the state of North Carolina for education in 1870 ever reached the schools. In South Carolina, at the same period, the schoolteachers were not getting their pay because most of the state appropriation went to pay the salaries of school commissioners in each of the districts of the state. There were, however, twice as many schools, and twice as large an attendance in 1870 as there had been the year before, according to the report of Superintendent Jillson.

As each of the new state governments was established, it devoted much time and attention to school matters, with a commendable devotion to the ideal of general education which usually found a fuller expression on paper than in fact.

The first session of the legislature of reconstructed Mississippi, for example, in May, 1870, "reconstructed" the State University at Oxford, which, since its reopening in September, 1865, had operated undisturbed under an able board of trustees. Radical members were added to the board, and there was some apprehension that, as in South Carolina and Louisiana, the university would be converted into a school for both races. No changes were made in the faculty, however, and the legislature, at the same session, created Alcorn University, a separate institution of higher learning for Negroes, with the same appropriation for its support as that granted to the University at Oxford.

On July 4, 1870, the legislature set up a new and elaborate mechanism of general public education, to go into effect in October. The intention of the act was good, and its administration was entrusted to the capable Captain Pease, elected superintendent of instruction. After a year of experience with the act, Superintendent Pease reported to the Governor and legislature that the law

"would operate successfully in Ohio or Massachusetts, but not in Mississippi. . . . Notwithstanding, we have succeeded in establishing a large number of schools, the work has been accomplished at the expense of an enormous and unnecessary outlay of labor and money."

One cause of the difficulty, and a serious one, was widespread apprehension among the whites that mixed schools were to be imposed upon them. This apprehension led to violent opposition, which sometimes took the form of burning schoolhouses and threatening, or even assaulting and whipping, teachers. Usually, the teachers so visited were of Northern birth. Sometimes, as in the case of R. W. Flournoy of Pontotoc, editor of *Equal Rights*, they were also advocates of the detested idea of "equality." But night riders, usually called Ku Klux, visited and threatened teachers of all sorts, women as well as men, Democrats and Republicans, even, in one case, a one-armed ex-Confederate soldier teaching a Negro school.

Neither the rigorous anti-Ku Klux law of the state, nor the substantial rewards offered under it, failed to check the lawless abuse. Lieutenant-Governor Powers told a congressional committee, in the spring of 1871, that in the county of Winston no one was permitted to teach a Negro school, and that all the schoolhouses but one had been burned. In that particular county, a mass meeting of solid citizens, held on April 6, 1871, condemned the outrages in the strongest terms, and the trouble ceased, as it did generally throughout the state with the passing of the early apprehensions as to the nature and purpose of the school law.

White taxpayers objected to what some of them considered the unnecessary and uncalled-for burden of education of Negro children, and what most of them considered its excessive cost. For the latter point of view there was some justification, as indicated in the report of Superintendent Pease and in a message of Governor Alcorn to the legislature, that "while the average pay of the teachers in northern schools is less than $300 a year, salaries here range from $720 to $1,920." Such disparities were looked upon by taxpayers as one of the reasons why state taxes in 1870, as reported by the Governor, were six times as high as before the war—"a startling comparison," observed Governor Alcorn.

The comparison of school salaries is hardly fair, however. There were social compensations other than money in teaching in the North which were conspicuously lacking for those who went south to teach in Negro schools. To a few unselfish and devoted souls, filled with missionary fervor, there were perhaps still greater compensations in the work in the South, but such persons, rare in all times and places, were but a small fraction of those who came down to teach. The others were entitled to receive higher salaries than they would have commanded in Northern schools at the same time.

Superintendent Pease's report for the first year of Mississippi's postwar school system shows, however, that progress was made in public education in spite of the extravagance in administration, construction and furnishing of schools which he deprecated; in spite of the loss of most of the ante-bellum sources of school revenue, through poor management of the public lands and the Chickasaw funds, formerly devoted to that purpose; and in spite of prejudice and opposition. As compared with 1,116 schools and 30,970 pupils in Mississippi in 1860, there were 3,000 schools, 3,600 teachers, of whom 399 were colored, and 66,257 pupils in 1871. Five hundred schoolhouses were built on donated sites during the first year, and 200 buildings erected by subscription. School expenditures were nearly $870,-000, more than half the total expenditures of the state.

Burning of Negro schoolhouses was one expression of resentment more or less common to the whole South. That the extent of it has been somewhat exaggerated is indicated, negatively, at least, by the Rev. A. S. Lakin, the Ohio missionary who became president of the University of Alabama during Reconstruction days. The Rev. Lakin was much given to general statements about the persecution of himself, of Northern men in general, and of Negroes by the "rebels." Pressed for particulars as to the numerous burnings of schoolhouses of which he had spoken, he was able to recall and list but six specific cases of incendiarism in all northern Alabama during the whole period of his residence in that section.

In Louisiana there was dissatisfaction with the school law which, theoretically, was for the benefit of all persons between six and twenty-one years "without distinction of race or color." In 1870, the Governor reported that the elaborate act of 1869 had been a "cumbrous and expensive" failure. W. L. McMillan said in the House of Representatives:

"There is not in my whole parish, as far as I know, a single schoolhouse, no sirs, not even a shed devoted to educational purposes. . . . We have a statute providing for a system of common school education, and under that superintendents have been appointed. The salary set apart for such officers has been punctually drawn."

The New Orleans *Republican*, in fact, intimated that salaries were the main object of the school law of 1869. "The sum of $262,000 would be required for the salaries of officers," it said, "leaving nothing with which to pay teachers, or build or rent schoolhouses."

In that state of educational affairs, Governor Warmoth recommended a new law, with fewer and larger school districts, and with more authority in the State Board of Education, including increased power over the school system of New Orleans, which had been in successful operation for more than a quarter of a century. Over the opposition of legislators from that city, the added power asked for was given the Governor. That any great benefits to the school system followed does not appear.

When the state superintendent of instruction requested co-operation of the Peabody Fund, in 1870, Dr. Barnas Sears, agent of the fund, pointed out that the benefit of the school funds went principally to the colored children, because of the unwillingness of most of the whites to send their children to mixed schools. The Peabody Fund, he said, was not concerned with the question of the propriety or impropriety of the course of the white people. He added:

"We wish to promote universal education—to aid whole communities. . . . If that cannot be, on account of peculiar circumstances, we must give the preference to those whose education is neglected. It is well known that we are helping the white children of Louisiana, as being the more destitute, from the fact of their unwillingness to attend mixed schools. We should give the preference to colored children were they in like circumstances."

The state superintendent in Louisiana, W. G. Brown, a Negro, reported, in 1871, that fraud and embezzlement were not unknown in the school system. Exhibiting "but a fraction of the frauds" he stated that in one parish, Plaquemines, $2,841.05 was embezzled out of total school revenues of $4,846.05, in the preceding year.

Everywhere in the South, even where there were good school laws well administered, there were fundamental difficulties in the way of public education which were hard for well-meaning persons in the North to realize. The necessity, as it appeared to Southern people, for separate schools for the children of the two races imposed upon the impoverished section the burden of a dual system. That might conceivably have been looked upon as an unnecessary obstacle due to ignoble race prejudice, but the sparseness of the population in the country districts was a very real difficulty, inescapable until long years

The "September Rebellion" in Louisiana.
(Left) Building the Barricades. (Right) The State House Surrenders.
From *Leslie's Illustrated Newspaper.*

The Disputed Election of 1876—United States Troops Encamped at Florida State House, Tallahassee.
From *Leslie's Illustrated Newspaper.*

afterward when it was somewhat overcome by consolidated schools, with long-distance transportation for the children.

Unsympathetic observers in the South after the war were inclined to lay the shortcomings of Southern public education to the influence and persistence of the old "slave spirit," or the spirit of caste among the so-called "planter class," and to the alleged conviction among the more ignorant whites that whisky, tobacco and snuff were necessities of life while reading and writing were not.

Edward King, however, observing conditions seven years after the close of the war, reported that

"the impoverished southern states managed to bring under the operation of a school system proportionally four-sevenths as many children as are at school in the North, and to keep them in school three-fourths as long. . . . The southern property holder is paying a much heavier school tax than his northern brother."

With special reference to Negro education, Mr. King observed:

"The negroes have been called the wards of the nation; yet we find the southern states and a few individuals and societies doing all that is done for them."

The remark was not entirely correct. The most astonishing of all contributions was that of the Negroes themselves, just out of slavery. In the five years following the war, according to the calculations of Dr. W. E. D. DuBois, the freedmen contributed in cash the sum of $785,700 to their schools.

The achievement, both of the Negro and of the Southern states in the education of the race, was disappointing, no doubt, to those who expected speedy and miraculous change with the passing of slavery. The testimony of Dr. J. L. M. Curry, Confederate congressman and colonel and the second general agent of the Peabody Fund, given thirty-five years after the war, is a wiser and juster estimate of the achievement. He said:

"I have very little respect for the intelligence or the patriotism of the man who doubts the capacity of the negro for improvement or usefulness. The progress made by the negroes in education, considering their environments, their heredity, the abominable scoundrels who have come here from other quarters to seduce and lead them astray, is marvelous. . . ."

"It is irrational, cruel to hold the negro, under such strange conditions, responsible for all the ill consequences of bad education, unwise teachers, reconstruction villainies and partisan schemes. To educate at all, slowly, was a gigantic task."

Education in the South, of blacks as well as whites, lost the quiet backing and inspiring example of Robert E. Lee with his death on October 12, 1870. The General looked upon schools and colleges as merely "laying the foundation for a good solid education," and in his own work at Washington College, to become Washington and Lee University after his death, he emphasized the development of courses to fit his young men to deal with the task of rebuilding Southern life. To the ancient classical courses at the college, his administration added scientific work and, in 1869, a school of commerce and what was probably the first "school of journalism," at which young printers on scholarships were given the training to enable them to become better editors—the arts of printing and editing being combined in many cases in one man in those days.

From the very beginning of Reconstruction, in his unobtrusively effective way, the South's great war leader urged, not only in Virginia, but through his correspondents in other states, that "the thorough education of all classes of the people is the most efficacious means, in my opinion, of promoting the prosperity of the South"— and by "all classes of the people" he meant Negroes as well as whites.

CHAPTER XLII

"Affairs in the Late Insurrectionary States"

THE prevailing public mind in the dominant North, at least as it was reflected in the sessions of Congress in the early months of 1871, was not yet concerned over the nature and record of the governments which had been imposed upon the states in the South. The North, in fact, was as yet but dimly aware of the failure of those governments to live up to their high promises of regenerating Southern life through the workings of democracy. Revelations of rascality, when they got attention at all, were likely to be looked upon as mere stock political denunciation by Democrats deprived of office.

The "outrage" story was the staple of news from the South. To the authentic outrages, of which there were more than enough to be reported from the vast and disturbed region between the Potomac and the Rio Grande, there were added the results of unconscious exaggeration, overactive imagination and pure invention. That in whole counties, indeed in the overwhelming majority of the counties in the South, there was not even a reported outrage from year's end to year's end escaped attention.

The Northern people naturally felt an interest in the freedmen. They had freed them from slavery and made them voting citizens. Humanity and politics joined in the demand for their protection, both in their rights of person and property and in their right to vote, and particularly their right to vote Republican.

When the Forty-first Congress met for its final session at the beginning of December, 1870, it was beginning to be apparent to their Radical sponsors that the reconstructed governments which Congress had set up could not stand alone without outside help, or rather that they could not be relied upon to remain safely Republican. Before the month was out that was made even more clearly apparent by the results of the Georgia election.

This election, which the Bullock administration had fought so hard to get postponed until 1872, was for members of Congress and one-half the legislature. The governor and the other half of the legislators were not to be voted upon, under the constitution, until 1872. The

437

election was to be held under a new law passed by the legislature early in October, with the final control centralized in the governor.

Having passed the new election law, the legislature closed its first Reconstruction session, after ten and one-half months of continuous sittings at a cost to the impoverished state of Georgia of nearly one million dollars in pay, mileage and legislative expenses alone. More than one-fourth of this amount was secured by diverting the poll tax levied for the educational fund from the pay of teachers to the pay of legislators.

The campaign was short, sharp and decisive. The Conservative keynote was struck by Benjamin H. Hill. The Thirteenth, Fourteenth and Fifteenth Amendments, he said, "are in fact and will be held in law fixed parts of the Constitution," not to be repealed "because the great body of the Northern people regard the freedom and the civil and political equality of the Negro as great national, philanthropic and religious results." Accept the situation, Mr. Hill advised the people of Georgia, and elect to the legislature "members whom feed lobbyists cannot buy. A black man who cannot be bought is better than a white man who can and a Republican who cannot be bought is better than a Democrat who can."

In an exceptionally quiet election held on three days, December 20-22, and with the help of no small number of Negro votes, the Democrats elected five of the state's seven congressmen, nineteen of the twenty-two state senators to be chosen, and seventy-one of the eighty-six members of the lower house. Even with the holdover Radicals, the new legislature was to be Democratic in both branches by a two-thirds majority. The next session of the legislature was not due to be held, however, until November 1, 1871, which left to Governor Bullock and his friends ten months more of administration.

Meanwhile, the newly-elected representatives from Georgia presented their credentials to the House of Representatives of the Forty-first Congress, and were accepted and seated. Two pairs of senators presented themselves to the Senate—those chosen in February, 1870, by the legislature as reconstituted after "Terry's Purge," and those elected by the legislature in 1868 but not seated. The Judiciary Committee, after investigation and study, recommended the admission of Joshua Hill, Democrat, elected in 1868 for the long term, and of Dr. H. V. M. Miller, Republican, elected at the same time for the short term. In February, 1871, both were seated—and, for the first time since December, 1860, every Southern state was represented by members actually sitting in both houses of Congress.

Joshua Hill was sworn in as a senator in time to take part in the debate on the Second Enforcement Act, which became a law on February 28, 1871. The First Enforcement Act, approved on May 31, 1870, obviously had failed in at least one of its purposes, to judge from the Republican losses in the South in the elections of 1870. The new law, entitled "An Act to enforce the rights of citizens of the United States to vote in the several States of this Union," gave to the United States officials wider authority and greater powers in connection with elections of congressmen, which, in practice, carried with it like control of the elections for state and local offices usually held at the same time and in the same boxes.

In a message to the new Congress, which went into session on March 4, 1871, President Grant urged further legislation to "effectually secure life, liberty and property and the enforcement of law in all parts of the United States." The result was the passage, on April 20, 1871, of an act "to enforce the provisions of the Fourteenth Amendment," by direct Federal action, just as the Enforcement Laws of 1870 and 1871 had been passed to enforce the provisions of the Fifteenth Amendment.

The constitutional power of Congress to enact legislation to punish individuals for offenses alleged to have been committed against other individuals, was gravely doubted at the time by such lawyers as Senators Lyman Trumbull and Allen G. Thurman, and was definitely denied when cases arising under these laws reached the Supreme Court of the United States. The arguments for such laws, of course, were that they were necessary for protection and for fair and peaceable elections, which the state governments in the South were not strong enough to secure; and that the constitutional grant of power to pass them was found in the enforcement clauses of the amendments themselves.

The argument against the bills was that the amendments themselves applied to the acts of states which should attempt to abridge the privileges and immunities of citizens of the United States, or to deny or abridge the right to vote on account of race, color or previous condition of servitude; while the bills sought to prohibit not the acts of states but the acts of individuals. Senator Trumbull, chairman of the Judiciary Committee, said:

"I am not willing to undertake to enter the States for the purpose of punishing individual offences against their authority committed by one citizen against another. We in my judgment have no constitutional authority to do that. When this government was formed, the general rights of person and property were left to be protected by the States, and there they are left today. Whenever the rights that are conferred by the Constitution of the United States on the Federal government are infringed upon by the States, we should afford a remedy."

Practical as well as constitutional difficulties were pointed out by Senator Thurman. Referring to the Election Law of 1870, he said:

"Here, sir, is a law which has been in force now nearly a year with Republicans everywhere in these states to execute that law, everywhere having power to execute it, the judges of your own appointment, the jurors selected by your own marshals, and they the appointees of the President of the United States, with every power with which government can clothe a judiciary, and now we are told that we must have some more law of the same kind."

In spite of constitutional objection and practical argument, the bills became law because they met, and, as far as acts on the statute books could, satisfied both the instinctive desire of the Northern public to protect the "wards of the nation" against what was represented as a systematic and well-nigh universal reign of terror, and the desire of Republican politicians for a greater degree of control over elections in states which were showing a disconcerting disposition to go Democratic. As the various Enforcement Acts came before the Supreme Court in appeals involving actual cases, they were in large part declared to be contrary to the Constitution, broadly on the grounds stated by Senator Trumbull.

Under the Second Election Enforcement Law, any two citizens in any town of twenty thousand inhabitants or more might call for the holding of a special term of the United States Circuit or District Court at the time of any registration or election. The court was to control the registration or election, scrutinize the results, and prevent or investigate frauds, intimidation or other violations of the act. Supervisors of election were to be appointed by the court, and special deputy marshals, with extraordinary powers, who were to be named on the application of any two citizens. The jurisdiction granted the Federal courts was intended to exclude that of the state courts, and to authorize the removal from them of election cases.

The Ku Klux law further extended the jurisdiction of the Federal courts by listing more than two pages of offenses newly declared "high crimes" under the Federal law with penalties of fines of from five hundred dollars to five thousand dollars and imprisonment of from six months to six years, or both; and by making the same offenses also causes of action in civil suits for damages. In addition to the powers and duties of the courts, the president of the United States was empowered to use the militia or the United States forces and to suspend the writ of habeas corpus, whenever and wherever necessary to suppress any "insurrection, domestic violence or combinations" which might deprive any person of his rights, privileges and immunities.

Events in North Carolina during the weeks in which Congress was considering the passage of the new "Force Bills" were looked upon as justifying the position that the governments of the Southern states must be kept Republican to insure the desired protection for the freed people, and that even Republican state governments lacked the power to carry out their good intentions in that direction.

On November 21, 1870, the "Reform Legislature" of North Carolina met in Raleigh, with Conservative majorities of well above two-thirds in both houses. The legislature met to make an end of the Radical regime in the state, insofar as it had power to do so. Its most immediate and pressing business was the removal of Governor Holden, whom the House of Representatives impeached on December 14, not on charges of personal dishonesty or peculation, but on charges of oppressive abuse of power and unlawful expenditure of state funds in connection with the Kirk-Holden War of the preceding summer. The nature of the charges led seventeen colored members of the House to issue a solemn protest against the whole proceeding as a mock trial of a man whose only offense was that he "thwarted the designs of a band of assassins."

Managers of impeachment for the House presented the articles to the Senate on December 20, when, in accordance with the constitution, Governor Holden was suspended from office and Lieutenant-Governor Tod R. Caldwell became acting governor.

The impeachment trial began on February 2, 1871, with the Chief Justice, who himself was under serious threat of impeachment, presiding, and continued until March 22, when the Senate sitting as a court of impeachment convicted the Governor on six of the eight counts against him, and "adjudged . . . that the said William W. Holden be removed from the office of governor and be disqualified to hold any office of honor, trust, or profit under the state of North Carolina."

Governor Caldwell, a native Republican of good personal standing, continued in office without molestation, while the legislature adjourned, in April, after electing Zebulon B. Vance to the United States Senate, in the place of the "carpetbagger" Senator Abbott, whose term expired on March 4; and after having called an election for August, 1871, on the question of holding a convention to write a new constitution in the stead of the constitution of 1868.

The Reform Legislature also paid its respects to the existence of secret political societies which had caused so much trouble in North Carolina, first by the repeal of the Shoffner Law, under which the Governor had declared the Kirk-Holden War, and then by the passage of its own stringent act against the existence or operations of secret political societies of both parties. On this subject the Raleigh *Telegram* expressed a general sentiment:

"The leagues of the Republicans and the klans of the Conservatives have already damaged the material interests of North Carolina beyond computation, and their influence will be felt for years to come. The impeachment trial, now progressing in the State Capitol, originated in the organization of these two opposing associations, and over one-half of the lawlessness of the State can be traced to their closed doors. It behooves the good men of both parties to repudiate and condemn them. Laws should be passed prohibiting them. They bode no good to a people. They are a nuisance and an utter abomination and, if continued, will undermine our liberties and subvert the government."

Reconstruction of North Carolina, in the sense of a rule imposed upon the state from without, was at an end; but the struggle between parties continued, with varying fortune, for another five years. The proposal to hold a new constitutional convention, generally favored by the Conservatives and opposed by the Republicans, was defeated at the election of August, 1871. At its session in October of that year the legislature exercised its right to make amendments by a three-fifths majority and struck from the constitution the provisions to which the Conservatives most objected.

Governor Vance, still under the disabilities of the Fourteenth Amendment, which could be removed only by a two-thirds vote of Congress, was not seated, nor did he resign to make way for some other Democrat who could qualify until nearly the end of the Forty-second Congress. When he resigned, M. W. Ransom, Democrat, was elected and seated, to complete North Carolina's representation.

During the discussion in Congress of the Ku Klux law, a special joint committee of twenty-one members was appointed "to inquire into the condition of affairs in the late insurrectionary states." In five of the states—Virginia, Tennessee, Arkansas, Louisiana and Texas—the committee took no testimony, but the testimony taken in the other six states fills twelve volumes. With the volume of reports of the majority and minority of the committee, they constitute the record of another great inquisition into Southern affairs comparable to that of the Committee on Reconstruction five years before. The testimony presents almost every degree of fact and shade of opinion but, as Professor Walter L. Fleming pointed out, to appraise most of it at anything like its true value would require a knowledge of the biographies and personalities of the witnesses.

In its report based on this testimony, the committee divided strictly on party lines—thirteen Republicans signing one report, eight Democrats the other. They agreed in their condemnation of the cruel crimes of bands of disguised men, but disagreed as to the extent, the purpose, or the cause of those barbarities. The majority held that the Ku Klux was systematically and generally organized and active in the South, and that it was a "political organization whose purpose is to put the Democratic party up and the Radical party down." The minority held that there was no concerted system of general outrage; that "there never was a disguised band" in as many as one-tenth of the counties in the six states examined; and that where they existed, they were without "political significance or the endorsement of any respectable number of the white people in any state."

The minority, while "neither justifying nor excusing" lawless violence, managed to get into the record much testimony about those features of Reconstruction government of which the Northern people had heard but dimly, if at all. From Republican witnesses, as well as Democratic, they were able to develop information about the actual workings of the new governments which showed why General Clanton of Alabama, for example, could say with bitterness:

"So far as our State government is concerned, we are in the hands of camp-followers, horse-holders, cooks, bottle-washers and thieves. . . . We have passed out from the hands of the brave soldiers who overcame us, and are turned to the tender mercies of squaws for torture."

From the Republican side, D. H. Chamberlain of Massachusetts, then attorney general of South Carolina, told the committee that while he thought "the ground of the Ku Klux movement was political," he thought also "that it has been greatly exaggerated by the misconduct of the Republican party."

The committee of Congress, taking testimony in the spring and summer of 1871 in Mr. Chamberlain's adopted state of South Carolina, undertook to find out what it could about the tangled fiscal affairs of the first three years of Governor Scott's administration.

To begin with no one could tell with any degree of exactness the amount of the state's debt. It had been approximately $5,800,000, net, when the Radicals took over the state government in July, 1868. Three years later, according to the report of a Republican committee of the state legislature, it was either $16,731,306, as "confessed" by the Governor and his associates; or $29,371,306, if the contingent debt and certain batches of bonds aggregating $6,000,000, already executed and ready for issue, be included. Of this amount, the legislative committee found $6,314,000 to be fraudulent and unauthorized. There were other outstanding claims in an undetermined amount, as well as certain vague and indeterminate credits. A taxpayers' convention, which met in Columbia on May 12, 1871, arrived at still another figure, of $20,045,151, while the congressional committee, with some uncertainty and doubt, figured the net debt at $15,968,000. Judge R. B. Carpenter, Republican, testified that it was "about $17,450,000," and Representative L. P. Poland, of the congressional committee, figured that the actual amount of the debt was an "unsettled problem."

Whatever the exact amount, it was concededly several times the figure of three years before. Some of the causes for that startling development were brought out in the testimony and reports of the congressional committee, the statements before the taxpayers' convention, and the messages and papers of Governor Scott himself. The Governor stated that he and the state's financial agent, Mr. H. H. Kimpton, with the assistance of Senator Sawyer and George S. Cameron, had disposed of South Carolina bonds in New York for

"what we could get for them. After much effort, and the most judicious management, I succeeded in borrowing money, through Mr. Cameron, at the rate of four dollars in bonds for one dollar in currency . . . or at twenty-five cents on the dollar."

For this loan, the Governor said, interest was paid at the rate of eighteen per cent a year, while later loans carried even higher interest rates, with commissions to Mr. Kimpton besides. To secure $3,200,-000 in money, the state gave $9,514,000 in bonds—a state of affairs which the Governor laid to the low credit standing of the state as a result of acts before his administration.

No matter what the cost, however, South Carolina had to have money to carry on the Reconstruction schemes of public welfare and private profit. One such project was the plan for the purchase of large blocks of land by the state, to be subdivided and sold to the Negroes, upon long and easy terms, in small farming tracts. For this praiseworthy purpose, $200,000 was appropriated in 1869 and $500,-000 in 1870. When F. L. Cardozo took over the office, two years later, he reported to the legislature that $224,620 of the amount appropriated was "totally unaccounted for;" that land had been bought at two and three times its value; and that most of the land purchased, though not all, was worth little or nothing for the purposes for which it was intended. The land bought in Chesterfield County, for example, was reported to be "one vast sand-bed from one end to the other, and, if sold at one dollar an acre, no set of people under heaven could raise enough to pay for it." The land in Colleton County was "better for fishing than farming purposes," and much of that in Charleston County was an "interminable swamp, utterly worthless." On John's Island, in that county, however, good land was secured and the resettlement venture was pronounced a success. In Edgefield County, also, excellent land was bought and the settlers did well but the agent in charge, it was reported, embezzled the money they paid to him for the state.

From witnesses, the committee of Congress developed that owners who sought to sell land to the state were forced to set a price two or three times more than they were willing to take. The excess price was for division among the middlemen and the state officials concerned, most of whom were members of the legislature. General M. C. Butler, being examined as to the practice, readily admitted that the land owners who submitted to it were, in most cases, native white South Carolinians. Asked if they had not at least given countenance to the fraud in such cases, he answered:

"Clearly so; and I think they are to blame for it; but it was human nature almost. I do not think a strictly honest man would do it.

If I had 10,000 acres of land to sell, and a senator would come to me and say, 'I will buy that if you will give me $500,' I would buy him up as I would buy a mule."

"Incompetency, dishonesty, corruption in all its forms . . . rule the party which rules the state," declared D. H. Chamberlain. And yet the Attorney General was a member of the ring of state officials and legislators who, in 1870, thimblerigged the state out of the stock it owned in the Greenville & Columbia Railroad; persuaded the legislature to subordinate the first lien on the road held by the state to secure itself against loss on its endorsement of $1,500,000 of bonds; and started on a career of extensions and consolidations, on state money and financing made possible by these maneuvers. "There is a mint of money in this or I am a fool," wrote the Attorney General to financial agent Kimpton. It turned out that there was not a mint of money in it but the state's loss on its investment was complete and entire.

Senator Beverly Nash afterward testified that for his vote on a bill involving one of the several angles of this operation, he received five thousand dollars in money and five thousand dollars in Blue Ridge Railroad scrip. He explained:

"I was supporting those Bills because I thought . . . that it was right, and I merely took the money because I thought I might as well have it and invest it here as for them to carry it off out of the State."

There was constant dissension over the division of what could be extorted from business concerns and embezzled from the taxpayers. Those engaged in one form of larceny not infrequently objected to the operations of others who had hit upon a different method of misappropriation. Then there was the constantly recurring resentment against the other fellow who "got more than his share," which culminated, before the end of 1871, in the proffer by C. C. Bowen of articles of impeachment against the Governor and the State Treasurer. The articles were brought to naught by judicious use of state's warrants and cash, placed in the hands of Speaker of the House Moses.

Investigations were not rare, including investigations of the investigators. When Joseph Crews, chairman of one investigating committee, became himself the subject of investigation on charges of excessive expenditure and padding his accounts with fictitious lawyer's fees, he dared his accusers to indict him, as there was talk of doing. They had first better make an appropriation to enlarge the penitentiary, he jibed, for he knew and would tell enough to put half of them there. The prosecution was dropped and the disputed bill paid.

In vetoing a deficiency appropriation bill which brought up to four hundred thousand dollars the total expenditure for the session of the legislature ending March 7, 1871, Governor Scott declared the amount to be

"simply enormous for one session of the Legislature. It is beyond the comprehension of anyone how the General Assembly could legitimately expend one-half that amount of money."

The point turned on what was to be considered "legitimate." C. P. Leslie, carpetbag senator who was also the first land commissioner, stated the prevailing doctrine among the legislators: "The state had no right to be a state unless it could pay and take care of its statesmen."

Acting on that doctrine, it became common to pay all the personal expenses of "statesmen" while in Columbia, under the elastic head of "supplies" or "sundries" in the contingent accounts of the houses of the legislature. The choicest of wines and liqueurs, cigars and tobacco, groceries and delicacies, were included, of course, not only for the refreshment rooms operated in the capitol building but for the soirees and personal parties of the members and their friends. At social affairs in the high political society of Columbia, as J. W. Alvord of the Freedmen's Bureau wrote to his chief, General Howard, there were "no invidious distinctions" between the few white and the one hundred and twenty-five colored members of the legislature. Governor Scott was particularly distinguished for the "graceful urbanity" of his entertainment for "all alike."

Furniture for the new capitol came to two hundred thousand dollars and included, along with such items as desks and chairs, and china spittoons at eight dollars each, bedsteads, marble-top bureaus, large shelf-back marble-top washstands, bed lounges, extra-large and heavy feather beds, pillows and bolsters, and other items which seemed destined for the bedroom and the boudoir rather than the halls of legislation—as, indeed, they were. Only seventeen thousand dollars' worth of the furnishings purchased was found in the capitol upon taking inventory after the Reconstruction period.

Literally, from the cradle to the grave, the state took care of its "statesmen," for in the list of purchases were one "fine cradle" and one "fine coffin." The state took care, also, of its statesmen's ladies, with fine imported gloves, hosiery, hoods, ribbons, skirt braids, whalebone, hooks and eyes, boulevard skirts, bustles, extra-long stockings, chignons, palpitators, garters, chemises, and parasols.

Jewelry purchased by the state for its "statesmen" and their ladies included gold watches and chains, diamond rings and pins, lockets, charms, necklaces and breastpins. Then there were perfumes and pocket pistols; artificial flowers from France, and extra-fine marble mantel clocks from Belgium; the "latest and most expensive library works" and one Webster's Unabridged Dictionary; albums and sets of the popular stereoscopes and views.

Resentment at corruption and inefficiency such as was developed in the testimony before the congressional committee had some bearing, no doubt, on Ku Klux activities, as suggested in the minority report of the committee. That it was a large direct cause of such activity, however, is doubtful. "They who lay the taxes do not pay them, and they who are to pay them have no voice in the laying of them," complained the taxpayers' convention which met in South Carolina in the spring of 1871, but the resentments which bred night-riding and masked terrorism do not appear to have been roused by matters of taxation and extravagance.

In spite of determined efforts to show political animus for every outrage, most of the operations ascribed to the Ku Klux in its latter days seem to have been more personal than political. The masked visitors were less exercised over matters of general welfare than over the chance to band together secretly to gratify grudges or perpetuate personal advantages. The masked bands lacked the general organization and the degree of discipline which the authentic Klan enjoyed, imperfect as those were. No longer able to create the ghostly illusions which gave the early Klan so much of its power, its decayed successor had to rely more on physical violence. It appeared to Mr. Somers, an outside observer not unsympathetic with the conditions which led to the original creation of the Klan, that the organization was "dying fast." He wrote:

"It is the deep vice of all such secret leagues to survive, in a more degenerate form, the circumstances which could give even a colourable justification to their existence, and to pass finally into the hands of utter scoundrels, with no good motive, and with foul passions of revenge, or plunder, or lust of dread and mysterious power alone in their hearts."

Henry Watterson, in the columns of the *Courier-Journal*, paid his most vigorous respects to disguised bands operating in Kentucky, in the spring of 1871. He wrote:

"The desperado who, calling himself a Kuklux, puts on a mask and mounts a horse at midnight to prowl about after the weak and unprotected is merely a brutal assassin, without one solitary picturesque or dramatic quality. He is an enemy of his race, a foe to society. . . . But, pretending to be a Democrat . . . he is the most fatal of Radical emissaries, who is mightily undermining the foundations of State authority and piling up fuel for the partisans of Federal usurpations."

The "Federal usurpations" which Mr. Watterson foresaw came promptly on the heels of the passage of the Ku Klux Act of April 20, 1871. On May 3, President Grant issued a general proclamation calling attention to the law and its provisions. Before the end of June, trials had begun in the United States Court at Oxford of habeas corpus proceedings as to the first twenty-eight of the more than six hundred persons indicted in Mississippi that year for violations of the Enforcement Acts or the Ku Klux Act. At the Oxford trials, conducted under the protection of a company of United States infantry and a troop of cavalry, the constitutionality of the law was sustained but the defendants were released on bond.

Six weeks later, in August, trials were held in the United States District Court at Greenville of the first twenty-three persons out of the eighteen hundred arrested that year in South Carolina. The Greenville trials resulted in only one conviction.

On October 12, President Grant issued a warning proclamation, addressed to those engaged in unlawful combinations and conspiracies against the United States and its laws in the nine upcountry counties in South Carolina—Spartanburg, York, Union, Chester, Laurens, Newberry, Fairfield, Lancaster and Chesterfield. Five days later, since the "insurgents engaged in such unlawful combinations and conspiracies" had not "dispersed and retired peaceably to their respective homes," and had not delivered to the United States authorities their "arms, ammunition, uniforms and disguises," the President declared the counties in a state of insurrection, put them under martial law, and suspended the writ of habeas corpus.

On November 28, before the United States Circuit Court at Columbia, the trials of indictments against five hundred and one persons charged with violation of the Ku Klux and Enforcement Acts began. Five of the prisoners were convicted and fifty confessed, at the first trials, while later convictions brought the whole number fined or imprisoned, or both, up to eighty-two.

Prosecutions under these acts continued to swamp the United States courts in the South for the rest of the period of Reconstruction, and afterward. For years, more than half the total expense of the United States Department of Justice was incurred in the South, much of it for the services of special marshals engaged in the enforcement of these acts. It is an interesting commentary on the strength of the Reconstruction governments, that in those states where the Radical state authorities were most entrenched, as in South Carolina and Mississippi, there seems to have been the greatest call for the supporting action of the Federal authorities.

The Federal campaign was effective. With the breakup of the weak and loosely organized bands which had inherited the name of the Klan dissolved two years before, the organization ceased to have any tangible effect on the course of public events. When the whites organized again for political action by the threat of force it was openly and by day, not secretly and by night.

CHAPTER XLIII

DIVISION AND COALITION

BY 1872 the national mind had begun to accept the fact of failure of the reconstructed governments in the Southern states, a realization in which publication of the report of the congressional committee, in February, had its part.

As to causes, whether they arose from the stubborn intractability of the governed, or the inherent incompetence of the new governing classes, there was plenty of dispute; but as to the fact that all was not well with the governments themselves, even as described by Republican witnesses, there could be no doubt.

Contributing toward a more open-minded and critical attitude on the part of Northern voters toward government in the South, were the scandals in the national administration and the schisms in the Republican party which made many citizens less willing to accept at face value protestations of purity and patriotism from anyone merely because he wore the label "Republican."

Still another contributing cause was a series of events in the South itself, including continued struggles between Republican factions, which raised doubts as to the fitness of the Reconstructionists to rule, even in the minds of some who approached the subject with the conviction that the heirs of the old "slave power" were unfit to rule in a democracy.

On October 30, 1871, two days before the new Conservative legislature in Georgia was to assemble for its first session, Governor Rufus B. Bullock fled the state. A week before, secretly, he had entered in the executive minutes of the state his resignation for "good and sufficient reasons," to take effect on the 30th. On that date, B. F. Conley, president of the Senate, took the oath of office as governor and began to lay plans to hold the office for the nearly two years remaining of the term for which Bullock was elected. His resignation, and the transfer of the office to Conley, was explained by Governor Bullock in an open letter made public on October 31, as the only way to block the designs of the incoming legislature to wrest the office from the hands of the Republicans by impeachment and removal.

451

The new legislature was not to be so easily balked in its design, however. Among its first acts was to pass, and to repass over the veto of Governor Conley, an act calling a special election on the third Tuesday of December, 1871, to choose a governor to serve out Bullock's unexpired term. Knowing that he had but a few more weeks in office, Governor Conley made the most of his opportunities by pardoning, in advance of their trials, those of his political associates who had been indicted on charges of divers frauds, and awaited with what resignation he could the end of the Reconstruction regime in Georgia.

On December 1, the legislature appointed a committee to investigate the record of that regime, with General Robert Toombs in the congenial rôle of special attorney without fee. The committee report, one hundred and sixty pages of it, charged the Governor and his associates with corruption in transactions so various as the purchase of an opera house for the new capitol building, the endorsement of state bonds for railroads, the management of the state's railroad, the settlement of claims against the state, and the issue of pardons. Waste and wanton extravagance were charged in the management of the state's prison affairs, in publishing proclamations and executive orders in forty-two friendly newspapers at an extra cost of more than one hundred and forty thousand dollars, and in excessive fees to lawyers employed by the state. Political dishonesty was charged in the efforts of Governor Bullock to bring about the second Reconstruction in Georgia.

Besides a legislative investigation, the grand jury at Atlanta looked into the affairs of Governor Bullock, and returned an indictment against him for larceny in connection with the purchase of the opera house for a capitol. In 1876, the former Governor returned to Georgia, was tried two years later, and acquitted by a jury of Democrats. Benjamin H. Hill, Jr., who prosecuted the case, wrote that "the most searching investigation failed to disclose any evidence of his guilt."

While the legislative investigation was under way, the voters of Georgia elected as governor, James M. Smith of Columbus, an anti-secessionist originally, who went with his state and served as an officer in the Confederate Army. On January 12, 1872, Mr. Smith, who was speaker of the new House of Representatives, was inaugurated governor of Georgia. The period of Reconstruction in that state was over.

The political struggle in Arkansas in the year 1871, leading up to the 1872 campaign, continued to center about Governor Clayton. The year started auspiciously for the Governor, with his election early in

January to the United States Senate, by the almost unanimous vote of supporters and opponents. The opponents did not vote for him out of a sudden rush of friendship, however, but because that was the quickest and easiest way, they thought, to get him out of the state and to get his bitter Republican rival, Lieutenant-Governor James M. Johnson, into the executive chair.

Governor Clayton shrewdly declined the election until some way could be found to get rid of the Lieutenant-Governor and so insure against his succession to the office. The first way tried was impeachment. That failed, to be followed by a bill palpably aimed at legislating him out of office. That failed, also, to be followed in turn by *quo warranto* proceedings against him before the state Supreme Court, which itself was reconstructed for the trial of the case by the resignation of two justices; the promotion of the third member, John Mc-Clure, to be chief justice; and the appointment of two new associate justices. And, after all that, the court decided in favor of the Lieutenant-Governor.

In the meanwhile, factional lines shifted until the House of Representatives became anti-Clayton. While the Johnson case was being tried before the Supreme Court, a counterattack was launched against Clayton, when the House of Representatives voted, forty-two to thirty-six, to impeach him on charges of arbitrary and improper removals from office, accepting "pecuniary consideration" for issuing state bonds in aid of railroads, and participating in the election frauds of 1870. There was not the slightest hope of conviction, the Senate being strongly pro-Clayton, but the voting of impeachment was intended to bring about his suspension from office, and the succession of the Lieutenant-Governor.

Governor Clayton, however, under his construction of the constitution, held on to the office, while his friends saw to it that there should be no quorum in the Senate before which the charges might be presented. Finally, after nine days, the Senate met with a quorum, received the articles of impeachment from the House, and laid down such rules for the trial that the managers of impeachment declined to proceed. New managers appointed by the House reported that the articles could not be sustained, and the House accepted the report and dropped the impeachment, by a vote of forty-nine to eighteen.

Compromise efforts, under way in the meanwhile, were successful before the end of March. The Secretary of State resigned. The Lieutenant-Governor resigned and was appointed secretary of state. Senator O. A. Hadley, a friend and supporter of Governor Clayton, was elected president of the Senate. Governor Clayton was elected United States senator for the second time, and this time accepted. Mr. Hadley became governor, and the government of Arkansas remained in the hands of the "regular" Republicans.

The session of the legislature was not entirely given up to these intricate and involved factional fights over office, however. Upon the recommendation of the Governor, the legislature submitted to the voters of the state an amendment enfranchising former Confederates, which was afterward ratified.

It authorized the issue of three million dollars of "levee bonds," to be redeemed by the proceeds of the sale of swamp and overflow lands improved by the construction of the levees. The work was done under contracts let by the Commissioner of Internal Improvements, at prices several times the usual cost of such work. The bonds, of doubtful validity, could be disposed of only at ruinous discounts, and by 1874 had ceased to have any value at all.

A more successful enterprise was the Arkansas Industrial University, authorized by the 1871 session of the legislature, and opened at Fayetteville, in January, 1872, with a student body of seven, which grew to one hundred before the end of the session.

In the summer of 1871, Joseph Brooks opened the Liberal Republican campaign for the following year, on the issues of "universal suffrage, universal amnesty, and honest men for office." The intensity of the factional fight led, even, to the arrest of Senator-elect Clayton by the United States Marshal, on a warrant issued on advice of the District Attorney, charging violation of the Federal Enforcement Acts. Governor Clayton fought back, with his usual vigor, and with success, both in the court, where the charge was dismissed, and in the field of politics, where one after another of his enemies found themselves separated from the public pay rolls.

In Florida, upon the eve of the campaign of 1872, the perennial fight between Governor Reed and his opposition entered into dark and devious intricacies. At the 1872 session of the legislature, as had come to be usual, a resolution of impeachment was introduced; but this time, at a hurriedly-called night session, to which members had to be dragged forcibly by the sergeant-at-arms to get a quorum, the resolution was adopted. On the next morning Governor Reed was notified that he was impeached and, under the constitution, suspended from office. Unlike Governor Clayton, he accepted the situation and retired to his farm near Jacksonville to await trial on the sixteen articles brought against him, charging fraud, embezzlement, bribery and misuse of state funds. Lieutenant-Governor Day, of the Osborn opposition faction, acted as governor.

On February 10, when the Senate met as a high court of impeachment, Governor Reed was ready and sought trial. The House managers refused to go to trial, however, and the Senate adjourned sine die, without action, with apparent intent to leave Governor Reed suspended and the Lieutenant-Governor in office.

Governor Reed was a pertinacious man, however, and not to be left hanging in such an indefinite fashion. Taking the not unreasonable position that the refusal of the Senate to try him amounted to an acquittal, he watched his time, caught Day away from the office at Tallahassee, and on April 8, took possession, and entered upon a war of proclamations and appeals to the courts. Defeated there, Day called an extra session of the legislature, with intent to push the trial against Reed and deprive him of his claim to the Governor's office.

Meanwhile, other forces were at work. William D. Bloxham, Democratic claimant to the office of lieutenant-governor, had his case before the Supreme Court with fair chance of success. Should a Republican Senate convict and remove Reed, and a Republican Supreme Court uphold the claim of Bloxham against Day, the Republicans stood to lose not only the Governorship but also the control of the Senate, which, at that time, stood at a tie, with the deciding vote in the presiding officer.

On May 4, the Senate again sat as a high court of impeachment, but there was to be no trial. The evidence against Reed was inconclusive and the political risks arising from his removal, if it should be accomplished, were too great to be run. An accommodation was reached, the charges dismissed, and the Governor restored to the undisturbed possession of his office. Truce was made between the factions for the 1872 campaign, which was upon them.

Surface harmony, more than a little strained and flawed, was maintained among the Republicans in Mississippi during the year 1871, only to break up in 1872 in violent altercation and abuse in the United States Senate between the two senators of the state.

The term of Governor Alcorn of Mississippi in the Senate was to have begun on March 4, 1871, but when that date came he preferred to remain in control of the state government, at least through the spring session of the legislature, and the campaign and election of the autumn. To judge from the tone of his message to the legislature, the Governor was somewhat encouraged about governmental affairs in

Mississippi and the progress of the colored people, particularly in rising "to the moral level of freedom." The number of Negro churches had trebled between 1865 and 1870, he reported, the number of preachers had increased even more, and the marriage ceremony was increasingly popular among a people striving for "a strict adherence to the formularies of sexual proprieties."

While only members of the legislature were to be chosen in the 1871 elections, the Governor made a canvass of the state, partly, it was supposed, to strengthen himself in the coming struggle with Senator Ames. Opposition speakers pointed out that state taxation was already five times what it had been before the war, while even greater increases were in effect in some of the counties and levee districts. Counties were operating on a basis of warrants, upon which the unfortunate holders sometimes realized as little as ten cents on the dollar.

In spite of complaints and protests, the Republicans retained safe control of the legislature. With the election out of the way, Governor Alcorn resigned to take his seat in Washington in December, as the successor of Senator Revels, who returned to Mississippi to become the first president of the new state college for colored students, Alcorn University.

The Governorship devolved upon R. C. Powers, lieutenant-governor, a Northern man and former Federal officer. "We know Governor Powers," said the West Point *Citizen*, "and although a carpetbagger, we really believe he will make us an infinitely better governor than Alcorn." The *Citizen* continued:

"He has no chronic hates to avenge, no old enemies to punish, nor ambitious projects to carry out as did Alcorn. In short, if our rulers must be carpetbaggers or scalawags, let us have the least of the two evils—the carpetbagger. May the good Lord deliver us from being ruled by such a miserable political Esau as the scalawag."

When the new legislature met in January, 1872, new prominence was given to the third element in the Reconstructionist combination in Mississippi, the Negro. The House of Representatives deadlocked over the election of a speaker. Both United States senators returned from Washington to Jackson to use their powers of persuasion to secure the election of the Republican caucus nominee, John R. Lynch of Natchez, a Negro of such character and ability that at a subsequent session he was presented with a watch by members, irrespective of party, accompanied by a resolution offered by a Democrat testifying to his "ability, courtesy and impartiality" as speaker.

The friction between Mississippi's two United States senators finally came to an open break during a debate in the United States Senate over a bill to extend the right to suspend the writ of habeas corpus, granted to the President in the Ku Klux Act of 1871 but expiring by its own limitation in a year. Democrats in the United States Senate were given the agreeable treat of hearing Alcorn say what he thought about Ames and Ames say what he thought about Alcorn—not only with reference to the question before the Senate but with reference to their past records, personal qualities, and fitness for office.

The General from Massachusetts, said Senator Alcorn, had taken advantage of his position as military and provisional governor to "seize a senatorial toga before taking off a military coat"; he was "not a citizen of Mississippi, has never contributed a dollar to her taxes, and is not identified with her to the extent of even a technical residence." To which Senator Ames replied that his colleague, too, had come from the free territory of the North but with the difference that he had come earlier and so considered himself one of the natives, one of the high-toned chivalric gentlemen of Mississippi. As for himself, Senator Ames declared, he had fought his way into the state and had a right to go there and to stay.

Senator Alcorn, denying that there was any necessity for the proposed extension of the President's right to suspend the writ of habeas corpus, gave a vivid account of government in the river counties of the state as he had left it:

"In all those Mississippi river counties, for three hundred miles, not a man holds an office unless he holds it at the will of the colored people, and . . . two-thirds of the offices . . . are held by the colored people. Is it possible that the courts cannot administer justice in a society like this? . . . Colored men sit upon juries, and it is frequently the case that the jury is entirely composed of colored men. . . . Colored men are sheriffs. . . . And yet it is said justice cannot be administered there, when every judge who sits upon the bench is Republican, appointed by a Republican Governor and confirmed by a Republican Senate."

But it was in turbulent Louisiana that the opposition parties in the campaign of 1872 found their most effective examples of the strife which attended the actual workings of Reconstruction. Trouble,

which was never long absent, began with the session of the legislature
in the early months of 1871. At first all was serene, with what appeared to be a coalition between Governor Warmoth and the Democrats in control. To be speaker of the House they elected Mortimer
Carr of Maryland, even younger than Governor Warmoth and, like
him, a newcomer to Louisiana. The Governor's message urged the
return of the state capital to Baton Rouge and the continuation of improvements, with economy. He returned also, with his vetoes, thirteen
bills passed at the previous session, some of them carrying heavy
appropriations. The state's indebtedness, he warned, was already such
as to preclude previous liberality.

As a matter of fact, property all over the state was being allowed to
"go for the taxes," which was one reason why the mere cost of collecting the revenues rose to twelve per cent by 1871. In many instances,
no buyers could be found at tax sales at any price. One witness assured
a congressional committee that not even the Chicago fire of 1871 was
as "devastating" as the continuance of current taxation and legislation
would be upon the city of New Orleans. "When the city of Chicago
was burned to the ground," he said, "the people had at least the
ground left."

The legislature, however, paid small heed to complaints as to taxation, or to recommendations of economy, no matter what the source.
The mere expenses of the legislature itself were just under a million
dollars, nearly ten times as much as the highest cost of any prewar
body. The services of the legislature cost the state, for each day it
was in session, $113.50 per member, a cost explained thus by Gover-
nor Warmoth in his message to the next session:

"It was squandered in paying extra mileage and per diem of members
for services never rendered; for an enormous corps of useless clerks
and pages; for publishing the journals of each house in fifteen obscure
parish newspapers, some of which never existed, while some never did
the work; in paying extra committees authorized to sit during the
session and to travel throughout the State and into Texas; and in an
elegant stationery bill which included ham, champagne, etc."

The "elegant stationery bill" and other public printing cost the state
$1,500,000 in the first three years of Reconstruction.

Bribery and accepting bribes likewise received the attention of the
Governor in his message, there being at that time no statute against
the practice in Louisiana. The legislature, however, was not disposed

to put unnecessary obstacles in the way of that pleasant accompaniment of legislative service. Charles Nordhoff, himself a staunch Republican, an abolitionist, and a thorough believer in the "capacity of the people to rule themselves . . . better than anyone else can rule them," obtained possession of an order drawn by one member on the "Finance Committee of the Louisiana Levee Company," authorizing them to pay to a colleague "the amount you may deem proper to pay on account of the Levee Bill," for which he "would have voted . . . had I been there," and authorizing the obliging colleague to sign a receipt for whatever sum was given.

The immediately inciting cause of the violent break between the Republican factions, as was so often the case, was a fight over the election of a United States senator early in the session. White Republicans refused to enter or be bound by the nominations of a Republican caucus. The Negro members, therefore, held a race caucus, and nominated P. B. S. Pinchback as their candidate for senator. The white Republicans united on General Joseph R. West, former Union soldier, and with the help of many of the Democrats elected him on January 10, 1871.

The Pinchback supporters were bitterly disappointed, of course, but there was another disappointment less obvious but in the long run more serious in its effects upon already strained Republican harmony. Collector Casey, so his chief deputy informed Governor Warmoth, wanted to be United States senator because the climate of New Orleans was too hot for Mrs. Casey, the "favorite sister" of Mrs. Grant. Failure to support this proffered candidacy of the President's brother-in-law, said the Governor, caused the Collector to break with him and join the forces of the "Custom House" faction of Republicans—a preliminary to the lurid developments of the coming campaign year.

The coalition between Warmoth Republicans and Democrats, like most of the other coalitions which the sorely tried Democrats made or attempted during the next five years, was at best an unstable combination. It lasted less than a month. On January 31, the House removed young Carr as speaker and put in his place George W. Carter, an elderly, slightly deaf ex-preacher, ex-president of two "female colleges," ex-Confederate colonel, and currently parish judge and representative in the legislature of the Parish of Cameron, created the year before to give him a job.

Speaker Carter, who had come into Louisiana politics as a protégé of Warmoth, entered into a new combination with Lieutenant-Governor Dunn, in alliance with the Custom House faction, in opposition to Warmoth. The struggle between the factions, and their forever shifting successors, and the charges and countercharges which they threw at each other with such abandon, contributed much to knowledge of the underside of Reconstruction. Some of the charges were proved to the hilt; many remained in the class of political accusations suspected but not proved. The Governor was freely charged with having become a wealthy man in three or four years, on a salary of eight thousand dollars a year. He consistently denied charges of accepting bribes for his political acts, however, and no specific charge of the sort against him was proved.

Attention was challenged to the amount of the state debt toward the end of the legislative session, when a long list of taxpayers advised the world, and especially European investors, that the debt of the state already exceeded the twenty-five-million-dollar limitation of the constitutional amendment of 1870, a position which was sustained by the Supreme Court of the state in May.

The immediate cause of the special efforts of these taxpayers, according to the Governor, was the desire of Charles Morgan, who operated a railroad from New Orleans to Berwick's Bay, with a line of steamers from that point to Galveston, to make it impossible to market more Louisiana bonds, and thus to block state aid to a proposed railroad direct from New Orleans to Houston, to be built by a new company headed by ex-Governor E. D. Morgan of New York, with financial backing in that city.

While Governor Warmoth was at Pass Christian, Mississippi, threatened with lockjaw from an infected foot, and variously reported as dead or *in extremis*, the Republican party convention was called to meet on August 9, 1871, to choose a new State Central Committee. Since two-thirds of the seats in the convention were in contest, the temporary organization was of controlling importance. Marshal S. B. Packard, the chairman, proposed to control it by having the meeting in the Custom House, with admission only by "tickets" issued by himself, and with United States officers on hand to see that none of the discouraged and leaderless Warmoth faction made their way in. On the day of the convention, the Governor dramatically appeared at the Custom House on crutches. He discovered the plan of operations; entered his protest against being excluded from the courtroom where the meeting was to be held; rallied his supporters, and led them to Turner Hall, for their meeting. The day's work resulted in two Republican organizations, with chairmen and central committees all complete, both appealing to President Grant for support.

On November 21, Lieutenant-Governor Dunn, the colored house painter who even his enemies said was incorruptible, died. The Governor was left in a potentially uncomfortable situation. The legislature was due to meet in January. If the House, under the leadership of Speaker Carter, should succeed in impeaching the Governor before the Senate could elect a new presiding officer, Warmoth would be suspended from office and Carter would serve as governor. The Governor, therefore, shrewdly called a special session of the Senate alone, to meet on December 6, to select a new presiding officer. By a vote of eighteen to sixteen, Senator Pinchback was elected president, as a Warmoth man. This time the Democrats lined up with the Custom House faction, such being the mutations of Louisiana politics of the time.

On January 1, 1872, the legislature met in a regular session which, in its irregularity and confusion, defies description. On the second day of the session, a test vote revealed that the anti-Warmoth forces controlled the House by a narrow margin which, by the next day, had been converted into a narrow margin for Warmoth. On that day, amid violent confusion, an unsuccessful effort was made to depose the Speaker. Meanwhile, the Senate was without a quorum. Three Democrats and eleven Custom House or "reform" senators were staying away from the sessions until arrangements could be perfected for action satisfactory to their side. They were not only staying away from the sessions but staying out of reach of the sergeants-at-arms, as guests of Collector Casey and Marshal Packard on the United States revenue cutter *Wilderness*, cruising upon the waters of the Mississippi.

On the morning of the fourth day, General W. H. Emory, in command of United States troops, marched them into the city to protect the numerous sergeants-at-arms of the Carter House of Representatives in the event of collision with the still more numerous "metropolitan police" of the Governor, who were in possession of Mechanics' Institute, the temporary capitol. Just before noon of that day, a United States deputy marshal appeared at the capitol and arrested the Governor, the Lieutenant-Governor, four senators and eighteen representatives on charges of violating the Enforcement Acts.

The Governor and his fellow prisoners were admitted to bail by the United States Commissioner, but they were held away from the capitol for about an hour. During that hour the opposition took advantage of their absence to unseat a few Warmoth men and replace them with Carter men in the House.

Later in the afternoon, however, after the House had adjourned and its members scattered through the city, the Governor called the assembly into extra session, to meet at four-thirty that day. The Warmoth faction, held together in the emergency, reported promptly, undid all that the Carter House of Representatives had done at noon, on the ground that it was done without a quorum, expelled Carter, elected O. H. Brewster as speaker, voted its confidence in the Governor and adjourned.

From the morning of January 5, three legislatures sat in Louisiana. At the Mechanics' Institute there were the Warmoth House of Representatives and the Warmoth Senate. At the Gem Saloon on Royal Street, was the Custom-House or Carter House of Representatives. On the United States revenue cutter, in the Mississippi River, was the "reformers" Senate, until January 6, when the President peremptorily ordered the *Wilderness* to land. Thereafter the seagoing Senate made port at Bay St. Louis in Mississippi, to await developments.

On Jackson Day, January 8, the anniversary of the Battle of New Orleans and a day of celebration there, the Democrats held a mass meeting in Lafayette Square, addressed by Democrats, Custom-House Republicans, and Negroes, with much denunciation of Warmoth. On the following day, a Warmoth member was killed when he refused to be arrested by Gem Saloon sergeants-at-arms. On the day after that, as excitement continued to mount, three hundred of Warmoth's police broke up the Carter House of Representatives sitting in the Gem Saloon, and took possession of the hall. The remnant moved its sessions to the Custom House, and then to a hall on Canal Street. On the 13th and 14th Carter made unsuccessful efforts to recover possession of the Hall of Representatives by force. And all the while, proselyting and swapping of sides went on between the rival Houses.

On January 15, came the first decided break in a tense situation. A Democratic senator came over to the Warmoth Senate, under an agreement that the registration and election laws, the constabulary acts and the printing act would be repealed. The repeal was voted by both houses the same day, but the bill was neither signed nor vetoed by the Governor.

On the 16th the "Mississippi" branch of the Senate came to New Orleans and, on January 20, resumed their seats at the capitol, believing that they had a majority and could capture the organization. One senator switched, however, at the last moment, and the Senate, instead of unseating Speaker Pinchback, ratified his election and recognized the Warmoth House of Representatives, and not the Carter House.

On that day, being Saturday, Speaker Carter announced his supreme effort to take place on the morning of Monday, January 22. Inflammatory posters and newspaper announcements screamed:

"TO ARMS! TO ARMS! TO ARMS!
COLORED MEN TO THE FRONT!"

Stating that "Warmoth's Slaves at the Mechanics' Institute" were expelling colored members from the legislature, he appealed for the citizens to meet at Rampart and Canal Streets, on Monday. "Let those who have dared to trample on your rights as freemen and citizens tremble until the marrow of their bones shakes. Let the cry be:

DOWN WITH WARMOTH AND HIS THIEVING CREW.
RALLY! RALLY! RALLY!
LIBERTY OR DEATH."

By Monday morning the stage was set in New Orleans for a bloody political riot, when General W. H. Emory, who had spent an anxious three weeks trying to stay within his orders and yet preserve order, appeared with a telegram from the President, directing him to "hold your troops in readiness to suppress a conflict of armed bodies of men, should such occur; and to guard public property from pillage or destruction."

The game was up for the Carter faction, upon which would have fallen the onus of attacking the heavily guarded Institute. Two days later, on the twenty-fourth, the Carter members sought to resume their places, only to be held in the ante-room and admitted one by one, as their cases were acted upon by the sitting Warmoth House of Representatives. Three were refused admission.

During the remaining month of the session, little was done toward carrying out the promises of reform made on behalf of the Warmoth faction in their efforts to get working control of the legislature. Several of the bills were passed by one house or the other, or even by both, but only one became law—an amendment to the election laws which made the Returning Board elective by the Senate.

Affairs in Louisiana attracted national attention. The House of Representatives appointed a special investigating committee, which arrived in New Orleans on January 29, took five hundred and fifty-three pages of testimony, and made a report which, in the main, sustained the things done by the fusion of Custom-House Republicans and Democrats, and condemned the Warmoth government. Much of the testimony is hearsay or opinion—"a subject of notoriety," as Marshal Packard said about certain charges against the Governor of which he had no proof. Governor Warmoth himself said afterward that he ought to have spent his life in the penitentiary if one per cent of the charges made against him in the investigation had been true.

But, regardless of the truth of the allegations, the events in Louisiana and the report of them gave to the Northern public a different and less favorable opinion of the workings of the governments they had imposed upon the South, even though they might be called Republican. Four years earlier, the same sort of continuous disorder probably would have been attributed to innate rebelliousness in the Southern people. General Emory, however, in his report on events laid the trouble to the fact that the state authorities were "distasteful to all parties, Republicans and Democrats, black and white. . . . The hostility here is not against the United States, but against the State government, which is odious beyond expression, and I fear justly so."

CHAPTER XLIV

THE ELECTIONS OF 1872

ON JANUARY 24, 1872, while the committee of Congress was on its way to New Orleans to investigate Louisiana's riotous factional rivalries, the Liberal Republicans of Missouri met at Jefferson City, under the leadership of General Carl Schurz, now United States senator, and Governor B. Gratz Brown. Two years before, the same group had turned Missouri from its postwar policy of proscription. Now, to all those of like mind with themselves throughout the nation, they proposed reform and reconciliation as rally cries for the campaign of 1872—reform in the administration of the national government, with reduction of the war-high tariff, and reconciliation with the people of the South.

Having no idea that these things could be accomplished under the administration of President Grant, and being without hope of defeating his renomination at the hands of the Republican party, the Missouri Liberal Republicans called a national convention to meet in Cincinnati on May 1.

It was understood from the beginning that, in all probability, the Cincinnati convention would nominate a candidate for president; would attempt to bring together behind its candidate the great group of Republicans who were disappointed or offended at the policies of the Grant administration; and would invite the co-operation of the Democrats. The great scandals of the Grant administration had not yet come into the open, but there was in the country an uneasy sense that the government was shot through with inefficiency and favoritism, if not corruption. The President's unconcerned nepotism; the "oriental nonchalance" with which he accepted valuable gifts from those who had, or might have, official favors to seek; his stubborn insistence upon the purchase and annexation of Santo Domingo, after negotiations carried on by unusual and extraordinary means; the enforced retirement from his Cabinet of Attorney General Hoar and Secretary of the Interior Cox, leaders in the movement for the extension of the merit system in government service—these were some of the things which the reform element in the party resented. And there were

465

enough of the reformers, together with disappointed practical politicians, to make the Cincinnati nomination for the Presidency worth something, particularly with the prospect of Democratic help.

The Cincinnati convention was a heterogeneous affair, with a huge attendance of men of all beliefs and all degrees of experience in the practice of politics, united only on the point of opposition to the Grant administration. Friends of half a dozen men of national standing and strength were at work seeking the presidential nomination. Partly behind the scenes, a group of self-constituted managers, including the heads of some of the principal newspapers of the country—Democratic as well as Republican—sought to find the candidate who could present the strongest and most united front. There was a general feeling that Charles Francis Adams, wartime ambassador to Great Britain and now in Geneva representing the United States before the Court of Arbitration on the *Alabama* claims, would be such a candidate, as would Lyman Trumbull, the Liberal senator from Illinois and chairman of the Senate Judiciary Committee. With either as a candidate, there would have been a basis for the adherence of Democrats and large elements of the Republican party.

On the second day of the convention a platform was adopted, with substantial agreement on three of the four major points—denunciation of the shortcomings of the Grant administration, a powerful declaration for an immediate and thorough reform of the Civil Service, and "the immediate and absolute removal of all disabilities imposed on account of the rebellion," with local self-government for the states. On the fourth major point at issue, the reduction of the tariff, the convention adopted a straddling plank, referring the whole matter to the people in their respective congressional districts—a concession demanded and secured by the unalterably high-tariff Horace Greeley, editor of the New York *Tribune*.

Mr. Greeley's victory on the one seriously disputed point in the platform presaged his victory in the race for the presidential nomination, which came on the third day and sixth ballot of the convention. The ticket was completed by the nomination for vice-president of Governor B. Gratz Brown of Missouri, who had been one of the serious contenders for the first place on the ticket.

From the standpoint of winning an election, there could hardly have been a more inept nomination than that of the distinguished editor of the *Tribune*. The very high priest of high protective tariffs, he was expected to win and hold the support of low-tariff Republicans and free-trade Democrats. The foremost exponent of the then widely held theory that any American, merely by virtue of his birth and without special training, could fill any office within the gift of the government, he was expected to win and hold the support of the Civil Service reformers devoted to the ideal of training and competence in public office. After a generation of trenchant editorial writing, with never a good word to say for the Democratic party, he was expected to win the support of Democrats, Northern and Southern. He had been outspoken for more generous treatment of the South, after the war hysteria passed, it is true, and it was not forgotten that he had come forward at Richmond to sign the bond of Jefferson Davis; but it was remembered that he had been for long years an evangel of what many looked upon as a crusade against the South and its institutions.

To these positive disqualifications should be added the fact that the new candidate, with all his great gifts as an editor and agitator, had few executive qualities and no reputation for sound common sense to commend him to substantial and thoughtful men in either party. That the nominee of the Cincinnati convention polled as large a vote as he did is striking testimony to the deep dissatisfaction with the administration of affairs.

The regular Republican convention, meeting in Philadelphia on June 5, pointed with pride to the achievements of President Grant's administration; viewed with alarm the threat of a Democratic or coalition victory to the preservation of the hard-won "results of the war"; renominated the President unanimously; side-tracked Vice-President Schuyler Colfax, and nominated in his stead Henry L. Wilson. As a senator from Massachusetts and colleague of Senator Sumner, Wilson was expected to strengthen the appeal to Negro voters and their friends who might have been alienated by the action of the Grant forces in deposing Sumner as chairman of the Senate Committee on Foreign Affairs the year before. With "safe" candidates, a platform which made the most of the party record on the "Southern question," and a disciplined organization ably directed and amply financed, the Republicans were ready to re-elect their President.

A month later, on July 9, the Democratic national convention met in Baltimore. The weakness of the Greeley candidacy was apparent to the discerning, but the Democrats had no real choice except that between Grant and Greeley. Greeley and Brown, therefore, were nominated by a vote almost unanimous, and the "Cincinnati platform," with its declaration against "any reopening of the questions settled by the Thirteenth, Fourteenth and Fifteenth Amendments," was adopted by a convention in which Southern Democrats were a most important element. Democrats who refused to swallow the nomination of Greeley met afterward, in August, at Louisville, and attempted to run a "straight-out" ticket, without success. The lines were drawn between Greeley and his supporters, preaching reform and reconciliation, and the Grant Republicans, standing for things as they were and the "preservation of the results of the war."

The Liberal Republican movement, even before the election was held and regardless of its result, was of immense service to the South in its struggle toward ridding itself of state governments described by Senator Schurz as "a combination of rascality and ignorance wielding official power." To many in the North the movement brought for the first time some realization of the results of the policy imposed on the South five years earlier. The policy of conferring political rights upon the freedmen, said Senator Schurz, was "well calculated and even necessary to protect their rights as free laborers and citizens," but it was a mistake to couple with it disfranchisement and disqualification of those more experienced and intelligent. As he put it:

"The stubborn fact remains that the negroes were ignorant and inexperienced; that the public business was an unknown world to them and that in spite of the best intentions they were easily misled, not unfrequently by the most reckless rascality. . . . When ignorance and inexperience were admitted to so large an influence upon public affairs, intelligence ought no longer to so large an extent to have been excluded. In other words, when universal suffrage was granted to secure the equal rights of all, universal amnesty ought to have been granted to make all the resources of political intelligence and experience available for the promotion of the welfare of all."

The point of view thus expressed found practical expression in the passage, on May 22, 1872, of the General Amnesty Act, which removed the political disabilities imposed by the Fourteenth Amendment from an estimated 150,000 supporters of the Confederacy, and reduced the number still under disabilities to not more than the five hundred or so who, before the war, had been members of the Thirty-sixth and Thirty-seventh Congresses, officers in the judicial, military and naval service of the United States, heads of departments or foreign ministers of the United States.

The passage of the General Amnesty Act of 1872 climaxed a year of effort to secure agreement by both houses on some one bill, with the two-thirds majority required by the Fourteenth Amendment. Such a bill passed the House in the spring of 1871, but was defeated in the Senate in January, 1872, when Senator Sumner succeeded in loading it down with a supplementary civil rights clause, providing by Federal law equal rights for Negroes in churches, hotels, theaters, railroad cars and like public places. After the Cincinnati convention, however, as a matter of practical party politics as well as good judgment, the Republicans joined with the Democrats in carrying out the earlier recommendation of President Grant for general amnesty, and so reducing the impact of one of the issues of the campaign.

After 1872, Congress was liberal in passing individual acts of amnesty for former Confederate leaders whom the Southern people elected to office. More than one hundred were relieved of their political disabilities by acts passed before 1880, but it was not until June 6, 1898, after the United States was at war with Spain, that Congress passed a general act granting full amnesty to all who had supported the Confederacy.

While Congress and the national party conventions were drawing the lines of the issues of the campaign of 1872, the state governments in the South and their political parties and factions were, in their various ways, lining up for their local struggles. To the "regular" Republicans in the South, the situation was satisfactory enough. Liberal or anti-Grant Republicans, notably Governor Warmoth who had headed a delegation of more than a hundred Louisianians at the Cincinnati convention, and Joseph Brooks in Arkansas, with his "reform Republican" or "brindletail" movement, were not so well satisfied with their prospects. The regular Democrats or Conservatives were least happy of all. They went into the fight to elect Greeley, rather ruefully, simply because it was the only possible chance to defeat Grant. To do that, according to the "solemn conviction" expressed by their convention in Mississippi, was "the one vital necessity of the hour." To that end, they declared their entire willingness to "lay down all prejudices"—or, in the political language of the day, to "eat boiled crow" by supporting their ancient enemy Greeley.

But no matter how ardent the desire to be rid of the Grant administration, it was not possible to work up any great enthusiasm for the Greeley ticket in the South. Political interest there centered more on the state elections in which governors were to be chosen, in most instances, and new legislatures and congressmen in others.

The first of the state elections to be held, that in North Carolina on August 1, was watched keenly as an omen of the national race. The national party organizations took an active part, with outside speakers and other political aids sent into the state, while the United States marshals demonstrated the political possibilities in the various Federal acts by arresting nearly three thousand persons under the Ku Klux, Election Enforcement and Internal Revenue Laws. Most of those arrested, the Democrats alleged, were promised that charges would not be pressed upon a sufficient showing of Republican support and zeal. "With pardon and the Radical party on the one hand and the Albany penitentiary on the other, the Ku Klux is not long in making up his mind how he will vote," wrote H. V. Redfield, of the Cincinnati *Commercial*, describing the dilemma of the voters under Federal arrest, as it was generally understood.

By a majority of less than two thousand out of a total vote of nearly two hundred thousand, North Carolina elected Governor Tod Caldwell, Republican, over August S. Merrimon, Democrat. The legislature remained Conservative, but the defeat of Merrimon, nominated by the Democrats and supported by such Liberal Republicans as there were in North Carolina, was widely and rightly looked upon as the first augury of the national result in November.

South Carolina's state election, on October 16, was not an indicator of national prospects, however. The fight was entirely between Radical factions, each outdoing the other in support of Grant and Wilson. For governor, the "regular" Republicans nominated the Speaker of the House of Representatives, Franklin J. Moses, Junior, most heartily despised of all South Carolina scalawags, while the "bolters" nominated Reuben Tomlinson—"carpetbagger," former superintendent of schools of the Freedmen's Bureau in the state, and state auditor. The Conservatives, disheartened by the result of their attempt to appeal to the Negro majority in the campaign of 1870, took no part in the contest, except as they voted for the more desirable of legislative, city and county candidates.

"The good people . . ." said the Edgefield *Advertiser*, "simply look upon the entire contest as a struggle between thieves and plunderers, and have no preference between the contestants. . . . Let us pray!"

To attitudes of this sort, whether they be called resigned indifference or disgusted defeat, has sometimes been ascribed the failure of the Southern whites to direct more effectively the course of events during the Reconstruction period. What they might have done in the very earliest days after the surrender, had broader wisdom and more determined purpose been shown, no one can say; but Daniel H. Chamberlain, last Reconstruction governor of South Carolina, was convinced that after 1867 the whites of South Carolina had no chance to accept Reconstruction and make an effective alliance with the Negro voters even if they had wanted to. Writing more than thirty years after the event, in the *Atlantic Monthly*, Governor Chamberlain said:

"It cannot be too confidently asserted that from 1867 to 1872 nothing would have been more unwelcome to the leaders of reconstruction at Washington than the knowledge that the whites of South Carolina were gaining influence over the blacks, or were helping to make laws, or were holding office. . . .

"Seventy-eight thousand colored voters were distinctly and of design pitted against forty-six thousand whites. . . . It was deliberately planned and eagerly welcomed at Washington."

The factional fight in South Carolina resulted in the election of Moses as governor and R. H. Gleaves, a Negro "carpetbagger" from Pennsylvania, as lieutenant-governor, by an overwhelming vote of nearly two to one.

In the November elections, Grant carried all but six states, with a total of two hundred and seventy-two electoral votes to sixty-six for Greeley, and a popular majority more than twice that over Seymour four years earlier. In the South, Grant carried Alabama, Arkansas, Florida, Mississippi, North Carolina, South Carolina and Virginia. Of the states carried by Greeley, three were former Confederate States—Georgia, Tennessee and Texas; and three were of the old group of border slave states—Kentucky, Maryland and Missouri. On the face of the returns, Greeley carried Arkansas and Louisiana, also, but the states were excluded in the final count on the ground of fraud and intimidation. Besides re-electing their President, the "regular" Republicans regained their overwhelming control of the House of Representatives and once more enjoyed a two-thirds majority in both houses of Congress.

Just before the election, Mrs. Greeley died. The strain of her illness, on top of the weariness and excitement of the campaign, grief at her death, and chagrin and disappointment at the election, all combined to unseat the reason of the never too well-balanced Greeley and to bring about his death before the month of November was out. One more link with the great crusading days of the early Republican party was broken.

Four of the states still under Reconstruction rule—Alabama, Arkansas, Florida, and Louisiana—elected new governors, legislatures and representatives in Congress at the same time as the national election in November. In Texas, Governor Davis held over, but representatives in Congress were elected and a new legislature. In Mississippi, where Governor Powers remained in office, members of Congress were elected.

The election of November, 1872, all but brought to an end the rule of the Radicals in Texas. At the postponed election for members of Congress a year earlier, the Democrats had elected three out of four representatives. At the 1872 election they made a clean sweep of all four, as well as carrying the state for Greeley, and named a majority of the members of the new legislature which was to take its seat in January, 1873. This thirteenth legislature of Texas was to undo much of the work of its predecessor, and to take the steps that, a year later, were to end what was left of Radical rule in the state.

In Mississippi the 1872 elections had no such immediate and direct result. The Republicans elected every congressional representative but one—but that one, chosen from the group of "white counties" in the northeastern corner of the state, was L. Q. C. Lamar, former member of the Congress of the United States and of the Confederate States, colonel in the Confederate Army, diplomatic representative of the Confederacy abroad, university professor and lawyer. Colonel Lamar, at the time of his election, was still disqualified for office by the Fourteenth Amendment, being of the class excluded from the General Amnesty Act of 1872. Political opponents, including Governor Powers and even Colonel R. W. Flournoy, the Mississippi Republican whom he had defeated, generously joined in the successful effort to secure the prompt removal of his disabilities by special act of Congress. So doing, they helped to place again on the national stage a man who later was to become a great power for reconciliation and peace.

The 1872 election did not disturb Radical rule in Florida. The new governor was O. B. Hart, justice of the Supreme Court of the state, and native white Republican, largely supported by the Negroes. His Democratic opponent, whom he defeated by a narrow margin, was the same William D. Bloxham who, according to a decision of Judge Hart's court in July, 1872, had been elected lieutenant-governor of the state two years before. With Governor Hart, there was elected as lieutenant-governor in 1872, Marcellus L. Stearns, who had come south as a Bureau agent and had later become the shrewd speaker of the House of Representatives. Both representatives in Congress,

Florida having become entitled to two after the census of 1870, were Republicans, and the Republicans held a slender but safe majority in both houses of the legislature.

Radical rule remained undisturbed in Florida except for its own internal factional fights, but that was not true of the three other states that elected governors in November, 1872—Alabama, Arkansas and Louisiana. In those states disputed elections brought into being dual governments, struggling and even fighting to make good the authority which they claimed.

In Alabama, there was no dispute over the election of the governor, the state officers, or the members of Congress. The Democratic nominee for governor was Thomas H. Herndon, a resident of the city of Mobile, and for that reason weak in the "white counties" of north Alabama, where the Republican nominee, David P. Lewis, lived and was strong. The contest was close, like all Alabama elections in the Reconstruction period after the first, with the Republicans winning by a narrow majority. The new Governor had been a Confederate congressman and judge, a Unionist since 1864, a Democrat in the time of President Johnson's restoration of the state government, and a Republican thereafter. Of the eight representatives sent to Congress, five were Republican, four of them "scalawags" and one a Negro.

Control of the legislature became the cause of dispute in Alabama. Extraordinary efforts had been made by George E. Spencer, whose term as United States senator was expiring, to insure the election of a legislature which would return him to Washington, as well as keep the state government Republican. United States troops, detailed ostensibly to help Federal revenue officers in the performance of their duties, had been marched to and fro in the state under the direction of Spencer appointees, to give the impression that the power of the United States government and the administration were behind the candidate who was able to command their presence. One ingenious revenue officer afterward testified that he had made use of the soldiers to work up a Ku Klux scare by the simple expedient of getting out of sight in advance of the detachment accompanying him, shooting a hole in his own hat and rushing back to the troops with the cry that he had been set upon from ambush by the Ku Klux. The troops deployed as skirmishers, he testified, and "advanced upon the supposed K.K.K.'s with an intrepidity which reflected credit upon the troops, who knew no better than that there was a real foe before them."

With the returns in from the closely-contested November election, both sides claimed control of the new legislature. The Democrats claiming seats met at the state capitol; the Republicans, at the United States courthouse in Montgomery. The retiring Governor Lindsay recognized as the legislature the Democratic bodies in the capitol which received and canvassed the ballots and declared the Republican candidates for governor and lieutenant-governor elected. The new Governor and Lieutenant-Governor thereupon recognized as the legislature the Republican bodies assembled at the United States courthouse. Both legislatures claimed a quorum in both houses, and both appealed to Washington. Before the end of November the new Governor, in addition, had asked for and secured United States troops, who came to Montgomery, went into camp on a vacant lot adjoining the capitol, and there, "quietly tented," awaited orders and developments.

The "courthouse" legislature, on December 3, bestowed upon Senator Spencer his desired re-election. The "capitol" legislature, a week later, named F. W. Sykes to the same seat, on the day before both parties received from George H. Williams, attorney general of the United States, a compromise plan for a joint organization of the two legislatures, avoiding the use of "military or other force" by either side. With misgivings of the result, but with a lively sense of the presence of the troops camped beside the capitol at the behest of the new Governor, the Democrats accepted the peace offer and went into the proceedings of the joint reorganization. The Republicans did likewise, but maintained their legislature at the courthouse also, to fall back on if they should fail to control the joint organization. The authorities at Washington, however, advised that "the extraordinary proceedings in the United States courtrooms" were a matter of "surprise and extreme regret," and that the United States courthouse was no longer to be used for such purposes. This admonition of the Attorney General put an end to the deliberations of the "courthouse" legislature, as a separate body. Its members joined the Democrats sitting in the capitol, but the election of Senator Spencer at the courthouse was accepted as valid by the Senate of the United States.

Under the Williams compromise, which involved accepting certain members as duly elected and rejecting others, the combined House was to be definitely Republican and the Senate precariously Democratic, by one vote, a majority which was to be lost to the Democrats in February, 1873, when a temporary majority of Radicals present unseated one Democrat and replaced him with a Republican. The short period of dual government in Alabama was at an end. When next the Democrats were to come into power, two years later, it was to be power undisputed.

The 1872 election in Arkansas, close and hard fought, did not result immediately in dual government; but from it came, nearly two years later, the split which was to be the end of Reconstruction rule in the state. The election closed a campaign of shifting alliances and bewildering and scrambled issues, national and state. The "regular," or Clayton Republicans were opposed by three factions or parties—"reform" Republicans, Liberal Republicans and Democrats, united only in objection to the Clayton-Hadley government.

In August, for a season, the three parties of opposition coalesced under the management of a joint committee of nine, in support of the Greeley-Brown national ticket and of Joseph Brooks, anti-Clayton Republican, for governor. Meanwhile, the "regular" Republicans supporting Grant named as their candidate for governor, Elisha Baxter, "scalawag," but a man of high type, who was more acceptable than Brooks to many Democrats. The apparent strength of the opposing coalition, in fact, had forced upon the "regular" Republicans a realization that such a man must be nominated. Both platforms declared for "reform," a word much used in the campaigns of 1872.

The confusion of issues was so great, the breakdown of party lines so complete, and the composition of both organizations so heterogeneous, that the opposing sides, by common consent, received new names—the "minstrels" being the political organization supporting Baxter, and the "brindletails" that supporting Brooks. Bestowed by each faction upon the other in derision, the names stuck but the factions themselves continued to dissolve and shift. On October 1, the Liberal Republicans split off from the "brindletails" and nominated their own candidate for governor, Dr. Andrew Hunter, like Brooks a preacher of the Methodist faith.

The Democratic element in the combination, likewise disgruntled at what they considered cavalier treatment by the controlling forces among the "brindletails," called on all members of the party to support Dr. Hunter. When the doctor refused to run, the Democrats attempted, only ten days before the election, to return to the original plan of supporting Brooks. With such division of counsel and blundering management by the opposition, and with the all-important election machinery securely in "minstrel" hands, Baxter received an apparent majority of three thousand over Brooks.

There was bitter complaint among the "brindletails" at the frauds and irregularities in the election, and much talk of seating Brooks as governor by force. Only the original Brooks supporters felt so strongly about it, however, while the friends of Baxter were busy making it clear that he intended to abide by his campaign promises for a broad and honest government. There was no great love for Brooks among the Democrats in the coalition, and there was considerable respect for Baxter. Consequently, they declined to go along with the "brindle-tail" plan, either to seat Brooks or to organize a dual legislature in Little Rock in January, 1873. Governor Baxter was inaugurated peacefully at that time, and the warfare between the factions deferred until the summer of the following year. When it did break out, it was to be under different circumstances and with an almost exact reversal of the forces behind the contestants.

The split in the government of Louisiana as a result of the election of 1872 was immediate and lasting, costly to the people of Louisiana and, eventually, disastrous to Reconstruction rule. The election closed a campaign of confusing shifts in political alliances, and opened a bewildering bag of politico-legal tricks—contested canvasses, contradictory court orders, unstable compromises—which cursed Louisiana with all the uncertainties, disorder and violence of a divided government.

The campaign opened in April, when the Democratic state convention denounced Grant and "Warmothism." Six weeks later, on June 3, the same convention assembled in New Orleans to consider the changes in their situation as a result of the national coalition between the Liberal Republicans and Democrats. At the same time, the convention of the "Reform" party, many of whom were Democrats, also met in New Orleans. Efforts to bring about a coalition failed, for the time being, and the Democrats nominated a full state ticket, headed by John McEnery of Ouachita as their candidate for governor.

Two weeks after the Democrats met in New Orleans, both wings of the Republican party convened separately in Baton Rouge, on June 19. Efforts at coalition on a pro-Grant and anti-Warmoth basis failed, whereupon the Pinchback wing of the party adjourned to their steamboat and returned to New Orleans, while the Custom House wing proceeded to nominate a state ticket, headed by Senator William Pitt Kellogg as the candidate for governor, and C. C. Antoine, colored, for lieutenant-governor.

By the end of June, four distinct parties were in the field—the "last-ditch" Democrats; the "Reform" party, most of whom were Democrats; the Custom-House Republicans headed by United States Marshal Packard as chairman; and the Republicans called "bolters," headed by the colored Lieutenant-Governor Pinchback as chairman. Besides these there was a fifth group, the Liberal Republicans, a remnant of the once all-powerful Warmoth following. Governor Warmoth, it seemed, was being left out of calculations by both factions of both parties—but he was still governor; he still controlled the machinery of registration, election and returns of state elections; and he had lost none of his resource, courage and political cunning.

Coalitions began on July 8, when the efforts of their central committees brought the Democrats and the "Reform" party together. Efforts were continued, without apparent success, to fuse into one organization all elements opposed to the Grant-Custom-House Republican ticket, during the five-day session of a convention of the Liberal Republicans, or Warmoth party, held in New Orleans August 5-9. This convention nominated a full state ticket headed by Colonel Davidson B. Penn, ex-Confederate, as the candidate for governor, but did not attract to itself, at the time, the support of the Democratic coalition.

Alliance was in the air, however, and was commonly discussed. To join forces with Warmoth was distasteful in the extreme to the last-ditch Democrats. Other Democrats, of whom the New Orleans *Times* was a notable spokesman, not only believed that fusion was necessary to have any chance of success but that Governor Warmoth's course of action in 1872 justified confidence in his intentions. The French-speaking New Orleans *Bee*, on the other hand, continued its warnings against Warmoth, addressed to the "*grand nombre de citoyens respectables qui croyaient honnêtement que le parti conservateur de la Louisiana ne pouvait réussir sans l'intervention du gouverneur.*" The drift of intention, however, was indicated by the remark of a Shreveport Democrat that, if the fusion of Democrats and Reformers with Warmoth was an "infamous alliance," as it had been called, he was "ready for the infamous alliance."

On August 27 the alliance was achieved, with the combined Democrat-Reformer-Warmoth forces backing a ticket composed of Greeley-Brown electors, the Democrat McEnery for governor, Penn for lieutenant-governor, and Warmoth or Liberal Republicans for other state offices. On the same day, two Republican factions came together, supporting the Kellogg-Antoine ticket for state offices, with the addition of Pinchback as a candidate for congressman-at-large, and with a new State Central Committee under Packard as chairman, and Pinchback as vice-chairman. A whole summer of negotiation and fusion, on both sides, had reduced the original five organizations to two, both of which gave recognition to the colored voters and candidates in the make-up of their tickets.

Perhaps the greatest strength which Governor Warmoth contributed to the fusion was his control of the election machinery of the state. That control was threatened once during the campaign, when Lieutenant-Governor Pinchback and the Governor raced from New York to New Orleans, the prize being the opportunity to act as governor for a few hours. During the stormy days early in 1872 the legislature passed a new election bill, but the Governor did not act upon it. Instead he held the bill without action as he could do under the peculiar constitution of the state, until the opening of the next session of the legislature. The Governor, in New York on unexpected business, there met Lieutenant-Governor Pinchback, who was in the East stumping for the Grant ticket. The unsigned election bill reposed in the executive office in New Orleans. That night, the Lieutenant-Governor started for New Orleans, with intent to sign the bill and set up new election machinery, free of Warmoth's control.

The next morning, suspecting what was afoot, the Governor started, half a day behind Pinchback in the race. He wired to New Orleans, however, to have him detained or delayed. As a result, when the Lieutenant-Governor's train reached Canton, Mississippi, at two o'clock in the morning, a messenger went through the train calling him, with word that an important message in the office could be delivered only to him personally. The sleepy Lieutenant-Governor went into the telegraph office unsuspecting, received his message, started to go back to his train, and found himself locked in while the train puffed away to New Orleans. Eight hours later, the train bearing Governor Warmoth arrived at Canton, to be met by a special car and engine upon which the two rivals traveled together to New Orleans amicably enough.

The voting, which took place on November 4, was exceptionally free from violent outbreaks. It was, wrote the *National Republican* two days after the election and before the strenuous contest over the count began, "remarkably quiet and orderly." The state election machinery was in the hands of Warmoth; the machinery of Federal supervision of elections, under the Enforcement Acts, in the hands of Packard. The election became, in reality, a contest of wits and skills between the two organizations, with both sides exhibiting what could be done in the way of fraudulent use of election machinery for partisan purposes. In the subsequent congressional investigation many of the simple and ingenious frauds practiced by both sides were set forth in considerable detail. Polls were not opened by the Warmoth forces in some sections known to have large hostile majorities, or were secretly transferred to remote and unknown spots. Boxes were opened before hours, to receive friendly ballots, or were closed ahead of time to prevent the long queues of waiting Republican voters from depositing their printed tickets. Tickets were switched and imitation Republican tickets, bearing the names of Democratic nominees, were imposed on ignorant voters. Poll lists were padded, and "tissue ballots" used, a dozen or a score of them being folded inside a regular ticket and deposited by one voter. Repeating was common. Further opportunities were found for fraud and irregularity in the counting and returning of the ballots.

But the Warmoth-Democratic combine had no monopoly on such practices. They had the better tactical position for executing them, but the Custom House-Pinchback party, through its control of the Federal machinery, had a powerful check and had tricks of its own. Numerous Federal supervisors were named in every parish, and more than six hundred special marshals in New Orleans. Affidavits made by voters who were alleged to have been wrongfully deprived of their right to vote, or to have their votes counted as cast, were the main weapons of the Federal forces. These affidavits were printed in blank by the thousands, before the election, and signed in bulk by obliging officers. The special marshals engaged to complete them had only to dig up names, from any convenient source, and fill in the blanks. Such affidavits, when put into the hands of the proper Returning Board, were looked upon and treated as if they had been votes cast in the box.

Special Marshal Jacques, operating in Plaquemines Parish, told the congressional committee that he got the names of three hundred men who had not gone to the polls and filled them in on his affidavit forms as having sworn that they were unlawfully prevented from voting. This was not enough to suit the candidate for Congress in that district, he said, so he dug up another thousand names from the poll lists of two years before; and, finally, was called on "to extend it to thirty-five hundred if the registration books would allow it. There were four thousand names on the books."

"Can't you make thirty-five hundred on that?" Jacques said he was asked by the anxious candidate for Congress. "The books ought to bear it."

"Has Plaquemines quit voting yet?" became a standing joke between Chairman Lynch, of one of the Returning Boards, and the witness, who gave the congressional committee another revealing glimpse of the political morality of the time and place. "If a man signs another man's name for the sake of money or anything of that kind," he said, "then we look upon that as forgery, but it is not so in political matters."

The returns from the election so conducted were, in due course, laid before the state Returning Board, consisting of the Governor, Lieutenant-Governor, Secretary of State, and state Senators Anderson and Lynch. Two of its members, Lieutenant-Governor Pinchback and Senator Anderson, were candidates in the election. The Secretary of State was F. J. Herron, holding office under a recess appointment by the Governor, who had removed George E. Bovee from the office on charges of improper publication, as an act of the legislature, of a bill which, in fact, had not become a law. At the time of the 1872 election, Bovee had a suit pending in the courts, claiming the office.

The Returning Board met on November 12, organized by electing Governor Warmoth president and Senator John Lynch secretary, and adjourned to the next day because of the absence of Senator Anderson. Chief Justice Ludeling, present to swear the members on the next day, ruled that Pinchback, being a candidate in the election, was not eligible to canvass the votes. Anderson, also a candidate, still was not present, and Pinchback departed. Three members remained, Warmoth, Lynch and Herron, when, to the astonishment of two of them, a new secretary of state, Jack Wharton, appeared to demand the seat held by Herron. The Governor, charging Herron with failure to make good a defalcation of public funds in a previous office, had again exercised his right of removal.

Political considerations had more to do with the sudden removal of Herron than protection of the public revenues. The Governor had learned that Herron and Lynch proposed to outvote him and fill vacancies on the board with Custom-House supporters. In fact, as Wharton, the newly appointed secretary of state, entered the office to claim his seat, Herron was in the act of nominating for membership on the board General James Longstreet, late of the Confederate Army, and Judge Hawkins, of the Custom-House faction. The Governor, however, recognized his new appointee, Wharton, instead, and with his help filled the vacancies by the election of Frank H. Hatch and Durant da Ponte. The new members, waiting in readiness, were called in and sworn, while Lynch and Herron, who in the confusion had attempted to carry through their plan also, left. On the next day, November 14, they met again, claiming to be the rightful board, and sought an injunction restraining the Warmoth board from acting.

The injunction issued by Judge Dibble of the Eighth District Court, the special tribunal created to determine political questions, was served on November 15. The Warmoth-Wharton canvass was discontinued, except for clerical tabulation, but on the following day that board likewise secured an injunction from the same Judge Dibble, restraining the Lynch board from canvassing returns.

On the same day, Senator Kellogg filed a bill in the United States Circuit Court, alleging, among other frauds and impositions, that ten thousand Negroes had been kept from voting because of their color, and praying an injunction restraining the Warmoth-Wharton board from canvassing returns; the Governor from placing returns in the hands of any board other than the Lynch board; and McEnery from setting up any claim or doing any act as governor. Judge E. H. Durell issued temporary injunctions as prayed. Political injunctions had become so common in New Orleans by that time that one official explained his apparent disregard of such process, a few days later, by saying: "I never looked at them much. I merely put them away."

On the nineteenth, Judge Dibble heard both the cases brought before him and decided that Herron was still secretary of state and a member of the Returning Board; that his vote and that of Lynch had prevailed to make General Longstreet and Judge Hawkins members of the board; and that the board so constituted was the rightful Returning Board for the state. From his decision an appeal was taken to the Supreme Court of the state.

On the next day, the ever-resourceful Warmoth reached into the executive desk, pulled forth the election law passed early in the year, which Lieutenant-Governor Pinchback had vainly raced back from New York to sign, and himself signed it. Its effect, he claimed, was to abolish all existing Returning Boards and to empower him, as governor, to appoint a new one.

On November 21, a motion was made in the Eighth District Court for rehearing of Judge Dibble's decision in favor of the Lynch board, handed down two days before—and on the same day, the Governor issued a certificate of election and commission to W. A. Elmore, the fusion candidate for judge of the Eighth District Court, not upon a canvass of the votes but "upon the general notoriety" of his election. The new judge, accompanied by a newly commissioned sheriff of the court, proceeded forthwith to the courtroom, took possession, and successfully defied Judge Dibble to regain it.

To add to the confusion, the Supreme Court of the state, on December 2, handed down its decision in Bovee's suit, sustaining his right to the office of Secretary of State and his right ex officio to serve as a member of the Returning Board. Bovee promptly joined himself to the Lynch board, which was making a canvass, using as "returns," affidavits, newspaper estimates, and even their own calculations, from general knowledge, of what the vote in a given parish might or should have been.

On the next day, December 3, the Warmoth forces won a round when their motion for a new trial of the cases in the state court was granted by Judge Elmore, the new judge on the bench of the Eighth District Court. Judge Elmore not only granted the new trial sought, but dissolved the injunctions and held that the new election law signed by the Governor on November 20 superseded the former board and authorized the appointment of a new one.

That night the Governor exercised the right claimed under the new law and named an entirely new board of five members, the De Feriet board. On the same evening he called a special session of the legislature, to meet on December 9. Another and more important event of the same day, not known publicly at the same time, was the receipt by Marshal Packard of a telegram from Attorney General Williams:

"You are to enforce the decrees and mandates of United States courts, no matter by whom resisted, and General Emory will furnish you with all necessary troops for that purpose."

On December 4, the new DeFeriet Returning Board met, quickly canvassed the returns as tabulated by the Warmoth-Wharton board, and declared the McEnery-Penn ticket elected by 65,579 votes against 55,973 for the Kellogg-Antoine ticket. Two days later, the Lynch board declared the Kellogg-Antoine ticket elected by a still larger majority.

But before the Lynch board acted, late in the evening of December 5, Judge Durell of the United States Court issued his famous "midnight order." The Governor's proclamation of the results of the election as determined by the DeFeriet board, he held, was a violation of the injunction of his court issued on November 16. The Judge therefore ordered the United States Marshal to take possession of the Mechanics' Institute, occupied as the state house of Louisiana, "to hold the same subject to the further order of this court" and to prevent "all unlawful assemblage therein." At two o'clock in the morning of December 6, the marshal, with two companies of United States soldiers as a *posse comitatus,* marched into the Mechanics' Institute and took possession, with troops quartered in the legislative chambers and the officers and the deputy marshal in charge quartered in the executive offices.

And there, for six weeks, they remained to sustain the taking over of the government of the state of Louisiana by a Circuit Court of the United States.

CHAPTER XLV

POLITICS AND PROGRESS

NEWS of the midnight seizure of the state house spread through New Orleans with the morning light of December 6, 1872. By midmorning, some three thousand persons had gathered about the building, to find a United States deputy marshal in charge, with a company of troops quartered in the Senate chamber and another in the House of Representatives, allowing admission to no one who did not hold a pass signed by the United States marshal. That official, under the terms of Judge Durell's order of the night before, was to hold the building against "unauthorized persons" and to prevent its use for "unlawful assemblages."

As the terms of the order became known there was a deal of indignation in the crowd but no disposition to resist an order so obviously backed up by the force of the United States government, regardless of what might be thought of its justification or its legality. At eleven o'clock in the morning the interest of the populace shifted to the United States courtroom, where Judge Durell, from the bench, contributed further to the whirl of decrees and injunctions. Governor Warmoth and his Returning Board were prohibited from canvassing the election returns in their possession, and ordered to turn them over to the Lynch board. On the same day, however, Samuel Armstead, the colored candidate for secretary of state on the McEnery-fusion ticket, went into the state court and secured an injunction to restrain the Lynch board from keeping on with the highly irregular canvass of estimates and guesses which it was making.

That night, paying no more attention to the state injunction than did the Warmoth board to the Federal, the Lynch board announced the result of its canvass of the votes for members of the legislature, with a list of senators and representatives overwhelmingly Republican. As Mr. Bovee, a member of the board, afterward testified, they "were determined to have a legislature."

Before the hectic day closed United States Marshal Packard wired his report of the canvass and its results to Attorney General Williams at Washington, while Revenue Collector Casey telegraphed to a more

484

important personage, his brother-in-law President Grant, that Judge Durell's decree, "if enforced will save the Republican majority and give Louisiana a Republican Legislature and State Government, and check Warmoth in his usurpations."

On the next day, December 7, some of those declared elected to the legislature by the Warmoth-Wharton and the DeFeriet boards met at the New Orleans City Hall, informally and in advance of the call for a special session to begin on the ninth. On the eighth, apparently in an effort to get everybody involved in one law suit, C. C. Antoine, claiming election as lieutenant-governor on the Kellogg Republican ticket, filed his bill in the United States court against the Warmoth board, the DeFeriet Board, all candidates claiming election to the legislature or state offices under their returns, the metropolitan police and the out-going officials, altogether more than three hundred defendants. The purpose of the vague and wordy bill seems to have been, as the congressional committee afterward put it, to ask the "United States court to do what no United States court had the right to do"— to use its process to organize a state legislature. The court, however, obligingly undertook the task through the issuance of a temporary injunction returnable three days later.

December 9 was the day set for the meeting of the legislature in special session, on the call of Governor Warmoth. At noon of that day, the United States marshals and troops admitted to the state house only known and approved Kellogg members. At the same hour, other members claiming election on the fusion ticket convened at the Lyceum Hall, in the New Orleans City Hall. And so, for the second time in the year 1872, the politics-plagued state of Louisiana found itself with two "legislatures" in session, each one claiming to be the original and only genuine body of lawmakers.

The first business of the Kellogg legislature was the adoption by the House of Representatives of a resolution impeaching Governor Warmoth; the presentation of the resolution to the Senate; the organization of the Senate as a court of impeachment, presided over by the Chief Justice; the announcement of the suspension of Warmoth as governor, and the accession of Lieutenant-Governor Pinchback to the office— all within six hours after convening.

The second business was to telegraph President Grant, and ask his military protection against "certain ill-disposed persons reported to be forming combinations to disturb the public peace and defy the lawful authority."

A third order of business was to rush through all the stages of enactment, in one day and under the continued suspension of the rules, of a bill to abolish the Eighth District Court, with its fusion-elected judge; to create a new state court for the consideration of public questions; and to appoint as its judge, Jacob Hawkins, a member of the Lynch Returning Board. Judge Hawkins was not the only member of the board to receive his reward promptly. General Longstreet was appointed levee commissioner by Governor Pinchback, at a salary of six thousand dollars a year. Mr. Herron was named recorder of mortgages, a post carrying fees of from ten thousand dollars to twenty thousand dollars a year, created for him by the legislature which he had helped to create. To Senator Lynch's son, the Governor offered a place as inspector of livestock, another fee-bearing office worth some twelve thousand dollars a year. No member of the Returning Board was overlooked.

The Warmoth-Democratic-fusion legislature, meeting in Lyceum Hall on December 9, did not organize until the following day and did not receive enough accessions to declare that it had a quorum until December 11. On that evening the Senate and House organized, elected speakers, heard a message from Governor Warmoth, and created a fourth Returning Board, known as the Forman board, to make the final and official canvass of the returns already tabulated by its Wharton-Warmoth and DeFeriet predecessors.

Through the eleventh, the day on which the fusion legislature secured its quorum, and the twelfth, the wires to Washington burned with appeals to President Grant and Attorney General Williams, from both sides. Acting Governor Pinchback urged that additional troops be furnished on his requisition, for the great moral effect it would have. Governor-elect, or claimant, Kellogg urged some indication of presidential recognition, after which "Governor Pinchback and legislature would settle everything." Both promised discretion on their part. Collector Casey likewise assured his powerful brother-in-law, on December 11, that "Governor Pinchback is acting with great discretion, as is the legislature, and they will so continue." Mr. Casey's first dispatch of that day was an almost despairing appeal. "Old citizens are dragooned into an opposition they do not feel," he wired, "and pressure is hourly growing; our members are poor and adversaries are rich, and offers are made that are difficult for them to withstand. There is danger that they will break our quorum. The delay in placing troops at disposal of Governor Pinchback . . . is disheartening our friends and cheering our enemies." A second dispatch during the day was less discouraging but no less importunate.

On the same day, Governor Warmoth wired the President a summary of the case and the situation, from the fusion point of view. On the next day, the twelfth, appeals continued, with wires from John McEnery, "claiming to be governor-elect of this State" and from Thomas A. Adams, chairman of a committee of one hundred citizens, "about to leave here for Washington to lay before you and the Congress . . . the facts of the political difficulties . . . existing in this State." Both wires requested no more than delay in action until the committee could reach Washington and state their case.

A more persuasive and effective wire went, on the same day, from Collector Casey. It recited the course of events as construed by the Kellogg forces; claimed the perfect legality of the steps taken; denounced the Warmoth organization as a "pretended legislature"; predicted conflict between the two governments; and expressed the opinion that a "decided recognition" of the Pinchback government, with the furnishing of Federal troops to support it, "would settle the whole matter."

"General Longstreet," added Mr. Casey, "has been appointed by Governor Pinchback as adjutant-general of State Militia"—a bit of news calculated to appeal to "Pete" Longstreet's old West Point and army chum, now in the White House.

In a telegram from the Attorney General, sent on December 12, the President recognized Pinchback as governor and the "body assembled at the Mechanics' Institute" as the lawful legislature of Louisiana, and promised "all necessary assistance . . . to protect the State from disorder and violence." The Attorney General wired, also, to General Emory, commanding United States forces, to use them to preserve the peace, under the authority of Governor Pinchback. To Mr. McEnery he wired:

"Your visit with a hundred citizens will be unavailing so far as the President is concerned. His decision is made and will not be changed, and the sooner it is acquiesced in the sooner good order and peace will be restored."

The Warmoth-fusion legislature, on December 13, adjourned to meet again in regular session on the first Monday in January, 1873. The Pinchback government, on the following day, secured control of the arms from the state arsenal, when they were handed over to General Emory. That evening, with rain pouring upon the heads of a monster throng of citizens turned out to see them off, the Committee of One Hundred entrained for Washington, regardless of the warning of the Attorney General, to go through the futile performance of presenting their case, on the nineteenth, to a cold and distant president.

But the "Louisiana question" was in no wise settled. It had moved out of the stage of writs and counterwrits into the field of realistic politics. The Pinchback legislature, whose members had had experience of Warmoth's resourcefulness before, feared to adjourn as the Lyceum Hall body had done, and await the beginning of the regular session in January. Troops remained in the state house and the legislature, too, remained "on guard," with daily meetings right up to the minute of the regular January session, upon which they entered without a break.

Meanwhile, throughout the nation the strange doings in New Orleans were the subject of attention. There was much editorial astonishment and indignation at the assumption of power by a Federal judge to take over the government of a state and replace it with another. The House of Representatives at Washington was equally outspoken. In a resolution adopted on December 16, it described the government of Louisiana as "administered by orders from the Federal courts, supported by Federal bayonets," and called upon the President for information. Not until after the regular sessions of the rival legislatures got under way, however, in January, 1873, did the question of recognition of the rightful government in Louisiana get squarely before the Congress.

On January 13, inauguration ceremonies were held by both governments, Governor Kellogg taking the oath at the Mechanics' Institute; Governor McEnery in LaFayette Square, before a great crowd. The resignation of Governor Kellogg from the United States Senate created an immediate vacancy. To that vacancy, the McEnery legislature, now meeting in Odd Fellows Hall, elected W. L. McMillan; the Kellogg legislature, John Ray. The Kellogg legislature also elected to the Senate, for the ensuing full term, Acting Governor P. B. S. Pinchback— who likewise claimed election as congressman-at-large in the November, 1872, elections. Upon the presentation of these conflicting certificates of election, the Senate found itself faced with the question of determining the true and lawful government in Louisiana by accepting, as a duly-elected senator, either McMillan or Ray.

To that end, the Senate named a special committee, strong in the Republican faith, with Senator Oliver P. Morton of Indiana, who had succeeded to the leadership of Thaddeus Stevens among the Radicals, as chairman. Other members were Senators Matt. H. Carpenter of Wisconsin, John A. Logan of Illinois, J. L. Alcorn of Mississippi, H. M.

Anthony of Rhode Island, Lyman Trumbull of Illinois and Joshua Hill of Georgia. Before the month of January was out, the committee had before it in Washington the members of the various Returning Boards, with trunks of papers and records. Other testimony was taken as well in an exhaustive investigation which ended on February 20 in a report to the Senate unfavorable to the legality of the Kellogg government.

Four members of the committee, Senators Carpenter, Logan, Alcorn and Anthony, held that Judge Durell's actions were "irregular, illegal, and in every way inexcusable"; that his orders and injunction were "most reprehensible, erroneous in point of law, and wholly void for want of jurisdiction;"that "the testimony abundantly establishes the fraudulent character" of the canvass of the Lynch board; and that:

"But for the interference of Judge Durell in the matter of this State election, a matter wholly beyond his jurisdiction, the McEnery government would today have been the *de facto* government of the State. Judge Durell interposed the Army of the United States between the people of Louisiana and the only government which has semblance of regularity, and the result of this has been to establish the Kellogg government, so far as that State now has any government. For the United States to interfere in a State election, and, by the employment of troops, set up a Governor and Legislature without a shadow of right, and then to refuse redress of the wrong, upon the ground that to grant relief would be interfering with the rights of the State, is a proposition difficult to utter with a grave countenance."

The majority of the committee reported that there was no state government existing in Louisiana, and recommended a new election to be held under the authority of the United States. Senator Trumbull went further and recommended the seating of McMillan as an express recognition of the McEnery government, while Senator Hill, reprobating the conduct of Judge Durell, suggested that the matter of organizing a state government be left to those members of the legislature whose election was conceded by both sides.

Even Senator Morton, the one member of the committee who recommended that the Kellogg government be sustained, had his word of condemnation for poor old Judge Durell, whose conduct, he said, could not be "justified or defended." The Radical leader's recommendation, as stated in the debate in the Senate in the closing days of the last session of the Forty-second Congress, was "masterly inactivity":

"I say let that government alone, and if Congress adjourns and leaves it just where it is now, all will be well. If McEnery attempts to make any trouble, Governor Kellogg is able to take care of him without any assistance from the Government of the United States; but if he requires it he will get it. The President has said he would give it."

The President had, indeed, given assurance of his support of the Kellogg government, but he was exceedingly anxious to have a congressional determination of the legal rights of the Louisiana situation. Despite a message from him to that effect, the Congress closed its sessions without action, unless the policy of "masterly inactivity" recommended by the Senator from Indiana could be so called.

The Forty-third Congress did not come into special session immediately upon the adjournment of its predecessor, as other Congresses had done since 1867, and the "Louisiana question" was left upon the hands of General Grant and the government which he sustained in the state. That government had, also, the sanction of the Louisiana Supreme Court, handed down on January 31, in a decision of one of the numerous lawsuits involving the question, but it did not have the support and obedience of the people of Louisiana. In fact, it can hardly be said that the unhappy state had a government in the early months of 1873. The majority report of the Senate committee thus described the situation:

"The McEnery government, so-called, approaches more nearly a government de jure, and the Kellogg government a government de facto.

"The Kellogg government is in possession of the State House, the seal, archives and records of the State, and its empty treasury. . . .

"The people of the State, as a whole, neither support nor submit to either government. Neither government can collect taxes, for the people have no assurance that payment to one will prevent collection by the other government. Business is interrupted and public confidence destroyed; and should Congress adjourn without making provisions for the case, one of two things must result: Either collision and bloodshed between the adherents of the two governments or the President must continue the support of the Federal authority to the Kellogg government. The alternative of civil war or the maintenance by military power of a State government not elected is exceedingly embarrassing. . . ."

Both of the ills feared by the committee came to pass. On the evening of March 5, unorganized bodies of citizens adhering to the Mc-

Enery government attacked the police stations in New Orleans, and were driven off by the metropolitan police, equipped with rifles and artillery, only after bloodshed. On the sixth, armed police seized the Odd Fellows Hall, the seat of the McEnery legislature, arrested its members, and marched them to the guardhouse. General Emory warned Governor McEnery that if any resistance were attempted, the action of the Kellogg metropolitan police would be backed up by the United States troops.

That sufficiently established the *de facto* character of the Kellogg government in the capital, although it did not end the spirit of resistance. In the parishes, however, the struggle continued, with mass meetings of taxpayers resolving that they would recognize and pay taxes to no government but that of McEnery. Still more acute, in spots, were the struggles between rival parish governments claiming election under certificates of the hostile Returning Boards.

In such a struggle the Colfax massacre had its origin. County officers, including a sheriff, were in the courthouse of Grant Parish, at the hamlet of Colfax, under fusion certificates of election, until March 25, 1873. On that day they were forcibly expelled by officers claiming place under Kellogg certificates. The parish, a remote and rural district up the Red River, was filled with members of a former Negro militia company which had been disbanded by order of General Longstreet because of its disorders, but whose members kept their arms. Claiming the need of protection, the new Kellogg sheriff summoned these armed Negroes as a posse. Deposing the sheriff, the bands took possession of the tiny courthouse town. For two weeks there was sporadic terror and violence in the parish, with unsuccessful efforts to establish peace. Governor Kellogg declined to interfere and perhaps could not have done so had he wished, although the Democrats claimed that he allowed the situation to drift dangerously, hoping for an "incident" which would give him a much-needed ground for appeal for Northern sympathy and support. They charged, also, that those who had stirred up trouble for two weeks left the parish before the explosion.

That came, with all the bloodthirsty ferocity that such affairs take on, on Easter Sunday, April 13, when the ousted fusionist sheriff, with one hundred and fifty men, marched on Colfax with the professed intent of putting down disorder. After a first brush, the Negroes fled to the courthouse. Two whites, sent forward to demand the surrender of the building, were shot, in violation of a flag of truce, the whites claimed. The whites charged the building, fired it, in spite of such evidences of surrender as a waving shirt and a fluttering page torn from a book, and shot the occupants as they tried to escape. Some were burned to death in the building; about thirty-seven were shot after they had surrendered, with revolting cruelty in some cases; fifty-nine bodies were counted about the courthouse, where they had been left, on the third day after the massacre. A common attitude among Louisiana whites was that the men of Grant Parish had acted as a unit to avert what was developing into a second Santo Domingo uprising among the Negroes. The opinion of the North, as expressed by the committee of Congress which investigated the affair, was that it "was without palliation or justification . . . deliberate, barbarous, cold-blooded murder."

President Grant's final reaction to the Louisiana situation was a formal proclamation, on May 22, 1873, reciting that Congress had tacitly recognized the Kellogg government by refusing to take any action to undo his own informal recognition; formally recognizing it as the lawful government of the state of Louisiana; and commanding "turbulent and disorderly persons to disperse and retire peaceably to their respective abodes" within twenty days.

President Grant was called upon, also, in the early months of 1873 to sustain by his recognition the government of Arkansas, when Joseph Brooks and the "brindletails" appealed to Washington against Elisha Baxter, inaugurated governor on January 6. Both Senators Clayton and Dorsey recommended, at Washington, the recognition of Baxter, who had been elected as the "regular" Republican, as the rightful governor. In the early days of the Baxter administration, it leaned heavily for support on the United States troops, but the new Governor, through his conservative and conciliatory course, soon developed strength among the Democrats who held the balance of power in the legislature—and who did not like their "brindletail" candidate, Brooks, any too well at best.

Rebuffed at Washington, Mr. Brooks petitioned the Arkansas legislature for leave to contest the election, which was denied by a vote of sixty-three to nine. After the adjournment of the legislature, he tried the courts. With the aid of Attorney General Yonley, he applied to the Supreme Court for a writ of quo warranto to contest the right of Governor Baxter to his seat. The court held that the question was not within the jurisdiction of the courts but was a matter for the general assembly to determine, whereupon, on June 16, Mr. Brooks filed his suit in the Pulaski Circuit Court at Little Rock under a section of the Civil Code of pre-Reconstruction days, to gain possession of an office "usurped" by his rival.

Governor Baxter remained quietly in possession of the office, pending a decision of the case, which did not come for nearly a year, and then only after the political re-orientation of Arkansas was complete. This re-orientation was speeded by the vote of the people of the state, on March 3, overwhelmingly ratifying the amnesty amendment to the state constitution, submitted the year before. Ratification of the amendment, which restored the right to vote to ex-Confederates, was supported by all elements, including Senator Clayton, Governor Baxter and would-be Governor Brooks. The ratification of the amendment was of immediate importance because before the legislature adjourned on April 25 there were nearly forty vacancies in its two houses—six by reason of resignation, and thirty-three by reason of the acceptance of appointments to state offices by twenty-eight Republicans and five Democrats. A special election to fill vacancies was called for November 8, 1873, by which time the total number of vacancies had risen to fifty. In that new election the Confederates, formerly disfranchised, would be able to vote, and, as it turned out, to carry the election.

The drift of events was made still more evident when, in July, Governor Baxter awarded the state printing contracts to a Democratic paper, the *Arkansas Gazette*. The Republican press of the state was outraged. Led by John McClure, the strange and brilliant chief justice of the Supreme Court who combined with his judicial office the editorship of the principal Republican paper, as well as the leadership of the "minstrel" faction, the party organs screamed with anguish at the perfidy of politics and at their "betrayal" by Baxter.

Governor Baxter's efforts were directed toward better and more economical government in Arkansas, and toward salvaging what he could of the state's credit. He vetoed an act of the legislature intended to relieve state-aided railroads of their liability to the state for bonds issued, upon payment by them to the state of an equal amount of their own capital stock, and successfully maintained the veto. Later, in March, 1874, he declined to issue more of the bonds already authorized. At that time there had been issued nine million nine hundred thousand dollars out of an authorization of eleven million four hundred thousand dollars. Some railroads, notably the Cairo & Fulton, had declined to accept the state bonds issued in their aid, which reduced the amount outstanding to about seven million dollars.

Judge O. B. Hart, inaugurated governor of Florida in January, 1873, like Governor Baxter, tried to improve the government of his state, but he proved to be helpless in the legislature against the Radical machine which elected him. To succeed Marcellus L. Stearns, elected lieutenant-governor, the House chose as its speaker Simon B. Conover of New Jersey, who, in a short while, was elected to the United States Senate, to succeed Senator Osborn, by a combination of Republican and Democratic votes. Another factional crack had developed in the structure of Reconstruction government in Florida.

At this session of the legislature there came to an end, finally, the three-year negotiation by which the state of Alabama had sought to enlarge its seaboard through the purchase of that part of Florida lying west of the Apalachicola River, paying for the territory acquired with bonds of Alabama. Commissioners visited Tallahassee as early as 1870, when they spent more than ten thousand dollars in entertainment of Florida legislators in one session. The negotiations came to an end in 1873, however, when, according to John Wallace's account, the Alabama commissioners failed to "talk turkey" to the Florida legislators. Another reason may well have been, however, that Alabama bonds had ceased to have enough value to tempt even an impecunious Reconstruction legislature—for before the year was out, Governor Lewis of Alabama was forced to report to his legislature that the state was "unable to sell for money any of the state bonds."

The new governor of South Carolina, Franklin Moses, Jr., had to inaugurate his administration by communicating to the legislature the melancholy fact that there was no money in the treasury. And he might have added, as well, that the state was wholly without credit. "The note of any negro in the State is worth as much on the market as a South Carolina bond," observed James S. Pike, a few months later, in *The Prostrate State*. Governor Moses was inaugurated in November, 1872, the same month in which the battle of writs and returns began in Louisiana. Like Louisiana, South Carolina was governed in 1873 not by any intrinsic strength of its rulers but by the sustaining power of the Federal authority at Washington—but with the difference that South Carolina to all outward seeming had come to accept its fate with what resignation it could muster.

The new Governor had the reputation at the time of spending each year not less than ten times his salary. He had, during his term as speaker of the House of Representatives, purchased for his own use the finest home in Columbia, of course at the greatly depreciated prices at which almost any property in South Carolina could have been purchased. Vague promises of "reform" and retrenchment had been made by the new Governor and on his behalf, in the campaign of 1872 against Reuben Tomlinson. Indeed even without such promises, South Carolina statesmen, in the early months of 1873, were somewhat put to it to find something to steal.

One of the colored officeholders told Mr. Pike, ingenuously, that everybody knew that the senatorial election was the only "money bill" before the legislature at the session. The seat in the United States Senate went to John J. Patterson of Pennsylvania, former newspaperman and political follower of Simon Cameron, who had come south in 1869 to become chief, in South Carolina, of the "railroad ring" which plundered the Blue Ridge and the Columbia & Greenville Railroads. Senator Patterson gloried in the name of "Honest John," his reputation consisting in a general belief that he was honest enough to "stay bought." To win election over Robert Brown Elliott, the Negro speaker of the House, and former Governor Scott cost "Honest John" an estimated forty thousand dollars.

This was not quite the only "money bill" in that legislature, however. There was the good old reliable item of "public printing," always an important opportunity for personal profit in the Reconstruction governments, which did not have so many avenues and outlets as have since been developed for the public expenditures necessary to keep political organizations going. The average charge for public printing in South Carolina during the first six years of Reconstruction, according to the figures of Governor Chamberlain, was one hundred forty-eight thousand dollars a year. In the fiscal year of 1871-72, this figure reached three hundred forty-eight thousand dollars. In the following session of the legislature the Republican Printing Company, which was a corporate name for Josephus Woodruff and A. O. Jones, the colored clerks of the two houses of the legislature, had the problem of collecting about two hundred fifty thousand dollars of this amount. To get the appropriation through to pay their bill cost them ninety-eight thousand dollars in bribery. The share of Governor Moses, as he himself afterward testified, was fifteen thousand dollars. A year later, to get the appropriation approved cost one hundred twenty-five thousand dollars.

"Justice in the lower and higher courts was bought and sold," wrote Governor Chamberlain in the *Atlantic Monthly* in 1901, "or rather those who sat in the seats nominally of justice made traffic of their judicial powers."

Clerk Woodruff, of the Senate, confided to his diary a plaintive story of his efforts to purchase "justice" from Supreme Court Justice Wright, in a suit in 1874 to secure a mandamus to compel the payment of charges made for public printing the year before. The Judge, he said, "had the decision in his pocket and would let me have it on my giving him the money" demanded—two thousand five hundred dollars in this case. The clerk was grieved and indignant at such venality, looking upon it as a "strike of the Judge to get money in advance of the decision." He sagely decided, "if the Judge can't trust us we ought not to trust him."

"The rule of South Carolina should not be dignified with the name of government," wrote Mr. Pike in *The Prostrate State*. The publication of that work was, in itself, an important event in the history of Reconstruction. It introduced into the Northern mind, with explosive force, the dynamite of an idea. James S. Pike was one of the ablest and most effective of the old abolition crusaders. He had been associate editor of the New York *Tribune*, second only to Horace Greeley himself in his fame throughout the land, and even surpassing him in the vigor and force of his attacks on the slave power and his devotion to the success of the Republican party in its crusading and war days. He had served as minister to the Hague under Presidents Lincoln and Johnson. In the spring of 1873 he visited South Carolina. He saw Columbia and Charleston. He saw the legislature in action and talked with its members and with all manner of men, white and black, official and unofficial. He read the records of the Committee on the Insurrectionary States which had made its report on the Ku Klux just a year before. He was appalled by what he saw and heard and learned. The result was *The Prostrate State*, a book which, at last, waked the North to the knowledge that all was not well with government in the South by remote control from Washington.

In his shocked reaction at the mess of government in South Carolina, the honest and ardent old abolition crusader probably went too far in his emphasis on the Negro's part in that government. That the government was, as he described it, "the rule of ignorance and corruption, through the inexorable machinery of a majority of numbers" is no doubt true. "We only say of them what they say of themselves," he wrote. "They are in the habit of charging one another with ignorance and venality and corruption without stint, and it is not deemed any offense."

The implication that this was peculiarly due to the fact that the government was so largely "black" is too strong. Even as Mr. Pike was writing his book revelations were beginning, in the national legislature, which demonstrated that corruption did not necessarily spring from ignorance, and that neither party, race nor color had a monopoly on political virtue or on corruption either.

Mr. Pike found the deliberations of the South Carolina legislature a "shocking burlesque upon legislative proceedings" but he noted that some of the colored members acted with dignity and decorum. Of the coal-black chaplain of the House he wrote that "in the dignities and proprieties of his office, in what he says, and still better, in what he omits to say, he might be profitably studied as a model by the white political parsons who so often officiate in Congress." Of the general run of members he observed:

"Seven years ago these men were raising corn and cotton under the whip of the overseer. Today they are raising points of order and questions of privilege. They find they can raise one as well as the other. They prefer the latter. It is easier and better paid."

Mr. Pike's book appeared at a time when the whites of South Carolina were, insofar as matters of government went, "gloomy, disconsolate, hopeless. . . . They endure, and wait for the night." The book had no immediate effect, of course, but *The Prostrate State* was the beginning of a new and more accurate sort of reporting of Southern affairs. While Mr. Pike was in South Carolina, Edward King, another Northern journalist of distinction whose words carried weight, was traveling through the South, keenly observant, writing a series of articles for *Scribner's* which were collected, in 1874, in *The Southern States of North America*. A year later, still, there appeared Charles Nordhoff's *Cotton States*—all books which showed something of the South besides the standard "atrocity" story of the political sheets.

Edward King, in the spring of 1873, was in Texas. The thirteenth legislature was in session, at the time, beginning the work of restricting the autocratic powers of the office of governor, and restoring more popular government, which was to earn for them the title of "The Liberators of Texas." A special election to choose a new governor was called for December, 1873, by act of the legislature. Nominating conventions, held in the summer, put forward Governor Davis for re-election on the part of the Republicans, and Judge Richard Coke for the Democrats. A violent campaign was beginning, with the Loyal Leagues active for the Republicans and intimidation rampant among the Conservatives.

But Mr. King did not concern himself so much with legislatures and politics as he did with developing agriculture, industry and transportation. At Galveston, he noted, three thousand immigrants were coming into the state each month by the steamer route from New Orleans alone—a "great silent exodus," as he called it, from the old states of the southeast. Overland, the immigrants came in streams, in wagons, but railroads were building, and the state watched eagerly for its new connections north and east by rail.

During Christmas week, 1872, the Missouri, Kansas & Texas Railroad had entered the state from the North, starting at Fort Riley in Kansas, and building across the Indian Territory, to span the Red River at Denison. Before the year 1873 was out, the Houston & Texas Central had completed its line from Houston to Denison, while in 1874, by way of connections with the Atlantic & Pacific at what is now Vinita, Oklahoma, Pullman cars were running through from Houston to St. Louis in a scheduled time of sixty hours.

Meanwhile, the International Great Northern was building northeastward from Houston toward a connection with the Texas & Pacific, building west from Shreveport, and the Cairo & Fulton, completed diagonally across the state of Arkansas, at the end of August, 1873. Through a branch connecting at Poplar Bluff with the Iron Mountain Railroad, the Cairo & Fulton also reached St. Louis. The Arkansas town of Fulton, the head of navigation on the Red River toward which this most important of Arkansas lines was projected, was soon to disappear as a commercial center of importance, as was the Texas town of Jefferson, and for like reasons. Fulton was the head of navigation of the Red River, and Jefferson, the head of navigation of a chain of lakes stretching westward from that stream. Below them, was a great natural "raft" of driftwood which obstructed the channel of the river, but acted as a sort of dam.

Jefferson was a town of ten thousand people receiving cotton from twenty thousand wagons and shipping out, over its chain of shallow lakes and the difficult channels of the Red River, more than one hundred thousand bales of cotton a year. In the following year, when government engineers removed thirty miles of the driftwood "raft" as a work of channel improvement, the lakes began to dry up—and Jefferson with them. The railroads came, to meet at Texarkana and afford another route between Texas and the states to the east and north.

From Texarkana, too, there started westward a Transcontinental line, while from Shreveport, the Texas & Pacific was already building west. Where the Texas & Pacific crossed the Texas Central, there grew up a little settlement called Dallas; where it met the Transcontinental, another called Fort Worth. From Galveston and the then important town of Harrisburg, near Houston, another line was building west to reach San Antonio.

Railroad building in the South—and in the nation as well—reached a new peak that summer of 1873. Even a great epidemic of cholera early in the summer, and yellow fever at Memphis, Montgomery, in Texas, along the coasts and elsewhere in the late summer and early fall, did not stop the activity. The effects of pestilence and the terror of mysterious death upon the commerce and life of Memphis were not entirely devastating. The panic of the autumn of 1873, however, put a check on the building of railroads to connect Memphis with Paducah, Kentucky, to the northeast, and Selma, Alabama, to the southeast—the latter being the line to which General Forrest was devoting his energies. Connection had been established with Little Rock, at last, through the medium of a ferry across the Mississippi, and a direct line to the Missouri River at Kansas City was contemplated, to meet the competition of St. Louis.

The new Air Line connecting Atlanta with the Piedmont section of Georgia and the Carolinas was nearing completion. A new railroad was building from Augusta to Port Royal, the deep-water harbor on the South Carolina coast which had attracted national attention as the base of the Union fleet blockading the South Atlantic ports. New lines were opening from Macon to Brunswick, on the Georgia coast, and to Opelika and Eufaula in Alabama. At Eufaula, one of these roads connected with a new line to Montgomery. A new line to Bainbridge, in southwest Georgia, opened up a rail route from Savannah to Jacksonville, by way of Live Oak, Lake City and Baldwin—a distance of 263 miles, with three changes of cars, accomplished at an average speed of twelve miles an hour.

Cotton factories and cotton-seed-oil mills were becoming more numerous in the southeast, and other industries were beginning to develop—the commercial production of lime at Calera, Alabama; coal mining in Tennessee and Alabama; iron furnaces in the Birmingham area, in southwestern Virginia and in Tennessee; slate and marble quarries, and the mining of ocher, manganese and iron pyrites in the remarkably diversified mineral section about Cartersville, Georgia, among others.

Florida had begun to attract the tourist. Mr. King noted, that winter, that it was "not invalids alone who crowd to Florida nowadays, but the wealthy and the well." Mrs. Harriet Beecher Stowe, author of *Uncle Tom's Cabin*, and many other New England people were at their winter homes along the St. John's River. Of the Northern people of this type settling in Florida, Mr. King noted that they found themselves gradually inclining to the side of the Conservatives in state political affairs, to protect themselves from the consequences of ignorance and demagoguery in government.

Most of the winter residents reached Florida by steamer from the North, landing at Jacksonville, whence river steamers went up the St. John's to Tocoi, where connection was made with St. Augustine by a horsecar railway running eighteen miles through the sandy pine and palmetto scrub; and to Palatka, where there were connections with local steamers up to Silver Spring and to Lake Dora, the extreme head of navigation. Passengers from the west might take steamer from Pensacola to Saint Mark's, from which port a railroad ran to Tallahassee and thence to Jacksonville. There was a railroad from Tallahassee to the Chattahoochee River also, but, because of the squabbles among its promoters, it was not in running order.

In industry and transportation, the South shared in a feeble way the great surge of national optimism which was coming to its crest in 1873. It was even urged in Florida for example, that a ship canal be cut across the peninsula, connecting the headwaters of the St. John's with the headwaters of the Withlacoochee, flowing into the Gulf of Mexico. There was to be no limit to expansion, and no end to the need of additional ways to transport increasing production—the usual state of mind of the boom.

But with the coming of autumn, and the pinch of demand for cash and credit to move the crops, there came the ominous cracking of the great postwar boom. On September 18, the financing house of Jay Cooke & Company failed. Two days later the Stock Exchange in New York closed its doors for a period of ten days. Reassuring statements were made in various quarters that the affair was a mere money panic affecting only the speculators of Wall Street, somewhat like the "Black Friday" of 1869 when the attempted Fisk-Gould corner on gold was broken. It was predicted that this affair, like that, would blow over with a return to better conditions of business in a country held to be fundamentally sound. Despite such reassurances, the country plunged into a long depression beginning with the Panic of 1873.

CHAPTER XLVI

WAR AND THE TOUCH OF REUNION

PERHAPS because they shared less in the great boom than had other sections; perhaps because, in 1864 and 1865, they lived through devastations which made a mere business panic seem mild; perhaps because they were already pretty well impoverished, the men of the South went into the Panic of 1873 and the years which followed with what Edward King aptly described as "an elastic spirit and a remarkable courage."

To those Southern states still under the rule of Reconstruction governments, the business depression had one positive value. It helped break the Radical control of Congress, and so allowed a better chance to break the hold of lesser Radicals in control of the states of the South. Even then, most of the states were to find ridding themselves of Radical government a process long-drawn-out, requiring remedies drastic and heroic.

The double burdens of business depression and of taxation which, in the language of Governor Kellogg in a message to his Louisiana legislature, was "not far removed from confiscation," produced in the minds of the taxpaying part of the Southern population a feeling thus described by Mr. King, as he found it in South Carolina:

"It is not taxation, not even an increase in taxation, that the white people of South Carolina object to; but it is *taxation without representation* and *unjust, tyrannical, arbitrary, overwhelming taxation,* producing revenues which never get any further than the already bursting pockets of knaves and dupes."

The inevitable "remedy" of scaling the state debt was the proposal of the Moses government in South Carolina. In April, 1873, D. H. Chamberlain, as attorney for Morton, Bliss & Company of New York, sued for a mandamus to compel the comptroller general of the state to levy taxes to pay delinquent interest on state bonds. The mandamus was granted by the Supreme Court, but, in October, Governor Moses called a special session of the legislature to defeat its operation by

501

depriving the comptroller general of the power to make a tax levy for such purposes. With South Carolina bonds selling at from fifteen to twenty-three cents on the dollar, the matter of scaling the state debt was then considered. Later, at the session in December, an act was passed authorizing the "exchange" of certain bonds, amounting to $11,480,000, for new bonds of half that face value; and declaring the "conversion bonds," $5,965,000 in amount, to be null and void because "put on the market without any authority of law."

Partly because Mississippi was pretty well without credit in the bond markets when Reconstruction began, as a result of its earlier repudiation of bonds issued to establish banks, and partly because of the fortunate inclusion of a clause in its Reconstruction constitution forbidding the loan of the state's credit, the state did not suffer such increases in its bonded indebtedness as afflicted most of the Southern states. Great increases in the current spending by the state government, however, and even greater increases by the local governments in important counties, imposed real hardships on the taxpayers of Mississippi.

County taxpayers' leagues were organized, sometimes with the support of the more thrifty and substantial Negroes. In the Delta county of Washington on the Mississippi River, a grand jury which included Negroes indicted, and a petit jury of like make-up convicted, one J. P. Ball, president of the Board of Supervisors, whom the league prosecuted for embezzlement. Upon the call of the case of his son, under a like indictment, counsel for the league gravely addressed the court at Greenville:

"Owing to your honor's adverse ruling on Ball senior's application for a change of venue, Ball, junior, applied to the ferryman for a change to Arkansas; which application, I am informed, was granted."

The campaign and election of 1873 in Mississippi was a fight between Republican factions, in which, curiously, the two United States senators left Washington to contest for the office of governor of Mississippi—an office which both of them had already held. Senator Adelbert Ames, who had the Republican nomination, made his appeal largely to the Negroes, of whom there were three on the ticket with him—Alexander K. Davis, barber, nominated for lieutenant-governor; James Hill, for secretary of state; and T. W. Cardoza, under indictment for larceny in Brooklyn, named for superintendent of education. Two capable carpetbaggers, Governor Powers, and Superintendent of

Education Pease, were discarded. The color line had been drawn in the Republican party in Mississippi and such men as Cardoza were nominated because they were aggressively colored. In his campaign Ames laid heaviest stress on the charge that Alcorn, as governor, would not protect Negroes in Mississippi but allow them to be killed "by the hundreds."

Senator J. L. Alcorn, running as an independent Republican, had the half-hearted endorsement of some of the Democrats whose convention at Meridian in September had hopelessly refrained from making nominations. His attack on Senator Ames was based on the charge that "He does not even live in Mississippi; he has no interest here, except simply to hold an office as long as the office continues; and when the office ends he is through with Mississippi." Senator Ames, in fact, did spend his summers in the North, and the peculiar timing of elections under Mississippi's belated Reconstruction constitution did favor his practically perpetual continuance in office after office. From the office of provisional governor he had gone to that of United States senator, without delay or lapse. Should he now be elected governor, he could be elected to the Senate again, in the stead of Alcorn, by the next legislature, and still retain his seat as governor until December, 1877, before returning to Washington as senator. On the surface it appeared that he was to have the doubly pleasurable satisfaction of blocking the desire of his rival Alcorn to be governor again, and then defeating him for re-election to the Senate. General Ames's thoughts were not entirely political, however, for he somewhat ruefully confided, after Reconstruction was over, that, ludicrous as it seemed to him afterward, he had gone to Mississippi with the "idea that he had a Mission with a big 'M'."

After a deal of judicial and legislative sparring over the question of whether the election was due to be held in 1873 or 1874, it was held, as Ames desired, in November, 1873. The Ames ticket won handsomely, by about seventy thousand votes to fifty thousand, while the new legislature elected at the same time was overwhelmingly Republican in both houses—approximately two to one. Only one-fifth of the senators were Negroes, however, and another one-fifth carpetbaggers. Of the membership of the House, one-eighth were carpetbaggers, one-half Negroes. The House, as the custom had come to be in Mississippi, elected as its speaker the colored Representative Shadd from Adams County, in the place of John R. Lynch, sent to Congress from the Natchez District.

Governor Ames, inaugurated on January 22, 1874, urged economy on the legislature, as well he might since the rate of taxation had gone up to fourteen times what it was under the restoration governments just after the war. The recommendation, however, got small attention from the legislature, as was the way with such recommendations. The mere expense of the legislative sessions themselves was a real burden but it proved impossible to persuade the legislators to abandon the pleasant habit of regular annual sessions with occasional extras, with compensation at seven dollars a day and travel pay at eighty cents a mile going and returning. In the last five years of Reconstruction in Mississippi there were nine sessions of the legislature, lasting a total of more than twenty-four months. In 1874, the assembly was in session from January through April, and then adjourned to meet again in the autumn. In the interim, Governor Ames went north for the summer and Lieutenant-Governor Davis took over the actual governing of the state, to display great activity in the granting of pardons and to add to the confusion by firing out the Ames appointees in non-elective state offices.

One of the duties of the new legislature was to elect a successor to Governor Ames as senator. The honor was conferred on Blanche K. Bruce, a Negro carpetbagger of ability, who came to Mississippi in 1869. He was elected sergeant-at-arms of the state Senate through Alcorn's influence, appointed assessor of Bolivar County by Alcorn, and elected sheriff and tax collector of the same county in 1871. Shrewdly refusing to allow himself to be sidetracked by the nomination for lieutenant-governor, he was elected as the second, and the last, of his race to sit in the United States Senate. Senator Bruce's election was not for a short term as Senator Revel's had been, but for the long term running to March 4, 1881. When he presented himself to take his seat, his angry colleague, Alcorn, declined to escort him to the desk to be sworn in. The service was performed by Senator Roscoe Conkling of New York, to be remembered by Senator Bruce in naming his first son Roscoe Conkling.

Early in his new term, Governor Ames removed Hiram Revels, first Negro to sit in the Senate, from his post as head of the state college for Negroes, because of his support of Alcorn in the election. The legislature expressed its further displeasure by cutting the annual appropriation for the institution from fifty thousand dollars to fifteen thousand dollars. As a result, the school, which was making a promising start under the wise leadership of President Revels, largely went to pieces.

Texas also held an election for Governor in the off-year of 1873, on the first Tuesday in December, but with results totally different from those in Mississippi. Judge Richard Coke, the Democratic nominee, received 85,549 votes to 42,663 for Governor Davis. Before the election the Governor had appealed to Washington for aid, without avail, predicting what would come to pass without it. After the election, he appealed to the courts, through the somewhat transparent device of a habeas corpus proceeding for the release of one Joseph Rodriguez, arrested on charges of fraudulent voting in Houston. The case, brought before the state Supreme Court in Austin, was based on the allegation that the whole election was illegal and invalid because the legislature had provided that polls should be opened at various places in each county and should remain open but one day, instead of the four days allowed when elections were held at but one place in the county, the county seat.

The Supreme Court sustained Governor Davis, released Rodriguez and declared the whole election void. Governor Davis proclaimed that he would hold his office until April 28, 1874, that being four years from his inauguration, but the Democratic legislature went right ahead with plans to inaugurate their new Governor.

Times were tense in Austin in mid-January, 1874. The Democratic legislative leaders met on the twelfth. On the same day, the Governor determined to seize the capitol with his militia, mostly Negroes, and to hold it with his own force, not having been able to persuade President Grant to support him as he had supported Governor Kellogg the year before. Both sides made a determined dash for the capitol, ending in the legislative leaders holding the upper floor, the Governor's militia holding the lower. A small spark, in such a situation, might well have precipitated a most serious explosion.

Fortunately, the spark did not come. The legislature met on the thirteenth, and called on the Secretary of State for the election returns so that they might be canvassed and the result declared. The Secretary of State, at first, refused to deliver the returns. On the fifteenth, however, he turned them over to the legislature, which promptly canvassed them, declared Judge Coke elected governor, and proceeded to inaugurate him that day. The Travis Rifles, a company of white militia ordered out by Governor Davis that day, supported the new Governor instead. Once more, on the sixteenth, Governor Davis appealed to President Grant for support in retaining his office; once more, the President refused—whereupon, on January 17, 1874, Governor Davis gave up the struggle and surrendered his office. Reconstruction in Texas was at an end.

Governor Davis, a man of personal probity, represented the Reconstruction spirit in its better manifestations. He tried zealously, according to his narrow lights, to make Reconstruction work and to give Texas good government. His failure lay in the spirit of vindictive proscription in which he approached the task, a spirit which bred hatreds where the need of the state was peace. Largely because of his personal honesty, good intentions, and courage, however, Texas was spared some of the more flagrant abuses of Reconstruction which afflicted other states in the South—even though the twelfth legislature, which came into office with him, did not often heed his admonitions toward economy and good government.

That, in fact, was a not uncommon relation between Reconstruction legislatures and their governors, whether "carpetbagger" or "scalawag." The divided responsibility and comparative obscurity of the legislator seems to have encouraged governmental extravagance and to have promoted rascality, which few Reconstruction governors were in position to halt or even check.

The Kellogg legislature, in Louisiana, was in its second session in the early months of 1874, with the Governor giving forth futile, almost pathetic, admonitions to economy and good government, and the corrupt legislature running over him whenever it desired to do so. The bankrupt condition of the state, and the excessive rate of its taxation, Governor Kellogg laid to the malfeasance of his predecessor, Warmoth. He charged that in the last year of the Warmoth administration more taxes had remained delinquent than had been collected; and that when he took over the government more than two and one-quarter million dollars of unpaid warrants were floating about, with a total state debt of fifty-three million dollars, from which, he declared, thirty million five hundred thousand dollars in unauthorized state guarantees should be deducted. The remedy which he recommended, in line with the recommendation of his fellow Governor Moses in South Carolina, was a virtual repudiation of the overwhelming debt.

While Governor Kellogg wrestled with his hopeless problems of debt in a state where his administration was recognized most grudgingly, if at all, his predecessor, Acting Governor Pinchback, was struggling for his seat in the Senate of the United States. Senator Oliver P. Morton of Indiana, who led the fight for him, planned to bring the matter to a vote on January 20, 1874, after a month of desultory debate, and to put all his great force behind the motion, which carried with it the inference of recognition of the Kellogg government.

On the day before, E. E. Norton, originally of New York, who had gone to New Orleans as a commissary officer and remained there as Judge Durell's assignee in bankruptcy, called on Governor Warmoth who was in Washington to oppose the seating of the Kellogg claimants. With Warmoth was George A. Sheridan, claiming a seat in the House of Representatives as congressman-at-large on the McEnery ticket. To them, Norton unfolded with great particularity the story of how he had procured the issuance of the midnight order by Judge Durell, upon the promise of the Kellogg seat in the Senate; how Pinchback developed such strength before the caucus that he and Kellogg had interviewed him, and Norton had bought him off with ten thousand dollars reimbursement for the expenses of his race; how Pinchback had accepted the ten thousand dollars but had taken the Senate seat also; and how it was only after much delay and with great difficulty that the disappointed Norton had managed to retrieve his money.

Sheridan, originally from Indiana, where he had been a political supporter of Senator Morton, went to the Senator, told him the story, and suggested to him that he verify it by asking the vain Pinchback to tell him all about how he had "defeated that fellow Norton for his nomination to the Senate." Pinchback, glad to display his superior cleverness to his great political patron, unbosomed himself in the Senate cloakroom on the morning of the twentieth. There came a time later when party considerations enabled Senator Morton to overcome his repugnance against seating one so nominated, but on that day, at the hour appointed for his motion to seat the Louisiana claimant, he moved instead that the matter be referred back to his Committee on Privileges and Elections.

Never again was Pinchback so close to being seated in the Senate, although his claim dragged along through April, when it went over to December; and then after another legislature had again elected him on January 13, 1875, and Governor Kellogg had given him another certificate, it dragged all through the year 1875 and until March 8, 1876, when he was finally rejected—one of the few reliably Radical claimants to meet that fate in a Congress of Reconstruction days. During the three years that his claim was before the Senate, he remained much of the time in Washington, where his handsome "Spanish" appearance caused him to be mistaken, occasionally, for an attaché of the Emperor Dom Pedro's Brazilian mission.

His claim for a seat in the Senate was not his only business in Washington during this time however. He sought a seat in the House of

Representatives also, claiming election as congressman-at-large on the Kellogg ticket. The House seated the other three Kellogg claimants in December, 1873, with small ado, and no doubt would have seated Pinchback also, had he not requested that action be deferred until he found whether he was to be accepted as a member of the Senate. The matter came before the House again, in June, 1874, when both Pinchback and his opponent, Sheridan, were allowed the unusual privilege of stating their own cases on the floor of the House. This feature of the debate was enlivened by Pinchback's account of his devotion to the Republican party, "from the first day when you clothed me with the right to vote," as particularly evidenced by his race against Warmoth from New York to New Orleans, two years before.

"There was but one way on earth" to save the Republican party in Louisiana at that time, he said, "and that was for me to take my life in my hands and start for New Orleans, and if I got there before Governor Warmoth, I could save it. . . . I knew the dangers I should encounter but was brave enough to risk it. . . ." The House, however, not being persuaded, followed the recommendation of the majority of its committee, that there had been no valid election.

The "Louisiana question," however, was little more than an incident in the long and dismal first session of the Forty-third Congress, which began in December, 1873, as panic hung over the land. Congress spent much of its time debating measures of relief—inflation of the currency through the issue of more greenback dollars being a favorite topic—and in explaining or defending its members and their political associates from the gathering clouds of suspicion and scandal which played so large a part in the closing years of the Grant administration. The "back-salary grab," whereby, in the exuberant spring days of 1873 before the panic came, the Forty-second Congress voted themselves five thousand dollars additional back pay for services already performed, had to be repealed in a storm of public indignation.

But in the long, dreary session there was one high note of reconciliation and "oblivion of past differences." It involved two men, Sumner of Massachusetts and Lamar of Mississippi, alike in qualities of wide scholarship, inflexible integrity, and devotion to a cause. Senator Sumner, long since out-distanced in Radicalism by men more practical in their politics and less scrupulous, died on March 11, 1874, almost a man without a party. At the opening of the last session of the Forty-second Congress in December, 1872, he had introduced a bill for "national unity and good will," prescribing that "the names of battles with fellow-citizens shall not be continued in the Army

Register, or placed on the regimental colors of the United States."
The immediate effect of the bill was to stir a storm among the "professional" ex-soldiers of the North, and furnish a convenient text to
orators of the school of the "bloody shirt." The legislature of Sumner's own state resolved that it was "an insult to the loyal soldiery of
the nation." Hurt by the storm of abuse, but abating nothing of his
faith, the Massachusetts Senator tried, through the last year of his
life, to secure enactment of his battle-flags bill, and of his supplemental civil rights bill—the same which, more than once, he had
tried to attach as a rider to acts of general amnesty.

One week before his death, he received from the legislature of
Massachusetts a record of the rescinding of the resolution of condemnation for the battle-flags bill. He died, calling on his friends
to "take care of the civil rights bill—my bill, the civil rights bill—
don't let it fail." And that, as a sort of memorial to the man, was done,
although the resulting act was found by the Supreme Court to be
beyond the power of the Congress of the United States, under the
Fourteenth and Fifteenth Amendments, in its purpose of detailed
regulation of affairs within the states.

But there was a more lasting memorial to Charles Sumner, a memorial in words, in a eulogy by the new Representative from Mississippi in the lower house of Congress, L. Q. C. Lamar. Lamar's eulogy
to Sumner struck far beyond and above the ordinary amenities of a
congressional memorial for a departed member. Speaking of Sumner's
battle-flags bill, he declared that while he and other Southerners cherished the recollections of sacrifices endured and battles fought, and
respected the prowess and devotion of the men of the North:

"They do not ask, they do not wish the North to strike the mementoes
of her heroism and victory from either records or monuments or battle
flags. They would rather that both sections should gather up the
glories won by each section; not envious, but proud of each other, and
regard them as a common heritage of American valor.

"Let us hope that future generations, when they remember the deeds
of devotion done on both sides, will speak not of Northern prowess
and Southern courage, but of the heroism, fortitude and courage of
Americans in a war of ideas; a war in which each section signalized its
consecration to the principles, as each understood them, of American
liberty and of the constitution received from their fathers. . . .

"It was certainly a gracious act toward the South—though unhappily it
jarred upon the sensibilities of the people at the other extreme of the

Union and estranged from him the great body of his political friends—
to propose to erase from the banners of the national Army the mementoes of the bloody internecine struggle, which might be regarded
as assailing the pride or wounding the sensibilities of the Southern people. That proposal will never be forgotten by that people as long as
the name of Charles Sumner lives in the memory of man. . . .

"Charles Sumner in life believed that all occasion for strife and distrust
between the North and South had passed away, and there no longer
remained any cause for continued estrangement between these two
sections of our common country. Are there not many of us who
believe the same thing? Is not that the common sentiment, or if it is
not ought it not to be, of the great mass of our people, North and
South? Bound to each other by a common constitution, destined to
live together under a common government. . . . Shall we not now at
last endeavor to grow *toward* each other once more in heart, as we are
already indissolubly linked to each other in fortunes? Shall we not . . .
lay aside the concealments which serve only to perpetuate misunderstandings and distrust, and frankly confess that on both sides we most
earnestly desire to be one. . . ."

The South, he continued, "accepts the bitter award of the bloody
arbitrament without reservation . . . yet, as if struck dumb by the
magnitude of her reverses, she suffers on in silence." The North, he
was assured, cherished "a heart full of magnanimous emotions toward
her disarmed and discomfited antagonist; and yet, as if mastered by
some mysterious spell, silencing her better impulses, her words and
acts are the words and acts of suspicion and distrust."

"Would that the spirit of the illustrious dead whom we lament today
could speak from the grave to both parties to this deplorable discord
in tones which should reach each and every heart throughout this
broad territory: 'My countrymen! *know* one another, and you will *love*
one another.'"

To utter such a eulogy upon such an occasion and at such a time,
required a courage on the part of Lamar equal to that of Sumner in
introducing his battle-flags bill thirty years ahead of its time. He was
attacked in the South by Bourbons and fire-eaters but the wiser elements, North and South, recognized in him and his speech those
qualities which were to make of Lamar such a power for genuine Reconstruction, in a career which took him into the Senate, into the
Cabinet, and finally to a seat upon the bench of the Supreme Court.

Different as they were in many ways, both Sumner and Lamar were exceptional men, with the breadth to fight for a cause without personal hatred of their opponents.

Even as Lamar spoke in Washington, and was acclaimed for his speaking, actual and literal war was on foot between the scrambled factions in Arkansas, struggling with force of arms for possession of the government of that state.

On April 15, 1874, the ouster suit of *Joseph Brooks v. Elisha Baxter*, came to life. It had slept quietly in the circuit court of Pulaski County at Little Rock ever since Governor Baxter, ten months before, had filed his demurrer to Brooks's bill claiming the Governorship until Judge John Whytock, without notice to the Governor and in the absence of his counsel, overruled his demurrer; sustained the bill, and declared Brooks elected and entitled to the office of governor.

Mr. Brooks, waiting conveniently with a small party, procured a record of the court's order; presented himself at once before the waiting Chief Justice McClure and was sworn in; proceeded immediately to the capitol of the state and ousted Baxter; took possession of the office and proclaimed himself governor of Arkansas.

So began the Brooks-Baxter war, sixteen months after Baxter had been inaugurated and recognized as governor by the administration at Washington. Those months had been, on the whole, peaceable and undisturbed, but the Governor had shown a strong leaning toward accommodation with the Democrats, and an inclination to agree with them that there should be a new constitution for the state. Because of his election as the nominee of the "regular" Republican party, such a disposition was peculiarly disconcerting. When it became apparent that those who nominated the Governor had ceased to direct his course, the moribund Brooks claims were recalled and revived. The official Republican attitude thereafter was that the Democrats and "brindletails" were right in 1872 when they claimed that Brooks had received a majority of the votes, and that, therefore, he should be seated as governor. The official Democratic attitude was to admit that while Brooks might have received a majority, Baxter had been seated and in undisturbed possession of the office for sixteen months, had been recognized by the United States government, and should not now be turned out.

While both sides made appeals to Caesar at Washington, and appeals to the people at home, they relied more immediately upon their military strength at Little Rock. Brooks, through his adjutant general, seized the state armory, and began to fortify the capitol and its grounds. Baxter, driven from the capitol, in a pouring rain, went to the St. Johns Military College for protection. President Gray, who had been a Confederate cavalry captain, organized a guard for the Governor among the older cadets who volunteered for the service. Later Governor Baxter established his headquarters near by at the Anthony House, and organized his forces. With the exception of J. M. Johnson, the secretary of state, the state officers elected on the Baxter ticket recognized Brooks as governor, as did the justices of the Supreme Court of the state, and the entire Arkansas delegation at Washington, except Representative W. W. Wilshire.

The President and the Attorney General moved cautiously in the matter, at first merely instructing Colonel T. E. Rose, in command of United States troops at Little Rock, to interpose his force between the hostile armed camps, so as to forestall the bloodshed which would follow an attempt by the Baxter forces to regain the capitol by armed attack. And there the matter stood at Little Rock for a month with both sides strengthening their earthworks and other defenses, adding to their arms from every possible source, public and private, and reinforcing their armies—but with the United States regulars between them to keep the peace. Outside Little Rock, where there was no such fortunate presence, clashes between armed parties in the Brooks-Baxter war took perhaps two hundred lives, in all.

Originally, when the line-up was reversed, the Supreme Court of the state had held that the question of the Governorship was not within the jurisdiction of the courts but of the legislature. Baxter, therefore, proposed a special session of the legislature to settle the question, and agreed to abide by its decision—just as Brooks agreed to abide by the determination of the courts. President Grant's position was that the United States government favored a peaceable settlement, whether by the courts, the legislature or otherwise, and would give all the protection which it was constitutionally authorized to do to those engaged in such an effort.

Governor Baxter thereupon called a session of the legislature, to convene on May 11, while the Brooks faction rapidly ran a case through the courts, and secured a decision of the Supreme Court, on May 7, that Brooks was the regularly elected governor of Arkansas. As the legislators were gathering, the partisans of both sides in Arkansas and in Washington worked away at some sort of a compromise adjustment. Attorney General Williams and President Grant suggested one, which neither side accepted in full. Brooks was less than tactful in the manner of his rejection, while Baxter's friends in Washington, among them the author and orator, General Albert Pike, were able to persuade the President and his advisers that the Brooks movement was using the courts of Arkansas for purely partisan ends.

On May 13, the legislature secured a "Baxter" quorum in both houses, and called on the President for help in restoring rightful government in Arkansas. On the following day, Brooks sent the President a long and scolding demand for support. On the fifteenth, Attorney General Williams ruled that the decision of Judge Whytock in the circuit court at Little Rock was void, and recommended that the President act immediately. That afternoon, just a month after the Brooks-Baxter war broke out, the President's proclamation recognizing and sustaining Baxter as governor, and commanding the dispersal of all armed resistance to his authority, was received in Little Rock—and the war was over. The two former Confederate generals who, by that time, were in command of the opposing forces got together at once, and by the following day troops of both sides were being transported home by the state. Another day, and Baxter was back in his office at the capitol. Still another day, and on May 18 the legislature passed an act calling an election to be held June 30 to decide whether the state should have a new constitutional convention, and to choose delegates to the convention should one be held. The date for the convention, if approved, was set for July 14, and machinery for holding the election, under a State Board of Supervisors elected by the legislature, was provided.

The Democratic-Conservative party, as they styled themselves, canvassed the state in thorough style through June, and on the last day of the month carried the proposition of holding a convention by a vote of fifteen to one, and elected seventy of the ninety-one delegates who were to make up the body. There were but four Negro members of the convention, and few carpetbaggers. The convention went to work promptly, completed its deliberations in six weeks, and submitted a new constitution to the state at a special election to be held on October 13. The principal changes in the constitution had to do with elections, taxation, centralization of executive power and restriction of the public debt.

While the constitutional convention was in session, the select committee appointed by the national House of Representatives "to inquire into the disturbed conditions of governmental affairs in the state of Arkansas" came to Little Rock. The committee, with Representative Luke Poland of Vermont as chairman, began its hearings in Washington, near the last of May, first hearing witnesses supporting the claims of Brooks. There was some disposition among Democratic hotheads in Arkansas to flout the committee as a partisan investigation but wiser counsel determined the Democratic-Conservative party to treat the committee with the utmost consideration. Upon the urgent and cordial invitation of Governor Baxter and his supporters, a sub-committee visited Arkansas, conducted hearings, and made first-hand investigations which extended, with interruptions, until mid-November, when the committee's activities were transferred back to Washington.

New state officers were to be chosen also at the special election on October 13 to pass on the new constitution. The Democratic-Conservatives offered their nomination for the office of governor to Elisha Baxter. When he declined, it was tendered, by unanimous vote, to Augustus H. Garland, onetime senator of the Confederate States of America, and now the wise and conservative leader of the Democrats of the state, who accepted. Among the Republicans who endorsed the nomination was the staunch old Unionist restoration governor, Isaac Murphy.

The "regular" Republican organization, however, at a conference at Hot Springs, participated in by Senator Morton, the leader of the Radicals in Congress, took the position that all that had been done by Elisha Baxter, or in his name, since the decision of Judge Whytock in April was null and void, and decided that they would make no nominations and take no part in the election in October. Under such circumstances, of course, the constitution was ratified and the Garland ticket elected by overwhelming majorities.

Victory in such an election, however, did not mean the unopposed acceptance of the Garland government in Arkansas, or its unequivocal recognition in Washington. The Republican secretary of state, Johnson, declined to issue commissions to those claiming election on October 13 but the board designated by the legislature to hold the election certified the result. Two weeks later, on November 13, Governor Garland and those elected with him quietly took over the government of Arkansas, under the terms of the new constitution which shortened the four-year term for which Baxter had been elected.

Governor Baxter cheerfully yielded, but local opposition was not entirely dead. Volney Voltaire Smith, lieutenant-governor under Baxter, attempted to keep up the fight. He had sided with Brooks in the "war," but had returned to his Baxter allegiance after the President's proclamation. He had presided over the Senate at the special session called by Baxter, had signed the bill calling a constitutional convention, sat in the convention as a member, and participated in the October election. Suddenly, however, he came to the conclusion that all these proceedings were null and void, and that the voluntary retirement of Baxter as governor transferred the office not to the newly-elected Garland, but to himself as Baxter's lieutenant-governor. Whereupon he issued a proclamation claiming the Governorship; procured an opinion from Attorney General Yonley of the state, supporting his pretensions; set up the skeleton of a government in Arkansas; and posted off to Washington to secure the Federal recognition to which, as a Republican, he felt himself entitled.

There the aspiring Smith found that the Brooks adherents were still pressing his claims, based on the 1872 election; that the Poland !committee had not yet made its report on the state of affairs in Arkansas; and that pending the report the President was not disposed to act. The Smith "government" quietly collapsed, for lack of recognition abroad or support at home and the Brooks "government" pinned all its hopes on Federal recognition, while the Garland government went quietly and strongly ahead, to the great benefit of the peace and quiet of Arkansas. And that, in the then condition of the state, was of paramount importance. "The sentiments of the people of Arkansas," according to a telegram sent to the President by a citizen made desperate by the prospect of the ruin of the year's crops because of the Brooks-Baxter war, could be compressed into the sentence: "We do not care who is governor. All we want is peace."

CHAPTER XLVII

The Landslide of 1874

BEFORE peace descended upon the Arkansas front, a new war was under way in harried Louisiana, where the summer of 1874 saw the organization of White Leagues—Ku Klux without the disguise and secrecy charged the Radicals; peaceable bodies formed for self-preservation and protection against "Republican Alliances" being organized among the Negroes, declared the Democrats.

In some parishes, the White Leagues were hardly more than another name for the Democratic party. Elsewhere, notably in New Orleans, they were organized, drilled and militant bodies. The Crescent City White League, headed by Frederick N. Ogden, numbered three thousand members before the end of the summer; the Leagues throughout the state, about fourteen thousand.

Everywhere in the state, the sense of outrage at the Kellogg "usurpation" persisted, and the 1874 session of the Kellogg legislature did nothing to allay it. The session was merely another act in what Edward King described as "a legislative farce . . . enacted for six weary years." It did little or nothing to improve the conditions of Louisiana or the reputation of its legislative bodies. Property values in New Orleans were down to one-third the level of 1868. The sheriff, with an income of sixty thousand dollars a year, was "the prosperous man in New Orleans," according to Mr. King, who added that it was no wonder there were White Leagues in Louisiana.

The state of mind which produced them may be glimpsed in the pages of the diary of David French Boyd, struggling to keep his state university alive, without supplies, money or credit, with a faculty down to two members besides himself, all three unpaid, and with a student body which averaged that year six cadets. The school, he wrote, had been brought "through 'Reconstruction,' and now we have the 'Usurpation.' To take it through Hell could not be much more. . . . If I thought the next eight years would be like the last, I would rather die now."

Editors of Northern newspapers, even friendly editors, were overwhelming in their criticism of the White League movement as unwise, if not positively wicked, but the evidence of the Leaguers themselves is that the movement was a spontaneous outgrowth of a deep popular sense of wrong. The White League, in its platform, recited the failure of efforts to enlist the political co-operation of the Negroes, declared that the Negroes "with scarcely an exception invariably voted like a body of soldiers obeying a word of command" from leaders known to be "unworthy and dishonest," and asserted that "a league of the whites is the inevitable result of that formidable, oath-bound and blindly obedient league of the blacks." The White League leaders were determined that there was to be no more "Fusion" on the pattern of 1872.

To add to the bitterness of the campaign, Governor Kellogg brought forth from his desk and signed, on July 29, a new Election Bill, passed by the legislature in January and held since without action, under the peculiar practice permitted by the Louisiana constitution. The new bill, declared the outraged Democrats, still further concentrated in the hands of the governor the machinery of holding, returning and canvassing elections.

No governor was to be elected in 1874 but representatives in Congress, members of the lower house of the state legislature, and a state treasurer were to be chosen. At a noisy four-day convention, beginning on August 5, the Republicans made their nominations. The Democrats, as a concession to the country members of the party, transferred their convention from New Orleans to the old capital at Baton Rouge. There, on August 24, the Democrats convened as

"the white people of Louisiana, embracing the Democratic Party, the Conservative Party, the White Man's Party, the Liberal Party, the Reform Party, and all others opposed to the Kellogg usurpation. . . ."

This vehement insistence on the color line was abandoned, however, before the campaign was a week old, in making nominations for local offices in the parishes.

The campaign went forward with less of widespread and general violence than might have been expected, considering the temper and tension of the times. The most atrocious instance of violence was the massacre at Coushatta in Red River Parish on August 28. After a pitched fight around the courthouse, peace was restored by the surrender of six white Republican officeholders, who received assurance of safe conduct upon their agreement to resign and leave the county. On the next day, as they were being carried to Shreveport, bound and under guard, they were set upon by an armed band and murdered in cold blood—murdered, said the New Orleans *Republican*, "for the crime of Northern birth and Republican principles."

The crime brought a proclamation of martial law in the parish, the offer of heavy rewards for the arrest and conviction of the guilty, which were never claimed, and an outburst of indignation all over the country. Less than three weeks later, however, the Coushatta murders were to be eclipsed in interest, locally and nationally, by events in New Orleans.

On September 12, reports ran through the city that the Kellogg government would act to prevent the steamer *Mississippi* from landing a shipment of arms—"arms," in this sense, being rifles, presumably intended for the organized White Leagues, and not the pocket pistols which formed so common a part of the personal equipment of the male Louisianian of the period.

On Monday, September 14, business houses in New Orleans remained closed, and the general run of people stayed indoors. At the Clay statue on Canal Street, three thousand determined men gathered at eleven in the morning in response to the call of posters and bulletins in the Sunday newspapers. Ranged about the little iron-railed enclosure in which the statue stood, they adopted resolutions demanding that Governor Kellogg abdicate, and sent a committee to the old Saint Louis Hotel, at that time used as a state house, to present and press the demand.

The committee failed to see Governor Kellogg. He had left the state house for the protection of the United States government within the massive granite walls of the Custom House, to which the demand of the mass meeting was forwarded. From this "House of Refuge," as it was dubbed by derisive Democrats, came back the Governor's refusal to abdicate, and his proclamation ordering the crowd to disperse.

Back at the statue of Clay, the assembled citizens heard Governor Kellogg's proclamation read with a howl of indignation, and listened with a roar of approval to the reading of another proclamation, issued by D. B. Penn, the ex-Confederate who claimed election as lieutenant-governor on the McEnery ticket. Colonel Penn, proclaimed himself acting governor, in the absence of McEnery, denounced the usurpations and misgovernment of the Kellogg regime, and called out the "militia of the state . . . for the purpose of driving the usurpers from power." To organize and command this effort, General Order No. 1 named Frederick N. Ogden, the White League leader, as provisional general of the militia.

Through the early afternoon hours, the rival forces pushed their preparations for the inevitable fight. Most of the Kellogg officials gathered at the Custom House, under the protection of a body of Kellogg militia commanded by General James Longstreet, the same who once had commanded the mighty First Corps of the Army of Northern Virginia. A few officials remained at the Saint Louis Hotel, under the protection of some two hundred of Captain Badger's New Orleans metropolitan police. Above Canal Street, the Penn militia were busy throwing up street barricades, in true Parisian style, using the Belgian granite paving blocks which came to New Orleans as ship ballast, lumber, boxes, carts, baled hay, even a few overturned horse-cars.

While preparations for battle went on leaders of both sides were telegraphing varying versions of the events of the day to President Grant. The Kellogg government called for succor, the Penn government asked only that the United States keep its hands off. The difference in requests was significant of their relative strength in New Orleans that day.

The battle did not begin until after four o'clock in the afternoon, when the Kellogg militia, made up for the most part of the metropolitan police of New Orleans, marched out from the Custom House, with their artillery, crossed Canal Street, and started up the levee toward the Poydras Street barricades. As the "metropolitans" advanced, they were taken in flank by two companies of the White League militia, advancing down the levee under protection of piled bales of hay, and attacked in front by the Penn forces along Poydras Street. The fight lasted hardly more than ten minutes, before the Kellogg militia broke and ran, demoralized, for the shelter of the Custom House, leaving their artillery in the hands of the enemy. In the fight, the Longstreet command lost forty-four killed, the Ogden forces, twelve killed.

Before dark the city was quietly in the hands of the Penn forces, except for the Custom House, the Saint Louis Hotel, the state armory and one police station. Before nine o'clock on the morning of the fifteenth all of these, except the Custom House held by United States troops, capitulated to the new government. By eleven o'clock barricades were cleared away, stores reopened, and business resumed. That afternoon, Penn was formally inaugurated as governor, others on the McEnery ticket were installed in office, and the government claiming election in 1872 was set up. At three o'clock, after a parade and a review, the Penn troops were dismissed by General Ogden. Order was restored in New Orleans.

"So ends the Kellogg regime," exulted the New Orleans *Picayune*, prematurely. "Big, inflated, insolent and overbearing, it collapsed at one touch of honest indignation and gallant onslaught." In the vivid phrase of H. V. Redfield, "the Kellogg government fell over one morning when a few armed men leaned against it." But, as Mr. Redfield added, "the general government set it up again"—and set it up promptly. On September 15, the day on which the McEnery-Penn government took control of New Orleans and of most of the parishes of the state as well, the President issued his proclamation again sustaining Kellogg and again ordering the dispersal of "the turbulent and disorderly persons combined together with force and arms to overthrow the government of Louisiana."

Two days later, on September 17, United States troops made the proclamation fully effective, when General Emory made formal demand for the surrender of the arsenal, state house and other state buildings. Governor McEnery, who had arrived in New Orleans, yielded to the demand backed up by the threat of the force of the army, because he had "neither the power nor the inclination to resist the government of the United States." Governor Kellogg came forth from the "House of Refuge" to resume his duties after another two days, and so far as New Orleans was concerned the September rebellion was over.

The rebellion, and the second setting-up of the Kellogg government by the President, at once became issues in the national campaign of 1874 for the election of a new national House of Representatives. By some in the North, the President was praised for his prompt and decisive action; by more, he was blamed for his usurpation in the affairs of a state, and for his persistence in support of a system of government which, as was coming to be more and more generally realized, had failed.

Less arresting than affairs in Louisiana, but perhaps even more effective in bringing about the realization of the incapacity of Reconstruction government in the South, was the campaign in South Carolina in the autumn of 1874, as the administration of Governor Moses wore toward its end. The fight there was not between Radical and Conservative, Republican and Democrat, but between factions of the Republican party, still so safely dominant that it could afford to split. The split, however, and the revelations from Republican sources of rascalities in South Carolina, added much to the disrepute of the whole Reconstruction regime in the minds of the more independent voters of the North.

Meeting in July, the executive committee of the party in South Carolina resolved that the time was at hand to "retrace our steps and vindicate the integrity of Republicanism." The "reformers" within the party not only controlled the executive committee but the state convention, which, after a stormy five-day session in September nominated as the candidate for governor the attorney-general of the state, Daniel H. Chamberlain—the same who had declared:

"I am a Republican by habit, by conviction, by association, but my republicanism is not, I trust, composed solely of equal parts of ignorance and rapacity."

As his running mate, for lieutenant-governor, the convention named R. H. Gleaves, the Negro from Pennsylvania who held the same place in the Moses administration.

On October 2, the "independent Republicans" held another nominating convention and put forward as their candidates the men whom Chamberlain and Gleaves had defeated in the "regular" convention—for governor, Judge John T. Green, native white Republican; for lieutenant-governor, Major Martin R. Delaney, one of the most remarkable colored men of the state. This ticket was endorsed, six days later, by a convention of "citizens in favor of honest and good government," called by General James Chesnut, chairman of the state Union of Taxpayers' Leagues.

Both factions made much of the issues of economy and reform, as well they might in South Carolina, where, as Mr. Chamberlain pointed out, the mere expense of holding legislative sessions had averaged three hundred twenty thousand dollars a year for the past six years, and reached a peak of six hundred seventeen thousand dollars in one flush session—as compared with an average of twenty thousand dollars per session before Reconstruction. From their inside positions both sides were able to make charges and countercharges about affairs during the administrations of Governor Moses and Governor Scott. From responsibility for these charges, Samuel J. Lee, the exceptionally able Negro who was speaker of the House of Representatives, felt moved to clear his own people. "We, as a people, are blameless of misgovernment," he said. "Bad men, adventurers . . . men we have elevated and made rich, now speak of our corruption and venality, and charge us with every conceivable crime."

After a campaign in which each of the diverse elements which went to make up the whole of the Reconstruction government sought to cast upon the others the blame for the admittedly wretched state of affairs in South Carolina, the "regular" Republican ticket, headed by Chamberlain, won by a vote of 80,403 to 68,818—the largest vote yet cast and the closest race yet run during Reconstruction.

But the "Southern question," and the Reconstruction policy of the Grant administration, were but one wave in the tide of resentment running against the Republicans in 1874. The party could not escape blame for the effects of the great Panic of 1873, just coming to its worst in many particulars in the campaign and election months of 1874. There were other and special causes of opposition to the party in power, also, arising out of the actual administration of the government. Civil service reformers resented the breakdown of the none-too-vigorous efforts at replacing the system of political patronage with merit appointments. Widespread frauds in the collection of the internal revenue, particularly the excise on spirits, came to light in the spring of 1874. So seriously compromised was Secretary of the Treasury Richardson that he resigned his post, to accept a judicial appointment at the hands of the President, then as always stubbornly loyal to those to whom he had given his friendship.

Early in the year, in February, the Freedmen's Savings Bank and Trust Company collapsed, with grievous loss to the great number of small depositors whose toilsome savings, to the amount of more than three million dollars, were on deposit in its thirty-four branches. The "Freedmen's Bank" was not an agency of the government but a separately chartered private institution. Public figures had been kept prominently to the front in its promotion and management, however, and it was identified in the popular mind with the government. Its failure added to the gathering load to be carried in the campaign by the administration.

Particularly was this true when it developed that an important element in the failure of the bank was the use of its funds in helping to finance the government of the District of Columbia in grandiose plans for the improvement of Washington. The ultimate value to the capital city of the plans carried out under the driving direction of A. R. Shepherd, first a member of the Board of Public Works of the District and then governor, was great. The committee of Congress which investigated the various charges in connection with them reported in June, however, that developments had been undertaken and carried out in such a way as to enrich a ring of real-estate speculators, associated with the District government; and that they had been accompanied by extravagance, corruption and a disregard of the rights of citizens, property owners and taxpayers.

The report of this committee of a Republican House of Representatives, composed of members of both parties, was unanimous in conclusions and in the recommendation that the territorial government of the District of Columbia be abolished. A feature of this government was Negro suffrage, voted by Congress only seven years before as a demonstration of political justice to the freedmen and an object lesson to the states. The mass of Negro voters in Washington, most of whom were not direct taxpayers, supported with enthusiasm the Shepherd government in its lavish use of tax-collected funds for public improvements. Congress, being unwilling to perpetuate the Shepherd government which it so severely censured, and equally unwilling to touch off the political dynamite of an attempt to deprive the Negroes of Washington of the right to vote, while leaving it to the whites, created a new form of government for the District in which all residents were disfranchised, impartially and alike.

There was so little in the immediate past record to which the Republicans could point with pride, that the managers of the campaign were almost compelled to fall back upon Southern "atrocities" for issues. To dramatize the "atrocity story" to the country, a convention of Southern loyalists was held at Chattanooga on October 13. Efforts to play up the sufferings of this persecuted class were handicapped, however, by such reporting of the convention as that of the *Nation*, which declared that it included "all the more prominent thieves, carpetbaggers and scalawags among southern politicians."

While the convention was no great success, the "atrocity story" remained standard in campaign material. In Indiana friendly newspapers were urged to give prominent space and display "until after election" to "the horrible scenes of violence and bloodshed transpiring throughout the South."

But even the old standard "atrocity story" seemed to have lost some of its political potency by 1874. Perhaps it was because it was beginning to be realized that intimidation was not exclusively a Democratic device in Southern politics. That it was "practiced in the last three years quite as much, and even more rigorously, by the Republicans," was noted by Charles Nordhoff, the intelligent Republican reporter whose book, *The Cotton States*, was published in 1875. Mr. Nordhoff found that intimidation by Federal officers was a peculiarly effective method to keep Negro voters in line, since to them "the lowest Federal officer was a very powerful being, armed with the whole strength of the Federal government." Such officials, often of the kind described as "Republicans by trade," made free use of the potent name of General Grant, and exploited the appearance of the United States troops put at their disposal.

But "the most savage intimidators of all," reported Mr. Nordhoff, were the Negroes themselves. "In their political relations among each other, they are as intolerant and unscrupulous as ignorant men suddenly possessed of political rights are sure to be." Political intimidation took various forms—the threat of re-enslavement for those who did not vote as "General Grant" ordered; the threat of social ostracism, including the dreaded possibility of being left alone in times of bereavement without the friendly comfort of mourners; the threat of religious excommunication or, as one South Carolina Negro testified, being "disbanded from the church"; and even other cruder and more direct deterrents to voting the Conservative or Democratic ticket.

Another handicap to getting full political value out of the "atrocity story" was a growing disposition on the part of Northern readers and hearers to scout generalities and to demand names, dates and places. Charles Hays, scalawag representative in Congress from Alabama, in a letter to his Connecticut colleague, General Joseph R. Hawley, obligingly undertook to furnish such specifications in a long and gory catalogue of assassinations, ambushes, whippings and outrages alleged to have occurred during July and August in certain specified Alabama counties. General Hawley, horrified at the recital, had the letter published. It rapidly became a campaign document of such importance that Senator Morton, among others, used it in his speeches.

But, unfortunately for the effectiveness of the Hays letter, the New York *Tribune* sent a trusted correspondent to Alabama to find out more about the events described. It developed that some of the men whose murders had been described in detail were alive, well and unmolested; that other homicides had not even the remotest connection with politics or race antagonism, but were the result of private quarrels, or of jealousy between husband and wife, or in one case, even, of suicide; and that the wholesale whippings and assaults simply did not occur. The *Tribune* correspondent investigated fourteen of the twenty-two homicides circumstantially catalogued by Mr. Hays; found that two had political implications; and that all the others either did not happen or had not the remotest connection with politics. Not only were the statements untrue, he reported, but "in the majority of cases Mr. Hays knew his statements were lies when he wrote them."

Behind the *Tribune* correspondent came another, from the then staunch Republican organ, the New York *Times*, to support what his colleague of the *Tribune* had written. Daily life was going on quietly in Alabama, he found, with whites and blacks working together peaceably. Even Mr. Hays, six weeks after his libelous letter was published, was allowed to go about the state unmolested, making inflammatory speeches to Republican political meetings.

To Governor Lewis, north Alabama Republican, conditions in the state did not seem to make it necessary to call out troops to keep the peace or protect his party associates. President Grant, however, acting under the provisions of the Election Enforcement Laws, sent in United States troops, whose presence the local Radical politicians used to strengthen their hold upon voters who might be suspected of weakening.

The year 1874 was the year of the supreme effort of the Conservative-Democratic party in Alabama. The issue drawn was one of race. The platform first adopted at Troy, in Pike County, and afterward ratified in county after county, affirmed that "the Republican party of Alabama, for years past, has distinctly made and tendered to the people of this State an open, square issue of race," put forward "at the instance of the thieving crew known as carpetbaggers, and the more contemptible and infamous gang known as scalawags." That "issue of race thus defiantly tendered and forced upon us," the "democrats and conservatives" accepted, and declared for "social ostracism of all those who act, sympathize or side with the negro party."

The organization and management of the campaign was in the capable hands of Captain W. L. Bragg. The Conservative nominee for governor was George S. Houston, the same whom the restoration legislature of the state had sought to send to the United States Senate in 1865. Mr. Houston was a north Alabama man, self-described as "a sort of Union man" during the war. The Republicans again nominated Governor Lewis, with whom they had won in 1874.

The Republicans had the advantage of possession of the election machinery but they had the disadvantage of factional splits, particularly on race lines, with incidental squabbles over patronage and public printing. The state treasury was empty; the administration disintegrating. The Democrats planned a peaceable campaign, to avoid the possibility of Federal interference, but there was about all their plans a deep determination to "break the chains" of "our starved and cursed land," as the Opelika Times described it.

The election in November was quieter than usual in Reconstruction Alabama. There was one considerable riot, at Eufaula, where four Negroes were killed and ten whites wounded. Federal troops on duty there openly sympathized with the whites in the trouble which led up to the fighting. There was probably the usual amount of election fraud, distributed on both sides, but the count of the ballots showed the undisputed election of Houston, by a majority of 107,118 to 93,928, and with him the entire Democratic ticket. In the Senate of the new legislature, the Democrats had twenty votes to thirteen Republicans, including six Negroes; in the House of Representatives, sixty to forty Republicans, including twenty-nine Negroes.

During the following year Alabama adopted a new constitution but the election of 1874, when for the first time since the beginning of military Reconstruction, all branches of the government passed into Democratic hands, marked the real end of Reconstruction in Alabama—except for liquidating the consequences.

The same election of 1874 marked the beginning of the end of the whole Reconstruction policy, as well. The Democrats elected a majority of nearly seventy members in the House of Representatives of the new Forty-fourth Congress, which was to take office on March 4, 1875. The composition of the new state legislatures was such as to insure that the two-thirds majority of the Senate which the Republicans had enjoyed would be broken in the new Congress, also. In the North, the Democrats carried such states as Pennsylvania, Ohio, Indiana, Massachusetts and New York. In the South, the Democrats carried every state except Mississippi, where no elections were held; South Carolina, where there was no Democratic ticket in the field; Florida and Louisiana.

In Florida, despite Republican factional fights, Governor Marcellus L. Stearns, controlling the "regular" organization, was elected to fill out the remainder of the term of Governor Hart, upon whose death the year before Stearns had succeeded to the Governorship. Both new representatives in Congress were Republican, also, although of opposite factional alignment. The state legislature, however, was to be Democratic in both houses, for the first time since Reconstruction began. By how slender a margin that was true, however, was to be demonstrated vividly at the beginning of 1875 when the legislature elected a successor to United States Senator Abijah Gilbert. On the twenty-fifth ballot, coming within one vote of election, Charles M. Jones, a great, gaunt, gangling Democrat, homely of speech and strong in his quick grasp of essentials, rose from his seat and announced:

"In behalf of the 1,500 voters of Escambia County whom I have the honor to represent, I cast my vote for Charles M. Jones."

The vote so cast was the one which, for the first time since 1861, sent a Democrat from Florida to the halls of legislation in Washington. But though the campaign of 1874 in Florida was hard and bitterly fought, and the margins of victory slight in all cases, the results were definite and were accepted.

Not so in unhappy Louisiana, where once more in 1874 there was a disputed election. The campaign was intense, although quieter than might have been expected after the flare-up of the September rebellion, and the reseating of Governor Kellogg by the President. The Governorship was not in issue, the term running to 1876, and the fight centered upon the state legislature. Charles Nordhoff, who was in the state during the campaign, reported that in spite of inflammatory talk "the attitude of the races toward each other is essentially friendly, and only the continuous efforts of white demagogues keep them apart." To judge from the extreme violence of some of the expressions of some of the Conservative newspapers of the time, not all the "white demagogues" were among the Radicals. The responsible management of the Conservative campaign, however, frowned on intemperate expression and provocative action, in an earnest and partially successful effort to have a campaign and election of such a sort that the results could not be overturned on charges of intimidation and violence. Even Chairman Packard, of the State Central Committee of the Republicans, testified afterward that "there were very few instances of parishes" in which intimidation was serious.

The election machinery, state and Federal, was in the hands of the Radicals, to such an extent that the *Nation* expressed the opinion, a week before the election, that the result would depend upon "how much fraud Kellogg believes himself to be in a position to commit." On election night, November 7, the Conservatives began celebration of victory apparent upon the face of the returns—but no victory in a Louisiana Reconstruction election could be counted upon until the Returning Board had done its work.

On November 14, a week after the election, the Returning Board went into session, with former Governor J. Madison Wells as chairman. Representatives of both sides were allowed to appear in open sessions but the real work of the Board was done in its numerous and prolonged secret sessions. Six weeks were required to complete a count which resulted in the announcement by the Returning Board, on the day before Christmas, that the Democrats had elected fifty-three members of the House of Representatives and the Republicans fifty-three, with five doubtful cases referred for decision to the House itself.

The Democratic State Central Committee, meanwhile, had carried out its own canvass, without the official returns in its possession, of course, and on December 23 declared that seventy-one Conservatives and thirty-seven Radicals had been elected to the House.

Louisiana, as the year closed, passed into another period of fevered political incertitude. The Committee of Seventy, leading and substantial citizens, declared to the world that the state was again to be turned over to "another mongrel herd of rapacious plunderers . . . claiming to be Republicans, elected by Radical returning-officers, and installed in the Legislature by the potential force of the Army and Navy of the United States"—a prediction to be borne out, as to the manner of election and installation, at least, and that speedily.

CHAPTER XLVIII

"Declare Them Banditti"

In the tense Christmas season of 1874, with the rival parties announcing their varying versions of the election results, Lieutenant General Philip H. Sheridan came south again. Ostensibly he came as escort to a party of ladies sailing from New Orleans for a Havana holiday; actually, he came armed with secret orders from the President to assume command if, in his judgment, the situation might warrant it.

President Grant, apprehensive of further disturbances in the South, was, as he said in his message to the expiring Forty-third Congress at the opening of its last session, fully determined to enforce Federal laws "with rigor . . . but with regret that they should have added one jot or tittle to Executive duties or powers." To carry out that determination he had chosen his favorite and most trusted military subordinate, the immensely energetic, impetuous, head-long Sheridan.

Although inclined to regard as revolutionary the proceedings in Arkansas which resulted in the transfer of the government of the state from Governor Baxter to Governor Garland, the President refrained from mention of Arkansas affairs in his message to Congress out of deference to the Poland committee, which had not completed its investigation and made its report when Congress convened on December 7.

Neither was Mississippi mentioned specifically, but on the very day on which the message was being read to Congress, Vicksburg's troubles broke out in open riot. With eleven thousand inhabitants in 1874, Vicksburg had seen its municipal debt grow in five years of Reconstruction rule from thirteen thousand dollars to one million four hundred thousand dollars. The city government was sustained politically by appeals, on the color line, to non-taxpaying Negroes, and supported financially by taxpaying whites. When, in the spring of 1874, the local Radicals nominated for mayor a white man under twenty-three indictments, and for aldermen, one illiterate white and seven Negroes of low type, the long-delayed revolt began.

The old white citizens, supported by half a hundred substantial Negro citizens and by such representative Republicans as General

529

C. E. Furlong and George McKee, the carpetbag representative of the district in Congress, undertook to carry the city election, to be held in August. When the campaign grew heated Governor Ames was in the North, but the colored Lieutenant-Governor Davis raised the alarm and called for United States troops. When the President declined to respond to his call, Governor Ames reinforced the request, first from his place of sojourn in the North and later from Jackson, upon his return to Mississippi at the end of July. Once more the President declined to interfere, with the result that in an exciting but peaceable election on August 4, the city government of Vicksburg was turned out of office.

Encouraged by their success, the same group of responsible citizens turned their attention to Warren County, in which Vicksburg is located. Government in the county was in the hands of a group of illiterate, incompetent and corrupt officials of both races, dominated by Peter Crosby, sheriff and tax collector. A grand jury made up of ten Negro citizens and seven whites exercised the immemorial inquisitorial rights of such bodies, investigated the affairs of the county, and returned indictments for various embezzlements and forgeries against the chancery clerk, the circuit clerk and a former clerk, T. W. Cardoza, then state superintendent of education. Charles Nordhoff, at this time, arrived in Jackson to investigate Reconstruction education in Mississippi, armed with a letter of introduction to School Superintendent Cardoza. He found that the head of the school system had gone to Vicksburg, "to look after an indictment." Arriving in Vicksburg, Mr. Nordhoff found that Cardoza was not merely indicted but, "as an indignant Republican told me, 'shingled all over with indictments' for embezzlement and fraud."

Before Cardoza and the other defendants could be brought to trial, they "looked after the indictments" against them with such success that the records essential to conviction disappeared from the courthouse, to be found later under the house of Davenport, the indicted chancery clerk.

Sheriff Crosby, whose official bond was without value as a protection to the county, was to collect one hundred and sixty thousand dollars in taxes during December, at rates which were fourteen times those of 1869. On the second day of the month, taxpayers met at Vicksburg, determined that no taxes would be paid to Crosby, and demanded his resignation and that of other county officials. When Crosby refused to give his resignation, a delegation of five hundred men went to the courthouse and got it. Crosby, however, went to the capitol at Jackson, enlisted the aid of Governor Ames, decided to treat his resignation as null and void, and returned to Vicksburg, backed by the Adjutant General of the state, whom the Governor sent with him. The Governor likewise instructed the local colored militia organization in Vicksburg to support the movement to return Crosby to office but did not call on the white militia, commanded by ex-Union officers. As he afterward explained, he knew they would not obey the call.

On Sunday, December 6, couriers rode through the county with handbills, calling the country Negroes to Vicksburg on Monday morning to see that Sheriff Crosby was allowed to exercise the right of his office at the opening of court week. The call was broadcast from the pulpits of the country churches, and the march on Vicksburg began. By noon Monday, the mayor had put the city in a state of defense, closed all the saloons as a safeguard, and sent parties out to meet the Negroes advancing to protect Crosby in his "rights." There were parleys on the roads leading into the city, the usual party or parties unknown began to shoot, with the usual result—fighting and riots, with the death of two whites and more than a score of Negroes. Crosby, whose tenacious desire to continue to hold office had brought together the ingredients for race war in Vicksburg, deserted his followers when the fighting began, and disappeared for the time being.

Ten days later, on December 17, the Mississippi legislature met in special session to consider the Vicksburg violence. The majority called on the President of the United States for troops, and secured, on December 21, a presidential proclamation calling on the "disorderly and turbulent persons" disturbing the peace to disband. The minority made direct appeal to the people of the nation for understanding of misgovernment in Mississippi, and sympathy in their efforts to correct it.

Two investigating committees were appointed to look into Mississippi matters—one by the state legislature; the other by the House of Representatives in Washington.

Still another special congressional investigating committee went south in December, 1874—a subcommittee of three, from the larger Committee on the Condition of the South named on December 15. The subcommittee arrived in New Orleans on December 22, as affairs were coming to one of their recurring crises, and went at once into what proved to be a rarity in congressional investigations of Reconstruction affairs—an investigation where numerous witnesses of repute from both sides were heard, documents were carefully examined, and, in the end, a conclusion reached which both Republican and Democratic members of the committee signed and supported. The principal reason for such an almost unparalleled result was found in the personnel of the committee, Charles Foster of Ohio and William Walter Phelps of Connecticut, Republicans, and Clarkson N. Potter of New York, Democrat—"three as honest, fair-minded and judicious men as could have been selected from the whole House of Representatives," said the *Nation*.

The state of affairs in the Louisiana which they came to investigate may be glimpsed in the report of Colonel Henry A. Morrow, of the United States Army, made to General W. H. Emory on the same day on which the Wells Returning Board certified to the election of a legislature to be controlled by the Kellogg faction. Colonel Morrow, after a two months' investigation of the rural sections of the state, assured his commanding officer that there was no idea whatever of resistance to the general government in Louisiana but that there was "a universal expression of contempt for the State government," with a fixed determination to bring about "the 'liberation of Louisiana,' to use the expression in common use." It was Colonel Morrow's conviction that "the present State government can not maintain itself in power a single hour without the protection of federal troops" and state authorities would be unable "to collect taxes and perform the functions of government after an early day in the new year." Even "a standing military force," he added, "cannot compel people to pay taxes and do a thousand things necessary to good government."

The result of this state of affairs, he reported, "is manifest in almost every department of business"; in "uncultivated fields, unrepaired fences, roofless and dilapidated dwellings, and abandoned houses"; in schools closed "for want of money to pay the teachers," after the "school funds had been stolen by State officials"; in rampant crime and judicial corruption, where "money, and not justice, is charged with turning the judicial scales"; in "exorbitant taxes . . . ruined credit . . . depleted treasury . . . enormous debts . . . multiplication of officers"; in a perfect contempt for the Kellogg government, both in the state and in the parishes, and a determination to be rid of it if ever the support of Federal troops should be withdrawn.

With affairs in that condition, and men in that dangerous state of mind, Louisiana came to the day appointed for the meeting and organization of the new legislature, January 4, 1875. State troops were in charge of the great pile of an old hotel which did duty as a capitol, under orders to admit no one to the building but state and Federal officials, and members of the legislature. Outside the building, the narrow streets of the old quarter of New Orleans were packed with a crowd of thousands, through whom the legislators had to push their way to gain entrance. At the hour of noon, the clerk of the House of Representatives called the roll, as made up by the Wells Returning Board. As he completed the roll call and began to announce the result—fifty-one Republicans and fifty Democrats present—a Conservative representative nominated L. A. Wiltz for temporary speaker. Almost immediately, as the clerk declined to put such a motion, the representative put his own motion and hurriedly declared it carried. Wiltz sprang upon the rostrum, seized the gavel, pushed the astonished clerk aside, took the oath of office before a justice of the peace conveniently provided for the purpose, swore in his Democratic colleagues in a moment, went through the form of electing a clerk and a sergeant-at-arms, and appointed a staff of assistants—all in a breath, as it were.

The assistant sergeants-at-arms, newspapermen and others who had obtained entrance by various devices, blossomed out with large and imposing badges, and went to work ejecting the old officials, while temporary Speaker Wiltz went ahead to complete his permanent organization. The temporary House promptly settled the five contested cases which the Returning Board had left unsettled by seating the Democratic claimants. With the Democratic majority so secured, they elected Wiltz as permanent speaker and declared the House duly organized and ready for business.

By that time, the Republicans began to do something more than shout "noes" to the quick succession of Democratic "ayes." They started out of the chamber with a rush to break the quorum, which transferred the focus of the struggle from the space about the rostrum to the doors, where members were pulled and hauled between Republican police trying to drag them out into the lobbies, and Democratic sergeants-at-arms struggling to save their quorum by holding them in the chamber. By keeping five unwilling Republicans in the hall the quorum was saved.

General P. R. DeTrobriand, commanding the United States troops stationed near by, came to the capitol in civilian clothes, upon the invitation of the Wiltz House, and quieted the mob milling about in the lobbies and corridors. For some two hours, in comparative peace, the Wiltz House went ahead with its organization, unseating eight of the contested members declared elected by the Wells board and replacing them with those whom the Democratic committee declared to have been elected. And then General DeTrobriand came back to the capitol upon the call of Governor Kellogg—this time not in mufti but in full uniform, followed by a detachment of United States soldiers with bayonets fixed.

With force and arms, but with great politeness, the General and his soldiers "expelled the intruders" as they were pointed out by the Republican members, and seated in their places the candidates returned by the Wells board. The Wiltz members withdrew, to continue their sessions in a private building on St. Louis Street, near by, while the fifty-two Radical members, under military protection, organized by electing as speaker, Michael Hahn, the same who had been governor of the state of Louisiana as restored by President Lincoln, a dozen years before. The five places left unsettled by the Wells board were filled by seating the Radical claimants, and the Hahn House was securely organized, although not securely organized enough to be willing to dispense with the protection of DeTrobriand's troops.

That night General Sheridan assumed command of the situation, under his secret orders from the President. On the next day, January 5, he reported to the Secretary of War, W. W. Belknap, by wire:

"I think that the terrorism now existing in Louisiana, Mississippi, and Arkansas could be entirely removed and confidence and fair-dealing established by the arrest and trial of the ringleaders of the armed White Leagues. If Congress would pass a bill declaring them banditti, they could be tried by a military commission. The ringleaders of this banditti, who murdered men here on the 14th of last September, and also more recently at Vicksburg, Miss., should . . . be punished. It is possible that if the President would issue a proclamation declaring them banditti, no further action need be taken, except that which would devolve upon me."

The startling suggestion that citizens should be declared "banditti," whether by act of Congress or proclamation of the President, and turned over to a military commission for trial and punishment, apparently received the approval of the President and most of his Cabinet, since, on the sixth, the message went back to Sheridan, from the Secretary of War, that "The President and all of us have full confidence and thoroughly approve your course."

In the country as a whole, however, the combination of DeTrobriand's "purge" of the legislature and Sheridan's "banditti" suggestion was too much. Indignation swept the North, including Republicans who were not hidebound party men. The New York Tribune declared that if Kellogg, backed by the United States Army, could decide who were the members of the Louisiana legislature, "might not President Grant better decide who shall belong to the next Congress and enforce his decisions by five or six regiments of United States troops, commanded by that truthful and just man, General Sheridan"? Senator Carl Schurz described the general state of mind:

"On all sides you can hear the question asked, 'If this can be done in Louisiana, and if such things be sustained by Congress, how long will it be before it can be done in Massachusetts and Ohio? . . . How long before a general of the Army may sit in the chair you occupy, sir, to decide contested election cases for the purpose of manufacturing a majority in the Senate? How long before a soldier may stalk into the National House of Representatives, and pointing to the Speaker's mace, say, take away that bauble.' "

Legislatures in several states passed resolutions of reproof. Mass meetings were held in many cities, culminating in great gatherings at Cincinnati, in Faneuil Hall at Boston, and in the Cooper Union at New York, where William M. Evarts, George William Curtis and the venerable William Cullen Bryant denounced the things done in Louisiana.

Generous indignation in the North was, in the South, a fury of resentment. No more business was done in New Orleans that week, while the city seethed, as the two legislative bodies went through the motions of public business. General Sheridan remained in the city, the object of execrations which seemed to do no more than heighten his joy in combat, while in Washington Louisiana affairs moved to the center of the stage. For a week after the sending of the "banditti" telegram debate raged in the Senate, over a resolution of inquiry introduced by Senator Allen G. Thurman of Ohio; an amendment to investigate armed organizations seeking to overturn the government by force, offered by Senator Oliver P. Morton; and finally, a resolution by Senator Schurz inquiring what Congress should do to secure to Louisiana the right of self-government.

On January 13, the President sent a message on the Louisiana situation, a long defensive document, upholding the course of Sheridan and his own course, and attacking the White Leagues—and still the debate went on, not only in the Senate, but in the House, where resolutions to hold a new election in Louisiana and to withdraw the United States troops were offered.

On January 15, the committee of three members of the House of Representatives sent to investigate Louisiana made their first report, covering the points on which they were unanimously in agreement. By good fortune, this extraordinarily fair and able subcommittee was in New Orleans when the Returning Board announced its decision, and was present in the Hall of Representatives on the day of the "purge." They had examined nearly a hundred witnesses, and numerous documents, and had had unusual opportunities to get at the truth. From those opportunities and their investigation came a document almost unique among congressional committee reports on the state of affairs in the Reconstruction South. They found unanimously, two Republicans and one Democrat, that the 1874 election was fair and peaceable; that what fraud there was, was preponderantly in favor of the Radicals who controlled the machinery of election; that the Conservatives won a clear majority of the seats in the legislature; and that the Returning Board, by methods described as "arbitrary, unjust, and illegal" had deprived them of that majority.

As to the testimony of "intimidation," the subcommittee reported that "there was hardly anyone who of his own knowledge could specify a reliable instance of such acts." No Negro was produced who had been threatened or assaulted or deprived of his livelihood because of political opinion, while "of the white men who were produced to testify generally on such subjects, very nearly all, if not every single one, was the holder of an office. . . ."

As to the general state of affairs in Louisiana, the background to the recurrent turmoil, the committee found that there was a general conviction that the Kellogg government was a usurpation; and a "general want of confidence in the integrity" of state and local officials, accompanied by "paralyzation of business and destruction of values. As the people saw taxation increase and prosperity diminish—as they grew poor, while officials grew rich—they became naturally sore."

The Conservatives in Louisiana, said the subcommittee, sought "peace and an opportunity for prosperity," and would support any form of government that would afford protection. "In their distress they have got beyond any mere question of political party. They regard themselves as without government and without power to form one."

The importance of government in its simple and essential functions appeared in the testimony before the subcommittee as to the conditions of the people in the country, depressed, almost in despair, partly because of the "unsparing depredations to which they are exposed, and to their utter lack of power to bring the culprits, whoever they are, to justice . . . they cannot raise anything because they cannot keep it; it is stolen from them."

The nature and extent of the distress in Louisiana was such as united "all white men and many blacks . . . absolutely all except the officeholders and their relations" in a "feeling of detestation for their rulers," as Charles Nordhoff put it. The details appear in the testimony taken by the subcommittee of Congress; in the careful study of Mr. Nordhoff; in the newspapers of the time. The poverty, distress, hunger and ruinous taxation contrasted with the high life of legislators who had their choice of placing their feet upon four-dollar a yard Brussels carpets or three-hundred-and-seventy-five-dollar desks, adorned with ten-dollar fancy inkstands and monogrammed stationery.

It was estimated that the state had realized only about fifty cents on the dollar of the face value of the huge increase in bonded indebtedness since 1865, and that of the money actually received by the state not more than half had reached the public works for which it was supposed to have been collected. In three years, four and one-half million dollars were appropriated for work on the levees, without discernible improvement in the levees. The famous Louisiana Lottery, chartered in 1868 and, by 1875, in the hands of New Jersey operators, was reputed to be making seven hundred and fifty thousand dollars a year on a capital of one million dollars, paying the state a few thousand dollars a year for the privilege of using its charter and its soil as a base of operations. The state had all the demoralization of a public lottery without even the excuse of a profit for public benefit.

There were a few parishes capably and honestly governed but, in most, local government was of the same pattern as that of the state. Taxes were delinquent, collectors were in default. Purchasers could no longer be found for land at tax sales, even though, as Mr. Nordhoff noted, three of the four "sides" of some parish newspapers were filled with advertisements of tax sales. The judiciary was venal and corrupt, even up to the chief justice, who was convicted by the Supreme Court of the United States of a knowing and fraudulent breach of trust. The school funds were stolen and the schools not held, according to the report of the colored state superintendent, while the constitutional provision requiring the mingling of the races in the schools was a constant source of friction and fighting.

The report of Messrs. Foster, Phelps and Potter to the House of Representatives, in mid-January, was a sympathetic statement of the demoralization of government and the distress of the people of Louisiana. It was, in truth, a new sort of committee report on Southern conditions, and one which the Republican leadership in the House felt must be counteracted. The other four members of the special investigating committee, therefore, arrived on January 22 in New Orleans, to take testimony and formulate another report. The new report, submitted to Congress on February 23, reverted to the familiar pattern of a majority and a minority presentation—but the majority, this time, was split in its recommendations. Three of the Republican members, Hoar, Frye and Wheeler, issued a report on the "bloody shirt" order, in which they accepted General Sheridan's "careful statistics" that in the years between 1866 and 1875, two thousand one hundred and forty persons had been killed in Louisiana because of political opinion—a figure which the General himself revised upward to thirty-five hundred within a few days.

It is impossible to know, exactly, the number of homicides in Louisiana in those years. Certainly it was higher than it would have been but for the prevalence of the custom of carrying arms. The best figures are those compiled by Mr. Nordhoff, who found that in the years 1868-1875, there was a total of three hundred and thirteen recorded homicides in approximately one-fourth of the parishes of the state, but that very few of these, except the Colfax and Coushatta affairs, were connected with politics. He found that ninety-three whites had been killed by white men and one hundred and forty-three colored men by colored. Twenty-eight whites were killed by colored men, and thirty-two colored by whites. Three colored men had been killed by peace officers, five by mobs and five by parties unknown. Five whites had been killed by mobs and five by parties unknown. It was not a pretty record of homicide, but it was not a record of wholesale political assassination such as General Sheridan described.

As to what should be done about Louisiana, the members of the full committee divided. Five members, three Republicans and two Democrats, favored seating the legislature shown to have been elected before the Returning Board got in its work. Three of the five Republicans recommended that Kellogg be recognized as governor. Two Republicans did not urge his recognition but did not oppose it, while the two Democrats objected strenuously.

The report of the majority of the committee, which was adopted by the House of Representatives in the closing days of the session, gave effect to an understanding which became known as the Wheeler Compromise, because of the effective diplomatic work of William A. Wheeler of New York, a member of the committee, in bringing the parties together.

The compromise, after a stormy history of negotiation, was finally agreed to by the Conservative caucus, by a vote of thirty-four to thirty-three, "under protest" only because the choice was between the compromise or "a condition of anarchy, in which event . . . the strength of the Federal forces would be used unrelentingly by the Federal authorities." The substance of the compromise was that Governor Kellogg should be left in office until the end of the term for which he claimed election, in 1877, and that the legislature should be made up of those members determined to have been rightfully elected by the committee of the National House of Representatives. The members of the caucus who agreed to these terms were roundly denounced by many Democrats but the compromise was put into effect and finally accepted on all hands.

The two legislative bodies which had been meeting intermittently, as either could secure the semblance of a quorum, ever since the stormy days in January, brought their sessions to a close on March 2. Later in the month, the committee of representatives in Congress went over the contested records of the election of 1874, taken to New York for the purpose, and on March 15 announced its list of members of the legislature, giving the House to the Conservatives, sixty-three to forty-seven; and the Senate to the Radicals twenty-seven to nine.

On March 24, Governor Kellogg, a warm supporter of the compromise, called the legislature in special session, as the plan provided. Two days later, Governor McEnery announced his acceptance of the compromise and the withdrawal of his claims to the office of governor. The special session of the legislature began on April 14, and continued for ten almost wholly useless days, in which partisans of each side sought to throw upon the other the blame for frittering away time and money without accomplishment. The special session, however, had one distinct value. Louisiana, after nearly four years of divided and disputed government, at last had, for a little while, only one government accepted by all parties and factions, and recognized in Washington, even if it was not much respected at home.

While the committee of the House of Representatives was in New Orleans patiently conciliating the Louisiana factions and bringing them together in the Wheeler Compromise, the final assurance of peace in Arkansas came through the report of another committee of the House, that headed by Luke P. Poland of Vermont.

On February 6, the Poland committee made its report—the majority recommending that the legality of the Baxter government and its successor, the Garland government, be accepted and that the Federal government not interfere in the affairs of the state; a minority, one member, declaring Brooks to be the rightfully elected governor of

Arkansas, and, by implication, recommending Federal interference to seat him.

Two days later, in response to a resolution offered by Senator Powell Clayton, President Grant submitted a message on the state of affairs in Arkansas, in which he inclined to support the claims of Brooks but asked only that Congress act so as to relieve the executive of determining such questions. On March 2, in the closing days of the last session of the Forty-third Congress, Chairman Poland called up his report on Arkansas and, after a long debate, carried it through to adoption. On March 5, Senator Clayton accepted the situation with good judgment and good grace. In a telegram from Washington, where the Senator remained in attendance at the special session of the Senate of the new Congress which opened on March 5, he advised his constituents:

"The action of Congress on Arkansas affairs is conclusive. The validity of the new constitution and the government established thereunder ought no longer to be questioned. It is the duty of Republicans to accept the verdict, and render the same acquiescence which we would have demanded had the case been reversed."

The action of Congress on the Poland report marked the end of Reconstruction in Arkansas. That action came about, as L. Q. C. Lamar gave the story to a young reporter on the Atlanta *Herald*, named Henry W. Grady, because Judge Poland sacrificed a lifelong ambition to close his career with a certain Federal judgeship when he put through his report on Arkansas, contrary to the wishes of the President. "I have a thorough and genuine appreciation of the Liberal Republicans who have rebelled against the power of the party in behalf of my people," said Mr. Lamar to young Grady, who, eleven years later, standing before the New England Society in New York, with General Sherman sitting at his right hand, was to thrill the country with the note of reconciliation in his oration on "The New South." "Take the case of old man Poland," Lamar continued, "the man who saved Arkansas. He absolutely put behind him a lifelong ambition when he made his protest against Grant's interference. . . . It was his pride and his ambition against his convictions. He buried his hope and saved a State."

The "saving" of the state of Arkansas was but part of the tide running strongly against the Radicals in the depression years of 1874 and 1875. The expiring Forty-third Congress, which still had its Republican majority in both houses, did pass, at last, the "Equal Rights Bill,"

so long and consistently urged by Senator Sumner, to whom passage
of the bill was in a sense, a monument. It undertook to define and
protect the equal rights of the races in places of public business and
resort within the states, basing its claim to constitutionality upon the
Fourteenth Amendment. It became, finally, a dead letter when the
Supreme Court of the United States decided, in 1883, that its provisions went beyond the grant of power to the Federal government in
the Fourteenth Amendment.

One other Radical measure, the "Force Bill" to give the President
of the United States increased power over elections in the Southern
states, passed the House of Representatives of the expiring Congress.
The bill grew out of the report of the committee of the House which
investigated the election of 1874 in which the Democrats had finally
captured all branches of the state government of Alabama. The frauds
and intimidations which the committee charged against the victors
were to be prevented, in future, by giving to the President the broad-
est powers to interfere in state election affairs, even to the extent of
suspending the writ of habeas corpus. The purpose of the bill was
vehemently and quite frankly stated by the *National Republican*, on
the day before its passage in the House. The bill, it said

"is required to preserve to the Republican party the electoral votes of
the Southern States. Remember that if the Democrats carry all the
Southern States, as they will if the White League usurpation in some
of them is not suppressed, it will require only fifty Democratic electoral votes from the Northern States to elect a Democratic President."

The bill intended to ward off this threat of a future Solid South was
driven to passage with venomous vigor by Benjamin F. Butler. It was
resisted, in a filibuster of extraordinary intensity and ingenuity, not
only by the Democrats in the House of Representatives but by such
Republicans as Luke P. Poland, James A. Garfield, Joseph R. Hawley,
Henry L. Pierce and even the Speaker of the House, James G. Blaine,
whose parliamentary advice and rulings were of decisive assistance in
delaying the passage of the bill until midnight of Saturday, February
27, which sent it to the Senate too late to be acted upon in the closing
days of the session, under the rules.

With the closing of the session of the Forty-third Congress and the
opening of the special session of the Senate of the Forty-fourth Congress, on March 5, 1875, there occurred one more portent of the decline of the Radicals—for on that day there marched down the aisle

of the Senate, to take the oath of office as successor to William G. Brownlow of Tennessee, that Andrew Johnson, whom, seven years before, the Senate had all but convicted on articles of impeachment and forever disqualified from holding a public position of trust. He was to serve only through the short and unimportant extra session of the spring of 1875, before his death in Tennessee on July 27, but the mere fact of his return to the Senate, of his vindication and justification by his own people, furnished one of the gratifying coincidences of our political history—for the only president of the United States who was ever brought before the bar of the Senate to stand trial was, likewise, the only president ever returned to the Senate as a member after his term in the White House.

How definitely the tide had set against Radical rule was not yet apparent to men in the South struggling to redeem their states from the conditions imposed upon them. To so sagacious an observer as L. Q. C. Lamar, the "future of Mississippi" seemed "very dark." The expenses of the state government had increased enormously; while the resources with which to meet the increase had declined. Much of the process of government appeared to a neutral reporter such as Mr. Nordhoff as "robbery pure and simple." Especially was this true in the administration of county and local governments, where the sheriffs, who were also tax collectors, added to onerous fees the still richer opportunity to speculate in the depreciated warrants in which most of the public business was carried on. The other county officers, often illiterate and sometimes corrupt, were to a greater or less extent satellites in schemes of the same sort.

The attempt to rid the important county of Warren of such a government ended in failure. Troops sent by General Sheridan in January, 1875, upon the call of the legislature and Governor Ames, ousted the sheriff chosen at a special election, and restored Crosby to the office from which he decamped during the Vicksburg riots in December. The state legislature passed, in the same month, a new militia law, authorizing the governor to void all commissions, call in all arms, and reorganize the state's armed forces so as to be more responsive to his will.

It was in such a state of affairs that Mr. Lamar on February 15, 1875, expressed his gloomy foreboding as to the future of Mississippi. "Ames has it dead," he wrote to his wife. "There can be no escape from his rule. His negro regiments are nothing. He will get them killed up and then Grant will take possession for him. May God help us!"

But almost as Mr. Lamar was writing, there began a movement among the despairing Democrats which, before the year was out, was to bring Reconstruction rule to an end in Mississippi. The Democratic minority in the legislature, on March 3, met in caucus to reorganize the Democratic party, disheartened after its disastrous attempt to back Alcorn in his race for governor against Ames. A Committee of Forty-two was created, with John M. Stone, who had supported the Alcorn alliance as the best that could be done two years before, as chairman. Organizing through the spring, the committee called a state convention of the Democratic-Conservative party for August 3, to nominate candidates for the November elections, when a new legislature, representatives in Congress, and county and local officers were to be chosen. The convention was a political gathering but the movement there organized, in the language of the Aberdeen *Examiner*, was not so much a political campaign as it was a revolution.

CHAPTER XLIX

THE MISSISSIPPI PLAN

THE Revolution of 1875 in Mississippi was no such aborted uprising as the September rebellion of 1874 in Louisiana. The "Mississippi plan," as it came to be called, was based not on the use of force but on the ever-present possibility that it might, and would be, used if necessary. Its leaders planned, with the greatest care, to avoid violence of the sort which might cause Federal intervention, or even serve as an excuse for it, and were able to exert a fair degree of control over their more impetuous followers. Their aim was to carry an election which was to be conducted by their opponents, and to carry it in such fashion that the result could not afterward be overturned.

The platform of the Democrats was a vigorous arraignment of the "utter incapacity," the "blunders and follies" of the state's rulers, and the "mass of confusion" which was the government of Mississippi. There was no denunciation of "negro domination" and no attempt to draw a color line in a state which had a Negro majority. Instead, the platform closed with a strong appeal to "both races to unite . . . in a determined effort . . . to secure . . . the blessings of an honest, economical government administered by able, efficient, and competent public officers."

To manage the campaign so outlined, the Democratic convention of August 3 chose James Z. George, a lawyer and scholar, a soldier and an organizer. General George had been a private in the regiment of Colonel Jefferson Davis at Monterey; an officer of the Confederate forces; and, for two periods totaling twenty-six months, a prisoner of war on Johnson's Island. The quality of the man is indicated by the fact that in the prison camp he organized and taught classes in law, an enterprise for which he was peculiarly well fitted because of his service as compiler of the official law reports of his state, as well as a practicing attorney. General George threw all his varied experience and rich gifts into a campaign as strenuous and determined as was ever made in Mississippi or elsewhere.

The color line, which the Democratic managers studiously tried to avoid, was the natural issue for the Ames forces. The Republican

544

voters were not without warning, however, of the consequences of drawing a color line, even in such a state as Mississippi. The Columbus *Press*, an anti-administration Republican paper, stated the case at the outset of the campaign:

"It became known to unscrupulous men of both colors that the voting mass of the Republican party being ignorant, an appeal to their prejudices upon the question of race was sufficient to secure a considerable political capital in the person who resorted to this base measure. The most unprincipled of white men . . . readily seized this device. . . . Swell-headed colored men who had gotten a little taste of office . . . applying the argument that colored men did the voting and colored men should have the offices, succeeded in molding and fastening a sentiment which . . . has finally brought the Republican party . . . up to the very verge of destruction."

The *Press* pointed out that the shocking losses of the party in the Northern states in the election of 1874 were due to "the scandal and disgrace" brought upon it by "shameless and corrupt management in many of the Southern states." The blame for this it laid, largely, upon the "black-liners." Warren County and Vicksburg, where the "black-liners" had succeeded for a time in their plans, were pointed to as

"but an example of the several Southern states that have been revolutionized and gone over to the enemy. It is but an example of what will become of the state of Mississippi if the same counsels . . . are allowed to prevail. . . . They will tell you to vote for your own color or die in the attempt. . . . They will have you rush upon an issue of race against race and plunge the country into strife and bloodshed if they perchance might ride safely upon the surging waves over the dead bodies of their countrymen to positions of profit."

Even Governor Ames, according to the statement of the Republican Attorney General of the state, suggested that "the blood of twenty-five or thirty Negroes would benefit the party in the state," in reply to his adviser's warnings of the consequences of raising Negro troops during the campaign.

The development of the "black line" in Mississippi made it increasingly difficult for the Southern white Republicans to continue with the party. One of them, Thomas Walton, testified to a congressional committee that the state of affairs in Mississippi

"had brought great reproach . . . upon every white man connected with the republican party, a reproach which requires an enormous weight of personal character to oppose and weigh down. . . . Indeed, . . . I may say that a white man must be very well known in the South for a true gentleman to overcome the presumption which arises there *prima facie* that he must be a rogue if he is a republican. And I find that even here (in Washington) when my friends present me even to northern republicans, there are signs of this same feeling, as they always feel it necessary to certify to my character after saying that I am a southern republican."

The Democrats campaigned with the utmost vigor. "Nearly all the Democratic clubs in the state were converted into armed military companies," wrote the colored representative in Congress, John R. Lynch. The clubs, which were at least semi-military in their character and organization, paraded by day and by torchlight. They held barbecues and speakings, and attended the speakings of their opponents. Some of the clubs borrowed a small field piece from the United States arsenal and dragged it about firing salutes. Other clubs, not so well equipped, fell back upon the ancient rural device of "shooting anvils" as a means of shattering the quiet.

That there should have been violent clashes in such a campaign, in spite of the earnest exhortations of General George and the leaders, was to be expected. One bloody fight took place at Yazoo City, on September 1, while A. T. Morgan, the Wisconsin soldier who was the sheriff and "boss" of the county, was speaking. In the first outbreak, one white and three Negroes were killed. Upon the report that the plantation Negroes were coming to sack the town in revenge, companies were formed of "Northern men and Southern men, Democrats and Republicans," with an ex-Union soldier in command. The invasion did not materialize but Sheriff Morgan fled to Jackson, where the Governor proposed to send him back to Yazoo with an escort of three hundred colored militiamen. The county was put in a state of defense to resist the expected invasion, but the Sheriff wisely declined to undertake it.

At Clinton, on September 4, shooting of obscure origin started at a political barbecue attended by twelve hundred Negroes and a hundred or so whites. In the first fight, three whites were killed. In the days of terror which followed, with race clashes going on over the county, not less than a score of Negroes lost their lives. On the seventh, Governor Ames proclaimed a state of riot and telegraphed to President Grant an urgent request for Federal troops.

In the nine months since General Sheridan had sent troops to Vicksburg upon the request of the Governor there had been changes in the state of affairs. There was a new attorney general in Washington, Edwards Pierrepont of New York, who came to the office in April, upon the resignation of George H. Williams, of whom the *Nation* remarked that "somehow it seemed to him that all states of facts and all emergencies called for the dispatch of troops." The new Attorney General, not so quick to send troops, inquired of Governor Ames if there was, indeed, an "insurrection *against the state government*," such as could not be put down by the state's own civil and military forces. A strong committee of anti-Ames Republicans assured the President that no troops were necessary, since a posse of citizens could keep order in any county.

Governor Ames declared that Federal aid was necessary, and again appealed for troops, expressing "the hope that the odium of such interference shall not attach to President Grant or the Republican party.... Let the odium in all its magnitude descend upon me." It was being represented to the President, however, by party leaders in Ohio that there was no way to avoid the odium of another intervention such as that in Louisiana, and that an immediate effect would be defeat of hopes to carry Ohio's off-year election for governor for the Republican candidate, General Rutherford B. Hayes.

As Attorney General Pierrepont quoted the President, in a dispatch to Governor Ames, he was not willing to send Federal troops to Mississippi because he felt that

"the whole public are tired out with these annual autumnal outbreaks in the South, and the great majority are ready now to condemn any interference on the part of the government."

The President added that if it should be necessary to send Federal troops, after all, the commander of the forces would be instructed "to have no child's play."

Denied the outside military aid which he so intensely desired, Governor Ames started to enlarge his colored militia organization and increase his armament. The new militia was to be largely colored, since the Governor declared that none but colored people had respect for the state government or would support it. Colonel Morgan of Yazoo was dispatched to the United States authorities at New Orleans to get the needed additional arms, while in the state the drilling of new companies started.

With affairs in this desperately dangerous state, there arrived in

Mississippi, a month before the election, George K. Chase of New York, commissioned by Attorney General Pierrepont to get the facts and report. On October 9, four days after he arrived, there was a bloody clash on the outskirts of the town of Friar's Point, in which United States Senator Alcorn and General James R. Chalmers led a force of whites which met and turned back Negroes summoned in from the country by the carpetbag sheriff of Coahoma County, with a loss of two whites and six Negroes killed. The Attorney General's emissary talked not only with Governor Ames but with Republicans who did not approve his course, and with General George, Ethelbert Barksdale and other Democratic leaders. Between the persuasive efforts of Mr. Chase, the genuine desire of the Democratic leaders for a peaceable election, and the anxiety of the Governor to avoid the threatening war, it was possible to make a treaty of peace, by the terms of which the militia were to be disarmed and their arms stored under guard; the Democratic committee was to guarantee order; and both sides were to guarantee a fair election. The agreement was reported to the Attorney General on October 16, was approved by the President and the Cabinet, and put into effect a week later.

General George and his committee redoubled their efforts to prevent violence, in the light of the treaty of peace, and with fair success. There was intimidation on the day of the election but it took the form, in most cases, of threats of discharge for the Negro who voted against his employer, or of devices to frighten the Negroes into staying away from the polls. In one county bands of mounted men, each with a rope hanging conspicuously to the pommel of his saddle, rode up to the polls before the boxes were due to open. In the hearing of the large crowds of blacks assembled for the purpose of voting early, if not often, they inquired when the voting would begin.

"In fifteen minutes," was the reply.

"Then," said the leader, speaking not to the assembled voters but to his own men, "the hanging won't begin for fifteen minutes."

Not another word was spoken but when the polls opened, a quarter of an hour later, the crowd assembled to cast their ballots had quietly melted away.

On election day, November 2, Chairman George was busy telegraphing his forces to forestall disorder and violence. "Faith must be kept in the peace agreement," he wired repeatedly, in protecting active Republicans from the attentions of hot-head Democrats. "We are nearly through now and are sure to win. Don't let us have any trouble of that sort on our hands." There were election riots and

oppressive tactics in several counties, however, perhaps ten or a dozen
out of the seventy-four in the state. Yazoo County, which had been
showing Republican majorities of some two thousand, returned only
seven Republican votes; Tishomingo, only twelve; Kemper County,
only four. That General George did his best to keep the peace was
conceded but without doubt many Republican voters were fright-
ened away from the polls, even where there was no actual violence. On
the other hand, many property-owning Negroes voted with the Democrats, in spite of the social ostracism which such a vote brought them
among their own people.

The result of the election was an overwhelming Democratic victory—a state treasurer elected by thirty-thousand majority; four out of
six representatives in Congress, the other two being an anti-Ames
Republican whom the Democrats supported, and a "regular" Republican, John R. Lynch; a majority of more than two to one in the new
state Senate, and of more than four to one in the House; and a sweep
of the county offices in sixty-two counties.

President Grant was convinced that the Mississippi officials were
"chosen through fraud and violence such as would scarcely be accred-
ited to savages" but Hiram Revels, the first Negro senator of the
United States, felt otherwise. Four days after the election he wrote
the President:

"At the late election men, irrespective of race, color, or party affiliation,
united and voted together against men known to be incompetent and
dishonest. . . . The bitterness of hate created by the late civil strife . . .
would have long since been entirely obliterated, were it not for some
unprincipled men who would keep alive the bitterness of the past, and
inculcate a hatred between the races, in order that they may aggrandize
themselves by office and its emoluments. . . ."

But regardless of any one's opinion of the methods used in Mississippi, there was to be no concerted move to overturn the results
by presidential action. Indeed, the President and his advisers had no
great time or attention to give to Mississippi or to the "Southern question" in general. They had more pressing matters nearer home.

There was, for one thing, the new Democratic House of Representatives, gathering in Washington for its first regular session at the beginning of December, 1875. This first Democratic House since 1860 was
eager to have its turn at making a few investigations of affairs governmental—and opportunities seemed really at hand. There were the
great Whiskey Frauds, whose trail led directly into the White House

when, on December 9, two days after Congress convened, a grand jury in St. Louis indicted General Orville Babcock, private secretary to the President, for complicity in the organized frauds uncovered by Benjamin H. Bristow, secretary of the treasury, in the spring of 1875. General Babcock was acquitted, on a sort of Scotch verdict, largely by the help of a deposition as to his good character furnished by his confiding friend, the President.

Within the week after Babcock's trial closed, the secretary of war, General W. W. Belknap, tricked the President into hurriedly accepting his resignation, in a highly informal way, just before a committee of the House of Representatives made public the fact that the secretary had, in effect, sold a post-tradership at Fort Sill, in the Indian Territory, from which he had received each year, through checks paid to his wife, a substantial share of the profits. Even though he had resigned, the House impeached Secretary Belknap and the Senate tried him. More than two-thirds of the senators believed him guilty as charged but several of them felt that his resignation had put him beyond the jurisdiction of the Senate in an impeachment trial and, on that ground, did not vote to convict.

And, finally, toward the close of the long session of the Forty-fourth Congress, in the early summer of 1876, there came the disclosure of secret commissions retained by James G. Blaine in connection with the sale of bonds of the Little Rock & Fort Smith Railroad to his friends in Maine, in 1869; and the charge that he had raised the money to protect some of them from loss and himself from exposure by sale of the securities received, at an artificial price, to railroad companies having dealings with the government at a time when he was speaker of the national House of Representatives.

The charges were neither proved nor disproved at the time, partly because Mr. Blaine got into his possession the Mulligan letters which contained his essential statements on the subject, and never allowed them to leave his possession or to be seen by the committee of Congress investigating the subject. He did, however, read to the whole House excerpts from some of the letters, with his own running comments, or misread them as he was charged, in a speech of such rhetorical power and superior showmanship as seemed to friendly hearers, at the time, a dazzling and complete refutation of the charges against him.

This was the easier to do because Mr. Blaine skillfully related the whole attack upon him to the everlasting "Southern question." The year was 1876, a presidential year, and the leading candidate for the

Republican nomination was Mr. Blaine, who had just retired as speaker of the House to become the very able minority leader. Adroitly, he had decided right at the beginning of the session that Republican hopes in 1876 rested not in defending the almost indefensible position into which the repeated failings of the Grant administration had led them but in exploiting the perennial issue of the "bloody shirt." Mr. Blaine had not been distinguished as a waver of that gory political banner, as had his two leading opponents in the forthcoming race for the nomination for president, Senator Roscoe Conkling of New York and Senator Oliver P. Morton of Indiana. Events of 1874 and 1875 had shown that Republican voters of the North were beginning to weary of the annual autumnal cry from the South, about election time. But the astute Mr. Blaine, crying back to an earlier aspect of the same issue, brought forward not the present-day persecutions of the carpetbaggers and their Negro allies, but the sufferings of the prisoners of Andersonville.

On January 6, 1876, the House had under consideration the bill of Samuel J. Randall of Pennsylvania to remove all disabilities of the Fourteenth Amendment. The same bill, in practical effect, had passed the previous House, with its two-thirds majority of Republicans, and had not then been objected to by Mr. Blaine. But the campaign year of 1876 was different. Mr. Blaine announced that he proposed to offer an amendment to the bill. Four days later he did so—an amendment to exclude from its provisions one man, Jefferson Davis. He wanted to exclude him, said Mr. Blaine, not because he was "the head and front of the rebellion" but because he "was the author, knowingly, deliberately, guiltily and willfully, of the gigantic crimes and murders at Andersonville. . . . And I here before God, measuring my words, knowing their full extent and import, declare that neither the deeds of the Duke of Alva in the Low Countries, nor the massacre of St. Bartholomew, nor the thumb-screws and engines of torture of the Spanish Inquisition begin to compare in atrocity with the hideous crime of Andersonville."

In the House which heard the speech were such ex-Confederates as Alexander H. Stephens and Benjamin H. Hill of Georgia; John H. Reagan, David B. Culberson and Roger Q. Mills of Texas; Eppa Hunton, John Randolph Tucker and George C. Cabell of Virginia; Randall Lee Gibson of Louisiana; L. Q. C. Lamar of Mississippi. At the other end of the capitol, in the Senate, were John B. Gordon of Georgia, Samuel B. Maxey of Texas and Francis Marion Cockrell of Missouri— every one a general officer of the Confederate Army. A major purpose of the speech was to goad the "Confederates" to reply, that the issue might be more sharply stirred up. The first reply came from Benjamin H. Hill—a reply which made clear the fact not then generally known that suffering and death in the prison camps of the North was like unto that in the camps of the South; and which closed with an appeal for reconciliation:

"Sir, There are no Confederates in this House; there are no Confederates anywhere. . . . But the South is here and here she proposes to remain. . . . We are here: we are in the house of our fathers, our brothers are our companions, and we are at home to stay, thank God!"

The controversy which Mr. Blaine's speech stirred up was to be useful to him in a collateral way, when his connection with the Little Rock & Fort Smith transaction was under investigation by the House. It gave him an opportunity, with the dramatic force of which he was a master, to charge the whole thing to prejudice and resentment against his "Andersonville" speech.

This defensive device of accusing the accusers became an essential part of the Republican strategy of the campaign of 1876, in fact. The Democratic House made it more effective than it might have been otherwise by its preoccupation with the investigation of Republican shortcomings to the neglect of the necessary positive legislation which the situation required. There could not have been, in any case, much of consequence done in a campaign year, with a Democratic House, a Republican Senate, and a president who had lost the leadership of his party—but the Republicans were able to put the blame for not "doing something" about conditions upon the Democratic House.

The Senate, still Republican, did not leave all the investigating to the new Democratic House, however. In the spring of 1876, it sent the inevitable committee to Mississippi, three Republicans and two Democrats, with Senator Boutwell of Massachusetts as chairman, to investigate and report upon the election of 1875. The committee's report, which divided strictly along party lines, was not made until midsummer, when it became a document in the campaign. The Republican majority found no sufficient causes for complaint at the Ames government in Mississippi; found that fraud and force had carried the election; recommended the passage of more stringent Federal laws to regulate affairs in the states; and proposed that such states as continued to have "disorders" be reduced to territorial status—to none of which did the Democratic minority agree.

Meanwhile, the Ames government had come to an end. The new legislature, Democratic in both branches, met in January. Governor Ames wrote that their purpose was "to complete the revolution" by clearing the state offices of Republicans and voting in Democrats, "to restore the Confederacy." Investigation looking toward impeachment was undertaken immediately. On February 14, Lieutenant-Governor Davis was impeached for accepting bribes in a pardon case, with ten colored members of the House voting aye. On March 13, he was convicted, overwhelmingly, with six Republican Senators, including one colored, voting aye. Superintendent of Education Cardoza, impeached about the same time, was allowed to resign on February 22, the same day on which impeachment articles against Governor Ames were proposed to the House.

On March 2, the House voted impeachment of the Governor on twenty-three counts. The trial of the Governor was set for March 28. On that date, upon the advice of his attorneys, he decided to avoid the trouble and expense of a trial by resigning his office, if the House and Senate were willing to give him the vindication he desired by withdrawing the charges. The plan was accepted by the legislative leaders, more concerned with bringing the Reconstruction regime to an end than with the mere matter of making a record against the Governor. The House withdrew the charges and the Senate dismissed them, almost unanimously in both cases. Governor Ames, addressing his resignation to the people of Mississippi, turned over the office to John M. Stone, president of the Senate, on March 29, 1876, and Reconstruction government in Mississippi was at an end.

Of the onetime Confederate States only three—Florida, Louisiana, South Carolina—remained under Reconstruction rule eleven years after Appomattox.

CHAPTER L

The Last Campaign

CELEBRATION of the centennial year of American independence coincided, in 1876, with the excited clamor of a presidential campaign of the sort calculated to wilt the pride of the patriot.

The Democrats, with a chance to elect a president for the first time in twenty years, nominated Samuel J. Tilden, governor of New York, whose reputation as an effective foe of corruption was based on his successful prosecutions of the Tweed Ring and the Erie Canal grafters in that state. For vice-president, the Democrats named the distinguished senator from Indiana, Thomas A. Hendricks. With candidates of such caliber, and with the vulnerable record of the Grant administration as a target, they went into the campaign on the issue of reform in government, with the blessing of many of the Liberal Republicans whom they had joined in the Greeley movement of 1872.

The Republican nomination for president went to a dark horse, Rutherford B. Hayes, governor of Ohio and brigadier general of volunteers during the war. For vice-president, the Republicans nominated William A. Wheeler, representative in Congress from New York and the conciliator whose work in Louisiana had brought about the Compromise of 1875.

Governor Hayes was nominated as a compromise candidate after a convention deadlock developed among the supporters of the three senatorial candidates—Blaine of Maine, Morton of Indiana, and Conkling of New York—and the reformers' candidate, Benjamin H. Bristow of Kentucky, secretary of the treasury and prosecutor of the whisky frauds. Governor Hayes, with a good war record and a successful administration in Ohio, was acceptable both to the reformers and to the practical politicians. Though obscure in a national sense before his nomination, he was far more than a mere political hack. He had strong views of civil service reform and honesty in government and expressed them in a sensible letter of acceptance of the nomination; but they, along with almost all other sensible ideas, were submerged in the straight-out "bloody shirt" campaign which the Republicans found it necessary to wage if they were to win.

554

The real keynote of the Republican campaign was struck in the famous "plumed knight" nominating speech in which Robert G. Ingersoll, speaking "in the name of all her soldiers dead upon the field of battle, and in the name of those who perished in the skeleton clutch of famine at Andersonville and Libby," placed in nomination James G. Blaine, "the man who has torn from the throat of treason the tongue of slander . . . who has snatched the mask of Democracy from the hideous face of rebellion."

The Democratic keynote was "Tilden and Reform," as the torchlight transparencies put it. The "urgent need of immediate reform" was the theme of the platform, with its recitals of the scandals clustered about the Grant administration. Such reform being impossible within the Republican party, according to the platform, the Democrats demanded for the nation a change of government, and for the South restoration of home rule.

Unable to stand on the defensive on current issues, the Republicans had no real choice other than to go back to the old reliable issues of slavery, secession, copperheadism, and the threat of rebel rule as exemplified in the fact that once more there was a Democratic majority in the national House of Representatives—or the "Confederate Congress," as campaign orators were fond of calling it. The nominee himself, writing to Senator Blaine, advised:

"Our strong ground is the dread of a solid South, rebel rule, etc., etc. I hope you will make these topics prominent in your speeches. It leads people away from 'hard times' which is our deadliest foe."

Such advice to Mr. Blaine really was not necessary. His "Andersonville" speech in Congress, at the beginning of the year, had already pitched the campaign along familiar lines which other Republican campaign orators took up willingly. "I prefer the old gray army shirt," declaimed Benjamin Harrison, governor of Indiana, "I prefer the old gray army shirt, stained with but a single drop of a dead comrade's blood, to the black flag of treason or the white flag of cowardice."

This sort of characterization of Democrats, Northern and Southern, reached what was probably its climax at a soldiers' and sailors' convention in Indianapolis, in September, where Robert G. Ingersoll delivered himself of his philippic against Democrats:

"Every man that shot Union soldiers was a Democrat. Every man that starved Union soldiers and refused them a crust in the extremity of death was a Democrat. Every man that loved slavery better than liberty was a Democrat. The man that assassinated Abraham Lincoln was a Democrat. Every man that sympathized with the assassin—every man glad that the noblest President ever elected was assassinated—was a Democrat. . . . Every man that helped to burn orphan asylums in New York was a Democrat. . . . Every man that tried to spread small-pox and yellow fever in the North . . . was a Democrat. Soldiers, every scar you have got on your heroic bodies was given you by a Demo-crat. . . ."

and so on with the pounding force of iteration, through a long cata-logue of crimes imputed to Democrats.

Mr. Ingersoll expressed a common theme of Republican campaign orators in his declaration that the election was "simply a prolongation of the war." The question, as he put it, was "Shall a solid South, a united South, united by assassination and murder, a South solidified by the shot gun; shall a united South with the aid of a divided North . . . control this great and splendid country?"

Whatever the causes, the methods by which it was effected, or the consequences, the South had become all but a solid unit in opposition to the Republican party—not only the old Confederate South of eleven states but the border states as well. Governors of the Radical persuasion still held on precariously, at the opening of the campaign of 1876, in the states of Florida, Louisiana and South Carolina, but only in the last was the government of the state still Republican in all its branches. In Florida, Governor Stearns was restrained by a Demo-cratic legislature and embarrassed by factional disputes with other leaders of his own party. In Louisiana, the hybrid government set up the year before under the Wheeler Compromise was failing to work, while blame for its failure was liberally bandied back and forth by the three elements involved—the Radical Governor Kellogg, the Repub-lican Senate and the Democratic House of Representatives.

Because of the impact of presidential policy on local government, both parties in the three states still under Reconstruction rule were concerned over the national election, but the deepest interest of Con-servatives was nearer home. They saw, at last, their chance to escape from a rule which to them was ruinous and intolerable—and of that chance they were determined to make the most.

In Louisiana, the line-up of factions for the campaign of 1876 was under way almost as soon as the legislature set up under the Wheeler Compromise adjourned its futile session, in the spring of 1875. Lou-isiana, complained the "Bourbon" wing of the Democratic party, had been without a true, straight-out Democratic party ever since the fusion with Warmoth Republicans in 1872. A summer and fall of agitation and demand for party reorganization brought a state Democratic convention, in January, 1876, which selected delegates to the national convention and went further with a resolution declaring the McEnery-Penn government to be the lawful government of the state, regardless of a compromise which had been negotiated by members of the legislature who, in their view of the case, had no authority to bind party members.

The legislature, going through another of its useless and expensive annual sessions at the time, responded to the sentiment with an attempt to remove Governor Kellogg from office, despite the protection afforded him by the Wheeler Compromise agreement. The movers of impeachment in the House of Representatives disclaimed any intention of repudiating the compromise to which they had agreed the year before, and based their charges against the Governor on acts subsequent to April 14, 1875, the effective date of the compromise.

The whole impeachment proceeding was farcical. The House of Representatives passed its resolution at five o'clock in the afternoon of February 28. Forty-five minutes later its committee appeared at the bar of the Senate, to give notice of the fact of impeachment. The Senate immediately organized as a court, with Chief Justice Ludeling, who was gaining a varied experience in such service, presiding. The court of impeachment allowed the House managers until seven o'clock, less than an hour, to prepare the definite articles, have them adopted by the House, and present them for trial. Without the authority of the House, which had adjourned, the managers rushed through the preparation of fourteen articles of impeachment, presented them for trial at the hour set, and saw the Republican Senate promptly acquit the Governor that evening on every count, by a vote of twenty-six to five. There was much indignation among the Democratic House members over the summary acquittal, but to many of the more level-headed Democrats the whole proceeding was distasteful.

"The House gets up an impeachment," wrote the strong Shreveport Times, "foolish and frivolous in design and unspeakably feeble in execution; and the Senate trumps up a trial and acquittal so monstrous, so arbitrary and so scornful as to shock and startle every reasoning mind."

On June 27, two weeks after the Republican national convention, the Republicans of Louisiana convened in New Orleans for a five-day factional free-for-all. Kellogg and Packard, as usual, stood together against Warmoth, with whom was joined once more the Negro leader

Pinchback, whose long struggle for a seat in the Senate had finally ended in failure only three months before.

After one whole disorderly day, and by a majority of but one vote, Pinchback was elected temporary chairman of the convention. Three more days of shouting and scuffling in the convention hall drew from the party organ, the *Republican*, the disgusted comment that not even the Democrats could have done worse. It thus described the fourth day's session:

"Nothing was done all day but howl, raise silly points of order, bully the chair, and each other, and listen to two or three windy orations from as many demagogues."

The chair, however, took the bullying to which he was subjected with appropriate nonchalance. With his feet on the table, the soles of his shoes presented to the noisy mob protesting his rulings, temporary Chairman Pinchback advised the delegates, "You might as well take it easy, for you've got to stand it."

The fifth day saw the development of enough harmony to elect Pinchback permanent chairman, and to adopt a platform. On the sixth day, really getting down to work, the convention made short work of the nominations. On the first ballot, Packard and Warmoth were neck and neck for governor. On the second ballot, Warmoth withdrew in the interest of harmony. Antoine, the Negro lieutenant-governor under Kellogg, was again nominated for the second place, and a full state ticket named, including Warmoth as the party nominee for one of the seats in Congress.

S. B. Packard, the Republican nominee for governor, a native of Maine, had come south during the war, and served throughout the Grant administration as United States marshal and leader of administration Republicans in the state. Charles Nordhoff found him to be

"reputed a man of unflinching courage, strong will, and no scruples. . . . His single idea is to keep Louisiana in Republican hands, and his only method is to mass the colored vote. To him is due largely the color line. . . . A part of his strength lies in that he is believed to be pecuniarily honest."

With the Republican nomination in such hands, the Democrats met at Baton Rouge, on July 24. The "Bourbon" wing of the party and the professional politicians soon found that the earnest and intelligent group of delegates had small concern with faction, and little patience with extremist views. No one of the active leaders of the past eight years who aspired to the nomination for governor could attract a majority of the delegates. On the fourth day of the convention, and the fourth ballot, the delegates turned to General Francis T. Nicholls, whom they nominated unanimously for governor, with L. A. Wiltz, mayor of New Orleans, as his running mate.

General Nicholls was a quiet man and a lover of peace, but a most courageous and unflinching man in a fight. A graduate of West Point, he had resigned from the army in 1856 to take up the practice of law in his home parish of Assumption. With the outbreak of war in 1861, he entered Confederate service, in which he soon became a brigadier-general, and to which he gave first an arm and then a leg, in Virginia. Quietly resuming the practice of law after the war, he possessed the liking and the trust of both races and all classes.

With such a candidate, the Democrats went into the 1876 campaign in Louisiana with determination and fervor. It was obvious, from the beginning, that grounds were being laid for the overturning of the results, as in 1872, if Nicholls and the Tilden electors should carry the state. As early as January, 1876, the *Republican* began to catalogue, under prominent headlines, "The Week's Record of Outrages," and continued such cataloguing throughout what it denounced as a "Shot-gun Campaign."

To a later investigating committee of the House of Representatives, the extreme and often exaggerated publicity given to disorders and outrages suggested the conclusion "that prominent Republicans considered the killing of a black man as equivalent to $50,000 of a campaign fund for the party."

Black men were killed, and some of the killings were political, without doubt. It was not a peaceable campaign, although the Democratic leaders urged that there should be "peace at all hazards, and perfect, thorough, universal organization in every neighborhood, for the purpose of preserving the peace." The local white organizations, sometimes known as Rifle Clubs, were denounced by the Republicans as White Leaguers or Ku Klux under another name, and their doings, real and imaginary, were made the meat of local campaign stories and of dispatches to show the Northern voters that the campaign argument of the Democrats in the South was violence and intimidation, "the shot-gun, the revolver, the bowie knife."

There was enough violence and intimidation in the Louisiana campaign to add a new word to American vocabulary—to "bulldoze." Like "scalawag" the word is of uncertain etymology, but there was never any doubt of its meaning. "Bulldozers" were those who undertook to carry the election by some violence and threats of more; "bulldozed parishes" were those in which, according to the Republicans, such tactics were decisive or influential in the result.

Governor Nicholls and the more responsible Conservative heads in Louisiana deprecated "bulldozing" and succeeded in confining its worst manifestations to a few of the more turbulent and disorderly parishes. Their effort was to break the color line in politics by securing the support of substantial Negro citizens, to whom they appealed with some success on the ground of the common interest of the races in good government. But behind the quiet-spoken, straightforward appeals of Governor Nicholls was determination to join Mississippi in its new-won freedom from Radical rule.

In Florida, perhaps even more than in Louisiana, with the election machinery in the hands of Radicals who had shown the ability to make use of their opportunities for fraud, the Democrats adopted force, and the threat of more force, as a campaign argument in 1876. Once more nocturnal regulators rode about, demanding cessation of Republican activities, or support of the Democrats. At the same time, poor bedeviled Negro voters who had no particular political predilections were under counterpressure from Republicans of their own race.

The campaign opened, encouragingly for the Democrats, with a four-day fight in the Republican convention at Monticello, ending in the nomination of Governor Marcellus L. Stearns for re-election, as was to be expected, and in a second convention of "Reform" Republicans, which nominated United States Senator S. B. Conover. From June to September, when peace was made between the factions in the face of the aggressive Democratic fight, Governor Stearns had no more vitriolic critic than Senator Conover. As a later by-product of this feud came those chapters of John Wallace's book, *Carpet-Bag Rule in Florida*, which give the liveliest version of the 1876 campaign. Wallace wrote:

"From the issuance of the call for the convention until and during its riotous sessions, whiskey was the strongest argument used to demoralize the colored people, with now and then a little money thrown in to keep up the hired loafers, who did nothing but follow up white carpet-bag ballot-box stuffers and halloo themselves hoarse for Stearns."

The Democrats made an expedient nomination for governor. Their candidate was George F. Drew, a native of New Hampshire, who had come to Florida more than thirty years before, had prospered in the lumber business, and had no prominent connection with either side during the war. For lieutenant-governor they named N. A. Hull.

The Democratic appeal was for reform and retrenchment. Their problem was to rouse discouraged Democrats, who felt it hopeless to fight against ballot-box control, and to bring to their support as many as possible of the Negroes. Nocturnal "regulators" not officially authorized, played some part in this latter work. Economic pressure, openly applied, probably played more. As the Democratic Club of Monticello put it, "first preference in all things" was to be given "to those men who vote for reform" and second preference to those "who do not vote at all." Against those who insisted upon voting the Republican ticket, a "distinction" was to be made in employment, in renting land, and in extending credit. As one Negro leader summed it up, "All colored people that voted the Republican ticket were to be starved out next year." The Democratic campaign was denounced as "the shot-gun policy pursued in Mississippi"—behind it was the same desperate determination to regain the rule of the state.

South Carolina had, when the centennial campaign year of 1876 opened, the best of Reconstruction governors, Daniel H. Chamberlain, and probably the worst of legislatures. The Governor and the legislature, both Republican, had been at war ever since the beginning of their terms of office, in December, 1874. In one of the nineteen vetoes which the Governor successfully used to defeat undesirable legislation during the first session of the legislature, he described certain certificates covering profligate legislative expenses as "the last culminating evidence of a prevailing system of corruption which had disgraced our state and offended the nation." The legislative expenses, he said elsewhere, were "stealing, pure and simple," while in an interview in May, 1875, he declared that "a very large number of the members of the South Carolina legislature come to the capital for the purpose of selling their votes and making all they can out of office."

The scholarly Massachusetts lawyer who became governor of South Carolina grew in strength and standing with the Conservative elements of the state throughout 1875, as he continued to oppose the clique which dominated the legislature, led by Robert B. Elliott, the Massachusetts-born Negro speaker of the House, C. C. Bowen, sheriff of Charleston County, Reverend B. F. Whittemore, Senator "Honest John" Patterson, and the like.

At the second session of the legislature, in December, 1875, the Governor met defeat when the legislature elected former Governor Franklin J. Moses judge of the Sumter circuit, and W. J. Whipper, Negro carpetbagger, judge of the Charleston circuit—"a horrible disaster" to good government, in the eyes of Governor Chamberlain. Moses, he wrote to President Grant, was "as infamous a character as ever in any age disgraced and prostituted public position," while Whipper differed in character "only to the extent to which opportunity had been allowed him."

To Senator Morton, he wrote that "no party can rule this State that supports Whipper and Moses. . . . There is but one way to save the Republican party in South Carolina and that way is to unload Moses and Whipper, and all who go with them." Overwhelming defeat, he declared, was inevitable, "unless we can persuade the people of this State that such things as these judicial elections will be undone, and never by any possibility repeated."

The Governor himself did his best to see that the elections were undone. He kept the newly elected judges off the bench by stern refusal to issue their judicial commissions, taking advantage of a technicality in the law, but he was not able to persuade the people of the state that such elections would not be repeated. The Governor himself said to the editor of the Charleston News and Courier that the election of such men to judicial office would bring about "the reorganization of the Democratic party within the State, as the only means left, in the judgment of its members, for opposing a solid and reliable front to this terrible crevasse of misgovernment and public debauchery."

As the Governor predicted, the fact of the election of Moses and Whipper to the bench brought about the rebirth of the Democratic party, dormant in South Carolina for eight years. The News and Courier, under the able editorship of Francis W. Dawson, believed in Governor Chamberlain, and was willing enough to see him re-elected in 1876, but it declared that the conduct of the legislature, which "had run over Governor Chamberlain as they have run over any other Republican who strives to check them" was such that they "must make way for the Democratic party."

Moves for the reorganization of the party went forward through the spring of 1876, with much sincere and earnest discussion between the "Co-operators," who believed with the News and Courier that the wise course was to concentrate on the election of a Democratic legislature and state officers and throw the support of the party to Cham-

berlain for governor, and the "Straight-outs," who were for fighting
it out with a full Democratic state ticket.

Most of the leaders, the men who remembered hopeless efforts
to elect Democratic tickets in the face of a hostile majority of thirty
thousand votes, with the whole machinery of conducting and returning elections in Republican hands, were "Co-operators." Their
position was strengthened by a demonstration of Governor Chamberlain's remarkable oratorical power over his party when, at four o'clock
in the morning of the last day of the Republican convention, in April,
he overturned a hostile combination against him with a speech, and
recaptured control of the party machinery. A month later, when the
Democrats met in convention, the argument still was not settled. A
thorough reorganization of the party was agreed upon, but no nominations were made.

Had affairs gone on undisturbed, there is every likelihood that the
policy of the "Co-operators" would have prevailed; that Chamberlain
would have been left unopposed in his race for re-election; and that
the Democrats would have concentrated on electing a legislature and
other state offices, and carrying the state for Tilden and Hendricks.
But on July 4, the very centennial day, in the decayed town of Hamburg on the Savannah River, opposite Augusta, there began a chain
of incidents inconsequential in themselves, culminating in another
riot of races which, in its effect, profoundly changed the history of
South Carolina and did much to determine the Presidency of the
United States.

Hamburg, forty years earlier, had been the busy western terminus of
what then was the world's longest railroad. It had been laid off on the
grand scale, as befitted a planned commercial metropolis, but its
glories had long departed; its brick warehouses had become the roost-
ing-places of birds and bats; its wide streets had become great expanses
of grass and weeds, through which ran a single sandy wagon track.
Along one of these tracks, in the afternoon of July 4, 1876, drove
Thomas Butler and Henry Getzen, of Edgefield County, returning
home from Augusta. Drawn across the one-hundred-and-fifty-foot
wide street stood, in line, a Negro militia company commanded by
Doc Adams, captain. Unable to pass, Butler went before Prince
Rivers, colored, who combined the functions of a justice of the peace
and a general officer of militia, and swore out a warrant against Adams
for obstructing the public highway.

Four days later, on the eighth, when the case came on for trial
before trial Justice Rivers, Hamburg was crowded with white men

from Aiken and Edgefield Counties, and with the Negro militia company, massed in the old brick warehouse which served as armory and drill hall. General M. C. Butler, representing the complainant whites, demanded the disarming of Adams' militia. The demand was refused. Lawyers, litigants and the Justice argued and maneuvered through the day, while some of the increasing crowd relieved the tedium with whisky. Late in the afternoon, the shooting began, for no discoverable particular reason, with the militia firing from their armory and the whites from any convenient shelter. The first man killed was white. From Augusta came white reinforcements. From somewhere, came an old field piece, loaded with slugs and stones, to be turned against the solid brick warehouse. The demoralized defenders broke and ran. Some were shot as they ran; others surrendered, were told to run, and shot as they ran. Seven were killed, altogether, and the Hamburg massacre, as was to be expected, became a major campaign issue. "A kilt nigger," as one practical Northern politician put it, "is worth twenty thousand votes to Hayes north of the Potomac."

Governor Chamberlain addressed President Grant in terms which, to white South Carolinians, seemed designed to bring the intervention of United States troops, once more, to secure an election for the Republicans. In his letter to the President, the Governor described the fight at Hamburg as one where the lines were marked by "race and political party," and as "only the beginning of a series of similar race and party collisions," foreshadowing "a campaign of blood and violence" of the sort "popularly known as a campaign conducted on the 'Mississippi plan.' " The letter closed with the request that the general government "exert itself vigorously to repress violence" by either party.

Governor Chamberlain's letter drew from the President an assurance of backing by the general government, in every constitutional way, and the opinion that the Hamburg riot was "cruel, blood-thirsty, wanton, unprovoked and uncalled for," although no more than "a repetition of the course that ·has been pursued in other Southern States in the past few years." The President disclaimed "any desire on the part of the North to humiliate the South; nothing is claimed for one State that is not freely accorded to all others, unless it may be the right to kill negroes and Republicans without fear of punishment, and without loss of caste or reputation."

In South Carolina, the Governor's letter and its invitation to Federal intervention spelled the end of the "Co-operators" movement. The Hamburg massacre was condemned but there was strong resentment at what was conceived to be Chamberlain's attempt to make political capital of it. Even the News and Courier, head and front of the "Co-operator" movement, protested the Governor's course as having "the appearance of taking advantage of a local disturbance to prop up the waning fortunes of South Carolina Republicanism."

In the four weeks between Governor Chamberlain's letter to President Grant and the meeting of the Democratic state convention, on August 15, county after county, especially in the upcountry, instructed its delegates to support the "straight-out" policy—a policy which prevailed in the convention on the second day, after a seven-hour secret session. Even then, perhaps, it might not have prevailed had not the Secretary of War, Don Cameron, on that day issued orders to General Sherman to hold all troops not engaged in the great Indian wars then in progress in the West in readiness to respond to the calls of state authorities for the protection of citizens—an order obviously aimed at the situation in South Carolina, Louisiana and Florida.

Those members of the party who had believed the chance of a straight-out victory too slight to justify taking the risk promptly fell into line when the majority discarded the name of "Conservative," went back to the older designation of "Democrat," and staked everything on their ability to do the impossible. "You gentlemen are all going straight to the devil," old Governor Perry was reported to have said, "but I'll go along with you."

For governor, the reorganized party named Wade Hampton, a leader whose strength, as Governor Chamberlain himself wrote twenty-five years later, "lay not in intellectual or oratorical superiority, but in high and forceful character, perfect courage, and real devotion to what he conceived to be the welfare of South Carolina . . . unselfish, resolute, level-headed and determined."

With General Hampton there was nominated a state ticket of real distinction. For lieutenant-governor, there was William D. Simpson, Harvard graduate, colonel under Stonewall Jackson, member of the Confederate Congress, later to be chief justice and governor of the state—as, indeed, were three others on that remarkable list of nominations. To manage the campaign, Colonel Aleck C. Haskell was elected chairman of the state committee.

The immediate effect of the nomination of General Hampton was Democratic unity and enthusiasm. General Martin W. Gary of Edgefield, leader of the militant "Straight-outs" and Captain Francis W. Dawson of Charleston, leader of the "Co-operators," whom Gary had challenged to a duel three weeks before, fell in line together for Hampton—action which was typical of what happened all over the state. At the same time, Democratic unity drove the warring Republican factions together behind Chamberlain, who was nominated for re-election in September. And so, behind the best men and leaders which each could put forward, the two parties went into the last desperate campaign of Reconstruction—the "Revolution of '76."

The odds were with the Republicans. There were more of them; they had the election machinery in all its branches, and the backing of the national administration with what Governor Chamberlain referred to in a letter to Senator Morton as "all its appliances, civil and military." But, despite Chamberlain's own good character, the party was burdened with a record of misgovernment, and suffered even more, perhaps, from a lack of the man power necessary to a party which would govern well. Governor Chamberlain himself put his finger on this weakness when, long years afterward, he wrote:

"There was no possibility of securing permanent good government in South Carolina through Republican influences. If the canvass of 1876 had resulted in the success of the Republican party, that party could not, for want of materials, even when aided by the Democratic minority, have given pure or competent administration."

At the time, however, the Governor threw himself into the campaign with zeal and earnestness, though with what inner bitterness at his failure to receive the coveted support of the substantial elements of the state as may only be imagined.

The Hampton men conducted their campaign "as if it were a life-or-death combat"—as it had come to be to them. They were not greatly concerned with national issues or the presidential canvass. As General Hampton put it, in one of his speeches: "I am not in the big fight. I am in this little fight to save South Carolina." His personal platform, repeated in one form or another from every stump, was "to bring the two races in friendly relation together," with "equal and impartial justice" to the "whole people of the State."

The plan of the Democratic campaign included appeals, by every sort of means, for the support of substantial, taxpaying Negroes, with assurance of protection for those who might join with the Democrats from the excessive zeal of some of the more extreme Republicans. The appeal met with some success, as evidenced by the several thousand "Hampton men" among the Negroes—who, incidentally, retained their right to vote in the Democratic party in South Carolina so long as they lived, even after the party became the white race politically organized.

Of greater effect upon the result was another phase of the campaign—to discourage from voting at all, all those who would not join with the Democrats. This result was to be brought about by a campaign of intimidation without violence. Actual violence was discouraged because of its probable effect in bringing Federal intervention, but throughout the campaign there ran the threat of potential violence, sensed beneath the surface of every maneuver.

No Republican speaking was free from Democratic demands for a "division of time." The Democrats punctiliously offered a division of time for speakers at their own meetings, it is true, knowing perfectly well that the offer would not be accepted. Joint discussion was not helpful to the Radical cause in South Carolina, particularly joint discussion forced upon an unwilling and unprepared speaker, but to refuse a division of time to a hundred, or five hundred, mounted men riding up to the platform in disciplined and watchful order, was more than most committees or speakers could manage.

The Democrats of the state were organized in Rifle Clubs—nearly three hundred of them, with some fourteen thousand members, under the leadership of General James Conner of Charleston. The Rifle Clubs, in the eyes of their own members, at least, were organized in answer to the Negro militia of the state. They were, too, an important part of the campaign organization which, as in General Johnson Hagood's county of Barnwell, undertook to call on every white man and "respectfully and cordially" invite his membership in the Democratic club of the county. If he should fail to join, a committee of two was sent to "urge him . . . not to desert his kindred and county in this supreme effort at deliverance; and to tell him that his decision will determine whether we regard him as friend or foe. . . . Should this last appeal fail, register that man as a radical and treat him as such."

Under the suasion of such calls, white Radicals almost ceased to exist in South Carolina. The process of transferring allegiance to the regenerated Democrats became known, in the evangelical fervor of the campaign, as "crossing Jordan."

From mid-August until the election in November, the county towns of South Carolina, one after the other, were the scenes of great Democratic processions, with bands and marching men and allegorical tableaux depicting the plight of South Carolina and her longing for

Liberty and Justice; with speakings, where General Hampton spoke quietly, earnestly, simply—always with a word for the Negroes in the audience, whether many or few. The roads leading into the county towns were filled with men, marching, riding, singing, shouting, shooting, doing everything to give the impression sought, relentless force in reserve, without violence.

And then, in the great torchlight procession in Charleston to celebrate the nomination of General Hampton, on the night of August 25, appeared the one thing needed to complete the campaign—a symbol. General Judson Kilpatrick, the same whom South Carolinians remembered as the commander of General Sherman's cavalry in 1865, wrote the Republican presidential nominee calling for a campaign of "the bloody shirt, with money" to carry Indiana. In derision, the "bloody shirt" appeared on a torchlight transparency in Charleston that night—to reappear at Aiken, on the night of September 5, on a whole company of men in a procession, wearing the Red Shirt, the distinctive emblem of a unique campaign.

On the night of September 6, a group of whites escorting Negro Democrats home from a meeting in Charleston had to fight to protect them from an infuriated mob of their own race. One white man was killed, and many of both races wounded. The organized Rifle Club of the city, held under discipline at its club rooms, took over the patrolling of Charleston, in spite of the extra-legal character of the arrangement.

On the fourteenth, at Newberry in the upcountry, the Red Shirt first appeared as the uniform of the whole body of four thousand mounted men in the great procession to greet General Hampton. From that day on the two ideas became inseparable, almost, in the minds of Carolinians—Hampton and his Red Shirts.

On the next night there broke out the Ellenton riots—five days and nights of terror and violence in remote sections of Barnwell and Aiken counties, with the women and children gathered together under guard for safekeeping, while in the swamps and the canebrakes bands of men hunted and fought. General Johnson Hagood, who restored order by the twentieth, reported the casualties as two white men killed, three wounded; at least thirty-nine Negroes killed. The Ellenton riots gave point to Governor Chamberlain's appeals to the President for aid in suppressing violence.

At the end of the first week in October, one month before the election, Governor Chamberlain proclaimed the lawlessness of the Rifle Clubs and ordered them to disband. The Democratic state committee denounced the order as an effort to irritate the people and "provoke collisions which may be the excuse for an appeal" to garrison the state with Federal troops, to which the Governor made reply that the "lawlessness, terrorism and violence . . . far exceed in atrocity any statements yet made public." Associate Justice A. J. Willard, able carpetbagger on the state Supreme Court, differed from the Governor as to the degree or extent of violence. There was, he said, less disposition toward personal bitterness than in any of the previous political campaigns which he had observed since coming into the state. A distinguished list of Charlestonians, including the bishops of three faiths, nine other ministers, and eight bank presidents, issued an address to the people of the United States denying that there was a "state of insurrection or domestic violence" in the state, but declaring that there was "a most active, earnest and excited canvass to overthrow corrupt rule. . . . It is not treason to defeat Chamberlain, nor is it insurrection or domestic violence to elect Hampton."

On October 17, at the request of Governor Chamberlain, the President issued his proclamation of insurrection in South Carolina, and the Secretary of War ordered into South Carolina "all the available force in the military division of the Atlantic." General Hampton and the Democratic committee counseled peaceable submission to military intervention, but the people of the state shrewdly went one step beyond. As United States troops arrived, they were not greeted as enemies but welcomed as friends and allies—a most disarming reception. The Rifle Clubs, too, disbanded as Rifle Clubs, although they frequently reappeared under other names—the "Mounted Baseball Club" of Allendale, for example, with one hundred and fifty members, the "Hampton & Tilden Musical Club," "Mother's Little Helpers" and the like.

On the sixteenth, the day before President Grant's proclamation, a political speaking at Cainhoy, a settlement on one of the coastal islands near Charleston, broke up in a fight in which five whites and one Negro were killed, and others wounded. There were other disturbances in the low country, some growing out of repeated strikes of laborers in the rice fields for higher wages; some out of political hatreds between black Republicans and black Democrats. There were assassinations and affrays in the upcountry and, especially around Aiken, numerous arrests of whites on Federal charges of violence and intimidation toward Negro voters. Yellow fever broke out in Charleston, but through it all the Red Shirt campaign went forward—great processions of red-shirted riders, some mounted on blooded horses, more on bony or lumpy work stock, many on mules, occasionally one on an ox; tableaux and floats; flowers, great bouquets bestowed upon the leader in whom all had such trust; hours and hours of oratory; and then, after all that, torchlight processions at night. Such was the never-forgotten campaign of Hampton and the Red Shirts.

Election came on November 7—election in South Carolina, in Louisiana, in Florida, in the nation; an election so desperately hard fought, so close, that it left in perilous division and uncertainty not only the government of the three states, but the Presidency of the United States.

CHAPTER LI

The Struggle for the State Houses

At three-forty-five o'clock in the morning of November 8, 1876, four weary newspapermen in the offices of the New York *Times* debated how they should treat the results of the election of the day before in their first edition of the morning. Already other newspapers, including the *Tribune*, had conceded the election to Mr. Tilden. In Columbus, Governor Hayes was in bed, believing himself defeated. In New York, workers and hangers-on had deserted Republican campaign headquarters. The nation had gone to sleep in the belief that a Democrat had been elected president for the first time in twenty years, with a majority of both the popular and the electoral votes.

Democratic headquarters in New York, however, remained open and active—too active. An over-anxious worker, of disputed identity, seeking quick confirmation of what was almost universally conceded to be true, telegraphed to the *Times*, then most rigidly Republican of New York journals: "Please give your estimate of electoral votes secured by Tilden. Answer at once." The message, with its obvious note of uncertainty, suggested to the resolute and resourceful council of editors who received it that the Democrats did not yet know their candidate was elected. It touched off a course of action and a chain of events which transferred the Presidency of the United States from Tilden to Hayes but, in so doing, secured the peaceful end of Reconstruction government in the South; and even, in a measure, secured Republican recognition of the rights of states to control their own elections.

Tilden had carried the big doubtful Northern states—New York, New Jersey, Connecticut, Indiana—and had a substantial popular majority. That much was known. It was assumed, too, that he had carried the border states and those of the South. On that assumption, he had two hundred and three electoral votes against one hundred and sixty-six for Hayes if the latter had carried every other Northern and Western state. But it was recalled that in the states of Florida, Louisiana and South Carolina there were Republican Returning Boards, with extraordinary powers to modify or even to manufacture

571

majorities, and Republican governors, to sign certificates of electors in accordance with the majorities so created and certified. If Governor Hayes should receive every one of the nineteen electoral votes of these three states, and keep every vote in the North which he had carried on the face of the returns, he would be elected president, with one hundred and eighty-five votes to one hundred and eighty-four for Tilden. And, obviously, Democratic headquarters did not know whether or not they had carried the doubtful Southern states.

While Edward Cary of the *Times* wrote an editorial cautiously claiming that Governor Hayes might be elected, John C. Reid, managing editor, posted off to the Fifth Avenue Hotel to arouse the Republican management to the possibilities of the situation. The only man he found awake was William E. Chandler of New Hampshire, secretary of the national committee, in the lobby of the hotel, hunched over a copy of the first edition of the *Tribune*, reading the announcement of the defeat of his candidate. Together, Reid and William E. Chandler hunted up Zachariah Chandler, who combined the functions of a Cabinet officer and Republican national chairman. Reid and the two Chandlers, one in his nightgown, quickly determined on a course of action and put it into effect by telegraphing, before dawn, to Republican leaders in the three states:

"Hayes is elected if we have carried South Carolina, Florida, and Louisiana. Can you hold your State? Answer immediately."

By afternoon of the eighth, Republican newspapers were claiming definitely that Hayes had received the votes of the three doubtful states in the South, and was elected. That night, Chairman Chandler issued a bulletin that if dispatches which "there was no reason to doubt" were correct should be confirmed, Hayes was elected by a majority of one, a claim which from that hour became Republican dogma.

Steps were undertaken immediately to see that the dispatches should be made correct. Secretary Chandler was already on his way to Florida, looked upon as the most doubtful and difficult of the states. Two days later, on November 10, four companies of soldiers were started to Tallahassee, while the President directed General Sherman to instruct military commanders in the South to preserve peace and good order, "and to see that the proper and legal boards of canvassers are unmolested in the performance of their duties." The President added a homily which, ironically, was to recoil on his party:

"Should there be any grounds of suspicion of a fraudulent count on either side, it should be reported and denounced at once. No man worthy of the office of President should be willing to hold it if counted in or placed there by fraud. Either party can afford to be disappointed in the result. The country cannot afford to have the result tainted by the suspicion of illegal or false returns."

On the same day on which the President sent orders for troops at the capitals of the three states, to protect and sustain the Returning Boards, party leaders of national standing, Republican and Democratic, started south to contribute their presence and their prestige to bringing about what each group conceived to be rightful results. Some of the "visiting statesmen," as they came to be called in the South, went "visiting" at the request of the President; some at the request of the Republican chairman or of Abram S. Hewitt, chairman of the Democratic national committee; some on their own motion.

On November 10, the day on which "statesmen" started south to persuade the Returning Boards, and troops were ordered to protect them in their work, the State Board of Canvassers of South Carolina met to canvass the returns of an election in which three of its five members were candidates. It was conceded on both sides that the board had no power directly to determine the vote for governor and lieutenant-governor, that being reserved for the incoming General Assembly. As to its other powers, the Democrats contended that the board could perform only the ministerial functions of aggregating the returns from the different counties to determine the persons having the largest number of votes for presidential electors, members of Congress, and members of the legislature, and report them to the secretary of state for the issuance of certificates of election. The board, on the other hand, claimed the right to exercise the judicial function of hearing protests and determining the rightful vote from each county.

On the face of the returns, the Democrats claimed the election of Hampton by the narrow margin of 92,261 votes to 91,127 for Chamberlain, and of the Tilden-Hendricks electors by the even smaller majority of 449.

On November 14, the Democrats transferred the struggle in South Carolina from the State Board of Canvassers to the Supreme Court, meeting at the other end of the unfinished, dilapidated state house in Columbia, with an application for a writ of prohibition against the exercise of judicial functions by the Board of Canvassers, and for a writ of mandamus to compel them to exercise their ministerial functions of aggregating the vote. Three days later, the aged chief justice,

Franklin J. Moses, Sr., issued the mandamus to the board, calling for the completion of the returns and their certification to the Supreme Court. This the board did, under protest, on November 21.

On the face of the returns, the Democrats had elected sixty-four out of one hundred and twenty-four members of the lower house of the legislature. In the Senate, including holdovers, the division was eighteen Republicans and fifteen Democrats. In joint assembly, the Democrats would have had, on the face of the returns, a majority of one. But the Board of Canvassers had not the slightest intention of certifying the election according to the face of the returns, with charges of fraud, repeating, violence and intimidation to be taken into account.

Without doubt such practices were common enough, and equally without doubt, they were not confined to any one party or any one section of the state. Alfred B. Williams, one of the last survivors of those who were close to the Red Shirt campaign, wrote fifty years afterward, in his glowing account of *Hampton and His Red Shirts*, that "the Democrats cheated and intimidated and bribed and bulldozed and repeated where they could and the Republicans did likewise." The Democrats received, in some places, the private and unauthorized assistance of United States soldiers who, when relieved from duty, changed to civilian clothes and went back to the polls to vote as often as they could for Hampton. In the low country, where the heavy Negro majorities were, "Hampton Negroes" met the same sort of threats and intimidations which confronted Republican Negroes in the upcountry.

With the election machinery in their hands, from top to bottom, the Republicans were enabled to place more reliance on fraud and less on intimidation, while the Democrats were forced to just the opposite practice. "Neither party," wrote Mr. Williams, "made more than the faintest and thinnest pretense of fairness and legality."

On the morning of November 22, the day after the returns had been transmitted to the Supreme Court under the compulsion of its writ of mandamus, the Board of Canvassers, acting on ex parte protests and without hearings, threw out all returns from Edgefield and Laurens counties—a procedure which converted majorities for Tilden, Hampton and a Democratic legislature into majorities for Hayes, Chamberlain and a Republican legislature.

On that afternoon, the Supreme Court, unaware that the Board of Canvassers had completed its work and adjourned, ordered it to transmit to the Secretary of State the returns as they stood, showing who had received the highest number of votes in each case. Three days later, on November 25, the Supreme Court, consisting of three Republican members, adjudged the Republican Board in contempt for its precipitate action contrary to the writs of the court, fined its members fifteen hundred dollars, and ordered them to jail at Columbia. There they spent a week end in comfortable confinement until the opening of the United States court on Monday, the twenty-seventh, when they were released under writs of habeas corpus by Circuit Judge Hugh L. Bond.

Acting under the returns as promulgated by the canvassers, Secretary of State H. E. Hayne, who was also a member of the Board of Canvassers and a candidate for re-election, issued certificates to all the Hayes and Wheeler electors; to the Republican candidates for five of the six state offices; and to fifty-nine Republicans and fifty-four Democrats in the new House of Representatives, leaving vacant the eight seats of Edgefield and Laurens. Under the Hayne certificate, the new legislature, including the Senate, was to have a Republican majority of seven on joint ballot, which meant that Chamberlain and Gleaves would be declared elected over Hampton and Simpson.

Monday, the twenty-seventh, was a day of perilous tension in Columbia. The little city was crowded with men, some there as defendants in Election Enforcement Law cases before the United States court; others, white and black, Democrat and Republican, as participants or spectators of the opening of the legislature, scheduled for noon of the next day. Saloons were closed as a measure of precaution, by order of the mayor. From General Hampton came quiet assurance and appeals that the peace be kept, no matter what the provocation.

Secretly and at midnight, the state house of South Carolina was garrisoned by United States troops, acting on instructions of President Grant, through Secretary of War Cameron to General Ruger, "to sustain Governor Chamberlain in his authority against domestic violence."

At noon on the twenty-eighth, the Democratic claimants to seats in the House of Representatives, holding certificates from the Supreme Court, marched in a body to the state house, with the members from Edgefield and Laurens at the head of the column, to find themselves barred from entrance to the House by United States soldiers, acting under instructions of the doorkeepers. Outside the building, a great crowd gathered, lacking only the spark to set South Carolinians once more into armed and violent opposition to the authority of the United States government. In that situation, at the request of the army officers, the ever-cool Hampton mounted one of the great granite blocks which had been lying on the grounds since the outbreak of hostilities sixteen years before interrupted the building of the new state house, spoke a hundred words or so of quiet confidence, and dispersed the threatening crowd. Violence was the one thing above all others which must be avoided.

While the Republicans in the House of Representatives held possession of the hall and organized by the election of E. W. M. Mackey as speaker, the Democrats retired to Carolina Hall and went into caucus. At the same time, the Senate, with a clear and undoubted Republican majority of three, organized and began its sessions, with Lieutenant-Governor Gleaves in the chair.

On the twenty-ninth, the Democrats organized as the House of Representatives of the state, with the election of William H. Wallace of Union County, late brigadier general, C. S. A., as speaker. On the thirtieth, which was Thanksgiving Day in 1876, they "stormed the state house." Leading the column as they reached the doors of the chamber were Colonel A. C. Haskell, who had managed the Hampton campaign, and James L. Orr, son of the former Governor. A Negro doorkeeper undertook to stop them. Colonel Haskell fixed him with his one good eye—the other was clouded by a bullet in the Confederate war—and spoke, coldly:

"You know me. You open this door and stand aside." The doorkeeper opened the door; Pat Shannon, the one white doorkeeper of the "Mackey House," rushed forward to stop the invasion; young Orr, standing six feet six inches, simply brushed him aside and opened the way for the "Wallace House" to enter.

General Wallace marched straight to the speaker's stand and took possession. In a moment the rival speaker, Mackey, rushed in to take possession also. Each speaker called on his sergeant-at-arms to remove the intruder, and on his clerk to resume the transaction of business. Neither speaker yielded an inch—both were men of exceptional personal courage and coolness—and both Houses went to work, as if the rival body were not present. Behind the two speakers, sitting comfortably in an ordinary chair, was Colonel Haskell. Speaker Mackey asked the reason for his presence:

"Mackey," he said, "you know I never go armed, but I'm armed now, and for the purpose of killing you if trouble starts in this House; and I tell you, as man to man, if trouble does start you'll be the very first to die."

And so passed the afternoon of Thanksgiving Day. Those members of the "Wallace House" who held certificates from both the Secretary of State and the Supreme Court could go and come at will, although few left the hall for any purpose. The others, from Edgefield and Laurens, being in the hall, stayed there. Night fell, dark and chill. The credit of the state with the gas company having long since expired, there were only a few guttering candles for light until the "Wallace House" members arranged to have the gas turned on, by agreeing to stand for the bill. Blankets were brought in to members of the "Wallace House," and in some instances shared with the "Mackey House" members. Breakfast came in from citizens of Columbia, on Friday morning, again to be shared with some of the "Mackey House."

So things stood, through Friday and Saturday and Sunday, peaceably enough, considering that two hostile legislative bodies were attempting to eat, to sleep, to live and to carry on business, all in the same hall at the same time. The composition of the two bodies indicates the extent to which the line of political division in South Carolina was becoming a racial line. In the "Mackey House," including the Republican contestants from Edgefield and Laurens whom they had seated, there were sixty-two members, of whom the Speaker and one other were white. In the "Wallace House," with sixty-six members, there were two Negroes.

The two Houses joined in singing together, at times, and in laughs at each other's expense, but on Sunday, December 3, there came a change. An anonymous letter, from a source never known, came to General Hampton that afternoon. Members of the "Hunkydories," a lawless gang of Charleston Negroes, it said, had been brought to Columbia to be made deputy sergeants-at-arms, and, at a signal, to clean out the "Wallace House." A little investigation showed that already a hundred of them were in the capitol building, and others were supposed to be on the way. Through the tense hours of the night, the two Houses, wary and watchful, lived in anticipation of the signal, even the unintended incident, which would start the fighting— fighting from which few men in the chamber would have had a fair chance to come out alive.

As the anxious men in the chamber waited, the Red Shirts rode their last great ride. They rode on horseback, from Richland and adjoining counties, and they rode by special train from the more distant counties whence they were called. By dawn of Monday, December 4, there were three thousand of them in Columbia; by night, nearly as many more. As they arrived, they were embodied and put under discipline; sent to quarters which had been provided for them; and there held under orders. There was to be no untoward violence so long as Hampton and his men controlled—but every man in Columbia knew, that day, what the starting of a fight would mean.

At noon, yielding to pressure from Washington and to the dictates of their own good sense, Hampton and Wallace decided that the "Wallace House" should vacate the capitol and resume their sessions at Choral Hall, in the city. To Democrats spoiling for a fight it seemed a retreat, but Hampton and his leaders were too wise to put themselves into armed opposition to the United States.

On the same day on which the "Wallace House" marched out of the capitol at Columbia, the Forty-fourth Congress met at Washington for its last regular session, with a Republican Senate and a Democratic House, and a problem to solve the like of which was never faced by a Congress, before or since—the problem of deciding a disputed presidential election under circumstances and conditions for which the Constitution made no provision.

Wednesday, December 6, was the day appointed for the meeting of presidential electors in the various states, to cast their ballots for president and vice-president, for transmittal to Washington. When Congress met, on the fourth, it was apparent that there would be at least two sets of returns from each of the three disputed Southern states. And there was nothing in the Constitution to tell what should be done with such duplicate returns except the brief sentence:

"The President of the Senate shall, in the presence of the Senate and the House of Representatives, open all the certificates, and the votes shall then be counted."

But who should do the counting? And who decide which certificate should be counted?

To these questions the Republicans were ready with an answer. Who but the president of the Senate—in this case Senator Thomas W. Ferry of Michigan, Republican, elected president pro tem upon the death of Vice-President Wilson the year before? And as to which certificate should be counted, why the one certified to by the governor of the state concerned, for in this matter the Republicans had become most zealous in their support of states' rights as sovereign and free from interference on the part of the general government.

The Democratic position was not so clear or so definite, except that they were quite sure that the president of the Senate had no such power as claimed, and that there lodged somewhere in the Congress the power to "go behind the returns" of the governors—for by the time that Congress convened, it was apparent that the governors of the three Southern states in dispute were going to certify the returns of the Hayes electors in every case.

To bring about that result had required no small amount of working over the returns as they came in from the counties and parishes. In South Carolina it had been achieved by the fairly simple device of throwing out entirely two heavily Democratic counties and defying the decree of the Supreme Court of the state. In the other states, more complicated calculations were necessary.

To the politicians of Louisiana, of course, there was nothing new or strange in Returning Board procedure. For the third time in three elections, the result of a state election was to turn not on the votes as cast, or as reported by the Republican election authorities in the parishes, but as revised by a state board in New Orleans. The new feature of the case was that this time the election of a president of the United States, as well as a governor of Louisiana, depended upon the action of the board.

"Visiting statesmen," a most impressive delegation of both varieties, arrived in New Orleans before the sessions of the board began, on November 15. The board consisted, at that time, of former Governor J. Madison Wells, now collector of the port of New Orleans, chairman; State Senator Thomas C. Anderson, who had amassed a competence in legislative service since the war; L. M. Kenner, operator of a faro bank and a brothel; and G. Casanave, a Negro undertaker who had the reputation of being the most honest member of the board but who was palpably ignorant. Oscar Arroyo, the one Democratic member, resigned and was not replaced in spite of the provisions of the statute.

Before this board came returns which showed that the Tilden electors had carried the state by majorities averaging above seven thousand votes, with slightly larger majorities for Nicholls, Democratic candidate for governor. The Louisiana election had been rather more peaceable than usual, because of the insistence of General Nicholls that no excuse be given for Federal intervention, but there had been violence in the "bulldozed" parishes, alleged to be five in number. On the strength of a mass of affidavits, of hearings from which all local representation was excluded, and of tabulations made in secret by clerks who were all Republican political workers, the Returning Board threw out all boxes from Grant and East Feliciana parishes, and sixty-nine selected boxes from twenty-two other parishes. The first compilation, completed on November 27, showed a sufficient change of votes to elect Packard governor, but failed to carry in two of the Hayes electors. More "affidavits" were sent for, and produced, and the board went into secret session, on December 2, to finish its work. The finish was predicted, on the next day, in a wire from United States Marshal Packard to United States Senator West: "Have seen Wells who says, 'Board will return Hayes sure. Have no fear.'"

On December 6, the Returning Board declared that Hayes had carried the state, according to the revised returns; that Packard was elected governor; that four of the six representatives in Congress were to be Republican; and that the new state Senate was to consist of nineteen Republicans and seventeen Democrats, and the House of seventy-one Republicans, forty-three Democrats and three Independents. On the same day, the Republican electors forwarded their vote for Hayes to Washington, under the certificate of Governor Kellogg. The Democratic electors, not to be outdone, forwarded their vote for Tilden to Washington, under the certificate of Governor McEnery, who for the purpose, revived his long quiescent claim to the Governorship under the election of 1872.

In Florida, as in the other states, the election passed off quietly, even in Representative Purman's county of Jackson, a storm center in earlier days. From Marianna, Mr. Purman himself telegraphed: "Election passing off gloriously. Everybody peaceable and unobstructed." But that was before Governor Stearns was advised from the North that "everything depended on Florida."

On the face of the returns, according to the Democrats, Tilden had carried the state by a hundred or so votes. According to the Republicans, Hayes had won by about half that majority. These returns were before the State Board of Canvassers at sessions beginning November 27. Samuel B. McLin, secretary of state, and Dr. C. A. Cowgill, comptroller, were Republicans; the third member, Attorney General William A. Cocke, a Democrat. The serious question of law before the board was as to its right to go behind the returns of the county boards. The Republican members insisted that they had such a right; the Democratic member, that they had not. Unfortunately for his position, however, as attorney general of the state he had given an opinion to the opposite effect two years before.

In general, the Democrats appeared before the board to charge fraud; the Republicans, to charge violence and intimidation, culminating, according to their account, in Mr. Purman's county of Jackson.

There was violence and intimidation, without doubt, and there was fraud, as well. One ingenious Radical improved on the "tissue ballot" by the preparation and voting of "little jokers," being tiny Republican tickets printed in small type which could be folded in numbers inside a regular ballot and deposited in the box by a friendly receiving clerk without attracting attention. Democrats attempted to distribute ballots bearing the Republican emblem and Democratic names, with the hope that illiterate voters would use them, but the device did not work well because of the vigilance of the Republican election officers. Their opportunities to prevent Democratic and to perpetrate Republican fraud, as described by Manton Marble of the New York *World*, one of the Democratic "visiting statesmen," extended from "the precinct ballot-boxes to the Tallahassee state house."

The final result, announced on December 6 just in time for the electors to play their parts, was arrived at by ingenious selection of precincts to throw out or to amend, whichever produced the greatest net Republican gain. Two of the three state canvassers gave the state to the Hayes electors and Governor Stearns' Republican state ticket, by majorities of less than a thousand votes in all cases. The third canvasser declared that the Democrats had carried the state in both national and state races. Both sets of electors transmitted their votes to Washington, but only the Hayes electors enjoyed the authority of the certificate of the Governor.

From Oregon, on the other hand, one of the Hayes electors held a certificate not from the Governor but from the Secretary of State. Oregon had gone for Hayes, without question, but had elected a Democratic governor. After the election, upon discovery that one of the Hayes electors was ineligible because of holding a Federal office, the new Democratic Governor certified a Tilden elector in his place. The Republican Secretary of State, however, equipped three Hayes electors with certificates.

With such contradictory returns and open questions to handle, Congress faced, in December, the absolute necessity of establishing some way to exercise its authority over the electoral count. By the middle of the month both houses had appointed able committees to devise some way out of the perilous position in which the government found itself. By the middle of January, after earnest consideration, the two committees were meeting jointly, trying and testing this plan and that, and finding them unacceptable either to the members of the committee or the members of the House and Senate. The work was carried forward in secret sessions, as such work had to be, until finally a plan was evolved to entrust the power of Congress over the election vote, whatever that might be, to an Electoral Commission, made up of representatives of the two houses and of the Supreme Court. The plan, which received the endorsement of every member of the two committees except Senator Morton, was adopted by the Senate, on January 24, 1877, with practically all the opposition to it coming from the Republican side and most of its support from the Democratic.

The essence of the plan was a commission of fourteen members, five from each House, and four from the Supreme Court, who were to be so chosen as to balance equally between the two parties. The four justices, named in the bill by reference to their judicial circuits, were to choose a fifth member from the court, who would be, in effect, the odd man on the commission. This fifth justice, it was universally assumed, would be Justice David Davis of Illinois, friend and appointee of Lincoln, but independent in politics.

On January 25 the House took up the Electoral Commission Bill—and on that very day, the Democrats of Illinois, with certain independents eager to defeat General John A. Logan for re-election to the Senate, found that they could agree on Justice Davis and elected him to the Senate of the United States. The man whose presence on the commission had made it acceptable to the Democrats was thus, by Democratic votes, removed from the list of possibilities. It was too late, however, to sidetrack the bill, which passed the House on January 26 and became law by the signature of the President three days later.

Before the commission was created, still another set of electoral returns came in from Florida, certified by the new Democratic Governor George F. Drew, and casting the votes of the state for Tilden. On December 13, a week after the State Board of Canvassers had declared Republican victory in Florida, the Democratic nominee for governor had gone before the Supreme Court of the state, Republican like the court in South Carolina, with a petition for a writ of mandamus to compel the board to count the votes as returned from the counties, not to revise them. The court sustained the Democratic position that the board could not go behind the returns, and ordered a recanvass by December 27.

Unlike the Board of Canvassers in South Carolina, the Florida board obeyed the court, retabulated the vote and declared Drew elected over Stearns by a majority of one hundred and ninety-five votes. The Democrats already controlled the Senate by one vote, and had elected a majority of the lower house of the legislature. On January 2, 1877, the legislature met in joint session for the formal inauguration of George F. Drew as governor. Reconstruction government in Florida was at an end, insofar as state affairs were concerned.

In national affairs, the new Democratic administration went to work promptly to undo, as far as they could, what their predecessors had done. A new State Board of Canvassers was created, through the election of new Democratic state officers. The votes for presidential electors were recanvassed by this board, in accordance with the decisions of the Supreme Court of the state; the Democratic candidates were declared elected by a majority of one hundred and four votes; and the new electors met, on January 19, and cast their votes for Tilden and Hendricks, to make the third set of presidential returns from Florida.

While Congress continued to wrestle with the disputed presidential election, South Carolina Democrats drove ahead with the transfer of actual power to the government which they were so earnestly convinced they had elected in November. On December 6, the day when presidential electors met to cast their ballots, the Supreme Court of the state sustained the legality of the "Wallace House." The "Mackey House," with the Republican Senate, the Supreme Court notwithstanding, canvassed the vote for governor that evening; declared Chamberlain elected; and, on December 7, conducted his inauguration, in the gloom of the dingy Hall of Representatives before an audience of sixteen senators, fifty-one claiming to be representatives, eighty-seven spectators, and six newspapermen.

A week later, the "Wallace House" canvassed the returns for governor, having secured certified copies of them from Secretary of State Hayne through a defeated Democratic candidate for the national House of Representatives who asked them, presumably, for purposes of contest in Congress. The set of returns before the legislature, which by inadvertence included those from Edgefield and Laurens counties, showed Hampton elected by 1,134 votes, which result was declared by the "Wallace House" and a Democratic fragment of the Senate.

General Hampton was inaugurated governor in an open-air celebration, viewed by cheering thousands, packing the streets, the windows and the roofs in the neighborhood of Choral Hall. South Carolina thus had two governors but no real and accepted government. The Democrats had a House; the Republicans a Senate; the Governorship was in contest—and the state was without a dollar in the treasury.

On December 15, the day after Hampton's inauguration, Dr. J. F.

Ensor, Republican superintendent of the state asylum for the insane, recognized him as governor, not on political grounds but on the simple ground of necessity. Several hundred insane men and women would have to be turned loose, or be confined, freezing and starving, if money could not be had from some source, and the doctor knew that it could not be had from Chamberlain's bankrupt government.

The Hampton government promptly proved its *de facto* character by meeting the needs of the insane. It had, as yet, no complete legal right to collect taxes but it had a stronger appeal. Pay us one-tenth of the taxes you have been paying, ran the program of the Hampton government, and we shall need no more. Mass meetings of taxpayers all over the state resolved to support the Hampton government, and to refuse to pay taxes to any other. "Starve out the thieves!" became the slogan.

Both legislatures adjourned, just before Christmas, but the test of strength between the two governments continued, quietly, day by day. Hampton pardoned Peter Smith, convict in the penitentiary. Superintendent Parmale of the prison refused to honor the pardon, and a habeas corpus case went before Judge R. B. Carpenter to determine the law of the matter. Meanwhile, the need for money to feed and keep the prisoners brought the superintendent to acknowledge in practical fashion that the Hampton government, which could collect taxes, was the government *de facto* of the state, regardless of the law.

Judge Carpenter decided, on January 28, that there had been no valid election and that Chamberlain was lawfully governor, holding over. The case was appealed to the Supreme Court but since the aged Chief Justice lay dying, the Hampton forces did not wait for what promised to be a delayed decision. They pardoned another prisoner, whose pardon was promptly recognized as valid by Judge T. J. Mackey, who was a brother of the chairman of the first Reconstruction constitutional convention, and so uncle of Speaker E. W. Mackey. By the time the Electoral Commission was created in Washington to determine the presidential election, there was no longer any doubt as to who was actually governor of South Carolina, and the Hampton strength continued to grow. On February 11, Senator Beverly Nash, as a trustee of the colored orphan asylum of the state, came to Hampton as governor, to get money to feed his charges. A week later, President Grant declared in an interview:

"The entire army of the United States would be inadequate to enforce the authority of Governor Chamberlain. The people have resolved not to resort to violence, but have adopted a mode of procedure much more formidable and effective than any armed resistance."

Like conditions prevailed in Louisiana through the winter months except that the state was again the scene of a congressional investigation, or rather of two, one by the Senate and one by the House which, as was to have been expected, reached exactly opposite conclusions about what had happened in the election and the canvass by the Returning Board.

But while the congressional committees took testimony in New Orleans, Washington and elsewhere, the Democrats of Louisiana went on with the business of taking over the government of their state. The new legislature was to convene at noon on January 1, 1877. On the night before, the Republican members and claimants took possession of the state house, the old Saint Louis Hotel, where they spent the morning barricaded, behind the protection of police and of United States soldiers. Just before noon, the Democratic members marched in a body down Royal Street toward the state house, where all except those who held certificates of the Wells Returning Board were refused admission. After formal protest, the Democrats marched to St. Patrick's Hall, where they went into session and organized as the legislature of the state. At the same hour, the Republican bodies organized in the Saint Louis Hotel, and entrenched themselves for the session.

On the next day, both legislative bodies canvassed the returns for governor and lieutenant-governor. The St. Patrick's legislature declared Nicholls and Wiltz elected, by eight thousand majority; the Saint Louis legislature declared Packard and Antoine elected by thirty-five hundred majority.

On January 8, "Jackson Day" in New Orleans, both legislatures inaugurated their candidates for governor—Packard in a dismal private ceremony in the barricaded hotel, already beginning to show the effects of continuous day and night occupancy by the legislature for more than a week; Nicholls, before ten thousand cheering spectators massed in the square in front of St. Patrick's Hall.

On the next day Nicholls adherents took possession of public buildings in New Orleans, a movement described by the *Republican* as the "Biennial Rising of the White League." In fact, an informal Nicholls police force, organized under the direction of General Ogden, took charge of the policing and good order of the city during the troubled times. Failing to receive active protection from the Kellogg-Packard metropolitan police, the Supreme Court presided over by Chief Justice Ludeling went out of business and the actual judicial authority of the state passed to the newly elected court composed of Democrats. By the middle of January, the Nicholls authority was spread well over the state, and into almost every phase of the government. The writ of Governor Packard and his legislature hardly ran beyond the walls of the state house, dubbed "Fort Packard."

On January 14, President Grant made it clear that he had no desire to interfere in Louisiana affairs while committees of Congress were investigating conditions but that it was

"not proper to sit quietly by and see the State government gradually taken possession of by one of the claimants for gubernatorial honors by illegal means. . . . Should there be a necessity for the recognition of either, it must be Packard."

By that time, and despite the President's position, the Packard legislature had proved unable to hold together. Its members were drifting over to the Odd Fellows' Hall, to which the Nicholls government had been transferred. Senator Pinchback, one of those who came over, declared that in the Packard legislature "today, no bill, no law, no measure" could be passed without a bribe. By January 30, there was no longer even the semblance of a quorum in either house of the Packard legislature, although the sessions continued to drag along wearily, from day to day, in the fetid and unwholesome atmosphere of the old hotel in which hundreds of men had been confined for weeks.

The Nicholls government, like that of Hampton in South Carolina, was collecting a small percentage of former state taxes through voluntary contributions, to sustain its work through the months of January and February.

On the last day of January, in Washington, the Electoral Commission was organized, with Senators Thurman of Ohio and Bayard of Delaware, and Representatives Payne of Ohio, Hunton of Virginia and Abbott of Massachusetts, as the Democratic members; Senators Edmunds of Vermont, Frelinghuysen of New Jersey and Morton of Indiana, and Representatives Garfield of Ohio and Hoar of Massachusetts, as the Republican members, from Congress. From the Supreme Court the commission drew Associate Justices Clifford and Field, Democrats, and Miller and Strong, Republicans. The fifteenth man was Associate Justice Bradley, Republican.

On February 1, the count of the electoral vote started in Congress, at a joint session of the two houses. Under the Electoral Commission plan, those states from which there was more than one return were to be referred to the commission, whose decision was to be final unless reversed by both houses, sitting separately. The first disputed state to be reached was Florida, with its three returns, each having certain elements of legality. For a week, the commission heard argument and gave consideration to the case of Florida. On February 9, by a vote of eight Republican members against seven Democratic members, the commission decided that it was incompetent under the law

"to go into evidence aliunde on the papers opened by the President of the Senate in the presence of the Houses to prove that other persons than those regularly certified by the governor of the State of Florida . . . had been appointed electors, or by counter-proof to show that they had not, and that all proceedings of the courts, of acts of the Legislature, or of the executive of Florida, subsequent to the casting of the votes of the electors on the prescribed day are inadmissible for any such purpose."

On February 10, the decision not to go behind the returns in Florida was reported to the two houses of Congress, immediately ratified by the Senate, and, on the twelfth, rejected by the Democratic House. The decision of the commission was to stand, therefore, and Florida to be counted for Hayes.

From that day forward, there was no possibility that the commission would decide otherwise than that Hayes should receive the votes of Florida, Louisiana and South Carolina, on what the Democrats denounced as the "aliunde doctrine," and the one disputed vote of Oregon, to which he was, of course, clearly entitled. That meant the election of Hayes, by a bare majority of one, an outcome bitterly resented by Democrats at the time but one which they accepted because they had to. There were too many among the Democrats of the South who had fought one war against the United States and who had not the slightest intention of forcing an issue to where they might have to fight another—and that was where recalcitrant opposition to the commission's decisions was heading. Henry Watterson might talk about a hundred thousand men marching to Washington to see that Tilden got his rights but Benjamin H. Hill and forty-two other Southern Democrats quietly banded together to see that no obstruction was put in the way of completing the presidential count. They did not propose to have "a second civil war if their votes could prevent it," observed Mr. Hill.

And so, with patience and restraint and patriotism the nation passed through a crisis intrinsically more difficult than that involved in the election of Lincoln by a minority of the popular vote, but a crisis faced by a generation of men who had seen civil war at first hand and wanted none of it. Not every Southern Democrat took this view. Many were bitterly opposed to leaders of the stature of Hill and Gordon of Georgia and Lamar of Mississippi, who did, but time has sided with those who accepted the compromise.

Louisiana and South Carolina, with the problem of their local governments still unsolved, watched the conduct of the electoral count with an interest different both in kind and in degree from that felt elsewhere. The Democrats of those states had made the best fight they could for Tilden and Hendricks. Hayes had carried South Carolina, in all probability, and the Returning Board had carried Louisiana for him, it seemed. There was nothing more the Democrats in those states could do about it after the Florida decision had shown so clearly how the case would end—but there was something they could do about securing the withdrawal of the Federal troops who kept the feeble spark of life in the Chamberlain and Packard governments. And that they proposed to do.

Even before the Florida decision, General Nicholls had sent E. A. Burke, of the New Orleans *Times-Democrat*, to Washington as special representative of the state, to work with the state's representatives in Congress, Ellis, Gibson and Levy.

Through close contact with President Grant, and with Northern members of Congress who were, in turn, close to Governor Hayes, the representatives of Louisiana were able to secure satisfactory assurances as to his Southern policy at a conference held in the room of William M. Evarts, who was to be in the Hayes Cabinet, at Wormley's Hotel on the night of February 26. With such assurances, indefinite as they were, the Louisiana representatives undertook to abate the filibuster in the House against the electoral count which threatened to delay its completion beyond March 4, with serious consequences to the country.

The count was completed at ten minutes after four o'clock in the morning of March 2, a Friday in 1877, and Hayes and Wheeler were declared elected. At noon of that day, there went forward from the White House a message from C. C. Sniffin, President Grant's secretary, to Governor Packard, that the President "does not believe public opinion will longer support the maintenance of State government in Louisiana by the use of the military. . . . The troops will hereafter, as in the past, protect life and property from mob violence when the State authorities fail; but . . . they will not be used to establish or pull down either claimant for control of the State. It is not his purpose to recognize either claimant."

At the same time, through General Sherman, a copy of the dispatch went to General Augur at New Orleans for his information and guidance.

On the following day, Saturday, March 3, being his last day in the White House, the President personally revised and approved a dispatch of the committee of Louisiana Conservatives in Washington to Governor Nicholls. The President, said the dispatch, "means the people of Louisiana are as free in their affairs from Federal interference as the people of Connecticut, and that there will be no disposition to interference with them, any more than with the people of New York."

That evening, the new President was quietly and privately sworn in in the White House, to avoid any possibility of the claim of an interregnum on account of the fact that March 4, 1877, fell on Sunday. On Monday, the fifth, he was inaugurated publicly with the usual ceremonies, and took up, under exceptionally trying and difficult circumstances, the task of reconciliation between the sections.

By many of the Southern Democrats, President Hayes was looked upon in the light of the comment of Joseph S. C. Blackburn of Kentucky on the Friday when the electoral count was concluded:

"Today is Friday. Upon that day the Saviour of the world suffered crucifixion between two thieves. On this Friday constitutional government, justice, honesty, fair dealing, manhood, and decency suffer crucifixion among a number of thieves."

Radical Republicans, on the other hand, saw in the whole series of informal understandings between friends and advisers of Hayes and Southern representatives, a betrayal of the governments which they had set up and so long supported in the South. To "unload" Packard and Chamberlain, they declared, was to repudiate the very process of election upon which depended the President's own title to his office.

But just as the Southern Democrats had to accept the seating of Hayes because they could do no better, so did the President and the Northern Republicans have to accept the end of the Chamberlain and the Packard governments, because they could no longer be held together.

On March 1, Associate Justice Willard, the "carpetbag" member of the Supreme Court of South Carolina, held that Hampton was "at least de facto" governor of the state. Chief Justice Moses, the "scalawag" member, lay dying, while Associate Justice Wright, the Negro member, held that Chamberlain was lawfully holding over as governor.

More potent than either of these decisions, however, was the treasury statement of the two governments. As of that date, General Johnson Hagood, "acting comptroller & treasurer" of the Hampton government, had collected $119,432 and paid out $37,794. The Chamberlain government had collected less than $1,000 and procured the money to pay the members of the "Mackey House" the two hundred dollars each which they had voted themselves, only through advances made by D. T. Corbin, Vermont "carpetbagger" who made a bad speculation in securing an election to the United States Senate by the Mackey legislature. The Wallace House and the Democratic Senators, meanwhile, had elected General M. C. Butler.

Stanley Matthews of Ohio, intimate friend of the new President, suggested to Governor Chamberlain, on March 4, that troops be withdrawn from South Carolina and each government allowed to stand or fall on its own strength. This suggestion Chamberlain indignantly repelled, as it would "permit Hampton to reap the fruits of a campaign of murder and fraud."

On March 23, both Chamberlain and Hampton were invited to Washington to see the President. There was some talk in Washington of compromise, even of a new election, to none of which would Hampton listen. His unwavering position was that the people of South Carolina had elected him to be their governor, and their governor he would be. On April 2, the Cabinet decided that troops would be withdrawn from Columbia. To Lieutenant-Governor Simpson, Governor Hampton wired:

"Everything satisfactorily and honorably settled. I expect our people to preserve absolute peace and quiet. My word is pledged for this. I rely on them."

There was no disorder except for a perfect riot of joy as the Governor's train brought him back to Columbia. The celebration started in North Carolina, at Charlotte, and continued all the way to Columbia, with locomotive and cars decorated with flowers, floral arches over the track at almost every station, bands and fireworks and, at Columbia, a welcoming procession headed by the band of the Eighteenth United States Infantry, the garrison of the city.

That was in the afternoon of April 7. Three days later, at noon, the troops marched out of the state house which they had held since midnight of November 27. On the next day, at eleven o'clock of April 11, after an interchange of polite notes between the two governors, Governor Chamberlain closed his office, handed the keys to his successor's private secretary, and walked out of South Carolina's state house. In South Carolina, Reconstruction was at an end.

Only in Louisiana, then, did there remain a dual and divided government. There, too, the Radical government was hemmed in until it ruled no more than the state house, and was supported only by the United States troops quartered in a building next door. The problem of the President, there, however, was more difficult than in South Carolina. It was possible to say, and probably it was true, that that state had actually gone for Hayes and Hampton. The title of Rutherford B. Hayes to the Presidency, however, rested on precisely the same foundation, in the action of the Returning Board, as did the title of S. B. Packard to the Governorship of Louisiana.

The President did not send for the two governors to come to Washington, as he had done in the South Carolina case, but he sent to Louisiana an extra-legal commission, charged with the difficult duty of working out some way to secure the establishment of one government, and only one, in the state. To execute this delicate task, the President sent down General Joseph Hawley of Connecticut, Judge Lawrence of Illinois, John M. Harlan of Kentucky, former Governor John C. Brown of Tennessee, and Wayne McVeigh of Pennsylvania—a group of distinction.

Instructions were issued by Secretary of State Evarts on April 2, the same day on which the Cabinet voted to withdraw troops from the South Carolina capitol. The members of the commission arrived in New Orleans on the fifth, for two weeks of conferences with General Nicholls and his legislature, in special session, and with Governor Packard and his legislature. They were, they insisted, merely advisers and negotiators. Their evident intent was to assist in bringing a majority of undisputed members into the vigorous Nicholls legislature, since it was obviously impossible to revive the moribund Packard assembly.

By April 19, not more than ten members were left in the Packard legislature. Something of the nature of the solvent which dissolved that body may be gathered from the comment of former Governor Warmoth, who was a member and had access to both legislatures. He wrote, in his memoir:

"Kellogg had to be bought off with a seat in the United States Senate. Packard was bought off with an appointment by President Hayes to the Consul-generalship at Liverpool. Pinchback was bought off with the appointment of his brother to a tax-collectorship by Governor Nicholls; and $60,000 from the Louisiana Lottery Company helped to satisfy a number of other members of the Packard legislature to move over to the Nicholls Legislature and give it a legal quorum."

At the same time, other appointments, or prospects of them, dissolved the Packard Supreme Court, which had made no attempt to hear cases for three months. The President's commission, having the satisfaction of seeing the government of the state united once more, after nearly five years of division and dispute, made its final report on April 21, and left New Orleans.

Three days later, on April 24, 1877, New Orleans and Louisiana being at political peace, the troops of the United States vacated their quarters adjoining the last state house of the last of the Reconstruction governments, and marched back to Jackson Barracks. Reconstruction in the South was over.

Over, that is, if such an experience in the life of a people may ever be said to be over—over, except for the consequences.

THE END

ACKNOWLEDGMENTS

ACKNOWLEDGMENTS

IN A SENSE, this book is a sequel to the *Story of the Confederacy*. Like that book, it is not so much an attempt to enlarge the knowledge of the period treated as to organize and present it in direct narrative form. The book is without footnote references, the source of information being indicated in the text itself where it seemed desirable. In general the text is based on published works, although in considerable part it is derived from contemporary newspapers, old railroad and business reports, and family records and letters, kindly made available for the purpose.

In the writings about Reconstruction there has been an alternation of emphasis that amounts almost to a rhythm. In the earliest period, in the congressional reports and atrocity stories which afforded the basis of most information about what went on in the South, the emphasis was on the unregenerate state of that section and its people—even, to some extent, in such substantial works as John T. Trowbridge's *Picture of the Desolated States;* Whitelaw Reid's *After the War;* and Sidney Andrews' *The South Since the War.*

In the latter years of Reconstruction there came a different sort of reporting of things Southern—Robert Somers' *The Southern States Since the War;* James S. Pike's *The Prostrate State;* Edward King's *Southern States of North America;* Charles Nordhoff's *Cotton States.*

With the passing of the Reconstruction period, interest in it seemed likewise to pass, except for the vogue of Albion W. Tourgee's novels, and for the publication of volumes of military and political reminiscence in which Reconstruction was discussed incidentally—such works, to take opposite examples, as S. S. Cox's *Three Decades of Federal Legislation* and James G. Blaine's *Twenty Years in Congress.*

Not until the middle 1880's did the South begin to tell its own story of the period, with *Why the Solid South?*, a collection of state studies edited by Hilary A. Herbert, a member of President Cleveland's Cabinet, and *The Ku Klux Klan: Its Origin, Growth and Disbandment,* by J. C. Lester and D. L. Wilson.

Fifteen more years of comparative silence on the subject and then, in 1901, appeared a remarkable series of articles in the *Atlantic Monthly,* for the most part presenting a view of Reconstruction strange to Northern minds of the time. Within half a dozen years there appeared John W. Burgess' *Reconstruction and the Constitution;* William A. Dunning's *Reconstruction, Political and Economic;* Walter L. Fleming's *Documentary History of Reconstruction;* David M. DeWitt's *Impeachment and Trial of Andrew Johnson;* Paul S. Peirce's *The Freedmen's Bureau;* William G. Brown's *The Lower South in American History;* Paul L. Haworth's *The Hayes-Tilden Disputed Presidential Election of 1876;* Mrs. Myrta Lockett Avary's *Dixie After the War;* the

Reconstruction volumes of James Ford Rhodes' *History;* and complete detailed studies of Reconstruction in the several states, to be mentioned more particularly hereafter. A new and different picture of Reconstruction was being presented.

After another fifteen years or so, with few general works on the subject other than Professor Fleming's brief *Sequel of Appomattox,* there came a striking revival of publication on Reconstruction, beginning in the late 1920's: Allan Nevins' *Emergence of Modern America;* Claude G. Bowers' *Tragic Era;* Howard K. Beale's *The Critical Year: A Study of Andrew Johnson and Reconstruction;* three new biographies of Andrew Johnson, by Robert W. Winston, Lloyd P. Stryker and George F. Milton, in three years; new biographies of William G. Brownlow by E. Merton Coulter; of *Ulysses S. Grant, Politician,* by William B. Hesseltine; of Hamilton Fish by Allan Nevins; of *Rutherford B. Hayes: Statesman of Reunion* by H. J. Eckenrode; of Benjamin H. Hill by Haywood J. Pearce; of L. Q. C. Lamar by Wirt Armistead Cate; of William Mahone by Nelson M. Blake; of Francis H. Pierpont by Charles H. Ambler; of Alexander H. Stephens by E. Ramsey Richardson—all within the space of little more than five years. During the present year two notable general works have been added to the list: *The Civil War and Reconstruction* by James G. Randall, and *The Road to Reunion* by Paul H. Buck.

Indispensable in the writing of any general story of Reconstruction are the books which give more complete and detailed accounts of the process in particular states, most of which were published in the first fifteen years of the present century. A partial list of such works referring to particular states follows:

FLEMING, WALTER L., *Civil War and Reconstruction in Alabama.*

STAPLES, THOMAS S., *Reconstruction in Arkansas.*

DAVIS, WILLIAM W., *Civil War and Reconstruction in Florida.*

THOMPSON, C. MILDRED, *Reconstruction in Georgia.*

WOOLLEY, EDWIN C., *The Reconstruction of Georgia.*

COULTER, E. M., *Civil War and Readjustment in Kentucky.*

FICKLEN, JOHN R., *Reconstruction in Louisiana.*

LONN, ELLA, *Reconstruction in Louisiana After 1868.*

GARNER, JAMES W., *Reconstruction in Mississippi.*

McNEILY, J. S., "War and Reconstruction in Mississippi." (From *Proceedings, Mississippi Historical Society.)*

HAMILTON, J. G. DeROULHAC, *Reconstruction in North Carolina.*

HOLLIS, JOHN P., *The Early Period of Reconstruction in South Carolina.*

REYNOLDS, JOHN S., *Reconstruction in South Carolina.*

SIMKINS, F. B., and WOODY, R. H., *South Carolina During Reconstruction.*

ALLEN, WALTER, *Governor Chamberlain's Administration in South Carolina.*

WILLIAMS, ALFRED B., *Hampton and His Red Shirts.*

BALL, WILLIAM W., *The State That Forgot.*

FERTIG, JAMES W., *The Secession and Reconstruction of Tennessee.*

PATTON, JAMES W., *Unionism and Reconstruction in Tennessee.*

RAMSDELL, CHARLES W., *Reconstruction in Texas.*
ECKENRODE, H. J., *Political History of Virginia During Reconstruction.*
AMBLER, CHARLES H., *History of West Virginia.*

There are numerous other works of special value on particular phases of Reconstruction, such, for example, as Eben G. Scott's *Reconstruction During the Civil War,* or the volume of *Studies in Southern History and Politics* inscribed to Professor Dunning by his former pupils. Most recent of such special studies is Otto Eisenschiml's thrilling piece of historical detective work, *Why Was Lincoln Murdered?*

Local histories, personal reminiscences, and the standard biographies of the principal figures of the time give additional material on the period.

The "carpetbaggers," like the Carthaginians, had their history written by their enemies, with few exceptions. Fortunately, however, a few of the groups known as "carpetbaggers" and "scalawags" have, within recent years, presented some part of the other side of the story. Just before his death, Governor Holden of North Carolina dictated a brief memoir. Governor Chamberlain of South Carolina has found adequate presentation, partly through his own articles and partly through Walter Allen's book. Governor Clayton of Arkansas and Governor Warmoth of Louisiana have each published vigorous presentations of their own stories.

Last of the major groups concerned in Reconstruction to be heard from in their own behalf were the Negroes—the truly tragic figures of that tragic time. Booker T. Washington's *Up From Slavery* is a classic human and historic record. John R. Lynch's *The Facts of Reconstruction* gives the views of an intelligent Negro state official and representative in Congress. A. A. Taylor's *The Negro in the Reconstruction of Virginia* and his similar work for South Carolina; Carter G. Woodson's *The Negro in Our History;* and, most important of all, *Black Reconstruction in America* by W. E. D. DuBois, present more directly the part of the Negroes in Reconstruction activities.

Personal acknowledgment for material and assistance in the development of this work is extended to the libraries of Vanderbilt University and the State of Tennessee, in Nashville; the Library of Congress and the library of the Bureau of Railway Economics in Washington; to Messrs. Gilbert Govan, E. Y. Chapin, and Garnett Andrews, to Senator Newell Sanders, and to Miss Alice Eloise Stockell, of Chattanooga; to Mr. Robert M. Hughes of Norfolk; to Mr. Alan S. Bedell of Greenville, South Carolina; to Mrs. John L. Cobbs, Jr., of Larchmont, New York; to Colonel Roane Waring of Memphis; to Mrs. West Morton, Mrs. John Trotwood Moore, Miss Isabel Howell, and Miss Mary Olivia Rutledge and Messrs. Charles Barham, Frank Slemmons and Stanley F. Horn of Nashville; to Mr. F. H. Caldwell of Tampa; to Mr. Joseph G. Kerr of Atlanta; to Mr. David Chambers Mearns of Washington; to Professor William O. Lynch of Indiana University, who has read the work in manuscript; and to Mr. D. L. Chambers of Indianapolis, who has been a model of patience.
Washington, D. C.   ROBERT S. HENRY
December 14, 1937.

INDEX

INDEX

Abbeville (S. C.), 24

Abbott, Gen. J. C., senator from N. C., 317

Abbott, Gen. Joseph V., Ga. senator, 442; pres. of N. C. Republican Convention, 1867-1868, 264, 288; quoted on spirit of South, 69

Abell, Judge Edmond, on 1866 convention in La., 187

Aberdeen *Examiner,* and Miss. politics, 543

Abolition, *see* Slavery, abolition

Adair, George W., 176

Adams, Charles Francis, 138, 466

Adams, Doc, captain of Negro militia, 563, 564

Adams, Maj. G. M., admission to 40th Congress, 253

Adams, Thomas A., wire regarding La. 1872 elections, 487

Adams, Thos. E., New Orleans' chief of police, 1866, 188

Adams County (Miss.), 1873, 503

African Colonization Society, 1866, activity, 176

Agricultural and Mechanical College, of Ga., established, 1866, 206

Aiken, William, of S. C., and Peabody Fund, 242

Aiken (S. C.), politics, and riots, 568, 569

Aiken Counties (S. C.), 564

Air Line R. R., 1873, 499

Akerman, Att.-Gen. Amos T., 397, 414; in Grant's cabinet, 284-285; ruling on oath, 379

Alabama, 91, 313, 345; and abolition, 89, 90; and cotton frauds, 64; and Fla. land purchase 1870-1873, 494; and the Omnibus Bill, 313, 319; and the Negroes, 65, 90-91, 119, 244, 433; and the Reconstruction Act, 219, 299; "Black" and "White" Counties, 90; bushwhacker trial, 1865, 86; congressmen seated, 320; Conservative convention, 1867, 263; constitutional convention, 1867, 89, 261, 267, 278, 280; destitution, 61; economic conditions, 429, 499; elections, 266, *passim* 471-475; Freedmen's Bureau, 60, 320; government, 34, 320; iron works, 174; mail-service, 124; Northerners in business in, 145; nullifies Ordinance of Secession, 89; planta-

Alabama, *Continued*
tions, number, 1860-1870, 428; politics, 366, 384, 417, 421, 525; provisional governor, 53; Radical government, 319; railroad service, 202, 247, 367, 422, 423, 427; ratifies Thirteenth Amendment, 107, 113; ratifies Fourteenth Amendment, 320; rejects Fourteenth Amendment, 207; repudiates Confederate debt, 89; Tuskegee Institute founded, 244; University, destruction by Federal army, 131

Alabama & Chattanooga R. R., 1870, 422, 423

Alabama River, 90

Alamance (N. C.), and the Klan, *passim* 410-415

Albany (N. Y.), presidential party's visit, 194-195

Alcorn, Gen. J. L., of Miss., 391; and riot, 1875, 548; governor of Miss., 1870, 409, 432; granted amnesty, 1868, 332; political activity, 1867, 263, 381, 392, 488-489, 503, 504; quoted, 392-393, 457, 503; succeeds Sen. Revels, 455-456

Alcorn University, for Negroes, 431, 456

Alden, Mayor, political defeat, 380

Alden, Sec., of Fla., 358

Aldrich, A. P., quoted, 87

Alexandria (Va.), 1866, Union Republican party organization, 173; constitution and government, 39, 112, 113

Alexandria County (Va.), 60

Allan, Gen. Edgar, and Va. politics, 1869, 377; Loyal Leaguer, quoted, 225-226

Allison, Governor of Fla., 95

Alston, James, Negro legislator, Ala., 1870, 417

Alvord, J. W., quoted on political society in Columbia, 447

American Missionary Assn., and establishment of Negro schools, 244

American Missionary Society, Negro education activity, 130

Ames, Gen. Adelbert, of Miss., 349, 353, 382, 391, 392; and race riots, 1875, 546; appointed governor of Mississippi, 325, 376; governor of Miss., nomination, election, administration, 502-504, 530, 531, 542, 552-553; impeachment, resignation, 553; quoted, 457, 545, 553; re-

601

Montgomery (Ala.), *Continued*
pute, 418; headquarters Ala. Freed-
men's Bureau, 60; political dispute,
474; race relationship in churches, 127;
Radical meeting, 300; railroad service,
202; transportation, 499
Montgomery (Tex.), 499
Montgomery-Mobile R. R., 423
Montgomery & West Point R. R., rates,
service, 71
Monticello (Ark.), 355
Monticello (Fla.), 295, 560, 561
Moore, Gov., 128
Moren, Lt.-Gov. E. H., 418
Morgan, Col. A. T., 287, 547
Morgan, Charles, 460
Morgan, Sen. E. D., 163
Morgan, Stokeley, execution, 342
Morgan, Sheriff, in Miss., flees, 546
Morganton (N. C.), 201, 413
Morrill, Sen. Lot, 162, 163
Morissey, James, 320
Morristown (S. C.), railroad service, 201
Morrow, Col. Henry A., 532
Morton, John W., and Nashville Klan,
230
Morton, Gov. Oliver P., 138, 376, 395,
506, 535, 551, 554, 582, 586; and Ark.
Republican convention, 514; and 1866
Ind. election, 198; and La. 1872 elec-
tions, quoted, 488-490; excerpt from
letter to Johnson, 81; quoted, 391-
392; quoted on Fifteenth Amendment,
354; supports President, 136
Morton, Bliss & Co., 501
Moses, Chief Justice Franklin J., Sr.,
574, 590
Moses, Gov. Franklin J., Jr., 290, 370,
446; adjutant and inspector general of
S. C., 313; administration, 494-497,
521; election, 1876, 562; government
in S. C., 501-502; granted amnesty,
332; S. C. election, 1872, 471; nomina-
tion, 1872, 470
Mountain Boy, 419
"Mounted Baseball Club" of Allendale,
569
Mower, Gen. Joseph A., 249, 258
Mudd, Dr. Samuel A., 36, 37
"Mule Team," 265, 294
Mulligan letters, and charges against
Blaine, 550
Murfreesboro (Ark.), 355
Murphy, Gov. Isaac, 55, 172, 312-313,
339, 514; and 1866 legislation, 205-
206; chosen gov. of Ark., 41; comments
on Ark. difficulties, 61; government,
9, 41-42, 172; quoted on rebels, 197
Murrah, Gov. of Texas, 26
Musgrove, Henry, 382
"My Policy," 192

Nash, Sen. Beverly, 292; and Hampton
government, 584; and S. C. railroad
fraud, 446; quoted, 416
Nashville (Tenn.), 12, 43, 66, 86, 201,
329; and Negro education, 130; Benevolent Society, 172; conventions, 42,
226, 237, 402; Freedmen's Bureau, 60;
Ku Klux Klan organizes, 1867, 230,
232; Klan disbanding, 388; liquor
shops, 128; martial law, 1869, 360; put
in receiver's hands, 380; railroads, 175,
247, 365, 424
Nashville and Chattanooga R. R., 21
Nashville (Tenn.) *Press & Times,* on Ne-
gro labor, 363
Nashville (Tenn.) *Union & Democrat,*
152
Natchez, Miss., 119
Natchez District (Miss.), 503
Natchez, Miss. steamboat, 427-428
Nation, on Kellogg fraud, 527; on
Southern atrocities, 1868, 339-340; on
Southern loyalist convention, 1874, 523
National Republican, on "Force Bill,"
541; on La. voting, 1872, 478
National Teachers' Assn., 31
National Union Clubs, in Arkansas, 172
National Union Convention, 42
National Union party, 1864, 43, 132, 133;
caucus, 133; see Union party
National Union Republican party, *see*
Republican party
Neagle, John L., comptroller general of
S. C., 313
Nebraska bill, 304
Nelson, James, 350
Negroes, 347; aid for urged, 140; Ala.
congressmen, 1870, 418; and Fla. Re-
publican convention, 1870, 406, 407;
and labor, 117, 119, 363, 364-365, 429;
and N. C. government, 368; and
Tenn. government, 368; and Tex.
election, 1874, 505; attend Montgomery convention, 1867, 263; attend
Richmond Republican convention,
1867, 261-262; attitude toward in
South, 1868, 336; churches in Miss.,
1865-1870, 456; civil rights, 76, 77, 78,
103-105, 138, 469; in Ala., 91; in Ark.,
1866, 205; in Fla., 95-96; in Ga. action,
94-95, 204; in La., 372; in Miss., 1865,
80, 97-100; in N. C., 93; in S. C., 89;
codes for, 149, 150; colonization advocates, 74-75, 176; conditions in South,
120, 121, 122; convention in S. C., 1865,
173; count for congressional representation, 88, 89, 90-91; crime and punishment, 1869, 355, 356; danger to
whites, 76; delegates to Ala. convention, 1868, 278; to Ark. convention,
286; to Fla. convention, 1868, 294; to